Up South

POLITICS AND CULTURE IN MODERN AMERICA
Series Editors: Michael Kazin, Glenda Gilmore, Thomas J. Sugrue

A complete list of books in this series is available from the publisher.

Up South

Civil Rights and Black Power in Philadelphia

MATTHEW J. COUNTRYMAN

PENN

University of Pennsylvania Press

Philadelphia

10   9   8   7   6   5   4   3   2   1

Published by
University of Pennsylvania Press
Philadelphia, Pennsylvania 19104-4112

Library of Congress Cataloging-in-Publication Data

Countryman, Matthew.
    Up south : civil rights and Black power in Philadelphia / Matthew J. Countryman.
        p.   cm. (Politics and culture in Modern America)
    ISBN-13: 978-0-8122-3894-5 (cloth : alk. paper)
    ISBN-10: 0-8122-3894-X (cloth : alk. paper)
    Includes bibliographical references and index.
    1. African Americans—Civil rights—Pennsylvania—Philadelphia—History—
20th century.   2. Civil rights movements—Pennsylvania—Philadelphia—History—
20th century.   3. African Americans—Pennsylvania—Philadelphia—Politics and
government—20th century.   4. Black power—Pennsylvania—Philadelphia—
History—20th century.   5. Philadelphia (Pa.)—Race relations—History—20th
century.   6. Philadelphia (Pa.)—Politics and government—20th century.   I. Title.
II. Series
F158.9.N4 C68   2006
974.8'110496073-09041—dc22   2005048450

For Rosie

Contents

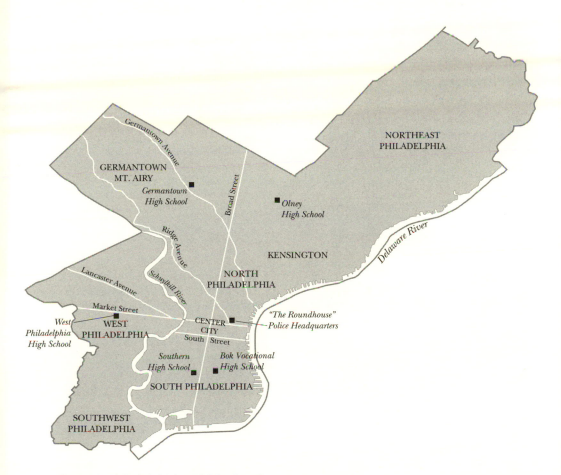

Figure 1. Philadelphia's neighborhoods.

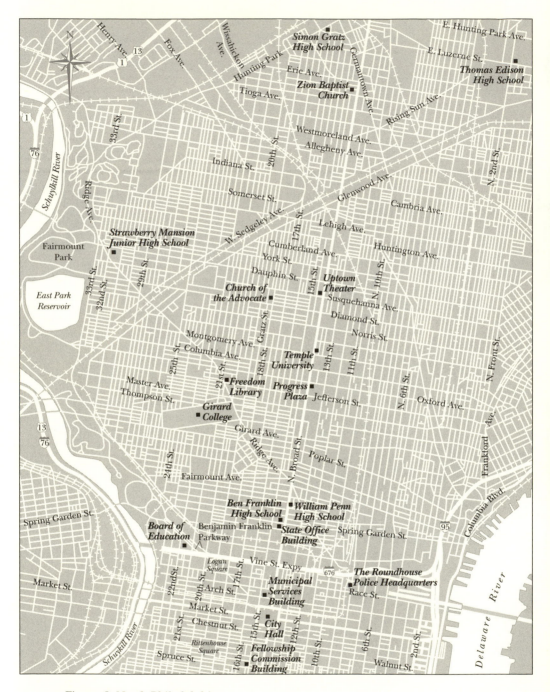

Figure 2. North Philadelphia.

Introduction: Liberalism, Civil Rights, and Black Nationalism in the Urban North

Philadelphia is rarely depicted as a significant place in the history of the modern civil rights movement. Most histories of the civil rights movement move from the Montgomery bus system to the Little Rock public schools, from Greensboro's five-and-ten lunch counters to the bombed-out churches of Birmingham, from Freedom Schools in the Mississippi Delta to the Edmund Pettus Bridge in Selma, Alabama. Even when the focus shifts away from the South, what we remember are the riot-torn streets of Watts, Harlem's Audubon Ballroom, Martin Luther King's open housing marches in Chicago, and Black Panther shootouts with the police in the black neighborhoods of Oakland. While some remember that Chaney, Goodman, and Schwerner—the three Freedom Summer volunteers—were murdered near Philadelphia, Mississippi, in the summer of 1964, few would think of the nation's then fourth-largest city as the site of important developments in the black freedom struggle.

Despite Philadelphia's invisibility within civil rights historiography, the city was home to one of the most successful campaigns for black civil rights in the nation during the 1940s and 1950s. In 1948, civil rights advocates convinced Philadelphia's Republican mayor and its Republican-controlled city council to enact one of the country's first municipal fair employment practices laws. Three years later, these same civil rights advocates, in alliance with a liberal reform movement inside the city's Democratic Party, succeeded in writing "human rights" provisions banning racial discrimination in all municipal employment, services, and contracts into the new city charter. The charter also provided for the establishment of a new agency within city government, the Commission on Human Relations, with responsibility for the enforcement of the city's antidiscrimination laws. For its advocates, the new city charter portended an era of steady progress toward the goal of racial equality in Philadelphia.

By the end of the 1950s, however, the commission's inability to substantively transform racial inequities within the city's labor markets, residential neighborhoods, and public schools led many in Philadelphia's black communities to begin to question the efficacy of government action in the struggle for racial equality. In 1960, the 400 Ministers, a group of black clergy led by a Baptist minister named Leon Sullivan, began a protest campaign they called selective patronage, a series of black consumer boycotts against private employers who failed to provide equal employment opportunities to black workers. By 1963, the ministers claimed to have convinced, through boycotts and the threat of boycotts, more than two hundred companies to change their employment policies.

That same year, selective patronage was superseded by a civil disobedience campaign led by local NAACP president Cecil Moore. Moore targeted the municipal government directly for failing to enforce the antidiscrimination provisions of the new city charter by continuing to contract with construction companies and building trades unions that excluded black workers. Not only did the 1963 protests force the local construction industry to begin to open skilled trades positions to black workers, they also set the stage for a comprehensive reevaluation of workforce desegregation efforts at the national level—a reevaluation that would culminate in the U.S. Department of Labor's adoption in 1967 of an affirmative action program famously known as the "Philadelphia Plan."[1]

Black Philadelphians would continue to mount protests against the failure of government agencies to enforce the principles of equality of opportunity and equal protection under the law in the years that followed. In August 1964, anger at police brutality and the perceived high cost and poor quality of goods in white-owned stores in the city's poor black neighborhoods led to three days of rioting in the large North Philadelphia neighborhood known as the Jungle. A year later, the Philadelphia NAACP led daily protests for more than six months to demand government action to desegregate Girard College, a city-founded but privately run boarding school for orphaned boys in the heart of predominantly black North Philadelphia.

By the mid-1960s, many within the Philadelphia movement had begun to question the efficacy of civil rights protest and the desegregation agenda. Even Leon Sullivan, the driving force behind selective patronage, decided to shift his focus from protest to self-help strategies. The selective patronage campaigns, he argued, had convinced the city's business community that it had to more fully integrate its workforce and therefore that the prime challenge facing the city's black working poor was to develop the skills and work habits necessary to take advantage of these new job opportunities. Preaching that "integration without preparation is frustration," Sullivan declared that it was time to bring "a whole new dimension to the civil rights picture, placing emphasis on production rather than protest."[2] Working within black middle-class traditions of self-help and racial uplift, he established a nonprofit job training program, the Opportunities Industrialization Centers (OIC), and a series of black-owned for-profit ventures. Within a year of its founding, OIC would become an important model for, and beneficiary of, President Lyndon Johnson's War on Poverty because of its emphasis on helping the poor to help themselves through the provision of social services—"a hand up"—rather than more direct forms of income redistribution—"a hand out."[3] Sullivan's for-profit companies would have an equally significant national impact. During the 1968 presidential campaign, Richard Nixon heralded them as models of "black capitalism," which he called the most important development in the struggle for racial justice in the country.[4]

In February 1966, four months before Stokely Carmichael of the Student Nonviolent Coordinating Committee (SNCC) popularized the slogan "Black Power," activists in Philadelphia formed the Black People's Unity Movement (BPUM). Their goal was to synthesize Malcolm X's call for black cultural pride and community control over the social, economic, and political institutions in the black community with SNCC's commitment to community organizing and indigenous leadership development. In 1967, BPUM activists helped to organize a school walkout by black high school students from across the city to protest the lack of black history courses and black administrators in their schools. A year later, BPUM hosted the Third National Conference on Black Power, and in 1970 the Philadelphia chapter of the Black Panther Party (BPP) served as the organizing committee for the BPP-sponsored Revolutionary People's Constitutional Convention at North Philadelphia's Temple University. It was during the 1970 Black Panther convention that four years of confrontations between Black Power activists and the Philadelphia police reached a crescendo. Following a police raid on the Panthers' North Philadelphia headquarters, police officers forced male party members to strip to their undershorts on the public sidewalk. But while confrontations with the police garnered the headlines, it was within black Philadelphia that the call for Black Power, and in particular the call for community control, had its greatest impact, inspiring a broad range of organizing initiatives designed to democratize black leadership in the city and guarantee a voice for the black working-class majority in the governance of their communities and city.

While distinctive in its timing, the Philadelphia experience was not unique among northern cities. In cities from Boston to San Francisco, civil rights and Black Power activists led protest movements against racial discrimination and oppression in employment, housing, education, and the criminal justice system. Indeed, recent scholarship has begun to rethink the chronological and geographic parameters of the modern civil rights movement. As the editors of *Freedom North*—a collection of historical essays on black movements in the urban North and West in the post-World War II era—have pointed out, the focus on the South and the decade between the Montgomery Bus Boycott and the passage of the Voting Rights Act in 1965 severely truncates our understanding of the civil rights movement and its impact on American life.[5] Racism was never just a southern problem. Nor were civil rights activists ever solely concerned with solving southern variants of racial segregation and inequality. The strategies and goals that we associate with southern civil rights activism were at the core of a vital political movement that challenged the racial status quo in Philadelphia and other cities of the urban North beginning in the 1940s.[6] This study of racial politics and activism in postwar Philadelphia constructs the history of a local civil rights movement that began in the 1940s and continued through the 1970s. And it argues that the modern civil rights movement was as much a product of the black experience of racial oppression in the urban North as it was of life in the segregated South.

What then happens to civil rights movement history when we broaden our chronological and geographic focus? First of all, the history of civil rights activism in the urban North during the 1940s makes it clear that the goals of the modern civil rights movement, far from being self-evident, were a product of the optimism of mid-century American liberalism about the uses of state power to protect individual rights and encourage upward mobility. Franklin Delano Roosevelt's New Deal had constructed the state as the facilitator of individual opportunity and upward mobility for white Americans, while largely excluding African Americans and other racial minority groups from access to the American Dream. Unlike the social democratic welfare states of western Europe, the New Deal sought to protect individual Americans against the vicissitudes of a capitalist economy by ensuring that opportunities to own a home, open a small business, and attend college were available to all. Of course, the New Deal state also provided temporary assistance in difficult times through programs like unemployment insurance, but these were less important than such programs as federal mortgage guarantees, the GI Bill, small business loans, and Social Security that could be and were trumpeted to the public as investments in individual opportunity and the American Dream.[7]

Inspired by the ideals of the New Deal, civil rights advocates began in the 1940s to see state action to protect the citizenship rights of individual "Negro" Americans as the key to achieving racial justice. Indeed, the expansion of federal power and of government interventions in daily life that took place under the New Deal made it possible to imagine the state—not just the courts, but every branch of government—working to guarantee that blacks and other racial minorities could enjoy the same rights and opportunities as white Americans. It is in this sense that the 1941 March on Washington Movement and President Roosevelt's subsequent Executive Order 8802 guaranteeing equal job opportunities to black workers in defense plants—not the 1954 *Brown v. Board of Education* decision or the Montgomery Bus Boycott—was the crucial opening salvo of the modern civil rights movement. Not only did E.O. 8802 promise equal opportunity, but it established a federal agency, the President's Fair Employment Practices Commission, whose sole purpose was to guarantee black rights in the workplace. It created a realm, no matter how limited, in which the government took as its responsibility the protection of black citizenship rights. And like the New Deal labor reforms that preceded it, it gave the government's seal of approval for popular action to insure equal opportunity in the workplace.[8]

Also fundamental to the developing liberal civil rights agenda was the intellectual redefinition of the "race problem" that took place in the 1930s and 1940s. As scientists began to discredit the idea that there were biological differences between the races, liberals in particular began to view race—to paraphrase sociologist Gunnar Myrdal—as a problem of white attitudes, not of black capacities. If in fact blacks were biologically the same as whites, then not only could white society be faulted for black poverty and underdevelopment but fair-minded whites would eventually recognize black equality if only given the opportunity to interact and compete with blacks on an equal basis. In other words, many liberals came to believe that state policies which brought the races together by providing blacks with the same social and economic opportunities as whites would inevitably lead to the erosion of racial fears and misconceptions that were at the root of interracial hatred and conflict.[9]

Simply imagining a liberal rights-based solution to the race problem was, of course, not sufficient. It would take a national political movement to enact the antidiscrimination laws, establish the regulatory agencies, and promulgate the integrationist ethos that were all necessary if the liberal vision of a colorblind society was to become a reality. As I show in Chapter 1, just such a movement was beginning to emerge across the country during the 1940s. For the most part, it was not a protest movement but rather a movement that emphasized the development of mass membership organizations—membership in both the NAACP and trade unions peaked in this period—and the formation of broad political coalitions. Civil rights advocates in this period focused their efforts on electoral action, legislative advocacy, and public education.[10]

Although they achieved very important national victories in this period, including the desegregation of the armed forces and the Supreme Court ruling banning racial covenants in housing, the power of southern congressional delegations for the most part forced northern-based activists to focus their energies on implementing the liberal civil rights policy agenda at the local and state levels. In cities like Philadelphia, black activists and their white allies had put in place large parts of the liberal civil rights agenda, particularly in the area of employment discrimination, by the mid-1950s. With each victory, the city's liberal civil rights community predicted rapid advancement toward their goal of a colorblind city.

The second way that a focus on the Philadelphia movement changes the national civil rights narrative is by reframing the relationship between the southern movement and northern activism during the late 1950s and early 1960s. In those years, local protest movements developed in Philadelphia and elsewhere in the urban North.[11] The Philadelphia movement sustained a series of local civil rights protest campaigns over a multiyear period not because of a desire among the city's black residents to mimic the southern protests but rather because these campaigns were rooted in black Philadelphians' direct experience with the limitations of civil rights liberalism. By the end of the 1950s, it had become clear to a great many black Philadelphians that civil rights liberalism could not fulfill its *promise* of equal opportunity for all. What is crucial here is the gap between what civil rights liberalism had promised and the actual changes it was able to bring to the daily lives of black Philadelphians. African Americans did make significant gains in Philadelphia during the 1950s. The city's antidiscrimination laws opened up to African American workers large numbers of jobs from which they once had been excluded. In particular, the expansion of job opportunities in the public sector made possible the emergence of a sizable home-owning black middle class, often in neighborhoods that whites were abandoning for the suburbs. But few in the city's poor and working-class black communities were able to benefit from these achievements. It turned out that by themselves, bans on explicit racial discrimination in employment and government services and the enforcement efforts of local human relations agencies could not achieve the kinds of structural changes in the local labor and housing markets that advocates of civil rights liberalism had expected. Moreover, the level of municipal investment in antidiscrimination efforts could not compete in their impact with policies that, at every level from the federal government to counties and municipalities and in every region of the country, institutionalized white privilege. In public housing and education, in mortgage subsidies and highway construction, in tax incentive programs for suburban industrial and residential development, in Social Security and immigration policies that excluded farm and domestic workers from the full benefits of citizenship, the preponderance of government activity in the postwar era exacerbated the persistent practice of racial discrimination in local labor and housing markets.[12]

What then emerged in Philadelphia and other northern cities in the early 1960s was a form of civil rights activism that—despite its similarities with the southern movement—constituted a protest movement against the institutions of liberal government for failing to fulfill their commitment to substantive racial equality. While SNCC and the Southern Christian Leadership Conference (SCLC) were appealing for the federal government and the national Democratic Party to intervene on behalf of black citizenship rights in the South, activists in Philadelphia increasingly turned away from state action and biracial coalition politics and toward traditions of black collective action and self-help to achieve substantive advancements in black employment, education, and housing. And while the southern movement proclaimed its belief in the beloved community and a colorblind future, in Philadelphia movement leaders such as Leon Sullivan and Cecil

Moore pursued all-black protest strategies in order to achieve what the city's liberal coalition could not. Twenty years ago, social movement theorist Aldon Morris reconceptualized the narrative of the civil rights movement by arguing that at its core the southern movement was made up of "indigenous" local movements—self-sustaining, locally led movements that were rooted in community-based institutions and employed their own strategies and tactics against local "system[s] of domination."[13] It was just this kind of social movement, albeit one drawing on different local contexts and traditions, that remade racial politics in Philadelphia during the early 1960s.

The third aspect of the civil rights narrative that is transformed by a community study of the Philadelphia movement is our understanding of the reasons for the emergence of Black Power and its impact on the civil rights movement and the broader context of racial politics in United States. In both popular memory and the historical literature of the civil rights movement, Black Power is usually depicted as an outside ideological influence whose incursion into the civil rights movement disrupted the movement's sense of common purpose and goals. Often Black Power activists are described as sacrificing the movement's commitment to mass protest and organizing strategies for the sake of ideological purity and an expressive politics of race pride and unrestrained rage at all things white.[14] Certainly, ideological analysis and debate were important both to the work of national Black Power figures such as Stokely Carmichael and Huey Newton and to many of the local activists who embraced the Black Power project. And there was a kind of psychological liberation at play in what Eddie Glaude has called Black Power's "politics of transvaluation," its subversive reversal of white supremacy's cultural pecking order.[15] What this study seeks to show, however, is that Black Power's cultural and ideological appeal would have meant little had it not provided the basis for the development of alternative movement strategies for challenging racial inequity in American society.[16] Civil rights strategy had been based on the liberal presumption that racism was an unfortunate distortion of American values and institutions and that it could be remedied through specific legal and political reforms. In contrast, the black nationalist tradition viewed racism as constitutive of the American social structure. And therefore, only movement strategies based on intraracial solidarity within the black community, not the goodwill of whites, and committed to the collective advancement of the black community as a whole, not just the liberal vision of equal opportunity and individual advancement, could solve the race problem in America.[17]

Black nationalism, however, served only as the starting point for the strategy and politics of the Black Power movement. Black Power in Philadelphia emerged out of the local experiences of the movement activists who became its most avid proponents. These activists drew on the lessons learned in a decade's worth of movement activism to build a local move-ment that fused a black nationalist analysis of the structures of racism in American society with the southern student movement's commitment to community organizing and indigenous leadership development. As SNCC had in the rural South in the early 1960s, Black Power activists in Philadel-phia sought to build organizations that were accountable solely to the black community and in which leadership was based not on professional degrees or middle-class status but on one's proximity to and ability to identify with poor and working-class blacks. While many historians have argued that the emergence of Black Power led movement activists to abandon their com-mitment to the democratic empowerment of local communities, in Phila-delphia it was Black Power activists who brought what Charles Payne has called "the organizing tradition" into the local movement.[18]

This community study thus confounds the usual narrative of Black Power in another way. As numerous scholars have documented, Black Power ide-ology was deeply patriarchal. Much of its critique of American racism focused on its denial of the fundamental prerogatives of manhood to Afri-can American men. To the extent that black women had been able to forge histories of self-reliance, work outside the home, and political activism, many male black nationalists regarded these aspects of black community life as evidence that white America had denied to black men their rightful roles as leaders and protectors—to the community's overall detriment. Moreover, a central component of the black nationalist critique of the civil rights movement focused on the insufficient manliness of its leadership as reflected in its commitment to nonviolence—even in the face of racist attacks on women and children—and the disproportionate representation of women in the movement's rank and file.[19] In Philadelphia, however, Black Power's masculinist ideology was contradicted by the commitment to community organizing and indigenous leadership. As had been true for SNCC in the rural South, the vast majority of neighborhood leaders with whom Black Power activists worked in Philadelphia were women. Thus, Black Power activists' commitment to promoting community-based leaders contributed to a significant shift in the gender balance of black leadership in Philadelphia. Before the mid-1960s, black political and movement lead-ership in the city had been dominated, with a few extraordinary excep-tions, by men from the black community's professional class. In contrast, the black movement organizations of the late 1960s produced a cohort of neighborhood-based working-class women activists with citywide constitu-encies and influence equivalent to the most prominent of male Black Power leaders.[20]

At its most fundamental, the Black Power movement in Philadelphia challenged the decision-making structures that controlled public and pri-vate investment in the city. Drawing on Malcolm X's call for community control, Black Power advocates argued that decisions that affected the city's black communities should be made within those communities, not in government offices. Philadelphia's Black Power activists faced a number of significant obstacles, including lack of a consistent vision of how a racially just city might look, inconsistent organizational structures, ongoing police surveillance and harassment, and an increasingly powerful and well-organized white conservative backlash against black activism. Still, the city's Black Power movement was able to present a formidable challenge to the weakened, though still powerful, liberal coalition. On issues ranging from public education and urban renewal to police brutality and welfare, advocates of Black Power rejected liberalism's faith in antidiscrimination laws and technocratic government in favor of the principles of community-based leadership, participatory democracy, and racial self-determination.

This study concludes by challenging the view that it was the overheated rhetoric of Black Power, and more generally the rising demands of black activists in the late 1960s and 1970s, that derailed the civil rights movement and contributed to the collapse of the New Deal coalition by precipitating white flight from the Democratic Party. As Thomas Sugrue and others have demonstrated, the roots of white working- and middle-class racial conservatism in the North and West can be found in a political backlash against the liberal civil rights reforms of the 1940s and 1950s, long before the racial militancy of the 1960s. This study of the Philadelphia movement extends this point in three ways: (1) Black Power activists constructed a vital and effective social movement that remade the political and cultural landscape in American cities during the late 1960s and 1970s in ways that postwar liberalism could and did not accomplish; (2) by the early 1970s, Black Power advocates across the ideological spectrum had begun to adopt a common political strategy based on the mobilization of black electoral majorities and pluralities in major urban areas; and (3) the failure of this urban political strategy was as much the product of urban deindustrialization and of suburban antitax politics—historical developments that can be directly traced to postwar liberalism's policy making—as it was the result of a white working-class backlash against the ethnic political strategies of Black Power.

* * *

Up South is divided into three parts. In Part I, "Race, Rights, and Postwar Liberalism," I trace the rise and fall of civil rights liberalism in Philadelphia during the 1940s and 1950s. Chapter 1 describes how black and white liberal activists built a civil rights coalition which, allied with New Deal reformers in the city's Democratic Party, was able to write the principles of nondiscrimination and equal opportunity into the governing charter of the city in 1951. Chapter 2 analyzes the impact of liberal policy making on race and its inability to transform the structure of race relations in the city. Part

II, "A Northern Protest Movement," discusses the reasons for the emergence of a black protest movement against liberalism in Philadelphia. Chapters 3 and 4 describe how local activists, most notably Leon Sullivan and Cecil Moore, drew on black nationalist traditions of collective action and self-reliance, as well as the strategies of the southern protest movement, to channel black Philadelphians' disillusionment with liberalism into a powerful local movement. Chapter 5 then shows how a group of local activists, many of them veterans of the southern movement, forged a vibrant Black Power movement in the city—one that effectively synthesized the black nationalist demand for community control with the grassroots democratic politics of the southern student movement. Finally, in Part III, "Black Power in the Postindustrial City," I analyze the local Black Power movement, its achievements and failures. Chapter 6 discusses efforts to achieve community control over the city's black public schools. Chapter 7 examines the gender politics of Black Power, both its commitment to establishing an explicitly masculinist leadership for the black community and its paradoxical support for the emergence of a new kind of community-based, working-class, and predominantly female leadership within black Philadelphia. Finally, Chapter 8 explores the complex relationship between the local Black Power movement and the War on Poverty and describes how the logic of community control led many Black Power activists to turn to electoral strategies in the 1970s.

*   *   *

"Up South" was the punch line to the many stories black Philadelphians, and their counterparts in other northern cities, told each other about their encounters with racism in the North. Charyn Sutton, a student activist who worked both in interracial movement groups during the early 1960s and in the emerging Black Power movement, describes the Southwest Philadelphia neighborhood in which she grew up as "Up South." In her childhood, racial segregation was enforced not by law, but by the unspoken rules that told you not to walk on that block or go to that public swimming pool. Another veteran of the student movement remembers SNCC activists joking about coming "Up South" when they headed north for a respite from the racial terror of the segregated South. And in his new memoir of his years in the Black Panther Party, Mumia Abu-Jamal described the culture of postwar Philadelphia as more akin to the jim crow South than to our public memory of the North as the promised land of freedom.[21] Racial oppression was, of course, not the same in Philadelphia as it was 'Down South.' Both the forces of racial domination—and the means they used against black people—were different than those faced by African Americans in the South. But to live "Up South" was to confront structures of racial inequality and exclusion on a daily basis. This is the story of the efforts of two generations of black Philadelphians to turn the city of "brotherly love" into a place of promise and opportunity for all.

Part I
Race, Rights, and Postwar Liberalism

Chapter 1
Civil Rights Liberalism in Philadelphia

> Within any given historical period, a particular racial theory is domi-
> nant . . . The dominant racial theory provides society with "common
> sense" about race . . . Challenges to the dominant racial theory emerge
> when . . . the racial policies it prescribes are challenged by political
> movements seeking a different arrangement.
>
> —*Michael Omi and Howard Winant*, Racial Formation in the United
> States

In the political history of Philadelphia, 1951 was a landmark year. In April,
city voters approved a new home rule charter for the city designed to transform the city's patronage-laden municipal government. The new city charter increased the powers of the mayor's and other executive-branch offices,
reduced the size of the city council, and shifted control over the vast majority of municipal jobs from the patronage operations of the city's political
parties to an independent civil service board. The new city charter was also
the first in the nation to include a ban on racial and religious discrimination in city employment, services, and contracts. Then, in the November
municipal elections, the Democratic ticket, headed by patrician reformer
and mayoral candidate Joseph Clark, swept the city's Republican machine
from office for the first time in the twentieth century. To Clark and his
supporters, the landslide victory signified a mandate for an end to municipal corruption, for urban renewal, and for the protection of civil rights for
all Philadelphians.[1]

The centrality of civil rights to the 1951 victories of Philadelphia's liberal
reformers can be explained in a number of ways. First, the civil rights victories can be seen as a product of changes in the structure of local Philadelphia politics, changes brought on by World War II and its aftermath. For
example, the industrial mobilization for World War II transformed the
racial demography of Philadelphia and other northern cities. African
American migrants from the South increased the city's black population by
fifty percent during the 1940s (see Table 1).

While these working-class migrants might seem a natural constituency

TABLE 1. PHILADELPHIA POPULATION, 1930–1950

Year	Total	Per-centage change	White total	White per-centage	White per-centage change	Black total	Black per-centage	Black per-centage change
1930	1,950,961		1,728,417	88.6		219,599	11.3	
1940	1,931,334	−1.0	1,678,577	86.9	−2.9	250,880	13.0	14.2
1950	2,071,605	7.3	1,692,637	81.7	0.8	376,041	18.2	49.9

Source: U.S. Census.

for New Deal Democrats, they were also refugees from the jim crow South where the Democratic Party was the party of segregation. The presence of a well-established Republican Party patronage operation in Philadelphia's black neighborhoods insured continued two-party competition for the city's black vote, thus necessitating a strong racial platform from the Democrats if the party hoped to win black votes in its efforts to unseat the city's Republican machine.[2] At the same time, the emergent anticommunism of the postwar period and, in particular, the growing pressure to demonstrate the superiority of Western-style democracy over Soviet communism to the peoples of the decolonizing third world provided a further incentive for Philadelphia's liberal reformers to embrace the civil rights agenda. To postwar liberals, the persistence of racial segregation in the United States was the Achilles' heel that threatened the nation's standing in the international community.[3]

Second, the 1951 civil rights victories in Philadelphia were the result of four decades of political organizing and legal initiatives undertaken by civil rights advocates. No matter how ripe the postwar political environment was for civil rights reforms, changes in public policy do not just happen; they must be organized. Like the better-known court victories won by the National Association for the Advancement of Colored People (NAACP), the Philadelphia reforms were based on liberals' optimism about the rule of law. Efforts to outlaw racial discrimination, liberals believed, would not only end the practice of racism, they would also enable blacks to enjoy substantive equality in an increasingly prosperous society. They genuinely believed, as Thurgood Marshall is reported to have predicted following the1954 *Brown v. Board of Education* decision, that all evidence of segregation would be eradicated by the time of the centennial of the Emancipation Proclamation in 1963.[4]

While the concept of civil rights as a remedy to racial discrimination and inequality extends back to the adoption of the Fourteenth amendment at the close of the Civil War, the twentieth century drive to establish legal guarantees of equal civil rights for racial minorities begins with the founding of the NAACP in 1909. Historians have rightly focused on the NAACP's efforts to use court challenges to establish a legal basis for overturning the Supreme Court's 1896 *Plessy v. Ferguson* decision upholding separate but equal segregation laws. Throughout its first four decades, however, the NAACP complemented its legal strategy with campaigns to pass civil rights legislation at the federal, state, and local level. For example, the Philadelphia chapter of the NAACP, which was first organized in 1912, joined with other NAACP chapters in the state to press the Pennsylvania state legislature to pass an equal rights bill banning racial discrimination in public accommodations in 1915, only to see the bill vetoed by the state's Republican governor. An NAACP-drafted public accommodations bill was finally enacted in 1935 after the Democrats swept to control over state government with the crucial support of black votes. Fourteen years later, a coalition of liberal civil rights groups convinced Philadelphia's Republican-controlled City Council to pass a fair employment practices ordinance, the city's first significant civil rights legislation. Over the years, these legislative campaigns, in conjunction with the NAACP's legal strategies, contributed to the development of a liberal consensus that legal protections of minority civil rights were the key to establishing racial equality in the United States.[5]

To argue that the civil right victories of 1951 were the product of the confluence of the opportunities created by postwar demographic change and cold war political concerns and four decades of civil rights advocacy in the city does not, however, explain how and why these factors combined to produce the liberal regime of civil rights protections that emerged in Philadelphia. Both black nationalists and advocates of the left-wing Popular Front were an active presence in Philadelphia's black neighborhoods in the immediate postwar years, as was the tradition of black Republicanism with its long-standing criticisms of the Democrats' alliance with southern segregationists. Why then did an overwhelming percentage of the city's black voters place their faith in the Democrats' reform agenda? And how were the Democratic reformers able to convince voters from the city's various New Deal constituencies—not just African Americans but also middle-class white liberals and white working-class Catholic and Jewish voters as well—to support the inclusion of civil rights protections in the new city charter?

Many social movement theorists see a process they call "discursive framing" as crucial to explaining the ability of activists to convert a favorable political context and their organizing activities into substantive achievements. Discursive framing is the process by which activists describe both their plans for changing public policy and why their proposed changes will lead to fundamental improvements in the social order.[6] It occurs not only in the formal pronouncements of organization leaders, but also in the one-on-one recruitment pitches of movement organizers and the informal banter of rank-and-file movement supporters. At their most successful, movement frames represent the movement's goals as a natural response to unacceptable defects in the social and political status quo. What had once been commonplace—for example, the categorization by race of help wanted ads in Philadelphia's daily newspapers—is now represented and decried as a violation of the society's most basic values. And what had once been unimaginable public policy—the regulation of employer advertising in privately owned newspapers by a municipal government agency in this example—becomes a commonsense response to a social ill.

Advocates of civil rights liberalism in postwar Philadelphia produced two distinctive, though related, discursive frames that represented the inclusion of antidiscrimination provisions in the new city charter and other civil rights reforms as essential to establishing a healthy and just city. To black Philadelphians, civil rights activists described the charter's antibias provisions, as well as the Democratic Party's commitment to enforce those provisions, as necessary first steps toward achieving socioeconomic progress for the race. By guaranteeing equal opportunity in the economic marketplace, the new charter and its Democratic proponents would enable black Philadelphians to participate as equals in the city's postwar economy. And to white constituencies within the city's reform coalition, from white middle-class opponents of the patronage system to working-class New Dealers, civil rights proponents depicted the charter's civil rights provisions as a necessary representation of the city and the nation's commitment to the American principles of freedom and democracy. In the context of the cold war competition between the United States and the Soviet Union for the loyalty of the emerging nations of the third world, Philadelphia's treatment of its religious and racial minorities became an issue of international importance. Sadie T. M. Alexander, one of Philadelphia's leading black attorneys and the author of the new charter's civil rights provisions, argued that "a city charter providing equal opportunity for everyone would . . . be the best possible answer to the demagogues of the left and right who exploit discrimination and segregation in the United States and mock our democratic ideals as being so much 'sweet talk.'"[7]

The impact of civil rights liberalism's discursive frames on race relations in Philadelphia went far beyond the electoral victories of 1951. By the 1950s, a new orthodoxy of race was emerging in the city to challenge an older view that saw African Americans' place at the bottom of the socioeconomic and political order as a natural outcome of their racial inferiority. As Michael Omi and Howard Winant have argued, political movements can and do contribute to the transformation of the dominant racial paradigms of a given historical moment.[8] Of course, liberalism's ethic of equal opportunity and colorblindness did not completely displace Social Darwinist notions of black racial inferiority in postwar Philadelphia. As Thomas Sugrue has demonstrated in his account of race relations in postwar Detroit, race prejudice not only remained pervasive in elite, middle- and working-class white neighborhoods in Philadelphia but it was one of the primary causes of the persistence of racial inequality and neighborhood segregation in the city.[9] The persistence of racial prejudice and discrimination in Philadelphia, however, did not prevent civil rights liberalism from emerging as the official race creed of the city in the decade following World War II. The 1951 elections not only certified that protection of the civil rights of racial and religious minorities was a prime function of city government in Philadelphia, but they signaled that the city's political and business elites had accepted the discourse of civil rights, with its emphases on equality under the law, equal opportunity, and colorblindness, as the commonsense response to the changing racial demography of the city.

What was not clear, however, in the events of 1951 was how these changes in racial language and policies would affect actual racial practices in the city. This chapter examines how civil rights liberalism became the racial orthodoxy in postwar Philadelphia. In the following chapter, I will discuss the impact of this new racial paradigm on government and business practices in the city and what difference it made in the everyday lives of black Philadelphians.

Black Philadelphia Before 1940

Before World War I, the African American population of Philadelphia was divided between a small elite made up of professionals, small business owners, and domestic servants to the city's leading white families and a much larger group of unskilled and often intermittently employed laborers. According to Sadie Tanner Mossell, the first black woman to receive a Ph.D. from the University of Pennsylvania and a member of one the city's leading black families, the city's "relatively small population of Negroes of culture, education, and some financial means . . . had always enjoyed the same social and education facilities as the whites, and courteous treatment from them." During the 1890s, many of these families were able to move across the Schuylkill River from Center City into newly built middle-class residential areas north of Market Street in West Philadelphia. The majority of black Philadelphians, however, resided in the city's oldest and poorest neighborhoods, particularly the Fourth, Fifth, Seventh, and Eighth wards on the southern border between Center City and South Philadelphia, where they lived, in the words of historian John Bauman, in "moldering roosts that honeycombed sweltering courts and narrow alleys."[10]

Before 1900, the small size of Philadelphia's black community constrained its ability to influence local politics. The 39,371 black Philadelphians counted by the 1890 census constituted only 3.8 percent of the city's population (see Table 2). Within twenty years, however, the city's black population had more than doubled to 84,459, 5.5 percent of the total population. The onset of World War I and the resulting labor shortage in the

TABLE 2. PHILADELPHIA POPULATION, 1890–1930

Year	Total	Per-centage change	White total	White per-centage	White per-centage change	Black total	Black per-centage	Black per-centage change
1890	1,046,964		1,006,590	96.1		39,371	3.8	
1900	1,293,697	23.6	1,229,673	95.1	22.2	62,613	4.8	59.0
1910	1,549,088	19.7	1,463,371	94.5	19.0	84,459	5.5	34.9
1920	1,823,779	17.7	1,688,180	92.6	15.4	134,229	7.4	58.9
1930	1,950,961	7.0	1,728,417	88.6	2.4	219,599	11.3	63.6

Source: U.S. Census.

city led to even more rapid growth in Philadelphia's black population. During the three years of American involvement in the war, the Pennsylvania and Erie Railroads actively recruited southern black workers to fill job openings in the city's defense-related industries. Between 1916 and 1918, 40,000 black southerners arrived in the city. Among the city's industrial producers, Midvale Steel hired 4,000 black workers during the war years, Atlantic Refining 1,000, and Franklin Sugar 700. By 1920, the city's black population had risen to 134,229, a 59 percent increase in just ten years.[11]

While African Americans represented only 7.4 percent of the city's population in 1920, the wartime in-migration of black southerners strained the racialized boundaries of working-class life in the city. As the growing black population sought improved job opportunities in the city's wartime industries and better housing outside of the city's overcrowded black slums, they were met with rising levels of white violence. For three days during the summer of 1917, groups of white rioters, including white sailors in military uniform, terrorized the black residents of Chester, Pennsylvania, an industrial suburb fifteen miles south of Philadelphia. Later that year, a black man who had just been hired to work at the South Philadelphia naval shipyard was lynched by a white mob whose members included uniformed soldiers. The following summer, mob attacks on black families who were attempting to move into neighborhoods near the shipyard left three whites and one black dead and many more injured.[12]

W. E. B. Du Bois and other NAACP leaders viewed World War I as an opportunity to demonstrate the race's fitness for full citizenship in American society. In the pages of The Crisis, the NAACP magazine, Du Bois urged African Americans to "forget our special grievances and close our ranks shoulder to shoulder with our fellow-citizens and the allied nations that are fighting for democracy." The racial violence that greeted black veterans returning from the war effectively deflated the hope that wartime patriotism would strike a blow against racial hatred. During the Red Summer of

1919, black soldiers were among the most prominent targets of the race riots that swept Chicago, Washington, D.C., Omaha, and Knoxville as well as the lynch mobs that terrorized African American communities throughout the South.[13]

Among the city's black elite, there was a marked ambivalence about the black southern migrants to the city. Sadie Tanner Mossell, in her 1921 essay, argued that "the increase in [black] population by a group generally uneducated and untrained" was the prime reason that the local black elite had begun to lose its access to the city's leading social and educational institutions. Still, as W. E. B. Du Bois documented in *The Philadelphia Negro*, the city's black elite was tied to the community's working-class majority by a web of interlocking churches, fraternal and social organizations, and political clubhouses. For example, the Citizens' Republican Club, the political clubhouse which delivered South Philadelphia's black working-class vote to the Republican machine in return for low-level patronage jobs, beer, and gambling, also served as a base for the civil rights activities of Arthur Mossell, Sadie Tanner Mossell's father and the city's leading black attorney. Moreover, members of the Philadelphia black elite organized a number of groups to provide services to, and defend the interests of, the growing number of black migrants to the city. In 1905, women activists formed the Philadelphia Association for the Protection of Colored Women to aid women in domestic service. Two years later, the Armstrong Association, which would become the local affiliate of the Urban League, was established to assist the migrants' efforts to find work in local industry. During the war, two progressive-era reform organizations, the Octavia Hill Association, a South Philadelphia settlement house, and the Philadelphia Housing Association worked to relieve overcrowding in black neighborhoods by pressing landlords to renovate tenements and to open up previously segregated areas near the city's defense plants to black families. And following the 1917 lynching of the naval shipyard worker, the Philadelphia NAACP successfully pressed for an end to segregated eating arrangements at the shipyard.[14]

As with the national organization, the Philadelphia chapter was founded by a coalition of socially prominent white reformers and African American professionals. Charter members of the Philadelphia branch included R. R. Wright Jr., the head of the black-owned Citizens and Southern Bank and Trust, Drs. J. Max Barber, Nathan Mossell, W. A. Sinclair, and Mrs. Frances Bartholomew. Elwood Heacock, the secretary of the Quaker Abolition Society, served as the branch's first president and then was succeeded by Dr. Barber. Among the branch's early financial supporters were the prominent Jewish philanthropists Dr. Jacob Billikopf and William Rosenwald. In addition to lobbying for the civil rights bill in the state legislature, the branch also convinced local movie houses not to show D. W. Griffith's *Birth of a Nation*, which depicted the Ku Klux Klan as saving the South from black misrule, and unsuccessfully pressed the Philadelphia Board of Education to employ black teachers at the junior and senior high school level. Branch members also organized fund-raising campaigns "to pay a fitting tribute to the memory of John Brown" and to support the national organization's legal defense of Dr. Ossian Sweet, a Detroit physician charged with murder for firing on a white mob that had surrounded the home that his family had purchased in an all-white neighborhood.[15]

The end of World War I once again closed off most of Philadelphia's industrial jobs to black workers. By 1927, only 6.1 percent of the city's black wage earners were employed in Philadelphia's industrial sector, including the many textile factories that had relied on black workers during the war. Still, African American migrants continued to flow into Philadelphia during the 1920s. By 1930, Philadelphia's black population had grown to 219,599, a 63.6 percent increase since 1920 (Table 2). Blacks now constituted 11.3 percent of the city population, up from 7.4 percent ten years earlier. Common laborers constituted 27 percent of black male workers, while 20 percent were employed as waiters, chauffeurs, cleaners, or porters. And 52 percent of black women workers were employed in domestic service.[16]

Population growth, however, did not lead to increased political clout. In 1899, W. E. B. Du Bois described the city's black vote as "the tool of the Republicans." In Du Bois's view, the city's black Republican clubs delivered voters to the polls in return for a disproportionately small share of the Republican machine's political patronage. In 1920, the Republicans finally agreed to slate black candidates in two state legislative districts in Philadelphia. As a result, John Asbury, an attorney, and Andrew Stevens, an insurance agent, became the first blacks to be elected to the Pennsylvania legislature. Rather than demonstrating increased black political clout within the city's Republican machine, however, Asbury and Stevens's short political careers proved an object lesson in the party's refusal to address black concerns. Shortly after their arrival in Harrisburg, the two black legislators sought to reintroduce the NAACP-drafted civil rights bill banning segregated public accommodations that Republican governor Mark G. Brumbaugh had vetoed in 1915. However, U.S. senators Boies Penrose and William Vare, who controlled the state and city Republican organizations respectively, opposed Asbury and Stevens's effort, reportedly at the request of the state's hotel and restaurant industry. In 1924, Penrose and Vare forced Asbury and Stevens to agree not to run for reelection, reportedly because they had refused to stop promoting the civil rights legislation, and replaced them with two more pliable black politicians. Still, the Citizens' Republican Club continued to deliver the black vote to the Republican machine through the 1920s. In 1928, for example, Republican presidential candidate Herbert Hoover received 82.1 percent of the vote in election precincts with at least 90 percent black population. So long as Republican candidates continued to receive overwhelming support from the city's black voters, the party felt little pressure to respond to black demands.[17]

The Origins of Civil Rights Liberalism

The NAACP was founded at the end of a period that historians have long called the nadir of postemancipation African American history. Following the collapse of Reconstruction, a consensus emerged in white America that the attempt to integrate blacks into the nation's civic and political institutions had been a mistake. In 1896, the U.S. Supreme Court ruled, in the *Plessy v. Ferguson* case, that the establishment of separate but equal public facilities for blacks and whites did not violate the Fourteenth Amendment's ban on racial discrimination. At the same time, Social Darwinism and other forms of "scientific" knowledge about innate racial differences provided intellectual justification for the exclusion of blacks from the American polity. In the South, black voters who had provided crucial support to the Reconstruction state governments were disfranchised through a combination of racial terror and restrictive suffrage laws. At the same time, films like *Birth of a Nation* naturalized the practice of racism for the nation by depicting blacks as inherently ignorant, amoral, shiftless, and sexually promiscuous.[18]

It was in this political and racial context that the NAACP was founded to pursue government protection of full constitutional rights for black Americans solely on the basis of their citizenship, not on the relative "fitness" of the race. Delegates to the 1909 National Negro Conference that led to the NAACP's founding resolved "that the Constitution be strictly enforced and the civil rights guaranteed under the Fourteenth Amendment be secured impartially to all . . . [and] that in accordance with the Fifteenth Amendment the right of the Negro to the ballot . . . be recognized in every part of the country." It was this constitutionalist stand—that blacks and other racial minorities benefit more from efforts to protect individual rights than from efforts to promote group interests—that came to form the core of civil rights liberalism. More than ninety years later, it is easy to underestimate how remarkable was the claim that the NAACP was making. The most dominant black figure of the time, Booker T. Washington, explicitly rejected the pursuit of political and civil rights in favor of a strategy of industrial education and economic self-help. Even W. E. B. Du Bois accepted the prevailing wisdom of contemporary race theory with its division of human beings into distinct races with shared physical, intellectual, and even cultural characteristics.[19]

A debate that took place in Pennsylvania throughout the 1920s over whether blacks should seek the total desegregation of the state's public education system or the creation of a system of state-supported black institutions from the elementary to postsecondary levels exemplifies the fierce divisions created by the NAACP's integrationist position. Even as the NAACP sought to define desegregation as the essential first step toward a racially just society, other black voices argued that the establishment of separate, black-controlled institutions capable of increasing the educational and economic capacities of the black community as a whole were essential to the progress of the race. While no black leaders publicly endorsed state-mandated school segregation, supporters of state support for designated black schools argued that such schools created job opportunities for black educators and a healthier learning environment for black students. In 1920, Leslie Pinckney Hill, the president of the Institute for Colored Youth, a Quaker-founded normal school (teachers' college), successfully lobbied for the school's conversion into Cheyney State College, a state-supported training institute for black teachers. Writing in *The Crisis*, Hill argued for "the right of any group of Negroes to organize by themselves . . . for any proper ends which they themselves may voluntarily choose to further. This right of self-determination is the very essence of democracy." Hill's critics in the NAACP responded that the establishment of Cheyney as a state-supported institution would only serve to justify the exclusion of black students from the rest of the state university system. Despite losing the battle over Cheyney, by the 1930s the Philadelphia NAACP would largely succeed in convincing the city's black educators to abandon their support for all-black elementary schools.[20]

During its first two decades, the NAACP experimented with a broad range of strategies for achieving these constitutional protections, from legislative and public education campaigns to legal defenses of figures like Dr. Ossian Sweet. In many ways, the NAACP's most visible initiative during the 1920s was its unsuccessful drive to pressure Congress to pass a federal anti-lynching law. However, the near-total exclusion of black voters from the electoral arena, and the hegemonic role of race science in justifying that exclusion, eventually led the NAACP to focus on the courts as the branch of government most responsive to the constitutional claims of a disenfranchised racial minority. Organized in 1912, the NAACP's National Legal Committee actively sought out cases conducive to constitutional challenges to racial discrimination. A grant from the American Fund for Public Service enabled the organization to hire Charles Hamilton Houston, the dean of Howard University Law School, in 1934 to coordinate a nationwide legal attack on segregation. For the next three decades, the NAACP pursued a legal strategy that sought to force the courts to enforce the Supreme Court's separate but equal standard in public education and other public facilities in order to demonstrate to the country's judicial and political establishment that such a standard was unattainable in the real world.[21]

The Great Depression and Black Politics in Philadelphia

Equally important to the development of civil rights liberalism were political developments in northern cities like Philadelphia during the Great

Depression. The popularity of President Roosevelt's New Deal within African American communities enabled the Democrats to break the Republicans' hold on the northern black vote. The first sign that a growing proportion of Philadelphia's black voters were willing to break from the party of Lincoln came during the 1932 presidential election. Despite the near-unanimous support of the black elite, Herbert Hoover's proportion of the city's black vote fell from 82.1 to 70.5 percent. With the black unemployment rate in the city at 56 percent, 26.7 percent of Philadelphia's black voters pulled the lever for Franklin Roosevelt. The fact that more than one in four black voters was willing to resist the blandishments of the Republican machine provided a new generation of aspiring black politicians with the opportunity to press for greater concessions from both of the city's major parties. In 1933, the Rev. Marshall Shepard, a Baptist minister from West Philadelphia, organized a group of black community leaders to demand greater black representation on the local electoral slates of each party. The group first approached Senator Vare, a testament to the Republicans' continuing domination of the city's political structure. Vare, however, refused the group's request to slate a black candidate for a position on the city's municipal court, telling the delegation that black voters would never abandon the Republicans.[22]

Shepard and his supporters decided to take up Vare's challenge. "Mr. Vare thinks blacks in this city don't have enough sense to switch parties," Shepard told a protest meeting, "now is the time to show him that he is mistaken." Each of the city's black newspapers endorsed Shepard's call for black Philadelphians to vote Democratic. The following year, Shepard was elected to the state legislature on the Democratic ticket, beginning a thirty-year career as one of the city's leading black Democrats. Shepard's victory was part of a revival of the Democratic Party in Philadelphia and across the state. That year, New Dealers led by John B. Kelly, a millionaire contractor and the father of actress Grace Kelly, won control of the city's Democratic organization from a Vare ally who had run the party as an appendage of the Republican machine. A year later, the Democrats swept both the governor's office and the state legislature for the first time since the 1890s. Eager to solidify their support among the state's black voters, the Democrats then pushed through the state legislature the NAACP-drafted ban on segregation in public accommodations nearly twenty years after Governor Brumbaugh first vetoed it. The Democrats also greatly increased the number of blacks appointed to state and federal patronage positions. According to one newspaper report, black political leaders claimed to have received more patronage positions from the Democrats in two years than the black community had received from the Republicans in more than forty. In 1936, the Roosevelt administration signaled its recognition of the increasing importance of northern black voters by asking Shepard to give the invocation at the 1936 Democratic National Convention in Philadelphia, making him the first African American to speak to a Democratic convention.[23]

Over the course of the 1930s, Philadelphia's black citizens rewarded the Democrats for their efforts with a growing proportion of their votes. In 1935, John B. Kelly, the Democratic candidate for mayor, received 44.2 percent of the city's black vote and narrowly lost the election amid widespread charges of Republican vote stealing. African American enthusiasm for the New Deal translated into even higher levels of black support for Democratic candidates for state and national offices. In both the 1936 and 1940 campaigns, President Roosevelt received 68 percent of black votes cast in Philadelphia. The Democratic candidates for governor and the U.S. Senate each won 57 percent of Philadelphia's black vote in 1938. The growth in support for Democratic candidates was matched by large increases in the number and percentage of registered black voters in the city. In 1932 only 46 percent of black adults were registered to vote in Philadelphia; by 1940 that figure had grown to 82 percent.[24]

Black support for the Roosevelt administration was largely a function of the New Deal's programs for the poor. Millions of black workers benefited from participation in New Deal programs like the Works Progress Administration (WPA) and from the commitment of the newly formed Congress of Industrial Organizations (CIO) to organize all workers into industrial trade unions, irrespective of race. Still, black Philadelphians continued to suffer disproportionately from the Depression. In 1939, 60 percent of the city's black residents were eligible for poor relief or public assistance, 89 percent of the city's black households were renters as compared to only 54 percent of white households, and 51 percent of black renters lived in substandard housing as opposed to only 14 percent of white renters.[25]

The popularity of the New Deal in black communities did not, however, translate into significant improvements in federal racial policy. As a number of scholars have shown, federal, state, and local officials, with few exceptions, implemented New Deal programs in ways that upheld and even reinforced existing racial inequities. Concerned that any explicit challenge to southern segregationist practices would result in a loss of southern Democratic support for the New Deal in Congress, the Roosevelt administration for the most part allowed local officials to administer the new federal programs with a minimum of interference. As a result, black sharecroppers in the South received little or no benefit from the 1934 Agricultural Adjustment Act and the 1935 Social Security Act explicitly excluded sharecroppers and domestic workers, two largely black occupations, from its provisions.[26]

Racial discriminatory patterns were also evident in the administration of federal programs in the North. While Secretary of the Interior Harold Ickes insisted that blacks share equally in the federal government's new public housing program, he also mandated that individual housing projects should reflect the "prevailing racial composition of the surrounding neighborhood." Moreover, as Thomas Sugrue has argued, "federal housing policy gave official sanction to discriminatory real estate sales and bank lending practices." Under the terms of the 1934 Federal Housing Act, federal officials worked with local real estate professionals and bankers to determine which neighborhoods would be eligible for federally insured home mortgages based on the quality and condition of the housing stock and the racial, ethnic, and economic homogeneity of the neighborhood population. In urban areas throughout the North, neighborhoods where there was even the possibility of racial integration were determined to be too risky for federal mortgage assistance.[27]

Still, it was clear by the end of the 1930s that the elite consensus that had sanctioned the attenuation of black citizenship rights in the years since Reconstruction was finally collapsing. No event better symbolized the shift in the nation's official racial discourse than the controversy over the Daughters of the American Revolution's refusal to allow Marian Anderson, the black contralto from Philadelphia, to perform in Constitution Hall in Washington, D.C. When Eleanor Roosevelt responded by resigning her membership in the DAR and her husband then agreed to sanction an NAACP plan to organize a concert for Anderson on the steps of the Lincoln Memorial, African Americans felt their faith in the Roosevelts rewarded.[28]

While black support for the New Deal did not lead to significant advances on racial issues during the Depression, two related political developments in northern cities like Philadelphia did advance the liberal civil rights agenda during the 1930s. First, there was the emerging alliance between the NAACP and white liberal activists from the city's Protestant and Jewish communities. Before the Depression, Philadelphia's white liberal communities had demonstrated little interest in racial issues, despite the financial support that the local NAACP branch had received from prominent figures in the city's Quaker and Jewish communities. Thus, leaders of the Philadelphia Housing Association (PHA), one of the city's most respected progressive reform organizations, had long accepted racial segregation as a necessary component of both public and private efforts to improve the city's low-income housing stock. As late as 1935, for example, the PHA's executive director Bernard Newman proposed "a separate slum clearance [program] in a Negro district, the new housing in which will be for Negroes." Others in the city's white liberal communities, however, became increasingly concerned during the 1930s that the Depression was leading to a dangerous rise in "antiblack sentiment" in the area. Leaders of the Friends Committee on Race Relations (FCRR), a Quaker agency, and the Race Relations Department of the Protestant Philadelphia Council of Churches (PCC) therefore began an effort to involve the city's Protestant congregations in efforts to combat racial segregation in local public accommodations. When their initial efforts to organize church members produced few results, the religious leaders shifted their focus to Protestant youth groups. In 1931, the FCRR and the PCC jointly formed the Young People's Interracial Fellowship (YPIF) as a forum for young people from black and white congregations to meet to discuss solutions to interracial tensions in the city.[29]

YPIF's emphasis on intergroup dialogue and study was rooted in the liberal Protestant belief that the roots of prejudice lay in ignorance and that education was the key to building intergroup harmony and understanding. In 1934, Marjorie Penney, a Methodist who had joined the group two years earlier, was named YPIF's first full-time director. Under her leadership, the "Fellowshipers," as they were called, developed an educational program to counter racial and religious prejudice in the city. According to Penney, the strategy was "to reach out and teach . . . people of all ages and all backgrounds who could reach and teach others and so help create communities where prejudice and discrimination gave way to opportunities and equal rights for all." In the late 1930s, YPIF acquired an old firehouse on Girard Avenue in the heart of North Philadelphia to serve as a center for intergroup relations training programs. Adopting the model of a settlement house, YPIF then changed its name to Fellowship House.[30]

At the same time, the Fellowshipers recognized that there were some threats to intergroup harmony that needed a more prompt response than educational programs could provide. In the latter half of the 1930s, membership in Philadelphia-area pro-fascist and racist groups grew significantly. According to a 1938 FBI estimate, there were eighty-three anti-Semitic and KKK-affiliated groups with ten thousand members in the Philadelphia area. That year, the Philadelphia NAACP, YPIF, FCRR, and the PCC joined with the newly formed Jewish Community Relations Council (JCRC) to form the Tolerance Clearing House to coordinate opposition to the growing racist and anti-Semitic organizing in the region. Founded by Maurice Fagan, a local schoolteacher, the JCRC's mission was to promote greater cooperation between the city's Jewish community and non-Jewish organizations committed to promoting interreligious and interracial understanding. While the Tolerance Clearing House lasted only a few months before it was derailed by disagreements over whether to include left-wing organizations associated with the Communist Party's Popular Front, the effort to establish the coalition set the stage for increased cooperation between a wide variety of secular and religious civil rights groups on efforts to achieve the liberal civil rights agenda.[31]

The second important political development during the 1930s was the increasing involvement of the socialist left in racial activism. African American participation in the American left grew significantly in the aftermath of the post World War I race riots, the 1918 Bolshevik revolution, and the collapse of Marcus Garvey's United Negro Improvement Association

(UNIA). The decision of the Soviet-led Communist International (Comintern) to define African Americans living in the Black Belt of the Deep South as an oppressed nation deserving of self-determination attracted both prominent black radicals and rank-and-file workers to the party. With the onset of the Depression, communist organizers built a growing following of unemployed black workers in both northern and southern cities and of black sharecroppers in the rural South. In particular, the party's vigorous defense of nine black teenagers falsely charged with rape in Scottsboro, Alabama, in 1931 earned it a national reputation for its commitment to racial equality.[32]

The rise of fascist movements in Europe, however, led to a major shift in communist strategy in the mid-1930s. While the Comintern had previously rejected cooperation with liberals and noncommunist leftists, it now promoted common cause with a broad range of progressive forces against the worldwide growth of fascism. During what became known as the Popular Front period, which lasted until the Hitler-Stalin pact of 1939, the Communist Party found allies among African American intellectuals and activists who were simultaneously critical of the NAACP for its failure to engage the black working-class in mass protest and impressed by the work of communist-affiliated organizations on issues like the Scottsboro case. In 1936, for example, the Communist Party endorsed and helped to organize the founding conference of the National Negro Congress (NNC). The brainchild of African American intellectuals and New Deal activists Ralph Bunche and John Davis, the NNC sought to unite a broad range of church, fraternal, labor, and civil rights organizations on a program of militant action against racial discrimination and support for the emerging multiracial industrial unions.[33]

During the second half of the 1930s, Philadelphia was a hotbed of left-wing antiracist activism. The chairperson of the Philadelphia affiliate of the NNC was Dr. Arthur Huff Fauset, an elementary school principal and member of one of the city's elite black families. In addition, a number of black Philadelphians served on the NNC's National Executive Committee, including Russell Watson, a black member of the Philadelphia branch of the Communist Party, and his wife Goldie Watson, a public schoolteacher. In 1937, the Philadelphia NNC played host to the NNC's second national congress. In addition, the Philadelphia NNC worked with two other Popular Front groups in the city, the Workers' Alliance and International Labor Defense, to organize a Tenants' League of slum dwellers to press for improvements in the housing stock in low-income neighborhoods and expansion of the city's public housing program. The desire of groups like the NNC to join the Tolerance Clearing House reflected both the strong similarities between their program of racial reform and the liberal civil rights agenda. Despite its ideological commitment to revolutionary social change, the left's support for desegregation and antibias legislation made the Popular Front's racial program virtually indistinguishable from civil rights liberalism.[34]

World War II and the Rise of Civil Rights Liberalism

It was during World War II that civil rights issues emerged as a major liberal priority. Nazi anti-Semitism and racialism destroyed what remained of scientific racism's political and intellectual respectability among the nation's elites. The release in 1944 of *An American Dilemma*, Swedish economist Gunnar Myrdal's study of American race relations solidified colorblind constitutionalism as the liberal orthodoxy on race. Commissioned by the Carnegie Corporation, Myrdal's encyclopedic study argued that the country's "black problem" lay not in the physical, mental, and cultural attributes of black bodies, but in "the minds of white Americans." According to Myrdal, the question was not whether blacks had the capacity for citizenship, but whether white Americans were prepared to live up to their national creed.[35]

Still, the liberal reaction against Hitler's racial policies would have had little impact on domestic racism had it not been for the persistent activism of the black community and its allies. In contrast to the NAACP's position in World War I, liberal civil rights advocates adopted the Double-V strategy during World War II, calling for victory over fascism abroad and racial bigotry at home. Even before the Japanese attack on Pearl Harbor, A. Philip Randolph initiated a nationwide drive to demand an end to racial segregation in the armed forces and the emerging defense industries. Having left the NNC, Randolph formed the March on Washington Movement (MOWM) to organize an all-black march on the nation's capital for June 1941. Concerned that such a march would disrupt the war effort, President Roosevelt quickly agreed to negotiations with Randolph and the NAACP. On June 25, 1941, just six days before the scheduled march, the president issued Executive Order 8802 banning racial discrimination in defense industries and establishing the President's Fair Employment Practices Committee (FEPC) to investigate and publicize discrimination complaints. In return, Randolph agreed to cancel the march. Though the FEPC lacked direct enforcement powers and was forced to rely on persuasion and publicity to remedy cases of racial bias in defense plants, the commission quickly became the focus of wartime civil rights advocacy.[36]

In wartime Philadelphia, both liberal and left-wing activists renewed their effort to establish a coalition of organizations working against racial and religious bigotry. On October 11, 1941, the JCRC's Maurice Fagan and Marjorie Penney of Fellowship House joined with representatives from the Philadelphia Council of Churches and the Friends Committee on Race Relations to establish the Philadelphia Fellowship Commission (FC). The purpose of the new organization would be to promote "intergroup understanding and equal treatment and opportunity for all racial, religious and nationality groups." Fagan volunteered to serve as the commission's unpaid executive director even as he continued to work as the JCRC's full-time and salaried director. Although the Philadelphia NAACP was not represented at this initial meeting, the local branch soon became the commission's fifth "constituent" or founding agency. In its first two decades, the FC grew to include nine constituent agencies, a board of fifty-four, five hundred cooperating organizations, and five thousand individual members.[37]

The Hitler-Stalin pact of 1939 and the subsequent left-wing opposition to U.S. involvement in the "European" war brought about a lull in left-wing civil rights activity in the city. With the collapse of the pact in 1941 following the German invasion of the Soviet Union, Arthur Fauset set out to reorganize the Philadelphia NNC and its Popular Front approach to racial reform. Delegates to a September 1943 conference on the "war and post-war problems of the Negro in Philadelphia" adopted a new name for the group, the United People's Action Coalition (UPAC). With Fauset as its chairman, the UPAC called on "people's organizations, trade unions, [and] civic organizations" to join its efforts to make the city "the strong citadel of democracy it was intended to be."[38]

Philadelphia's civil rights community, including the UPAC, the local NAACP, and the Fellowship Commission's Council for Equal Job Opportunity (CEJO), focused its wartime efforts on fighting racial discrimination in the local defense industry. At a July 1942 conference on "the integration of colored workers into the [local] war effort," a representative of the local Urban League charged that a number of local firms, including Bendix Aviation, refused to hire blacks to any skilled positions; others, including General Electric, only hired enough black workers "to satisfy government regulations," and still others, including Philco and Westinghouse, failed to train or upgrade the black workers they did hire. That month, a CIO local union charged that a private contractor at the U.S. Army's Frankford Arsenal fired thirteen "Negro girls" after the women workers complained of racially discriminatory treatment. In October 1942, civil rights groups filed a complaint with President Roosevelt's FEPC, charging that Bendix Aviation had placed an order to the federal government's United States Employment Service (USES) for "light-skinned" women to work as matrons. Earlier, Sun Shipbuilding in Chester, south of Philadelphia, had announced plans to hire 9,000 black workers but to maintain a rigidly segregated workplace.[39]

Black maintenance workers at the Philadelphia Transit Company (PTC) filed the most significant complaint with the FEPC. The PTC workers charged that the company refused to hire blacks to the positions of "motorman" or conductor on the company's trolleys and subway cars. The company did employ 537 black maintenance workers out of a total work-force of 11,000. Shortly after the maintenance workers filed their complaint, the local NAACP invited members of both CEJO and UPAC to join an "Action Committee" to promote the cause of the PTC workers. Even after the FEPC issued two directives ordering the PTC to employ black motormen and conductors and the Wartime Manpower Commission ruled that the company was an essential wartime service provider and therefore must establish nondiscriminatory employment policies, the company continued to refuse to hire blacks for what it called platform jobs. The Philadelphia Rapid Transit Employees Union (PRTEU) actively supported the company's segregated employment practices and its refusal to comply with the government order. Only after a rival union, the CIO-affiliated Transport Workers Union (TWU), ousted the PRTEU in a labor representation election in March 1944 and insisted that the company include a nondiscrimination clause in its collective bargaining agreement did the PTC agree to train eight black motormen.[40]

The black trainees were scheduled to begin their new duties on August 1, 1944. On that day, however, a group of white employees began a wildcat strike with the support of the now-displaced PRTEU leadership. Initially, the strike only involved a small group of workers. The PTC, however, quickly decided to shut down its entire operation, suggesting that the company and its former union had jointly planned the strike. The shutdown had an immediate impact on a city in which wartime rationing of gasoline forced even those defense workers who owned cars to use public transit to commute to and from work. According to one newspaper, military production in the city declined by more than 50 percent after the strike's first day. By the end of the day, the National War Labor Board and the secretaries of the army and the navy had all ordered the strikers to return to work. The strike, however, continued for a second day. On August 3, President Roosevelt authorized Secretary of War Henry Stimson to seize control of the transit company. The strike leaders, however, refused to call off the strike after the War Department made it clear that it intended to continue the black training program. On August 4, the streetcars were still running at only 30 percent capacity. Finally, on August 5, Stimson ordered the arrest of four strike leaders for violating the wartime ban on strikes in defense industries. In addition, the War Department announced that PTC workers who did not appear for work on Monday, August 7, would risk having their draft deferments and their defense industry work permits revoked. Ninety percent of the PTC's employees arrived for work on Monday morning. Five days after it started, the PTC strike was over.[41]

For a week, however, racial tensions had divided the city. Groups of hostile whites rampaged through the city's black neighborhoods; crowds of black youth retaliated by breaking the windows of white-owned businesses and by attacking whites in cars in black neighborhoods in North and South Philadelphia. Eleven people had to be hospitalized and more than three hundred were arrested on the first day of the strike alone. Throughout the week, the NAACP and Fellowship Commission worked hard to prevent full-scale racial rioting from breaking out, while charging that "the Mayor of the city made himself unavailable, and his 'Interracial Committee' refused to meet." All told, the two groups distributed 100,000 copies of a leaflet and recruited fifty civic groups to sign a newspaper advertisement calling on Philadelphians to support the FEPC order.[42]

The successful campaign against the PTC strike provided a tremendous boost to civil rights groups in Philadelphia. The Philadelphia NAACP reached a membership peak of 16,700 in 1945. And Maurice Fagan credited the effort to prevent a race riot with enabling the Fellowship Commission to achieve "a degree of cooperation" among its member groups that it had lacked previously. "The agencies," he would argue later, "found a process whereby they could come together to agree where they could, disagree where they couldn't, but to find out why, in such cases, they couldn't agree." Following the PTC strike, the Fellowship Commission was able to raise funds to purchase a small Center City office building at 260 South Fifteenth Street to house the commission's offices as well as those of the Philadelphia chapters of the NAACP, the JCRC, and the American Civil Liberties Union (ACLU). The building, Fagan believed, was crucial to the Fellowship Commission's emergence as a permanent coalition of the city's leading civil rights and civil liberties groups.[43]

At the same time, the PTC victory solidified a renewed alliance between the liberal and Popular Front wings of the local civil rights movement. For the next two years, liberal and left activists worked together on campaigns to establish permanent fair employment practices committees at the federal, state, and municipal levels. On September 15, 1945, the Bi-Partisan Committee for a Pennsylvania FEPC, whose members included the Philadelphia NAACP, the Fellowship Commission's Council for Equal Job Opportunity (CEJO), and prominent left-wing activists like Arthur Fauset and local Communist Party lawyer Morris Shafritz sponsored a public meeting to call for a federal FEPC that featured a keynote speech from left-wing congressman Vito Marcantonio of the American Labor Party. The executive secretary of the Bi-Partisan Committee was former national NNC board member Goldie Watson. Two months later, Republican city councilman Louis Schwartz announced that he was sponsoring a municipal FEPC ordinance on behalf of a "Citizens Committee" that included Shafritz and Watson along with representatives of the NAACP, CEJO, and the local chapter of the American Jewish Committee (AJC). And on November 29, the local NAACP and AJC chapters sponsored another mass meeting to protest the closing of the federal FEPC's Philadelphia regional office and to demand that the U.S. Congress pass FEPC legislation. Speakers at the meeting included Councilman Schwartz, Arthur Fauset, and Charles Shorter of the Philadelphia NAACP.[44]

The left-liberal FEPC alliance of 1944 and 1945 demonstrates the extent to which the Popular Front had come to accept the liberal argument that the constitutional guarantee of individual rights was the key to ending racial inequality in the United States. Like civil rights liberals, the left believed that passage of antidiscrimination legislation and court tests of jim crow practices were the key to ending racial discrimination in public accommodations, employment, education, and housing. However, this agreement on goals could not mask significant differences in the postwar liberal and Popular Front strategies for achieving a colorblind society, differences that were evident in the lessons drawn from the PTC victory. In a column written a month after the abortive PTC strike, Arthur Fauset wrote that the victory proved that mass action was the key to "we Negroes" becoming "first-class citizens." Comparing civil rights advocates to "John Hancock, Benjamin Franklin and George Washington," Fauset concluded that "if we would be free—that is, if we would be first class Americans— then we must willingly pay the price of believing that we are Americans, whether this be shrunken bellies, depleted purses or even . . . smeared reputations." This belief in the necessity of mass action was evident in UPAC's public campaigns for fair employment practices laws, defense reconversion, public housing construction, the continuation of wartime price controls, and peace with the Soviet Union.[45]

In contrast, the liberal leadership of the NAACP and the Fellowship Commission viewed the PTC campaign as proof that there were two keys to achieving racial progress in Philadelphia: discreet lobbying by human relations professionals and their middle-class supporters for incremental gains for black workers, and second, the careful maintenance of interracial peace in the city's working-class neighborhoods. In the PTC campaign, the black transit workers and their supporters in the NAACP and the Fellowship Commission had made deliberately modest demands. Rather than seek a complete overhaul of the PTC's racially segmented workforce, they asked only that the PTC symbolically eradicate racial barriers to employment in the company by upgrading small numbers of black workers who were already employed by the company. Five months after the PTC strike, the Philadelphia NAACP reported that "less than 25 blacks are employed" in PTC platform jobs "but the door is definitely open, and other public utilities are beginning to 'set their house in order' as indicated by the recent hiring of black clerks by the Bell Telephone Company in Philadelphia." As important, liberal activists believed that maintaining racial peace in the city's working-class neighborhoods was a necessary precondition to achieving racial gains in the city. When even the small-scale changes they were working for at PTC greatly exacerbated racial tensions in the city, the civil rights coalition undertook emergency actions to prevent racial violence. When the strike came to an end, the NAACP and its allies celebrated the restoration of interracial peace and the successful upgrading of the black workers at PTC as evidence that quiet advocacy, not mass action, was the key to achieving racial progress in the city.[46]

Civil Rights in Postwar America

As World War II came to a close, a number of factors gave civil rights liberals hope that they were on the verge of making significant progress toward their goals. In a postwar world in which colonialism was collapsing and scientific racism had come to be identified with genocide, liberals would increasingly see American claims to global leadership—and the nation's effort to halt the spread of Soviet-style communism—as resting in large part on the country's ability to extend its democratic principles to the treatment of the nation's racial and religious minorities. At the same time, the war had reignited black migration to the North. While the black population of Philadelphia had grown by only 13.6 percent during the 1930s (see Table 1), the rapid expansion of defense industries combined with the wartime labor shortage to draw unprecedented numbers of black migrants to the city. In the first year of the defense buildup alone, the federal government provided $131 million for the expansion of defense plants in Philadelphia. Between 1940 and 1943, the city's black workforce increased from 74,000 to 130,000. And the migration did not slow with the close of the war. By 1950, Philadelphia's black population had grown to 378,968, an increase of 49.9 percent since the beginning of the decade. Meanwhile, the city's white population remained nearly 36,000 below its 1930 peak.[47]

The rapid growth of the black population in the urban North during the 1940s turned black voters into a crucial constituency for the Democratic Party's New Deal coalition. Following Franklin Roosevelt's death in 1945, the Democratic Party's national leadership would come to view black voters as essential to the party's efforts to remain in power. These two factors—the growth of the national black electorate and the importance of racial issues in the international arena—were evident in President Harry Truman's decision to appoint a blue ribbon committee on civil rights in December 1946. Named one month after the Democrats suffered a devastating defeat in the 1946 congressional elections, the committee's ten members included two African Americans, Philadelphia's Sadie T. M. Alexander and Channing Tobias of the New York-based Phelps-Stokes Fund (see Figure 3).[48] The committee's final report, *To Secure These Rights*, based its appeal for black civil rights not only on the American constitutional tradition, but also on the demands of the emerging global competition between the United States and the Soviet Union. The United States, the committee argued, must counter the charge that American "democracy [is] an empty fraud, and our nation a consistent oppressor of underprivileged people." During World War II, Gunnar Myrdal had argued that racial segregation and discrimination was a violation of the country's democratic promise;

Figure 3. Sadie T. M. Alexander with President Harry Truman and members of the President's Committee on Civil Rights, 1947. Collections of the University of Pennsylvania Archives.

now, in the context of the cold war, President Truman was prepared to endorse the argument that such policies threatened the nation's global interests. What had been a radical challenge to the natural order of the races in the early decades of the century had become by midcentury a central element of the official creed of postwar liberalism.[49]

To Secure These Rights would prove a crucial component of the Truman campaign's efforts to shore up its support in black communities in the urban North, particularly in the face of Henry Wallace's left-wing Progressive Party candidacy. An estimated 69 percent of black voters supported Truman. Black votes provided Truman with his margin of victory in Philadelphia as well as in the crucial swing states of Ohio, California, and Illinois. Moreover, the committee's report demonstrated the extent to which racial equality had become a central tenet of the liberal creed by the late 1940s. In its recommendations, the commission called on the judicial, legislative, and executive branches of government to interpret the Bill of Rights as guaranteeing citizens protection not simply from the coercive power of the federal government but also from discrimination by local governments, private businesses and organizations, and their fellow citizens. Such an interpretation, the committee argued, would make it incumbent on Congress and the president to bring an end to segregation in public accommodations and schools and to prevent racial discrimination in employment and housing in both the public and private sectors. While *To Secure These Rights* had only a minimal impact on federal policy in the short run, its recommendations served as a virtual blueprint for the liberal approach to resolving the race question and thus foreshadowed every civil rights advance of the next two decades.[50]

Making Progress: Civil Rights Advocacy in Postwar Philadelphia

Southern domination of the United States Congress meant that there was little hope that the federal government would adopt the liberal program for achieving racial justice.[51] Liberal and left-wing civil rights activists were therefore forced to return their attention to the federal courts and to northern cities and states with growing black electorates. The increasing importance of black voters to the electoral fortunes of Philadelphia's Democratic Party provided the city's left-liberal civil rights coalition with the political influence it needed to implement its agenda. By 1946, however, the emerging cold war and the resulting hysteria over the internal communist threat was beginning to cause irrevocable damage to the coalition. The history of the left-wing coalition that controlled the Philadelphia NAACP from 1945 to 1951 is illustrative not only of the damage that the postwar red scare did to the movement for black civil rights, but also of how a vigorous postwar left might and might not have changed the civil rights movement at the local level.

A left-wing slate headed by a prominent local journalist named Joseph Rainey won an upset victory in the December 1945 Philadelphia NAACP branch election. Rainey was a former columnist for the city's leading black newspaper, the *Philadelphia Tribune*, who had been elected to the post of city magistrate on the Republican ticket a year earlier. Twelve other members of the Rainey slate, including Goldie Watson, were also victorious in the branch election, thus giving the Popular Front activists control over the branch. According to a supporter of outgoing branch president Judge Theodore Spaulding, Rainey's forces won the election by turning out one hundred newly paid-up branch members to what was usually a poorly attended election meeting.[52]

At the programmatic level, Rainey's election brought little change to the branch's activities. In 1946, the branch actively lobbied for passage of federal, state, and municipal FEPC legislation, successfully prosecuted a downtown hotel for refusing service to blacks, negotiated with a number of local companies and unions to overcome racial barriers to employment for blacks, established a counseling service to help individuals solve problems with their housing, protested a number of police brutality cases in the city, successfully advocated for the appointment of the first black interns at Philadelphia General Hospital, and staged a series of rallies against incidents of racial violence in the South.[53]

Still, Rainey and his supporters' approach to civil rights advocacy differed from their predecessors in important ways. First, they framed their call for racial justice in the language of the international movement against fascism and colonialism rather than the language of the Bill of Rights. In contrast to Arthur Fauset's wartime references to the revolutionary tradition of the American founding fathers, Rainey portrayed the struggle for racial equality in the United States as part of a global effort to fulfill the promise of the Allied victory in World War II. In the "months since V-J Day," he argued in his inaugural speech as branch president, black Americans had learned that "Fascist minded groups are in our midst in our very nation." Rainey saw fascism in conservative attacks on the labor movement, in attacks on "working people [in] Indo-China and Indonesia," and in the decision to keep American marines in China. "Could it be," he asked, "that we are interested in saving estates and prerogatives of a handful of Chinese landlords or even to make China safe for American dollar diplomacy?" He also found evidence of fascism in the persistence of racial discrimination in the United States. "Fascism comes in the restricted covenants in real estate . . . in the depriving [of] the colored child from swimming in the pool . . . in [the] Jim-Crow cars we are forced to use in the South . . . in the second rate jobs and homes we are forced to take over."[54]

The second difference between Rainey and his liberal predecessors was strategic. While the liberals continued to advocate elite-oriented legislative and litigative strategies that relied on their alliance with the liberal wing of the Democratic Party, the Rainey faction called for the mass mobilization of the city's black working-class majority to insure that liberal political leaders fulfilled their professed commitment to racial equality. Once in office, Rainey set out to transform the NAACP from the organization of the black middle class into one that was more representative of the black community's working-class majority. He charged that the branch had been little more than a paper organization under his predecessors' leadership. "There were 16,241 members on the books, but less than 500 . . . ever took an active part in any association activity." The average "black on the street," Rainey maintained, felt that "his participation was unwanted." Moreover, "the branch's failure to have mass character prevented it from playing the role it should—that of leadership on every front in the struggle to advance the interests of colored people." While black contributions to the defense of democracy should have guaranteed "secure jobs of a skilled nature . . . thousands of black veterans returned to the city and were unable to find homes or jobs."[55]

Finally, Rainey differed with his predecessors on the question of alliances, a perhaps inevitable conflict in the increasingly anticommunist postwar political environment. The new leadership of the Philadelphia NAACP shared with prominent left-wing black activists including W. E. B. Du Bois and Paul Robeson the belief that the organizations of the Popular Front were the most reliable allies for the civil rights struggle, not the increasingly anticommunist liberal wing of the Democratic Party. In October 1946, Rainey announced that the Philadelphia branch was withdrawing from the Fellowship Commission's Council for Equal Job Opportunity (CEJO) because, he charged, it had failed to make sufficient headway in its efforts on behalf of FEPC legislation. Rainey's decision to break with CEJO was a pointed swipe at Judge Spaulding, his predecessor in the branch presidency, who was one of a number of branch activists serving on the CEJO executive committee. Rainey also declared that the Philadelphia branch would maintain its affiliation with the national Bi-Partisan Committee for the FEPC. The national NAACP and other liberal civil rights groups had pulled out of the Bi-Partisan Committee because of its affiliation with National Negro Congress (NNC) and the Civil Rights Congress, both of which welcomed the participation of communists, and instead formed the National Committee for a Permanent FEPC under the leadership of A. Philip Randolph.[56]

From the very beginning of his tenure, Rainey's liberal opponents sought to have him removed from the branch presidency. In January 1946, the national office received a request from eleven members of the Philadelphia local that Rainey be removed as branch president for violation of the chapter's bylaws. The eleven charged that Rainey had sought to stack the branch executive committee and a number of its subcommittees with his supporters, that he was "using his position as president of the NAACP to foster personal . . . political ambitions," and that he had misused $500 of the organization's funds. In addition, an anonymous report to the NAACP's national board charged that Goldie Watson "was reputed to be a communist," that she was leader of the pro-communist "faction" on the Philadelphia board, and that she and Rainey were conducting secret caucuses of their supporters who then arrived at board meetings "with a cut and dried program." The author was forced to admit, however, that "there has been no overt act on which I actually point a finger other than the taking over of leadership." Of course, Rainey and his allies had not "taken over" the Philadelphia branch; rather they had defeated the Spaulding "faction" in the branch's annual leadership election. Throughout Rainey's tenure, his opponents trumpeted the 17,000 membership figure enjoyed by the branch in 1946. But the Rainey faction was able to win branch elections in 1946 and 1947 with roughly 300 votes, thus revealing just how narrow was the base of support for its opponents. What seems to have been most disturbing to Rainey's opponents was that he had wrested control over the branch from the circle of prominent black Philadelphians that had run it for the previous forty years.[57]

Though the national NAACP was eager to trumpet its opposition to communism and to Popular Front organizations, the national office was hesitant to take action against the duly elected leaders of a local branch. In April 1946, the NAACP's national board ruled that there was insufficient evidence to charge that communists were in control of the Philadelphia branch. Instead, it appointed Thurgood Marshall, head of the NAACP's legal defense fund, and Ella Baker, the national field secretary, to help resolve the factional differences within the branch. Rainey's response was to demonstrate that his program both conformed to the national organization's policies and enjoyed broad support in the city's black communities. The branch, he wrote to Walter White, the NAACP's executive secretary, was working for the establishment of both a federal and a city FEPC, to convince Bell Telephone to hire "black girls as operators," and to end police brutality and racial discrimination in local trade unions. By the summer of 1947, the branch's list of accomplishments included "the cessation of discrimination" at one of Center City's leading hotels, the organization of a "Day of Mourning" following a Monroe, Georgia lynching, mass rallies in support of the victims of the Columbia, Tennessee race riot, the integration of "sales girls" in local department stores, the employment of blacks as gas company meter readers, and the appointment of the first black intern at Philadelphia General Hospital.[58]

Still, tensions between the liberals and the left only increased after Rainey was reelected in December 1946. By the end of the following summer, Rainey's supporters were charging that a clandestine effort had been mounted to disrupt the branch's annual membership drive. As evidence, they pointed to a series of articles that had appeared in the *Tribune* charging that communists were now in control of the branch. Headlined "NAACP Faces Probe of Reds" and written by James Baker, a prominent local black attorney, the article reported that the Philadelphia NAACP was one of three large urban branches of the organization that "may be investigated by the National Office . . . on a suspicion of having strong Communist influences in their official machineries." According to Baker, "observers active in NAACP circles" were concerned that the NAACP was the target of a left-wing campaign to dominate national black organizations. Even though they were able to force the paper to print a retraction, Rainey's supporters charged that the damage done to the membership drive could not be repaired.[59]

In a series of reports, the field secretaries assigned to Philadelphia by the national office described the toll that the faction fight was taking on the branch's membership drives. In June 1947, Marion Bond charged that public resentment of "communist domination of the branch" had caused the branch membership to fall from nearly 17,000 in 1946 to 8,211. Bond cited three specific factors as causes of the membership decline: the exclusion of long-term local board members from the current leadership, Rainey's political activities, and rumors of an "immoral relationship" between Rainey and Elizabeth Young, the branch's full-time executive secretary. A year later, Leroy Carter blamed the branch's membership problems on "a well-organized movement on the part of forces in opposition to the incumbent administration to discredit the present administration although it means destroying Branch membership." While Carter initially set a goal of 15,000 for the drive, he later reduced the goal to 7,500.[60]

While some in the Philadelphia branch continued to press the national NAACP to remove Rainey and his supporters, longtime NAACP activist (and husband of Sadie Alexander) Raymond Pace Alexander argued that a national takeover of the branch would simply enable the current leadership to accuse "the national office . . . of dictator tactics, or fascist rule." With the support of Walter White, the national NAACP's executive secretary, Alexander proposed to recruit a group of twenty to twenty-five leaders "of both races" to organize an opposition slate to challenge Rainey in the 1947 branch elections. With the support of the national office, Alexander argued, such an opposition slate could marshal the 400-plus votes necessary to defeat the Rainey slate, which had received between 300 and 350 votes in the previous two elections. Just such a slate, called the Citizens Committee to Save the NAACP, challenged Rainey and his supporters in the December 1947 branch election. Headed by Eustace Gay, the editor of the *Tribune*, the slate included Theodore Spaulding, Maurice Fagan, Dr. Harry Greene, a dentist and Spaulding's predecessor as branch president, attorney William Coleman, James H. Jones, a black UAW activist, Lenerte Roberts, a real estate broker, and Harold Pilgrim, a postal supervisor. The Gay slate, however, failed in its effort to unite black Philadelphia's leadership class. Supporting Rainey were two of the city's leading black Republicans: E. Washington Rhodes, who as publisher of the *Tribune* was Gay's boss, and Austin Norris, Raymond Pace Alexander's former law partner.[61]

Despite its impressive roster, the Gay slate could neither deliver on its claim to represent "the substantial, clear-thinking [black] citizenry of Philadelphia" or meet Alexander's turnout goal for the election meeting. Rainey won reelection by a nearly three-to-one margin, 480 to 164. Not only had the Gay slate failed to reach even half of Alexander's goal, but the vote for Rainey had exceeded Alexander's prediction by more than 100. Still, the total vote of 644 was less than ten percent of the branch's membership. As impressive as Rainey's vote was, he could not yet claim to have reached his goal of significantly raising the number of black Philadelphians who took an active role in the branch.[62]

Divisions among the chapter's liberals were probably more important to Rainey's reelection than his efforts to turn the branch into a mass organization. Norris and Rhodes may have decided to support the left faction because as journalists and political activists (Norris was editor of the Philadelphia edition of the *Pittsburgh Courier*, a leading *Tribune* rival) they valued

Rainey's mass popularity. Or they may have shared the branch president's view that the only way for the black community to achieve its goals was to build a popular movement against racism. So long as the left-wing faction's Popular Front discourse continued to win significant liberal support, it would remain in control of the Philadelphia branch. Even supporters of the Gay slate remained divided over how best to respond to Rainey's victory. Some called for renewed unity within the branch and the civil rights community. Theodore Spaulding, for example, sent the branch president a congratulatory letter promising to "work in whatever way I can toward great accomplishment . . . in this coming year." Others, however, continued to attack the left faction. Shortly after the election, twelve of Gay's supporters protested the election result to the national office. They charged that they had been prevented from distributing materials in support of the Gay slate in the election meeting and that, as a result, less than half of the members who attended the meeting chose to vote. However, observers from the national office did not support these charges. They reported that the election had been managed fairly and that the result accurately reflected the division of support in the election meeting.[63]

In 1948, Rainey attempted to take his Popular Front coalition into the electoral arena. With the support of prominent liberals like Rev. Luther Cunningham, who was both treasurer of the Philadelphia branch and a leading figure in the Fellowship Commission, he announced his candidacy for the U.S. Congress on the Progressive Party ticket of Henry Wallace. The Communist Party's enthusiastic support for the Wallace campaign along with Wallace's outspoken opposition to the emerging cold war made it inevitable that Rainey's campaign would provide even more fuel for the factional tensions within the Philadelphia NAACP. Rainey's unsuccessful candidacy and his subsequent resignation from the branch presidency, however, did not undercut the left's strength within the branch. In Rainey's place, Rev. E. Theodore Lewis was elected without opposition on a combined left-liberal slate, while Goldie Watson and her allies won a majority on the local's executive board for the fourth straight year. The Lewis/Watson slate would remain in control of the branch through 1950.[64]

The Divided Civil Rights Community

By then, cooperation between the NAACP's left-wing leadership and the rest of the city's liberal civil rights groups had completely broken down. The local branch, for example, played almost no role in CEJO's successful campaign for passage of Philadelphia's municipal Fair Employment Practices ordinance on March 11, 1948. "We NAACP members cannot be proud," one branch activist wrote to the national office, "that our organization was not part of the important group (largely . . . white Protestant[s] and Catholics, and Jews) which was influential in having the legislation passed."[65]

In fact, a number of black activists were active in the FEPC campaign, but as members of CEJO and the Fellowship Commission, not the NAACP. In effect, the left faction's control of the Philadelphia branch enabled the Fellowship Commission to solidify its position as the preeminent liberal civil rights organization in the city and simultaneously to become the activist home for most of the prominent black anticommunist liberals in the city, including Raymond Pace and Sadie T. M. Alexander, and Judge Theodore Spaulding. The Fellowship Commission would serve as the strategic locus of the city's liberal civil rights community through the 1950s and into the early 1960s. It convened activists from a broad range of organizations to develop, debate, and refine the coalition's legislative and political strategy, while its various subcommittees and task forces provided a forum for activists to meet with officials from both the city and state governments to urge them to enact and enforce antibias policies. Specifically, the Fellowship Commission forged a three-pronged civil rights strategy in the postwar years: (1) passage of state and local legislation banning racial discrimination in public and private labor and housing markets; (2) integration of blacks into the city's leading political institutions, including the agencies of city and state government, the Democratic Party, and major civic organizations; and (3) development of a working alliance of city agencies, civic and neighborhood groups, and private social service organizations committed to defusing racial and ethnic tensions in the city's working-class neighborhoods. Civil rights liberalism flourished in Philadelphia so long as these three principles seemed to be contributing to the social and economic advancement of the city's black communities.[66]

At the core of the Fellowship Commission's strategy for achieving racial equity in Philadelphia was the municipal FEPC. The FEPC ordinance prohibited employers, employment agencies, and labor unions from making "any inquiry concerning, or record of the race, color, religion, national origin or ancestry of applicants." It also established a five-member Fair Employment Practices Commission, with three members appointed by the mayor and two by the city council, to enforce the law. Like the wartime federal FEPC, the Philadelphia FEPC lacked formal enforcement powers; it could only investigate complaints of employment discrimination. On the premise that public exposure would shame employers into following the law, the FEPC was empowered to hold public hearings if, and only if, it determined that a complaint had merit *and* was unable to negotiate a proper remedy with the employer.[67]

Meanwhile, the faction fight within the local NAACP continued to hurt its membership drives and its resources. By the fall of 1949, membership in the branch had fallen to 8,000. Critics of the branch faulted Lewis for maintaining Rainey's policy of not participating in the Fellowship Commission. In addition, they charged that the city's labor leaders refused to work with the branch "as long as the Communist Party elements dominate the administration." In February 1949, Judge Spaulding reported to Walter White that rumors were circulating through the city that the branch was about to be placed on the attorney general's list of subversive organizations because of its participation in left-wing civil rights meetings and because its executive board included Goldie Watson, Morris Shafritz, and "six others [who], if not Communists, are faithful followers of the Communist Party line." Early in 1949, the national NAACP took its first direct action against the left leadership of the Philadelphia branch, ordering it to withdraw its endorsement of a Washington, D.C. conference sponsored by the left-wing Civil Rights Congress. A year later, the organization's national convention passed a resolution giving the national office the authority to investigate and remove all supporters of "the Communist Party line" from the organization. On October 24, 1950, the NAACP's national board voted to give Lewis fifteen days to "show cause why" the branch's charter "should not be suspended or revoked." Still, the board carefully avoided the issue of communist influence, instead charging the branch with failing to pay its debts to the national organization, operating "in excess of its income," not carrying out the NAACP program, and causing the organization to suffer "a great loss of prestige in the community."[68]

In the end, the national board chose not to suspend the branch, instead accepting a four point proposal that Judge Spaulding and E. Washington Rhodes had submitted for revitalizing the branch. At the core of Rhodes and Spaulding's proposal was their pledge to organize for the December 1950 branch elections "a complete slate of non-partisan, non-faction, non-clique persons" that would seek to prevent the reemergence of the factional fighting in the branch. Ironically, however, the Spaulding-Rhodes slate lost the election to an all-liberal anti-Lewis slate that was led by former branch president Harry Greene. The years of anticommunist attacks on the Rainey and Lewis administrations had finally eroded the left's strength in the branch.[69]

While Harry Greene's election as NAACP branch president restored liberal control of the local NAACP and returned the branch to the city's civil rights coalition, the branch could not reestablish its position as the preeminent civil rights group in Philadelphia. As just one civil rights group among many in the Fellowship Commission, the local branch repositioned itself as the representative voice of the city's black residents within the commission. Under the leadership of President Greene and Charles Shorter, who was rehired as branch executive secretary six years after he quit in a dispute with Joseph Rainey, the branch sought to mobilize black Philadelphians to support the liberal coalition's legislative initiatives. Greene and Shorter viewed the branch's members as constituents who periodically required the services of the branch's professional staff rather than as a collective force

capable of pressuring government agencies and private companies to provide equal employment opportunity. According to the branch's 1954
annual report, 3,072 persons had visited the branch office in the previous
year, the office had received 3,701 phone calls, and 1,699 individuals had
sought the branch's "advice and counsel." Mittie Jennings and Bette Love,
for example, each sought the NAACP's assistance after receiving what they
felt was unfair treatment from their employers. According to the report,
the branch leadership was able to secure for Jennings the promotion she
had been denied at the U.S. Army's Frankford Arsenal and to have Love
reinstated to the position she had been fired from at Kaiser Metal Products.[70]

The postwar factionalism within the Philadelphia NAACP was ostensibly
focused on whether civil rights activism would be helped or hurt by working in coalition with the Communist Party and its Popular Front allies.
More fundamentally, the two sides disagreed on whether progress toward
racial equality was possible within the consensus liberalism that was emerging in the postwar years. With its insistence that popular mobilization
rather than alliances with liberal Democratic politicians was the key to
achieving civil rights reforms, the left faction of the Philadelphia NAACP
prefigured the black protest movement that would emerge in the city during the 1960s. While supporters of the Philadelphia branch's traditional
middle-class leadership shared in the postwar liberal faith that the New
Deal coalition of liberal, labor, and black voters was capable of eradicating
racial discrimination from the nation, Popular Front activists believed that
a complete restructuring of society was necessary to end American racism.
For them, the New Deal welfare state remained incomplete. Not only civil
rights, but also workers' rights, the trade union movement, and the government institutions formed to protect citizens from the dual threats of fascism and big business were at risk unless a progressive coalition of workers,
blacks, and liberals could be mobilized to protect each group's interests.

In the immediate postwar years, noncommunists like Joseph Rainey were
attracted to the Popular Front by its commitment to popular mobilization
as well as its linking of the fight against American racism to international
struggles against fascism and colonialism. Even such anticommunist liberals as Theodore Spaulding and E. Washington Rhodes recognized that they
shared common goals with Popular Front advocates like Goldie Watson
and Morris Shafritz. They believed that finding a basis for internal unity
within the NAACP was more important than protecting the organization's
anticommunist reputation. Of course, the fact that Rainey and Watson
could mobilize a core of active NAACP members larger than the branch's
liberal wing explains much of Spaulding and Rhodes' pragmatism. By the
early 1950s, however, the cold war and the red scare had so effectively isolated and demoralized the pro-communist left that advocates of anticommunism within the Philadelphia NAACP were finally able to win a branch

election. Once out of office and with the bylaws of the national NAACP now reflecting the national political consensus that communists were not deserving of basic democratic civil liberties, Goldie Watson and her allies found themselves unable to operate effectively within the branch.

Civil Rights Liberals and Urban Reform in Philadelphia

The collapse of the left during the cold war was not the only factor that enabled liberals to emerge as the dominant black leadership in postwar Philadelphia. Equally important was the growth of the city's black population in the postwar years and the resulting importance of the city's black vote in municipal elections. The Republican majority on the city council understood this new reality. Its decision, in 1948, to approve the FEPC ordinance by a unanimous vote was an obvious attempt to demonstrate to the city's black voters that they were as ready to support racial equality as their Democratic opponents. It was the Democrats and their liberal reform wing, however, which would reap the benefits of the growing black electorate.

Concerned that the city's reputation for political corruption was hurting its business climate, a generation of upper-class reformers from traditionally Republican families but influenced by the New Deal founded a number of civic organizations committed to political reform and to using government to revitalize the city's economic infrastructure. Among these groups the most important were the Greater Philadelphia Movement, which promoted the use of urban planning to revitalize the city's central business district, and a local chapter of Americans for Democratic Action (ADA), the national organization of anticommunist liberals whose local agenda was focused on ending political corruption. The city's civil rights coalition was drawn into this liberal reform milieu as these reformers actively participated in the Fellowship Commission and built alliances with such prominent black liberals as Raymond Pace Alexander and Rev. Marshall Shepard. At the same time, these activists, who were known originally as the Young Turks, convinced the local Democratic Party organization that it could add middle- and upper-class Protestants to its base of working-class New Deal supporters if it adopted a program of government reform and urban renewal.[71]

As recently as 1943, the Republicans had scored a landslide victory in the municipal elections. In the 1947 campaign, however, a Democratic ticket led by prominent civic reformers and running on an anticorruption platform was able to cut the Republican victory margin to 100,000 votes. The architect of the alliance between the civic reform movement and the Philadelphia Democratic Party was James Finnegan, who was elected chairman of the Democratic city committee in 1946. Finnegan recognized that a plurality of Philadelphia's voters were still white Protestants and that an anticorruption and urban renewal platform would give the Democrats the best opportunity to add enough of these voters to its New Deal coalition of Catholic, Jewish, and black voters. Finnegan tapped Richardson Dilworth, a patrician lawyer who was a leading figure in the local ADA, to lead the Democratic ticket in the 1947 municipal elections. Dilworth's defeat did not prevent his attacks on the corruption of the Republican machine from making what one observer described as "an impression on the public mind that was both fresh and vivid." Two years later, Dilworth ran successfully for the district attorney's office, while his fellow ADA leader Joseph Clark was elected city controller. The reformers' victories were achieved by splitting the city's mostly white working-class wards, winning eleven of the twelve middle-class wards that had histories of independent voting, and by sweeping the nine predominately black wards that had developed in North Philadelphia since 1940.[72]

It was, however, the passage in 1948 by the state legislature of a bill providing for the establishment of a commission to write a new Home Rule Charter for Philadelphia that provided the Democrats with the opportunity they needed to successfully challenge the Republican machine. Advocates of good government reforms had been lobbying the state legislature for a new city charter for Philadelphia since the late 1930s. However, it was not until they won the support of the Greater Philadelphia Movement (GPM), a business reform group whose members for the most part lived outside the city limits, that they were able to overcome the Republican machine's opposition to any effort to limit political patronage in the city. Unlike the industrialists who had traditionally supported the Republican machine, GPM's leadership was drawn primarily from the city's new corporate sector—for example, law firms and the so-called FIRE industries (finance, insurance, and real estate)—and therefore more likely to be concerned that the city's corrupt reputation would dampen private investment in the downtown business core. In an effort to appease both the reform movement and the city's business community, Mayor Bernard Samuel and the Republican city council filled the commission with nominees suggested by the GPM. Freed from party interests, the commission was able to develop a blueprint for city government that reflected the reformers' faith in technocrats and rationalized planning to solve urban problems.[73]

The civil rights coalition viewed the reformers' control of the charter commission as providing a great opportunity to establish the principle that a basic function of city government was to protect its citizens from racial and religious discrimination. In the fall of 1949, the Fellowship Commission board asked Sadie Alexander, who was then a member of the Philadelphia FEPC, to chair a committee to draft human rights language that it could propose to the charter commission. Alexander proposed, and the charter commission adopted without amendment, that the new city charter include a human rights section with provisions that included bans on discrimination in the use of all city property, facilities, and services as well as in civil service employment, and a requirement that all city contracts over $2,000 include a nondiscrimination clause. In addition, the charter provided for the establishment of a Commission on Human Relations (CHR) to replace the current FEPC. The new commission would be responsible for administering the fair employment practices ordinance as well as all future antibias laws adopted by the city government. In addition, it would have the mandate to investigate all cases of racial or religious discrimination within the city limits and to carry out educational programming against racial and religious bias. By establishing the CHR as part of the city charter, Alexander hoped to ensure that the new commission would have the resources and legal mandate that the original FEPC had lacked in its efforts to enforce the FEPC ordinance.[74]

The restoration of liberal control of the Philadelphia NAACP in December 1950 began what would be civil rights liberalism's most successful year in Philadelphia. Over the next twelve months, the city's liberal reformers and their allies in the Democratic Party would win two elections that would fundamentally alter the political structure in the city. First, in an April referendum, the city's voters approved a new Home Rule Charter that greatly increased the powers of the mayor and the agencies of city government at the expense of the political parties and their patronage bosses. In the process, the city's civil rights coalition also won its two most important victories: (1) the inclusion in the city charter of antidiscrimination language and provisions for the establishment of a human relations commission to enforce all of the city's current and future antibias laws, and (2) the creation of a politically independent Civil Service Board, which would ensure for the first time that black workers would have equal access to city employment by ending patronage control over thousands of municipal jobs. Then, in the November general election, the Democratic ticket swept to its first victory in a municipal election in more than fifty years. With strong support from the city's black electorate, the Democratic mayoral candidate, Joseph Clark, defeated his Republican opponent by 122,000 votes. Also victorious on the Democratic ticket was Raymond Pace Alexander, who was elected to represent North Philadelphia on the city council.[75]

* * *

Race relations in Philadelphia underwent a radical transformation in the first decade after World War II. Scientific racism, once a key element of the nation's ruling ideology, was reduced to the ideology of a discredited and dangerous far right wing. Segregated public accommodations substantially disappeared from Philadelphia. Where once Philadelphia's ruling elites had accepted the virtual exclusion of blacks as a given, a new generation of patrician reformers and their New Deal allies now endorsed a city charter that banned racial discrimination and promised equal treatment to all the city's residents. Black Philadelphians had moved from being the unseen dependents of a corrupt Republican machine to an important constituency of the Democratic reform coalition that now ran City Hall.

Philadelphia voters' approval of a new city charter in 1951 did not end the efforts of the liberal civil rights coalition to achieve its vision of a city free from racial bias. Contrary to the image of the politically somnolent 1950s, liberal advocates of civil rights in Philadelphia continued to press for the adoption of antidiscrimination legislation as well as for the effective enforcement of the human rights provisions within the new city charter. Activists lobbied for federal and state fair employment practices laws at both levels and for the city and state governments to enact bans on racial discrimination within private housing markets. At the same time, they worked to increase the enforcement powers and capabilities of the government agencies that were mandated to implement antidiscrimination legislation as well as to encourage black residents of the city who felt that they had been discriminated against to bring their cases to the proper agencies. However, it would be their ability to translate legal and legislative gains into substantive improvements in the treatment of blacks within local labor and housing markets, the city schools, and the local judicial system that would determine the level of black support for the liberal civil rights agenda and the city's new Democratic regime over the long term.

Chapter 2
The Other Philadelphia Story

> The men and women who make the Twice-A-Week Tribune present
> with great pride "The Other Philadelphia Story." We hope you will . . .
> become inspired to greater and nobler achievement. This is the real
> down-to-earth story, the true story of Negro life in America's third
> largest city.
> —Philadelphia Tribune, *April 26, 1955*

The *Philadelphia Tribune* devoted its entire April 26, 1955, issue to "The
Other Philadelphia Story," a photo essay on African American owned
homes in the city. In part, the essay was motivated by anxieties about white
perceptions of black behavior in the city. "Many have heard," the paper
wrote, "about the shocking housing conditions . . . the disproportionate
number of juvenile delinquents, the unmarried mothers, and the dope
addicts." But the essay was as much a celebration of racial progress as an
attempt to refute stereotypes of black pathology. It sought not so much to
change the perceptions of whites as to raise the racial esteem of its black
readership. "It is our desire that, after reading, you will hold your head
up high with full knowledge that the majority of the 400,000 Negroes in
Philadelphia are NOT criminals, alcoholics and buffoons." To the *Tribune*'s
editors, the untold story of black life in Philadelphia was the "large number
of thrifty, hard-working Negro home-owners . . . their values and importance to the city." The 40,000 black-owned homes in the city, the *Tribune*
told its readers, ranged from "$40,000 mansions" to "$3000 modest
homes." Wherever they stood in this spectrum, these homes symbolized
the ways in which refinement and respectability were bound up with prosperity in the culture of the post-World War II economic boom. Black-
owned homes, the *Tribune* crowed,

have every modern convenience. The bathrooms are spic and span and the kitch-
ens glisten. The furnishings and decorations prove that the owners are refined and
cultured. There are television sets and radios, magazines and newspapers. Book-
cases filled with books written by the best authors line the walls. These citizens are
members of neighborhood organizations which have as their purpose the proper

upkeep of their area. They plant flowers and shrubs. They paint-up and fix-up their properties. They mow their lawns. In short, they are first-class Americans, proud of their homes, proud of their country.[1]

Following the introductory essay, the *Tribune* featured seven pages of photographs of black-owned homes, from the stately mansions recently purchased by members of the black business and professional elite in the city's integrating Northwest to rowhouses and duplexes (known in Philadelphia as "twins") in working- and middle-class areas of North and West Philadelphia. Here was irrefutable evidence not only of the character and values of the city's black residents, but also of the community's progress in the decade since World War II. Each photo was accompanied by a caption extolling the condition of the home, the modernity of its appliances, or the sophistication of its owners and their artistic taste. A photo of a kitchen urged readers to note the "latest time and work-saving equipment" and "the arrangement . . . which conserves the housewife's steps." Another caption described the library of a North Philadelphia physician as representative of "the culture and refinement which is present in the majority of Philadelphia Negro homes."

The *Tribune*'s optimism was the product of the civil rights victories of the first decade of the postwar era and the improved economic opportunities that those victories seemed to be creating for blacks in the urban North. Nationally, the median income of blacks and other nonwhite minorities in the country rose from \$3,563 to \$4,344 between 1947 and 1952.[2] Similar progress seemed evident in Philadelphia. In 1950, only 2 percent of the city's black workers earned more than \$4,000 per year. By the end of the decade, that figure had risen to 12 percent.[3]

Driving this growth in black incomes were increased employment opportunities in the public sector. During World War II, government agencies lost white workers to the labor demands of military service and the defense industries. And in the postwar economic boom, white government workers left for better-paying private-sector employment. At the same time, the growing importance of northern black voters to the Democrats' electoral fortunes created a political imperative for hiring black workers to government jobs. Moreover, the Philadelphia fair employment practices ordinance and the 1951 charter reform movement further opened up municipal employment opportunities for black workers. Not only did the new Home Rule Charter's antidiscrimination provisions commit the city to fair hiring practices, but it shifted thousands of municipal jobs from the control of the political parties' patronage operations to an independent civil service board. Black workers could now compete on even terms (through "colorblind" merit exams) for jobs that had previously been closed to them. They may even have enjoyed a competitive advantage on the civil service exams as whites with similar levels of skill and education were drawn to better-paying private-sector jobs that were closed to blacks. By 1963, blacks made up 39 percent of the municipal workforce and 30 percent of the city's public school teachers. Many political observers cited the rapid growth in black municipal employment as a major factor in the popularity of the 1950s reform administrations among black voters.[4]

The *Tribune*'s decision to devote a special section to black homeownership demonstrates how improved employment opportunities for black Philadelphians led to rapid growth in black home buying in the city. During the 1940s and 1950s, rates of black homeownership in Philadelphia grew even faster than the overall rate of black population growth. In 1939, only 11 percent of black homes in the city were owner-occupied. By 1950, the rate of black homeownership in Philadelphia had more than tripled to 37.4 percent. Homeownership rates continued to grow during the first half of the 1950s. Between 1950 and 1956, the number of black-owned homes in the city grew by 84.7 percent from 30,000 to 55,411, raising the black homeownership rate to 43.8 percent. By 1960, 38 percent of black families in Philadelphia had combined annual incomes that qualified them to buy a $9,000 house.[5]

These signs of economic progress, however, masked significant barriers to black economic progress in Philadelphia. Much of the private-sector labor market—both white-collar and blue-collar—remained closed to black workers. Moreover, changes in the regional economy in the years following World War II exacerbated the impact of persistent racial segmentation on black workers. The Philadelphia economy began its shift from a mixed industrial base to a service-sector economy almost as soon as World War II came to an end. Between 1950 and 1965, Philadelphia lost 90,000 industrial jobs. The proportion of the private labor force in manufacturing in Philadelphia declined from nearly 50 percent in 1947 to 40 percent in 1970. At the same time, in-migration and natural population growth continued to increase the city's black population even as the city's total population began to decline. During the 1950's, the number of black Philadelphians increased by 41 percent—to 529,240—while the white population fell by 13 percent. A decade later, the city's total population had fallen below two million for the first time since 1940, but the black population continued to grow, reaching 653,791 in 1970 (see Table 3). As the latest migrants to arrive in the city, poorly educated and unskilled black workers were most vulnerable to these changes in the labor market. For example, two of the defense firms that had hired black workers during the war, Budd Trucks and Cramp Shipbuilding, either left the city or closed in the late 1940s. As a result, black un- and underemployment in the city rose precipitously throughout the 1950s. One 1956 study of black workers living near the corner of Girard and Poplar in the heart of North Philadelphia found that 37 percent of workers surveyed were unemployed and 42

TABLE 3. PHILADELPHIA POPULATION, 1950–1970

Year	Total	Per-centage change	White total	White per-centage	White per-centage change	Black total	Black per-centage	Black per-centage change
1950	2,071,605		1,692,637	81.7		376,041	18.2	
1960	2,002,512	−3.3	1,467,479	73.3	−13.3	529,240	26.4	40.7
1970	1,948,609	−2.7	1,278,717	65.6	−12.9	653,791	33.6	23.5

Source: U.S. Census.

percent had irregular employment as common laborers, domestics, and service employees.[6]

Changes in Philadelphia's textile industry demonstrate the impact of deindustrialization on black workers in the city. Since the very beginnings of the industrial revolution, the textile industry had been the largest employer in the city. While the city's textile manufacturers suffered through the Great Depression, the demands of military mobilization proved a boon for the local industry during World War II. Throughout the war, black southern migrants flocked to the textile industry's entry-level jobs. However, the city's mixture of aging factories, mixed industrial and working-class residential neighborhoods, high rates of unionization, and relatively high land costs and taxes left it ill-equipped to compete with land-cheap suburbs, nonunion southern and western states, and low-wage foreign countries, for the benefits of postwar industrial expansion. While textile employment remained steady in Philadelphia into the early 1950s, textile jobs began to disappear in the years following the end of the Korean War. In 1951, 28 percent of the city's private labor force had been in non-durable manufacturing; by 1959, that figure had fallen to 25 percent and by 1970 to 20 percent.[7]

Urban renewal was the primary economic development strategy of Philadelphia's 1950s reform administrations. Like most economic development initiatives of the era, urban renewal was premised on the view that the proper economic role for government was as a facilitator of private enterprise. Operating through public-private development corporations, the Philadelphia Redevelopment Authority spent the decade clearing land and developing the infrastructure for the city's shift from a blue-collar industrial economy to a white-collar service economy, with an emphasis on finance, insurance and real estate firms. In order to facilitate the construction of modern (white-collar) office buildings, the redevelopment authority removed from the Center City business core outdated industrial facilities as well as the tenderloin (red-light) district and the so-called "Chinese Wall," the Pennsylvania Railroad viaduct that bisected the western

TABLE 4. THE BLACK POPULATION IN NORTH PHILADELPHIA, 1930–1960

Year	Black population	Percentage increase	Percentage of neighborhood population
1930	77,930		22
1940	97,155	24.7	28
1950	164,107	68.9	45
1960	215,554	31.3	69

Source: U.S. Census; Nancy Kleniewski, "Neighborhood Decline and Downtown Renewal: The Politics of Redevelopment in Philadelphia, 1952–1962," Ph.D. dissertation, Temple University, 1981.

half of Center City. It also replaced the sprawling nineteenth century Food Distribution Center with a modern facility built on swamp land on the city's southern edge and began a program of slum clearance in the impoverished communities (many with large black populations) that ringed Center City in hopes of attracting up-scale developers and residents to the historic neighborhoods surrounding Independence Hall.[8] Later in this chapter, I will discuss the impact of these policies on black employment and residential patterns in the city. For now, though, it is sufficient to point out that these policies were targeted solely at the aggregate economic health of the city and in no way addressed the structural inequalities that disadvantaged black workers in the local labor market.[9]

Thomas Sugrue has argued that the origins of the postwar urban crisis— with its high rates of concentrated black poverty in northern inner cities— lay in the unintentional racial impact of postwar corporate decision-making processes that removed entry-level industrial jobs to the suburbs and the Sun Belt. In combination with institutionalized systems of racial privilege and discrimination in employment, housing, and education, Sugrue argues, this shift in industrial jobs disproportionately affected black working-class communities, thus setting the stage for the pandemic levels of inner-city unemployment and social disorganization so well documented by underclass theorists like William Julius Wilson. By World War II, it was evident that the focal point of black ghettoization in Philadelphia was shifting from the old Seventh Ward of Du Bois's *Philadelphia Negro* to North Central Philadelphia, a collection of neighborhoods bounded by Spring Garden Street to the south, Ninth Street to the east, Lehigh Avenue to the north, and the Schuylkill River to the west. As early as 1896, Du Bois had noted that blacks were beginning to move north of Center City. In 1890, 7,694 blacks were living in all of North Philadelphia, fewer than in the Seventh Ward alone. By 1930, the area's black population had grown to 77,930 (see Table 4), 35 percent of the city's black population, and 22 percent of the population of North Philadelphia. Over the next decade, two-thirds of the black population growth in the city occurred in North Philadelphia. By 1940, North Philadelphia's black population had grown by 25 percent to 97,155, 94 percent of whom lived in the cluster of neighborhoods just north of Center City. These neighborhoods, an area that city planners began to call North Central Philadelphia, were now 39 percent black, while less than 30 percent of South Philadelphians were black.[10]

It was during the 1940s and 1950s, however, that residential segregation in Philadelphia increased most dramatically (see Figures 4 and 5). The black population of North Philadelphia more than doubled during those decades; by 1960, blacks constituted 69 percent of this area's total population. A 1953 Commission on Human Relations study found that two-thirds of the city's black households were concentrated in 40 of the city's 404 census tracts and that 40 percent of the black households in those census tracts were living in substandard housing. During the 1940s, 13,000 white families moved out of those 40 tracts and 23,000 black families moved in. By 1950, 24.9 percent of black Philadelphia households lived on blocks that were 90 percent or more black, 49.9 percent on blocks that were 50 percent or more black. That year, "nonwhite dwelling units" were eight times more likely than those inhabited by whites to be dilapidated, three times more likely to lack a private bath and one-half as likely to be owner-occupied. "Unless sufficient suitable housing is provided for dislocated families," the CHR warned, "redevelopment may result in a decrease in the total living space available to Negroes or to a further reduction in the quality of their housing."[11]

Meanwhile, an industrial boom was taking place in Philadelphia's northeastern suburbs. In the decade's first three years, seven large industrial producers, including U.S. Steel, Philco, Rohm and Haas, and Minnesota Mining and Manufacturing (3M), opened new plants in Bucks County, Pennsylvania. Without a state fair employment law, black workers found themselves unable to take advantage of the growth in job opportunities in the suburbs. In 1953, only 70 of the 3,000 employees, and none of the skilled workers, at U.S. Steel's Bucks County plant were black. Even after a statewide coalition of civil rights groups succeeded in pushing fair employment legislation through the state legislature in 1955, those percentages did not improve substantially, despite pledges made by U.S. Steel to the NAACP to increase the number of black workers it employed.[12]

A major factor in black workers' near-total exclusion from the suburban industrial boom was the lack of suburban housing available to blacks. While 85 percent of the black population increase in Philadelphia's metropolitan area during the 1940s occurred within the city limits, 96 percent of white population growth was in the suburbs. Racial exclusionary sales policies were commonplace in postwar suburban housing, despite the 1948 U.S. Supreme Court ruling that racial covenants were unconstitutional. Only three subdivisions built in suburban Philadelphia between 1946 and 1955

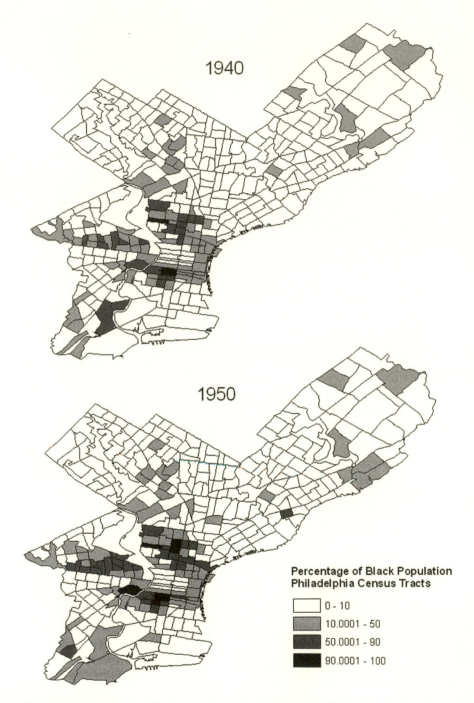

1940

1950

**Percentage of Black Population
Philadelphia Census Tracts**

☐ 0 - 10

▨ 10.0001 - 50

▨ 50.0001 - 90

■ 90.0001 - 100

Figure 4. Philadelphia's black population by census tract, 1940–50. U.S. Census.

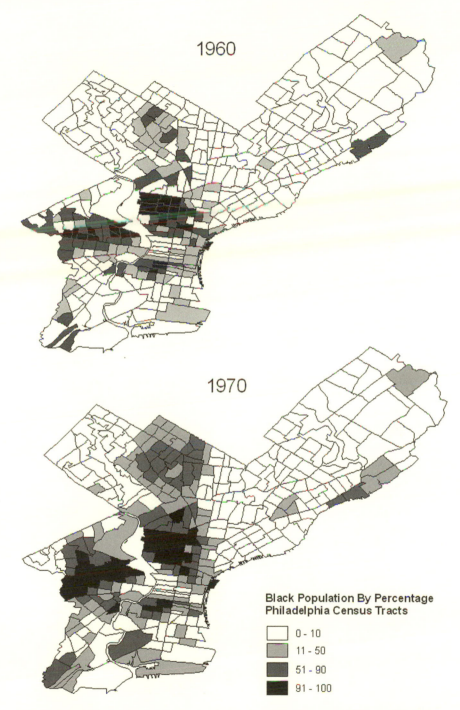

1960

1970

Black Population By Percentage
Philadelphia Census Tracts

☐ 0 - 10
▨ 11 - 50
▨ 51 - 90
■ 91 - 100

Figure 5. Philadelphia's black population by census tract, 1960–70. U.S. Census.

were made available for sale on a nonracial basis. And of the 919 new housing units built for blacks in Philadelphia's suburban counties during this
period, the vast majority were in small, working-class cities like Chester and
Camden, New Jersey. It was even difficult for blacks to find housing in those
segments of the city that were nearest to the new factories in Bucks County.
Even as the number of black homeowners in Philadelphia grew precipitously during the 1940s and 1950s, blacks were completely excluded from
the suburban-style tract developments being built in the Greater Northeast,
an expansive section of former farmlands that borders Bucks County.
Instead, blacks were restricted to buying homes in the older residential
neighborhoods that whites were fleeing for the suburbs. Of the 150,000
new housing units built in postwar Philadelphia, only 1,022 were made
available to black families. And of these, only 28 were detached houses in
residential areas. In 1959 alone, an average of ninety black families per
week moved into previously white-owned homes in the city.[13]

The case of the Levittown development in Bucks County demonstrates
how the exclusion of blacks from the suburban housing boom contributed
to the black employment crisis in northern cities. In 1951, U.S. Steel asked
Levitt & Co., the developers of Levittown, a massive suburban development
on Long Island, to build two large housing developments near the company's Bucks County plant. The company turned to William Levitt because
of his company's demonstrated ability to mass-produce affordable homes
on a rapid scale. While the county's abundance of undeveloped land made
it ideal for the expansive, modern facility the company desired, it lacked
sufficient housing to accommodate the influx of new workers. The plan
was for Levitt to build 20,000 homes for the thousands of production workers who would be needed at the county's new factories. Levitt, however,
had a policy of not selling his homes to black families. In a 1952 letter to
the NAACP, Levitt declared that "he personally did not want an all-white
policy in his developments but that the white public which he served"
demanded it.[14]

It was not simply Levitt's company policy, the real estate decisions of U.S.
Steel, or white consumer demand that limited black access to the Bucks
County industrial boom. Not only did the segregationist practices of postwar housing developments violate no federal, state, or local laws, they were
in fact encouraged by federal housing policy. Since the 1930s, the mortgage assistance programs of the Federal Housing Administration and the
Home Owners' Loan Corporation had subsidized neighborhood segregation by limiting their lending to new housing construction, by favoring
racially homogeneous neighborhoods, and by declaring integrated and
predominately black areas to be poor risks for private financing. By the
1950s, the impact of federal policy on residential patterns in Philadelphia
was dramatic. "The white slum," read a 1953 Philadelphia Housing Associ-

ation report, "has disappeared and substandard housing occupied by whites is scattered . . . The concentrated slums today are largely Negro."[15]

Thus, there was little civil rights advocates could do to protest the exclusion of black home buyers from William Levitt's Bucks County developments. The national NAACP did file a suit against Levitt, charging that the company's use of federal mortgage assistance programs made its racially discriminatory marketing policies unconstitutional. Without an explicit federal ban on racial discrimination in housing, however, the suit had little chance of success. While a campaign led by the American Friends Service Committee (AFSC), a Philadelphia-based Quaker organization, would eventually enable a small number of black families to purchase Levittown homes from their original owners, most black workers seeking jobs in Buck County had to be able and willing to make the long commute over secondary roads from Philadelphia or Trenton, New Jersey. As a result, the vast majority of black workers remained effectively excluded from the Bucks County industrial boom.[16]

During the 1950s, the only protection Philadelphia's black workers enjoyed against the disparate racial impact of industrial flight were the city and state's FEPC laws. But while these laws would prove effective at banning explicit racial discrimination in hiring and promotion—thus enabling small groups of black workers to enter into occupations previously barred to them—they proved woefully inadequate to the task of overcoming racial segmentation in the local labor market. The story of efforts to enforce the 1951 city charter's antidiscrimination provisions is a cautionary tale for those who argue that vigorous enforcement of the nation's laws against racial discrimination in employment should and would make affirmative action unnecessary.

More important for this book, however, is the impact that this policy failure had on black attitudes toward the liberal civil rights agenda. Liberal activists, and their reform Democratic allies, had promoted the 1951 city charter as the remedy to racial discrimination in the workplace and, by extension, black poverty in the city. However, Philadelphia's civil rights liberals badly misjudged their ability to maintain the support of the city's Democratic Party and its base of New Deal voters for racial reforms in local employment, housing, and education issues.[17] To many black Philadelphians, the inability of civil rights liberalism to fulfill its promise of a truly colorblind city was a profound political betrayal. It was this sense of liberalism's failure that would lead many local black activists to begin a search for alternative approaches to achieving racial equality. The results of this search, I will argue in later chapters, was the emergence in Philadelphia of protest movements modeled first on the southern nonviolent movement and later on Black Power and its black nationalist critique of racial integration.

Civil Rights Liberalism After 1951

It is hard to overstate the optimism that Philadelphia's civil rights community felt following the passage of the city charter. In its first annual report, the Philadelphia Commission on Human Relations declared that the city "had very nearly assembled . . . the ideal combination of legal authority, organization, funds and community support for an effective attack on racial and religious prejudice and discrimination and for building rich and wholesome relationships among the racial, religious and nationality groups that make up America." According to the commission, that combination included its own "substantial powers of investigation," the "vigorous support" of the city's reform administration, "strong community backing mobilized by the Fellowship Commission," and "a substantial, although not entirely adequate budget." While the commissioners and their allies in the city's liberal civil rights organizations did not believe that enforcement of the charter's antidiscrimination provisions would cause racism to disappear from the city overnight, they did expect that they could eradicate the most blatantly discriminatory employment practices. The commission's initial targets were racially specific help-wanted ads and the exclusion of blacks, Jews, and other minorities from entire job categories. The commission's emphasis on placing black workers in positions to which they had previously been excluded reflected the so-called "breakthrough" jobs strategy common to civil rights groups of the 1950s. Giving just one individual the opportunity to do a job that was widely deemed inappropriate for people of their race or religion, the commissioners believed, would lead white employers to recognize that even subtle barriers to minority advancement were unnecessary and counterproductive.[18]

Philadelphia's civil rights community maintained this faith in the Commission on Human Relations despite the limited achievements of its predecessor agency, the Fair Employment Practices Commission. The first commission had suffered from limited enforcement powers and an inadequate budget. Its executive director, Frank Loescher, had sought to compensate for these limitations by appealing to the moral conscience of employers.[19] In the Philadelphia FEPC's first annual report, Loescher described the commission's enforcement strategy as premised on the "the proposition that prejudice cannot be legislated out of existence," a somewhat ironic position for the head of an agency charged with enforcing antibias legislation. Thus, when the commission succeeded in negotiating back pay for a group of black piece workers in the garment industry who complained that they were given heavier garments to sew than their white co-workers, thus depressing their wages, Loescher argued that the specific resolution was less important than the investigation's inherent educational value. "When a charge is brought, the law becomes the occasion for explaining the goals of the Ordinance." In Loescher's view, the result of such educational efforts was that "the likelihood that other incidents of discrimination will arise in the same place is reduced, and employment opportunities are opened for others."[20]

Loescher's commitment to conciliation and the educational value of behind-closed-doors consultations with employers was reflected in the fact that the FEPC did not hold a single public hearing on a case of employment discrimination during his tenure. Between 1948 and 1951, the commission received 807 complaints of racial or religious discrimination and found evidence to support such a claim in 247 cases, more than thirty percent of the complaints received. In every one of these cases, however, Loescher and his staff agreed to a negotiated settlement with the offending employer, employment agency, or labor union, even if that settlement required only that the employer promise to follow the dictates of the ordinance in the future. During Loescher's tenure, the local Woolworth stores, three grocery chains, two large insurance companies and one major bank all formally adopted nondiscriminatory hiring policies. In addition, the large Center City department stores all hired blacks for clerical and sales positions for the first time and Bell Telephone and AT&T both employed their first "colored operators."[21]

What the Philadelphia FEPC had not been able to achieve during Loescher's tenure was to make any significant impact on the structure of racial segmentation in the Philadelphia labor market. Still, the city's civil rights community had three reasons for believing that the new Commission on Human Relations would make a much larger impact on job discrimination than had the FEPC. First, the new commission was established within the new city charter as a permanent city agency, insuring, its supporters believed, that it would receive a larger and more consistent funding stream from the city council and greater cooperation from other city agencies. Second, the new mayor, Joseph Clark, and his administration had made civil rights enforcement a major priority within their reform agenda. And finally, the commission had succeeded in hiring George Schermer, the former director of the Mayor's Interracial Committee in Detroit, to be its first Executive Director. While acknowledging that Loescher had been "devoted to the cause," commission member Sadie Alexander later described feeling frustrated by Loescher's conciliatory approach. "He moved like a snail and we needed action." Schermer, in contrast, had a reputation for aggressive advocacy of antidiscrimination practices. "We were really flying high when we got George," Alexander remembered in a 1976 interview.[22]

During Schermer's first years as CHR executive director, the commission did compile an impressive list of accomplishments. According to its 1953 annual report, for example, the commission was instrumental in the decision of the Pennsylvania Railroad to become the first railroad in the country to hire a black to a "class A clerical position," a decision that Schermer predicted would lead to additional job opportunities for blacks at the railroad. In addition, the CHR persuaded a meat products firm to end its bar to black employment; over the course of the year, the company placed twenty-two black workers in four departments. The commission also claimed responsibility for convincing a large restaurant chain to end its practice of not hiring Jewish waitresses, a chemical firm to hire its first black clerical and technical workers, and a large publishing firm to employ its first black workers in editorial, mechanical, and clerical positions. The breakthrough jobs strategy seemed to be producing results.[23]

These achievements, however, were not the result of a major shift in the CHR's enforcement strategy. In fact, Alexander greatly exaggerated the differences in approach between Schermer and Loescher. For example, Schermer maintained his predecessor's policy of using voluntary behind-the-scenes negotiations to resolve job discrimination cases and thus continued to eschew the provision of the FEPC ordinance that enabled the commission to hold public hearings when it found evidence of bias. Once the commission's staff investigators had determined that a violation had been committed, they would seek a private conference with the employer in order to negotiate a "conciliation agreement." While some of these agreements required the employer to hire, promote or reinstate the complainant or otherwise rectify their violation of the ordinance, others simply asked for changes in the company's stated employment policies or a general commitment to uphold the "letter and spirit of the law." As a result, the CHR was able to continue its record of success in individual cases of explicit discrimination and in opening up job categories that had previously been closed to black workers. In 1954, for example, the CHR took credit for ending employer and union discriminatory practices against black truck drivers, plasterers, and carpenters and for convincing two national loan companies to desegregate their Philadelphia storefront offices. In addition, the commission passed a resolution banning all references to race, color, religion, national origin or ancestry in help-wanted newspaper advertisements and convinced the city's daily papers to submit to the CHR staff all ads it received that might violate the ban. In 1955, the CHR convinced a public utility, a restaurant chain, and a maker of precision instruments to hire black workers for the first time.[24]

These successes, however, masked the fact that neither the fair employment practices ordinance nor the Commission on Human Relations had achieved their desired impact on the Philadelphia labor market. "Qualitatively," the CHR wrote in its annual report for 1956, "the achievements are impressive. Quantitatively, the size of the job is so great that at year's end the job ahead seems as great or greater than before." A year later, the commission report acknowledged that "the complaint procedure alone cannot accomplish the objective of full equality of opportunity . . . discrimination is becoming increasingly subtle. It is becoming harder to establish that race

TABLE 5. EMPLOYMENT DISCRIMINATION COMPLAINTS RECEIVED BY THE
PHILADELPHIA COMMISSION ON HUMAN RELATIONS

Year	Total complaints received	Cases closed	Cases where evidence of discrimination was found	Percentage of cases where evidence of discrimination was found
1949	260	216	114	53
1950	215	241	118	49
1951	258	235	60	26
1953	174	146	24	16
1954	170	151	42	28
1955	111	139	31	22
1956	99	117	33	28
1957	117	76	17	22
1958	101	111	17	15
1959	78	71	7	10
1960	109	88	12	14

Source: annual reports of the Philadelphia Commission on Human Relations.

is a decisive factor in many cases where it seems clear that it was among the factors affecting the actions of the person against whom the complaints are made." The CHR's own statistical analysis of its efforts reveals the declining impact of its case-by-case approach to enforcing the FEPC ordinance over the course of the 1950s. As Table 5 shows, the number of complaints of employment discrimination received by the CHR fell from an average of 244.3 per year between 1949 and 1951 to 174 in 1953, Schermer's first year as the commission's executive director, and then to an average of 101.2 over the last five years of the decade. More significantly, the number of cases where the FEPC/CHR found probable cause of a violation fell from 118 in 1950 to 42 in 1954 and then to 7 in 1959. In fact, the CHR averaged only 22.9 findings of probable cause per year in employment discrimination cases during the first eight years that Schermer ran the commission.[25]

Had these statistics been evidence of declining levels of employment discrimination in Philadelphia, they would have been cause for celebration. But, as a 1959 CHR survey found, 93 percent of black workers believed that employers in the city practiced racial discrimination in hiring and 25 percent reported that they had been denied a job or treated unfairly because of their race. What in fact the decline in complaints to the CHR revealed was that the city's employers had learned how to avoid blatant violations of the FEPC ordinance while not fully integrating their workforces. "In the framework of the present-day administration of the fair employment law," the CHR's 1960 annual report concluded, "the employer who does not 'refuse to hire' because of race may, with impunity, continue to conduct his recruitment, training and advancement of employees with only rare and nominal deviation from the traditional pattern." As the CHR report acknowledged, the decline in the number of complaints received was evidence that black workers had become increasingly aware of the limited utility of the FEPC ordinance. After an initial period of enthusiasm, fewer and fewer black workers viewed the commission as capable of providing a remedy for the barriers they found in the city's labor markets. The commission's commitment to negotiating "conciliation agreements" in private, the CHR staff had come to believe, had convinced "the minority public . . . that nothing is happening under the fair employment law."[26]

The Persistence of Racial Segmentation in the Philadelphia Labor Market

Three employment discrimination cases from the 1950s demonstrate how the limitations of the FEPC ordinance and the CHR's reliance on conciliation agreements kept the commission from having a significant impact on African American employment in Philadelphia. In 1952, the Philadelphia NAACP's Labor Committee and the Philadelphia CIO's Antidiscrimination Committee agreed to support a group of black maintenance workers from the local Philco radio and television plant who were demanding that the company hire blacks for production jobs. The city's largest industrial employer, Philco only employed blacks in unskilled maintenance positions. In the view of the protesting workers, Philco and Locals 101 and 102 of the International Union of Electrical, Radio and Machine Workers (IUE-CIO) had a tacit agreement to protect the company's white women assembly workers from having to work side by side with blacks. With the assistance of the national NAACP's labor secretary, Herbert Hill, the local activists threatened to file a formal complaint with the CHR against the company and the union. However, they ultimately decided to make use of what they believed would be a more effective mechanism for forcing Philco to change its hiring policies. Since they understood that the commission would not be able to take action without explicit evidence that blacks had been refused employment, they instead sought to pressure the IUE's national leadership to demand that the Philco locals uphold the antidiscrimination provisions in the international union's constitution. Within a month, the two Philco locals had issued a "policy statement" calling on the company to practice "equal treatment of all workers." Shortly thereafter, the company agreed to upgrade twenty-seven black male employees to production jobs and promised that black women would be included in the next group of assembly-line workers hired.[27]

The victory at Philco, however, was a hollow one. The plant had recently laid off 2,000 white women production workers. Seniority provisions in the plant's collective bargaining agreement required the company to rehire those women before it could add any new workers. Moreover, Philco was on the verge of opening a new production facility north of the city in Bucks County. In an economic context in which manufacturers like Philco were in the midst of shifting the bulk of their production to modernized facilities in the suburbs and the Sun Belt, promises of future hiring at facilities like Philco's Philadelphia plant, whether dictated by an FEPC ordinance or a union constitution, meant little for efforts to establish equal opportunity in the city's labor markets. And, as we have seen, blatant discrimination in housing markets combined with a weak state fair employment practices law prevented all but a handful of black workers from finding employment in the new suburban industrial plants.[28]

Even when the CHR found evidence of discrimination at local companies with stable or expanding workforces, however, the liberal commitment to the principles of merit hiring, race blindness, and behind-the-scenes negotiations made it difficult for the commission to force employers to sizably increase job opportunities for black workers. For example, in 1955 the CHR conducted an investigation into hiring practices at the Philadelphia-based Atlantic Richfield Oil Company (ARCO) after it received a complaint from two black job applicants who charged that they had been denied jobs with the company because of their race. ARCO, however, contended that the complainants had been refused employment because they had failed to score well on the test given to job applicants. After reviewing the test papers and other records from the company's personnel files, the commission agreed with Atlantic's contention that the complainants "had done poorly in the examination as compared with those employed." As a result, the CHR was forced to close its investigation "in favor of the company" even though blacks were underrepresented in well-paying production and managerial positions at ARCO's corporate headquarters and at its Philadelphia refinery. Instead of producing substantive improvements in job opportunities for black workers at Atlantic, the commission settled for publicizing the company's "verbal assurances that [it] will follow a policy of merit employment." The CHR would later report that ARCO had promoted four black refinery workers to the position of subforeman and had begun to hire blacks to clerical positions in its corporate headquarters. But here again, these were hardly numbers that would have had a significant impact on the structure of black employment in the city.[29]

Thus the commitment to race-blind merit hiring, which had helped to open up city government jobs to thousands of black workers by converting patronage jobs into civil service positions, proved a double-edged sword. Simple reliance on merit hiring in a labor market in which most white workers enjoyed a competitive advantage in educational background, skill training, and family and community networks made it nearly impossible to prove that a given company maintained racially discriminatory hiring policies. So long as companies like Atlantic Richfield could cite test scores as evidence that they had not discriminated against a specific individual, they could justify their failure to desegregate their workforces.

Even more devastating to black hopes for equality in the labor market was the CHR's inability to end racially discriminatory employment practices in the city's unionized construction industry. Officially, racial discrimination was outlawed on all publicly financed construction projects—the largest local source of construction contracts—in Philadelphia. Not only did the new city charter ban racial discrimination in all municipal government contracts of more than $2,000, but a 1948 federal directive dictated that there could be no racial discrimination in the expenditure of federal construction funds or in the administration of federally funded vocational education programs. By relying exclusively on contractors who employed union labor on a closed-shop basis, government agencies were not only ignoring their own antidiscrimination rules but were providing a captive market for the racially discriminatory construction unions. As late as 1963, not a single black skilled craftsperson was employed on city construction projects and the 7,300 combined members of the local plumbers, electricians, and steamfitters' unions included only one single black electrician. Even the Philadelphia Board of Education allowed the building trades unions to exclude black students from the federally financed apprenticeship programs that they ran in the city's three vocational public high schools. According to a 1962 NAACP report, only 4 percent of "apprenticeable trades" in Philadelphia were open to black workers. Given the central role of publicly and privately financed office construction to the city's postwar transition from an industrial to a postindustrial economy, the exclusion of black workers from some of the best-paying working-class occupations in the local economy was no small matter.[30]

Despite the overwhelming evidence that Philadelphia's building trades unions and union contractors were using union membership regulations and apprenticeship programs to exclude black workers from the skilled construction trades, the city government never undertook a serious effort to enforce the city charter's ban on racial discrimination in city contracts during the reform administrations of either Joseph Clark or Richardson Dilworth. The Commission on Human Relations began its first investigation into the employment practices of the local construction industry in 1953. After more than a year of consultations with other city departments and representatives of the local construction industry, the commission adopted what it called "new and stricter" enforcement provisions for city contractors in the summer of 1955. Despite a commission news release which touted the new provisions as "a great step forward in advancing equal job opportunity for all Philadelphians," the provisions themselves constituted a tacit admission that the CHR lacked the power to enforce the charter's nondiscriminatory clause on city contractors. In effect, the new

provisions did little more than require contractors to post "in a conspicu-
ous place" notice of the nondiscrimination clause and insert it in all subcontracts. In addition, the CHR began a policy of early morning visits to
construction sites to insure that foremen hired day laborers on a racially
equitable basis. However, the limited size of the commission's staff prevented it from conducting anything more than random inspections.[31]

In fact, it can be argued that the CHR's inspections of day laborer hiring
served only to reinforce the racial segmentation by job category that
existed within the construction industry. As Thomas Sugrue has shown,
black construction workers, particularly those who had migrated from the
South, often possessed high levels of skill in specific trades. More than 10
percent of black male workers in the city had experience in construction,
most in either non-union or unskilled jobs. They were, however, prevented
from joining the skilled crafts unions by strict apprentice requirements and
other arcane membership practices and thus could not find work in their
skill area on union construction sites. What these workers could find was
day laborer work if they were willing to accept the designation of unskilled
laborer and to join the racially integrated Laborers' Union. With the postwar housing boom and Center City urban renewal greatly increasing the
demand for skilled construction labor, the presence of day laborers with
significant construction skills enabled the skilled trade unions to meet the
demand without having to increase the size of their membership and thus
risk diluting their bargaining power.[32]

Unable to force the building trades unions to change their membership
policies, the CHR staff resorted to exhortations to "the minority worker"
to demand fair treatment from unions and union contractors and to file
complaints with the commission when their entreaties were rejected. In a
1955 workshop for church leaders on how they could best assist members
of their churches "to get the greatest benefit from" labor unions, the
emphasis was on the responsibility of black workers to participate fully in
their unions. "Being admitted into a union [i]s only the first step," the
commission declared in a newsletter. "Black workers should attend meetings, and . . . in order to gain the full benefits a union has to offer them,
they must be prepared to assume some of the responsibilities for setting
the policies and practices of the union." Despite widespread awareness of
the exclusion of black workers from the skilled trades, it would not be until
March 1963 that the CHR would publicly condemn racial discrimination in
the local construction industry. Following a four-month investigation, the
commission accused four local unions—the electricians, the steamfitters,
the plumbers, and the sheet metal workers—of maintaining segregated
employment policies on municipal construction sites. "We have drawn the
conclusion," George Schermer finally announced twelve years after the city
charter banned racial discrimination in municipal contracts, "that the total
absence of Negroes in skilled jobs is evidence of Negro exclusion."[33]

From Antidiscrimination to Affirmative Action

The CHR's exhortations to black workers to demand equal treatment from the city's trade unions constituted a significant shift in the commission's discursive representation of its efforts to establish equal employment opportunity in Philadelphia. As the decade progressed, the CHR increasingly abandoned its optimistic declarations about the city's vanguard position in the movement toward a colorblind society. The commission's 1956 annual report acknowledged for the first time that it lacked both the legal and fiscal resources necessary to confront the racial challenges facing the city, challenges that included high rates of black in-migration, "the suburbanization of advantaged groups," and "continuing limitations upon [black] economic opportunity." A year later, the CHR argued that its initial view of what it would take to eradicate racial discrimination in the city had been deeply flawed. At its founding, the commission wrote in 1957, it had seen the struggle against discrimination as primarily a government responsibility. The "responsibility" of the citizen was limited to "complain[ing] or to report[ing] discrimination." It "was up to the Commission . . . to investigate, educate, conciliate, enforce the law and thus resolve the discriminatory practices." Six years later, the CHR now believed that only a massive cooperative effort "of all agencies of government, of business and industry . . . of community organization and of individual citizens" could achieve the goal of a colorblind city. The "function" of the commission, it asserted, was "primarily that of planning, communicating and organizing."[34]

At first, the CHR saw an increase in educational programming as the solution to persistent racial discrimination and segmentation in Philadelphia's labor markets. Beginning in 1954, the commission's staff set out to encourage both employers and black workers to be more aggressive in their pursuit of equal employment opportunity. For employers, the CHR organized a series of conferences targeting those who still possessed "unscientific attitudes about the employment capabilities of certain minorities." The purpose of these "Employer Conferences" was to convince individual employers "that traditional patterns of employee utilization are not beneficial, either to their business[es] or to the economic health of the community at large."[35]

For much of the 1950s, however, the commission focused on educational and skill deficits within the black community as the prime cause of persistent racial segmentation in the city's labor markets. "Fair employment," the CHR announced in 1954, "is a two way street . . . it involves both the responsibility of the employer to hire without regard for race, religion or national origin and the responsibility of the job applicant to qualify himself for employment and to apply for jobs where he is qualified." Declaring that "more and more Negro job applicants are meeting industry's standards for education and ability," the commission blamed black workers' "lack of confidence and skill in 'selling' themselves to employers" for continued high levels of black un- and underemployment. "The minority worker," one CHR news release read, "has a responsibility. Workers who don't apply for jobs . . . aren't likely to be handed those jobs." In addition to its efforts to encourage black workers to apply for union membership and to take "an active role in their unions," the CHR also initiated a youth employment program to prepare "young minority group job seekers" with "suitable attitudes toward employment . . . [and] adeptness in the . . . job interview" and to inform them of job training opportunities and of "occupations with the best opportunities for employment." While these educational efforts may have helped individual black youth find better employment opportunities, the commission's emphasis on the need for black workers to better prepare themselves for job opportunities served only to justify employers' reluctance to aggressively desegregate their workforces.[36]

By the end of the decade, however, the CHR was finally prepared to acknowledge that the problem of persistent labor market segmentation was more the result of limitations inherent in fair employment practices legislation than of skill deficits in the black workforce. As I have said, the commission's 1959 annual report highlighted survey data on black workers' continued experience of discrimination. In the early years of the FEPC ordinance, the report concluded, "a rather large backlog of well-trained underemployed Negroes in Philadelphia" had enabled the commission to make a number of important breakthroughs in the local job market. Since then, however, "the Commission's almost exclusive use of private conciliation procedures" meant that large numbers of black workers were completely unaware of the ordinance and were therefore locked into low-paying unskilled occupations. Declaring that the CHR could no longer accept employer "pleas of evolutionary intent toward full merit employment," the 1959 report promised to use the commission's public hearing mandate to highlight continuing cases of employment discrimination in the city. In that year alone, the CHR held more public hearings than it had in the previous decade. One series of twelve public investigative hearings on employment policies and practices in Philadelphia's hotel and restaurant industry led to the negotiation of a 1960 consent agreement with the Greater Philadelphia Restaurant Operators Association that provided for the internal promotion of currently employed black personnel, the development of written job specifications in the industry, the modification of union seniority requirements, and the integration of referral lists from union hiring halls.[37]

In 1960, the CHR introduced new language into the struggle for employment equity in Philadelphia. Employers must take "affirmative steps," the commission declared, "to compensate for the fact that the discriminatory patterns have been 'frozen' into the economic, social, political and cultural structure of society." Specifically, the CHR began requiring that employers found guilty of racial bias take "affirmative measures with regard to recruitment, training and supervision to assure the inclusion of minority persons in more and higher levels of employment." The commission acknowledged that it was adding "a new dimension" to its program "for equal opportunity" and that many in the fair employment community viewed efforts to require employers to act affirmatively as "discrimination in reverse." However, this new approach was necessary, the CHR argued, because "the framework of the present-day administration of the fair employment law [had allowed] the employer who does not 'refuse to hire' because of race [to] continue to conduct his recruitment, training and advancement of employees with only rare and nominal deviation" from practices that had long disadvantaged black workers. Unfortunately, the commission could only mandate more aggressive measures "where unlawful practices can be proven." Still, the CHR's call for employers to take "affirmative steps" to integrate their workforces can be seen as part of a liberal reevaluation of fair employment legislation that would eventually lead institutions from the federal government to Fortune 500 companies and elite universities to adopt the mix of outreach initiatives and racial diversity goals that has come to be known as affirmative action. In the short term, though, the CHR's initiative had little immediate impact on the lives of Philadelphia's black workers. Rather, as I shall discuss in Chapter 3, it was black anger at the failure of the commission to transform the racial segmentation of the city's labor markets that would lead to the emergence of a mass protest movement for civil rights in Philadelphia.[38]

Black Housing in Postwar Philadelphia

The postwar paradox of racial progress and persistent racial discrimination and inequality was also evident in the housing of black Philadelphians. As the 1955 *Tribune* photo essay demonstrated, some black middle- and working-class families had begun to enjoy unprecedented opportunity for homeownership outside of the traditional black ghettos of South and lower North Philadelphia. In addition, the rapid development of public housing complexes in the postwar years gave even lower-income families the opportunity to live in modernized and well-maintained apartments with stable rents and a seemingly reliable landlord. Still, housing discrimination remained pervasive in Philadelphia so long as neither the federal, state nor municipal governments passed fair housing legislation. A 1958 CHR study of apartment rentals in Center City, for example, found only two nonwhite tenants in 4,202 units surveyed. "Restrictions on the base of race and ancestry were found to be widespread," the commission concluded. "Relief of persons aggrieved by these restrictions was not possible in the absence of legal sanctions." Two years later, a commission public hearing

TABLE 6. POPULATION AND HOUSING CHARACTERISTICS OF PHILADELPHIA CENSUS
TRACT 32A, 1930–1950

	1930	1940	1950
Total population	5,944 (100%)	7,437 (100%)	9,571 (100%)
White population	3,376 (56.8%)	2,802 (37.7%)	260 (2.7%)
Black population	2,568 (43.2%)	4,635 (62.3%)	9,311 (97.3%)
Occupied dwelling units	1,365 (100%)	2,315 (100%)	2,950 (100%)
Owner occupied	386 (28.3%)	222 (9.6%)	289 (9.8%)
Tenant occupied	979 (71.7%)	2,093 (90.4%)	2,661 (90.2%)
Dilapidated or no private bath	NA	1,743 (83.3%)	2,122 (79.7%)
Avg. rent	NA	$20.87	$30.15

Source: U.S. Census, "Philadelphia's Negro Population: Facts on Housing"; Commission on Human Relations (CHR) papers, box 148, folder 4, Philadelphia Municipal Archives (PMA).

found evidence that real estate offices were inundating homeowners in racially transitioning neighborhoods with as many as eight to ten mailings per week. One homeowner submitted a total of thirty-nine mailings that he had received from sixteen firms over eighteen months. One realtor admitted to mailing out 500 cards per week, another to more than 3,000 per year. By the end of the 1950s, it was clear that the hope that stable integrated neighborhoods would emerge from the spread of black home-owners into middle-class residential areas had been little more than a pipe dream. In all but a couple of neighborhoods, the vast majority of white families decided to move to the suburbs or to the still lily-white Northeast section of the city once the black population reached a "tipping" point that the CHR identified as a 30 to 40 percent black population on a given block.[39]

Meanwhile, the continued in-migration of black southerners had created ideal market conditions for real estate interests to pursue disinvestment strategies in the city's black ghettos. As white families fled to the suburbs from middle-class residential areas on the city's periphery, the white working-class communities that bordered the inner-city ghettos continued to resist black incursions. As a result, black migrant families joined with the poor majority of black Philadelphians in the search for housing in the constricted areas of the black ghetto. Growing demand thus collided with the limited supply of rental units in impoverished neighborhoods, enabling landlords to raise rents and subdivide the neighborhoods' aging housing stock.

North Philadelphia census tract 32A, on the east side of North Broad Street just to the south of Temple University, provides a classic example of the disinvestment process. In 1930, 5,944 people lived in 1,365 "dwelling units" in census tract 32A (see Table 6). The tract was 57 percent white and 43 percent black and 386 of the 1,365 dwelling units were owner occupied. By 1950, the tract's population had nearly doubled to 9,571. It was now 97 percent black; only 260 whites remained in the area. Although there had been no new housing construction in the tract since 1930, the number of dwelling units had more than doubled to 2,950. Of these only 289 were owner occupied. Of the 2,661 rental units in the area, 2,122 were either dilapidated, lacked a private bath, or both. Moreover, average rents in the tract had jumped from $20.87 per month to $30.15 per month, an increase of 44.5 percent, between 1940 and 1950 even as the number of rental units increased from 2,093 to 2,661.[40]

Urban renewal and slum clearance further exacerbated the black housing shortage by removing dwelling units from poor neighborhoods. While urban renewal advocates' primary emphasis was on the revitalization of Center City, they believed that their efforts to modernize Center City would have little impact if the business district were to remain surrounded by "blighted" inner-city neighborhoods. Adopting the view of contemporary sociologists that the decaying physical structures of the ghetto bred pathological behaviors, the reformer-led Philadelphia Redevelopment Authority adopted a policy of aggressive slum clearance. By clearing the slums, the authority's leadership hoped to create open space that would attract private housing developers eager to revitalize the city's inner-city neighborhoods by building modern housing for the poor. Although this program of slum clearance led to the displacement of large numbers of black families, the city's liberal civil rights coalition supported the urban renewal program as the best solution to the problem of black ghettoization. In fact, the Fellowship Commission and other civil rights groups offered their services to assist the Redevelopment Authority's efforts to find new housing for the displaced families.[41]

But the private investment that the Redevelopment Authority expected to occur in the slum clearance areas did not materialize. Real estate developers and lenders, including the federal government's home loan agencies, viewed older urban neighborhoods, particularly those with large minority populations, as a significant investment risk. Thus, Philadelphia's inner-city neighborhoods were simply not eligible for the federal mortgage assistance that was fueling the suburban housing boom. While all of the city's working-class neighborhoods suffered from the federal government's housing priorities, the predominately black communities of North, South, and West Philadelphia were particularly hard hit. A 1957 Redevelopment Authority study found that 90 percent of the families displaced by slum clearance in the previous seven years had been black and 56 percent earned less than $399 per month. Moreover, only 21 percent of displaced families found satisfactory housing; 26 percent found unsatisfactory housing and 52 percent disappeared or refused to cooperate with the survey. The authority concluded that the city lacked sufficient funds to complete the clearance of the most blighted areas or to provide adequate housing for the families already displaced. It ascribed the failure of slum clearance to two factors: the inadequacy of federal aid to the city and the paucity of financing available for private investment. Ensuing plans for reviving the city's black ghettos would continue to suffer from these weaknesses. In place of slum clearance, the Redevelopment Authority adopted a much more modest program of conserving the relatively stable neighborhoods that bordered the cleared areas. While these older neighborhoods had once been seen as an asset to the city, their stability was now threatened by an influx of poor families displaced from the now empty slums. Rather than continuing slum clearance, this new policy ended public investment in the most blighted areas and instead focused on strict enforcement of the housing code for privately owned rental properties in the more stable border areas. The impact of the city's urban renewal program thus was to exacerbate rather than lessen the process of black isolation into decaying ghetto neighborhoods. To the extent that liberal civil rights groups failed to protest the impact of these policies on the city's black poor and working-classes, they appeared unconcerned with the day-to-day challenges facing most black Philadelphians.[42]

The work of historians Arnold Hirsch, Kenneth Jackson, and Thomas Sugrue places prime responsibility for the failure of residential integration and the growth of black ghettos in the urban North on federal housing policy, the business practices of the real estate industry, and the racial attitudes and anxieties of white homeowners.[43] An examination of three liberal housing campaigns of the 1950s—(1) the Commission on Human Relations' Neighborhood Stabilization Program (NSP) which sought to convince white homeowners to remain in racially transitional neighborhoods, (2) the efforts of liberal civil rights groups to integrate public housing in the city, and (3) the statewide campaign to pass fair housing legislation—demonstrates how Philadelphia's liberal civil rights community moved from extreme optimism on housing issues at the beginning of the 1950s to a gloomy assessment of the very same issues by the end of the decade.

The Neighborhood Stabilization Program

Neighborhood stabilization became a prime goal for the Commission on Human Relations following George Schermer's appointment to run the agency in February 1953. That year, the commission staff began to establish relationships with community leaders in neighborhoods going through racial transition. The goal was to prevent racial tensions and curb white panic selling. During 1954, the CHR received twenty-eight reports of vandalism targeted either at blacks moving into all-white neighborhoods or at whites for selling their homes to blacks. Between 1954 and 1956, black Philadelphians purchased homes in twenty-eight previously all-white neighborhoods, with the most activity occurring in Strawberry Mansion, a one-time Jewish neighborhood on the western edge of North Philadelphia, Germantown, a middle-class neighborhood in the Northwest section of the city, and West Philadelphia south of Market Street. By the end of 1955, the commission believed that its Neighborhood Stabilization Program had succeeded in averting panic selling and unethical real estate practices in many areas experiencing racial change. The following year, the CHR received not a single report of vandalism or violence directed at black move-ins.[44]

Based on the principles of community organizing and intergroup education, the goal of the NSP was to convince white homeowners that it was panic selling, not the presence of black neighbors, that threatened their property values and therefore it was in their interest to limit white flight from their neighborhoods. Specifically, the CHR's field representatives sought to bring together "old and new [white and black] neighbors" to establish permanent working committees to monitor racial tensions and to work with local real estate agents to discourage block busting initiatives. Each NSP initiative began with a meeting between a CHR field representative and concerned white neighborhood residents. The field representatives were to respond with "facts," not "preaching," to the residents' concerns that the presence of black families would lead to falling property values, increased crime, and neighborhood deterioration. The field representatives were instructed to point out that blacks were becoming increasingly middle-class, that they were making advances in employment and education, and that they were moving into white neighborhoods across the city. Not only were their new black neighbors likely to be as committed as they to maintaining respectable homes and safe, crime-free communities, but there was no evidence that residential integration led to declining property values. Appealing to the residents' sense of civic pride, the field representatives were also to point out the city's interest in maintaining neighborhood stability during this period of black population growth. Finally, they were to encourage their listeners to establish a neighborhood group whose mission would be to squelch rumors that might inflame racial tensions, to monitor housing standards and zoning changes in the community, to notify the city of possible housing code violations, and to serve as a welcoming committee for new residents. To concerns that residential integration would place white residents in the minority and would eventually lead to intermarriage, the field representatives were to respond with "humor."[45]

According to the CHR's 1955 annual report, the most common initial response to the field representatives' presentations was "contempt." White residents insulted the commission staff "in the hot folk language of the big city" and condemned the city government for not acting to preserve their property values and the racial integrity of their neighborhoods. Still, the

CHR believed that it had "apparently stabilized the situation" in most areas where it had undertaken a NSP initiative, by preventing neighborhood turnover and allowing for intergroup understanding to grow. Only in one neighborhood had the white residents remained completely unresponsive to the NSP program, largely as a result of the presence of a "neighborhood improvement group" committed to using "veiled threats and intimidation" to keep out black families.[46]

Two examples from 1954 demonstrate the range of neighborhood and class contexts in which the CHR was forced to respond to racial tensions resulting from the move-in of a black family. On Slocum Street in Germantown, the commission's staff helped to form an integrated neighborhood committee after a new black family received a number of anonymous letters. According to the CHR, the neighborhood committee's efforts to prevent panic selling helped to insure that of four homes placed up for sale that year, two were bought by whites and two by blacks. In a more dangerous incident, a crowd of 300–500 whites battered down the windows and doors of a rundown rowhouse near Judson and Cambria Streets in Kensington, a white working-class neighborhood, just hours after a black family with a lease-to-purchase agreement moved in. After the police intervened to prevent further damage to the home and to prevent the crowd from attacking black passersby, the CHR initiated a week of intensive negotiations with white community leaders and black ministers from surrounding areas. Finally, an agreement was reached in which the local community agreed to recognize the property rights of the black family and civil rights groups agreed to raise the funds necessary to enable the family to bring the home up to the housing code. Three months later, the black family returned to their home without incident.[47]

By 1956, however, the CHR had grown increasingly pessimistic about its ability to prevent white flight and the resegregation of transitional neighborhoods. Too many neighborhoods were simply changing too fast for the commission to implement the NSP program on a sufficient scale to meet the challenge. That year, the commission published a pamphlet detailing eight observations about neighborhood stabilization. The problem of neighborhood transition, the commission now argued, could not be solved solely at the neighborhood level. Rather, the root problems of racial injustice in the housing market and intergroup hostility needed to be solved first. The local housing market was pushing black demand into changing neighborhoods while discouraging white demand for those same neighborhoods, thus eroding the basis for stable integration. Even in areas that avoided panic selling or overt racial tensions, the normal process of housing turnover inevitably led to racial change. Once the black population of a given block reached between 30 and 40 percent, the CHR concluded, the possibility of maintaining stable integration was lost. In the commission's view, stabilization efforts remained important only insofar as changing neighborhoods were test cases for the possibility of racial integration in the society as a whole. From this perspective, stabilization efforts were more likely to succeed in neighborhoods characterized by higher education levels, greater economic security, lower population density, and a greater distance from ghetto areas. Still, stabilization efforts could help to educate allies for the cause of residential integration even in neighborhoods that were destined to be incorporated into what the commission called the "advancing ghetto."[48]

Beginning in 1956, therefore, the CHR increasingly turned its attention to issues of racial bias in the real estate industry. Part of this effort focused on working with the city's civil rights coalition to press for fair housing legislation at the state and municipal level, an effort that I will discuss later in this chapter. At the same time, the CHR initiated a major educational program directed at the city's real estate industry. Specifically, the commission hoped to use "education rather than punitive means" to convince real estate agents to abandon their racially divisive practices. To achieve this goal, the CHR established a Housing Industry Advisory Committee in order to involve "housing industry representatives in a cooperative approach to solutions of the racially restricted market." Specifically, the commission identified five human relations problems in the local real estate industry: (1) the refusal of housing interests to make new, suburban-style housing available to blacks or to open "unbroken" neighborhoods to black home buyers, (2) the channeling of white home buyers to the suburbs, (3) the belief that once blacks entered a previously all-white neighborhood, the re-segregation of that community as an all-black neighborhood was inevitable, (4) racial discrimination in the home mortgage industry, and (5) overcrowding in black neighborhoods. The city's black residents, the commission believed, were not the only ones harmed by these practices. The inability to disperse the city's black ghettos made urban renewal efforts more difficult. The real estate industry opened itself to more government regulation because of its inability to curb its own "unethical practices." And the level of racial prejudice and tension in the city was exacerbated.[49]

The CHR real estate program was premised on the belief that the industry was a "willing tool of prejudice" and that it was just "doing what most of its customers want it to do." The focus of the real estate program was to provide educational materials with hard data on the size and growth of the "Negro housing market" to homebuilders and real estate brokers on the assumption that "members of the industry, armed with factual information . . . [will] undertake constructive measures toward developing a non-restricted housing market throughout the city." In 1956, the CHR sent letters to four thousand local realtors asking them to notify the commission when the first black family moved into a white block so that the commission could take preventive action against vandalism, racial hostility, and panic selling. The commission also began distributing complimentary copies of *Currents*, its newsletter, to local realtors.[50]

Two years later, however, the CHR's efforts to work cooperatively with the real estate industry came to a sudden halt when the real estate professionals on the commission's Housing Industry Advisory Committee rejected all four of the CHR staff's proposals, including the publishing of a real estate trade association brochure on home buying and racial change, the organization of an industry conference on open housing, the establishment of a housing clinic jointly sponsored by the industry and the municipal government to examine racial discrimination in housing, and an effort to develop alternatives to legislative remedies to housing discrimination. In 1959, the CHR abandoned an attempt to revive the real estate initiative when the Philadelphia Board of Realtors failed to take action against seventeen realtors whom the commission had found to be "pursuing panic and/or tension inducing activities." Once again, the CHR had devoted, to little effect, significant resources to a program of education and moral suasion directed at the practitioners of racial discrimination. Not only did the effort have little impact on actual real estate industry practices, but it further signaled the agency's ineffectualness in the struggle against racial discrimination to the city's black residents. "Hundreds of cases of community tension, discrimination and vandalism," the CHR concluded in its evaluation of its neighborhood stabilization efforts, "have demonstrated that discriminatory practices and segregation cannot be eliminated through case by case treatment or educational efforts alone. The need is for fair housing legislation."[51]

The Campaign to Integrate Public Housing

In its origins, federally funded public housing, like federal support for home mortgages, was explicitly designed to reify patterns of residential segregation. Federal funding for slum clearance and low-income housing construction was first included in President Roosevelt's National Industrial Recovery Act (NRA) to create employment opportunities in "the 'sick' building trades." The 1937 Wagner-Steagall Act formed the U.S. Housing Administration, established public housing as a job creation and slum clearance program, and limited it to poor families unable to afford "sanitary" housing in the private sector. Harold Ickes, Roosevelt's secretary of the interior, decided that the racial composition of individual housing projects should be determined by the "prevailing racial composition of the surrounding neighborhood" as part of his efforts to deflect the real estate industry's opposition to public housing. In addition, the Interior Department gave local governments the power to determine both housing project site and tenant selection. The first federally funded housing project in Philadelphia was not even designed for low-income families; its white tenants were either middle-class professionals or skilled workers. When the local housing authority did begin to make plans to build projects for the chronically ill-housed residents of the city's black slums, they made it clear that they intended to do so on a strictly segregated basis. One white supporter of public housing was "delighted" to hear that the Philadelphia Advisory Committee on Housing was "contemplating the establishment of a Harlem section for Philadelphia." Relieved that the city was finally showing a willingness to open its public housing program to blacks, leaders of the Philadelphia chapters of the NAACP, the NNC and the Urban League all endorsed plans to build all-black projects in the city. Thus, when the 535-unit James Weldon Johnson Homes opened in West Philadelphia on October 1, 1940, 95 percent of its 1,800 tenants were black.[52]

By the time the second black project, Richard Allen Homes, in the West Poplar section of North Philadelphia, was ready for occupancy in 1942, more than 4,000 African American families had applied to live there, including 764 who had been displaced from their tenements in order to clear land for the project. Of the residential units that were torn down to make room for the project, 68 percent lacked indoor toilets and almost half were without central heat. The city's Republican administration, however, asked the U.S. Housing Administration for permission to convert it to housing for white defense workers and their families. That same year, similar controversy over Detroit's Sojourner Truth housing project would lead to a race riot. In Philadelphia, however, a concerted campaign by the city's civil rights organizations successfully preserved the project for African Americans families. However, as John Bauman has pointed out, the success of the Allen Homes campaign says less about the strength of the civil rights community than about the city government's "desire to preserve the existing boundaries of the emerging black ghetto." Of the families selected to move into the project, 40 percent were headed by laborers, 25 percent by domestic or service workers, and 15 percent by workers in shipbuilding or munitions factories.[53]

Following the war, Philadelphia's civil rights community made it clear that it was no longer willing to accept racially segregated housing projects. In 1946, for example, an NAACP delegation unsuccessfully pressed the Philadelphia Housing Authority (PHA), the municipal agency responsible for managing public housing projects, to abandon the "neighborhood formula" for determining the racial composition of specific projects. Three years later, the U.S. Congress passed and President Truman signed the Federal Housing Act of 1949. Strongly opposed by the real estate industry, the 1949 act revived public housing construction and required that new projects be developed "on a nondiscrimination and non-segregated basis, without regard to race, religion and national origin." Still, the PHA continued to refuse to change its racial policies, despite the lobbying efforts of Democratic reformer Joseph Clark, who had just been elected city controller for

Philadelphia, and the Fellowship Commission's Committee on Democracy in Housing. The PHA would not agree to begin to integrate the city's housing projects until 1951, the year of Clark's election to the mayor's office and the passage of the new city charter. That year, the PHA enlisted the support of the city's civil rights community in a campaign to press the city council for a zoning change that would enable the authority to build a new interracial housing project in a predominately Irish and Italian section of South Philadelphia. In addition, the PHA announced the formation of a Neighborhood Relations Committee, made up primarily of representatives of civil rights groups, to aid in the process of integrating housing projects. By July 1952, Arch Homes, the city's first integrated housing project, had opened near the University of Pennsylvania in West Philadelphia with thirty white families, many of whom were the families of veterans currently attending the university, and forty black families whom the PHA defined as "stable." A month later, the Fellowship Commission convinced the housing authority to allow a black veteran and his family to integrate North Philadelphia's Abbotsford Homes, despite the opposition of many of the project's white tenants.[54]

Despite the PHA's announced commitment to integration, only two of the eleven projects that it was building in 1952 were slated for integration. Moreover, only black tenants who conformed to a "middle-class profile" were selected to integrate projects. As a result, Arch Homes remained the only project whose tenants were evenly split between the races in 1954. In that year, three of the city's projects were at least 99 percent black and one other was 90 percent. And though the first black families moved into the all-white Bartram Village project in Southwest Philadelphia that year, five of the city's housing projects were still less than 5 percent black and two more less than 20 percent black.[55]

Still, the civil rights community enthusiastically supported a 1956 PHA proposal to build twenty-one scattered-site small-scale public housing projects as a crucial opportunity for increasing neighborhood integration. Under the scattered-site plan, half of the new projects would have been built in all-white outlying areas of the city and the rest in racially transitional neighborhoods. The PHA and its supporters hoped that the smallness of the projects would minimize white opposition to their proposed locations. Instead, the decision to spread the proposed projects throughout the city had the ironic effect of uniting opposition to the plan. Despite a concerted campaign by civil rights liberals to promote the virtues of scattered-site projects, homeowners in the targeted neighborhoods attacked the proposal as an attempt by middle-class elites to impose their political ideals on white neighborhoods without consideration of the impact on property values. Charging that renters were inevitably less responsible neighbors than homeowners, opponents of the PHA plan argued that public housing should be restricted to slums where it was needed. Backed by the Democratic Party councilmembers and ward leaders from the slated neighborhoods, the homeowners' groups were able to force the city to shift the proposed sites to areas of the city that were less white and therefore less controversial in order to save the promised federal housing dollars. As a result, every housing project built in Philadelphia between 1956 and 1967 was located in either a predominately black ghetto or a racially transitioning neighborhood. The mission of public housing in the city had become providing housing for poor black families displaced by slum clearance. Rather than contributing to neighborhood integration, the public housing program in fact exacerbated—along with the city's slum clearance program and white suburban flight—residential segregation in the city. By 1960, nine of Philadelphia's housing projects were at least 95 percent black and two others, including the once-integrated Arch Homes, were more than 85 percent black. In contrast, the number of projects that were less than 5 percent black had dwindled to two, while four others were between 10 and 20 percent black.[56]

By the end of the decade, even liberal civil rights activists had begun to give up the hope that the city's working- and lower-middle-class neighborhoods could be effectively integrated. Two years after the Fellowship Commission called on the PHA to increase "markedly . . . the pace of integration" of its housing projects, a 1957 independent study committee commissioned by the PHA and chaired by FC board member Jefferson Fordham, the dean of the University of Pennsylvania Law School, argued that public housing should not be used to promote racial integration. Like the homeowner opposition to the scattered-site plan, the city's civil rights community had come to see the sole purpose of public housing as meeting the housing needs of the (black) poor.[57]

*   *   *

For the many black Philadelphians who were able to secure well-paying government jobs and purchase single-family homes in the middle-class residential neighborhoods within the city's northern and western boundaries, civil rights liberalism's promise of racial progress became a tangible reality during the 1950s. Income from public-sector employment—or, for a small number of self-employed professionals and retailers, from the growing black consumer market—enabled the educated middle-class and some blue-collar workers to enjoy the benefits of desegregated public accommodations and, at least temporarily, racially integrated neighborhoods. Improved economic opportunity encouraged these black Philadelphians to view the persistent racial bias in employment, housing, police practices, and other parts of daily life as an unfortunate part of a gradually disappearing and anachronistic world.

The majority of the city's black residents, however, remained trapped in tenements and housing projects in deteriorating neighborhoods, were unemployed or stuck in unskilled jobs, and were forced to send their children to overcrowded, underfunded all-black public schools. In many ways, of course, life in the urban North was vastly preferable to the segregated South. But for many in Philadelphia's black communities, the promise of postwar liberalism had begun to fray by the late 1950s. In the early 1960s, black activists in the city would experiment with both the nonviolent protest strategies developed by the southern civil rights movement and the self-help doctrines of the black nationalist tradition. In the context of a northern city that had adopted the official creed of civil rights liberalism, the turn to mass protest and self-help reflected the belief that grassroots initiatives rooted in the black community, not political coalitions with white liberals and the goodwill of government bureaucrats, were the key to advancing the cause of black freedom.

Part II

A Northern Protest Movement

Chapter 3

Don't Buy Where You Can't Work

Philadelphia had a Commission on Human Relations, but it seemed
helpless. . . . I wrote to the mayor . . . but nothing happened. The same
for the governor and the president.

—*Rev. Leon H. Sullivan, Pastor, Zion Baptist Church*

During the second half of the 1950s, a new generation of black community
leaders emerged in Philadelphia who explicitly rooted themselves in the
city's black working-class neighborhoods rather than in the Center City
offices of the liberal reform organizations. These neighborhood-based
leaders did not openly question civil rights liberalism's faith in the legal
protection of individual rights and interracial coalitions as the keys to ending racial injustice. Instead, these critics of civil rights liberalism questioned
the exclusive focus on legislative goals and the sole reliance on the leadership of middle-class professionals. The city's civil rights leadership, they
believed, was too focused on the achievement of abstract legal rights and
had willfully ignored issues like urban decay and juvenile delinquency that
were equally important to the residents of the city's black working-class
communities. Inspired by the emerging southern civil rights movement,
this new generation of black activists came to believe that only the mass
mobilization of black Philadelphia's working-class majority could achieve
real progress toward racial equality in the city—ironically, the very same
position that the by-then-discredited left-wing faction of the Philadelphia
NAACP had taken a decade earlier.

The Neighborhood Challenge to Philadelphia's Civil Rights Leadership

The most prominent black community activist in 1950s Philadelphia was
Rev. Leon H. Sullivan, pastor of the prestigious Zion Baptist Church in
North Philadelphia. A West Virginia native, Sullivan was named pastor of
Zion Baptist in 1950 when he was only twenty-eight years old. He came to

Philadelphia from South Orange, New Jersey, where he had served as the pastor of a small Baptist church for five years. Prior to his time in South Orange, Sullivan had served as Adam Clayton Powell Jr.'s assistant pastor at Abyssinian Baptist Church in Harlem for two years, while also working for A. Philip Randolph's March on Washington Movement and helping to found the Coordinating Council on Juvenile Aid in Harlem.[1]

Like Martin Luther King, Jr., and many other black ministers of his generation, Sullivan defined his ministry in the language of the social gospel, the Protestant theological school which commanded the church to work to remedy social injustice in the here and now.[2] Sullivan's version of the social gospel was particularly materialist. "While some think of the church as a place to get people into heaven," Sullivan wrote in the late 1960s, "I think of it as the place to preach hell out of men. I long to see the kingdom of God a reality in the everyday lives of men. Some people look for milk and honey in heaven, while I look for ham and eggs on earth." By then, Sullivan's social ministry had come to resemble the wealth building strategies of Booker T. Washington. In the early years of his career, however, Sullivan's focus was on combating the crime and violence that plagued the black neighborhoods that housed his churches. In both South Orange and North Philadelphia, he sought to find ways to help young black men, whom he felt were particularly prone to delinquency, overcome racial barriers in the job market.[3]

The issue of juvenile delinquency provided an opening for Sullivan to address the full range of obstacles facing working-class African American young men. In March 1953, he founded the Citizens Committee Against Juvenile Delinquency and Its Causes (CCAJD). Sullivan envisioned CCAJD as a citywide coalition of African American block associations and neighborhood groups committed to identifying and solving the root causes of juvenile delinquency. CCAJD organized homeowners and renters in black working-class neighborhoods to maintain their properties, keep track of local teenagers, build relationships with police officers working in the area, and "resist the concentration of bars in our neighborhoods." At CCAJD's peak, Sullivan claimed a membership of 100,000. The organization's Clean Block campaign won the attention of the National Junior League which named Sullivan the first African American recipient of its Young Man of the Year award in 1955. And in July 1958, CCAJD hosted the National Grass Roots Assembly to Combat Juvenile Delinquency and Its Causes.[4]

The 1950s were a time of heightened anxiety about juvenile delinquency. Much of CCAJD's program mirrored the national drive for increased judicial and police attention to the problem of youth crime. In October 1953, Sullivan blamed the leniency that local magistrates showed to adult criminals for the rise in the number of youthful offenders. In 1954, he endorsed the local police union's campaign against juvenile delinquency. At the same time, CCAJD's analysis of juvenile delinquency in the black community drew on a long tradition of black elite anxieties about the behaviors of the black urban poor. In contrast to liberals who blamed delinquency on external factors like housing and employment discrimination and inadequate recreational opportunities, Sullivan focused on factors internal to the black community such as "a lack of parental concern for their youth" and "places of ill repute within the community." The group's program for 1957 declared that "first and foremost among the causes of Juvenile Delinquency and Crime is a breakdown of the home life." In addition, "bars and taprooms [were] pulling into [our] communities that low and cheap element of our population . . . [whose] vulgar language and obscene conduct . . . corrupt the morals of our children." At the same time, the group faulted the black middle-class for not fulfilling its responsibilities to the less fortunate members of the community. The 1957 program blamed "people of means . . . who spend millions on selfish pleasure" for not contributing "time and money to the solution of this problem."[5]

CCAJD's focus on the moral condition of the race and the promotion of intraracial community solidarity as the key to improving life in black neighborhoods, rather than on government action and interracial alliances, placed it firmly within what Wilson Moses has called the conservative nationalist tradition. In language that both harked back to Garveyism and prefigured the Black Power era, Sullivan's CCAJD argued that the inculcation of pride in black historical accomplishments was key to reducing juvenile delinquency in black communities. "We feel," the 1957 program declared, "that a knowledge of Negro history by white and Negro children is vital . . . Without such a knowledge no group can be proud of itself and there will be an absence of respect for that group by others."[6]

Of course, CCAJD had little in common with the Nation of Islam, the leading black nationalist group of the immediate postwar period. But while the hegemonic position of civil rights liberalism within black political life had pushed explicitly nationalist ideologies to the margins, the logic of the conservative nationalist tradition, with its emphasis on intraracial institution building and cross-class solidarities, remained evident throughout the nation's black communities, and in particular in the organizational and cultural life of the black church. The mix of moral and material uplift that black ministers from Martin Luther King to Leon Sullivan preached drew more on the ethic of intraracial self-help promoted by Booker T. Washington and his nineteenth century black nationalist predecessors than on the integrationism of the postwar civil rights movement.[7]

In 1957, Sullivan decided to step aside as CCAJD president to focus on establishing an employment agency for black teenagers in his North Philadelphia neighborhood. Neither his successor, Rev. H. J. Trapp, nor the group's executive secretary, Mildred R. Seption, was able to maintain the CCAJD citywide network of neighborhood activists. In the early 1960s, new

CCAJD president, Cecil Moore, a criminal attorney and fellow West Virginia native whom Sullivan had initially recruited to run the CCAJD's law enforcement committee, shifted the group's focus from neighborhood organizing to public education on the sociopolitical causes of delinquency. While CCAJD's tenure as a mass organization was brief, both Sullivan and Moore would emerge in the 1960s as leading proponents of movement strategies that relied on intraracial solidarity and the mass mobilization of the black community.[8]

CCAJD's most significant legacy was the increasing number of community protests against "taprooms" in Philadelphia's black neighborhoods. Throughout the 1950s and into the 1960s, antitavern pickets drew attention to the issues of poor police protection, deteriorating buildings, and high rates of crime and violence in the city's working-class black neighborhoods.[9] Antitavern protests, with their emphasis on neighborhood mobilization and intraracial solidarity, provided an important contrast to the interracialism and legalism of civil rights liberalism as well as crucial organizing experience for a number of activists who would emerge as important community-based leaders in the mid- to late 1960s.

CCAJD's demise did not diminish Leon Sullivan's growing prominence in Philadelphia's black community. By the late 1950s, the success of the Montgomery Bus Boycott and the subsequent founding of Martin Luther King's Southern Christian Leadership Conference (SCLC) had created new opportunities for ministerial leadership in the civil rights movement. On April 29, 1957, Sullivan hosted the founding meeting of the Philadelphia Committee of the May 17 Prayer Pilgrimage for Freedom at Zion Baptist. King and Sullivan's former mentor A. Philip Randolph had issued the call for the pilgrimage, which they scheduled to take place on the third anniversary of the Supreme Court's *Brown v. Board of Education* decision, to demand congressional and presidential action on black voting rights and school desegregation.

Randolph's longtime aide Bayard Rustin opened the meeting at Zion Baptist with a speech that demonstrated the impact that the bus boycott was having on civil rights advocacy across the country. Rustin argued that activists should look to the black church as the key to building a mass movement for civil rights. "The dynamic, militant action of Negroes," he told the meeting, "must be developed in the churches." And for Rustin, the church's most important resource was not the clergy. "The power of women in the movement," he concluded, "must not be minimized." Following Rustin's speech, the meeting bypassed a number of long-serving local civil rights leaders, including local NAACP president Harry Greene, to elect Sullivan and newspaper columnist Evelyn Reynolds as co-chairs for the local pilgrimage committee.[10]

Black Nationalism in Postwar Philadelphia

Neighborhood activists were not the only voices critical of civil rights liberalism in black Philadelphia during the 1950s. On street-corners and in meeting halls in the city's black working-class communities, black nationalists argued that white supremacy was so constitutive of American society that liberalism's goal of a colorblind society could never be achieved. While nationalist groups had won significant followings in black communities in the urban North during the 1930s, in large part for organizing "Don't Buy Where You Can't Work" campaigns, as well as for protesting the Italian invasion of Ethiopia, they suffered a significant decline in popularity during the 1940s and 1950s. Two factors seem to have been most important in this decline. First, the victories achieved by civil rights liberals convinced the vast majority of African Americans that the country was fast making progress toward according first-class citizenship for all. Second, the postwar rise in domestic anticommunism, along with increased southern repression of even the most moderate of civil rights activists, left most black Americans eager to demonstrate their support for the patriotic orthodoxy of the cold war.[11]

But if black nationalism appeared invisible within the broader political culture, its advocates continued to exert influence in the growing black ghettos of the urban North. The Muslim Brotherhood of America, remnants of Marcus Garvey's Universal Negro Improvement Association (UNIA) and independent proponents of African solidarity were among the black nationalist groups with an active presence in postwar Philadelphia.[12] The most prominent black nationalist voices in the city, however, were the ministers and members of the Nation of Islam (NOI). W. D. Fard, an itinerant merchant and preacher, founded the Nation of Islam, or the Black Muslims as the religious sect was called by hostile scholars and journalists, in Detroit in the early 1930s. Among Fard's converts was a factory worker named Elijah Poole who had migrated north from Georgia with his family. Fard appointed Poole to run the sect's second mosque in Chicago and gave him the honorific surname Muhammad. In 1934, Fard mysteriously disappeared and Muhammad proclaimed himself the movement's new prophet. For the next decade, the Nation of Islam remained a small regionally based religious sect. During World War II, Muhammad and a number of his chief aides were imprisoned for draft evasion. The Nation of Islam's fortunes improved significantly after the minister's release from federal prison in 1946. The NOI pitched much of its postwar evangelizing at those members of African American urban communities who were benefiting least from civil rights liberalism. Not only did the Muslims actively proselytize in the nation's prisons, but they also targeted ex-convicts, drug addicts, and street hustlers living in the nation's black ghettos. Elijah Muhammad's message

of economic self-help had an obvious appeal for those who had grown discouraged by liberalism's failure to deliver on its promise of economic
opportunity to black urban migrants.[13]

Much of the NOI's growth in this period can be attributed to Malcolm
X, Muhammad's most charismatic aide. Malcolm Little joined the Nation
of Islam in 1947 while serving a prison sentence for burglary. Following his
release in 1952, he rose rapidly through the NOI hierarchy. As assistant
minister of Detroit's Temple No. 1, Malcolm's persistent recruitment
efforts contributed to a significant growth in the mosque's membership.
He was then sent to Boston where he helped a small group of Muslims to
establish a NOI mosque there. From Boston he moved to Philadelphia in
March 1954. There are conflicting accounts of the origins of Philadelphia's
Temple No. 12. In his autobiography, Malcolm took credit for the founding of the Philadelphia mosque. Another account suggests that the mosque
had existed before Malcolm's arrival but had been hampered by internal
divisions. Whatever the case, within three months of Malcolm's arrival, the
Philadelphia mosque was sufficiently strengthened that he was able to
move onto New York City where he became minister of Harlem's Temple
No. 7. Still, he continued to serve as minister of the Philadelphia mosque,
traveling to the city from New York each week for Wednesday night meetings.[14]

The reports of FBI informants on Malcolm X's preaching in Philadelphia during the 1950s demonstrate how the NOI's teachings combined
belief in black racial and religious superiority with explicit attacks on the
liberal notion that colorblind individualism would enable the full integration of African Americans into American society. In November 1954, the
FBI informant in the Philadelphia mosque described Malcolm's message
as follows: "The white man is the devil and . . . the black man is God of the
earth and the only supreme being." A 1955 FBI report quoted Malcolm as
rejecting the possibility that white Americans might be willing to treat
blacks as fellow citizens. "If you were citizens of this country," he told his
listeners, "they would not have to sign bills for your rights."[15]

Despite the group's critique of civil rights liberalism, the Nation of Islam
made no attempt to directly challenge the political hegemony of civil rights
groups during the 1950s. Instead, Elijah Muhammad offered his followers
a messianic vision of African American redemption. Allah, the prophet
taught, would destroy "the white man and his evil government" once
blacks gave up Christianity, "the slavemaster's religion," and returned to
the black man's true religion, Islam. Rejecting the liberal faith in interracial political coalitions as an illusion, the Nation of Islam demanded that
its members limit their contacts with white society and instead focus on
maintaining personal discipline and building up the NOI's religious and
economic institutions. Malcolm X, the FBI's Philadelphia informant

reported, preached that NOI members should not only "obey the law" but also "keep out of controversy with the 'devils.'"[16]

Elijah Muhammad's teachings on proper gender roles also reinforced this inward focus. The prophet offered his disproportionately male and young converts the opportunity to reclaim patriarchal prerogatives over black women. According to an FBI informant, Malcolm told his Philadelphia congregants that "Muslims respect their women and demand that everyone else respect them," while, at the same time, he criticized black women for wearing revealing clothes and for imitating white standards of beauty. As Clayborne Carson has argued, Malcolm's discourse on women taught that "not until all 'the lost-found sisters' awaken to the teaching of Elijah Muhammad will the Nation of Islam be complete, for only then will all the black brothers be fully free of such black women's evil influence and able finally to save themselves."[17] In a society that denied African American men the privileges of whiteness and of maleness, the Nation of Islam promised black men that as Muslims they would be able to resume the place of the patriarch in the black family.

The Nation of Islam faced enormous obstacles as it sought to rebuild mass support for black nationalism within black urban communities. Much of the NOI's difficulty resulted from the internal logic of its own theology. In contrast to Garveyism, which had embraced black Christianity and cited biblical allusions to Ethiopia as the basis for its vision of a resurgent Africa, Elijah Muhammad and his followers called on African Americans to abandon not only their Christian faith but also the musicality that has long been at the core of African American religious practice. Moreover, the NOI's message of racial separatism encountered a very different social and political context from the 1920s. Marcus Garvey built the UNIA in a period of racial retrenchment in which the Ku Klux Klan was a significant political force and black workers were unable to hold onto the gains they had made during World War I. In contrast, the Nation of Islam's growth came in a postwar world in which liberalism seemed to be making significant progress toward the creation of a racially just society.

Despite these obstacles, the Nation of Islam experienced significant membership growth in Philadelphia and other northern cities during the late 1950s and early 1960s. George X had succeeded Malcolm as minister of the Philadelphia temple after Elijah Muhammad promoted his best-known follower to the position of national minister. In 1959, George X was succeeded by Wallace Muhammad, Elijah Muhammad's eldest son and expected successor. On August 14, 1960, the prophet made his first public appearance in Philadelphia. According to the *Tribune*, 2,000 Muslims and another 1,500 black spectators attended the rally. While most of black Philadelphia's prominent political and religious leaders stayed away, Congressman Robert N. C. Nix, the city's highest black elected official, did attend the rally and publicly praised the Muslims' work. Nix's words were further testament not only to the growth of Philadelphia's Temple No. 12, but to the growing support in the black community for the ideals of racial separatism and self-reliance.[18]

Still, the Muslims' proselytizing remained largely on the margins of black political life in Philadelphia. The small number of black Philadelphians who joined the Nation of Islam or otherwise counted themselves as supporters of Elijah Muhammad and Malcolm X were, for the most part, those least able to take advantage of the opportunities created by civil rights liberalism. In the Nation of Islam, they found an organized expression of the long tradition of black skepticism toward white promises of racial justice. Even among those who fully embraced liberal integrationism, the Muslim critique of the American commitment to white supremacy resonated with their experiences of persistent racism. Michael Simmons, who would later become a prominent Black Power student activist in the city, remembers as a teenager being intensely curious about the Garveyites and Black Muslims he encountered in his North Philadelphia neighborhood even as he actively participated in a number of avowedly integrationist youth programs.[19]

The NAACP Institute for Organizations of the Community

In the late 1950s, the Philadelphia NAACP embarked on an ambitious campaign to strengthen its ties to community organizations in the city's black neighborhoods, in part because it feared that the growth of organizations like the CCAJD and the NOI signaled an emerging frustration in black Philadelphia with the liberal civil rights agenda. The branch's first such initiatives took place in the summer of 1957. Hoping to energize its annual membership drive, the branch organized a series of twelve neighborhood public information meetings. NAACP branch president Harry Greene's description of the meetings' purpose—to help "our citizens understand that the NAACP is a tremendously important community organization"— clearly suggests concern about the organization's standing in the community. The meetings sought to use the excitement created by the southern protest movement to the local branch's advantage by promising "those attending the meetings the latest information in civil rights matters."[20]

The second initiative, begun early in 1958, was designed specifically to increase the involvement of black community leaders in the work of the NAACP. Coordinated by Calvin Banks, the second project's stated "aim [wa]s to determine [the] Fundamental Position of the Negro Citizen on crucial community problems" by reaching out to "churches, social and civic groups, fraternities, sororities, Elks, Masons, [and] neighborhood clubs." To coordinate the initiative, Banks organized a special project committee within the Philadelphia branch whose members included Leon Sullivan as well as Lenerte Roberts, a black community activist and realtor from West Philadelphia. Banks and the special project committee organized a one-day institute for organizations of the community at South Philadelphia High School on March 29, 1958. The importance that the national NAACP gave to the institute was reflected in the prominence of the day's three keynote speakers: Roy Wilkins, the executive secretary of the national NAACP, Channing Tobias, the chairman of the NAACP's Board of Directors who had served with Sadie Alexander on President Truman's Committee on Civil Rights, and Mordecai Johnson, president of Howard University. In their promotional materials, conference organizers made it clear that the primary purpose of the meeting was for the NAACP's leadership to hear from representatives of the community organizations. The conference flier urged organizations to send representatives to the conference, "where together we'll Blueprint the Future for the Negro Citizen." In addition, the flier asked "Where Do Philadelphia's Negroes Stand? Who really knows?" and then concluded, "Let's find out!!!" Here was implicit recognition that the NAACP had lost touch with the concerns of the majority of black Philadelphians.[21]

150 delegates representing 86 community organizations attended the one-day institute. The conference program, however, demonstrated that neither the national nor the local NAACP leadership were ready to alter the organization's civil rights agenda in response to community concerns. In addition to the three keynote speeches, the day was divided into four workshop periods, each one with the word "problem" in the title: "The Housing Problem," "The Education Problem," "The Political Problem," "The Economic Problem." In each workshop session, the conference delegates were asked to discuss six or seven questions. The focus of the politics session, for example, was on how to "enlist the aid of local and state political machines to achieve the goal of first class citizenship" and what "the Northern Negro" could do to combat the power of southern politicians in national politics. While there was discussion of the failure of the schools to teach the "languages of Asia and Africa" and of the ways "economic pressures" could be used to advance the cause of civil rights, neither juvenile delinquency nor the issue of neighborhood taprooms—two sets of concerns that had so motivated black neighborhood groups during the 1950s—made it onto the conference agenda.[22]

The special project committee's final report praised the Institute for creating "closer ties between the Branch and those agencies and organizations represented" and urged the NAACP to make use of both mass protest and self-help strategies. The report called not only for "a comprehensive legislative campaign" to pass fair housing legislation, but also for "the use of boycotts, picketing, and other economic pressures" against employers who practiced racial discrimination, for "close monitoring of taproom licenses," for the creation of programs to "equip Negro parents" to volunteer in their children's schools, for "credit unions and other cooperative financial plans," and for job training programs. The report concluded by urging the local branch to establish "a coordinating council of organizations" to develop "effective cooperation between" the NAACP and "other Philadelphia community organizations."[23]

The 1958 Fair Housing Campaign

Following the conference, however, the leadership of the Philadelphia branch did little to implement the committee's recommendations. Branch president Harry Greene and executive secretary Charles Shorter seem to have seen the Institute more as an opportunity to improve the branch's public image than as a first step to making the branch more responsive to the concerns of the majority of black Philadelphians. Thus, the branch focused most of its efforts during the summer and fall of 1958 on a state-wide campaign to pass fair housing legislation. The drive to pass the state FEPC legislation—as well as the ambivalence of many liberal civil rights organizations about the use of legislation to regulate the private housing market—had kept housing issues off of the civil rights legislative agenda for most of the 1950s. A 1952 Fellowship Commission memorandum, for example, urged the Commission on Human Relations to use its powers to end segregation in the city's public housing projects, but argued that purely educational means should be used to promote "democratic practices by private builders, apartments, realtors, home owners, finance agencies, office buildings." Toward that end, the Fellowship Commission issued a voluntary fair housing code for all involved in private housing transactions that described as "unethical practices" all forms of racial or religious discrimination. It would take until the fall of 1956 for the commission board to endorse the concept of fair housing legislation.[24]

Finally in 1958, two years after the passage of the FEPC bill, the forty-two member groups of the Pennsylvania Council for a State FEPC agreed to take up the issue of fair housing legislation and to rename their coalition the Pennsylvania Equal Rights Council (PERC). Even then, there was a ferocious debate within PERC over how extensive a fair housing bill the group should advocate. The local and state branches of the NAACP favored a bill that would cover the vast majority of private housing transactions, including the sales of owner-occupied existing homes. In contrast, the Fellowship Commission argued that the legislation should be limited to new housing and other housing transactions that benefited from some form of government assistance. Limiting the legislation in this way, the Fellowship Commission contended, made sense not simply for political and constitutional reasons—some in the commission wondered whether the government had the right to regulate how an individual citizen chose to dispose of her or his property—but also because government aid to suburban housing developments had been crucial to increasing residential segregation in the state.[25]

PERC initially adopted a compromise between the positions of the NAACP and the Fellowship Commission. On June 15, 1958, the council's member organizations voted to draft fair housing legislation that would exempt all owner-occupied single family homes and duplexes. While such a formulation would cover only 50 percent of the private housing market (primarily new housing developments and apartment buildings with three or more units), its advocates argued that it would still promote neighborhood integration by giving black families access to suburban housing developments. In September, the Fellowship Commission board endorsed the PERC draft by a vote of nine to seven. The NAACP leadership, however, continued to press for broader legislation. They argued that PERC's narrowly crafted bill would fail to cover 85 percent of the homes purchased by blacks, most of them in racially changing urban neighborhoods. Only a fair housing law that covered sales of owner-occupied homes handled by real estate agents, the NAACP supporters argued, would promote integrated neighborhoods. And to those who argued that a more extensive bill would not pass, the NAACP responded that "it is [a] poor legislative tactic to begin with a bill that represents a compromise."[26]

On November 14, 1958 PERC approved, by a seventeen to eleven vote, a NAACP proposal to add language covering the sale of owner-occupied homes by real estate agents to the fair housing bill. Leading the opposition to the change were the Fellowship Commission representatives to the PERC. The NAACP's language, the commission argued, could delay passage of the housing bill for five years or more and thus would "so enlarge and freeze segregated housing that [Philadelphia] will suffer from its evil effects for years longer than would be true if 'strategic coverage' were enacted into law." In contrast, passage of the narrower bill, the Fellowship Commission leadership insisted, would give the state "the strongest Fair Housing Law in the United States," and would thus "end the problem of discrimination in housing." For the next four months, commission leaders sought to work out a compromise with the NAACP that would "have kept the PERC family united," while the PERC executive committee urged the Fellowship Commission not to publicly break with the statewide coalition. PERC's Pittsburgh-based vice-chair sent a telegram to the Fellowship Commission's Maurice Fagan, arguing that "a break in civil rights ranks now will assure defeat of any fair housing legislation in 1959."[27]

On March 13, 1959, the Fellowship Commission's board of commissioners voted to publicly break with PERC and to work for the passage of the original, more narrow bill. Only the Philadelphia NAACP's representative to the board of commissioners opposed the decision. Through its Council on Equal Housing Opportunity (CEHO), the Fellowship Commission then issued a call for an emergency conference for Philadelphia-area groups to support the original bill.[28] The NAACP responded with an open letter to the commission charging that "the change which the Fellowship Commission advocates would so decimate the bill as to make it completely ineffective." PERC had formulated its position, the letter concluded, "in a democratic forum" and it was "inconceivable that a member agency would then take a unilateral action and seek to influence . . . the legislation by external means."[29]

The disagreement between the NAACP and the Fellowship Commission reflected the significant changes that were taking place in the civil rights movement as a result of the limited racial progress of the 1950s. The expectations of black Philadelphians had been significantly raised by the passage of the city's new Home Rule Charter in 1951 and by national victories like the Supreme Court's 1954 school desegregation decision. By the end of the decade, however, these rising expectations were increasingly matched by frustration with the pace of reform. As the liberal civil rights group with the closest ties to the city's black communities, the Philadelphia NAACP was the most vulnerable to the pressure for more rapid civil rights gains. "Could it be," Walter Gay, PERC's executive vice-chairman and chair of the Philadelphia NAACP's housing committee, wrote in a letter to the Philadelphia Housing Association, "that the predominately mainline board membership of some of our civic organizations are underestimating the strident call now sweeping America . . . for the elimination of taboos and second-class citizenship?"[30]

However, the NAACP's outrage at the Fellowship Commission's unilateral decision masked the fact that neither organization was really prepared to shift its civil rights strategy in a more militant direction. After a state house committee amended the fair housing bill to exclude all owner-occupied residences, just as the Fellowship Commission had proposed, the NAACP and PERC continued to lobby for its passage. The bitter public squabble between the NAACP and the Fellowship Commission was in reality little more than a tactical debate over when to compromise with political reality. On August 6, 1959, the Pennsylvania House of Representatives passed House Bill 322 by a vote of 131 to 66. Although the state NAACP worried that the amended bill might "create for . . . real estate brokers the opportunity to escape effective control by the law," it congratulated the governor and legislators from both parties for its passage. The civil rights groups, however, were unable to convince the Committee on Labor and Industry in the Republican-controlled state senate to release the bill. Even a last minute effort to revive the legislation, highlighted by an NAACP and PERC-led "March on Harrisburg" to "dramatize serious displeasure with the arrogant contempt exhibited by some political figures," failed to move the senate to take action.[31]

Pennsylvania would finally enact a fair housing bill with the exemptions favored by the Fellowship Commission in February 1961.[32] By then, however, the damage had been done to the credibility of the civil rights coalition's legislative strategy. As Walter Gay predicted, the legislative campaign for a fair housing bill was soon eclipsed by the emergence of a mass protest movement for civil rights. Nor did the NAACP's support for the broader version of the housing bill protect it from criticism that it had relied too heavily on elite-oriented lobbying strategies. Internal critics of the branch leadership had already begun to argue that the mass mobilization strategies of the southern protest movement, not PERC-style coalition lobbying, was the best hope for advancing the cause of civil rights in Philadelphia

In the short term, however, branch president Harry Greene and executive secretary Charles Shorter were thrilled by the impact that the fair housing drive had on branch membership. Throughout the first half of the 1950s, membership in the Philadelphia branch had hovered around 5,000. By the end of 1958, it had risen to 6,797. Real growth came in 1959. On May 14, the branch issued a press release announcing that it had already surpassed its membership goal of 10,000 for the year. By the year's end, the branch's membership had reached 16,949, making the Philadelphia branch the largest NAACP chapter in the country. The success of the 1959 membership drive validated what Greene and Shorter believed had been one of the branch's most successful years. The "special emphasis" that the branch had placed "on fair housing legislation, employment expansion, and the elimination of police mistreatment and brutality" had all produced important victories. In addition, the branch had opened negotiations with two local retail baking companies on their failure to hire "Negro driver-salesmen," taken action on "many complaints of unfair dismissal practices against Negro workers," provided "scores of job referrals," and successfully handled the first case to come before the city's new Police Review Board, resulting "in disciplinary action being taken against the Officer."[33]

The 1959 NAACP Branch Election

Neither the branch's growth nor its newfound commitment to mass mobilization in the black community could forestall the emergence of the first challenge to Greene and Shorter's leadership of the local branch since 1951. As in the 1940s, the insurgent faction consisted of a mix of disgruntled branch insiders and activists with little previous involvement in the branch's day-to-day work. Unlike the 1940s, however, the outsiders were drawn not from left-wing popular front organizations but from the wide range of community and civic groups that had emerged in postwar black Philadelphia. Cecil Moore, Leon Sullivan's CCAJD protégé, was widely acknowledged to be the driving force behind the insurgent challenge. The most prominent insider to join the insurgents was *Tribune* publisher E.

Washington Rhodes, a one-time ally of the Lewis-Watson left-wing faction, who had been the co-chair of the branch's 1959 membership drive.

At a November 1959 branch meeting, Rhodes and other critics of the Greene-Shorter regime won control of the nominating committee for the December 8 branch elections. The nominating committee subsequently passed over Greene and instead endorsed an avowedly activist slate headed by a well-known civic activist named Harold Pilgrim. Pilgrim was an elected member of the Philadelphia branch's executive board who had been a member of the Greene slate that had defeated the left faction in the branch's 1951 election. A fifty-seven year-old veteran of World War I, Pilgrim was active in a number of black service organizations, a lay leader in the Episcopal Church, and a prominent figure in the National Alliance of Postal Employees. As a postal superintendent, Pilgrim was more representative of middle-class government workers than of black Philadelphia's working-class majority. Still, he lacked the professional status of the doctors and lawyers who had traditionally led the local NAACP. For the positions of first and second vice president, the Pilgrim slate chose two members of the branch executive board: Viola Allen, a leader of a number of service groups in the black community, and Mabel Turner, an assistant U.S. Attorney. The Pilgrim slate's list of executive board candidates included NAACP stalwarts like Rhodes and Gertrude Barnes, a teacher who had been selected to co-chair the 1961 NAACP national convention in Philadelphia, and community activists like Cecil Moore and Lenerte Roberts.[34]

Rather than face his first contested election in eight years, Harry Greene decided to retire from the branch presidency. He and Shorter threw their support to a slate headed by A. Leon Higginbotham, a partner in one of the city's leading black law firms, co-chair of the local NAACP's Legal Redress Committee and a former assistant district attorney in the Dilworth administration. The election quickly became a referendum on Greene and Shorter's leadership of the branch. Pilgrim's supporters called the branch's incumbent leadership spineless and charged that it had fostered an "apathetic attitude within the local branch." In contrast, Higginbotham's supporters defended the NAACP's traditional approach. "The present record membership of nearly 20,000 persons," Shorter told the *Tribune*, "should speak for the . . . esteem and regard in which the public holds our present policy of action."[35]

As the election approached, Pilgrim's supporters sought to portray it as a contest between representatives of the black elite and what the *Tribune*'s political columnist Dorothy Anderson termed "a group of so-called 'little people.'" In a column published on the day of the election, Anderson, who like Rhodes was a prominent Republican, accused the branch's "present leadership" of being primarily concerned with maintaining its social status and its ties to the politically powerful. The Pilgrim slate was, she wrote, determined to . . . place in power people who are NOT interested in "getting along," NOT interested in appeasement, NOT concerned about their so-called "social prestige" but who ARE concerned with the multitudinous daily injustices which beset the colored man and woman in this city and want to do something about it. . . . If our NAACP will fight for us we shan't have head-whippings and suspicious arrests in such number as we have had. . . . The recent successful membership campaign . . . was a mandate from the people for the local NAACP to become once again a militant, dare-devil organization fighting ACROSS THE BOARD for OUR rights."[36]

The Pilgrim slate's campaign platform further demonstrated the impact that the southern protest movement had on northern expectations for the pace of racial reform. Rhodes's *Tribune*, in particular, had given prominent attention to the Montgomery Bus Boycott and the Little Rock schools crisis. In the midst of the Pilgrim-Higginbotham race, the paper announced the establishment of the Daisy Bates Fund to help the Little Rock NAACP leader to continue publishing the newspaper that she owned with her husband in the face of racial harassment.[37] While the southern movement shared traditional civil rights liberalism's commitment to integration and the protection of individual rights, its use of mass protest strategies and its insistence on an immediate end to segregation provided a new model of civil rights advocacy. In comparison to the militant and courageous leadership of figures like Martin Luther King and Daisy Bates, Greene and Shorter's leadership of the Philadelphia NAACP seemed entirely too cautious.

Despite its advocacy of a more militant civil rights strategy, the Pilgrim slate badly misjudged its support within the branch. In response to the branch's rapid growth, the branch election committee printed more than 6,000 ballots for the election. However, less than 400 NAACP members (out of a total membership of more than 16,000) turned out for the election. By 210 to 162, Higginbotham was declared the winner. In addition, Higginbotham's slate won twenty-seven of the forty seats on the branch executive board. Rhodes and Gertrude Barnes were the most prominent members of the Pilgrim slate elected to the board; Cecil Moore and Lenerte Roberts did not make the cut.[38]

Instead of viewing the low turnout as evidence that its message of civil rights militancy had not reached the branch membership, the Pilgrim slate filed a formal complaint with the NAACP's national office, charging that its defeat was the result of election irregularities. Written by Cecil Moore, the complaint accused Shorter of purposely seeking to suppress turnout by failing to notify branch members of the election in writing at least seven days in advance as the organization's bylaws required.[39]

In response to the Moore complaint, the national NAACP agreed to open an investigation of the election and to delay Higginbotham's installation as branch president. Dr. Greene was to remain president until the investigation was completed. The hearing on the election was held in New York on February 3, 1960. However, the NAACP's board of directors did not issue its final ruling until March 14 when it upheld Higginbotham's victory. During the three-month investigation, tensions within the branch only increased. In February, Charles Shorter offered his resignation as branch executive secretary, an offer that the outgoing executive board decided to accept by a vote of 14 to 13.[40]

The 1960 Sit-In Movement and Civil Rights Protest in Philadelphia

On February 1, 1960, four black college students at North Carolina A&T in Greensboro began a sit-in at a Woolworth's lunch counter. The sit-ins quickly spread to other black college campuses, first in the Carolinas and then across the South.[41] The impact of the sit-in movement in Philadelphia was twofold: (1) it prompted the first citywide civil rights demonstrations in a generation, and (2) it further exacerbated tensions within the Philadelphia NAACP and between the city's liberal civil rights community and advocates of a more aggressive civil rights strategy.

Within a week of the first sit-in, the *Tribune* had begun to devote significant coverage to the southern student campaign. The first photograph of the Greensboro sit-ins ran on February 6, and the first article appeared on the front page of the February 9th edition. For the next three months, nearly every issue of the *Tribune* included an update on the sit-in movement.[42] When students from a number of Philadelphia-area colleges began to organize to support the sit-ins, the *Tribune* also provided extensive coverage of their efforts. A February 23, 1960, story, headlined "Pickets Empty Woolworth's At Peak Store Hour," reported that forty members of the Philadelphia Youth Committee Against Segregation had picketed the Woolworth's at Fortieth and Lancaster in West Philadelphia on the previous Saturday "to protest against the company's segregation policies in the South." The students carried signs with slogans like "Philadelphians! Join the Fight to End Segregation!" While hailing the picketers, the article also expressed concern about the small number of blacks on the picket line, quoting one observer who worried that local black students lacked "interest . . . in a situation which concerns their own race." Only ten of the forty student protesters were black.[43]

On the second Saturday of picketing, the Youth Committee expanded to a second Woolworth's at Fifty-Second and Market in West Philadelphia and doubled the number of picketers at the two stores. According to the *Tribune*, thirty-eight of the forty picketers at Fortieth and Lancaster and a significant minority of the protesters at the second store were black. Two black students were the first of the five-and-ten picketers to be arrested for preventing customers from entering the Market Street store. Following the second day of picketing, the Youth Committee announced plans to expand the picket lines to at least six Woolworth's stores, including the city's largest at Chestnut and Juniper in Center City. In addition, the *Tribune* reported that a number of black neighborhood activists, including Leon Sullivan and John Clay, president of the 5,000-member Cobbs Creek Civic Association in West Philadelphia, had discussed joining the five-and-ten pickets.[44]

By the end of March, four different groups were leading Saturday morning pickets at Woolworth stores in areas of the city with significant black populations. In addition to the Philadelphia Youth Committee's West Philadelphia pickets, an interracial student group from Fellowship House was organizing picket lines at a North Philadelphia store, the Temple University NAACP college chapter led pickets in Germantown, the middle-class residential neighborhood with a growing number of black homeowners, and a youth group from Ebenezer Baptist Church had begun to picket the Center City Woolworth's. On March 26, the Youth Committee picketed the West Philadelphia Woolworth stores, which it described as "90 percent effective" in keeping patrons from entering the stores, and then headed to the Center City store where one hundred pickets passed out pamphlets in front of the store.[45]

Throughout this period, Philadelphia's liberal civil rights community maintained a studied indifference to the five-and-ten pickets. However, after a spate of interracial violence left a white high school student dead and a black ten-year-old with a shotgun wound, the Commission on Human Relations grew concerned that the five-and-ten pickets might contribute to racial tensions among the city's youth. CHR director George Schermer thus called on the student groups to cancel their plans to picket on Saturday, April 2. While stressing that the commission had remained "neutral" during the first six weeks of picketing, Schermer reported that many people had complained to the CHR offices that they were tired of the picketing. "They take the attitude," the *Tribune* quoted Schermer, "that the Woolworth stores here are not discriminating and so why should they be picketed." Just as the civil rights community had done during the 1943 PTC hate strike, Schermer was defining racial peace as necessary to the achievement of racial progress.[46]

The Temple NAACP acceded to Schermer's request, but the Youth Committee maintained its weekly West Philadelphia picket line. Although the CHR withdrew its request for a picketing moratorium the following week, it issued a memorandum "for the many community leaders" who had requested "some guidance as to their role in the situation." Though the memo took "no position favoring or opposing the demonstrations," it speculated that "a 'new Negro' is emerging—one of great dignity, quiet courage, stubborn determination and self-discipline. The potential appeal of the demonstrating southern Negro students to young people, Negro and white, around the nation should not be underestimated." Most of the liberal civil rights groups, for whom face-to-face lobbying, not street protests, was the core of civil rights advocacy, surely shared the CHR's ambivalent view of the five-and-ten pickets.[47]

As the declared representative organization of black Philadelphians within the civil rights community, the NAACP could not maintain a hands-off attitude toward the pickets. On March 15, 1960, the *Tribune* reported that supporters of the Pilgrim slate—including the *Tribune*'s Rhodes and Anderson—were pointing to the branch's lack of involvement in the pickets as further evidence that the local NAACP leadership was insufficiently aggressive in its pursuit of civil rights. Four days later, the paper criticized "leaders of the Philadelphia NAACP," in a front-page article, for failing to offer any "active support to students . . . who have been picketing Woolworth stores here." According to the article, two local NAACP representatives had attended a recent meeting of the Philadelphia Youth Committee but had failed to speak or to commit the branch to supporting the committee's efforts. In a move that could only have been designed to embarrass the local branch leadership, a second front-page article reported the national NAACP's decision to call for "Negroes throughout the nation not to spend their money in chain stores that refuse them service at lunch counters."[48]

Of course, the controversy over the branch election was a major reason for the local NAACP's lack of support for the five-and-ten pickets. Moreover, it had taken the national NAACP six weeks to endorse the sit-ins and urge its local branches to boycott northern stores.[49] When Leon Higginbotham took office in late March, his first act as branch president was to appoint two branch activists, Florence Farnum and Eversley Vaughn, to head a protest committee to organize a citywide boycott of Woolworth, Kresge, Kress, and Grant stores. On April 14, the protest committee sent a letter headlined "Flash Bulletin" to African American ministers throughout the city, asking their congregations to join the NAACP "in a nationwide protest in support of the sit-down student strikes in the South." Specifically, the committee asked the ministers to announce to their congregations that the branch was planning to picket "25 Five & Ten Cents Stores" on Saturday, April 23. In addition, the letter asked the ministers to send "a captain-spokesman" to an April 19 meeting and "to volunteer a minimum of 30 pickets" to join the NAACP picket lines. According to the *Tribune*, the first Saturday of NAACP picketing drew 1,500 protesters to thirteen Woolworths, Grants, and Kresges across the city. Among the ministers who joined the picket lines on that day were Leon Sullivan and two leading members of the Fellowship Commission board, Luther Cunningham and Jessie Anderson.[50]

Throughout the spring of 1960, the protest committee held "briefing sessions" on the five-and-ten boycott every Wednesday evening in private homes in Germantown and North and West Philadelphia. By May 7, the NAACP pickets had handed out more than 10,000 leaflets in front of the city's five-and-tens. According to the *Tribune*, the West Philadelphia Woolworth stores where the pickets began were nearly empty that Saturday, while patronage of the Germantown Woolworth's was down by 75 percent. In addition to the picketing, the local NAACP also sponsored a series of talks by student activists from the southern sit-in movement.[51]

For a three-month period in the spring of 1960, the Philadelphia NAACP mobilized a broad cross-section of the city's African American community to support the southern sit-in movement, precisely the goal of Calvin Banks's coordinating council project. However, the branch could not sustain the momentum that the picket lines had generated. President Higginbotham and his allies were unwilling to make the fundamental shift from the organization's traditional legislative and legal strategies. Over the next two years, the Philadelphia NAACP used liberal advocacy methods to pursue a number of goals, including fair housing legislation, more aggressive prosecution of police brutality cases, and desegregation of the local roofers' union. Most importantly, Higginbotham filed suit against the Philadelphia Board of Education, charging that school system's policies and practices promoted segregated schooling in the city. Specifically, the NAACP suit charged that the school board and administration "have conspired, are now conspiring, and will continue to conspire" against black students and teachers solely on account of race and accused the school system of maintaining discriminatory school boundary, student transfer, and teacher placement policies.[52]

As much as the Higginbotham administration could claim that it had significantly increased the branch's civil rights activities in comparison to the previous administration, its efforts paled when compared to the rapidly growing southern protest movement. The enthusiastic response of black Philadelphians to the NAACP's five-and-ten boycott made it clear that any group claiming civil rights leadership in Philadelphia would now have to make mass protest a central component of its strategy for improving the status of African Americans in the city. As the Higginbotham administration retreated from mass protest, a new group of ministerial activists eager to apply the lessons of the southern movement to the fight against racial discrimination in Philadelphia emerged to challenge the NAACP's leadership on civil rights issues. Inspired by the role that the church was playing in the southern protest movement, this ministerial group set out to mobilize the city's black congregations in a protest campaign designed to improve employment opportunities for the city's black working-class.

Selective Patronage

In March 1960, Leon Sullivan convened a meeting of fifteen black pastors to discuss strategies for extending the sit-in movement to the problems of "the North and East." Sullivan and his colleagues recognized that the broad support in black Philadelphia for the sit-ins was in part a result of growing frustration with the failure of liberalism to bring an end to racial discrimination in the city's private labor markets. In the years since he left CCAJD, Sullivan had struggled to establish an employment service for black youth. Despite the gains in the government sector and the enforcement efforts of the Commission on Human Relations, Sullivan found black workers, particularly younger black workers, to be significantly disadvantaged in the city's private labor markets. "Thousands of Negro boys and girls," he later recalled, "were walking the streets of Philadelphia unable to obtain jobs, [while] white boys and girls who had just graduated from the same high schools were working." According to Sullivan, black workers held less than 1 percent of the "sensitive, clerical, and public contact" jobs in the city. "In all the banks in the City of Philadelphia there were only a few colored tellers," no blacks were employed as "salesman-drivers of trucks for such major soft drink companies as Pepsi-Cola, Coca-Cola, and 7-Up" or for any of the local baked goods, ice cream, or fuel oil companies, and "there were few black clerks in supermarkets, few colored sales girls in departments stores, and few black clerical . . . workers in the large office buildings downtown."[53]

By 1960, there was increasing evidence of the failure of the city's liberal institutions to provide equal employment opportunity for black workers. During the first seven months of 1960, black Philadelphians watched as the CHR conducted public hearings on racial discrimination in the hotel and restaurant industry and unions. Three years after the NAACP first raised the issue, the commission had still not taken action against the industry. When the hearings opened, *Tribune* political columnist Dorothy Anderson accused the commission members of "just now learning that there are discriminatory hiring policies in this city," and of holding "conferences . . . in local hotels where the colored people are not permitted to work." "WHAT GOOD IS A HUMAN RELATIONS COMMISSION," she asked in her trademark all capital letters, "which hides its collective head in the sands?"[54]

By June 1960, Sullivan and his fellow ministers had founded a new civil rights organization, the 400 Ministers, and had formulated a new strategy for using black consumer power, rather than the city's liberal civil rights networks, to press private employers to improve job opportunities for black workers. On Sunday, June 6, 1960, the ministers took to their pulpits to announce their new civil rights strategy. On a case-by-case basis, they explained, they planned to negotiate with local businesses that failed to hire or otherwise discriminated against black workers. In cases where the businesses were not prepared to negotiate, the ministers announced that they would then call on black Philadelphians to withhold their "patronage" from the company. A week later, the ministers told their congregants that they had selected their first target for "selective patronage," the name the ministers gave to their campaign in order to avoid antiboycott laws: the North Philadelphia-based Tastykake Baking Company. Since Tastykake had failed to respond to their entreaties, the ministers declared, they intended to stop buying the company's snack goods and they hoped their congregants would join them.[55]

While the 400 Ministers were never explicitly critical of civil rights liberalism or its proponents, the selective patronage campaign implicitly rejected the notion that government action was necessary to improve employment opportunities for African Americans in Philadelphia. Sullivan's decision to build a new organization to break racial barriers to employment within the city's private industries arose from his belief that liberal civil rights groups lacked a feasible strategy for solving the employment problems of the black poor. He would later write:

The Philadelphia NAACP was one of the largest in the nation and it did commendable work, but it could not move the giant enterprises to act on any significant scale. The Urban League was trying with some small success, but in proportion to the conditions its efforts were negligible. Philadelphia had a Commission on Human Relations, but it seemed helpless. It had no enforcement powers. I wrote to the mayor . . . but nothing happened. The same for the governor and the president.[56]

The ministers drew from the "Don't Buy Where You Can't Work" boycotts of the 1930s and 1940s and the church-based organizing of the southern movement to forge a protest strategy rooted in black consumer power. The ministers were most interested in what they called "sensitive" positions, jobs that were visible to the public—white-collar accountants and bank tellers, salesman and truck drivers. As one black journalist put it, "the public must be conditioned [to see] Negroes . . . doing more than menial jobs . . . The Negro in turn must become conditioned [to] holding such jobs and also [to] knowing . . . that opportunities for better job categories do really exist."[57]

As a member of the Philadelphia NAACP's executive board in 1959 and 1960, Sullivan had direct experience with the branch's inability to force changes in the hiring practices of local employers. Beginning in the fall of 1959, the local branch had approached the management of the General Baking Company, makers of Bond Bread, and Tastykake, which made snack pies and other baked goods, about employing black workers in the lucrative position of "driver-salesmen." Driver-salesmen both drove the companies' delivery trucks and sold the firms' goods to grocery stores and other retail outlets and thus were able to earn lucrative commissions on top of their salaries. Although the talks with the companies were cordial, both refused to change their employment policies.[58]

Selective patronage had a second purpose. The ministers were testing their ability to use their prestige and organizing abilities to mobilize a

united African American community. In the words of one boycott leader,
"people want to see whether the Negro community will be strong enough
to stand together in a cause that we know is right . . . Negro consumers,
storekeepers and restaurants could prove that every industry in Philadelphia that discriminates will have to change its job policy."[59] To the 400 Ministers, the key to achieving racial progress in Philadelphia was not the
cultivation of white liberal allies but the mobilization of the black community.

Organizing Selective Patronage

The ministers' strategy was to target employment discrimination in a single
industry at a time. To begin with, they selected the same retail baking companies, Tastykake and General Baking, that the NAACP had unsuccessfully
negotiated with in 1959. In mid-June, shortly after the 400 Ministers first
announced their new strategy, General Baking reached an agreement with
the group in which it promised to hire a number of new black workers,
including two salesman-drivers. Thus, the ministers announced that they
would defer "withholding patronage" from the company. However, negotiations with Tastykake did not go as well. On June 16, the ministers
announced that Tastykake was to be the target of the first selective patronage campaign and that Leon Sullivan would serve as spokesperson and
chief negotiator for the campaign.[60]

The Tastykake boycott provided a dramatic test of the ministers' ability
to control the consumption patterns of their congregants and of the black
community as a whole. Tastykake was known for hiring a large number of
black workers, even though it restricted them to certain production departments and was rumored to require them to use segregated restroom and
locker facilities. Furthermore, Tastykake products were very popular in,
and therefore profitable for, the black-owned corner groceries that were
ubiquitous in the city's black neighborhoods. Thus, key to the success of
the first campaign was the ministers' ability to convince 150 black grocery
store owners to stop carrying Tastykake products during the lucrative
school summer vacation. Soon stores across town began displaying handmade signs declaring their refusal to sell Tastykake products and the city's
black press was reporting that word of the boycott was spreading among
nonchurchgoers in the black community. It seemed that the ministers were
in fact capable of forging a unity of purpose and action among black Philadelphians.[61]

When negotiations with Tastykake remained deadlocked at the end of
June, the 400 Ministers decided to publicly announce their five demands:
(1) the assignment of "fixed" routes to three black salesmen-drivers currently working as substitute drivers;(2) a commitment to hire additional
black salesmen-drivers in the near future; (3) the placement of two "Negro

girls" on the company's clerical staff; (4) an end to the policy of segregated locker rooms for women workers, and a commitment to giving black women workers in the company's production departments the same opportunities for upgrading as white women workers; and (5) the adoption of a written policy of "nondiscrimination in employment assignments in all departments." Tastykake responded to these demands with a spirited defense of its employment policies in two full-page advertisements in the *Tribune* that promoted the company's hiring and treatment of black employees. In the first ad, Tastykake asserted that the ministers' demands would force the company to change its colorblind policy of hiring only qualified employees. "The future would be quite dim for either race or employee relations," the company insisted, "in any company which would succumb to pressure favoring one group over another." The company also invited a *Tribune* reporter to tour its production facility. To Tastykake's satisfaction, the reporter wrote a story which listed all the Tastykake departments that employed black workers and repeated the company's insistence that its policy was "to train and hire" from within. Finally, the company sought support within the city's liberal community for its efforts to defuse the boycott. Through the Greater Philadelphia Chamber of Commerce, the company asked the Commission on Human Relations to investigate whether selective patronage was an illegal attempt to impede commerce. The CHR agreed to investigate, but said it could find no evidence that the ministers were violating the law.[62]

When its public relations campaign failed to break the boycott, Tastykake finally agreed to negotiate with the ministers. On Sunday, August 7, the ministers were able to announce to their parishioners that Tastykake had met all of their demands and that the boycott was over. The company's black salesmen-drivers now had fixed routes, black women were working in the formerly all-white clerical, wrapping, and packaging departments, and all of the plants' facilities had been desegregated. At the same time, the ministers announced they were investigating other companies and that the community should "stand ready."[63]

"After the Tasty victory," Sullivan remembers, "black people were walking ten feet tall in the streets of Philadelphia." The 400 Ministers were particularly proud that they had maintained the Tastykake boycott without the benefit of any coverage from white-owned media outlets. A spokesperson for the *Bulletin*, Philadelphia's afternoon daily newspaper, would later explain that: "we didn't want to be put in a position of helping with publicity something we don't know whether we can agree with . . . morally or legally." The press blackout on selective patronage extended to the national media as well. In late June, the *Tribune* quoted an unidentified minister as saying, "we have information that a letter to the *New York Times* dealing with the [selective patronage] program has been rejected for publication." Rather than hurting the ministers' efforts, the media blackout only further emphasized the fact that the campaign's success was dependent solely on the actions of the black community.[64]

After the Tastykake settlement, Freihofer's, another local baking company, avoided a boycott by reaching an agreement with the ministers. The ministers then turned their attention to the soda bottling industry. On October 2, black pastors in pulpits throughout the city announced that selective patronage's next target would be the local bottlers of Pepsi-Cola. The Pepsi bottlers employed only two nonwhite workers out of a total workforce of several hundred. The boycott would continue, the ministers announced, until the bottlers started hiring black clerical workers, salesmen-drivers, and production workers. Having closely followed the Tastykake boycott, the company chose not to fight. Within a week, the *Tribune* was reporting that "a highly reliable source" had told the paper that the ministers had reached an agreement with the Pepsi bottlers that included provisions for the hiring of a large number of driver-salesmen. The following morning, the ministers called off the Pepsi boycott. Shortly thereafter, the local Coca-Cola and Seven-Up bottlers also reached settlements with the ministers.[65]

The success of the Tastykake campaign demonstrated just how much black Philadelphians had come to question the effectiveness of civil rights liberalism. It also reflected the organizational and tactical advantages that the 400 Ministers had over the Philadelphia NAACP and the rest of the city's civil rights coalition. The most important advantage was the central role that the church played in the lives of large numbers of the city's black residents. The church gave the ministers the ability to speak to black Philadelphians of all classes on a weekly basis. The churches also gave the ministers access to a broad range of women's social and community networks that would prove crucial to spreading the word about the boycott. Finally, the ministers also brought to selective patronage the visibility and prestige among poor and working-class black Philadelphians that the local NAACP leadership had not been able to develop. Not only did the pulpit make each minister the dominant voice within his congregation, but a number of the pastors had citywide reputations for their oratorical skill and organizational ingenuity. The prominence of the clergy in the southern movement had also led black Philadelphians to expect ministers to take leadership in the civil rights struggle. Shortly after Sullivan announced the formation of the 400 Ministers, the *Tribune* editorialized that: "in our opinion the greatest constructive force in America today is the Negro church . . . this latest movement reveals the type of positive leadership which makes this city a better place in which to live."[66]

Despite the expectation of leadership that the southern movement had thrust upon them, Sullivan and the other leaders of the 400 Ministers had to overcome a number of obstacles to build a citywide coalition of black ministers. First, they had to convince the ministers that organizing a series of consumer boycotts against local retailers would not make them vulnerable to prosecution. In their public pronouncements the ministers consciously avoided use of the word "boycott"—hence the euphemism "selective patronage." Rather than announce a boycott of a company, each minister told his parishioners of his personal decision to withhold patronage from the company and then urged them to join him.

In addition to concerns about legal liability, Sullivan also had to overcome the fear of individual ministers that leaders of the new ministerial organization would use it to advance their own ambitions, or worse, to raid other congregations. To offset this concern and to insure that as many clergy as possible would participate in selective patronage, Sullivan created what he called a "structureless" structure for the 400 Ministers. The group had no elected officers or formal decision-making processes. Instead, a "priority" committee with a rotating membership selected targeted companies and appointed a different spokesperson and negotiating committee for each campaign. The lack of structure limited the potential for internal divisions or turf battles between ministers of different denominations, political views, and potentially competing ambitions. In this way, the 400 Ministers upheld the primacy of each minister within his own congregation. The lack of formal organization made the success or failure of selective patronage dependent on the ability of each minister to control the consumption patterns of his congregation. To quell fears that the group's leaders might use their newfound prestige to raid other congregations, the 400 Ministers even refrained from organizing the kind of weekly mass meetings that had proved so important to the southern movement.[67]

While this "structureless" structure enabled Sullivan to put together an impressively broad ecumenical coalition of clergy, it would have hampered the ministers' organizing efforts had it not been for the women's organizing and communications networks that linked the church congregations to an extended network of civic, social, and service organizations. Particularly in a consumer boycott, women's networks were crucial to spreading the word not to buy. In order to reach beyond the churchgoing population, selective patronage's organizers sought to access other social and civic networks in black Philadelphia. In fact, one of selective patronage's key supporters was George Searles, the publisher of *Nite Life*, a free weekly that was distributed in black-owned bars and taverns throughout the city.[68]

Having successfully changed hiring policies in the city's baking and bottling industries, the ministers next challenged petroleum retailers. Just as the ministers had targeted Tastykake in the summer months when children were out of school and therefore most likely to patronize the corner groceries where the company's products were sold, they timed their effort to change hiring practices in the petroleum industry in the winter months when demand for home heating oil hit its peak. The first two companies approached, Atlantic Richfield and Standard Oil, entered negotiations will-ingly and reached settlements before a boycott was called. The agreement with Atlantic Richfield was particularly significant given the fact that Commission on Human Relations had not been able to force the company to change its hiring policies in either its corporate headquarters or its Phila-delphia plants. As a result of the agreement, the number of African Ameri-can white-collar employees at Atlantic Richfield grew to twenty-five. Company officials claimed to be pleased that their agreement with the min-isters had given them access to new sources of qualified personnel. To the ministers, the successful negotiations with Atlantic were evidence of "how smoothly their project goes when everyone cooperates."[69]

Gulf Oil, on the other hand, refused to even negotiate with the 400 Min-isters. After three weeks of trying unsuccessfully to schedule an appoint-ment with Gulf executives, the ministers urged the parishioners to stop buying Gulf products on January 15, 1961. By the next day, Gulf's switch-boards were jammed with customers calling to cancel their contracts for home heating oil. One newspaper reported that many black families in the city went without heat for a few days in the middle of January while they waited for other companies to fulfill contracts that they had canceled with Gulf. Even black-owned and operated Gulf stations were reported to be hard hit by the loss of customers. Within a week, Gulf had agreed to meet the ministers' minimum demands and had added four black clerical work-ers, an accountant, and several salesmen-drivers and sales representatives.[70]

The ministers' next target, Sun Oil, would test their ability to mount a full-scale boycott. Negotiations with Sun began on February 3, 1961. The company was quite proud of its record of hiring African American employ-ees in the Philadelphia area. Sun's three hundred black employees included two foremen at the Marcus Hook refinery just south of the city. Moreover, the company had contracted with Leon Sullivan and Hampton University, a black college in Virginia, a year earlier to establish a program to increase the number of black white-collar employees in its Philadelphia offices. This arrangement had led the company to hire two black clerks and to add three black colleges to its annual search for executive trainees. The ministers, however, were neither impressed with this hiring record nor with Sun's argument that an economic downturn had slowed its plans to add additional black employees. Citing Atlantic Richfield's addition of twenty-five blacks to its office staff, the ministers demanded that Sun hire nineteen black office workers, three truck drivers, and a motor products salesman. The company objected that it could not add that many office workers in a month and that it would be unfair to hire three new truck drivers at the same time that it was laying off thirty-five drivers because of the close of the heating-oil season.[71]

As the mid-March boycott deadline approached, Sun reported that it had upgraded an African American mechanic to the position of truck

driver and had hired a salesman and one of nineteen potential office workers referred to it by the local Urban League. The ministers, however,
rejected Sun's employment efforts as insufficient. Declaring that "token
employment is no employment," the ministers announced a boycott of Sun
on March 19, 1961. The next day leaflets headlined "No More Dollars for
Discrimination" and calling on black Philadelphians to stop buying Sun
Oil products appeared throughout the city.[72]

Sun proved to be the first company since Tastykake willing to aggressively
fight the boycott. The company quickly sent out a letter defending its hiring policies to its motor products salesmen, local newspapers, and a number of ministers. In particular, the letter trumpeted the fact that "a recent
publication of The Pennsylvania Fair Employment Practices Commission
on job opportunities for Negroes featured one of the company's Negro
supervisors." By late April, company officials were telling reporters that
they had met about half of the 400 Ministers' demands. The new hires
included seven female clerical workers, two salesmen, and three upgraded
drivers. In addition, Sun offered assurances to the ministers that it would
institute a nondiscrimination policy for all its future hires.[73]

The ministers still refused to lessen their demands. A letter mailed to
pastors and worshippers during the last week in March acknowledged the
progress that Sun had made, but declared that "it is still slow and they still
have a long way to go." At an April 9 press conference, the 400 Ministers
kicked off the second phase of their campaign against Sun with the
announcement that the state leader of the Negro Masons had ordered
Pennsylvania's 25,000 masons to stop buying Sun products. The ministers'
spokesperson said that the group was also prepared to ask churches across
the state to join the boycott if the company did not meet their demands by
the end of the month. Sun, however, continued to refuse to maintain its
position even when the ministers announced in May that they had asked
black churches in thirty cities across Pennsylvania, including Reading,
Scranton, and Pittsburgh to join the Sun boycott. Only when the ministers
threatened to call for a nationwide boycott did the company agree to meet
their demands. The boycott finally came to an end on June 11.[74]

Over the next three years, the 400 Ministers would lead five more selective patronage campaigns against companies in the ice cream, newspaper
and supermarket industries. An additional three hundred companies, Sullivan would later claim, had avoided boycotts by meeting the ministers'
demands. The success of the selective patronage campaigns went far
beyond the relatively small numbers of employees hired or promoted as a
result of the ministers' efforts. Selective patronage taught black Philadelphians that, if united, they could successfully attack racial discrimination
without the aid of either government agencies or white allies. The ministers
were particularly proud that they had achieved their success without the
mainstream media attention that was so critical to the southern movement.

While not explicitly black nationalist, selective patronage prefigured the Black Power movement in its emphasis on the power of intraracial solidarity and in the ministers' conscious decision not to seek the aid of white allies. In a political environment that dictated that African Americans could only achieve their social and political goals by building alliances with the white majority, selective patronage demonstrated that black nationalism might, in fact, provide a practical basis for developing new strategies for the movement for racial justice.[75]

Among the activists to take notice in Philadelphia was Max Stanford, the founder of the Revolutionary Action Movement (RAM). RAM was a black nationalist student group inspired by the self-defense doctrines of Robert F. Williams, the former leader of the Monroe, North Carolina NAACP. Williams developed a national following after a series of armed confrontations between members of a rifle club that he had organized and the local police and Ku Klux Klan. Shortly after its founding in the summer of 1962, RAM began to actively promote selective patronage. "RAM is asking all Black Americans to support the selective patronage program," the group wrote in a newsletter it entitled *The "A" Train.* "Your support for the 400 Afro-American ministers got 90 new jobs for Black men and women in this city as the largest movement ever launched by the Black community rolls on." For RAM, selective patronage provided proof that the black masses, not civil rights liberals, were the key to black liberation.[76]

From Selective Patronage to Self-Help

Ironically, Leon Sullivan drew a very different lesson from selective patronage than Max Stanford and RAM. Despite the 400 Ministers' claim to have opened up more than two thousand skilled jobs to black Philadelphians, the group's founder had come to believe that selective patronage's victories were insufficient to address the economic crisis in the city's black neighborhoods. Sullivan had never been eager to take protest into the streets. Despite the demonstrated appeal of pickets at the city's five-and-ten stores, he designed selective patronage to work without picket lines or street protests. And while the 400 Ministers hoped that the boycott strategy would demonstrate their ability to control consumption patterns within the black community, Sullivan also sought to develop working relationships with the targeted companies by avoiding making excessive demands. By showing that the ministers could "launch a Selective Patronage Program against a company," and then "call . . . one off effectively in a minimum period of time," Sullivan believed that he could convince the city's business community to work with the ministers to insure the "employment of colored men and women in all categories of the company's structure." Along with his refusal to appeal to government agencies to enforce existing anti-discrimination statutes, Sullivan's efforts to build alliances with private employers foreshadowed his shift toward economic self-help rather than mass protest.[77]

Like Booker T. Washington, Sullivan believed that blacks would remain a dependent class until they became owners of property, businesses, and industry within their own communities. Black Americans, he wrote in 1969, owned only 0.5 percent of the nation's "business and entrepreneurial wealth," despite constituting twelve percent of the American population. Sullivan was particularly disturbed by his belief that blacks' growing access to public sector employment was having little impact on the economic structure of the ghetto. "Administrative and supervisory" jobs in government, he argued, were creating "a tissue-paper middle-class . . . living on a different kind of plantation." Government jobs may have paid well, but they left black families and communities dependent on whites. Black Philadelphians, Sullivan preached to his congregants, owned "not a single apartment building of any size," not "a single shopping center . . . not a single factory, or an industry of any consequence, that employed large numbers of black people." Economic self-help, not political action, Sullivan believed, was the key to overcoming black poverty and fully integrating blacks into the life of the nation. "Mine is perhaps the premiere self-help movement in the world," he declared. "Black people helping themselves. And poor people helping themselves . . . because politically [we] only can go so . . . far." Sullivan was not a racial separatist. He rejected "the creation of a black economy" as counter to "the realities of economic development." For Sullivan, as for Booker T. Washington, full citizenship was not a birthright but rather something that had to be earned. "We black folk must become partners at the helm of the national economy, and not continue just in menial roles, for in the final analysis black men will be respected only in proportion to what they produce to strengthen the nation."[78]

Sullivan traced the origins of his economic development strategy to the peak of the selective patronage campaigns. In June 1962, he called a meeting of what he described as "a small group of young men" from his Zion Baptist church "to initiate a new kind of experiment in racial economic emancipation." To this group, Sullivan proposed the establishment of a cooperative investment program that would "demonstrate what could be done by consolidating the economic resources of a dedicated few." The following Sunday, Sullivan preached a sermon on Jesus' feeding of the five hundred and then announced that he needed fifty volunteers to help him establish a "10-36-50 Plan." Each volunteer would invest ten dollars a month for thirty-six months in the program. For the first sixteen months, the money would be invested in the Zion Non-Profit Corporation, a charitable trust that would provide educational scholarships for children of the black community "so that we could develop the psychology of giving before receiving." Contributions over the final twenty months would be used to establish a for-profit investment corporation "with each participant receiv-ing one common share of stock in all of the 10-36 Plan enterprises." Enthu-siasm for the investment program quickly exceeded Sullivan's goal of 50 volunteers. All told two hundred members of Zion Baptist joined the 10-36 program. By 1964, the program had raised enough funds to place a down payment on a $75,000 apartment building in an all-white neighborhood. A year later, it broke ground on a new apartment complex in the heart of North Philadelphia.[79]

Sullivan's shift in emphasis demonstrated how strategies designed to open up "opportunities" for African Americans came to be seen as insuf-ficient in the North. For Sullivan, it was no longer enough to open up "sen-sitive" white-collar jobs for relatively well-educated members of the black community. Black Philadelphians now needed a strategy that promised to solve the employment problems of the many thousands of unskilled black workers who were entering the Philadelphia job market every year. Every time selective patronage succeeded in desegregating the public face of an important retailer in the city, it helped to shift the concerns of black Phila-delphians from questions of equal opportunity to ones of socioeconomic equality. Thus, Sullivan saw the strategy of collective business investment as an explicit alternative to both civil rights liberalism and nonviolent protest. "If in the future," he would later write, "there were those who did not want us to rent an apartment because of the color of our skins, we would not argue about how to get into the apartment, or run to the Commission on Human Relations for help, but would be in a position to buy the place."[80]

Sullivan had already begun to shift his attention from selective patronage by the summer of 1963. Preaching that "integration without preparation is frustration," he declared that it was time to bring "a whole new dimension to the civil rights picture, placing emphasis on production rather than pro-test." Concerned that most black Philadelphians lacked the job skills they needed to take advantage of the job opportunities created by selective patronage, he invited what he described as a group of "Negro technicians" to attend a meeting at Zion Baptist in July 1963 to discuss "a bold new pro-gram of Afro-American industrialization." What Sullivan envisioned was a job training program that offered both badly needed job skills and a self-help ideology that taught that hard work and belief in self were the key to solving the problems facing the black community. The program would be run by and for black people. "We had to build a training program," he would later write, "to fit the needs of the man who had to be helped, and we could not read books about how to do it, because the man whose needs we wanted to meet had never been written about in any vocational training books."[81]

On January 26, 1964, Sullivan opened the first Opportunities Industrial-ization Center (OIC) in an abandoned North Philadelphia police station that he was able to purchase from the city for a dollar (see Figure 6). No

Figure 6. Leon Sullivan announces the establishment of the Opportunities Industrialization Center, 1964. Urban Archives, Temple University Libraries.

longer, he declared, would employers be able to use the excuse that they could not find black workers with the skills to fill their job openings. To start the program, he had received an anonymous gift of $50,000 from a Philadelphia businessman. General Electric, Bell Telephone, Philco, Smith, Kline & French, Western Union, Westinghouse, IBM, and the International Ladies' Garment Workers Union all donated equipment for OIC's job training programs. It would take OIC's inexperienced staff a number of months to realize that much of the donated equipment was completely outdated. Still, the ninety members of OIC's first class received training in restaurant work, electronics, drafting, and sewing. By May 1964, OIC had enrolled three hundred workers in eight different training programs—including drafting, sheet metal work, power machine operating, electronics assembly, teletype operations, and restaurant services—and had five thousand people on its waiting list. Within two years, OIC would claim to have trained and placed in jobs 1,500 black workers.[82]

OIC's training philosophy reflected both Sullivan's commitment to economic self-reliance and his willingness to accommodate the realities of the capitalist marketplace. On the one hand, he offered a Horatio Alger vision of economic opportunity in America. "Get a man to build his ambition, help his attitude, feed him into an OIC Skill Center, give him a skill, build his self-respect, find him a job, and . . . then watch him rise." On the other, he offered employers well-disciplined workers. "The OIC trainee gives a good day's work for a good day's pay. He is punctual and dependable. He recognizes that he represents an investment to an employer and that he is to return that investment in performance."[83]

As part of Sullivan's commitment to serving people who lacked the literacy and math skills necessary to participate in traditional vocational programs, OIC developed a program of providing remedial education. However, convincing adults to attend remedial classes was a challenge. As Sullivan would later remember, "people didn't want to learn [anything] that had to do [with] reading, writing, and arithmetic . . . they wouldn't come. It was too debasing. So I called it communications skills and computation skills. And people by the thousands came because they were learning something that had more of an elevating sound and purpose than reading, writing, and arithmetic." In order to minimize the stigma of remedial education, OIC required every trainee to start in what it called the "Feeder Program" and later "Opportunities Schools." Begun in September 1964 with five hundred students, the Opportunities Schools also included a black history curriculum designed to address the trainees' learned sense of racial inferiority. "The primary aim in teaching minority history," Sullivan would later write, "is to provide the individual with sufficient knowledge of his background to increase his pride and self-respect and develop self-reliance." For Sullivan, instilling racial pride was a distinctly gendered project. "Black women are taught that it is not necessary to be blond to be beautiful, and black men are taught that it is not necessary to be white to be smart."[84]

Sullivan organized networks of black supporters to donate their expertise to and raise funds for OIC. OIC's training curriculum was designed with the help of three hundred volunteers with expertise in various technical fields. After OIC's initial grant proposal to the U.S. Labor Department was rejected, a network of one thousand black women organized a community fund drive for the fledgling organization. By May 1964, the drive had raised $102,000: $52,000 from within the black community and $50,000 from local business leaders. During OIC's first year of operations, Sullivan was forced to take a second mortgage on his home and to draw funds from his church to meet payroll. Nonetheless, the mobilization of the financial resources of the black middle and working-classes enabled OIC to develop an ethic of self-help and racial pride even as Sullivan won large financial grants from both government agencies and large corporations.[85]

In this sense, Sullivan's advocacy of economic self-help was an attempt to synthesize the black middle-class desire to integrate into the nation's economic and political life with the era's reemergent race pride. Of course, black enthusiasm for a program of economic self-reliance was hardly unique to Leon Sullivan or Booker T. Washington. Much of the grassroots popularity of Marcus Garvey and Elijah Muhammad can be ascribed to their advocacy of race-based business schemes. What Sullivan shared with Washington was an ability to win unprecedented levels of financial support from white corporations and government agencies for his job training and entrepreneurial programs. In its specifics, Sullivan's effort to build programs to prepare blacks to integrate into the economic mainstream differed significantly from Washington's call for agricultural production and political accommodation with the segregated South. Sullivan, for example, never downplayed the importance of voting rights. Still, Sullivan's privileging of job training over protest strategies was as attuned to the thinking of political and business leaders during the era of the War on Poverty as Washington's accommodationism was to post-Reconstruction political and economic elites.

The enduring irony of OIC is that it grew into a national self-help program thanks to the financial support of white government officials and business leaders. OIC received its first significant external funding, a $200,000 grant from the Ford Foundation in March 1964. Then in December 1964, the Office of Economic Opportunity (OEO), the agency created to administer the War on Poverty, made one of its first grants to OIC, $458,000 for job training and remedial education programs. A year later, OEO head Sargent Shriver announced that he was prepared to provide more than $5 million to replicate OIC in eight cities across the country. By 1967, $16.8 million in federal grants was supporting twenty-four OICs nationwide. In December 1966, Senator Robert F. Kennedy made a well-publicized visit to OIC to examine it as a potential model for how public and private monies could be combined to stimulate economic development in inner-city New York. And after visiting Philadelphia in June 1967, President Johnson declared that OIC was "an example of how successful the whole war on poverty can be."[86]

Sullivan was equally effective in soliciting funds from business leaders. In May 1965, OIC dedicated a West Philadelphia training center in a building donated by a local businessperson. In June, Sullivan announced donations from Philadelphia-based Smith Kline & French and Fidelity-Phil Trust. "We must have a partnership with industry," Sullivan said, "if OIC hopes to continue to exist." In 1969, Thomas McCabe, chairman of Scott Paper Company and former chairman of the Board of Governors of the Federal Reserve System, helped OIC to establish a National Advisory Council of corporate leaders with Gerald Philippe, General Electric's Chairman, as its head. By the end of the 1960s, government and corporate support had enabled OIC to grow into a national job training program operating in more than 150 cities.[87]

Sullivan's overtures to the corporate sector, even as he touted self-help and black entrepreneurship, made him popular with many in the Republican Party. During his 1968 presidential campaign, Richard Nixon traveled to Philadelphia to promise Sullivan that he would do everything possible to support black capitalism if elected. As a slogan, "black capitalism" allowed Nixon to imply support for the moderate elements of Black Power even as he sought to distinguish himself from the integrationist agenda of liberal Democrats. For Sullivan, Nixon's support meant that OIC was able not only to survive the end of President Johnson's War on Poverty but to prosper in the 1970s. By 1978, OIC employed four thousand workers and had "more managers and executives than most businesses." "Don't underrate Richard Nixon," Sullivan would later write. "In terms of black enterprise, he did more than any president."[88]

Sullivan was not simply trying to prove that government and business funding could achieve what protests against government and business practices could not. Rather he was asking government and business leaders to support a program based in black self-improvement, self-help, and entrepreneurship. By 1966, the 10-36 Plan had accumulated sufficient capital for Sullivan to divide its resources into two investment funds. Zion Investment Associates (ZIA) became the plan's for-profit arm, providing venture capital for retail business and manufacturing while the Zion Non-Profit Charitable Fund focused on nonprofit housing development and educational programs. In 1965, Zion Non-Profit used $20,000 in collateral to secure a $1 million loan to build a 96-unit garden apartment complex on Girard Avenue in North Philadelphia. In 1968, ZIA opened Progress Plaza, a shopping mall on North Broad Street in North Philadelphia, built with a $1.3 million loan secured with capital from the 10-36 Plan, which by 1968 had grown to six thousand members. For Sullivan, the mall was a symbol of what black economic development could achieve. Progress Plaza's tenants included eleven black-owned stores, an A&P Supermarket, and branches of Bell Telephone and First Pennsylvania Bank. In addition, the Ford Foundation made a $400,000 grant to Zion Non-Profit to develop a training program for the plaza's black business owners.[89]

At the same time, Sullivan began to move his constellation of economic development programs into manufacturing. After the Greater Philadelphia Chamber of Commerce awarded him its William Penn Award, he declared, "that the day must come when I must not only go to another man's factory for a job, but when I must build factories to employ people for myself." Sullivan was able to use his prominence as a promoter of black capitalism to win subcontracts from some of the nation's largest industrial concerns for the ZIA's start-up manufacturing companies. In August 1968, ZIA's Progress Garment Manufacturing Co. opened for business in North Philadelphia with twenty-five OIC-trained women workers making skirts for Villager, Inc. A month later, Sullivan delivered the first terminal box produced by Progress Aerospace, another ZIA subsidiary founded with a loan from General Electric, to the defense contractor's missile space division, calling it "the first piece of aerospace equipment made by black hands." In 1972, Sullivan was appointed to the board of General Motors. A year later, the re-named Progress Investment Associates (PIA) opened Progress Products, an auto parts manufacturer, with a contract from General Motors. PIA recorded a net profit for each of the next three years. However, Progress Garment and a chain of neighborhood grocery stores owned by PIA failed in the early 1970s. By 1975 the holding company had been forced to renegotiate its bank debts. In 1980, Progress Aerospace went out of business after it was unable to fulfill a contract to produce padlocks for the U.S. Army.[90]

*   *   *

Selective patronage and the five-and-ten demonstrations showed that a significant segment of Philadelphia's black residents had begun to question the effectiveness of the antidiscrimination bureaucracy for which civil rights liberals had fought so long and hard. No longer willing to wait for the Commission on Human Relations to investigate charges of racial discrimination on a case-by-case basis, black Philadelphians were now eager to use the protest tactics popularized by the southern movement. The moral power of mass protest had replaced the political power of electoral alliances and the legal power of the courts as the key to achieving racial progress in the city. While the eagerness to protest reflected the influence that the southern movement had had on African Americans throughout the country, civil rights protest meant something very different in a northern city like Philadelphia. In the South, the tactics of mass, nonviolent protest were developed specifically in order to win the support of northern liberals for efforts to end legal segregation. In Philadelphia, the 400 Ministers' boycott strategy rejected appeals for white liberal support in favor of building intraracial solidarity within the city's black communities.

It is within the vacuum created by the failure of the liberal civil rights coalition to respond to the emerging crisis of black poverty in Philadelphia that we can find the origins of Black Power in the city. Hidden behind the formal civil rights advocacy of the 1950s, one can find forms of collective activity within the city's black working-class neighborhoods that sustained both traditions of grassroots protest and the black nationalist view of white supremacy as intrinsic to American society. By the beginning of the 1960s, the locus of civil rights activity in Philadelphia had shifted to the city's black churches and neighborhoods.

For the 400 Ministers, selective patronage had a didactic as well as a strategic purpose. By relying entirely on black support for the boycotts, the ministers were seeking to convince the city's black residents that the cause of racial equality was not dependent on white support. Selective patronage taught that the economic power of a united black community could achieve what appeals to liberal politicians and government bureaucrats had not: improved employment opportunities in the city's private sectors. The ministers were thus consciously engaged in what George Lipsitz has called the "social learning" function of protest movements. By involving people "in acts of social contestation," social movements provide every participant, from the nationally recognized spokesperson to the only sometime involved rank-and-filer, with an experiential education in the nature of political power and the process of, and possibility for, social and political change.[91]

It is in the ministers' decision to pursue a solely intraracial boycott strategy that the influence of black nationalism is most evident. In one sense, selective patronage may seem to have been little more than an innovative application of the strategies and tactics developed by the emerging civil rights protest movement in the South to the realities of black life in the North. But while the leaders of the southern movement celebrated the possibility of interracial coalitions, the 400 Ministers abandoned the discourse of interracialism in favor of a rhetoric and strategy based in intraracial solidarity and mobilization. In a northern city like Philadelphia governed by a supposedly biracial coalition, the decision to pursue a black-only protest strategy was to reject, at least in part, the logic of civil rights liberalism. The ministers' decision to pursue a boycott strategy was motivated by the belief that the civil rights coalition's approach to ending racial discrimination in the city's private labor markets had failed. The ministers' boycott strategy implicitly rejected the liberal argument that the building of interracial political alliances was the key to achieving racial progress in Philadelphia in favor of a strategy rooted in the development of racial solidarity and cohesion in the black community. Selective patronage literally shifted the physical locus of civil rights protest from the Center City office buildings where integration seemed a reality to all-black churches, civic groups, and neighborhoods.

Wahneema Lubiano has argued that black nationalism should be seen less as a codified political theory than as a "common sense" ideology that emerges from African Americans' daily experience with white racial privilege. Rooted in the collective experience of racial oppression and betrayal, rather than in a specific textual canon, the black nationalist tradition is, in Lubiano's words, "plural, flexible, and contested." In a similar vein, Michael Dawson has argued that the most popular form of black nationalism among African Americans is a variant he calls "community nationalism." As defined by Dawson, community nationalists reject both integration and black separatism as equally detrimental to the collective interests of the black community, but view intraracial unity and the development of black-controlled institutions as essential to advancing the race within a white supremacist society. What then does it mean to view selective patronage as an expression of the black nationalist tradition? Selective patronage resonated with a cross section of black Philadelphians because their daily experiences of continued white racial privilege in the city's labor and housing markets had convinced them of the limitations of the liberal campaign to inscribe racial equality into law. And while the 400 Ministers remained committed to desegregation and few would have identified themselves as black nationalists, their advocacy of an all-black protest strategy conforms to two of what Manning Marable has called "the ideals of black nationalism": "a commitment to create all-black political structures to fight white racism" and "a deep reluctance to participate in coalitions which involved a white majority."[92]

In the context of Black Power, it is easy to depict Leon Sullivan's shift from protest to self-help, social service delivery, and entrepreneurship as the work of a conservative apologist for American capitalism. But to label him as a conservative no more explains the mass support that OIC enjoyed among large segments of the black community than it would explain Booker T. Washington's enduring popularity. Rather than an ideological contradiction, Sullivan's ability to combine race-based economic self-help with continued support for integration reflected the worldview of many in a black community confronted with persistent racial discrimination and increasing residential and economic ghettoization. Sullivan and his supporters did not reject liberalism's vision of a color-blind society; they simply viewed liberalism's interracial coalitions as incapable of making that vision into a reality. At the same time, Sullivan's self-help organizations reaffirmed the value of black economic and institutional autonomy that had been at the core of African American community life at least since Richard Allen founded the African Methodist Episcopal church in eighteenth-century Philadelphia.

Chapter 4
A False Democracy

I am the goddamn boss.
—*Cecil Moore, President, Philadelphia NAACP*

As much as selective patronage represented a strategic and ideological break from the liberal civil rights tradition in Philadelphia, its critique of liberalism remained implicit—all the more so because of Leon Sullivan's decision to abandon intraracial protest strategies for job training and interracial cooperation with the white business community. Into the vacuum created by Sullivan's change in strategy strode Cecil Moore, Sullivan's former protégé at the Citizen's Committee Against Juvenile Delinquency and Its Causes and the newly elected president of the Philadelphia NAACP (Figure 7). A charismatic personality, jazzy dresser, and self-avowed heavy drinker, Moore would, over the next three years, draw on the black nationalist tradition of street populism to mobilize working-class black Philadelphians in a series of protest campaigns against the city's liberal institutions—even as he held onto liberalism's core commitment to institutional desegregation and the legal protection of individual rights. It was, in large part, Moore's charisma that convinced large numbers of working-class black Philadelphians to join explicit and collective racial protest. Perhaps only Adam Clayton Powell, Jr., one of Moore's political heroes, was better able to synthesize the liberal civil rights agenda with the unabashed demagoguery and backroom politics of old-style ethnic politicians.[1]

Moore's charisma and his commitment to representing working-class interests, however, should not blind us to the other important factors that contributed to the explosion of civil rights protest in Philadelphia during the middle years of the 1960s. The protest era in Philadelphia was also a product of black Philadelphians' growing disillusionment with the failure of the city's reform liberal coalition to deliver on its promise of substantive improvements in the quality of life for the city's working-class black majority. At the same time that the southern protest movement was raising expec-

Figure 7. Cecil Moore, president of the Philadelphia NAACP, 1963. Urban Archives, Temple University Libraries.

tations for the pace of racial change in the nation, black Philadelphians were confronted on a daily basis with the reality of persistent inequality in the city's job markets, residential neighborhoods, and schools. The success of the Philadelphia NAACP's mid-1960s protest campaigns lay in the group's willingness to target city government, which for more than a decade had claimed nondiscrimination to be one of its highest priorities, as the institution most responsible for failing to fulfill the local promise of civil rights liberalism.

Finally, successful protest campaigns require more than charismatic leadership and the discursive ability to demonstrate why change is possible in the existing political context. In the end, protest movements must be organized. People must be convinced to act and the resources found to meet the inevitable needs of protest. Were it not for the ability of Cecil Moore and his supporters to mobilize preexisting civic and social networks—from church women's groups and black-led trade unions to North Philadelphia youth gangs—to participate enthusiastically in the protest campaigns of 1963 to 1965, the victories of that period would not have been won.

Civil Rights Protest, Philadelphia-Style

In 1963, the target of civil rights protest shifted to the very government agencies that had been at the center of liberalism's strategy for ending racial discrimination in Philadelphia. First, the recently reorganized Philadelphia chapter of the Congress of Racial Equality (CORE) began a protest campaign against City Hall for failing to enforce the city charter's fair employment provisions on municipal construction projects. Shortly thereafter, the Philadelphia NAACP—under the leadership of its new president Cecil Moore—initiated its own series of protests against the municipal construction program. Both CORE and the NAACP directly blamed the persistence of racial discrimination in local labor markets on the Commission on Human Relations' inability to enforce the city's antidiscrimination laws and, more generally, on the city's Democratic Party for failing to fulfill its commitment to racial equity. The transformation of the Philadelphia NAACP from a key institution within the liberal reform coalition into a locus of movement criticism of civil rights liberals for their failure to eradicate structures of racial discrimination and privilege was an important signal of the growing frustration in the city's black communities.

The 1963 construction protests represented a significant tactical escalation for the Philadelphia movement. The leaders of selective patronage had relied entirely on a particularly passive approach to civil rights protest. They asked their parishioners to "withhold" their patronage from racially discriminatory retailers, but there were no picket lines, protest marches, or even mass meetings. In contrast, CORE and the NAACP utilized the full range of protest tactics developed by the southern movement. What distinguished the two chapters of these national civil rights organizations was that while CORE's protest tactics remained steeped in Gandhian nonviolence and the vision of a fully integrated beloved community, the NAACP, under the leadership of Cecil Moore, rejected Martin Luther King's philosophy of nonviolent protest in favor of all-black protests that used confrontational language and tactics on trade-union-style picket lines.

The protest campaign against employment bias in the Philadelphia construction industry marked a major turning point in efforts to end racial discrimination in the local labor market. While only a small number of black construction workers were hired to skilled positions as a result of the protests, the campaign forced the city's liberal civil rights bureaucracy to acknowledge that case-by-case enforcement of antidiscrimination laws was insufficient to the challenge of ending the racial discriminatory practices of private employers. At the height of the protests, George Schermer, the longtime head of the Commission on Human Relations, publicly called on the city to develop more "affirmative" methods for ending employment discrimination. The construction protests also drew the attention of the federal government. Within a month of the Philadelphia construction demonstrations, President Kennedy would issue Executive Order 1114 which required employers on federal construction projects to take "affirmative action" to desegregate their workforces. Three years later, the U.S. Department of Labor announced that from then on it would require Philadelphia-area contractors and building trades unions seeking federal contracts to submit affirmative action plans for raising the number of blacks in the skilled building trades to match the proportion of black workers in the local labor market. What became known as the "Philadelphia Plan" would serve as a model for local, state and federal government efforts to use the contracting process as a lever to pressure private employers to integrate minority and women workers into their workforces.[2]

It would take until the early 1970s for the shift in government policy from antidiscrimination to affirmative action to have a significant impact on employment patterns in the Philadelphia construction industry. However, the impact of the construction protests on the racial politics of the city's ruling Democratic coalition would be felt much sooner. For black protest leaders like Cecil Moore, the lesson of the construction protests had less to do with the inherent limitations of legal bans on racial discrimination than with the seeming superficiality of the Philadelphia Democratic Party's commitment to civil rights. When forced to choose, the leadership of the Philadelphia party had decided to remain loyal to the racially exclusionary policies of the construction industry rather than to their professed support for equal employment opportunity. Increasingly, Moore and his allies would come to see the formation of a black political power base independent of the ward heelers, business interests, and labor bureaucrats who controlled the Democratic Party as essential to forcing City Hall to uphold the nondiscriminatory principles of the city charter. By the time the U.S. Department of Labor was prepared to demand changes in the employment policies of the local construction industry, the focus of black activism in the city had shifted toward achieving black political and economic power.

Ironically, the construction protests also fueled the continuing decline in white support for the Democrats, particularly among so-called "white ethnic" voters. In municipal elections, Democratic vote totals in working and lower-middle-class neighborhoods had first begun to decline in the mid-1950s. In this context, the construction protests served as a set piece which once again demonstrated the willingness of liberal Democrats to meet black demands by extracting concessions from white working families. The ability of the construction unions and contractors to fend off demands that they change their membership and hiring policies was less important to these white voters than the fact that the city's leading politicians had defined those policies as racially discriminatory. It is the paradox and ultimate tragedy of the 1963 protests that both sides would come to believe that they had lost. From that point on, Democratic politicians in Philadelphia would find it nearly impossible to find satisfactory compromises between the competing interests of their black and white constituencies.

The "New Messiah" and the Reemergence of the Philadelphia NAACP

Cecil Moore's mass popularity in black Philadelphia's working-class communities sprang from his ability to synthesize the NAACP's commitment to institutional desegregation with a black nationalist-influenced critique of the civil rights movement's alliance with white liberalism. Moore had long argued that the ethnic mobilization strategies of traditional urban political machines had more to offer poor and working-class blacks than the interracial coalitions of liberal reformers. By 1963, however, he was voicing his attacks on civil rights liberals—both black and white—in language that sounded very much like Malcolm X. "We remain unalterably opposed," he announced shortly after his election as president of the Philadelphia NAACP, "to the antebellum practice of some white individuals and groups . . . deciding who our leaders will be and to what extent, if any, Negroes will be involved in community and governmental projects." Moore's antiliberal discourse, however, had more in common with the critique of nonviolence offered by Robert Williams, the exiled dissident NAACP activist from Monroe, North Carolina, than with the Nation of Islam's more comprehensive black nationalism. For Moore the discourse of black nationalism remained a means to very traditional civil rights goals. Like Williams, Moore believed that protest was an important strategy in the struggle for black civil rights, so long as it was shorn of Martin Luther King's preoccupation with nonviolence and interracial reconciliation. He attacked civil rights liberals not for their advocacy of equal opportunity in public accommodations, employment, education, and housing but rather for the strategies that they used to achieve those ends.[3]

Cecil Moore's election as president of the Philadelphia NAACP and his subsequent emergence as the dominant protest leader in the city reflected the rapid growth of a constituency for militant civil rights action in the years since the Pilgrim slate was defeated in the 1959 NAACP branch elections. In the immediate aftermath of Leon Higginbotham's installation as branch president in March 1960, Moore appeared willing to work with the new branch leadership, agreeing to serve as chair of the branch's North Philadelphia campaign committee. The new branch president clearly hoped that Moore could help the branch strengthen its membership recruitment efforts in black Philadelphia's largest and poorest black neighborhood. Of the branch's 15,000 members, only 700 lived in North Philadelphia. During the summer of 1960, Moore's committee organized a series of street-corner rallies in North Philadelphia in an effort to recruit new members to the branch. In his new role, Moore also announced that the branch would restore the NAACP membership of Goldie Watson, the former leader of the branch's left-wing faction who was now the owner of a popular dress shop in North Philadelphia.[4]

Moore and Higginbotham's alliance, however, was short-lived. They soon engaged in a bitter public fight over whether the branch should provide financial support for a fund-raising concert that Moore had proposed. By the fall of 1960, Moore had decided to challenge Higginbotham in that year's branch elections. The local chapter, he declared, was in need of "new and dynamic leadership." Despite a much less contentious election than the previous year's battle between the Higginbotham and Pilgrim slates, inclement weather contributed to an even lower turnout. Once again, Higginbotham emerged victorious, this time by a vote of 134 to 51. For the second year in a row, Moore had overestimated his ability to mobilize support within the branch membership for his militant program.[5]

In September 1962, Higginbotham resigned as branch president to accept a Kennedy administration appointment to the Federal Trade Commission. Three months later, Moore was elected president of the Philadelphia NAACP over two other candidates, despite not receiving the endorsement of the branch nominating committee. The 1962 presidential campaign demonstrated how much the discourse of militancy had come to dominate civil rights politics in Philadelphia during the early years of the decade. In his campaign, Moore repeated the themes that had created such controversy during the Pilgrim slate's 1959 campaign. He charged that a middle-class "clique" had kept the local NAACP from truly serving the needs of Philadelphia's black population for more than a decade, specifically citing "inactivity" in the areas of housing, police brutality, and public education. Moore's victory, however, was based on more than militant rhetoric. In 1959, he had complained that the branch leadership had actively sought to keep the majority of the city's NAACP members from voting in the election. Three years later, Moore organized a campaign to insure that his working-class supporters made it to the election meeting rather than rely on the branch staff to inform the local membership of the election. His campaign-style voter turnout operation included a phone bank coordinated by Dorothy Howard, the candidate for branch secretary on the Moore slate, and a pool of twenty cars that shuttled Moore's supporters from North Philadelphia to the West Philadelphia polling site. Superior organization and a divided opposition paid off as Moore received 296 votes, 124 more than his closest competitor.[6]

From the start of his presidency, Moore made clear his determination to radically alter the Philadelphia branch's approach to civil rights advocacy and its relationship to the city's liberal coalition. "We are serving notice," he told a standing room-only crowd at the January 12, 1963 inaugural of the new branch officers, "that no longer will the plantation system of white men appointing our leaders exist in Philadelphia," an obvious reference to Malcolm X's comparison of middle-class civil rights activists to the "house niggers" of slave plantations. Determined to remove the "plantation" from black politics in Philadelphia, Moore demanded "that a colored person be named to the executive level" of the Philadelphia Council for Community Advancement (PCCA), a Ford Foundation-funded agency whose mandate was to study methods for reducing black poverty in North Philadelphia. Four days later, Moore called for the removal of Samuel Dash, a former assistant district attorney with strong ties to the city's liberal reform community, as PCCA's executive director. Moore called Dash "a fine lawyer," but argued that he was not "qualified to solve the social ills of Negroes in North Philadelphia." "No white person can do the job properly," he told a press conference, a job that requires "inquir[ing] into the most intimate relationships and problems in North Philadelphia." Moore threatened to picket the PCCA offices and to urge blacks "not to cooperate" with the study if Dash was not replaced by a black sociologist or social worker.[7]

Moore's injection of black nationalist discourse into his critique of PCCA drew a firestorm of protest from liberal black activists and politicians. On January 21, thirteen black civic and political leaders issued a statement attacking Moore for abandoning the NAACP's commitment to interracialism. While conceding that the PCCA's board should have consulted more fully with leaders of North Philadelphia's neighborhoods and that the project should employ "a substantial number of qualified Negroes," the thirteen criticized Moore's "silly threats and other ineffective antics." The statement concluded that Moore's call for blacks to boycott PCCA was "more consistent with the program of the Black Muslims than with the approach and method of the NAACP." The statement's signatories included a mix of Moore's longtime rivals, including common pleas court

judge Raymond Pace Alexander, Sadie T. M. Alexander, chairwoman of the
Commission on Human Relations, Congressman Robert N. C. Nix, and
longtime NAACP president Dr. Harry Greene, and some of his most important mentors and allies, in particular *Tribune* publisher Washington Rhodes
and Hobson Reynolds, a leading black Republican in the city. Buoyed by
this support, Dash told the *Tribune* that Leon Higginbotham, a PCCA executive board member, had approved his appointment and claimed that
efforts to replace him with a Negro could lead the Ford Foundation to withdraw its support for the project.[8]

By linking Moore's attacks on PCCA to the racial separatism of Malcolm
X and the Black Muslims, the statement's authors were clearly trying to iso-
late the new NAACP president outside the circle of acceptable leadership
in black Philadelphia. Each side of the debate over PCCA insisted that the
other had violated fundamental interests and values of the city's "Negro"
community. For Moore's critics, black Philadelphia was made up of its institutions—its churches, fraternal organizations, hospitals, and newspapers—
and was ably represented by the leaders of those institutions and various
other professionals (lawyers, doctors, and government officials). Signed by
a cross-section of black political, civic, religious, and business leaders, the
statement confidently assumed the authority to speak for the city's black
residents. Moore's actions, they wrote, were "an insult to the Negroes of
this area." In contrast, Moore injected the concept of place into his evocation of Philadelphia's black community. Like Malcolm X, he accused his
professional-class critics of living in integrated neighborhoods outside the
ghetto and therefore of knowing little and caring less about the realities of
life for poor and working-class black Philadelphians. When the PCCA
board selected Dr. Howard Mitchell, a black assistant professor of psychology at the University of Pennsylvania, to be the project's associate director,
Moore criticized the appointment for not "solv[ing] the problem. . . . He
never lived there [North Philadelphia]. He had no experience with these
people." Moore's insistence that one must live among the poor to understand their problems was a particularly pointed attack on Raymond and
Sadie Alexander. Throughout Raymond Alexander's years on city council,
the Alexander family had lived in a brownstone on Jefferson Avenue in the
heart of North Philadelphia. Shortly after he gave up his city council seat
in 1959 to accept a judgeship on the city's common pleas court, however,
the family sold the brownstone to Moore and moved to a large Victorian
house on a wooded lot in Mount Airy, a middle-class neighborhood in
Northwest Philadelphia that had become the area of choice for the city's
black professionals.[9]

In less than a month, Cecil Moore had succeeded in polarizing the city's
black leadership. Even some of Moore's supporters on the branch's new
executive board found themselves unable to support his confrontational
style. Two days after Harold Pilgrim was sworn in as branch treasurer,

Moore's former ally resigned, saying that he "wanted to give Mr. Moore the opportunity to appoint another cabinet member more compatible with his policies." Board member Isabel Hoggard was less diplomatic. Calling Moore "a dictator," she too resigned. By late February, Edward K. Nichols, who had been elected the branch's first vice president on Moore's ticket, and branch executive secretary Thomas Burress had also resigned.[10]

In the short run, however, Moore's critics were outnumbered, or at least outshouted, by those who supported his critique of interracial liberalism. A *Tribune* poll found strong support among its readership for Moore's criticisms of PCCA and its failure to consult with existing community organizations in North Philadelphia. One reader accused the signatories of the anti-Moore statement of "keep[ing] themselves above the masses of Negroes." The *Philadelphia Independent*, a *Tribune* competitor, provided an even larger forum for Moore's supporters. On February 2, it ran a full page of letters under the headline "Readers Overwhelmingly in Favor of Cecil B. Moore in NAACP-PCCA Fight." One letter repeated Moore's charge that "not one" of the signatories "lives in the area in question" and another questioned "the signers' loyalty to the Negro and his problems." A third letter charged that the anti-Moore statement had been "aimed" at pleasing the city's "white power structure" and pointed to the fact that "eleven of the . . . signers are in public office or on the public payroll." This letter concluded by calling on black leaders to "remember that there is no correlation between their own 'arrival' and the status of the mass of Negroes."[11]

Moore's ability not only to resist the liberal attacks on his presidency but to use them to promote his militant style of leadership in the city's black working-class and poor neighborhoods provides a dramatic testament to black Philadelphians' growing skepticism about civil rights liberalism. Far from being cowed by the mix of former mentors and longtime enemies who signed the statement criticizing his leadership, Moore used the opportunity to shift the terrain of debate over PCCA from the paternalism of white liberals to the racial betrayal of middle-class black liberals. Moore accused his critics of caring more about maintaining alliances with the city's white leadership than with meeting the needs of the black poor. "For too long," he declared, "many Negroes have felt that our local branch has pursued some fancied notion of respectability at the expense of militancy, and status-seeking at the expense of integrity." Middle-class activists and politicians, he charged, had cynically given the city's black vote away to the Democratic machine in return for "the acceptance of whatever crumbs may be offered to Negroes in the name of charity." Pointing out that no black had ever been elected to public office in Philadelphia without the support of one of the white-controlled major party organizations, Moore argued that his election as branch president made him the only black elected official in the city who did not owe his office to a white-controlled political machine. His election was a "mandate that our organization be rededicated to the ideals of improving the condition of all Negroes." Only he, not the city's black elected officials, not the Fellowship Commission, not the Commission on Human Relations, and not the Democratic Party, could be trusted to represent the residents of the city's black neighborhoods.[12]

Beginning in late February, Moore set out to use the branch's annual membership drive to demonstrate the support in the black community for his campaign against PCCA and liberal interracialism. In a series of dramatic mass meetings, large numbers of black Philadelphians thrilled to Moore's militant oratory. An estimated three thousand people attended the membership campaign's kick-off rally on February 24 at North Philadelphia's Cornerstone Baptist Church. Speakers at the rally included Goldie Watson, who made the fund-raising appeal ("if you want freedom you must be prepared to pay for it"), and a representative of the NAACP's national office. However, it was Moore whom the standing-room-only crowd came to hear. The branch president attacked job discrimination in City Hall and in Philadelphia's main post office, segregation in the public schools, and police brutality in the city. The highlight of the evening came when Moore asked for volunteers willing to picket the PCCA and the Ford Foundation's New York offices. Thousands of hands were raised in response. According to the *Tribune*, Moore's forty-five-minute speech was interrupted by applause "two dozen times. " One woman told the paper that "that man's going to be Philly's new Messiah . . . it's about time the Negroes in this city got a Negro leader who isn't going to be afraid to open his mouth." Moore continued to draw large crowds to NAACP freedom rallies throughout March and April, concluding with another three thousand-person freedom rally on April 28. The enthusiastic response of the crowds at these meetings confirmed that there was a growing constituency for both Moore's brand of antiliberalism and his calls for militant civil rights protest.[13]

On March 23, Moore led twenty-five pickets outside PCCA's Center City headquarters and announced that five hundred volunteers would soon picket the homes of those who signed the statement critical of his attacks on PCCA. The mass protest campaign against PCCA never materialized, however. While Moore was able to generate enthusiastic outrage at PCCA's liberal paternalism, he was not able to convince large numbers of black Philadelphians to join a protest campaign against the organization. Unlike the five-and-ten pickets and the selective patronage boycotts, the demand that PCCA appoint more blacks to its senior staff and executive board offered no prospect of tangible gains for the black community. Moore would have to find a target more relevant to the immediate needs of black working-class families in Philadelphia if he were to build a mass movement on his synthesis of protest tactics and nationalist critique of civil rights liberalism. The NAACP president would find just such a target in a protest campaign initiated by Philadelphia CORE in April 1963.[14]

Protesting Job Discrimination in the Construction Industry

Throughout the 1950s, the Commission on Human Relations, hampered as it was by the building trades unions' insistence that there was nothing in either their membership or apprenticeship policies that explicitly barred black workers from the skilled construction trades, had chosen to focus its enforcement efforts on other industries. As a result, Philadelphia's liberal civil rights community had been forced to rely on its persuasive abilities as it sought to end job discrimination in the local construction industry. In 1954, for example, the Philadelphia NAACP, along with the Fellowship Commission's Council for Equal Job Opportunity, the Philadelphia Urban League, and the American Friends Service Committee, mounted an educational campaign to pressure the city's building trades unions and union contractors to integrate black workers into the industry. A year later, the merger of the American Federation of Labor (AFL), the national parent organization of the construction unions, with the Congress of Industrial Organizations (CIO), whose member unions had a more racially progressive reputation, raised hopes of a renewed commitment to racial equality in the labor movement. The new AFL-CIO constitution pledged "to encourage all workers without regard to race, creed, color or national origin to share in the full benefits of union organization."[15]

By the end of the decade, however, national civil rights leaders had begun to publicly criticize the AFL-CIO for failing to fulfill its commitment to racial equality. For example, a 1960 national NAACP report charged that "discriminatory racial practices by trade unions are not simply isolated or occasional expressions of local bias against colored workers, but rather . . . a continuation of the institutionalized pattern of anti-Negro employment practices that is traditional with large sections of organized labor." The report singled out a number of building trades unions, including the electricians, ironworkers, plumbers, and sheet metal workers, for particular criticism for their exclusionary practices. That same year, A. Philip Randolph, president of the Brotherhood of Sleeping Car Porters and AFL-CIO vice president, chose to go public with his criticisms of racial bias in the craft unions' apprenticeship programs. Specifically, he formed the Negro American Labor Council (NALC) to press the AFL-CIO's executive board to take action against those unions that maintained blatantly discriminatory policies against black workers. "Unless Negro workers," Randolph wrote in a 1961 NALC report on race bias in crafts unions, "are able to break though the racial barriers to . . . participation in apprenticeship programs . . . they are doomed to become the denizens of the black ghettos of the great metropolitan centers living off the dole."[16]

While the NALC achieved little at the national level, Randolph's efforts did lead the Philadelphia AFL-CIO to establish a Human Rights Committee (HRC) in 1960 to fight discrimination within the city's union locals. James Jones, a member of the Steelworkers' international staff and the only black member of the Philadelphia AFL-CIO's executive council, became the chair of the HRC in 1961. Jones, however, believed strongly that issues of racial discrimination within the labor movement should and could be resolved within the AFL-CIO's internal mechanisms. Rejecting all efforts to form a black "power-politics caucus" within the labor movement, he refused to join Randolph's NALC and instead formed the Negro Trade Union Leadership Council (NTULC) of Philadelphia and the Delaware Valley. Trade union activists, Jones argued, should only turn to external grievance mechanisms when behind-the-scenes persuasion failed and only then to agencies like the Commission on Human Relations.[17]

Jones's close ties to the city's civil rights groups made the HRC's efforts to desegregate the building trades unions a crucial test of the liberal civil rights community's strategy for ending racial discrimination. In February 1963, however, the HRC was forced to admit that its "efforts to get certain labor unions to change the pattern of discrimination has failed." Labor's "failure to meet the problem" of racism in the building trades unions, Jones predicted, would endanger "its influence . . . in the whole community." The HRC's fears reflected the damage that the national NAACP's campaign against racism in the AFL-CIO had done to the labor movement's reputation in Philadelphia's black community. From the beginnings of the squabble between the national NAACP and the AFL-CIO, the *Tribune* followed the dispute closely. In 1962, the paper began to devote significant attention to the membership policies of the local craft unions. On June 19, it kicked off a series of articles on the craft unions with an editorial entitled "The Honeymoon Between Negroes and Biased Labor Bosses Must End." "Negro leadership," the paper argued, "must get on the job and end the myth . . . about the fairness of labor." The accompanying article by George D. Johnson, a leader of the NALC's Philadelphia chapter, charged that the craft unions' membership policies were to blame for the fact that black workers accounted for fifty-two percent of the city's unemployed.[18]

In February 1963, *Greater Philadelphia Magazine* became the first local white-owned publication to give the issue extensive coverage when it published an article entitled "Jim Crow's Sweetheart Contract." The article extensively detailed racist practices in the local labor movement, including the racially discriminatory membership policies of the local plumbers, electricians, roofers, steamfitters, ironworkers, and sheet metal workers. The article's author placed the blame for the persistence of trade union discrimination on Philadelphia's liberal Democratic regime. "City Hall['s] . . . color conscious Democratic politicians," the article concluded, "refrain from pressuring unions on desegregation because labor has for so long been the faithful ally of the Party." The article also included James Jones's first public criticism of the building trades unions. "More pressure will have to be exerted," Jones acknowledged, if the apprenticeship programs of the skilled trades were to be opened to blacks.[19]

Jones's decision to cooperate with the magazine article signaled a new determination among Philadelphia's liberal civil rights groups to challenge racial conservatives within the city's Democratic coalition. On March 15, 1963, the Commission on Human Relations issued a report, based on a four-month investigation, accusing four crafts unions—the electricians, steamfitters, plumbers, and sheet metal workers—of maintaining segregated employment policies on municipal construction sites. "We have drawn the conclusion," George Schermer, the CHR's executive director, told the *Tribune*, "that the total absence of Negroes in skilled jobs is evidence of Negro exclusion." Then, on April 4, James Jones and the HRC took their complaint against the building trades unions to the floor of the Pennsylvania State AFL-CIO convention. Jones and Walter Reeder, another member of the Steelworkers' staff and the NTULC's vice president, presented evidence that blacks had been effectively excluded from seven construction craft apprenticeship programs that were housed in two public high schools in the city.[20]

CORE in Philadelphia

It was, however, the decision of Philadelphia CORE to mount a protest campaign against the city government for failing to enforce its ban on discrimination in city contracts that transformed the construction industry's racial practices from an internal struggle within the liberal reform community into the most explosive racial issue in the city since the 1943 PTC strike. Founded in the late 1940s to apply Gandhian principles of nonviolence to the struggle against racial segregation in the United States, CORE only grew into a major national civil rights organization after it initiated Freedom Rides on interstate buses across the South in 1961. In April 1961, Philadelphia CORE initiated its first protest campaign against the Horn & Hardart restaurant chain for its "unfair distribution of jobs." The restaurant's management quickly agreed to negotiate and, by the end of the month, had reached a fair hiring agreement with CORE.[21]

In 1962, Louis Smith, an African American vacuum cleaner salesman, was elected chairman of Philadelphia CORE on a pledge to develop a stronger base for the chapter in the city's black working-class neighborhoods. In July 1962, Smith led a series of sit-ins against Allen Brothers realtors for refusing to rent a Center City apartment to a black army private. Later that summer, a second CORE sit-in produced an antidiscrimination agreement with a local homebuilders association. Despite enthusiasm for Smith's leadership, Philadelphia CORE remained a minor force in civil rights activism in the city at the beginning of 1963. The chapter's visibility increased significantly, however, after Smith announced that the chapter had given Mayor James E. Tate an April 5 deadline to end discriminatory hiring on the construction site of the city's new Municipal Services Building (MSB) across from City Hall. If its demands were not met, Smith declared, CORE would begin to picket both City Hall and the mayor's home. In response, the mayor insisted that he was powerless to act but did order the city's Labor Relations Board to investigate whether the MSB contractors had violated the nondiscrimination clause.[22]

On Saturday, April 13, CORE members began picketing outside City Hall and outside the mayor's home.[23] CORE's protest campaign was a direct challenge to the Commission on Human Relations and the liberal strategy for guaranteeing equal employment opportunity in the city. Moreover, it was timed to take advantage of the May 1963 mayoral primary. That year's elections were the city's most significant since the alliance of liberal reformers and organization Democrats first won control of City Hall in 1951. A year earlier, reform mayor Richardson Dilworth had resigned to run for governor. According to the order of succession in the city charter, Dilworth was replaced by city council president James Tate.[24] A stalwart of the Democratic machine and the city's first Catholic mayor, Tate had never before been a candidate in a citywide election. His decision to run for a full mayoral term signaled that the party organization no longer felt that it needed the support of the liberal reformers to win citywide elections.[25]

Determined to reestablish liberal control over the mayor's office, Walter Phillips, the original leader of the "Young Turks" reform group and a founding member of the Philadelphia ADA, decided to challenge Mayor Tate in the May 21 Democratic primary. Phillips's candidacy motivated Mayor Tate to diffuse the CORE protest campaign as quickly as possible. By April 16, he had ordered the Labor Relations Board, the city solicitor, and the Commission on Human Relations to recommend what might be done to end racial discrimination on city construction sites. CORE, however, refused to reduce the pressure on the mayor. On the morning of April 19, CORE members began a sit-in in the mayor's City Hall office suite and in the offices of the CHR. Before the end of the sit-in's first day, CHR Executive Director George Schermer had delivered to the CORE protesters a letter from the mayor ordering the CHR to conduct an investigation of hiring practices on the MSB site. The letter required the CHR to report its recommendations for ending the exclusion of black workers from skilled positions on the MSB site to the Mayor within thirty days. As a result, CORE agreed to suspend its protest.[26]

The Commission on Human Relations began public hearings on

employment practices on municipal construction sites on May 1, 1963. During the four days of testimony, numerous witnesses provided dramatic evidence of discriminatory practices in the city's construction industry. One independent contractor charged that he had suffered union reprisals for his antibias views and that the CHR had a "do nothing attitude" toward evidence of discrimination in the construction industry. The commission's own investigator testified that he had found a "definite pattern of membership discrimination" in the craft unions but had been unable to convince any of the union leaders to confer with him.[27]

Coverage of the CHR hearings was overshadowed, however, by two more dramatic events. First, Mayor Tate declared, on the first day of the hearings, that "nothing can be done to remove discrimination on current city contracts," clearly implying that he would take no steps to integrate the MSB workforce. At the same time, images of young children being attacked by police dogs and fire hoses during civil rights demonstrations in Birmingham, Alabama began to flood the city's newspapers and television stations. On Saturday, May 11, Cecil Moore and the Philadelphia NAACP organized a City Hall rally to support the Birmingham movement that was attended by an estimated two thousand people. The *Tribune* called the rally "the largest and most successful civil rights demonstration in the history of Philadelphia." At the same time, a CORE-organized picket line drew two hundred people to the MSB construction site across the street from City Hall. With support for protest at its peak in black Philadelphia, fifteen CORE members returned to the mayor's City Hall office suite three days later, this time vowing to continue their sit-in until construction on the MSB building was halted. Mayor Tate's initial response was to try to convince the building trades unions to enter into emergency negotiations with the CHR. Key union leaders, however, refused to join the negotiations. Finally, on May 15, the mayor ordered construction on the MSB site halted until the unions agreed to allow the employment of black workers in skilled positions on municipal construction sites.[28]

Still, the MSB contractors and unions continued to refuse to enter into negotiations. On May 20, the CHR publicly released its finding that six local craft unions—two electricians' locals along with the plumbers, steamfitters, sheet metal workers, and roofers—and three contractors had violated the nondiscrimination clause in their city contracts. Within days, the commission was able to announce that industry and union officials had agreed to hire at least one black skilled worker at the MSB site, that the contractors had pledged to hire every qualified black craftsmen who applied for a position, and that the unions would accept membership applications from those who were hired. When work resumed on the Municipal Services Building on May 27, a single black electrician was working on the site, though International Brotherhood of Electrical Workers (IBEW) Local 98 had yet to accept his membership application.[29]

In just over a month, a small group of civil rights protesters had achieved what neither the liberal reform coalition nor the Commission on Human Relations had been able to do. They had successfully forced the city to enforce the city charter's nondiscrimination clause against the Democratic Party's supporters in the construction industry. Furthermore, the CORE sit-ins were the first civil rights protests to publicly target the Philadelphia city government for failing to fulfill its promise of equal opportunity.

Philadelphia CORE's break with civil rights liberalism remained partial in much the same way that selective patronage had. Just as civil rights protests in the South were designed to force the federal government to fulfill its commitment to enforce the constitution, CORE's goal was to force the city government to enforce its own laws and regulations. The group's protesters criticized liberalism not for its reliance on government enforcement of antidiscrimination laws but for the strategies it used to enforce those laws. By the 1960s, the liberal view that African American progress had to come through enforcement of legal protections of individual rights and interracial coalition-building seemed no less obvious to most civil rights activists than the racist dicta of the early twentieth century had seemed to most white Americans. Even for those frustrated by the slow pace of progress, it was hard to imagine an alternative approach.

Ironically, the success of the CORE sit-ins brought an end to the group's leadership of efforts to end racial discrimination in the local construction industry. One day after the mayor issued the order halting construction of the MSB, James Jones and Walter Reeder of the Philadelphia AFL-CIO's Human Rights Committee called a meeting of twenty-five "Negro leaders," to develop a common strategy for the campaign against racism in construction employment. While they included CORE chair Louis Smith, thereby acknowledging the success of mass protest strategies, the clear purpose of the meeting was to reassert the leadership of civil rights liberals in the negotiations with the construction industry. Toward that end, Jones and Reeder invited Andrew Freeman and Donald Hill of the Philadelphia Urban League, three leading black Democrats, city councilman Thomas McIntosh, state representative Sarah Anderson, and Austin Norris, secretary of the Philadelphia Board of Revision of Taxes, and Rev. Henry Nichols of the 400 Ministers, to the meeting.[30]

Cecil Moore Recasts Civil Rights Protest Strategy

"NAACP Chief 'Not Invited' to Negro Leaders' Meeting," screamed the *Bulletin* headline. By restricting the meeting's invitation list to black activists—a significant break from the usual practices of the civil rights liberals and trade unionists invited to the meeting—Jones and Reeder were seeking to diffuse the appeal of Cecil Moore's critique of interracialism among black Philadelphians. And, in a further sign of Moore's growing influence, the Commission on Human Relations asked the Negro Leaders' group, not the Fellowship Commission or any other of the city's liberal reform groups, to publicly endorse its agreement with the construction industry. Even as Moore's public attacks on the PCCA and its defenders made him persona non grata in the liberal civil rights community, he was helping to push the locus of civil rights advocacy from the Center City liberal reform groups to networks of civic and religious leaders within the black community.[31]

In their attempt to circumvent the NAACP president, Jones and the Negro Leaders failed to account for Moore's ability to mobilize large numbers of working-class black Philadelphians to reject the pace of reform promised by the CHR agreement. In the two weeks following the announcement of the CHR's agreement with the construction industry, Moore successfully pursued a protest strategy that both forced the building trades unions to make more substantial concessions and reasserted the NAACP's position as the leading civil rights group in Philadelphia. The key to Moore's success was his synthesis of CORE's tactics of nonviolent protest with the nationalist-influenced appeals to racial solidarity that had earned him the nickname the "new messiah" during the PCCA controversy.

Moore based his strategy to reassert the primacy of the NAACP within the Philadelphia movement on his decision to shift the focus of the construction protests from the MSB to the Board of Education's $58-million school building program. On Friday, May 17, just one day after the Negro Leaders' meeting, the NAACP president held a press conference at the construction site of a new junior high school at Thirty-First and Dauphin Streets in the Strawberry Mansion section of North Philadelphia. At the press conference, he announced that the NAACP pickets would seek to halt work at the site in one week if the school board did not end racially discriminatory hiring practices at eighteen different construction sites around the city. An NAACP investigation, Moore declared, had discovered that not one of the skilled craftspeople employed at the Strawberry Mansion site was black.[32]

By targeting employment discrimination in the school construction program, Moore was trying to link the question of construction jobs to long-standing black concerns about school segregation. For years, civil rights activists in the city had complained that the Board of Education continued to locate new schools in racially segregated neighborhoods, rather than use its school construction program to promote school integration. According to a *Tribune* analysis, the school board was devoting $31 million, or more than half of its school construction program, to building schools that would inevitably be all-black because of their location in black neighborhoods.[33]

Moore's strategy for protesting the exclusion of skilled black workers from the school construction program clearly demonstrated his determina-

tion to break with the orthodoxy of civil rights liberalism. Despite their criticisms of the school board's racial policies, Philadelphia's civil rights
groups had always positioned themselves as staunch supporters of public
education. On Monday, May 20, Moore broke with that tradition by calling
on the city's black voters to reject a $15 million school bond issue on the
following day's primary election ballot, charging that the money would be
used to maintain job segregation in its construction program. Moore's
silence about the mayoral primary between James Tate and Walter Phillips
further distinguished him from the city's liberal civil rights coalition. While
none of the reform groups could openly endorse candidates, they had long
supported the liberal wing of the Democratic Party. Moore, however, was
more interested in demonstrating his ability to influence black voting patterns than in supporting Phillips's candidacy.[34]

The results of the May primary validated Moore's claim to have significantly more influence over the city's black voters than the liberal reform
groups. In the mayoral election, Tate recorded a landslide victory. Phillips
received less than one-quarter of the total Democratic vote, only 15 percent
of the vote in the city's black wards and just 5 percent in the lowest-income
white wards. While Moore failed to defeat the school bond, the measure
passed by only a two-to-one margin—a significant decline from previous
school bond issues that had passed by margins of up to four-to-one. The
Tribune described the bond results as "a moral victory [for Moore] accomplished within the short space of 24 hours."[35]

Two days after the election, School Board President Harry LaBrum sent
Moore a telegram pledging "to invoke penalties" against contractors if the
NAACP could "substantiate any specific instances where hiring discrimination has occurred." Moore, however, rejected LaBrum's contention that
discrimination had to be proven in individual cases in order for the school
board to take action against the contractors. Charging that "the evidence
of discrimination is at his fingertips," he accused LaBrum of employing
stalling tactics. In the fifteen years since Philadelphia first enacted its FEPC
law, both public officials and civil rights advocates had presumed that prov-
ing racial discrimination required demonstrating that a specific individual
had been the victim of unfair treatment. To the city's emerging protest
movement, however, the absence of black workers in a specific occupation
was sufficient proof of discrimination.[36]

On May 24, the NAACP began picketing the Strawberry Mansion school
site following a small midday march from a nearby Baptist church. At the
end of the school day, students from public schools in the area swelled the
number of picketers to at least three hundred. In contrast to the CORE
sit-ins, which had drawn an interracial group of middle-class activists, the
majority of the Strawberry Mansion picketers were blue-collar workers and
working-class youth. Moreover, the NAACP picketers emulated the confrontational picket line tactics of the trade union movement rather than

Figure 8. NAACP pickets in front of the Strawberry Mansion Junior High School construction site, May 1963. Urban Archives, Temple University Archives.

the passive resistance preached by leaders of the southern civil rights movement and practiced by Philadelphia CORE at the MSB site. Following a weekend break, seventy-five protesters arrived at the site at seven o'clock Monday morning to resume picketing. Every day for the remainder of the week, small groups of protesters arrived at Thirty-Third & Dauphin Streets before seven, seeking to prevent workers from entering the construction site. And each afternoon, the number of picketers grew into the hundreds as teenagers arrived from school and blue-collar workers came from their jobs (Figure 8).[37]

By shifting the location of civil rights protest to a site deep within the ghetto, Moore was able to solidify his claim to be the only movement leader in the city with a black working-class base. One *Tribune* reporter described the many "Average Joes" on the picket line:

a 79 year-old woman [who] picketed for at least two hours . . . an uncountable number of mothers [who] marched with . . . small children . . . hipsters [who] came off the corner . . . ignoring the sun . . . on their processes . . . one of our "violent" brothers who kept on referring to the ancestors of white people . . . laborers [who] came from other jobs to join the line . . . and hundreds of children [who] marched as if they realized that bias protests were necessary to open up opportunities for them.[38]

Construction workers played a particularly important role on the Strawberry Mansion picket line. The *Tribune* quoted one laborer as declaring "this is a false democracy when qualified colored people can't get a job building schools for their own kids." On the first full day of picketing, sixty-six black (unskilled) laborers scheduled to work on the site refused to cross the picket line. By the next day, the number of laborers refusing to report to the site had grown to 106. In addition, a black bricklayer refused to cross the picket line even though his union had told him he would lose his job if he failed to appear for work. The bricklayer complained that the union's policy of not crossing picket lines had suddenly changed when the picket lines were set up by the NAACP. Among the strongest supporters of the Strawberry Mansion protests were Mr. and Mrs. Arthur Bradley. A laborer and a factory worker respectively, the Bradleys allowed the NAACP to use their home, which was less than a block from the construction site, as a picketing headquarters. "Although many persons are entering and leaving our home during the day," Mrs. Bradley told the *Tribune*, "it has in no way affected our everyday living." Her husband added that "for the advancement of the black man, my wife and I are willing to cooperate in any way. The little working man's condition must be made better." Living with the childless couple was William Leach, a high school senior who often remained on the picket line into the early morning hours even though he had to go to school the following day.[39]

On Monday, the first full day of picketing, the NAACP successfully repulsed the first group of workers that attempted to enter the construction site. Led by an official from the Bricklayers' union, the workers responded by forming what the *Tribune* described as "a flying-wedge formation." When scuffles broke out between protesters and union workers, helmeted police entered the melee, swinging blackjacks. By the time the police finally restored order, the Bricklayers official, three police officers, and two demonstrators had suffered cuts that required medical treatment. The police, however, first arrested the two demonstrators, Revolutionary Action Movement (RAM) activists Max Stanford and Stanley Daniels, for attacking the police officers who were trying to separate the NAACP pickets from the construction workers. Stanford and Daniels, the police charged, had sought to provoke the crowd by yelling, "nonviolence doesn't work; you have to fight for what you want." Daniels, however, insisted that the police had beaten them without provocation. He told the *Tribune* that he had been taking pictures for their newsletter, *The RAM Speaks*, while Stanford had simply been marching in the picket line. "I was shooting pictures of the line when . . . these construction workers . . . tried to crash through. The police came from everywhere. I never saw so many of them . . . I saw one of them pull a blackjack and hit Stanford twice on the head. I was still taking pictures when I felt a blow on the back of my head."[40]

Two weeks earlier, NAACP leaders had asked Stanford and Daniels to leave its rally in support of the Birmingham movement because they were carrying signs that proclaimed "All Afro-Americans Do Not Advocate Non-Violence." Now, however, Cecil Moore's response to their arrest was quite different. Speaking to the still angry crowd, Moore charged that the police bore most of the responsibility for the altercation and announced that he would represent the RAM activists in their criminal case. Moore also urged the protesters not to be provoked into violence, telling them that the deputy police commissioner in charge of the police detail had already expressed regret for the beatings and would soon withdraw the helmeted police. Still, he continued to call on the protesters to continue their efforts to halt work on the construction site. When a flatbed truck loaded with bricks arrived at the site soon thereafter, Moore asked for volunteers to keep it from being unloaded. Fifteen protesters immediately climbed aboard the truck. Later in the week, Moore would use a military analogy to highlight how his approach to civil rights protest differed from Gandhian nonviolence. "We waded into the beaches of Saipan together," he told the picketers, "we waded into the beaches of Okinawa together, and now we're going to wade into the beaches of segregation together." Martin Luther King based his call for nonviolent protest in the biblical admonition to love thy enemy; for Moore, the NAACP's campaign against racism in the local construction industry derived its legitimacy from the sacrifice of black soldiers in World War II.[41]

The violence between the picketers, police, and construction workers led to renewed efforts to negotiate a resolution to the school construction crisis. Within hours of Stanford and Daniels's arrest, the CHR's George Schermer convened a meeting with officials from the NAACP, the school board, and the building trades unions. In the meeting, school officials repeated their intention to cancel the contracts of any contractors found to be discriminating against black workers while the union representatives offered to extend the MSB agreement to the school construction sites. Moore, however, continued to insist that promises of nondiscrimination were insufficient; the unions and contractors had to agree to hire a specific number of skilled black workers. As the 400 Ministers had done during selective patronage, the NAACP was demanding that employers meet specific hiring goals in order to demonstrate their commitment to equal opportunity. By the time the meeting came to an end, Moore believed that the contractors had agreed to hire a black plumber, a steamfitter, and two electricians onto the Strawberry Mansion site.[42]

On Tuesday morning, however, Moore and the NAACP pickets found not a desegregated workforce in Strawberry Mansion but rather a significantly larger police presence with orders from Mayor Tate to insure that workers were able to enter the site. The NAACP, Tate told the news media, should have given the MSB agreement a chance to work instead of picketing unions that had demonstrated a willingness to open their ranks to "non-white craftsmen." Furthermore, he charged that Monday's violence was the result of the protesters' "overzealousness" and that therefore he was legally required to order the police to prevent the protesters from blocking access to the worksite. At 7 A.M., helmeted police officers broke through the forty-one picketers amassed in front of the construction site. "Picketers were thrown to the ground," the *Tribune* reported, "as the officers in flying wedge formation swept everything before them." Eighty-six workers followed the police onto the site and Moore was forced to implore the crowd of spectators that had gathered not to retaliate against the police (Figure 9). "Two wrongs don't make a right," he told the crowd, "we must not let ourselves be goaded into a fight we can't win." Accusing the mayor of a "double-cross," Moore concluded that "they may break our heads, but they can't break our spirit." Whether or not the mayor's order was the result of union lobbying, his decision clearly undercut the CHR's efforts to end discrimination in the construction industry. From that point on, Moore would refuse to negotiate with the CHR or any other city agency, insisting instead on direct negotiations with the unions and contractors.[43]

On Wednesday morning, the NAACP campaign suffered a setback when fifty black laborers joined more than one hundred white skilled tradesmen in following the police charge onto the construction site. The previous evening, the black business agent of the local Laborers' Union had publicly threatened to deny job placements to any laborer refusing to work the Strawberry Mansion site. By midmorning, however, a second group of blacks laborers had arrived at the site to publicly denounce the "Uncle Tom leadership" of their union local and join the picket line. Then, at 10:20 A.M., four black carpenters walked off the construction site and joined the picket line. The carpenters questioned why they had been assigned to the Strawberry Mansion site, saying that they rarely received work, and when they did, they were the first fired. Despite heavy rain, the NAACP picketers were able to block truck deliveries of construction materials throughout the day by repeatedly staging sit-ins on the streets surrounding the construction site. More than three hundred protesters stayed on the picket line until well past midnight in order to prevent evening truck deliveries. Finally, that afternoon, Leon Sullivan and the national NAACP's executive secretary Roy Wilkins announced their support for the construction protests. Wilkins promised that the NAACP would organize similar

Figure 9. Cecil Moore speaks to protesters at Strawberry Mansion construction site, while white construction workers watch from behind the police line, May 1963. Urban Archives, Temple University Libraries.

demonstrations in other cities where it found evidence of union bias. Sullivan announced that the 400 Ministers had formally endorsed the protests and declared that if the NAACP's demands were not met by Friday, "the ministers will issue a call . . . and by Tuesday, 31st and Dauphin will look like Yankee Stadium."[44]

Thursday, May 29 was Memorial Day, so no work was scheduled at the site. Still, a crowd of at least three hundred spent their holiday on the picket line. In his speech that day, Moore continued to emphasize his differences with civil rights liberals. The Commission on Human Relations, he told the crowd, "has sold the Negro a bill of goods." The CHR has "known about these Jim Crow unions and [has] done nothing about it. If they had, we wouldn't be here today." At the same time, he announced that Jimmy Hoffa, president of the Teamsters' Union, had promised that union truckers would not make deliveries to the site as long as the NAACP continued to picket. Round-the-clock picketing would continue, Moore promised, until the NAACP's demands were met.[45]

The growing support for the demonstrations increased the pressure on the unions and contractors to find a solution to the school construction crisis. On Thursday evening, Cecil Moore met in a downtown hotel with school board president Harry LaBrum, Building Trades Council president Joseph O'Neill, and other representatives of the construction industry and unions. O'Neill would later say that it was the 400 Ministers' threat of a mass march and fear of the havoc that such a march might provoke that led the unions to reopen negotiations with Moore. In the negotiations, O'Neill told Moore that the unions were prepared to allow the hiring of five "qualified Negroes" to skilled positions at the Strawberry Mansion site in return for an NAACP commitment to end the protests. With the support of Mayor Tate, however, the construction industry representatives continued to reject Moore's demand for the formation of a committee to monitor the agreement that would include representatives of the NAACP, the Board of Education, the Building Trades Council, and the two local contractors associations. As a result, the negotiations continued well into the night.[46]

Meanwhile, forty volunteers were maintaining an all-night vigil at the construction site. Their purpose was to insure that the NAACP picket line was in place before the police arrived Friday morning to escort workers onto the construction site. At 6 A.M., they confronted two hundred helmeted police officers, arms locked and singing "we shall not be moved." An hour later, the police drew their billy clubs and charged the demonstrators. In response, a group of black spectators began throwing bricks and bottles at the police. Bricks also greeted police who tried to force their way into the NAACP's protest headquarters a block from the construction site after someone yelled that a woman had a gun. When order was restored after twenty minutes, twelve picketers and nine police officers required hospital treatment. The *Tribune* reported that it was only the efforts of a small group of black police officers that prevented the situation from growing even worse. The fury on both sides of the conflict reflected the tensions that had accumulated over the course of the week. A *Tribune* reporter was hit by a police blackjack just after he heard a police officer yell "get that nigger cameraman." Police Commissioner Howard Leary blamed the violence on the demonstrators. His officers, he told a *Tribune* reporter, had been "kicked . . . in the groin . . . spit on . . . . The police are not throwing bricks."[47]

The renewed picket line violence finally convinced the school board and the construction industry to agree to the NAACP demand for a joint monitoring committee. The agreement signed that morning provided for the hiring of five black skilled workers on the Strawberry Mansion site, as the contractors and unions had offered the day before. In return, the NAACP promised both to halt its construction protests and to actively seek to prevent "any interference by way of picketing . . . at any construction site by any group or groups allegedly representing the Negro people in the Philadelphia area." Finally, the agreement provided for the establishment of a joint monitoring committee that would meet before June 12 to develop a plan to increase black employment in the skilled crafts, first on public school construction projects and then on all government and private construction sites throughout the region. This provision reflected Moore's insistence that the NAACP was the only civil rights group truly capable of representing the interests of the black community.[48]

At 9:30 A.M., just two hours after the latest skirmish between the police and the protesters, Cecil Moore arrived at the construction site to announce the agreement. The contractors' concessions represented "just a first step in the march to freedom," he told the cheering crowd. Moore then introduced four black workers—a steamfitter, plumber, and two apprentice electricians—who had already been hired to skilled positions on the Strawberry Mansion project. The fifth position was not to be filled until the sheet metal contractor began work on the site the following week. "This is true Americanism," Lewis Washington, the steamfitter hired, told the crowd, "I'm grateful to Cecil Moore, the NAACP, the pickets and all the people responsible."[49]

Just one week earlier, the Commission on Human Relations had negotiated an agreement with the construction industry that included little more than promises of nondiscriminatory employment. In that week, a sole black electrician was hired onto the MSB site. Now, the NAACP's protest strategy had forced the unions and contractors to agree to meet specific hiring goals. Overnight, four black workers had been hired to skilled positions. The NAACP had also prevented Mayor Tate, who still faced a difficult general election campaign, from taking credit for settlement of the construction crisis while simultaneously assuring his supporters in the building trades that they could maintain their racially exclusive hiring policies with, at worst, minimal adjustments. Three years after selective patronage had first begun to raise questions about the CHR, Cecil Moore and the NAACP had successfully discredited the city government's commitment to insuring equal opportunity for black workers.[50]

All This for Five Jobs? Negotiating with the Construction Industry

Despite the euphoria that followed the triumph over the construction unions, the NAACP's victory would soon prove more symbolic than substantive. As with selective patronage, the Strawberry Mansion campaign demonstrated that protest strategies were a more effective means to winning the symbolic employment of small numbers of black workers in previously white-only occupations than to creating procedures to enforce meaningful equal opportunity throughout an industry. The same liberal premises that limited the impact of the human rights provisions of the 1951 city charter also hampered selective patronage and the construction protests. All three presumed that removal of the blatant racial barriers within the local labor market would resolve the problems of black un- and under-employment. And like their liberal counterparts, Cecil Moore and the 400 Ministers lacked a strategy for addressing the multiple causes of the black employment crisis, including employers' use of token hires to stay in compliance with antidiscrimination laws, the decline of the city's manufacturing sector, and educational deficits within the local black workforce.

The end of the Strawberry Mansion campaign removed the pressure that the Building Trades Council (BTC) felt to make additional concessions. Determined to maintain their white members' privileged position within the local construction industry, the union leadership had long believed that its political influence would enable it to withstand the threat posed by the NAACP's protest strategy. Less than a month after they had sought to avoid testifying before the CHR's public hearings, the BTC negotiators used the language of civil rights liberalism to defend their refusal to meet the NAACP's additional demands. Not only were their membership policies colorblind, they insisted, but it would violate the rights of individual union members, as well as the unions' seniority rules, to grant black workers special treatment. The BTC's intransigence reflected the economic value that its member unions ascribed to their racially exclusionary membership policies. Throughout the postwar period, government had been the driving force behind almost all public and private development within Philadelphia's city limits. The liberal reform movement's commitment to urban redevelopment had led the city not only to invest in schools and government offices but also to provide infrastructure improvements and direct financial incentives for private development.[51] As the largest and most consistent contractor of construction labor in Philadelphia, the city government thus set the standard for employment policies throughout the local industry. In an urban economy suffering from the effects of deindustrialization, the building trades unions viewed both public sector investment in the construction industry and their lily-white membership policies as essential to the economic survival of their members. Efforts to pressure the city to enforce its nondiscrimination clause were thus a threat to the livelihood of unionized construction workers.

Significant opposition to the NAACP-BTC agreement emerged from within the construction unions almost from the moment Moore declared victory to the Strawberry Mansion demonstrators. Within hours, ten members of Steamfitters Local 420 walked off the construction site. While publicly disavowing the walkout, the local's business agent, Thomas Dugan, not only declared his opposition to the agreement but also threatened to withdraw the local from the Building Trades Council. In an interview with a local reporter, Dugan made clear the economic logic at the root of racial exclusion in the construction crafts. While admitting that the local had no black members, he insisted that its membership policies were nondiscriminatory. If the black steamfitter hired to work on the Strawberry Mansion site were to apply for membership in the union, he claimed, his application would be dealt with like any other. However, high levels of unemployment in the construction industry meant that the local was not currently taking new members since four hundred of the local's members had been out of work for as many as seven months. Even if Dugan was overstating the crisis, public sector investment was clearly crucial to the economic health of the construction industry and its unions in an economy struggling with private capital disinvestment. The NAACP's demands were thus a direct threat to the benefits that political influence had brought to the crafts unions.[52]

Union opposition to the NAACP agreement extended well beyond the steamfitters. While none of the other BTC member unions directly repudiated the agreement, the speed with which the BTC leadership moved to reassure the city's craft unionists that major changes in the unions' membership policies were not imminent suggests that there was significant displeasure among the rank and file. On June 3, Joseph O'Neill, president of the BTC, met with two thousand members of building trades union members to defend the agreement. O'Neill told the group that the BTC's leaders had acceded to the NAACP's demands in order "to stop a riot." Moore, he told the assembled, had depicted the Strawberry Mansion protests as "a loaded shotgun, a loaded rifle" and threatened the union leaders that "it is going to be my agreement and if you don't make up your minds now, you'll pay for it." By conceding to the hiring of a black plumber on the Strawberry Mansion site, O'Neill insisted, he had acted "in the interest of the union and the citizens of Philadelphia."[53]

Even before reopening negotiations with the NAACP, the BTC leadership moved both to quiet its internal critics and to neutralize those within the local labor movement who had been pressing the craft unions to enact more extensive racial reforms. On June 7, the BTC announced that it was withdrawing from the AFL-CIO's Philadelphia Labor Council to protest the local council's support for the Commission on Human Relations' investigation of the crafts unions' racial practices. A week later, Joseph Burke, president of Sheet Metal Workers' Local 19, accused the local council of failing to oppose a plan supposedly favored by George Schermer to strip the control of apprenticeship programs from the unions. James Jones and Joseph Schwartz of the Philadelphia AFL-CIO's Human Rights Committee, Burke declared, were "disturbers of the peace" within the labor movement. The threat of a split in the local labor movement was forestalled when the Philadelphia AFL-CIO formed a "unity" committee of the local labor council's officers and leaders of the BTC to resolve their differences. Not surprisingly, there was significant overlap between the two groups. In fact, Philadelphia AFL-CIO president Norman Blumberg was also the president of the local painters union. Blumberg signaled that the purpose of the committee was to quiet the crafts unions' internal critics when he called on labor activists to protect the right of the building trades unions to control hiring within their crafts.[54]

On June 10, 1963, negotiations on a comprehensive plan to increase black representation in the skilled trades began between the NAACP and the construction industry. Two weeks removed from the threat of mass demonstrations, the BTC refused to offer a substantive proposal for integrating its union membership. Instead, the council released a public statement affirming their opposition "to any policy of discrimination that interferes with any qualified workman to obtain work because of race, color, creed or national origin." To both the NAACP and the press, the industry representatives insisted that they could not continue the negotiations because they were required by law to cooperate with the CHR, which had announced the previous week that it was establishing a referral system to identify black construction workers for the skilled trades. Before the construction protests began, of course, the skilled crafts unions had resisted every effort by the CHR to investigate their membership practices.[55]

The BTC's intransigence forced Cecil Moore and the NAACP to once again pursue a protest strategy, this time in conjunction with Philadelphia CORE and the 400 Ministers. In a joint statement, the three groups demanded that fifteen percent of craft union jobs on city contracts and sixty percent of union apprenticeship slots be reserved for black workers. When the city failed to respond, a group of CORE activists resumed their sit-ins in City Hall and the CHR offices. After another fifty-five hours, Mayor Tate finally agreed to cancel the contracts of two contractors if they did not comply with the city's antibias laws within 48 hours. The mayor's action led the construction unions and contractors to return to their negotiations with the CHR. By the end of the summer, the CHR had reached agreements with the plumbers, the roofers, the steamfitters, and two electrical workers' locals to admit black journeymen and desegregate apprenticeship programs. In addition, seventeen local construction contractors, with a combined $17 million in city contracts, agreed to hire black journeymen.[56]

Ironically, the CHR negotiated this agreement without the benefit of its longtime executive director George Schermer. In the midst of the NAACP protests, Schermer penned a memo calling for a complete overhaul of the city's efforts to promote nondiscriminatory hiring practices. Specifically, Schermer called for a significant increase in the CHR's powers to "remedy . . . the injustices and inequities resulting from racial and religious discrimination." He argued that the city's antibias laws were insufficient to meet the just demands of black activists because they "require[d] proof of an overt act of discrimination and provide . . . little remedy beyond . . . requiring that discriminatory acts cease." In his search for ways to strengthen the CHR's regulatory powers, Schermer drew on President John F. Kennedy's 1961 Executive Order establishing the Equal Employment Opportunity Commission. Kennedy's order had mandated "affirmative action to assure results" in efforts to increase black employment in the federal government. "Experience demonstrates," Schermer wrote, that more was needed to "affirmatively enable groups long excluded to . . . become established in new jobs and new skills." If the commission and its allies were not able to craft such affirmative legislation, he concluded, "organizations concerned for social justice" would continue to be "persuaded that in the absence of legal machinery they must use their own extra-legal devices." Even as Schermer called for new antibias legislation, he also faulted Mayor Tate for the Commission on Human Relations' failure to defuse the construction crisis. "By intent or default," Schermer charged, the mayor had "undermined the prestige, the power and the morale of the Commission." Five days later, Schermer announced his resignation as executive director of the CHR. The mayor, he wrote in his resignation letter, was responsible for the commission's descent from "the finest, best equipped and most vigorous . . . in the country" to one "too weak to cope with the new challenges that have arisen in our community."[57]

Schermer's memo would prove a hauntingly prophetic analysis of the weaknesses inherent in the CHR's agreement with the BTC. According to the commission's own figures, only six black workers were hired to skilled positions on major construction projects in the city during the summer of 1963. A 1966 federal survey of the seven highest paid construction trade unions in the Philadelphia area—the ironworkers, plumbers and pipe fitters, steamfitters, electrical workers, sheet metal workers, roofers, and elevator constructors—found that the situation had improved only slightly in three years. The seven local unions reported a combined membership of nearly nine thousand. Less than fifty of those were racial minorities, a rate of less than one percent. As Schermer had feared, the CHR lacked the necessary legal powers to force the city's building trades unions and union contractors to abandon their exclusionary practices in anything more than token ways.[58]

In the end, it would take federal action to end racial discrimination in the Philadelphia construction industry. In September 1965, President Lyndon B. Johnson signed Executive Order 11246 which gave the Department of Labor the power to terminate federal contracts with firms that did not implement "affirmative action" hiring policies. In 1966, the Office of Federal Contract Compliance (OFCC) implemented its first two affirmative action plans in St. Louis and and San Francisco. The following year, the OFCC announced plans to implement its "Philadelphia Plan," including the requirement that all Philadelphia area recipients of federal construction contracts of more than $500,000 set goals for minority employment in the seven highest paid trades. Opposition from contractors and the building trades union would prevent full implementation on the Philadelphia Plan until 1969 when it was reaffirmed by the Nixon administration.[59]

Cecil Moore's Philadelphia

Cecil Moore, not the liberal architects of affirmative action, emerged from the Strawberry Mansion protests as the most important civil rights leader in Philadelphia in the summer of 1963. For the next four years, Moore would continue to position himself as a local version of Malcolm X, the only black leader in the city unwilling to censor his words and actions to conform to white liberal sensibilities. Increasingly, he would combine outspoken opposition to liberal interracialism with calls for black political independence from the Philadelphia Democratic machine. In its purest form, black nationalist ideology questioned the possibility, even the desirability, of legal equality for Americans of African descent. In contrast, Moore, like many of the Black Power activists who followed him, maintained his commitment to institutional desegregation and the legal protection of individual civil rights even as he drew from black nationalism a commitment to racial solidarity and a belief in the intractability of white racism.

Still, it was Moore's commitment to using protest as a civil rights strategy that most excited his supporters in the summer of 1963. Combined with the Southern Christian Leadership Conference's successful Birmingham campaign, the victory over the construction industry seemed to confirm that mass protest had the potential to achieve what years of legislative and court victories had not. The Philadelphia NAACP sponsored a series of rallies during June to highlight the mass support that the construction protests had won for the branch. At the June 9 rally, the national NAACP's executive secretary Roy Wilkins told the crowd that they were "lucky to have a man like Moore," and local disc jockey Georgie Woods declared that "the eyes of the city, the state, and the nation" were on the Philadelphia NAACP. Following the June 11 assassination of the NAACP's Mississippi field secretary Medgar Evers, Moore called on black workers in the city to stage a four-hour work "moratorium" on the morning of Monday, June 24. The moratorium, Moore declared, would serve as a "vivid portrayal of the Negroes' economic power as well as a memorial to the valiant martyr." When Fred Corleto, the city's managing director, and Philadelphia AFL-CIO president Norman Blumberg both announced that employees who joined the moratorium without authorization from their supervisors would be punished, Moore charged that the two were "anti-Negro."[60]

The black community's response to Moore's call for a work moratorium demonstrated how significantly the Philadelphia NAACP's class base had shifted to the city's black working-class neighborhoods. Despite Corleto and Blumberg's threats, 75 percent of the city's predominately black sanitation workers failed to appear for work and 50 percent of black postal workers on the day shift took the morning off. Corleto, in fact, was forced to retract his threat to punish city workers who were absent from work without authorization. The manager of a South Philadelphia bar told the *Tribune* that "the whole neighborhood's a graveyard." White-collar workers seem to have been much less supportive of the moratorium, however. The school board reported that only 12 percent of black schoolteachers stayed home, while Corleto insisted that the total absentee rate for the city's black workers was less than 25 percent.[61]

Over the remainder of the summer, the Philadelphia NAACP led a series of protests against discriminatory employers in the city. In July, Moore announced that the NAACP had reached an agreement with the Greyhound Bus Company to hire two black telephone operators and a baggage handler, positions that had previously been restricted to whites. Greyhound also pledged to hire additional black workers as jobs opened up in previously all-white occupations. In late August, following a month-long picket campaign at Philadelphia's main post office, the NAACP reached an agreement with local postal officials that allowed the branch to review postal promotions in the city for one month for evidence of discrimination.[62] The summer of protest reached another crescendo on August 28 when an estimated thirty thousand Philadelphians traveled on NAACP-sponsored trains and buses to the 1963 March on Washington.[63]

Throughout the summer, Moore continued to blame the persistence of racial discrimination and black poverty in Philadelphia on the perfidy of the city's liberal leadership. So long as black voters continued to support liberal politicians, Moore believed, the black community would remain powerless to address institutionalized forms of racial discrimination in the city. During the construction protests, Moore charged that Robert N. C. Nix, the long-serving representative of North and West Philadelphia's Second Congressional District, was a "racial apologist . . . [who] has never identified himself with the Negro community; he has never made any contribution to the welfare of Negroes." At a June 9 rally to honor those who "sacrificed their blood, their time, and their jobs" to walk the Strawberry Mansion picket lines, Moore accused the members of the Commission on Human Relations of using "their positions purely as a means of self-advancement to the detriment of those whose rights they are sworn to protect."[64] By attacking Sadie Alexander and Christopher Edley, the CHR's two black members—whom he called "part-time Negroes and Uncle Toms"—Moore insinuated that black liberals had betrayed not just the interests of the black community but their very racial identity in pursuit of the status and financial rewards that liberalism had to offer. Moore's attacks on Alexander, in particular, dismissed the entire history of civil rights liberalism as an effort to win the privileges of whiteness for a small group. When Alexander responded by citing her role in the passage of the state's Public Accommodations Act, as a member of President Truman's Committee on Civil Rights, and as the author of the human rights provisions of the city charter, he called her defense "another dreary recital of her dismal record of tokenism and gradualism which only further illustrates how out of step she and her associates are with the tempo of the times."[65]

Moore's willingness to offend powerful figures in the city, no matter their race or liberal credentials, appealed to black Philadelphians frustrated by the pace of racial change in the city. His outspoken attacks on liberals and their civil rights record differentiated Moore from those who appeared to place their own status above the needs of the black community. Moore's agile use of outrageous comments to demonstrate his loyalty to working-class black interests is evident in the controversy created by an interview he gave to the *Pennsylvania Guardian*, a weekly newspaper published by the Philadelphia ADA. In the interview, Moore accused "'phony white liberals,' 'part-time Negroes,' and people of 'Semitic origin'" of hypocrisy in their professed support for civil rights. He then went on to criticize "Negroes who owe their position to the fact that they are Negroes, rather than for what they would do for Negroes" as well as "those white men who call themselves liberal, but in fact do nothing but bleed the Negro." In his view, "so-called northern white liberals" were "a bunch of phonies" and he would "rather deal with any Southern racist than the unscrupulous bigots living in Chestnut Hill" (the upper-class neighborhood that was home to many of the city's liberal reformers, including Mayors Clark and Dilworth). Most disturbing were the comments that the paper attributed to Moore on the commitment of the Jewish community to black civil rights. The *Guardian* quoted Moore as saying that he knew of no Jewish civil rights activist in the city who was not a "goddamn phony." Specifically, Moore charged that the brother of Joseph Schwartz, leader of the city's garment workers locals and a local ADA activist, had opposed efforts to desegregate the city's motion picture operators locals. And of Schwartz himself, Moore said "I believe in guilt by relationship." "If people of a Semitic origin continue to exploit Negroes," he concluded, "I'll exploit them as anti-American. If you want to call that anti-Semitic, then I'm anti-Semitic." In his concluding remarks, however, Moore suggested that his inflammatory comments were designed, at least in part, to motivate his supporters. "The Philadelphia Inquirer calls me anti-white," he said. "The Jewish Times said I was anti-Semitic. They're trying to get the Negroes in this city up against me . . . but what they've done has helped me."[66]

The national NAACP was swift to condemn the reported remarks. Bishop Stephen Gill Spottswood, chair of the NAACP board, immediately wrote to Moore reaffirming the organization's opposition to anti-Semitism. "The NAACP," Spottswood wrote, "which has based its whole campaign for justice for the Negro minority . . . upon the thesis that a whole group cannot be indicted for the derelictions of any individual . . . cannot countenance anti-Semitism on the part of any official empowered to speak in the name of the NAACP." In particular, the NAACP chair criticized Moore's use of the phrase "guilt by relationship," a phrase which he argued "forms the basis of the mob psychology and the mob murders that have been visited upon Negro Americans for generations."[67]

Moore's response to the controversy surrounding the *Guardian* article reflected his contradictory desire both to maintain good relations with the NAACP's national leadership and to solidify his position as the one black leader in the city not afraid to offend white sensibilities. On June 20, Moore released a letter to the media that repudiated the most bigoted of his statements to the *Guardian*. He insisted that he had never used the phrase "guilt by relationship" and had "never said nor do I believe that 'all' of any group is guilty en masse of anything." Still, he defended the substance of his attack on liberals. He was, Moore wrote, "unalterably opposed to anyone who exploits Negroes. Some Negroes exploit Negroes, some do not. Some Jews exploit Negroes, some do not. Some Negroes are not sincere followers of civil rights movements, some are, and . . . some Jews are sincere in civil rights and others are not."[68]

From Protest to Politics

Despite the enthusiasm that the NAACP's protests had generated in black Philadelphia, Cecil Moore had been no more able than Leon Sullivan to force the necessary changes in the local labor market. The limitations of selective patronage led Sullivan to abandon protest as a strategy to solve the employment problems of the black poor. For Moore, on the other hand, the solution was not to abandon protest altogether but rather to combine it with a range of other legal and political strategies. Moore was now seeking to forge a very new role for the Philadelphia NAACP. By establishing the NAACP as an independent force in electoral politics in the city, Moore hoped to establish a basis for civil rights activism that was not dependent on maintaining alliances with either white liberals or the Democratic machine. While the decision to involve the NAACP more actively in electoral politics did not inherently move the chapter in a nationalist direction, Moore's approach to racial and ethnic relations within the electoral arena reflected his belief that blacks could not expect public officials to support their interests until they developed an electoral base independent of both the liberal coalition and the Democratic machine.

The collapse of the Democrats' reform wing following Richardson Dilworth's defeat in the 1962 gubernatorial race and Mayor Tate's defeat of Walter Phillips in the 1963 mayoral primary made Moore's call for an independent black politics particularly timely. For more than a decade, civil rights causes had benefited from the competition between the reform and organization wings of the Democratic Party. Democratic politicians in Philadelphia were forced to pay attention to black concerns so long as there was the potential for meaningful competition in the all-important Democratic primaries. By confirming the collapse of the Democrats' liberal wing, Tate's landslide victory raised the specter of the loss of all black leverage within the party. As a longtime Republican, Moore had argued that black voters would be better served if they demonstrated increased independence from the Democratic Party. But as president of the local NAACP, Moore's goals had necessarily changed. Rather than seeking to shift voter loyalty from one party to the other, Moore sought to position himself as the community leader who could deliver the black community's votes to whichever party or candidate had the most to offer.

As the November 1963 general election approached, Moore hoped to be able to establish the NAACP as an organization able to deliver a sizable block of black voters to either party. In early August, he wrote to both Mayor Tate and his Republican challenger, Jim McDermott, asking that they pledge if elected to increase the number of black appointees to the city's police force and zoning and park commission boards. In addition, he asked the respective parties to increase the number of blacks slated to run for the state legislature and city magistrate.[69]

Whatever the impact of the NAACP's efforts, Tate would not have defeated McDermott if not for the support he received from black voters. The 85,214 vote margin that Tate enjoyed in the city's seventeen predominately black wards exceeded his citywide margin by nearly 19,000. One study estimated that Tate received only 45.3 percent of the white vote as compared to 73.5 percent of the black vote. In the four years since Mayor Dilworth was reelected in 1959, the Democrats' share of the white vote had declined sixteen percentage points. The black Democratic vote, in contrast, had declined by less than a point. Black Philadelphians had clearly become the most loyal Democratic voters in city.[70]

Moore's goal, of course, had not been to prove the loyalty of the city's black Democrats. In the days following the election, therefore, Moore continued to insist that the black electorate was motivated by racial self-interest, not party loyalty. It was incumbent on the mayor, he argued, to reward the black voters who had returned him to office by appointing blacks to five major posts in his new administration: the commissioners of welfare, recreation, and licenses and inspection, the deputy commissioner of police, and the director of the personnel office. Moore threatened that if Tate failed to meet this demand, the NAACP would punish him through picketing, boycotting, and "intelligent use of the ballot." Moore's demands scandalized most other black leaders in the city. While acknowledging that the "Mayor certainly has an obligation in filling positions to consider qualified Negroes," city councilman Thomas McIntosh insisted that "I don't go along with the idea for designating any particular job for a race." Even more outraged was an unnamed "prominent Negro" quoted by the *Philadelphia Inquirer.* "You don't merely come forward and say X should have the job because he's Negro. We have been fighting for years to have Negroes hired on qualification."[71]

The irony of Tate's victory was that it was black votes that assured the election of the city's first Catholic mayor precisely at the point that a significant number of white ethnic voters were beginning to abandon the Democratic Party over racial issues. Still, the inability of the NAACP to crack the racism of the construction unions demonstrated the extent to which a Democratic machine led by Mayor Tate would continue to steer most of the city's resources toward white working- and lower-middle-class communities. Despite these realities, most of the city's African American leadership remained committed to the nonracial ideals of civil rights liberalism. For them, appointments based solely on qualifications provided the best opportunity for African American advancement. Instead of making outright demands, suggested the unnamed leader quoted by the *Inquirer,* Moore should have said "to the Mayor, 'Your Cabinet is all Caucasian. Don't you feel this [making black appointments] would be a judicious thing to do—and if you would like me to assist in finding somebody, I would be glad to help.'"[72] For Moore and his supporters, on the other hand, politics in Philadelphia were essentially an ethnic contest. To act otherwise was to fail to adequately protect the interests of the black community. Although Moore and his critics shared a commitment to increasing the number of African American city officials, their differences in approaches reflected divergent views on whether the racial divide in American society could be overcome.

Riot!

On the evening of October 29, 1963, just days before the mayoral election, a small crowd of black residents began throwing bricks at police and looting stores along North Philadelphia's Susquehanna Avenue retail district. Hours earlier, a police officer had shot and killed a twenty-four year-old man named Willie Philyaw on that stretch of Susquehanna, allegedly for stealing a watch from a local drugstore. According to the police, Philyaw had lunged at the officer in question with a knife; as a result the department would later rule that the shooting was justified. Witnesses to the shooting, however, saw something quite different. They saw Philyaw, who couldn't run because of a previous leg injury, attempting to hobble away from the officer and ignoring his order to stop. Another man then stepped between Philyaw and the officer and raised his hand as the officer shot at the fleeing suspect. The bullet passed through the bystander's hand before it killed Philyaw. To the crowd, the shooting was a prime example of the unnecessary violence that the police carried out with impunity on North Philadelphia's ghetto streets. While swift police action and the urgings of neighborhood clergy quickly dispersed the crowd and prevented the vio-

Figure 10. Teenagers surround a police car during the 1964 riot. Urban Archives, Temple University Libraries.

lence from spreading, Philyaw's death portended the ways in which issues of police brutality and economic underdevelopment in northern cities would disrupt the vision of racial progress and harmony that had been so successfully propagated by the mainstream civil rights movement during the early years of the 1960s. Less than a month later, President Kennedy was dead along with much of the nation's self-confidence and liberal faith in the inevitability of social progress.[73]

In Philadelphia, the threat of racial rioting came to fruition on Friday, August 28, 1964, almost a year to the day since the March on Washington (Figure 10). For three days, crowds of black Philadelphians attacked the police and looted white-owned businesses throughout North Philadelphia. The riot raised serious questions about the ability of either the protest or liberal wings of Philadelphia's civil rights movement to effectively address the problems of black poverty in the city. Like the more famous urban riots that would occur later in the decade, the North Philadelphia riot served as a metaphor for the lack of connection that many of the city's black poor felt to both the national and local leadership of the civil rights movement. Moreover, the events of August 28, 29, and 30, 1964, destroyed the myth of racial progress that had been so carefully crafted by Philadelphia's liberal-reform coalition. For two decades, the liberal civil rights coalition had worked for nonracial solutions to the problem of racial discrimination in the city. Antidiscrimination laws, intergroup relations workshops, and the creation of interracial political coalitions were all designed to ensure equal treatment for the city's residents regardless of race. In its spontaneity, violence, and lack of specified goals, the North Philadelphia riot was the exact antithesis of the city's liberal civil rights tradition. It was, however, the explicitly racial nature of the riot that was its most significant challenge to liberalism. By venting their anger on white police officers and white-owned businesses—and by sparing black-owned businesses—the rioters articulated a demand not for equal treatment but for the exclusion of white wealth and power from their neighborhoods.

As much as the riot symbolized black frustration with civil rights liberalism, it also exposed the contingent nature of mass black support for protest strategies like selective patronage and the NAACP's construction demonstrations. As James Williams, the new president of Philadelphia CORE pointed out, the rioters greeted Cecil Moore's pleas that they return home with the same "rocks" that they threw at more "moderate" leaders such as Raymond Pace Alexander and Leon Sullivan. "Nobody leads these people," Williams told the *Bulletin*, "Nobody quiets them down. We don't have a leader."[74]

The North Philadelphia riot began shortly after two police patrolmen, Robert Wells and John Hoffer, responded to a report that there was a car stalled in the intersection of Twenty-Second Street and Columbia Avenue at 9:35 on the evening of Friday, August 28, 1964. When Wells, who was black, and Hoffer, who was white, arrived at the intersection they found what appeared to be a drunk couple arguing in a car. After failing to convince Mrs. Odessa Bradford to move the car, Hoffer tried to forcibly remove her from the car so that the intersection could be cleared. As he attempted to do so, however, James Mettles emerged from the crowd that had gathered and attacked the white police officer. Officer Wells then immediately radioed for additional police assistance. By the time Mettles and Mrs. Bradford were taken away in a police wagon, bricks and bottles were raining down from nearby rooftops onto the police cars that were responding to Wells's call. A contingent of twenty-five police officers finally dispersed the crowd, but not before the rioters had broken the windows on one police car and ten other cars.[75]

Just one block away, however, at the corner of Twenty-Third and Columbia, a twenty-five-year-old neighborhood resident named Raymond Hall—who was known for racially militant views—began to yell that "a pregnant black woman's been beaten and shot to death by a white policeman." By 11 P.M., a crowd had gathered at that corner to throw bricks, bottles, and stones at the police. From Twenty-Third Street, the crowd then moved down the Columbia Avenue retail strip toward Twenty-First Street, smashing windows and looting stores. At Twentieth Street, refuse was thrown through the window of a police car.[76] Shortly after midnight, six hundred police officers descended on the riot area with guns drawn and with police dogs and fire hoses. One member of the police force compared the first night of rioting to "being in a war. . . . There were so many rioters. Most of them women, teenagers, or even younger. . . . We'd chase one way and another group would come on us from another direction throwing bricks, trash cans, anything." The police did little to stop the looting that night. Instead, the department implemented Police Commissioner Howard Leary's riot control plan, a plan that emphasized the avoidance of violence and casualties even at the cost of allowing extensive property damage.[77]

By 2:30 A.M., the looting had spread to Fifteenth and Columbia and to stores along the Ridge Avenue business strip between Norris and Jefferson Streets. By then, many of black Philadelphia's leading political and civic figures had descended on Columbia Avenue in an effort to disperse the crowds. Those urging the rioters to go home ranged from Judge Raymond Alexander, who had represented the area on city council for most of the 1950s, to Georgie Woods, the city's most popular black deejay and concert promoter. The looters, however, proved unresponsive. Voices in the crowd called the community leaders "handkerchief-headed Uncle Toms." The rioters even booed Stanley Branche, an NAACP leader from nearby Chester who had earned a reputation for militancy for his leadership of a protest campaign against school segregation in April 1964.[78]

At 3:45 A.M., Cecil Moore arrived from Atlantic City where he had been attending the Democratic National Convention. "I understand your problems," the NAACP leader told a crowd at one corner, "but this is no way to solve them. It's late. Everybody go home to bed." However, Moore's efforts to position himself as the voice of North Philadelphia's black poor meant little on this night. A woman was heard to respond to Moore's pleas: "listen, man, this is the only time in my life I've got a chance to get these things." As the police dragged two looters into a paddy wagon, someone yelled, "See this, Cecil? See this? What are you going to do about this?" And then the crowd began to chant, "We want freedom." One observer reported that the crowds threw rocks at Moore's sound truck. Fifteen minutes later, a twenty-three-year-old woman who worked as a secretary in the office of a local charity and had no previous police record stood on an overturned refrigerator at Seventeeth and Columbia, fourteen blocks from her home. "We don't need Cecil Moore," she yelled to the crowd that had assembled at that corner. "We don't need civil rights. We can take care of ourselves." Minutes later, the crowd surged onto Columbia Avenue and started looting and plundering stores. The crowds did not begin to thin until after sunrise.[79]

The Jungle

The North Philadelphia riot was centered in an area that had come to be known as "the Jungle" for its grinding poverty and racial homogeneity. The annual income of the vast majority of the residents living in the two-and-one-half-square mile area bounded by Poplar, Lehigh, Tenth, and Thirty-Third Streets—an area that encompassed the riot zone—was less than $3,352, thirty percent below the city average. Two-thirds of the black male workers living in the area were semiskilled or unskilled. Blacks living in North Philadelphia had an unemployment rate two to three times the city's rate. The high school graduation rate for black residents of North Philadelphia was 50 percent, while the unemployment rate for black male neighborhood residents between the ages of sixteen and twenty-one who were not in school was 60 percent. Families in North Philadelphia paid 35 percent or more of their income for shelter costs—as compared to the U.S. Labor Department recommendation of 20 to 25 percent—even though 53 percent of the houses in the riot area failed to meet the city's housing code. The city's urban renewal program had actually exacerbated housing problems in the area. Racial discrimination and high rental costs prevented most displaced families from finding new housing in other parts of the city and so they remained, further contributing to the problem of overcrowded housing in the area. According to one survey, 72 percent of those displaced by urban renewal were unable to find satisfactory housing.[80]

Community leaders, civil rights activists, and law enforcement officials worked feverishly throughout the day Saturday, hoping to prevent a second night of rioting. The Commission on Human Relations convened a mid-morning meeting of community leaders from North Philadelphia and civil rights activists at Emanuel Baptist Church on Twenty-Second Street. Following the meeting, CHR chairperson Sadie Alexander held a press conference to call on the mayor to enforce law and order in the riot area. Five thousand 'responsible' Negro leaders, she announced, were prepared to be deputized in an effort to support the police. Leon Sullivan called for the National Guard to be sent into North Philadelphia. Other black liberals bemoaned the riot's impact on white attitudes toward blacks. The *New York Times* quoted Judge Alexander as saying, "in my day, every home was a Christian home. We had no riots then. I feel very much as if our race has been diminished," while Congressman Robert Nix called the riot "the most disgraceful thing I ever saw."[81]

Cecil Moore, however, boycotted the CHR meeting. "The people we had to talk to wouldn't be there," he told the *New York Times*. "It's not the churchgoers who riot." Instead, the NAACP president went that night to a concert sponsored by Georgie Woods at the Uptown Theater just north of Columbia Avenue. A key figure in the promotion of black rock and roll and rhythm and blues groups on the East Coast, Woods had used his daily radio show and weekly concerts and dances to promote NAACP protests and other civil rights activities ever since Moore was first elected to the NAACP presidency. At the concert, Moore told the teenage audience that "nobody wins in a riot except the bondsman, the lawyers and the doctors." Moore also rejected concerns about the riot's impact on white attitudes toward the black community. "White leaders are not embarrassed by the Cosa Nostra. I'm not going to be embarrassed by hoodlums."[82]

Early on Saturday afternoon Mayor Tate, citing the concerns of the black leaders who attended the CHR meeting, invoked an 1850 state law that allowed him to place a curfew on a 410-square-block area of North Philadelphia. The curfew order required that all bars and liquor stores in the area close and subjected to arrest anyone refusing a police order to return home. The efforts of law enforcement officials and community leaders, however, failed to prevent a second night of looting. As darkness fell, 1,800 cops began to battle looters all across the riot area. One business owner described a crowd that moved "methodically from Columbia to Ridge on 31st breaking windows and looting all white-owned business establishments. What they couldn't carry, they threw into the streets." Forty-eight police marksmen were dispatched to rooftops along a six-block strip of Columbia Avenue. Police helicopters searched for people throwing debris from rooftops onto cops. At Seventh and Columbia, a group of fifty teenagers threw stones at the cops. A television cameraman filmed a man holding up a bag of looted groceries for the camera.[83]

Sunday brought a third night of rioting. Over the course of the weekend, two people were killed, 339 wounded—100 cops and 239 black residents—and 308 arrested, including 108 who resided outside of the riot area. Of those arrested, 200 were charged with burglary, 30 with breach of the peace and rioting, and the rest with violation of the mayor's curfew. The city estimated property damage from the riot at $3 million. Of the 170 business properties in a five-block radius of the intersection in which Odessa Bradford was arrested, only 54 survived the weekend undamaged. And of those, 52 were identifiable as black-owned or -operated. The other two were a Chinese restaurant with sign reading "we are colored too" and an osteopathic physician who was later indicted for conducting abortions. The only black-owned stores to be damaged over the course of the weekend were those that failed to identify themselves as such. "The enemy," wrote Lenora Berson, a journalist commissioned by the American Jewish Committee to study the causes of the riot, "was not all merchants, or even all bad merchants, but the white merchants; not all owners of property, but the white establishment, most visible, best symbolized and most vulnerable behind the plate glass windows in the black ghetto."[84]

Liberal efforts to contain and defuse the evident restiveness in the city's black ghettos began months before the August riot. Following the October

1963 police shooting of Willie Philyaw, the staffs of the Commission on Human Relations and the Fellowship Commission worked closely with the police department's top leadership to develop a new riot control plan for the city. By June 1964, Mayor James Tate had issued an order requiring that all citizens' complaints against the police be forwarded to the Police Advisory Board, the citizen review board established by Mayor Dilworth in 1958. That month, Police Commissioner Howard Leary also approved a proposal by Cecil Moore to place black lawyers from the Philadelphia NAACP in neighborhood police precincts on summer weekends. Moore believed that the presence of the NAACP lawyers, who had been specially trained to investigate charges of police brutality, would both pressure police officers to improve their treatment of black suspects and lessen the likelihood that black suspects would resist arrest or that onlookers would seek to violently protest police action. After continued lobbying from Moore—who called Leary "the most enlightened police man in America"—Leary agreed to order patrol officers to stop pulling over "suspicious" cars and raiding "disorderly" houses unless they received a citizen complaint, practices that were particularly inflammatory in black communities. By then, however, five days of rioting had hit Harlem after a police officer fatally shot a fifteen-year-old whom the officer claimed had attacked him with a knife. Similar incidents of police violence led to riots in Rochester, New York, and Paterson, Jersey City, and East Orange, New Jersey, during the month between the Harlem and North Philadelphia riots.[85]

Ironically, many national civil rights leaders had previously pointed to Philadelphia as a model for managing tensions between the black community and the police. In its study of the Harlem riot, for example, the New York Civil Liberties Union argued that Philadelphia's Police Advisory Board "has been good for the 'image' of the police force" in the city's poor black communities. Similarly, Cecil Moore predicted that the NAACP's volunteer lawyer program and its other efforts to cooperate with the police department would exempt the city from the summer's wave of riots. And the police department praised the NAACP's lawyers for helping to reduce tensions between the police and the black community. According to the department, the program had reduced the number of blacks arrested for offenses against a police officer from an average of thirty each weekend to just two during the first weekend in August.[86]

The Liberal View: The System Worked

It was not so much the actual riot as the debate over its meaning—its causes, its implications for the future—that helped to shape the future of racial politics in the city in the weeks, months, and years that followed. For liberals, the failure to prevent the riot was less important than the fact that the system had worked to prevent further damage to human life and prop-

erty. Not only was the police response restrained but political and community leaders of every race and religion had joined together, under the
direction of the Commission on Human Relations, to urge calm inside the
riot area and across the city. In this view, the effort to contain the 1964 riot
was as much of a liberal success as the campaign to prevent outbreaks of
racial violence during the 1944 transit strike that had enabled the Fellowship Commission to establish itself as the coordinating agency for the city's
civil rights community. The liberal civil rights coalition began a public relations campaign to praise the city's response to the riot almost as soon as
the rioting came to an end. In the week following the riot, the Fellowship
Commission issued a press release that "commended Mayor James H. J.
Tate, Police Commissioner Howard Leary, clergy and other civic officials
for the restraint used in handling the riot," while admitting that the "anti-
white feeling in much of the looting . . . makes the disturbance much more
than a question of . . . hoodlumism."[87]

For liberals, restoring racial peace in North Philadelphia was the essential first step toward finding solutions to the area's problems. And the key
to restoring racial peace was to bring together leaders from the various constituencies that had a stake in the neighborhood's future. "Leaders and
organizations of all races and faiths," Maurice Fagan told a meeting of the
Fellowship Commission's Committee on Community Tension, "must come
up with effective long-term solutions to the conditions to these outbreaks."
In the weeks following the riot, therefore, civil rights liberals focused their
efforts on forging an alliance between North Philadelphia's black leadership and the area's primarily Jewish storeowners. By September 3, the Citizens Emergency Committee of North Philadelphia, a group of black
neighborhood leaders that emerged from the meeting called by the CHR
following the first night of rioting, had invited white business owners,
including Walter Zwickel, president of the Susquehanna Avenue Businessmen's Association, to join the group. "Businessmen play an important part
in our community," said the group's chair, Rev. Joshua Licorish, pastor of
the Zoar Methodist Church and an active member of the 400 Ministers.
"We want them . . . to share in our organization and make our community
what we believe it ought to be." Black leaders of the citizens' committee
like Licorish and longtime Fellowship Commission board member Rev.
William Gray rejected the view that the area's white merchants were
engaged in a racist conspiracy against their black customers. According to
Gray, retail fraud was no more common in North Philadelphia than elsewhere in the city. "Bait advertising and high-pressure techniques," he told
Lenora Berson, "are used on everybody. Negroes are [just] more likely to
succumb."[88]

For the citizens' committee, the challenge was to find solutions to the
problems of North Philadelphia that met the concerns of both the neigh-

borhood's black residents and its white business and property owners. At the first meeting of the citizens' committee, Jules Cohen, Maurice Fagan's successor as executive director of the Jewish Community Relations Council (JCRC) of Philadelphia declared: "Some Negroes complain that businessmen gouge and rob them. And on the other hand, some businessmen complain that some people buy $1 worth of goods and steal $3. Some people complain that landlords don't provide the necessities for tenants. Some landlords complain that when they put in a new sink it's torn out. We need a joint approach to problems . . . so we can build a good neighborhood."[89]

In the tense post-riot political environment, however, the Fellowship Commission model of bringing together a cross section of political and civic leadership to mediate intergroup tensions would prove outmoded. By choosing to work with the white storeowners rather than with militant activists who could be said to be more closely attuned to the rioters' anger, the black leaders of the citizens' committee were clearly revealing the depth of their commitment to the colorblind ideal. Thus, it is not surprising that the citizens' committee had little success reaching out to black militants who believed that the merchants' use of fraudulent practices was a prime cause of the riot. Cecil Moore publicly excoriated the black ministers who were leading the committee. "Not one of those bastards," he complained, "even asked me to attend" the citizens' committee's first meeting. Moore described the committee's leaders as part of the "cocktail-party, tea-sipping, fashion-show attending group [that] . . . divide the Negro, separate him into classes." The committee's "professional part-time Negroes" were more interested in currying favor with white liberals than in addressing the real needs of black people. "Those bastards don't want to help the Negro," he concluded. "They just want to perform."[90]

Storeowners, the Police, and the "White Backlash"

The failure of civil rights liberals to engage black militants in their post-riot organizing process was just one of many signs that the Fellowship Commission model of intergroup relations, with its emphasis on top-down alliance building, was inadequate to the challenge of resolving the city's racial tensions. Within two other constituencies that liberals saw as central to their strategy, North Philadelphia's Jewish business owners and the Philadelphia police department, there was evidence of a growing backlash against civil rights liberalism. While the liberal coalition trumpeted its working relationships with the police department's top leadership and leading Jewish businessmen, among rank and file police officers and storeowners, the riot sparked very public anger at the racial policies of the city's ruling Democratic coalition and its civil rights allies.

It was this anger that provided an emerging generation of white ethnic political leaders the opportunity to use the riot as a metaphor for their coded appeals to white voters anxious about the trajectory of racial and ethnic change in the city. White racial conservatives charged that the real cause of the riots was the misguided efforts of liberals to restrain aggressive police action against criminal activity in black neighborhoods. The refusal of the police department's top command to use all the means at their disposal to clear the streets of North Philadelphia, conservatives argued, had turned the white storeowners whose businesses were looted and the rank-and-file police officers who were injured into the true victims of the riot. This criticism of the city's response to the riot reflected an emerging form of conservative political discourse, a discourse that linked black militancy and street crime as fundamental threats to law and order in the city and that depicted liberal efforts to respond to black concerns as inevitably leading to the violation of white civil and property rights.

Given that the majority of businesses affected by the riot were Jewish-owned, it is not surprising that many in the city's Jewish communities viewed the riot as an anti-Semitic pogrom. Soon after the riot, the JCRC's Jules Cohen distributed a memorandum to Jewish leaders in the city that clearly reflected his concern that a racial backlash was emerging in the city's Jewish communities. "The Jewish Community," Cohen wrote hopefully, "will not blame the entire Negro group for the acts of some hoodlums. . . . We must not give aid and comfort to extremist elements who would like nothing better than to foster a 'white backlash.'" In a similar vein, the local chapter of the Anti-Defamation League pointed out that "a maximum of a thousand persons were involved [in the riot] . . . out of the Negro population of more than a quarter of a million in North Philadelphia." The regional office of the American Jewish Committee was sufficiently concerned by the widespread perception that the riot was in fact a pogrom that it commissioned Lenora Berson to study the riot. While Berson's report acknowledged that the disproportionate presence of Jewish merchants, landlords, lawyers, and doctors in North Philadelphia had led to what she called "a particularly irrational Negro anti-Semitism," she concluded that the predominate feeling in the riot—as measured by the kinds of epithets yelled—was antiwhite rather than anti-Semitic.[91]

Conservative critics of the liberal approach to race relations had their largest impact within Jewish and other white communities on the question of the police response to the riot. One North Philadelphia merchant complained that the police should have protected "honest businessmen, not thieves"; another called on "the police to shoot [the looters] with machine guns." At a City Hall meeting to discuss reimbursement of storeowners for property damage, a third merchant demanded to know "why weren't [National Guard] troops used to save our businesses." Both city officials and Jewish civil rights activists sought to defend the city's approach to riot control from criticism that not enough had been done to protect the property of Jewish business owners. The mayor responded to these complaints by establishing a special committee to develop an aid program for riot-affected businesses. Meanwhile, the Anti-Defamation League suggested that Philadelphia could "be said to be much more fortunate" than the other riot-torn cities that summer. "In those communities where the police did use pistol fire, tear gas and other means of force, the riots lasted longer than in Philadelphia."[92]

Equally strong criticism of Police Commissioner Leary's riot control strategy came from within the police department. Rank-and-file officers were frustrated that the commissioner had insisted that they not use their weapons unless they were directly threatened and had refused to allow them to disperse the crowds that had gathered during the riot. Leary's most important internal critic was Deputy Police Commissioner Frank Rizzo, head of the department's uniformed division. Although he remained publicly quiet at the time, Rizzo was well positioned to encourage rank-and-file discontent within the department. In a story recounted by his biographer, S.A. Paolantonio, Rizzo unsuccessfully demanded that Leary allow him to deploy his officers to stop the looting during a confrontation on a North Philadelphia street corner early on the second day of the riot. And throughout the three days of rioting, he made sure that he was the most visible member of the department's top command on the streets. "It seemed like there was no chain of command," one officer remembered. "It was just Rizzo and the cops."[93]

Mayor Tate had appointed Rizzo, a twenty-year veteran of the police force, deputy commissioner shortly before the 1963 election in an effort to counter his Republican opponent's law-and-order campaign. As a beat cop during the 1940s, Rizzo earned his law-and-order reputation and the nickname "Cisco Kid," the name of a popular television cowboy, for his crack down on the numbers rackets and prostitution. He began his rapid rise through the department when he was promoted to sergeant in 1951 and to acting captain in 1952. For the next decade, Captain Rizzo would lead the fight against vice and gambling as the commander of police districts first in West Philadelphia, where his harassment of black-owned bars and private clubs led to charges of racism, and then in Center City. Rizzo's reputation for racism in the black community grew throughout the 1950s and early 1960s. In fact, Cecil Moore had denounced Rizzo's appointment as deputy commissioner, charging that he was known for making racist remarks and had used "storm-trooper tactics" against black-owned businesses in the city.[94]

"I Am the Goddamn Boss"

Cecil Moore initially responded to the 1964 riot in ways that might have been expected for any NAACP branch president. Over the course of the riot weekend, he traveled the streets of North Philadelphia urging crowd members to return to their homes. Many credited the NAACP president with preventing even more serious violence. "The swaggering former Marine," the *New York Times* wrote, "moved tirelessly through the area coaxing the people into cooperation with the police." To Sam Evans, a black concert promoter who had coordinated the local organizing for the 1963 March on Washington for the NAACP, Moore was the sole reason that the rioting had not been more extensive. "The Negro citizens of Philadelphia," Evans told the *Times*, "have had an opportunity to express themselves in the last year . . . that they never had before. Nobody has any yardstick for measuring what could have happened here this weekend if it hadn't been for Cecil Moore."[95]

For Moore to maintain his position as the most popular black movement figure in Philadelphia, he had to prove that he could move North Philadelphia's black residents from looting to more disciplined forms of protest. Soon after the riot, Moore set out to consolidate his position as sole spokesperson for working-class black Philadelphians. In an interview published in the September 11, 1964, issue of *Time* magazine, Moore returned to his rhetorical war on civil rights liberals. The riots, he insisted, proved that middle-class leaders "don't speak for the Negro. I do." He was, Moore declared, "the goddamn boss" of black Philadelphia. His use of the metaphor of the political boss was clearly meant to distinguish his leadership style from both the black community's traditional middle-class leadership and the reform politics of the city's liberal coalition. To compare his style of movement leadership to machine politicians was to identify with working-class forms of political action. In contrast to reform liberals' commitment to government rationalization and efficiency, political machines serviced the specific and parochial needs of individual communities. By declaring himself boss of black Philadelphia, Moore was thus pledging to deliver tangible improvements in the lives of the residents of the city's black ghettos, in contrast to the abstract civil rights laws that had been the primary accomplishment of the liberal civil rights coalition.[96]

To contrast his leadership with his liberal adversaries, Moore drew on the black nationalist critique of black middle-class elitism. Unlike the " 'professional Negro' who doesn't come into contact with the masses," Moore declared that he stood for a racially unified "one-class Negro community." Moore rooted his claim to racial authenticity and identity with the majority of the city's blacks in his decision to keep his family in North Philadelphia. "I'd be lost if I had to move up to [middle-class and integrated] Mount Airy . . . where I'd have to be so damned respectable that I couldn't . . . stand on a street corner on Saturday night. The Negro is always on the corner on Friday or Saturday night. That's where you go to talk." It was not enough for a movement leader to represent the black poor, he or she must live in and identify with the culture of the black working-class neighborhood.[97]

The machine analogy also served to accentuate Moore's independence from the white-controlled Democratic Party. Since he was first elected president of the Philadelphia NAACP, he had repeatedly reminded his liberal black critics that he was the only black elected official in the city not dependent on the endorsement of white party bosses. When *Time* asked for Moore's comments on the charge that he had declared himself "the self-appointed savior of the Negro in Philadelphia," he replied: "I'm not self-appointed. I was elected." As a leader who was not beholden to either the institutions or the ideas that defined civil rights liberalism in Philadelphia, Moore declared himself free to represent the concerns and interests of the city's black poor and working classes.[98]

In the days after the riot, Moore linked his rhetorical attacks on liberalism with the black community's concerns about police brutality. Thus, the NAACP president denounced Mayor Tate's decision to increase the police presence in the riot area. Declaring that he had collected 258 legitimate claims of police brutality since the riot, he called the police "an inhuman bunch of sadists bent on revenge" and threatened to organize a boycott of North Philadelphia merchants if the mayor did not remove the extra police details from the area.[99]

The first important test of Cecil Moore's ability to reestablish himself as the leader of working-class black Philadelphians came in the 1964 NAACP branch elections. In November of that year, Rev. Henry Nichols of the 400 Ministers announced that he would run against Moore for the branch presidency, a direct challenge to Moore's claim to being the most popular civil rights leader among Philadelphia's black masses. Could the black churches serve as a base for creating an effective mass-based opposition to Cecil Moore's antiliberal and nationalist-influenced protest discourse? The emergence of a black ministerial challenge to Moore's leadership of the Philadelphia NAACP can be traced directly to his comments in the *Time* interview. Soon after the interview, the Baptist Ministers Conference of Philadelphia demanded a meeting with Moore to discuss his attacks on the clergy. When Moore refused to meet with them, the ministers announced that they had decided to submit all NAACP membership dues raised in their congregations directly to the organization's national office. The ministers' threat was clearly intended to suggest the potential for a convergence between the Philadelphia NAACP's traditional middle-class base and the churches' rank-and-file membership. Henry Nichols's decision to challenge Moore in the 1964 branch elections carried with it the potential to build an effective anti-Moore alliance between middle-class liberals and rank-and-file churchgoers. Nichols, the pastor of Janes Memorial Church in middle-class Germantown, declared his candidacy in the name of the

more than one thousand local NAACP members he claimed were now paying their membership dues directly to the national organization to protest
Moore's attacks on interracialism and the city's black clergy.[100]

Moore's campaign against Nichols exemplified his ability to combine
support for the NAACP's integrationist goals with racially solidaristic
appeals to black Philadelphia's poor and working classes. Nichols's candidacy provided Moore with another opportunity to demonstrate that he,
and not his black liberal opponents, enjoyed the popular support of the
city's black masses. Throughout the fall of 1964, Moore publicly criticized
what he viewed as a liberal conspiracy to dislodge him from the NAACP
presidency. He told the *Bulletin* that "the big Negro power structure—
comprised of divisive 'Uncle Tom' hatchet boys—are attempting to . . .
unseat me as president of the Philadelphia branch." And to the *New York
Times,* he repeated some of his favorite phrases, "I'm the God-damned
boss. I run a grassroots group, not a cocktail party, tea-sipping, fashion
show-attending group of exhibitionists."[101]

The NAACP branch election, originally scheduled for December 1964,
had to be postponed when Moore ruled that Nichols was ineligible to run
for the branch presidency because Nichols had joined the protesters who
had sent their membership dues directly to the national office. Nichols
immediately appealed Moore's ruling to the national office which agreed
to hold a hearing on the matter. On January 4, 1965, the national NAACP
board ruled that Nichols was a member in good standing with the Philadelphia NAACP and was therefore eligible to run for the branch presidency.
The election was then scheduled for February 6, 1965, from 2 to 9 P.M. at
the National Guard armory at Thirty-Second and Lancaster in West Philadelphia. Nichols targeted his campaign at those who were put off by
Moore's confrontational style and his attacks on civil rights liberalism. The
NAACP president, he charged, had set class against class and race against
race in Philadelphia. At a four-hundred-person rally, Nichols blamed
Moore for dividing the black community into factions and for "creating
bitter feelings" that made it more difficult to create a multiracial society. If
elected, he promised to establish a coordinating council of all civil rights
groups in the city in an effort to promote more cooperative relationships
within the movement. Nichols conceded the charge of Moore's supporters
that he was close to many in the city's white power structure, but insisted
that it was better to work with whites than to have the races fight with each
other. At the same time, he rejected the notion that his commitment to
racial liberalism would lead him to be less aggressive in pursuit of the black
community's interests. Nichols called himself a "militant moderate
leader."[102]

Moore continued his attacks on civil rights liberalism and the black community's middle-class leadership, even as he sought to repair some of the

damage caused by the criticisms that he made of black clergy in the *Time* interview. His comments, he insisted, were meant for only specific ministers; he was not critical of the clergy as a whole. As the incumbent, Moore was eager to demonstrate that he had specific plans for fighting racial discrimination in the city. Moore's platform combined calls for cross-class racial solidarity with promises to initiate protest campaigns against local institutions that continued to deny blacks equal opportunity in employment and education. Specifically, he promised to maintain pressure on the Board of Education to desegregate the city's schools and on City Hall to appoint black officials to policymaking positions, to initiate protest campaigns against racially discriminatory landlords and real estate brokers, to advocate for apprenticeship and on-the-job training programs for unemployed youth, and to lobby for lower tuition rates at area colleges and trade schools.[103]

The centerpiece of Moore's campaign platform was a proposal to lead a combined legal and protest campaign to desegregate Girard College, an all-white boarding school for fatherless boys that was located in the heart of North Philadelphia. Separated by ten-foot-high walls from the black working-class neighborhoods that surrounded it, Girard had become by 1965 an anachronistic symbol of the black community's exclusion from the city's opportunity structure. Established by the City of Philadelphia in the mid-nineteenth century with income from the will of a local banker named Stephen F. Girard, the school had been a target of local civil rights activism since the 1954 *Brown v. Board of Education* decision outlawing segregation in public schools. Unable to convince the quasi-public Board of City Trust to desegregate Girard—the board insisted it lacked the authority to violate the provisions of the banker's will—then-city councilman Raymond Pace Alexander filed suit to desegregate Girard. In 1958, the U.S. Supreme Court ruled that the city could not continue to run a segregated school even if it was maintained entirely with funds from the estate of a private citizen. The court's decision, however, did allow that the school could remain all white if it were privately administered. In response, the Board of City Trust turned control over the school to a private board of trustees made up primarily of school alumni.[104]

The decision to focus his reelection campaign on the unfinished drive to integrate Girard thus further emphasized Moore's long-standing argument that his "machine-style" mass-oriented approach to leadership, not the rarefied liberalism of the black community's middle-class elites and their white allies, was the most effective means for achieving the meaningful desegregation of the city. In this sense Moore's target was as much the Alexanders as it was Girard's all-white board of trustees. Having demonstrated that his militant leadership, not the investigative fact-finding of Sadie Alexander's Commission on Human Relations, was the key to opening up jobs for the city's black workers, Moore now promised to show that he could accomplish what Raymond Pace Alexander's social prestige and legal gradualism could not, the desegregation of an educational institution founded by one of white Philadelphia's founding fathers. It was no accident that Moore—the self-declared leader of the city's post-World War II migrants—had purchased the Alexander's North Philadelphia home when the most prominent of black Philadelphia's old families left for liberal, middle-class, and integrated West Mount Airy. For Moore, his opponent in the 1965 NAACP election was not Nichols, it was the entire traditional leadership of black Philadelphia.

The February 6 election took on more of the appearance of a political election than an intraorganizational leadership contest. Each side had a campaign manager and focused a major proportion of its resources on getting its supporters to the polling site. For Moore, turning out unprecedented numbers of NAACP members to the branch election site was as important as defeating Nichols. Never before had more than 5 percent of the branch members voted in a branch election. A record turnout would demonstrate that Moore's "machine" model of leadership had succeeded in transforming the Philadelphia branch into a mass organization. Despite the advantages of incumbency, it was not at all given that Moore would win the turnout battle. Almost as many branch members lived in Germantown (2,100), Nichols's middle-class base, as lived in North Philadelphia (2,900). Located in West Philadelphia—itself a mix of middle- and working-class black neighborhoods—the polling site was moreover a significant distance from Moore's North Philadelphia base. Would his poor and working-class supporters make their way across the town to vote? Certainly, it would be easier for Nichols's middle-class supporters to find the time and transportation necessary to get to the polling site.[105]

In fact, the branch's middle-class base did turn out in unprecedented numbers. Nichols received 474 votes, more than any candidate had received in the three previous presidential elections. But the makeup of the Philadelphia NAACP had changed radically during the two years of Moore's presidency. The branch president's efforts to transform the branch into a protest organization and to strengthen its base in working-class neighborhoods had significantly increased the size of the branch's activist core. Moreover, Moore's campaign placed special emphasis on getting his supporters to the West Philadelphia polling site. It arranged for a bus to transport voters to the armory from specific street corners in North Philadelphia. In addition, fifty cars supplied by Teamsters Local 107 transported Moore supporters to the polls on election day. Moore's election day transportation system produced a turnout of historic proportions. So many branch members turned out that they were forced to line up outside and around the corner of the armory. All told, 2,215 branch members voted for Moore, giving him 82 percent of the vote. The total vote of 2,689 was the largest turnout for any branch election in Gloster Current's eighteen years as NAACP national field secretary.[106]

For Cecil Moore, the five-to-one victory over Nichols was a vindication "against the opposition of 'crybaby' conservatives," and a mandate for "two more years of intensive militancy." In his 1965 inaugural address, Moore declared that the branch's "motto in the next two years is going to change from 'We Shall Overcome' to 'We Shall Overrun'—the forces of bigotry."[107] Moore's unprecedented mandate, and in particular his demonstrated support among the city's black poor and working-classes, left him in a position to mount what could have been a major campaign against the social causes of black poverty and ghettoization in the city. President Johnson had just declared his "War on Poverty." Just four days after Moore's reelection, criticisms from both the Office of Economic Opportunity, the federal agency established to administer War on Poverty funds, and local advocacy groups forced Mayor Tate to announce that he was reorganizing the local antipoverty agency to allow for more input from community groups and social welfare organizations. Of the community leaders appointed by Tate to the fifteen slots reserved for civil rights and social welfare organizations on the new antipoverty board, Cecil Moore was the most prominent.[108]

Moore, however, would not make the War on Poverty or any of the other pressing issues facing the city's ghetto residents the central focus of the Philadelphia NAACP's activity in 1965. Instead, the NAACP president made the desegregation of Girard College the group's top priority for the year. Targeting a boarding school for fatherless boys would certainly seem an odd choice for a movement leader eager to demonstrate that his focus was on the interests and needs of the ghetto. Even a fully desegregated Girard would serve only a tiny portion of black schoolchildren in the city. Moore's primary concern, however, seems to have been to prevent a recurrence of the 1964 riot. Determined to provide a disciplined outlet for the legitimate anger felt by ghetto youth during the summer of 1965, Moore believed that Girard's location in the heart of North Philadelphia and the school's walled campus made it an important symbol of racial exclusion for young people growing up in the surrounding neighborhoods. For Moore, the goal of desegregating Girard College was thus less important than finding a protest target that would attract the black youth of North Philadelphia, and in particular the teenage members of the area's street-corner gangs, to join the NAACP picket line in front of the ten-foot walls. While Johnson's War on Poverty emphasized job training and educational enrichment programs, Moore believed that only a protest campaign could provide working-class young people with a constructive means for expressing their anger at a racist society, something that social service agencies would never be able to do.

Thus, it was young men, many of them members of the area's largest gangs, who maintained the daily picket line in front of the Girard College walls from May 1 to December 18, 1965. Georgie Woods played a crucial role in the recruitment of gang members to the picket line on the radio, in the concert hall, and on the picket line. Moore's ability to recruit members of North Philadelphia's street-corner gangs was rooted in his adoption of the discourse of self-defense popularized in the early 1960s by figures like Malcolm X and Robert F. Williams. The language of self-defense enabled Moore to cultivate a public persona as the one movement leader in the city willing to place the concerns of young ghetto residents above the sensibilities of black middle-class and white liberal leaders. After non-violent marchers were viciously beaten by state troopers in Selma, Alabama, in March 1965, Moore rejected a call from Martin Luther King for civil rights supporters to travel to Alabama to continue the march from Selma to the state capitol in Montgomery. At an NAACP-organized "mourners-march" in Philadelphia, Moore told the crowd of seven thousand that "I am not going to Alabama until I can take a rifle with me . . . It is the official policy of the NAACP not to be aggressively violent, but we have never given up our right to defend ourselves."[109]

The Masculinist Discourse of Self-Defense

Central to the success of Moore's self-defense discourse was his call for men to fulfill their leadership responsibilities within the black community. Moore's masculinist appeal for self-defense against racist violence came at a time of heightened public anxiety about the status of black masculinity. In the spring of 1965, for example, Daniel Patrick Moynihan's policy memorandum entitled "The Negro Family: The Case for National Action" emerged as a central rationale for President Johnson's War on Poverty. "Ours is a society which presumes male leadership in public and private," Moynihan wrote. "A subculture, such as that of the Negro American, in which this is not the pattern is placed at a distinct disadvantage."[110]

Nor were liberal policymakers the only ones concerned about the supposed emasculation of the black community. Racially biased labor markets and both legal and extralegal forms of racist violence had long heightened black male anxiety about fulfilling their responsibilities as breadwinners and family protectors. As E. Frances White has pointed out, black nationalists have often valorized patriarchal family forms in response to the ways that both state- and market-based racial discrimination have denied normative and respectable domestic roles to black men and women.[111]

Such gender anxieties were only further heightened by the ever increasing levels of racial violence directed at the civil rights movement. When the primarily male national civil rights leadership responded to events like the Birmingham church bombing that killed four little girls and the murder of three civil rights workers in Mississippi with continued advocacy of nonviolence, their credibility as leaders of the race was only further compromised—just as Robert F. Williams had predicted half a decade earlier. When the staff of the Commission on Human Relations set out to survey community attitudes in North Philadelphia in the aftermath of the 1964 riot, what they found were young people drawn to Malcolm X's call for self-defense by their anger with Martin Luther King and other advocates for nonviolence for their failure to respond to racist attacks on movement activists. In the view of the CHR staff, the rioters were seeking a way to participate in the civil rights movement without having to conform to the ethos of nonviolence. "Those that couldn't march, rioted," the staff told Lenora Berson.[112]

It was no coincidence that it was a rumor that the police had killed a pregnant woman that triggered the 1964 riot. During the first night of looting, one young woman was reported to have yelled "there are enough of you to kill all those . . . cops. Are you mice or men?" Within this context, Cecil Moore's critique of nonviolence defined street protests as the purview of "real" black men. From the beginning of what Moore called Operation Girard, the daily protests were as much about the articulation of resistance to police brutality as about school desegregation. The picket line became a free space in which the young demonstrators could violate, with a much greater chance of impunity, the etiquette of deference required in their usual confrontations with the police on the streets of North Philadelphia. Through chants and catcalls directed at the police, the protesters announced their readiness to physically resist police violence. To the tune of "We Shall Overcome," the protesters sang "We Shall Overrun." One favorite chant promised violent revenge on the police: "Jingle bells / Shotgun shells / Freedom all the way / Oh, what fun it is / To blow a bluecoat man away." Another, which began "Cecil's got a shotgun," enabled the teenage protesters to symbolically resolve their anxiety that racism would prevent them from claiming the prerogatives of masculinity. Much as Frantz Fanon argued that anticolonial violence would free the colonized from their internalized racial inferiority, the violent talk on the picket line exposed the violence of police practices in the black ghetto while perhaps psychologically liberating the demonstrators from the pressure of constant police harassment.[113]

Eight hundred police officers, including helmeted motorcycle cops greeted the twenty NAACP pickets who arrived at the Girard College wall to begin the protest campaign on May 1, 1965. The protesters' confrontations with the police quickly escalated from the verbal to the physical. On the fourth day of demonstrations, the police arrested eight protesters, all men between the ages of eighteen and thirty, and seized three ladders that the police charged had been used in an attempt to scale the campus walls. Eleven more demonstrators were arrested the next day, six at the wall and five others after they were chased through the surrounding neighborhood by motorcycle cops. With each confrontation with the police, Operation Girard was transformed from an issue of the integration of a single educational institution into an opportunity for young people to express their anger at police violence. Just after 11 P.M. on June 22, the police arrested nineteen young protesters after nearly one hundred demonstrators decided to move the protest from the wall into Girard Avenue. For fifteen minutes, the demonstrators succeeded in blocking traffic for several blocks. As the police attempted to clear the street, the crowd at the wall grew to more than one thousand. In what one reporter described as a "wild scuffle," roving groups of protesters clashed with police, throwing bricks and bottles.

Moore blamed the violence on the police's "apparent unequal enforcement of the law," a reference to the police department's failure to arrest striking local members of the Teamsters Union who had blockaded the street in front of a local truck depot in an effort to keep trucks from entering. Tensions with the police reached their peak on July 11 when Deputy Police Commissioner Frank Rizzo punched a demonstrator whom he said called his officers "dirty dogs." In the ensuing melee, Rizzo was punched and a second police officer was kicked in the groin before a group of police officers used their billy clubs to beat one of the male protesters into unconsciousness. All told, three picketers and two police officers were injured in the clash.[114]

Young men were not the only protesters to respond to the NAACP's call to demonstrate at the Girard wall. Cecil Moore made sure to publicize the fact that a vast majority of the Girard picketers came from working-class backgrounds, though sizable numbers of middle-class activists of all races did join the Girard picket line, usually on weekends and during the visits of prominent national civil rights leaders including CORE's James Farmer. Moore told the *New York Times* that the class make-up of the protesters was proof that preachers and other middle-class activists within the civil rights movement had grown lax. Among the heroes of the Girard picket line were two women with homes near the school. A member of the branch executive committee, Birdie Palmer took responsibility for making sure that there were picketers at the wall every night during the seven months of demonstrations. And on the last day of protest, the stalwarts of the picket line gave Mrs. Miles a standing ovation for "opening her house to people she had never seen before, for giving food, help and word of counsel and advice."[115]

Operation Girard was neither the most ideologically—or strategically—developed example of self-defense politics in the black movements of the 1960s. For this reason, however, it provides a window into understanding why the language of violence proved so compelling to the movement's militant wing despite its limited utility in the face of police firepower. While provocative chants and momentary skirmishes with the police had limited direct impact on everyday police practices in North Philadelphia, they had enormous performative value. Robin Kelley has described how public city buses provided a free space for working-class blacks to assert equal rights in Birmingham during World War II. In a similar way, the Girard picket line served as a public canvas for working-class youth to collectively assert their claims to equal rights within the criminal justice system.[116] Moreover, to talk violence on the picket line was to reclaim the prerogatives due men in a male-dominated society. Central to the crisis of black masculinity was (and is) the way that police practices constantly challenged and circumscribed black male access to the street and other public spaces. By talking violence, the Girard protesters were simultaneously claiming their constitutional rights as American citizens and the privileges of manhood.

The intersection of Americanness and masculinity must be at the center of any explanation of the militant fixation with violence talk in the late 1960s and early 1970s. The tendency of advocates of armed struggle, whether they were civil rights reformers like Robert F. Williams and Cecil Moore or explicit revolutionaries, to emphasize the public performance of self-defense rituals over the hard work of creating underground paramilitary organizations closely resembles the role of violence talk on the Girard picket line. In *The Crisis of the Negro Intellectual*, Harold Cruse called on black nationalists to abandon their search for solutions to the racial crisis in third world revolutionary ideologies and to "come to terms with themselves as American products, created out of American conditions and ingredients, requiring, in the final analysis, an American solution."[117] And yet, Cecil Moore and the Girard picketers were doing exactly what Cruse called for: staking their claim to the prerogatives and responsibilities of "manhood" in an American vernacular.

Fending Off the Next Liberal Challenge

In the midst of Operation Girard, Moore was faced with a renewed liberal challenge to his movement leadership. In July, a group of local supporters of Martin Luther King and nonviolent protest strategy sought to bring the SCLC leader to the Girard wall as part of their effort to convince King to make Philadelphia his next protest target. Following President Johnson's signing of the Voting Rights Act in March 1965, King had announced that SCLC would mount its next major protest campaign in a northern city. And that summer, he embarked on a tour of six northern cities—Chicago, Cleveland, New York, Newark, Philadelphia, and Washington D.C.—as part of his effort to decide where to begin his northern protest campaign. Even though the local host committee for the King tour had been careful not to publicly criticize Moore's leadership of the Philadelphia NAACP, Moore was quick to declare that the country's most famous civil rights leader was neither needed nor welcome in the city. The NAACP president characteristically charged that his liberal opponents were attempting to use King's visit and the SCLC leader's mass appeal to undercut his dominant position within the local movement. While Moore was not able to prevent King from visiting either the city or the Girard wall, the SCLC leader would eventually decide to make Chicago the target of his first northern protest campaign. In this sense, the Girard campaign had served Moore's purpose of enabling him to maintain his predominant position within the Philadelphia movement.[118]

The first meeting of the Philadelphia Committee for Dr. King's Tour was convened by Fellowship House's Marjorie Penney, who had known the SCLC president since his days as a seminary student in nearby Chester, Pennsylvania. Penney and her allies were careful to insure that the local host committee was composed of representatives of a wide range of civil rights and community activists. The inclusion of a number of neighborhood activists on the committee demonstrates how radically the locus of civil rights leadership in Philadelphia had shifted during the first half of the 1960s. The civil rights activists who hoped to bring King and SCLC to Philadelphia recognized that they could not hope to challenge Moore's preeminence in black working-class communities unless they included well-known leaders of those communities.[119]

The decision to appoint William Meek, a black social worker at the Wharton Centre, a North Philadelphia settlement house, as the chair of the host committee reflected the organizer's desire not to challenge Moore's leadership directly. Meek had strong ties to the city's pacifist and liberal civil rights groups but also considered himself a supporter of both the local NAACP and Operation Girard. He agreed to chair the committee because he believed that he could not pass up the opportunity "to have somebody like a Martin Luther King come here, select this city as being where he'd be turning on the heat, and making things happen, beyond what Cecil and the NAACP were ready to do." Meek believed that "there was a lot of things that [the two leaders] could have worked [on] together." A number of other activists with strong ties to Moore also actively supported the host committee, including Georgie Woods, who had traveled to Alabama for the Selma to Montgomery March, Goldie Watson, and Matthew Adams, the longtime head of the NAACP's labor committee. In retrospect, however, Meek believed that there were others on the host committee who viewed King's visit as their last, best chance to counteract Moore's popularity in the city's black ghettos and to insure "that Cecil and the Girard College folks were kept under control."[120]

The host committee hoped to make a visit to the Girard wall the centerpiece of King's visit to the city. Eager to prevent a public clash between King and Moore, the committee convinced Georgie Woods to ask Moore to personally invite King to join the Girard protesters. Moore immediately rejected Woods's entreaty. "He's a black man," he replied, "Why does he need an invitation?" Instead of issuing an invitation, Moore announced that he was asking King to stay out of the Girard College campaign, charging that it "appears as if the white power structure is using [King] to divide Philadelphia Negroes." He called King "a divisive force" interested only in "headlines and money." Moore also used the opportunity to reaffirm his critique of nonviolent protest. "The imported Gandhi philosophy of nonviolence," he declared, "will not be accepted in Philadelphia where we believe in self-help and self-defense."[121]

Moore's opposition threatened King's entire visit to the city. Two days before the visit was due to begin, King informed the host committee that he would not come unless Moore retracted his public opposition to his visit. He didn't want, King told the committee, "to create dissension in the city." As the committee met in emergency session at Fellowship House, Moore agreed to meet with Rev. Walter Fauntroy, the coordinator of King's northern tour, and Meek in the offices of Samuel Evans, the black concert promoter and Democratic Party activist. Finally, in the early morning hours of August 2, Evans announced to the press that he had brokered an agreement between King and Moore that would allow the visit to take place. According to Meek, it was a group of young protesters from the Girard picket line who finally convinced Moore that he had to invite "Doc" King to the wall.[122]

Martin Luther King began his two-day visit to Philadelphia on Monday, August 2, with a breakfast meeting attended by nine hundred people at the Fellowship House on Girard Avenue, just blocks from the wall. While Moore failed to appear at the breakfast meeting, he joined King the next day at a 10,000-person rally in West Philadelphia. King urged the crowd to support the formation of a new coalition of civil rights groups in Philadelphia. In his speech, Moore retracted his earlier criticisms of King and promised to cooperate closely with the SCLC leader in the future. Both men then traveled to the Girard College wall where each spoke to a large crowd.[123]

Despite their public rapprochement, King and Moore remained at odds over the SCLC leader's interest in playing an active role in the Philadelphia movement. Within days of King's departure, Moore was denying any interest in participating in "any coordinating council or summit conference." He insisted that "the NAACP was a big enough umbrella for everyone interested in solving the city's racial problems." King meanwhile continued to call for the formation of a coordinating council of civil rights groups in Philadelphia. "The problems in the North are so complex," he told a Philadelphia journalist, "that nothing short of a coalition of forces working toward the resolution of civil rights for all people can make a dent in Philadelphia." If such a coalition were established, King argued, Moore would have little choice but to align the NAACP. The host committee renamed itself as the Coalition for Equality in hopes of establishing such a coalition.

However, it never succeeded in propelling itself to the forefront of civil rights efforts in the city, in large part because it could never win the cooperation of Moore nor overcome his popularity among working-class black Philadelphians. And it lacked the breadth of support necessary to convince King to make a commitment to working in Philadelphia. Although he was forced to accede to King's visit to the Girard College wall, Moore had succeeded in preventing SCLC's entrance into the city.[124]

When Mayor Tate asked Sadie Alexander, as chair of the Commission on Human Relations, to seek a solution to the Girard crisis, Moore charged that the CHR was more interested in stopping the demonstrations than integrating the school. Alexander did seek to arrange a meeting with the Girard trustees in hopes of convincing the board to "voluntarily integrate" the school. In a letter to the trustees, she wrote of her concerns "that interracial misunderstanding and hostility are being intensified" by the Girard crisis. The trustees, however, refused to meet with her. Instead, they issued a statement which read in part that "under our free enterprise system, it is any man's prerogative to give his money . . . for the benefit of Negroes exclusively . . . it must follow that poor white male orphans may also be the exclusive beneficiaries of a man's bounty."[125]

Alexander's inability to engage the trustees in negotiations proved to be a major turning point in the Girard crisis. In late June, she called on the city administration to sue for the integration of the college. In response, Mayor Tate sought to shift responsibility for the crisis to the state government. On July 8, city solicitor Edward G. Bauer, Jr. called on the Republican governor, William Scranton, to lead a joint city-state legal initiative to desegregate Girard, arguing that previous court decisions made it virtually impossible for the city to sue successfully on its own. Heavy lobbying from the Fellowship Commission and prominent liberals like Richardson Dilworth finally convinced Scranton to invite Mayor Tate, the Girard trustees, and representatives of the U.S. Department of Justice's Community Relations Service to meet to discuss possible solutions to the Girard crisis. The parties met on July 11 at the State Office Building at Broad and Spring Garden Streets on the southern edge of North Philadelphia. While the trustees rejected a request from Governor Scranton and Mayor Tate that they voluntarily admit black students, they agreed in principle to join the state and city government in a renewed court test of the requirement in Stephen Girard's will that the school be restricted to whites.[126]

The Philadelphia NAACP continued its daily pickets at the Girard wall for five more months while state officials continued to debate how best to force the trustees to desegregate the school. By September, it was clear that the school's trustees had little intention of following through on their pledge to join the state in a renewed court test of Stephen Girard's will. Finally, on September 22, Governor Scranton announced that he had appointed two prominent Philadelphia lawyers, William Biddle and William T. Coleman, as special state attorneys to file suit to force the trustees to break the will and allow for the admission of black boys to the school. When Coleman and Biddle finally filed suit in federal court on December, 16, 1965, Cecil Moore declared a nine-month moratorium on picketing at the wall. The pickets would be back, he promised, if the suit was not settled favorably by the next September. From then on, the demonstrators would make only periodic and symbolic reappearances at the Girard wall, even though it would take until May 19, 1968, for the U.S. Supreme Court to rule the segregationist provisions of the Girard will unenforceable, even by a private board.[127]

* * *

No activist in the Philadelphia movement better demonstrates the complex ways that black nationalist themes could be and were synthesized with the traditional goals of civil rights liberalism to create dramatic and compelling new forms of black protest than Cecil Moore. Moore utilized the language of black nationalism to accentuate class resentment against black middle-class leaders and their white liberal allies, even as he maintained an unshakeable commitment to the NAACP's goal of a desegregated society. By depicting intraracial class tensions as the inevitable result of middle-class betrayal of "real" black interests and cultural practices, Moore was able to encode in a nationalist discourse black working-class resentment of the black community's liberal leadership.

The construction protests of 1963, and the mayoral election that followed, signaled the fragmentation of the liberal coalition that had dominated political discourse in postwar Philadelphia. For two decades, it had appeared self-evident that legislative action, government regulation, and interracial coalition building were the keys to achieving racial progress in Philadelphia. The construction protests, however, had challenged the hegemony of civil rights liberalism by demonstrating that a protest strategy based on intraracial solidarity could achieve what interracial alliances and legislation had not—jobs for skilled black workers in the construction trades. In the years that followed, black activism in Philadelphia would be characterized by a range of strategic initiatives, from mass protest and collective self-defense to self-help programs and independent electoral politics, all rooted in the racial mobilization strategies that had proved so effective during the selective patronage and construction protest campaigns.

As effective as selective patronage, the 1963 construction protests, and Operation Girard were in revealing the failure of civil rights liberalism in Philadelphia, they also demonstrated the limitations of protest as a strategy for creating substantive economic opportunity for poor and working-class blacks. Without an independent political base, the NAACP lacked the means to insure that these short-term gains would have a significant impact on the structure of the construction industry over the long term. The ability of the construction unions to prevent all but the most cosmetic changes in the racial distribution of jobs in the municipal construction program demonstrated that politics, not protest, was the key to determining who benefited from the distribution of public dollars in Philadelphia.

The NAACP's protest campaigns signaled more than the weakening of black ties to the liberal coalition in Philadelphia. In the early postwar years, the political discourse of liberalism—with its emphasis on economic growth and opportunity through urban revitalization—had forged an electoral coalition that crossed racial, ethnic, religious, and class differences in Philadelphia. To poor blacks, white working-class Catholics, and Jewish and white Protestant professionals and businesspeople alike, the city's liberal Democratic coalition promised economic prosperity and a decline in social conflict. The events of 1963, however, made it clear that it would be virtually impossible for the Democrats to simultaneously protect the interests of their various constituencies. As Felicia Kornbluh and Thomas Sugrue have argued, the roots of the white backlash against liberalism can be found much earlier than the urban riots of the 1960s and President Johnson's declaration of a war on poverty.[128] One observer of Philadelphia politics found "smoldering resentment" of black gains in city employment and civil service exams to be the cause of declining white working-class support for local Democrats as early as 1959.[129] Rank-and-file anger within the building trades unions at the construction agreements and the unexpected success of Jim McDermott's law-and-order campaign for mayor signaled that Democratic politicians in Philadelphia could not meet black demands while continuing to rely on a base of support in white working-class communities.

Operation Girard confirmed the predominance of Cecil Moore and Frank Rizzo in the racial politics of Philadelphia. Both men had positioned themselves as working-class heroes, rejecting both the middle-class constituencies and the reform ethos that had dominated local politics through the late 1950s. The Girard campaign had demonstrated Moore's ability to mobilize black working-class anger around an agenda that synthesized traditional civil rights issues with neighborhood concerns like police brutality. It was in this context that Deputy Police Commissioner Rizzo became the focus of black anger about the persistence of racial inequities in the city. Rizzo simultaneously emerged as the key figure in the resurgence of a racialist politics in Philadelphia's white working-class neighborhoods that demonized black activism as the main threat to the local social order. Moore and Rizzo's emergence as the dominant figures in Philadelphia's racial politics simultaneously signaled and escalated the racial, ethnic, and class tensions that were eroding the electoral coalition that had kept the Philadelphia Democratic Party in power since 1951.

Chapter 5
Black Power and the Organizing Tradition

I was offended by the notion that the only way that blacks could
develop was by being around white folks.

—*John Churchville, founder, the Freedom Library*

At the same time that Cecil Moore and the Philadelphia NAACP were rein-
venting civil rights protest, a small group of community activists began
meeting in a North Philadelphia storefront called the Freedom Library to
discuss how to shift the focus of the movement to what they viewed as the
fundamental causes of racial inequality and oppression in the city and
nation. John Churchville, a twenty-three-year-old Philadelphia native who
had worked as a Student Nonviolent Coordinating Committee (SNCC)
field secretary in Georgia and Mississippi, founded the Freedom Library in
1964 in order to bring the community organizing principles he had
learned while working for SNCC to the issues facing the black poor in the
urban North. Modeled on SNCC's Mississippi Freedom Schools, the library
sponsored educational programs for neighborhood children that combined basic educational skills with black history during the day. And in the
evenings, Churchville convened a series of lectures and discussions on
black political and historical topics that were intended to attract activists
who shared his frustration with the mainstream movement's integrationist
agenda.

The Freedom Library's evening session drew a core group of community
activists who were neither active in the student movement nor prominent
in local civil rights activism. Rather they were longtime neighborhood activists—in their thirties and older—who shared an adamant opposition to
what they saw as white and black middle-class domination of the mainstream civil rights movement. Inspired equally by Malcolm X's vision of a
movement politics rooted in the black nationalist tradition and SNCC's
commitment to developing movement leadership from within poor black
communities, these activists set out to formulate and act on a movement
politics that linked the fundamental black nationalist principles of race

consciousness, intraracial unity, and black control over the social, political, and economic institutions operating within black communities to SNCC's radical democratic faith in indigenous political leadership.[1]

A Black Nationalist in the Beloved Community

Even in its early years, SNCC's commitment to the discourse of the "beloved community" masked important similarities between its brand of movement activism and the black nationalist tradition. "By making southern blacks more confident of their capacity to overcome oppression," SNCC historian Clayborne Carson has written, "SNCC workers revived dormant feelings of racial consciousness." SNCC's deep suspicion of traditional black elites also had much in common with the nationalist critique of the black middle class. As early as 1962, SNCC activists were actively debating black nationalist criticisms of nonviolence and integration. In that year, for example, SNCC's Howard University affiliate sponsored a debate between Malcolm X and Bayard Rustin.[2]

John Churchville was among the most vocal advocates of black nationalism on the SNCC staff in the organization's early years. Born and raised in North Philadelphia, Churchville attended Temple University before dropping out in 1961 to pursue a career as a jazz composer and pianist in New York. While in New York, he frequented the Harlem headquarters of the Nation of Islam where he met Malcolm X and became "enthralled by the Black Muslim movement." Having grown up in a single parent family, Churchville identified with Malcolm as a positive "male role model . . . the only black man who could stand up and say what he wanted to say and everybody just backed off." According to Churchville, he never formally joined the Nation of Islam in this period, though he was known around the mosque as John X. "The black nationalist thing," Churchville remembers, "moved me emotionally at the very core of my being."[3]

In April 1962, Churchville attended the Inter-Collegiate Conference on Northern Civil Rights, the founding convention of the Northern Student Movement (NSM). Held at Sarah Lawrence College, just north of New York City, the conference brought together students from campuses in the Northeast "to provide . . . support—moral, physical and financial—[for] the southern student movement . . . information . . . on the dilemma of the Northern urban areas," and "opportunit[ies] for . . . action upon local problems: discrimination in housing, employment, public accommodations, slum redevelopment, [and] education." According to Joan Cannady, a black Philadelphian who was student body president at Sarah Lawrence, the central mission of the conference was to present racial issues as a national, rather than just a southern, crisis. Thus, the conference's keynote speaker was Leon Sullivan, who not coincidentally was Cannady's uncle. Still, developments in the southern movement remained a major concern of the conference. In fact, the conference speakers included two SNCC staff members, Chuck McDew, the group's chairman, and Charles Sherrod, director of SNCC's Southwest Georgia Voter Registration Project.[4]

During the conference, members of the SNCC staff recruited Churchville to drive a donated bus to the group's headquarters in Atlanta. Once in Atlanta, Churchville decided to join SNCC's field staff. Despite his philosophical opposition to integration—"I was offended by the notion that the only way that blacks could develop was by being around white folks"—he was excited by SNCC's commitment to taking civil rights activism into the most isolated and dangerous areas of the South. "A lot of people who were nationalists," he remembers, "were very good at being nationalists on the corner of 125th and Seventh Avenue, but you couldn't find them . . . taking on responsibility" in the South. "I was more on the Booker T. Washington side . . . that's what attracted me to Malcolm X . . . but activism was important to me." Moreover, he was able to distinguish between the racial separatism favored by the Nation of Islam and state-enforced jim crow segregation. "The problem with segregation," he remembers believing, "is that somebody else is in charge . . . somebody else controlled it." For Churchville, there was nothing "mutually exclusive" between the self-help philosophy of Booker T. Washington and Du Boisian opposition to segregation.[5]

SNCC and the Organizing Tradition

As practiced by SNCC, community organizing was premised on the existence in black communities of what Charles Payne has called "the organizing tradition"—the presence in every community of "informal" leaders whose leadership was based not on their class status or educational degrees but rather on their commitment to helping others and the trust and respect of their neighbors. Under the influence of Ella Baker and Septima Clark—two longtime activists who because of their gender and their commitment to democratic forms of leadership had largely been shunted aside from the leadership of the national civil rights organizations—SNCC developed a philosophy of community organizing in which the role of the organizer was not to provide leadership for the local movement but rather to help the "local people" to develop the skills to lead themselves. Baker, who as the executive director of the Southern Christian Leadership Conference organized the student conference that led to the founding of SNCC, encouraged the student activists to eschew top-down models of movement leadership. In place of the charismatic leadership style of Martin Luther King and other movement preachers, Baker urged SNCC to develop what she termed a "group-centered" form of leadership. "It was a handicap for oppressed peoples to depend upon a leader," she would later tell an interviewer. "The charismatic leader usually becomes a leader because he has found a spot in the public limelight . . . he has been touted through the public media, which means the media made him, and the media may undo him." In Baker's view, a top-down approach to leadership encouraged people to view individual leaders rather than their own participation as crucial to the movement's success. Charismatic leaders, she argued, "get so involved with playing the game of being important that they don't do the work of actually organizing people."[6]

As SNCC began to shift its focus from protest strategies toward voter registration, it was Septima Clark who guided the student activists' growing commitment to the leadership development model of community organizing. A former South Carolina schoolteacher who gave up her job rather than comply with a law banning state employees from belonging to the NAACP, Clark had served since 1956 as the coordinator of the Citizenship Schools program for the Highlander Folk School, a movement training center in Tennessee. Established to encourage rural blacks to register to vote, the Citizenship School program was designed to, in Clark's words, "broaden . . . the scope of democracy to include everyone and deepen . . . the concept to include every relationship." Specifically, the program recruited "nonteachers"—local people who were not part of the traditional black elite but who had earned the trust and respect of their neighbors—to organize adult literacy programs to prepare their neighbors to take the literacy tests that many southern states required for voter registration. More important to Clark, these literacy programs were to be laboratories of democracy in which teachers and students jointly developed their democratic skills by working together to find solutions to problems in their communities.[7]

Having decided to conduct voter registration in some of the most dangerous and repressive parts of the rural South, SNCC faced the dual dilemma of convincing poor rural blacks to undertake the risk of registering to vote and of preparing poorly educated and often illiterate adults to take the infamous literacy tests.[8] Clark's Citizenship Schools model encouraged SNCC to see voter registration campaigns not as an end in and of themselves, but rather as a means to promote the collective political development of entire communities with a particular emphasis on identifying and developing the leadership skills of influential "local people," often older women who became known in the SNCC lexicon as "mamas." In 1962, Charles Sherrod described one such local leader as "a gray-haired old lady of about seventy, who can pick more cotton, 'slop more pigs,' plow more ground, chop more wood, and do a hundred more things better than the best farmer in the area." "There is always a 'mama,'" Sherrod concluded, "She is usually a militant woman in the community, outspoken, understanding and willing to catch hell, having already caught her share."[9]

It was this organizing philosophy that drew John Churchville to join the staff of Sherrod's Southwest Georgia Voter Registration Project even though he "fundamentally disagreed" with Sherrod's commitment to interracialism. Determined not to use his "ideology as an excuse not to go to work," Churchville saw voter registration work as a crucial way to develop the ability of black folk to solve their own problems rather than having to depend on white goodwill. Still, Churchville continued to debate Sherrod on issues of interracialism, in particular lobbying to be exempted from the project's policy of only sending out integrated canvassing teams. In Sherrod's view, only by maintaining integrated teams could the project "strike at the very root of segregation . . . the idea that white is superior. . . . We can only do this if they see white and black working together, side by side, the white man no more and no less than his black brother." Churchville, however, believed that integrated teams had exactly the opposite effect. When faced with a white canvasser, he argued, black southerners were more likely to agree to try to register out of deference "to white authority" than because they were convinced by SNCC's message of political activism. "If I'm with a white partner, I'm not going to talk . . . about 'we as black people.' . . . You can really move to a level of identification . . . that is actually inhibited by the presence of a white person." In other words, the use of integrated teams undercut the project's commitment to developing local leadership within disenfranchised black communities. In the end, Churchville was able to convince Sherrod to give him a black canvassing partner, though the two were assigned to the town of Americus, forty miles up the road from the project's base in Albany.[10]

In March 1963, Churchville and many others on the Southwest Georgia staff were temporarily transferred to Greenwood, Mississippi, as part of an effort to overcome the violent repression of black voters and voter registration workers in the Mississippi Delta. Churchville calls his time in Greenwood his most important experience on the SNCC staff. In Greenwood, he shifted from canvassing to working in the Citizenship Schools, helping to train prospective voters to take the state's literacy test. In his classes, Churchville found that he was doing "two things . . . you're trying to get people to pass this literacy test, but . . . you're giving a skill at the same time." As a result, he came to believe that the movement must be equally committed to grassroots organizing for short-term political goals and to efforts to develop the basic skills of residents of poor communities. He recognized that voter registration in Mississippi meant more than giving southern blacks the right to vote for one of the major parties; it meant that "if there were a lot of black people registered to vote and . . . there was organization in that community about how one can vote, folks would begin to look at you better and treat you better because you could control whether they got in or out." It was not enough to win the right to vote, Churchville came to believe, blacks also needed to develop the skills and organizations that would enable them to use the political process to strengthen the communities in which they lived. He now viewed education

as essential "to getting fundamental rights [and to] building an infrastructure for freedom."[11]

Community Organizing with a Black Nationalist Agenda

As significant as the Greenwood experience was for Churchville, he
remained fundamentally uncomfortable with what he saw as SNCC's continued reliance on the support of white liberals. "The TRUTH," he would
later write,

is that the civil rights movement is not and never was our movement. The civil rights
struggle since slavery (except for the revolts during slavery and the riots now) has
been one of advancing our position as slaves, but not abolishing slavery. All white
people are racists; that is, no white person . . . can stand to deal with black people
as humans, as men as equals. . . . They can't stand the thought of black people
ruling over them or ruling independently of them."[12]

Churchville left Mississippi and the SNCC staff in the summer of 1963 and
moved to Atlanta where he had maintained a "solid relationship" with Jeremiah X, the minister of the local Nation of Islam mosque. Eager to make
use of the community organizing skills that he had learned from SNCC,
Churchville began to work closely with members of what he called the
mosque's "brain trust" on a project to improve the Muslims' image in the
local community. As in other cities, relations between the Atlanta mosque
and the city's black churches were very tense. In addition, mosque members had developed a reputation for using intimidation to fulfill sales quo-
tas for *Muhammad Speaks*, the Muslims' national newspaper. To remedy this
situation, Churchville began teaching classes on community organizing
skills and strategies to mosque members. "The theory," he remembers,
"was we do not need everybody to be a member of the Nation of Islam.
What we need is respect. What we need is that if we walk into a community
and there are ten of us, then we've got five hundred supporters." As a
result of this new approach, local sales of *Muhammad Speaks* increased significantly. "And the people who didn't buy, [began] looking up to Muslims, because they act like gentlemen . . . they are strong and masculine."
According to Churchville, the results of these efforts helped to convince
the Atlanta braintrust "that we could do a lot of things to help a lot of
people."[13]

Growing divisions within the Nation of Islam derailed Churchville's
organizing work in Atlanta, however. After NOI leader Elijah Muhammad
suspended Malcolm X in December 1963, ostensibly for his public comments blaming President Kennedy's assassination on the violent nature of
white American society, the national headquarters in Chicago ordered the
Atlanta mosque to end its outreach efforts. According to Churchville, the
NOI's national leadership was simply not interested in efforts to create "a

base of support" for the Muslims among blacks not yet willing to formally join a mosque. By the summer of 1964, Churchville had returned home to Philadelphia. As he remembers it, he felt himself "outgrowing" the Muslims and was eager to find a new setting to try out his ideas for using educational programs and community organizing strategies to build racial solidarity in the black community.[14]

Back in Philadelphia, Churchville started the Freedom Library Community Project in a Ridge Avenue storefront in North Philadelphia. Drawing on his work in the Mississippi Freedom Schools, he envisioned the Freedom Library as a community center that would simultaneously provide educational programming for neighborhood children and adults and serve as a staging point for community organization. Located just blocks from where the North Philadelphia riot would start, the Freedom Library was sufficiently well known by the weekend of the riot that it was one of the few Ridge Avenue storefronts not to have its windows smashed. "The notion," Churchville remembers, "was we could come up with a freedom library that would have books by and about black people. We could have black history lectures. We could then begin to develop programs, deal with the problems in the neighborhood." Soliciting donations from figures as diverse as Jeremiah X and Leon Sullivan, Churchville quickly amassed a library of "2000 books by Negroes and/or about Negroes," with a particular emphasis on "Negro history and contemporary problems."[15]

Where the Freedom Library differed from the Freedom Schools was in Churchville's belief that the most important problem in the black community was the lack not of civil and political rights, but of a "rich and meaningful identity." To counteract the "sense of worthlessness and self-hatred" endemic in black communities, Churchville believed you had to both promote community awareness "of the positive aspects of the history of the Negro race" and involve ghetto residents "in constructive activities," enabling them to "assum[e] positive roles in the community." Rejecting integration as an expression of the middle-class desire to assimilate into white culture, Churchville viewed blacks' lack of racial pride as a prime cause of the political apathy and negative social behaviors evident in black ghettos of the urban North. "It is very easy," he wrote in the Freedom Library newsletter, "for those of us who live in the ghetto of North Philadelphia to become frustrated to the point that we begin to doubt ourselves and our own ability as black people to achieve anything at all in this society . . . after all these years of persecution and abuse, it doesn't take very much to make us feel that way." The first step thus was "to stimulate Negro pride in self and in the community." Only then could activists work on "the broader goal of creating political and social awareness."[16]

Churchville opened the Freedom Library with a tutorial program that matched black college student volunteers with neighborhood schoolchildren. The Freedom Library's tutoring program took a very different approach from the usual focus on homework assistance. Traditional tutoring programs, Churchville believed, were "doing a disservice" to black students by treating them as if they could not meet the same standards as white children. "They would [say] don't push the black kids. Let them work at their own pace. My philosophy is, 'we don't have the time, guys!' If the kids are in the fifth grade and there's a fifth grade curriculum and the kid can only read at a second grade level, stop tutoring and go back and teach." The Freedom Library tutoring program thus sought to overcome the children's lack of racial pride with a curriculum that promoted self-esteem through black history.[17] Churchville's pedagogical approach emphasized rote memorization and strict discipline. Charyn Sutton, one of the volunteer tutors remembers the program as "very rigid, very regimented. . . . We were really strict on teaching them and having them do their alphabets." A similar method was used to teach lessons in black history. "We programmed those poor little kids," Sutton recalls, "to [say] things like, 'I am black and powerful.' . . . They're just spouting it off and they don't know what they're saying."[18]

Churchville's commitment to developing a sense of capacity and self-esteem within the local neighborhood eventually led him to shift the focus of the tutorial program from college students to community residents. In particular, he recruited neighborhood high school students to tutor the elementary and junior high school students in the tutorial program. Among the high school tutors were members of the area's teenage gangs. "I would get the gang guys to come in and [say] 'Look, man, you only read at the fifth grade level, but you read more than this kid. So teach him what you know.' And it would help his reading." Churchville's work with gang members exemplified his belief that a combination of race pride and community involvement could counteract the negative social identities of the ghetto. It also reflected his desire to establish the Freedom Library as an institution capable of solving community problems.[19]

For Churchville, however, the Freedom Library was to be more than a black nationalist-influenced educational program. Rather, he saw his efforts to promote black consciousness as the first step in a strategy to redirect the civil rights movement toward an agenda based on racial pride and black self-determination. "My perception of black power was never straight separatism," Churchville remembers. "It was come apart and be separate and get your act together . . . then you've got to get out there in the real world where other people are and you've got to argue with them." The next step was to create spaces in which black activists could come together free from the interference of well-meaning whites. To promote this vision of a black nationalist social movement, the Freedom Library sponsored an evening lecture and discussion series on issues ranging from black history to the current state of the civil rights movement. As Churchville remembers it, the lectures drew audiences of up to 150 people. "People would come from the bar and lend us [their bar] stools for people to sit on." Among those in attendance "were old Garveyites, people who remembered Marcus Garvey, who said . . . 'I'm ready to come out and do something now. It's been years.'" Mattie Humphrey, a frequent participant in the evening discussions, remembers them as "history lesson[s] on our glorious past . . . in the sweltering summer [heat]."[20]

The success of the Freedom Library's evening discussions reflected the growing appeal within movement circles of Malcolm X's attempt to define a black nationalist political project in the months following his expulsion from the Nation of Islam. "The political philosophy of Black Nationalism," he had declared in a March 1964 press conference, "means we must control the politics and politicians of our community. . . . We will organize, and sweep out of office all Negro politicians who are puppets for outside forces." Specifically, he promised that his new political organization, the Organization of Afro-American Unity, would lead "voter-registration drive[s] to make every unregistered voter in the Afro-American community an independent voter . . . run independent candidates for office, and . . . support any Afro-American already in [public] office who answers to . . . the Afro-American community."[21]

Churchville's attempts to build a community organization along the lines of Malcolm X's black nationalist project brought him back in contact with the Northern Student Movement, the organization that had first encouraged his involvement in the student movement. In 1964, NSM was also moving in the direction of black nationalism, in large part as a result of the group's efforts to work in poor black communities in the urban North. Following its April 1962 founding conference, NSM had focused most of its efforts on establishing tutoring programs that matched college students with inner-city youth. By the summer of 1963, NSM was running tutorial programs in five northern cities, including Philadelphia. NSM's leadership believed that the group's strong identification with the southern student movement differentiated its tutorial programs from more traditional kinds of student volunteerism. "Apart from the effect on individuals," NSM's white executive director Peter Countryman wrote in a 1962 article on the Philadelphia Tutorial Project, "the tutors and tutees sense that they constitute a 'movement' which has no less a goal than the complete alleviation of educational problems in North Philadelphia." Similarly, Joan Cannady Countryman, who married Peter Countryman and joined the NSM staff in 1962, remembers drawing a parallel between the tutorial programs and SNCC's determination to register voters in the most dangerous areas of the rural South. "SNCC by going into Mississippi and choosing voting was [making] the most dramatic statement about the hypocrisy of the society. And that was what we were about, too, trying to point out that there were inequities in society that could be addressed."[22]

Soon, the NSM leadership were looking for ways to implement more explicit forms of educational advocacy, including efforts to organize parent organizations. At the same time, there was a growing feeling that NSM should have a black director. In September 1963, Peter Countryman, who had dropped out of Yale to start NSM two years earlier, stepped aside to return to school and was replaced by Bill Strickland, a black Harvard graduate and former marine.[23] What attracted Strickland to NSM was its commitment to working in the black ghettos of the urban North. Like Churchville, he believed SNCC's organizing philosophy could be utilized in the North to establish community-led political organizations capable of challenging liberal dominance within both the civil rights movement and black electoral politics. "The poor," Strickland argued, in a January 1965 article coauthored with NSM newsletter editor Dan Schecter, "must become involved in this process of change. It is they who are oppressed and must end their oppression. As organizers, we must help by encouraging the development of political forms through which the poor can challenge and change those institutions which so limit their lives. This is the task to which NSM, SDS, and SNCC . . . have committed themselves."[24]

Strickland was also like Churchville in that he had become a committed black nationalist under the influence of Malcolm X. In Strickland's first year as NSM executive director, the group thus made what Charyn Sutton, who at the time was on the staff of the organization's New York headquarters, has described as "a conscious decision to move [from its interracial roots] into a black organization." The purpose of the move was, as Sutton puts it, "to say that African Americans needed to control our own destiny in . . . the Freedom Movement." Like Malcolm, NSM now took the stance that interracialism was little more than a device for insuring white control over the black agenda. "Whites were always partly controlling the movement, thinking that they knew how best to help blacks . . . [without] a lot of recognition of black leadership." By becoming a black organization, NSM would have the "opportunity to . . . step out and be positive and show black people that we really could run things and could do things in a very positive way." As part of this effort to demonstrate what an all-black organization could achieve, Strickland asked Churchville to affiliate the Freedom Library with NSM in the fall of 1964. The Freedom Library thus became the NSM Freedom Library and from his New York office Strickland played an active role in Churchville's efforts to build a black nationalist political movement in Philadelphia.[25]

The Freedom Library and the Organizing Tradition in Philadelphia

While NSM sponsorship of the Freedom Library gave Churchville a forum for promoting his views on movement goals and strategies to black (and white) students activists across the region, it did little to raise the library's local profile outside of its immediate neighborhood. In fact, the Freedom Library might well have remained a largely self-contained neighborhood project had not Churchville had the good fortune to meet a thirty-eight-year-old hospital administrator and community activist named Mattie Humphrey. Excited by the Freedom Library's mix of youth programming and nationalist critique of mainstream black leadership, Humphrey recruited to the library's evening sessions many of the neighborhood activists who would work with Churchville to build the city's first Black Power organization, the Black People's Unity Movement (BPUM).[26]

A nurse and hospital administrator, Humphrey and her teenage son had returned to her native city from Detroit in 1962 to be nearer to family. As someone who "had done some volunteer work all of my life," she quickly became involved in community work in her Germantown neighborhood while working as an administrative assistant at Mercy-Douglass Hospital, the city's only black-run hospital. In 1964, Humphrey's reputation as a committed, responsible, and creative community worker led Sylvia Meek, the education director of the Philadelphia Urban League, to recommend her for the position of youth development coordinator for the Philadelphia Council for Community Advancement (PCCA), the Ford Foundation-funded antipoverty pilot program. The position's job description, as PCCA executive director Samuel Dash described it to Humphrey, was to combat the gang problem in North Philadelphia by developing programs that would encourage neighborhood youth to become involved in efforts to improve their community.[27]

Despite never having held a leadership position in a civil rights or social service organization, Humphrey quickly developed a citywide network of neighborhood-based youth workers. Among those she met was John Churchville. Humphrey first learned of the Freedom Library from Prathia Hall, the daughter of a family friend who had worked with Churchville in southwest Georgia. Having admired the southern student movement from afar, she was immediately taken with what Churchville had established at the library. "John's operation at the library," she would later remember, "was a total thing . . . kids doing school and tutoring and . . . all kinds of activities; he . . . made it the hub."[28] Humphrey was so impressed with Churchville's approach to working with young people that she recommended him for a "gang worker" position at the nearby Church of the Advocate.[29] But it was the evening sessions, which she remembered attending a couple of times a week, that spoke to Humphrey's concerns about the impact of the civil rights movement on the collective well-being of the black community. Working as an administrator at black hospitals in Detroit and Philadelphia, Humphrey had grown angry at what she saw as the tendency of black doctors and other "professionals" to abandon the institutions that had taken responsibility for the collective strength of the black community as soon as they were given the opportunity to integrate "prestigious" white institutions. "I'm giving up everything on the basis of principle," she remembered thinking, "and here's a bunch of people laughing at the principles . . . for their personal gain."[30] It was this worry that for most African Americans integration would mean the deterioration of community that drew Humphrey to Churchville's vision of a social movement based in black nationalist principles.

A conference on inner-city schooling organized by Humphrey and Churchville in October 1965 demonstrates how the Freedom Library activists sought to use the tutorial program as a basis for community organizing. The purpose of the conference was to promote the tutorial program curriculum as a model that could be integrated into the public schools. Churchville's goal had always been "to impact public education. . . . You should be able to say, 'this is how the curriculum should look, look at how it's working with these kids.' . . . This is what we ought to have in the public school system." Humphrey's call to the conference cited the need for "massive change . . . in the potentially explosive . . . situation" in the schools in black neighborhoods. "Black people, Spanish-speaking people, and poor people are crammed into the oldest and most decayed [schools]."[31]

Among Humphrey's most significant recruits to the Freedom Library's evening sessions were a medical technician and autodidact named Walter Palmer, an insurance executive named Edward Robinson, and an Episcopal priest named Paul Washington. Publicly identified with efforts to promote the teaching of black history, Palmer and Robinson were natural recruits to Churchville's black nationalist project. Washington, in contrast, was pastor of the Church of the Advocate, an integrated Episcopalian parish in North Philadelphia, and had a history of organizing nonviolent civil rights protest.

Born in Atlantic City in 1934, Walter Palmer moved with his family to the West Philadelphia neighborhood then known as the "Black Bottom" on the eve of World War II.[32] His father, who had been forced to send Walter's five older stepsisters to live with relatives during the Depression, had finally found work as a janitor in Philadelphia's City Hall. Walter, his father and mother, and Walter's two brothers thus moved into a two-room flat at the back of a beauty shop run by one of Walter's stepsisters. When Walter was twelve, his father died and the family was forced to go on welfare. As the oldest son, Walter felt a strong sense of responsibility for his mother and siblings. As an adolescent, Palmer would extend this sense of responsibility to his friends and his community as a member of his neighborhood—or "corner" as it was known in local slang—gang. His first arrest came at the age of twelve for burglary of a University of Pennsylvania dormitory. During frequent run-ins with rival gangs as well as the police, Palmer survived a couple of stabbings, one gunshot wound, and repeated arrests.

An indifferent student, Palmer managed to graduate from West Philadelphia High School in 1952. It was following his high school graduation that Palmer's concern for family and community began to take him in new directions. Working as an orderly at the University of Pennsylvania Hospital, he was recommended by his supervisor for a four-year training program for medical technicians in cardiopulmonary care. Palmer remembers being reluctant, but his supervisor convinced him that he "could study that stuff." After completing the training, he was hired as a technician in the cardio-pulmonary unit at the Children's Hospital of Pennsylvania, eventually rising to the position of unit director. During a decade of work at Children's Hospital, Palmer would earn two college degrees, an associate's degree in business from Temple and a teaching degree from all-black Cheyney State College in the Philadelphia suburbs.[33]

While still in the training program at Penn Hospital, Palmer also threw himself into community activism, motivated, he would say later, by the same set of concerns that had led to his gang involvement. As he remembers it, there was no single point in which he shifted from being a gang leader to a community activist. Moreover, he believes that the skills that he had developed as a gang leader were crucial to his success as a community activist. "Later on, I am able to recognize . . . that what I am doing [as a gang leader] is working with, organizing neighborhood guys to have some purpose . . . those skills will eventually translate into youth activities." He began by helping many of his friends find work at the hospital. At the same time, he started an after-school program for young people in his West Philadelphia neighborhood. Just as John Churchville would do a decade later, Palmer developed a curriculum that taught racial pride through what he called "hero-identification." Drawing on stories he had learned from his father and "other men" in the community, as well as the works of African American historians J. A. Rodgers and Carter Woodson, he sought to use the lives of great black historical figures like Frederick Douglass and Marcus Garvey to counteract a culture that mocked the possibility of black achievement. By 1957, Palmer's youth program had a name, the Black People's University, and a permanent meeting space in the back of a dry-cleaning store that his family had purchased with his brother's GI Bill benefits.[34]

The confluence of the organizing and black nationalist traditions is evident in Palmer's efforts to reach the young people of his community with a positive message of black struggle and achievement. Within the black nationalist tradition, Palmer found the same collectivist ethic—the sense of duty toward family, community, and race—that drove his organizing efforts as a gang leader and then community activist. As a child, Palmer had listened to his father—whose own formal education had stopped after the eighth grade—tell "stories of struggle" and recite the poetry of Paul Laurence Dunbar. And as a teenager and young adult, he was deeply influenced by "men in the community" who were both capable of fulfilling their responsibilities to family and community and knowledgeable on matters of race and society. Thus, it was two older men—one his landlord, the other his barber—who convinced him to go to the Philadelphia Arena at Forty-Sixth and Market Streets to hear a speech by a local Muslim minister named Malcolm X. Though he found little of interest in the Nation of Islam's religious teachings, Palmer was deeply impressed by Malcolm's strength, by his message of self-reliance and self-knowledge, and by the discipline he exerted over young men that Palmer had known "from the street."[35]

To this point, Palmer's activism had largely been confined to his immediate neighborhood and to educational and self-help efforts. In the early 1960s, however, he began to make use of social movement tactics and to articulate public policy goals. Not surprisingly, neither the nonviolent strategies nor the integrationist goals of mainstream civil rights groups held any appeal for him. "I never supported the idea of subjecting yourself to abuse without fighting back." Still, he was clearly influenced by the achievements of the protest movement. In 1963, he formed the Society for the Preservation of Afro-American History and began to organize "street corner" rallies "calling for black history to be put inside the schools." On the day of the 1963 March on Washington, for example, fifteen members of Palmer's society marched on City Hall with placards with the names and portraits of African American scientists and leaders of slave revolts. In its demands, the Society for the Preservation of Afro-American History sought neither integration into nor separation from white America. Rather, in ways that prefigured the political stance taken by Malcolm X following his departure from the Nation of Islam, Palmer and his group were demanding the reshaping of public institutions to meet the specific needs and concerns of African Americans.[36]

Palmer met Mattie Humphrey—whom he would later call an "activist par excellence . . . a brilliant women"—in 1964 at a meeting of the Philadelphia chapter of the Medical Committee for Human Rights, an organization founded to provide medical assistance for SNCC's Freedom Summer project in Mississippi. Within months, she had recruited him to the evening sessions at the Freedom Library. To the now thirty-year-old Palmer, Strickland and Churchville were "southern movement guys," "kids" who had been caught up in a nonviolent movement whose tolerance of violent attacks made little sense to him. But the library's discussions offered him the opportunity to work with others who shared his commitment to building a social movement on the principles of racial consciousness and a sense of collective responsibility for the black community.[37]

A decade older than Palmer, Edward Robinson came to the Freedom Library from a very different part of black Philadelphia. A native Philadelphian and graduate of Virginia State College in mathematics, Robinson began selling insurance for the black-owned Provident Mutual Insurance Company in 1940. After serving in Europe during World War II, he rose steadily through the ranks at Provident, becoming manager of the sales division in the late 1950s, and president of the company in 1969. As befitting a successful business executive, Robinson lived with his family on Gowen Avenue in the Mount Airy section of Northwest Philadelphia.[38]

Robinson's true passion, however, was African history—in particular the achievements of the precolonial empires of West Africa—and one of the main benefits of working in insurance was the flexibility it gave him to pursue his historical interests. Like Palmer, Robinson credits his upbringing for his commitment to the study and teaching of African history. In Robinson's case, he grew up in a family that traced its ancestry to the last of the precolonial empires of West Africa. According to the family history, his great-great-great-grandfather was a lawyer and sculptor in Benin City, Nigeria, who raised an army to fight British and Dutch raiders who were accused of stealing the city's artistic treasures. In the ensuing battle, he was killed and his pregnant wife and infant daughter captured and placed with 266 other captives on a slave ship headed for the Americas. Before the ship could reach its destination, however, it was headed off by abolitionists seeking to enforce the U.S.'s 1808 ban on the importation of African slaves and towed to New Jersey. Instead of arriving at a slave market where she would surely have been separated from her daughter, Robinson's great-great-great-grandmother thus arrived a free woman in Trenton, New Jersey, where she raised her two children. Eventually, Robinson's great-grandmother, who was born in 1842, would move to Philadelphia, where as an old women she would tell the story of her mother and grandmother and the wonders of "the beautiful city" of Benin to Robinson and his two siblings.[39]

As Robinson grew up, he came to believe that this family history had inoculated him against the sense of racial inferiority that was so debilitating to most African Americans. "I was raised as an African in America . . . a Nigerian in America." Cut off from "the sophisticated cultures from which they came," the descendants of slavery were defenseless against white supremacist myths about life in the jungles of "darkest" Africa. For Robinson, then, teaching about the glories of the African past was more than a feel-good antidote to the eurocentric bias in American education; it was as essential to the development of intellectually confident and culturally assured black children as the knowledge of the political and cultural achievements of ancient Greece was to white children's sense of cultural heritage and identity.

Robinson began his efforts to promote the teaching of African history shortly after his return from military service during World War II. When his efforts to convince the school district to incorporate African subjects into its social studies curriculum fell on deaf ears, he shifted his focus to making presentations on African history and culture to school classes, churches, and community groups. Incorporating music and art into his presentations, he developed a citywide reputation as a dynamic presenter of historical narrative. Through the 1950s and into the 1960s, Robinson continued to sell insurance while also completing evening programs in business and law at Penn's Wharton School of Business and Temple's Law School respectively. As a fellow World War II-era veteran and with a shared history as an entrepreneur marketing to black consumers, Robinson was not surprisingly a strong supporter of Cecil Moore during his leadership of the Philadelphia NAACP. During the Strawberry Mansion protests, for example, he responded to a call from the NAACP for volunteers to sit in front of bulldozers at the construction site, one night filling the 2 to 4 A.M. shift by himself. Still Robinson's primary focus remained on his efforts to promote the teaching of African history when he was invited by Mattie Humphrey to attend an evening discussion at the Freedom Library.[40]

In contrast to Palmer and Robinson, Paul Washington was a most unlikely recruit to black nationalist causes when he became involved in the Freedom Library (Figure 11). As I have said, the rector of the Church of the Advocate first met John Churchville when Mattie Humphrey recommended Churchville for a position in the church's anti-gang program. In more than a decade as an Episcopal priest in Philadelphia—first in a Southwest Philadelphia parish and then at the Church of the Advocate—Washington had been actively involved in a number of integrationist protest campaigns. In 1960, for example, he joined with neighborhood activist Charles Sutton, Charyn Sutton's father, to lead a series of "planned swims" by an interracial group of children and adults that successfully integrated a public swimming pool in Southwest Philadelphia. Writing for the *Tribune,* Washington and Sutton described how they trained the young protesters in the method of nonviolent protest, instructing them in "how important it was that they behaved well in the pool, how essential that there be no violence on their part, no matter what was said to them, no matter how they were provoked."[41]

A similar commitment to interracialism was evident in Washington's work within the Episcopal Church. The Church of the Advocate presence in North Philadelphia predated the neighborhood's evolution into a black ghetto. Called "the finest specimen of French Gothic architecture" in the city, the church was built in the 1890s to serve the families of prosperous white industrialists who originally built and settled the area. For much of its history, the parish had actively discouraged black worshippers. By 1962, the church had been designated a "pilot parish," which meant, as Washington would later explain, that the church leadership saw it as an experiment to see "whether a WASP denomination . . . could minister meaningfully and effectively to Negroes, and in particular to those who were handicapped by . . . unemployment and poor education." To lead the experiment, the local Episcopal bishop appointed Washington to be the Church of the Advocate's first black priest. Still, the parish's six-hundred-

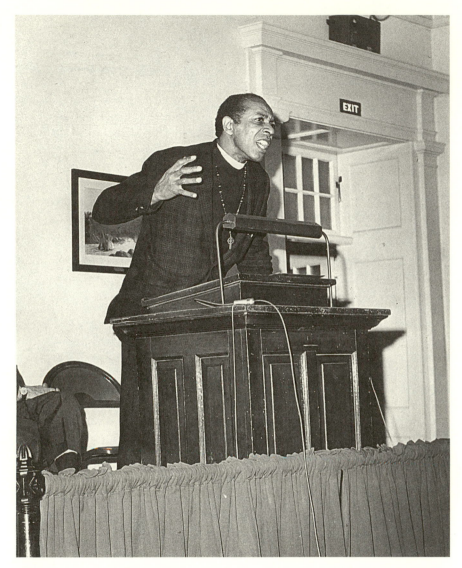

Figure 11. The Rev. Paul M. Washington, 1969. Urban Archives, Temple University Libraries.

member congregation, while interracial, remained disproportionately middle class, including large numbers of doctors, teachers and other professionals. Moreover, it remained proudly disconnected from black church traditions of social activism. Thus, a white member of the vestry, the congregation's lay leadership, reprimanded Washington for announcing a selective patronage target in one of his first sermons at the church. "We never talk about race in this church," the vestry member said.[42]

By the time he hired John Churchville to work in the church's antigang program, Washington was feeling profoundly ambivalent about his place in a denomination that continually reminded him that "though I was a priest of the Episcopal Church, I was still a Negro." He would later describe himself as having "learned to accommodate myself" both to everyday racial slights and institutional racism within the church until Churchville challenged him "to question those compromises and the sacrifices of our real integrity as human beings." For example, he had not objected when the bishop appointed a special committee of three white lay leaders of suburban congregations to oversee the management of the Church of the Advocate at the same time he was appointed to be the parish's first black pastor. For Washington, his own reaction to the use of "that word 'black'" symbolized the need for a change in racial consciousness. "I had cringed the first time I heard Malcolm X say 'black' on the radio . . . when I used the term from the pulpit for the first time, it was received like profanity."[43]

Washington had also grown disillusioned with the capacity of Philadelphia's liberal institutions to solve problems of racial inequity. "We have looked upon integration as being the highest good," he would come to argue, "but . . . whenever I got too close . . . I was always told I could solve my problems, but not much credence was ever given to my own solutions to my problems." During his time in Southwest Philadelphia, he had sought unsuccessfully to force the city to guarantee alternative housing for black working-class families displaced by the city's largest urban renewal scheme. Following his transfer to the Church of the Advocate, Washington became a prominent critic of police practices in North Philadelphia. As an eyewitness to the November 1963 police shooting of black robbery suspect Willie Philyaw near the church, he both saved a white motorist from an angry crowd and publicly challenged the assertion that Philyaw had lunged at a police officer with a knife.[44]

Shortly after the Philyaw shooting, Mayor Tate appointed Washington to the Commission on Human Relations (CHR). An Episcopal priest with a strong commitment to integration must have seemed a very safe appointment to a mayor beset by activist critiques of the CHR. But for Washington, it increasingly seemed that the black community could look only to itself to solve the interlocking problems of racism and poverty. Thus he opened the Church of the Advocate, following the 1964 riot, to a group of neighborhood residents who had organized a citizen patrol that sought to prevent police brutality and illegal arrests by tracking and observing police activity on Friday and Saturday nights.[45]

It was, however, an extended conversation that he had with John Churchville and Bill Strickland while Churchville served on the staff of the church's youth gang program that led Washington to abandon his commitment to integration. In particular, Churchville's analysis of gangs as a product of "the feeling of powerlessness among black people" resonated with conversations that the Episcopal priest had had with gang members in the neighborhood. "They always saying we ain't worth nothing," one had told him, "so when we kill somebody, it's like we ain't killing nothing." Churchville and Strickland were particularly concerned that NSM's use of white tutors in its tutorial programs would only confirm the black children's internalization of notions of white superiority. A member of the advisory board of NSM's Philadelphia Tutorial Project, Washington also found the relationship between well-meaning white tutors and their black students to be reminiscent of psychologist Kenneth Clark's famous research on black children's attitudes toward white dolls. "These little black kids used to like to run their hands through [the white tutor's] hair." How does one challenge the notion that "everything . . . white . . . [is] beautiful" in a movement that celebrates the presence of white activists. As a result of his conversations with Churchville and Strickland, Washington increasingly came to question the value of integration for the black community. "Black unity, to the end of achieving black power and ultimately self-love and respect" now seemed to him the essential goal of black movement activism.[46]

The Black People's Unity Movement

By the fall of 1965, the activists who had been convening at the Freedom Library were ready to present to a larger audience their vision of a new kind of movement politics, one committed to the black nationalist principles of racial unity, black consciousness, and community control over the key political and economic institutions operating within black communities. Drawing on Malcolm X's call for "all Afro-American people and organizations [to] henceforth unite so that the welfare and well-being of our people will be assured," the Freedom Library activists announced plans to start an all-black political organization—which they called the Black People's Unity Movement (BPUM)—that would unite black Philadelphians across both class and ideological divisions free from the gaze of white allies and opponents alike. The discourse of racial unity had long been a powerful rhetorical weapon in the black nationalist critique of liberal interracialism. In a white supremacist society, black nationalists argued, the failure to establish intraracial unity meant that the interracial coalitions favored by liberal integrationists were little more than tools for white control over the black agenda. Thus the purpose of BPUM would be, as John Churchville described it, "to try to get every group . . . of people . . . represented." The message to "black professionals" was that "it's okay to make money . . . We're not here to make you feel guilt about what you have. It is to make you a good steward of what you have and that you should share some things." Churchville was equally committed to fostering ideological diversity within BPUM. "We took a position that we didn't have to have an ideological program that required everyone to be at the same level." Walter Palmer would later describe BPUM's goal as "operational unity," not complete agreement on every point.[47]

To announce the formation of their new organization, the Freedom Library activists decided to hold a Black Unity Rally much like one Churchville had helped Jeremiah X to organize in Atlanta in 1963. Washington not only offered the Church of the Advocate for the rally but also gave Churchville permission to use the remainder of the funds for the church's youth gang program to organize the rally. To promote the rally, Churchville convinced the Episcopal priest to join him and Bill Strickland as guests on Joe Rainey's nightly talk show on WDAS-AM, a black-oriented radio station. In an early reflection of J. Edgar Hoover's concerns about the threat that black radicalism posed to the nation, FBI agents dutifully recorded a transcript of Rainey's radio interview with the three BPUM activists. Churchville, Strickland, and Washington each urged the talk show's listeners to support organizations committed to intraracial unity across class, religious, and ideological lines. Drawing on Malcolm X's analogy of house and field niggers, Churchville called on middle-class blacks to join in a cross-class coalition with the black poor and working-classes. "I'm not suggesting that the nigger in the house get out. I'm saying he should stay in there so he could tell us where the things are in the house when we come through." And in place of liberalism's emphasis on enabling individual blacks to escape the segregated ghetto, the founder of the Freedom Library declared that blacks must collectively "own, control and regulate the affairs of the so-called ghetto."[48]

The BPUM call for racial solidarity, however, only thinly masked the group's criticisms of the mainstream civil rights movement's liberal leadership. Churchville, for example, told the listeners to the Rainey show that: "The civil rights movement was never the black man's movement. It was a movement of white liberals . . . using us . . . as a tool to get power for themselves. It was a trick. . . . We must own and control the black movement." As an example of white domination of the movement, he cited the pressure that was placed on SNCC chairman John Lewis to drop criticisms of the Kennedy administration from his speech to the 1963 March on Washington.[49] Strickland further argued that white domination of the movement had blinded blacks to the fact that "American society and the entire white western world is basically racist" and had led them to believe that they could find "individual solutions" to their problems. "Black people are treated the same north, east, south, and west," he insisted, "the so-called progress of the Negro, the so-called advance in the middle class, these individual attainments do not in any way deal with the real prejudices of . . . white society." Strickland also synthesized the critique of white domination of the movement with the student movement's long-standing opposition to the mainstream civil rights organizations' dependence on charismatic leadership. "The question of black liberation, the freedom of black people, is not finding the proper leader," he told the radio audience. "We need to have a movement of all the people that tells the leaders what to do."[50]

In their respective comments, the three BPUM founders argued that a revolution in black self-consciousness was necessary if the black community was to achieve its goals. "There is a need for a change in our own consciousness of ourselves, a need for a change in our image," Washington told the radio audience. "There is no reason why we should look upon blackness as being a stigma. But you mention the word 'black' and people's stomachs turn." Such a change in racial consciousness would naturally result in the growth of true intraracial unity, thus enabling the black movement to move beyond its dependence on white liberals. "We have been taught that we are nothing," he concluded, "We have no worth . . . but this land was built with our labors. . . . We are not asking for favors. . . . We can do it if we are united."[51]

It was, however, Churchville and Strickland's comments about the Vietnam War that drew the biggest response from the show's listeners. Calling on black people not to support the war "until we are treated . . . as human beings," Churchville compared the struggles of the Vietnamese people to the black movement in the United States. "What is happening in this case," he told the radio audience, "is that our slave master is having a fight with another guy who used to be a slave [and] is struggling for his freedom and here we are slaves of the slave master fighting other slaves who are attempting to be free." In similar fashion, Strickland described U.S. involvement in Vietnam as "a racist war . . . a simple extension of the war that white Americans fought against the Indians, the Philippines, and the Guatemalans, and the people in the Dominican Republic." Pointing out that many of the strongest supporters of the Vietnam War in the U.S. Senate were also staunch segregationists, including the likes of John Stennis and Strom Thurmond, he concluded that "the crackers who were calling for more war . . . regard the Vietnamese the same way they do us, as niggers."[52]

Churchville and Strickland's comments on the Vietnam War reflected the growing desire of movement radicals to identify their efforts with anticolonial movements in Africa and elsewhere in the third world. In the months following his split from the Nation of Islam, Malcolm X, for example, simultaneously worked to develop ties with nationalist leaders in Africa and with SNCC and others in the militant wing of the civil rights movement. There was, he declared in a November 1964 speech at the Audubon Ballroom in Harlem, a "direct connection between the struggles of the Afro-American in this country and the struggle of our people all over the world."[53] SNCC's interest in African nationalist movements greatly increased after a number of its leading figures conducted a tour of newly independent nations in Africa in the fall of 1964 during which they had met unexpectedly with Malcolm. Just a month before the Black Unity Rally in Philadelphia, SNCC's executive committee passed a resolution declaring that the organization had "a right and responsibility to dissent with . . . United States foreign policy" and accused the government of being "deceptive in its claims of concern for the freedom of the Vietnamese people, just as the government has been deceptive in claiming concern for the freedom of colored people in such countries as the Dominican Republic, the Congo, South Africa, Rhodesia, and in the United States itself." The Georgia state legislature refused to seat SNCC Communications Secretary and newly elected state representative Julian Bond when he declined to disavow the SNCC resolution. To emphasize the connections between the black American struggle against racism and third world anticolonial movements, as well as Bond's community organizing approach to electoral politics, Strickland and Churchville invited the longtime SNCC leader to be the keynote speaker at the Black Unity Rally.[54]

Churchville, Strickland, and Washington's ability to convey black nationalism's ideology and program into simple phrases like "unity," "power," and "self-love" reflected the growing effectiveness of the nationalist challenge to the orthodoxy of civil rights liberalism. During the 1940s and 1950s, civil rights activists had been able to forge a coalition of black and white liberal voters with a simple message that invoked African Americans' historic desire to claim their Americanness and that promised that the passage of antidiscrimination laws would eradicate racial discrimination and second-class citizenship. But just as civil rights liberals were achieving their goals in the federal enactment of the 1964 Civil Rights Act and the 1965 Voting Rights Act, black nationalists were establishing the basis for a new kind of black social movement with an equally simple message that spoke to very different African American traditions. Words like "unity" and "self-love" celebrated a shared African cultural heritage, a common history of resistance to oppression, and the quest to forge a prideful racial identity.

A Rally for Black Unity

By selecting Julian Bond to be the unity rally's keynote speaker, the Freedom Library activists were signaling their continued belief in political action as the key to liberating the black community from white control. Bond described his campaign for the Georgia state legislature in classic community organizing terms: "We would go around to people, knock on their doors, and ask them what they wanted their state representative to do."[55] The Bond campaign represented the kind of independent political organizing that black nationalist activists hoped could free the civil rights movement from its dependence on coalitions with white liberals. Six months before Stokely Carmichael won national notoriety for his use of the "Black Power" slogan, the BPUM rally demonstrated that the growing interest of black student activists in black nationalism and its analysis of the intractability of American racism did not represent a decline in their commitment to the community organizing tradition and the political empowerment of the black poor.

The media response to the rally, however, presaged that it would be the racial imagery of the militants' discourse, not the strategic content of their message, which would dominate public debate over Black Power. A standing-room-only audience gathered at the Church of the Advocate to hear Bond and the BPUM organizers on February 5, 1966. The group's desire to build a new kind of movement organization outside of the gaze of white activists proved immediately controversial. Noticing that twenty or so whites were seated in the church's front rows, Churchville asked them to give up their seats to blacks who were standing in the aisles. As Paul Washington remembers it, Churchville told the audience that although church policy prevented him from asking the whites to leave, it was obvious from the rally's publicity—which stated that the rally was "for, of and by BLACK youth"—that they were neither invited nor welcome. According to both an FBI informant and Steve Gold, the white former director of the Philadelphia Tutorial Project, the white audience members acceded to this request without objection. Reaction in the city's white and black newspapers, however, was swift and angry. The *Bulletin* charged that Churchville had "ordered" the whites to give up their seats, while both WDAS radio, which was white-owned despite its black-oriented programming, and the *Tribune* accused BPUM of practicing "reverse segregation." To the *Tribune*, the fact that "many whites . . . remained standing even though there were still empty seats when all the Negroes had sat down" was proof that the whites in the audience had felt insulted.[56]

BPUM's organizers could not have been surprised by the mainstream press' depiction of the rally as a racially separatist hate fest. Nor were they surprised by criticisms they heard from within the movement. The ensuing debate over the proper approach to race relations within the movement reflected an emerging "generation gap" among movement activists. Washington's longtime friend, Rev. Jesse Anderson, Sr., the black rector of a West Philadelphia Episcopal parish and a prominent figure in the Fellowship Commission, spoke for many black liberals of the post-World War II generation when he published an open letter expressing his "shock and horror [at] segregation and hatred in the House of the Lord." To the white audience members, Anderson offered "as a Negro and an Episcopalian . . . my apology and heartfelt chagrin at this attempt to vilify a set of people because of the color of their skin."[57] Equally scathing was the front-page editorial that ran in the next issue of *Nite Life*, the black tavern weekly whose publisher George Searles was a longtime supporter of Cecil Moore. *Nite Life*'s editorial complained that there had been a 'lynch whitey' mood at the rally. With the exception of Julian Bond, Searles wrote, "the platform speakers" conveyed the attitude that "we must be brain-washed until we

. . . are willing to hate and fight 'whitey'." The editorial insisted that the speakers had "enraged some of the Negroes present that they called out in protest. One young man yelled, 'what shall I do about my white wife,' while a black girl asked, 'how do you teach hate in a Christian Church?'" In his conclusion to the editorial, Searles sought to distinguish BPUM's call for black unity from the "race-first" discourse used by Cecil Moore and his supporters. Perhaps, Searles's real concern was not BPUM's black nationalist oratory but rather the rally's implicit challenge to Moore's preeminence within the local movement:

Those of us who are concerned about Philadelphia have often used phrases that sound very much like black unity. We've talked about Negroes working together, blacks voting . . . for our own interests. . . . We had better take time out to explain . . . that we believe that all people should enjoy basic human and constitutional rights, that freedom for black Americans does not depend upon our taking away the rights of any other group. And let us . . . revere those members of the white race who have struggled and are still working . . . to aid us in our fight for freedom. We welcome them as allies.[58]

In their response to these criticisms, BPUM's founders combined a reasoned defense of the rally with a call to their supporters to rally to the organization. In a letter to the *Tribune*, Mattie Humphrey argued that it was no more discrimination for Churchville to ask the white audience members to give up their seats to blacks than it would be for the Sons of Italy to reserve seats for Italian Americans. "Those who came were fortunate enough to be permitted to remain," she wrote, "and there is no indication that they asked for more." Humphrey concluded by remarking that white critics of the civil rights movement often called on blacks "to get together and help themselves" rather than look to the government for aid. "Now . . . some Negroes got together and . . . confused and worried those very same people who have been criticizing black people for being unorganized, without common aims and common programs." On March 8, WDAS ran a response to its critical editorial from a "spokesman for the Northern Student Movement." "Why is white unity all right and black unity racial discrimination in reverse?" asked the NSM spokesperson who was not identified in the FBI transcript of the counter-editorial. "Why does WDAS not attack the Sons of Italy or the B'nai B'rith?" Finally, Churchville mailed a letter to BPUM's supporters in which he insisted that "these attacks only mean we are on the right track." BPUM's critics feared "a real Unity Movement" because it "would threaten their interests." While "certain of our people . . . have labeled us a 'hate group,'" he argued that BPUM's focus was on black self-love, not racial hatred. "If you say that you love your family, does that mean you hate others?" "Why," he asked in conclusion, "are they so afraid of our doing what comes naturally?"[59]

As much as the controversy over the role of whites dominated the Black

Unity Rally, BPUM's organizers were able, in the ensuing months, to pursue their goal of building a political organization attuned only to the needs of the black community. Monthly mass meetings at the Church of the Advocate brought together a diverse group of community activists and ideological nationalists while a number of subcommittees met regularly at the Freedom Library to work on issue areas such as education, economic development, and cultural consciousness. The group also sponsored a four-session training program, designed primarily for young activists, which combined the basics of community organizing with an introduction to black and precolonial African history. In its organizing campaigns and public events, BPUM strove to link the concerns of cultural and political nationalists. BPUM rallies always featured African drumming and dancers as well as speakers in African attire. Calling African Americans "the chosen people of the world," Walter Palmer declared at an August 1966 rally that: "White Anglo-Saxon Protestant culture is a dead thing. The only original thing it's produced is ice cream."[60]

BPUM's fluid organizational structure (Washington called it "more a movement than an organization") produced a democratic model of leadership in stark contrast to the hierarchical style of charismatic figures like Cecil Moore and Leon Sullivan. Churchville was particularly proud that BPUM was able to attract people from across the class spectrum in the black community, bringing together "teachers, doctors, at least one lawyer . . . professional and non-professional people . . . people on welfare." Claims to leadership within BPUM were based in an ability to speak for the black community rather than professional status or the ability to mobilize a specific group of constituents. In this sense, BPUM differed significantly from SNCC's vision of a community-controlled, collectively led freedom organization. Where BPUM did not differ from its predecessors in either the adult or student wings of the movement was in its assumption of male leadership. Charisma, masculinist bravado, rhetorical ability, and the declaration of a ghetto and/or African identity were central to the assumption of leadership in BPUM. As Cecil Moore had during Operation Girard, BPUM activists offered the movement a strong masculine leadership unafraid to fulfill its responsibility to defend black families and communities from racial terror.[61]

Although BPUM never achieved its goal of becoming a mass-based black nationalist organization, the group's members worked with others in the local movement's growing Black Power wing to make issues of racial consciousness and community control the focus of black activism in the city. During the summer of 1966, even protests that differed little from earlier civil rights campaigns were transformed into Black Power moments. On July 13, three hundred people attended a Philadelphia CORE protest against alleged discrimination in promotions in the city's post office; nine activists, including Bill Mathis, the new president of the local CORE chapter, were arrested for blocking entrances to the post office. Of course, protesters demonstrating against job discrimination had been a common sight in Philadelphia since 1963. By the July 1966 protests, however, Philadelphia CORE, like the national organization, had endorsed Stokely Carmichael's call for Black Power. Thus, the CORE protesters now chanted Black Power slogans and carried Black Power signs and local president Mathis gave a speech declaring, "some think 'Black Power' means violence. But the Democratic and Republican Parties have 'White Power.' . . . We just want to control the police, merchants, [and] loan companies . . . in our communities." The protests also demonstrated the multiple affiliations of the mostly young activists who now identified themselves with the movement's Black Power wing. Those arrested included veterans of the 1965 Girard protest campaign; Barry Dawson was now a member of the Philadelphia SNCC staff, while Kenneth "Freedom" Smith and Carole West were both active in the Young Militants, the youth activist group that had emerged from Operation Girard.[62]

Three Black Power rallies organized during the summer of 1966 highlighted efforts to shift the focus of the local movement from integration to race consciousness and community control. Alternately sponsored by BPUM, the Young Militants and the local chapters of CORE and SNCC, two of the rallies featured Stokely Carmichael, the SNCC national chairman whose June 1966 Black Power speech had made him into a national icon of black militancy; the third was a memorial tribute to Malcolm X which featured speeches from Malcolm's widow Betty Shabazz, the poet Le Roi Jones (later known as Amiri Baraka), and, most interesting, given the circumstances of Malcolm's assassination, Churchville's former mentor Jeremiah X, minister of the Nation of Islam's Philadelphia mosque. Carmichael's first speech took place on July 17 in the parish hall of the Church of the Advocate. Chaired by BPUM's Walter Palmer, the rally featured jazz singer Nina Simone and speakers from the local chapters of CORE and SNCC. In his keynote speech, Carmichael called on "black people in this country . . . to talk to each other and stop talking to and for white people" and urged whites in the movement to shift their focus to organizing against racism in white communities. He told blacks to pool their resources to buy out white-owned ghetto businesses. If the owner refused to sell, he concluded, "boycott him out of existence." In addition to Jones's poetry, the Malcolm X tribute included a performance by the Arthur Hall Afro-American Dance Ensemble. BPUM leaders Walter Palmer and Mattie Humphrey both spoke. American blacks, Humphrey declared, "know better than any other group that white people are not the best looking and not the best behaved people on earth." Finally on August 30, Carmichael returned to Philadelphia to protest police raids on the NSM Freedom Library and SNCC's Philadelphia office. "Philadelphia," he told a crowd of two thousand on the front steps of Church of the Advocate, "is a racist city run by police Gestapo." According to the *Bulletin,* the crowd responded to the SNCC chair's speech with chants of "Black Power" and "down with white people."[63]

At each of these rallies, cultural concerns received as much attention as political ones. Overturning the racial imagery that naturalized white superiority and black inferiority was of central importance to the primarily young activists of the emergent Black Power movement. In his first speech, Carmichael mocked notions of the superiority of Euro-American culture with sarcastic references to legendary historic figures and icons of pop culture. "No longer," he declared, "must we say the white man is Alexander the Great, but instead Alexander the Barbaric. I'm getting tired of looking at . . . Tarzan beating up black people. I want to see some of those black people beat the hell out of Tarzan and send him home." In the tradition of Malcolm X, he also drew on images of black criminality to condemn American policies in the third world. "Whites are right," he joked, "when they say Negroes act as savages when they riot in Watts . . . because to be civilized means to drop bombs on your enemy as America is doing in Vietnam." The rallies also sought to challenge racialized notions of physical attractiveness. Carmichael described civilization as "nappy haired, broadlipped, wide-mouthed black people," while local SNCC staff member Louella Scott urged her listeners "to recognize that there is a beauty in blackness."[64]

The peak of BPUM's influence came when the group hosted the Third National Conference on Black Power at the Church of the Advocate on the weekend of August 29, 1968. The conference brought together many of Black Power's leading national figures, including Dr. Nathan Wright, an Episcopal priest who had hosted the previous summer's conference in Newark, New Jersey, the poet and playwright Amiri Baraka, Maulana Karenga of the Los Angeles-based US Organization, Richard Henry of the Detroit-based Republic of New Africa, and the Revolutionary Action Movement's Max Stanford. According to Wright, the purpose of the conference was to forge a unified program for the Black Power movement. The conference delegates, Wright declared in a July press conference at the Church of the Advocate, would consider the question of "reform or revolution as the only alternative for humanizing this society." The conference, he promised, would "deal with methods, techniques and strategies to forge a black nation in thought, experience, and commitment by unifying all black brothers and sisters."[65]

Paul Washington served as host committee chair and Walter Palmer as conference coordinator. The most challenging issues facing the host committee had to do with relations with the media and the police. The 1967 conference had ended in a small riot after conference delegates angry at inflammatory news coverage of the gathering had attacked white reporters. The planning committee for the Philadelphia conference therefore decided to bar reporters from all conference sessions except a workshop on blacks and the media and instead to form a communications committee to inform the public of conference developments. To coordinate the communications effort, Palmer recruited Frankie Davenport, a political reporter for the *Tribune*.[66]

The Newark conference had also been plagued by tensions with the Newark police. As I shall discuss shortly, by 1968 Philadelphia also had a two-year history of conflict between Black Power activists and the police. To prevent a reoccurrence of the Newark fiasco, therefore, Palmer negotiated with Philadelphia police officials to keep white officers a significant distance from the conference site and to allow off-duty members of the Guardian Civic League, the local organization of black police officers, to provide conference security. All went well until the conference's final day when three white police officers shouted racial obscenities at conference delegates as they stood on a street corner. The crisis was averted, however, when police officials announced that they had suspended the three officers.[67]

An estimated two thousand people attended the conference plenaries and workshop sessions on subjects like education, politics, economics, and culture. Still, ideological differences and personality clashes between the conference's leading figures prevented the conference from adopting a unified Black Power program. Wright was a proponent of what would become known as black capitalism and recruited a number of companies to serve as corporate sponsors for both the Newark and Philadelphia conferences. Wright's brother was an executive with Clairol Company and he was able to convince Clairol's president to write a letter of invitation to the Philadelphia conference. Still, acceptance of corporate sponsorship did not mean endorsement of capitalist economic strategies for many of the conference's most prominent figures. Differences also emerged between cultural nationalists and revolutionary nationalists over whether the Black Power movement should focus its efforts on reviving black consciousness or on achieving political control over black communities and identifying with third world revolutionary movements. Most damaging to the conference's goals were suspicions that various of the Black Power leaders in attendance were angling to control the conference so as to establish themselves as the movement's most powerful figure, suspicions that may well have been exacerbated by the covert activities of police agents. The Third National Conference on Black Power would also prove to be the last.[68]

The disarray within the conference leadership did not prevent the conference from having a significant impact on Black Power activism in Philadelphia. The housing workshop, for example, emphasized strategies for accessing government funds for building and renovating low-income housing. The workshop led directly to the formation of a number of nonprofit housing corporations, including the Advocate Community Development

Corporation which Christine Washington, Paul Washington's wife, ran from the offices of the Church of the Advocate.[69] In the political workshop, activists began planning for a local Black Political Convention that would play a crucial role in the development of an independent black Democratic movement in the city.[70] Finally, the work of the communications committee led Frankie Davenport (who would soon change her name to Falakha Fattah) to establish an underground black newspaper, the *Voice of Umoja,* to serve the city's black activist community. Fattah would go on to build a network of black nationalist-influenced social service agencies in West Philadelphia, including the House of Umoja, a nationally known urban boys town for former gang members.[71]

SNCC Moves North

At the same time that the Black People's Unity Movement was establishing itself as the leading local advocate of the black nationalist politics of racial unity, SNCC's national leadership decided to make Philadelphia the test site for its effort to bring its particular mix of community organizing and black empowerment to the urban North. Disillusioned by the unwillingness of the Democratic Party's liberal wing to support fundamental political reform in the South, SNCC's community organizers had increasingly come to identify with Malcolm X's black nationalist political vision. In "The Angry Children of Malcolm X," a 1966 essay on SNCC's evolution from an interracial to a Black Power organization, Julius Lester, a member of the group's field staff, argued that "Malcolm X was responsible for the new militancy that entered The Movement in 1965. Malcolm X said aloud those things which Negroes had been saying among themselves . . . He spoke directly and eloquently to black men, analyzing their situation, their predicament . . . what it all meant for a black man in America."[72]

Following the 1964 Democratic National Convention, SNCC had begun to shift its political strategy from building coalitions with northern liberals toward Malcolm X's vision of an independent black politics. Specifically, SNCC's community organizing projects in the rural South shifted their focus to strategies for winning black political office independent of the traditional political parties. In Lowndes County, Alabama, for example, the SNCC-organized Lowndes County Freedom Organization (LCFO) ran candidates for county political offices against the white-only Democratic Party. LCFO drew national attention for its use of the black panther as a symbol for the campaign. As described by LCFO chairman John Hulett, the panther was chosen to distinguish the LCFO from the turn-the-other-cheek pacifism of mainstream civil rights leaders. The panther "never bothers anything, but when you start pushing him he moves backward . . . into his corner, and then he comes out to destroy everything that's before him."[73]

With the election of Stokely Carmichael, the director of the Lowndes

County project, as SNCC's national chairman in May 1965, the LCFO became the model for SNCC's efforts to promote independent black electoral politics. At the same time, Carmichael and his supporters saw the Harlem, North Philadelphia, and Watts riots as evidence that SNCC's brand of community organizing and independent electoral politics could win a significant following in the ghettos of the urban North. In 1965, Fred Meely, a longtime member of SNCC's Mississippi staff, arrived in Philadelphia to establish a full-fledged SNCC-sponsored community organizing project in the city. James Forman, who was SNCC's executive secretary from 1961 to 1966, would later write that the Philadelphia project was "the first attempt, in a major metropolitan area, to develop the concept of a national Freedom organization with the panther as its symbol."[74]

Before Meely's arrival, the Philadelphia SNCC office had focused solely fundraising for the group's southern campaigns. Local support work for SNCC began in April 1960, when the Fellowship House's Marjorie Penney and Joyce Barrett, a Temple University student who ran the settlement house's college student group, made a tour of southern campuses that had been active in the sit-in movement and then attended the SNCC-founding conference at Shaw University. Over the next four years, the Fellowship House would send a constant flow of volunteers, funds, and supplies to SNCC.[75] Most dramatically, Prathia Hall, a Temple graduate and Fellowship House activist, was shot and wounded while working as a volunteer in SNCC's Southwest Georgia project in September 1962.[76]

The fundraising and publicity efforts of Philadelphia Friends of SNCC reached their peak during the Freedom Summer campaign in Mississippi. Led by Barrett, the local committee recruited and trained twenty local college student volunteers to travel to Mississippi. Central to the strategy of Freedom Summer was the placement of articles about the northern volunteers and their families in their hometown newspapers. Shortly after the three civil rights workers disappeared from a Neshoba County, Mississippi, jail in June 1964, the parents of the Philadelphia volunteers announced the formation of the Parents Emergency Committee for Protection of Students in the Mississippi Summer Project and issued a public call for the federal government to provide protection for the summers volunteers and other civil rights workers in Mississippi.[77]

Philadelphia Friends of SNCC continued to focus its efforts on supporting the group's southern efforts in the year following the defeat of the SNCC-sponsored Mississippi Freedom Democratic Party (MFDP) at the 1964 Democratic National Convention.[78] But with Fred Meely's arrival in Philadelphia, the focus of SNCC's work in Philadelphia turned to local organizing. Meely recruited an all-black project staff made up of veterans of SNCC's southern projects, NSM members, and local youth activists. All of the project staff worked at SNCC's famous field secretary wage of $10 per week.

The End of the Beloved Community

Charyn Sutton's progression from a high school Gandhian to an organizer on the staff of Philadelphia SNCC is instructive in what it reveals about the process that led many young black movement activists to abandon the ideal of the beloved community for the politics of black nationalism. As I have said, Sutton's first taste of civil rights protest came as a preteen when her father and Paul Washington organized a group of black neighborhood children to protest their exclusion from a Southwest Philadelphia municipal swimming pool. As a high school student, Sutton was an active participant in By Youth Itself, a Fellowship House-based interracial high school activist group, and Student CORE, the youth wing of Philadelphia CORE. The CORE students, she remembers, were very proud to be one of the few CORE youth chapters in the country and to be invited to participate in many of the adult chapters' protest campaigns. As a high school senior, Sutton was "just absolutely devastated that I couldn't go south . . . for the Mississippi Freedom Summer. But they were requiring that you had to be eighteen."[79]

While still in high school, Sutton also worked as a tutor in NSM's Philadelphia Tutorial Project. And when she moved to the Boston-area to attend Brandeis University she joined the group's Boston tutorial program. It was while working in Boston that she first remembers becoming concerned by the role white activists were playing in black communities. "What I saw in the NSM tutorial projects was a lot of the white people helping poor little black people but yet some of those same whites . . . were upset about interracial dating [and] felt that affirmative action wasn't really good . . . It was very paternalistic . . . nice white people helping dumb black people."[80] It was not simply the character of the relationship between the white tutors and the black children that led Sutton to rethink her commitment to interracialism. It was also the kind of relationships that emerged between black and white activists in the organization. Given the social taboos surrounding interracial sex, it is not surprising that there was a significant amount of cross-racial dating and relationships within the student movement of the early 1960s. The focus on interpersonal relationships and sexual activity contributed to the sense of black activists like Charyn Sutton that many of their white counterparts were not sufficiently serious about the movement's mission, that they had the movement version of what Spike Lee would later call "jungle fever." "There also was a lot of playacting," Sutton remembers, "people involved in the movement because it was interesting and daring and . . . a chance to get back at daddy or mommy by dating a black or dating a white. . . . I think there was a sense that . . . that kind of non-serious behavior . . . would dissipate if it was an all-black movement."[81]

After one year at Brandeis, Sutton dropped out to join the staff of NSM's New York headquarters. By then, she saw herself as a committed black nationalist and full-time community organizer. "My politics [were] shifting . . . I was becoming much more black nationalist, much more focused on Africa." The strategic component of the student movement's turn toward nationalism was also evident in NSM and SNCC's continued emphasis on electoral politics. As a member of the NSM staff, Sutton was posted to SNCC's Atlanta headquarters to work on Julian Bond's state legislative campaign. Sutton's time in Atlanta was part of an ongoing "effort to coordinate work between SNCC as the southern link of the movement, and NSM as the northern link." The continued close working relationship between the two student groups would have important implications for the emergence of Black Power in Philadelphia.[82]

The Philadelphia Freedom Organization

From Atlanta, Charyn Sutton returned to Philadelphia and soon thereafter joined the staff of SNCC's Philadelphia project. Under Fred Meely's leadership, Philadelphia SNCC sought to build a local version of the Lowndes County Freedom Organization. Thus, Meely trained the staff in an organizing "model" in which, as Sutton describes it, "the organizer . . . goes into the community, mobilizes the community, but does not make him or herself a permanent part of that structure, the idea being that you could walk out of it, and it would continue." Meely also taught that community people had to be allowed to make their own mistakes. "Even if you knew certain kinds of activities were not going to pan out," Sutton remembers him arguing, "if you just simply told people that and forced them to go in the direction you thought they needed to go, then they wouldn't learn. The best you could do is to kind of speed that process, and at least be ready to redirect folks when things didn't work . . . to help them get the lessons out of it, so the people just didn't give up when they had failures."[83]

Specifically, Meely and his staff envisioned the Philadelphia Freedom Organization (PFO) as a community-based organization led by and for residents of Philadelphia's black working-class communities that could serve as an independent alternative to the city's mainstream political parties. The PFO's membership card listed eight "purposes and aims" including "to unify the people"; "to see that black people can participate freely in a true democracy"; and "to assure that the Negro community selects [its] candidates." Canvassing the city's black working-class neighborhoods, the staff sought, in Sutton words, "to use the southern model to get people registered to vote and . . . involved in electoral politics. We'd give little booklets that . . . talked about . . . the Freedom organization." One booklet included sections on "What Is The Vote?," "What Is Politics?," and "Why Come Together?" The answers that the booklet gave to these questions were remarkably sanguine about the possibilities for achieving black political power through the American electoral system. "When you vote," the book-

let read, "you speak for yourself about things concerning your own welfare.
. . . When we come together we can determine who from our . . . area can
best represent us in getting the things we want done . . . If we don't come
together, the people who have been running the show will put their own
candidates up . . . and we will have no say at all."[84]

From the start, the staff of Philadelphia SNCC made clear their commitment to promoting leadership from within the city's poor and working-
class black neighborhoods. In an interview with the *Tribune*, staff member
Morris Ruffin declared that "there has never been a legitimate black grassroots movement that has come out of the city. What has happened traditionally is that the bourgeois has constantly spoke incorrectly for the black
community. . . . What we will do is assist in bringing out the true black
community." The PFO booklet asked, "Do you know someone who lives on
your street who would make a good city councilman, a good state senator, a
good congressman, a good mayor or a good judge?" As Ruffin's comments
suggest, Philadelphia SNCC saw poor black communities as the site of an
authentic black identity. "If we could elect people who are not ashamed of
us or of being black or Negro," the booklet continued, "they would work
for us." Charyn Sutton remembers the challenge of building an organization that encompassed the entire community as "stressful." At twenty years
of age, she was working "with the longshoremen . . . go[ing] into bars. . . .
I remember my uncle calling my father and being very upset because I was
showing up in bars. But we figured we had to organize the people who were
drinking." At the same time, the staff encountered tensions between the
very people that they were trying to organize, in Sutton's words, " 'nice people' not wanting to organize with 'low-lifes.' " But even these tensions were
treated as an organizing opportunity. "You've gotta be able to let people,"
Sutton argues, "go through some of that stress. If you short-circuit it, then
they wouldn't be able to keep those organizations together after you've
left."[85]

In their canvassing, the Philadelphia staff sought to identify the Freedom
Organization with the rage that had been expressed in the 1964 North Philadelphia riot. A poem in one PFO leaflet mocked white anxiety about the
urban riots.

If you were president
And if you were white
And if there were riots in your cities
And if the people rioting were black
Well, you would probably try to destroy those black power people
The ones who keep saying that . . .
Black people riot because they are the last hired and the first fired
The ones who keep saying that . . .
Black people riot because they are fighting for their lives against this white racist
society.[86]

As part of their effort to demonstrate the relevance of electoral politics to the daily lives of black Philadelphians, SNCC canvassers focused on the issue of police brutality and, in particular, on "how damaging and dangerous" Deputy Police Commissioner Frank Rizzo was to the black community. They believed Rizzo's reputation for brutality, the threat that police violence posed to black lives in the city, and the fact that he had been appointed by a mayor who owed his election to black voters could provide the same object lesson of the importance of voting that the small-town sheriff had for SNCC's voter registration projects in the South.[87]

Philadelphia SNCC, of course, faced a vastly different political terrain than the group had found in the Mississippi Delta and other areas of the rural South. While southern blacks had been excluded from the political process for generations, Philadelphia's black voters had played an active and increasingly important role in the patronage-based machine politics throughout the twentieth century. To promote its vision of an independent black political organization, Philadelphia SNCC had to convince the residents of the city's poor black communities not only of the relevance of the electoral process but also to stop giving their votes to the Democratic machine. Much of SNCC's canvassing therefore focused on "how you put together a political party, how you get on the ballot, how you get enough votes, how you go through the paperwork."[88]

Beginning their efforts at the height of the NAACP's Girard College campaign, Philadelphia SNCC also had to confront the popularity that Cecil Moore enjoyed within the black community and the NAACP president's reluctance to share the mantle of civil rights leadership within the city. Sutton remembers that the SNCC staff was "very much opposed to" the Girard protests as "just another effort . . . to get white folks to let us come into their" institutions. SNCC's critique of Operation Girard was couched in language reminiscent of Moore's attacks on his liberal critics. "We were very much about," Sutton recalls, "self-determination and . . . ownership of our own programs, ownership of our own politics." To achieve its goal of building a mass community-based organization committed to independent politics, SNCC was thus committed to "splitting . . . the [black] community [between] the Cecil people and the NAACP and . . . the black nationalists." SNCC had long feuded with charismatic civil rights leaders like Dr. King and the Philadelphia staff was confident it could overcome Moore's popularity in the city's black neighborhoods. "We had a lot of support in the community," Sutton remembers. They "thought we were great kids."[89]

The effort to build the PFO reflected SNCC's continued belief that political action within the American electoral system was the key to ending racial oppression in the country. In the historiography of the civil rights movement, SNCC's effort to build mass community organizations like LCFO and PFO are usually seen as a brief interlude in its transformation from a group committed to liberal reform to one believing in the necessity

of revolutionary change. From a local perspective, however, SNCC's enduring legacy was this effort to develop black community-based organizations
and political parties capable of enabling the residents of majority black
communities to take control of local political institutions and their atten-
dant financial resources. In "The Philadelphia Black Paper," an analysis of
the impact of the Philadelphia Freedom Organization, James Forman
wrote that the continuing process of white flight made northern cities
"obviously a growing base of black political power." In this sense, SNCC's
embrace of Black Power and community control represented not an abandonment of the electoral process but a shift from the coalition model of
interracial liberalism to the ethnic mobilization model of urban political
machine. "Black power," SNCC Chairman Stokely Carmichael wrote in
1966, "means the creation of power bases from which black people can
work to change statewide or nationwide patterns of oppression. . . . Politically, black power means what it has always meant to SNCC: the coming-
together of black people to elect representatives and *to force those representatives to speak to their needs*" (emphasis Carmichael's). Just as urban political
machines had historically harnessed the resources of local government to
support the economic advancement of European immigrants, SNCC
believed that the mass organizations that it was building could use black
votes to win control of the public resources necessary to fuel the economic
development of poor black communities.[90]

Constructing the White Backlash Against Black Power

At the same time that SNCC was attempting to challenge the Democratic
machine's control over the black vote, its attacks on the machine and the
police provided racial conservatives with an opportunity to mobilize the
Democrats' white working- and lower middle-class constituencies against
the party's commitment to liberal reform. The more movement activists in
groups like SNCC and BPUM effectively demonstrated the ineffectualness
of liberal efforts to create a racially just society, the more conservatives were
able to position themselves as the only ones able to defend white working-
class jobs, schools, and neighborhoods. If, in fact, the turn toward black
nationalism was a response to the ways that the defense of white privilege
remained an unspoken organizing principle in Philadelphia's politics,
labor markets, and neighborhoods, then it is ironic, though not surprising,
that black activists' efforts to use race as the explicit basis for political and
community organization provided the rationale for the reemergence of an
avowedly white racial politics in the city.

The central institution in the resurgence of conservative politics in Philadelphia was the Philadelphia police department. As early as the local elections of the mid-1950s, there had been evidence of white support for racial

conservatism in Philadelphia. Following the 1963 construction pickets, members of the all-white building trades unions clearly resented Mayor Tate's unwillingness to defend the membership policies of their craft unions. And in the aftermath of the North Philadelphia riot, the Fraternal Order of Police was able to win significant support both from rank-and-file officers and in white working-class neighborhoods for its campaign against the Police Advisory Board. However, it was only after top officials in the police department made surveillance of black movement activists a major priority that conservative approaches to managing racial conflict emerged as a viable alternative to the liberal ethos that had dominated City Hall since 1951. Frank Rizzo not only rose from the rank of captain to police commissioner between 1963 and 1967 but he positioned himself as the most important articulator of racial conservatism in the city by seeking to prove to the residents of the city's white working-class neighborhoods that only aggressive police action could prevent black militants from overrunning their neighborhoods, schools, and workplaces.

Ironically, it was under the leadership of Howard Leary, the liberal commissioner whose support of the Police Advisory Board and cautious handling of the 1964 riot would lead to his appointment as police commissioner for New York City in 1965, that the police department established a special unit to monitor civil rights demonstrations. The civil disobedience squad as it was known soon expanded its mission to maintaining extensive surveillance on civil rights militants and other radical activists in the city.[91] Still, it was not until the series of clashes between protesters and the police during the 1965 Girard College protests that culminated in the incident in which Deputy Commissioner Rizzo punched a demonstrator that the department shifted its focus from monitoring demonstrations to developing strategies for preventing what it perceived to be a growing potential for movement-inspired violence in the city.

By 1966, Deputy Commissioner Rizzo—with at least the implicit consent of the new commissioner Edward Bell—had embarked on a concerted drive to discredit Black Power activists in the city. Rizzo proved particularly adept at citing the increasingly militant rhetoric of black nationalist activists to inflame concerns among a white public that the city was under threat of an impending wave of black political violence. Just as developments outside Philadelphia often motivated changes in the strategies and tactics utilized by civil rights activists in the city, so too Rizzo was able to use the pronouncements of national movement figures to justify intensification of the police department's antimovement initiatives. Thus, in the weeks after Stokely Carmichael's June 1966 call for Black Power made national headlines, Rizzo focused his public concern on Philadelphia SNCC's organizing project rather than on groups like the Young Militants that had been at the center of previous police-movement confrontations.[92]

According to Charyn Sutton, Philadelphia SNCC's staff and office became the subject of almost constant police surveillance during the summer of 1966. "A lot of the surveillance operations were so . . . obvious," she recalls, "that it seemed that the effort was not as much to . . . get information on us, as to terrorize us and to frighten us, to give us the sense that we're always being followed . . . always being traced, that nothing that we say is private . . . and that they're just in control of everything." Sutton remembers believing that the police placed undercover officers in the taxicabs that served the area near Philadelphia SNCC's headquarters. More than once, the drivers of the cabs that she flagged down seemed to know her destination without having to ask. Members of the civil disobedience squad openly patrolled the August 4 tribute to Malcolm X. What SNCC believed to be a campaign of police harassment reached a peak on August 10, 1966 when project staff member Barry Dawson was followed and then beaten unconscious by a car full of unidentified whites. Dawson's assailants called him by name, leading him to believe that they were police officers.[93]

In the early morning hours of Saturday, August 13, eighty "heavily armed" police, backed up by one thousand uniformed officers, raided four buildings: SNCC's Center City office, the NSM Freedom Library, and two North Philadelphia apartments, one belonging to Fred Meely and the second to "Freedom" George Brower, the leader of the Young Militants, a protest group founded on the Girard picket line with close ties to Cecil Moore and the NAACP. At the time, John Churchville and his wife were living in an apartment above the Freedom Library. He remembers that the police banged on his door in the early morning hours. "They came in with . . . sawed-off shotguns and bulletproof vests." A white officer whom Churchville believed to be the squad leader pushed him up against a kitchen cabinet, apparently "trying to start something." In a press conference held later that morning, Deputy Police Commissioner Rizzo announced that the police had raided the "four SNCC offices" based on an informant's tip "that the meeting places for the militant civil rights groups were becoming storehouses for arms, ammunition and dynamite." The police, he continued, had confiscated two and a half sticks of dynamite from the Brower apartment as well as important documents from all four offices. Four SNCC members, Rizzo announced, had been arrested and were being held on $50,000 bond: Barry Dawson, Eugene Dawkins, and Carole West, all of whom were in Brower's apartment, and Brower himself when he turned himself in later in the morning. Rizzo's charge that the raids had thwarted SNCC's efforts to amass ammunition for a plot to blow up Independence Hall was duly reported on the front pages of the city's daily newspapers.[94]

Rizzo seems to have been deliberately misleading in his efforts to pin the dynamite case on SNCC. In fact, the police had failed to find any evidence of dynamite or any other weaponry in their searches of the SNCC office, Meely's apartment, or the NSM Freedom Library, a group that had at least some demonstrable connection to SNCC. Furthermore, Brower, Dawkins and West not only had no ties to SNCC, but they were well known to police as leading figures in the Young Militants. Of the four, only Dawson was a member of the SNCC staff. A native Philadelphian, he had been arrested for spitting on a police officer during the Girard protests long before joining the SNCC staff.[95]

The media offensive against SNCC continued through the weekend and into the next week. By Saturday evening, Rizzo was able to announce that Dawson had signed a voluntary confession and that warrants had been issued for four other SNCC members, Fred Meely, Morris Ruffin and George Anderson, both of whom were members of the Philadelphia staff, and Winston Ealy, whom Rizzo described as "a member of SNCC's national board." Meely, Ruffin, and Anderson managed to get out of town before they could be arrested. On Sunday, however, the police detained Ealy and a second man, James Jenkins, and charged them with delivering the dynamite to Dawson. Only after Ealy's arrest did the police publicly acknowledge that he was not a SNCC member and that the only civil rights group to which he belonged was the NAACP. By Monday, Brower, Dawkins, and West had been released from custody on their own recognizance. Shortly thereafter, a black police inspector arranged for prominent local black leaders to see a collection of police photographs that allegedly showed people carrying bags of dynamite in and out of the SNCC office.[96]

Rizzo seems also to have had the tacit cooperation of Cecil Moore in his efforts to publicly discredit SNCC. After volunteering to represent the four arrested during the raids, Moore publicly called on the three SNCC fugitives to surrender. In his comments, Moore appeared to be blaming the dynamite on those members of the SNCC staff who were not native Philadelphians. They were, he told the *Tribune*, "cowardly treacherous people who are not concerned about Negroes." He further asked "what can nine sticks [of dynamite] do but hurt our own people?" and called on Morris Ruffin to "come out of a hole and tell where the rest of the dynamite is because all he's doing is using my folk as pawns to pull his funny little games." As former SNCC Executive Secretary James Forman would later comment, in an internal memorandum, it was certainly unusual for an attorney to publicly presume the guilt of a client. Forman, in fact, charged that Moore had convinced the police to release Brower, West, and Dawkins—the three Young Militants—in return for a voluntary confession from Dawson. According to Forman, Moore then told Dawson that "the only way that the other people could get off" was for him to confess. Whether or not these charges were true, Moore and Rizzo did seem to form an unlikely alliance during the dynamite case. After an assistant district attorney acknowledged to the *New York Times* that the four who had been arrested were all members of the NAACP, not SNCC, an unnamed police official told the *Times* that "the largest and most influential civil-rights organiza-

tion in Philadelphia, the local chapter of the NAACP, was in no way identified with any of those sought or arrested persons."[97]

With Dawson in jail and Meely, Ruffin, and Anderson in hiding, only
Charyn Sutton, Lenore Moore, and four other women were available to
staff the Philadelphia SNCC office. Unlike southern police forces that were
quick to arrest both female and male SNCC workers, the Philadelphia
police seemed to view SNCC's women workers as inconsequential to the
project's organizing efforts. Ironically, the cops' implicit male chauvinism
seems to have been shared by SNCC's national leadership, which did not
believe that the Philadelphia women could manage the situation on their
own. In the early morning hours of Sunday, August 14, the SNCC national
office decided to send James Forman, the group's former executive secretary, and four other longtime male staff members to Philadelphia when
they discovered "that there were only six girls in the SNCC office." Before
Forman could arrive, the women staffers successfully prevented the police
from conducting a second search of the SNCC office. Still, they were quietly encouraged to leave town once Forman had arrived, though not before
they had finished cleaning the office from the aftereffects of the raid. As
Sutton remembers, the concern was that the police might try to "get us,
arrest us, grill us, maybe try to implicate us."[98]

Not surprisingly, SNCC believed that the raids represented the beginning of a deliberate campaign to depict it as a terrorist organization in
retaliation for its endorsement of Black Power and the right to self-defense.
Shortly after the raids, Stokely Carmichael, Ruby Doris Robinson, and
Cleveland Sellers, SNCC's top three elected officials, issued the following
warning to the group's staff. "We feel there is a growing trend of 'plants',
frames, indictments, and other attacks, intended to destroy not only the
effectiveness of SNCC as a political force but to completely destroy the
organization. In short, the WORD IS OUT and WAR HAS BEEN
DECLARED against us." On August 19, Forman held a press conference
in Philadelphia in which he claimed to "have good evidence that the dynamite was planted by the police" and charged that Rizzo, whom he called
the "Cisco Kid" and the "real Mayor," had orchestrated the frame-up.[99]

While Forman refused to provide evidence for his charges to the Philadelphia press, *The Movement*, a monthly newsletter published by SNCC's
San Francisco Bay Area office, soon published an analysis of the dynamite
conspiracy that focused on contradictions in the public statements made
by police officials about the case. For example, the police first claimed that
Dawson had confessed that he and Ealy had removed the dynamite from a
construction site, then reported that Jenkins confessed to having stolen the
dynamite. Even more embarrassing to the police was their failure to find
more than two and a half sticks of dynamite or any blasting caps necessary
to explode dynamite. Even when Jenkins led them and an army ordinance
expert to the backyard of his home where he claimed to have buried the

dynamite and blasting caps and dug a four-feet-wide, fifteen-feet-long, and two-feet-deep trench, they were only able to find "several pieces of doorbell wire." As a result, the only evidence that the police were able to offer to corroborate the confessions was a photograph that *The Movement* dubbed "The X-Ray Photo." Taken by a member of the police department's civil disobedience squad, the photograph showed Dawson and Ruffin holding paper bags in front of the SNCC office. While the bags' contents were not visible in the photograph, the police insisted that Dawson had told them that they were full of dynamite.[100]

The dynamite case dropped from the headlines of the Philadelphia newspapers after SNCC lawyer Len Holt managed to raise a number of questions about Dawson's confession in a bail hearing on August 21. In November, Meely, Ruffin, and Anderson quietly surrendered to the district attorney's office and the charges against them were dismissed the following April. In his 1972 memoir, Forman cited Dawson's confession to ridicule the police claim to have uncovered a violent conspiracy. Dawson acknowledged receiving the dynamite from Jenkins and Ealy and said he brought it to the SNCC office while Meely was out of town. When Meely returned, however, he insisted that Dawson remove the dynamite from the office. Meely, Dawson, and Morris Ruffin each then left the office carrying a bag containing one-third of the dynamite. This seems to be the moment that the police photographers took the photo of Dawson and Ruffin holding the paper bags. Meely and Ruffin were able to dispose of their bags of dynamite into one of the city's two rivers. According to Dawson's confession, however, he panicked when he believed he was being followed by people he assumed to be police officers and took his bag of dynamite to George Brower's house. As Forman put it, the only thing Dawson seems to have been guilty of was "a serious error in judgment."[101]

Despite the exoneration of the SNCC staff, the Philadelphia project had been brought to a standstill by the concerted efforts of the Philadelphia police department and would never recover. "The police had won a larger battle," James Forman conceded in his memoir. "The momentum generated by our activities in the black community declined and SNCC lost its base in Philadelphia." In an internal memorandum written in 1966, Forman argued prophetically that the events in Philadelphia were "symptomatic of the increasingly open and avowed fascist tactics of police departments. . . . The police forces are the arm of the most reactionary elements in the city . . . these reactionary ideas tend increasingly to ensure that the police operate to suppress the legitimate aspirations of people within the inner city . . . the legitimate aspirations of black people."[102]

What is most extraordinary about the police campaign against SNCC was that it was directed at a group explicitly committed to working within the electoral process. For SNCC's young organizers, the police harassment served as an object lesson of white society's determination to prevent substantive racial change from taking place. In that context, it is not surprising that the political wing of the Black Power movement would increasingly turn to revolutionary means for achieving its goals.

*   *   *

The emergence of BPUM and the Philadelphia Freedom Organization and the transformation of the local CORE chapter into a Black Power group portended the emergence of a significant generational challenge to the liberal reform coalition that, though weakened, continued to dominate political discourse in Philadelphia. Over the course of the late 1960s and early 1970s, a new generation of activists—black and white and influenced by both the civil rights and antiwar movements—would emerge to challenge the liberal orthodoxy that had animated reform efforts in postwar Philadelphia. In their efforts to more justly distribute power and wealth in the city, this new generation of activists turned to the principles of community-based leadership, participatory democracy, and racial self-determination to replace liberalism's faith in antidiscrimination laws, technocratic government, and the New Deal coalition.[103]

Perhaps the most important legacy of the Black Power movement in Philadelphia, however, was its impact on the nature of black political leadership in the city. During the first half of the 1960s, selective patronage and Cecil Moore's reign as president of the Philadelphia NAACP had helped to shift the locus of black leadership from the Center City offices of liberal reform organizations to the city's black working-class neighborhoods. But it was the Black Power movement's commitment to community-based leadership that truly democratized black leadership in Philadelphia. While charismatic national Black Power leaders conducted an endless search for more and more media attention, black student organizing and other forms of community-based activism in Philadelphia served to decenter the structure of black leadership in the city. No longer could a Leon Sullivan or a Cecil Moore operate as the city's most dominant black movement leader. Nor could movement leadership be restricted to middle-class professionals. As will be evident in Part 3, the leadership of future black movement organizations and campaigns in Philadelphia would include significant and substantive representation of working-class activists from the city's poor black neighborhoods.

Part III
Black Power in the Postindustrial City

Chapter 6
Community Control of the Schools

> Give the white-dominated school system an eviction from the black community.
>
> —*Philadelphia CORE leaflet, November 17, 1967*

On the morning of Friday, November 17, 1967 at 9:50 A.M., someone pulled the fire alarm at Bok Vocational High School at Ninth and Mifflin Streets in South Philadelphia. By the time, students and faculty were allowed back in the building, a group of about two hundred students had begun to march the ten blocks to Southern (South Philadelphia) High School at South Broad and Snyder Streets where another hundred students joined their march. From Southern, the students headed north, some on foot, some on the Broad Street subway, toward Center City. Their destination was the Board of Education's main administration building at Twenty-First Street and the Benjamin Franklin Parkway, on the far northwestern edge of Center City. A second stream of marchers began at Germantown High School in the Northwest section of the city. More than 200 students walked out of Germantown during the 10 A.M. lunch period and began marching down Germantown Avenue, many wearing skullcaps in the school's green and white colors and gold "Black Power" buttons. Just before reaching the corner of Broad and Erie, the Germantown students met up with a group of marchers from Gratz High School. Some of the now nearly five hundred students then took the Broad Street subway to City Hall, while others marched south on Broad toward William Penn and Ben Franklin High Schools, twin single-sex schools located just north of Center City, before heading west to the parkway (Figure 12). A third stream of fifty marchers began at Kensington High, an all-girls school in the lower northeast section of the city. The Kensington marchers walked three miles to Edison High, their all-male counterpart, before heading to the school board building. From the west came marchers from West Philadelphia, West Catholic, Overbrook, and Bartram High Schools.[1]

By 12:30 P.M., the crowd of demonstrators had swelled to more than

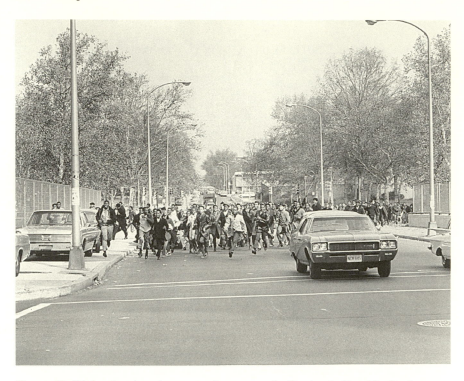

Figure 12. High school students running across the Benjamin Franklin Parkway toward the Board of Education, November 17, 1967. Urban Archives, Temple University Libraries.

3,500 students from at least twelve high schools marching around the Board of Education building.[2] According to a number of observers, the mood within the crowd of student protesters was festive as they waited for their leaders to return from the negotiating session. Like a number of adult activists, Paul Washington had arrived early in the demonstration "to show my support and to be of assistance." He left midmorning because he felt that "everything was proceeding so peaceably that my presence would not be needed." The *Bulletin* described the demonstrators as treating "the affair as a picnic." The students "laughed, asked news cameramen to take their pictures and danced before television cameras." Others chanted "beep, beep, bang, bang, boom, boom, Black Power" and carried signs calling for "more Black Power in the School System." Joan Countryman, who had just begun working in the school district's community relations division, remembers students calling out to their friends from different schools. "Who's here from West?" CORE activists distributed a leaflet that called for "Community Control" of black public schools as the only way to fix a school system in which the black dropout rate was nearly three times that of white students. "If the Philadelphia school system defeats your child now," the leaflet read, "he will remain defeated for the rest of his life . . . . Give the white-dominated school system an eviction from the black community."[3]

Shortly after the first demonstrators arrived at the Board of Education building, a committee of student activists, representing twelve high schools, and a number of adult advisers—including BPUM's Mattie Humphrey and Edward Robinson and Paul Vance from a black teachers group called the Educators' Roundtable—entered the building to meet with the school superintendent, Dr. Mark Shedd, and Richardson Dilworth and the Rev. Henry Nichols, the president and vice president of the school board respectively. There are conflicting stories as to how this meeting came about. According to Walter Palmer, the meeting was pre-arranged. The student committee had developed a list of twenty-five demands and had rehearsed its presentation to the school board officials with his and Humphrey's help. Others suggest that the request for the meeting came from school board officials who, impressed with how orderly the student protesters were, asked Humphrey if she would identify a group of student leaders who would be willing to meet with Dr. Shedd.[4] What is clear is that the student leaders and school board officials met for most of the morning in a room with large windows that overlooked the still-growing crowd of students in the streets below. In the meeting, the students presented a number of demands, including the addition of black history courses taught by black teachers, the assignment of black principals to black schools, increased black representation on the school board, exemption from the requirement that students salute the flag, and the removal of police and nonteaching assistants from all schools. According to Palmer, who was not in the meeting, at one point a student leader from Bok opened one of the large windows to yell out to the student protesters that the school board officials had agreed to twenty-four of their twenty-five demands.[5]

Despite the festive atmosphere on the student picket line, police officials seem to have become increasingly uneasy as the size of the crowd continued to grow. Palmer believes that police officials had not expected a very large group of students to show up that morning and thus made no attempt to keep cars from the metered parking spots in front of the building. He also remembers the police radios crackling with increasingly desperate reports of large numbers of students departing high schools across the city. At Dilworth's request, the only police officers on the scene when the morning began were members of Lieutenant George Fencl's plainclothes civil disobedience squad which had earned a reputation for maintaining cordial relations with black protesters. Dilworth and Shedd were clearly eager to maintain a dialogue with the students. Commissioner Rizzo, however, had urged a more aggressive approach, recommending that the school board seek a court order banning Walter Palmer and CORE's William Mathis from leading the rally. While Mathis would claim that Lieutenant Fencl had repeatedly complimented him on the students' good behavior throughout the morning, there was clearly concern within the police department over the size of the crowd.[6]

The only violent incident of the morning occurred just before noon. While reports differ, it seems that one male demonstrator began running over the tops of cars parked in front of the administration building. When members of the civil disobedience squad moved to arrest the young man, a group of about two hundred demonstrators surrounded the plainclothes officers. A young woman attempting to free the young man was then beaten and arrested. And when Rev. Marshall Bivins, a white Episcopal priest, sought to protect the young women, he too was beaten and arrested.[7]

What happened next continues to be a matter of some dispute. CORE's Bill Mathis would later testify that he successfully convinced Fencl to order his officers to retreat in order to give Mathis time to calm protesters who were moving dangerously close to the police lines as they played to the local news television cameras. According to Commissioner Rizzo, however, he received reports from Fencl that the protest "was getting out of hand," that the number of demonstrators was continuing to grow, and protesters were banging on parked cars and windows of the school board building. The commissioner, who had spent the morning at City Hall for the swearing-in of 111 new police sergeants, decided to load the sergeants into two police buses and head for the school board building. Rizzo and the sergeants arrived just as school board vice president Nichols was coming out of the building to investigate the disturbance. According to Nichols, he asked the commissioner to put away his nightstick and move the uniformed officers back from the school district building. Believing that Rizzo had agreed to this request, he then began trying to move the student demonstrators back. Rizzo, however, suddenly ordered his officers to charge the demonstrators with billy clubs drawn. The commissioner would later contend he ordered the charge because he saw the group of protesters surrounding the plainclothes officers begin to throw sawhorses that were used to reserve parking spaces for school board officials at the police. However, none of the journalists or other independent observers who were at the scene were ever able to confirm the commissioner's account. What local television news footage did seem to confirm was the charge of Nichols and a number of demonstrators that they had heard Rizzo order his officers to "get their black asses."[8]

The police charge was so vicious that many who witnessed it, including school board workers on their lunch hour, were reduced to tears. At its center, swinging his billy club freely, was Commissioner Rizzo. Most of the demonstrators, of course, had no idea of the events that led to the police charge. As Walter Palmer describes it, riot police with batons drawn suddenly, "without warning [and] without provocation," began pushing the students from the parkway toward the building, essentially trapping them. According to the police, Palmer yelled out to the crowd, "If they fight you, hit them back," a charge that Palmer now confirms. The police would also claim that Mathis began to shout "Kill Rizzo! Kill Rizzo!" through a bullhorn. Some students began to throw stones and bottles. Most, though, simply ran. Many were beaten as they ran from the charging police officers. According to a Fellowship Commission report, between twenty and thirty black students and adults were treated for injuries following the demonstration. Kenneth Blake, a sixteen-year-old student at Ben Franklin High, would receive five stitches under his left eye after being clubbed by this group of officers. One black school board employee was knocked to the ground and had his right sleeve torn off for urging the police to retreat. There were reports that some police officers laced their violence with racial epithets. One officer beat Dozier Smith, a seventeen-year-old school board maintenance worker, as he tried to enter the building. When he tried to explain that he had only come to pick up his paycheck, he was told to "shut up, nigger." From a window in the school board meeting, BPUM's Ed Robinson called out to two officers to stop beating a girl. One officer yelled back, Robinson would later testify in a police brutality suit, "Come on down here, nigger, and you'll get it."[9]

Many of the students, running from the police charge, headed into the midst of the Center City business district where they literally ran into office workers walking to and from their lunch hours. As they ran, some groups of demonstrators broke car and store windows and attacked white passersby, some as far as twelve blocks from the school board. A thirty-five-year-old telephone engineer was hospitalized with facial fractures and impaired vision in one eye after being attacked by two teenage boys as he walked toward his office five blocks from the school board. Two blocks further away, an eighteen-year-old white female college student was attacked by a group of black girls. A punch loosened two of her front teeth and her hearing aid was broken. One girl then helped her to her feet while telling her friends that they "shouldn't have done this." Another group of demonstrators ran through the City Hall courtyard chanting Black Power slogans where they were met by police with submachine guns and dogs. A number of buses, subway cars, and subway stations were vandalized by students as they headed back to their neighborhoods. According to the police, a total of twenty-seven pedestrians were treated for minor injuries after being assaulted by black youths. In addition, twelve police officers were treated for injuries.[10]

By the end of the afternoon, the police had arrested fifty-seven people for actions related to the demonstration. For their comments in the midst of the police charge, Bill Mathis and Walter Palmer were charged with inciting a riot and held on $50,000 bail, while BPUM youth leader Richardson was accused of leading the crowd of 200 to 300 demonstrators that sought to prevent the initial arrest of the young man on the car roof. According to Ed Robinson, who was Richardson's uncle, he saw the police club and arrest his nephew after he sought to throw himself over a girl who was being beaten on the sidewalk. Robinson himself was beaten at police headquarters at Ninth and Arch Streets when he went to inquire about his nephew.[11]

BPUM's High School Organizing

The November 17, 1967 demonstration was the culmination of a three-month organizing campaign carried out by BPUM's education committee and a network of student activists that the group had helped to organize. Continuing the curriculum reform efforts of the Freedom Library, the BPUM education committee promoted the efforts of black parents and teachers to win greater community say over the workings of the public schools that served the city's black communities, while seeking to bring BPUM's message of self-love and intraracial solidarity to young people across the city. Among the school reform organizations with whom BPUM worked was the Educators' Roundtable, a black teachers group whose members often invited BPUM's Ed Robinson and Walter Palmer to speak to their classes on black history topics, and the Educational Self-Help Centers, a War on Poverty-funded network of neighborhood-based and parent-run tutorial centers that the Philadelphia Tutorial Project had organized.[12]

BPUM's student organizing efforts also benefited from an explosion of interest among young African Americans with all things black nationalist. The November 17 demonstration came at the end of a three-year period that had seen Malcolm X's assassination, Muhammad Ali's refusal of induction into the military and subsequent loss of his world boxing title, the national furor over SNCC's embrace of the "Black Power" slogan, and the Black Panther Party's armed march into the California state legislature.[13]

By 1967, BPUM had become the center of black youth organizing across the city. At BPUM rallies and workshops, teenage activists from black neighborhoods in South, West, and North Philadelphia and Germantown were introduced to the cultural politics of race pride, black history, Africanist practices and values, and intraracial unity. And BPUM's adult activists encouraged the students to take these lessons back into their high schools, to press for the introduction of black studies courses into the curriculum, and to demand recognition of their right to form black student clubs and to wear African-oriented clothing. As Walter Palmer describes it, BPUM was equally committed to recruiting "corner kids"—leaders of the "corner" youth gangs in black working-class neighborhoods across the city—and members of student government to its events. "These corners," he argues, were "not gangs, they were neighborhood and community . . . young people who protect[ed] their entire community. Their turf [was] their mothers, their fathers, their brothers, their sisters, the elderly, their neighbors and themselves. They look[ed] forward to the time when they will protect the community, the turf." In fact, there was significant overlap between the corner kids and student council activists. "Some corner kids were in student government, some weren't." As an example, he points to Ronald White, a member of the student council at Ben Franklin High School who as "Billy-Boy" ran the Tenth and Poplar corner. White represented Franklin in the November 17 meeting with Dr. Shedd.[14]

BPUM thus presented movement activism and the politics of racial unity as an alternative to gang battles, much as Cecil Moore had done in 1965. The key figure in BPUM's youth organizing was Edward Robinson's nephew, David Richardson. A 1965 graduate from Germantown High School, Richardson's parents divorced when he was young and he grew up very close to his two uncles, Edward and his brother Calvin Robinson, who also worked as a sales agent for Provident Mutual Insurance. According to Richardson's mother Elaine Richardson, her son first began working to reduce gang tensions in East Germantown when he was in junior high. After high school, Richardson enrolled at Temple University, but soon dropped out to work for his uncles in the insurance business. And like his uncles, he used the flexibility offered by work in sales to pursue his interest in community activism. His mother, Edward Robinson, and Walter Palmer all agree that David Richardson saw Palmer as a mentor. "Dave want[ed] to know everything I know," Palmer recalls. Donning Palmer's uniform of a dashiki and a kufi, Richardson not only brought young men from the Germantown 'corners' into BPUM, he also used Palmer's connections to network with young activists throughout the city.[15]

The decision to organize a student campaign to press for the adoption of black history curricula, recognition of black student unions, and other school reforms seems to have been the result of at least two overlapping conversations within BPUM. First, a group of high school students led by David Richardson approached Palmer for help in challenging school dress and behavior codes that banned African clothing, 'afro' haircuts, and African names. At roughly the same time, members of BPUM's education committee were debating the relative merits of establishing independent schools to teach black history and culture—the classic cultural nationalist position—versus working to implement black history curricula in the public schools attended by most black children. A year earlier, an attempt to establish a black independent school in the city had failed to attract enough tuition-paying children to survive, thus buttressing the argument of those like Edward Robinson and John Churchville who had long argued for a focus on public school reform. But, of course, the school board had been ignoring the efforts of Robinson and others to lobby for black history curricula for decades. As Robinson remembers it, it was Palmer who argued that organizing high school students was the way to win changes in the public school curriculum.[16]

The Summer of 1967

BPUM began the student campaign in the summer of 1967 with a series of training sessions.[17] At the same time, BPUM activists participated in a series of Black Power rallies and confrontations with the police that drew large numbers of black youth into the local Black Power movement. For six straight Saturdays in June and July, street-corner rallies in different parts of South, North and West Philadelphia attracted hundreds of young people to hear Black Power speakers denounce the racism of the Philadelphia police department and of white-owned stores in black neighborhoods.

The street-corner rallies were the result of a surprising alliance between BPUM and Cecil Moore who until this point had been an avowed integrationist. Over the previous year and a half, however, Moore had become increasingly isolated within both the Philadelphia and the national NAACP. In October 1965, the NAACP's national office had announced plans to divide the Philadelphia branch into five neighborhood units and to replace the position of local branch president with a citywide council of branch leaders. Gloster Current, the NAACP's national director of branches, would repeatedly insist that the purpose of the breakup was not to undercut Moore, but to make the local organization more responsive to "individual problems" and to enable it "to stimulate the development of area leaders." Not surprisingly, Moore and his supporters viewed the national office's real intention as "to discredit and destroy militant, independent-thinking chapters." Moore's suspicions were confirmed in June 1966 when Kivie Kaplan, the NAACP's national chairman, blamed Moore for the decline in branch membership from more than 20,000 in 1963 to 7,000 in 1965. "It's apparent," Kaplan declared, "that Moore's job here hasn't been good." In response Moore accused Kaplan and the rest of the NAACP's national leadership of seeking to destroy Negro unity in Philadelphia, "the capital of the civil rights movement in the North," and vowed to challenge the national organization's actions at the 1966 NAACP convention.[18]

After failing to overturn the national board ruling at the 1966 NAACP convention, Moore turned to the courts to maintain his position as president of the Philadelphia NAACP. For nearly a year, he would succeed in delaying the breakup of the branch with a series of temporary court injunctions. In May 1967, however, the Pennsylvania Supreme Court ruled that it lacked jurisdiction over the NAACP because the organization was headquartered in New York. Shortly thereafter, the national NAACP announced that it had transferred the Philadelphia branch charter to the new North Philadelphia branch, which would remain under Moore's leadership, and that it planned to form new neighborhood branches in West, South, Northwest, and Northeast Philadelphia. Then, in July, the national office suspended Moore from the North Philadelphia branch presidency for allegedly diverting branch funds, including membership dues that were owed the national office, to his legal practice and to partisan political activities. By the time a subcommittee of the national board heard Moore's appeal of his suspension in the summer of 1968, the breakup of the Philadelphia NAACP was a fait accompli.[19]

Throughout the two-and-a-half-year battle over the plan to divide the Philadelphia branch, Moore directed a constant barrage of criticisms at his opponents in both the national organization and the local branch. His opponents, Moore charged, were "part-time Negroes" interested only in defending the interests of the black elite. By this point, however, Moore had adapted his attacks on liberals to the new language of Black Power.

Hell, I've been preaching and practicing black power . . . for years. When I took over the leadership of the NAACP, I put most of the whites out. If they are liberal and really want to help, let them walk one pace to the rear and one pace to the right. I think the so-called white liberal is a phony anyway. The only reason he gives money to the civil rights movement is to salve his conscience.[20]

Faced with the loss of his organizational base, Moore began to reach out to Black Power advocates in the city. In the spring of 1967, Moore announced the formation of a new civil rights group, the Society of United Leadership (SOUL), whose stated mission—"to preserve black unity in Philadelphia"—explicitly mimicked BPUM. In part, Moore's outreach to BPUM was motivated by his desire to run as a third-party candidate for mayor in that November's general election. In March, the one-time Republican had announced plans to lead an all-black third-party ticket, the Political Freedom Rights Party (PFRP). Moore's goals for the PFRP were less to win the election than to demonstrate the potential appeal of black independent electoral campaigns. Without significant campaign funds or a paid campaign staff, Moore's campaign consisted of a series of street-corner rallies in black neighborhoods. Young people were thus at the center of Moore's campaign strategy. Shortly after declaring his candidacy, Moore appeared at the 1967 Freedom Show, a rock-and-roll benefit show sponsored by WDAS and Georgie Woods, where he was greeted with chants of "We want Cecil" as he told the mostly young audience, "if you're really interested in Negro pride, vote for me for mayor, and I'll make you proud."[21]

What really solidified Moore's alliance with Black Power activists, however, was Mayor Tate's May 22, 1967, announcement that he was appointing Frank Rizzo to be the city's new police commissioner with a mandate to crackdown on black militancy and street crime. Tate was facing a difficult reelection campaign against Arlen Specter, the thirty-seven-year-old Republican district attorney who combined a strong law-and-order record with a commitment to government reform that had demonstrated appeal to the liberal reform community. By promoting Rizzo—and supporting the new commissioner's "get-tough" policies—Tate clearly hoped to reinforce his support in the city's white working- and lower middle-class neighborhoods as a buffer against the loss of liberal Democrats to Specter.[22]

Having attained the office he had long sought, Rizzo immediately set out to demonstrate his aggressive approach to containing black protest. "If Stokely Carmichael comes to town," he told a meeting of media executives, "we're ready for him. We'll put him away. We've got a whole roomful of tapes on this guy as evidence." What the commissioner's threats meant in practice became evident a few weeks later when five hundred helmeted riot police descended on a South Philadelphia black neighborhood after a dispute between the owner of Royal Hardware on South Street and a black customer led to a mini-riot of bottle tossing. This show of force, a black lawyer told *Greater Philadelphia Magazine*, "demonstrated to the Negroes of this city that [Rizzo] has special plans for them should trouble develop in a Negro area. The only way he could convince them that all those blue steel helmets are not for exclusive use in Negro neighborhoods is to do the same thing in a white area protecting the rights of a Negro."[23]

Not surprisingly, the city's black militants could not let Rizzo's show of force pass. Cecil Moore, Walter Palmer, and Nation of Islam minister Jeremiah X immediately called for a rally on June 17, the following Saturday, in front of Royal Hardware to protest both the store's treatment of black customers and Rizzo's draconian police tactics. On that day, two hundred mostly young protesters chanted "We want Cecil Moore" as they waited for Moore and the other scheduled speakers to appear. When the speakers arrived, however, Lieutenant Fencl served them with an injunction banning them from speaking on South Street that evening. Declaring their intention "to stay on the streets," Moore and the BPUM activists then announced plans for a series of Black Power rallies to take place on streetcorners around the city every Saturday for the remainder of the summer. The first two rallies took place on June 24—one at Seventeenth and Columbia near the epicenter of the 1964 North Philadelphia riot and the other at Sixteenth and South, just one block from Royal Hardware. The *Bulletin* estimated that two hundred people turned out for the Columbia Avenue rally and three hundred for the one on State Street. The following Saturday, there were rallies in West Philadelphia and at a different South Philadelphia site. For the remainder of July, Moore and BPUM held rallies at various sites throughout North and West Philadelphia; a second injunction prevented them from organizing gatherings along the entire South Street business corridor.[24]

In one sense, the street-corner rallies resembled the hundreds of mass meetings that Moore had led during his four and a half years as NAACP president, complete with crowd-pleasing attacks on his black middle-class and white liberal opponents. On July 1, for example, Moore described his former mentor, Austin Norris, as "a professional police informer and a professional traitor." But in a more fundamental way, these rallies represented a major shift in Moore's approach to movement leadership. Whereas Moore had always dominated the NAACP's rallies, now he shared almost equal billing with representatives of the city's growing Black Power movement. The emerging alliance between Moore and the Black Power advocates conveyed instant credibility on emerging figures like Walter Palmer. At the June 24 rally on South Street, Moore declared: "We got unity here. We got everybody here today. We got the Black Muslims, the Black Unity movement, and we got my brand of the NAACP, not the absentee brand." That same day, Palmer urged those at the Columbia Avenue rally not to "be fooled by these Uncle Tom Negroes . . . these superior Negroes . . . these white folks Negroes, because one day they are going to wake up and we are going to be like Jomo Kenyatta, leader of the Mau Mau, we will kill Uncle Tom first." For Moore, the Black Power themes of racial unity across class and ideological lines reinvigorated his anti-elitist discourse. The one-time integrationist told his supporters in West Philadelphia on July 1 to "vote black, buy black, eat black, be black."[25]

Tensions remained high between the police and black activists throughout the month of July. On July 26, for example, the police dispersed a crowd that had gathered at a South Philadelphia police station to protest the arrest of a black teenager following another protest outside a white-owned store. As he was being placed in a squad car, the teenager called out to others on the street to come to his aid. By the time the squad car arrived at a nearby police precinct, an estimated two hundred people had gathered to demand his release. When two hundred riot-helmeted police reinforcements arrived at the police station, the crowd broke into small groups, some of which raced through neighboring streets breaking windows. Over the next three hours, twenty-three people were arrested as 350 uniformed and plainclothes cops spread through the area.[26]

But it was the riots that erupted that month in Newark and Detroit that provided Rizzo with the rationale he needed to take extraordinary measures against black activism. On July 27, Mayor Tate announced that, on the recommendation of his police commissioner, he was issuing a "proclamation of limited emergency." Citing "the violence that has flared in other cities throughout the country," the mayor declared that the proclamation would prohibit gatherings of twelve or more in the city until August 11 "unless further extended." The mayor used a recognizable racial code to signal that black activists were the proclamation's real targets when he promised that it would only be enforced against crowds where there is a "potential" for violence. Rizzo, on the other hand, did not bother with racial codes. Police "intelligence," he told a press conference, "indicates that . . . militant Negro groups" were planning to incite a riot in Philadelphia. A black bar owner, Rizzo reported, had told the police that "members of a militant Negro group" had urged him to turn up the volume on a jukebox in order to bring the police to the bar. Their plan was to initiate a riot when a police officer arrived to investigate the noise. According to the commissioner, there had been thirty-two violent incidents—including fire-bombings and attacks on policemen—in the city since the beginning of June and the police had confiscated two hundred firebombs and fifteen rifles in that period.[27]

In Rizzo's view, the most dangerous of these militant groups was Max Stanford's Revolutionary Action Movement (RAM). In 1966, J. Edgar Hoover had publicly described RAM as "a highly secret all-Negro, Marxist-Leninist, Chinese Communist-oriented organization which advocates guerilla warfare to obtain its goals." Shortly thereafter, Stanford and fifteen other RAM members were arrested in New York for an alleged plot to assassinate the NAACP's Roy Wilkins and the Urban League's Whitney Young. Following his release in the New York case, Stanford announced his return to Philadelphia with a series of articles describing RAM in *Nite Life*, the black tavern weekly. His purpose in returning to Philadelphia was to establish the Black Guard as RAM's youth and self-defense wing. "The purpose of the Black Guard," Stanford wrote, "is to stop our youth from fighting among themselves, teach them a knowledge of our history . . . [and] prepare them . . . to protect our community from racist attacks." Not surprisingly, Stanford's return quickly came to the attention of the police department. During the summer of 1967, the police would undertake a campaign of surveillance and harassment against RAM that would lead to the group's demise in the city. In a memorandum to J. Edgar Hoover, the special agent in charge (SAC) of the FBI's Philadelphia office reported that "police units . . . controlled by the FBI" had carried out the campaign against RAM and argued that the success of the campaign suggested that "similar operations" could work "in other cities where close police[-FBI] cooperation exists."[28]

Publicly, the police department insisted that it had decided to take action against RAM only after receiving information from an informant that the group hoped to incite a riot in Philadelphia on July 21, 1967. According to the police, a teenager had flagged down a police car to report that RAM activists had told him that he "better get [his] blackjack out and get Molotov cocktails out . . . because there was going to be a riot Saturday." Within hours, the police raided a North Philadelphia home belonging to the family of George Anderson, the former Philadelphia SNCC staff member who had recently been exonerated in the dynamite case, and arrested his two teenage brothers for mimeographing posters that urged blacks to unite and "kill the real enemy—the white American and the Uncle Toms." Then, on July 26, Stanford was arrested along with six teenagers in front of the Black Guard's North Philadelphia headquarters on charges of conspiring to incite riot. Acting as the attorney for Stanford and the other six, Cecil Moore charged "that the concern for a riot was politically inspired by the mayor and an incompetent police commissioner who were trying to capitalize on what happened" in Newark. "Jim Tate and Frank Rizzo," he declared, "told policemen to go find me information about a riot."[29]

Over the next month, the police would arrest a total of thirty-five alleged RAM activists. Four were arrested at a West Philadelphia theater "for trying to stir up a crowd" at a jazz concert. According to the FBI memorandum, others "were arrested and released on bail [and then] were re-arrested several times until they could no longer make bail." One activist who was arrested for "passing out RAM literature at a local school" was interrogated and then charged with illegal drug use because of "alleged needle marks." In addition, the police stopped all cars that visited a specific residence and identified their occupants, who then, in the words of the Philadelphia SAC, "became . . . target[s] of harassment." One unnamed police official told the *Bulletin* that Rizzo had vowed to "break the back" of RAM by arresting all of its members. These police tactics were necessary, the police commissioner insisted, because the department had uncovered evidence that RAM was planning two terrorist attacks on government institutions. The first involved a fantastic plot to foment a race riot and then put cyanide in the food distributed to the police officers and firefighters placed on riot duty. The second was a more conventional plot to bomb City Hall, the city's federal courthouse, and the Police Administration Building and to assassinate Mayor Tate, Commissioner Rizzo, District Attorney Arlen Specter, President Lyndon Johnson, and FBI Director Hoover.[30]

Two characteristics of revolutionary Black Power organizations made them vulnerable to agent provocateurs and other forms of police subversion. First was the widespread fascination with tactics of guerrilla warfare utilized by third world revolutionary movements. Frantz Fanon and Malcolm X, perhaps the two most influential theoreticians on the Black Power movement, both argued that violence had to be a central component of the struggle against white supremacy.[31] In a leaflet entitled "Arise! Awake! Your Future Is at Stake," RAM declared that "as other oppressed peoples of the world push toward freedom, their struggle will inspire the Afroamerican to become more militant in the fight against the universal slaveholder." RAM's membership of college students and working-class teenagers, however, lacked both the discipline and the military know-how to turn their revolutionary rhetoric into anything resembling effective action. Second was the eagerness of Black Power activists to identify with the "brothers on the block," the petty criminals and underemployed workers who congregated on the street-corners of the ghettos of the urban North. Stanford, for example, declared that RAM "saw the need for a movement that would give our brothers and sisters from the street a voice and positions of leadership." Black Power activists were often so predisposed to believe the militant ardor of brothers with authentic "street" credentials that informants recruited from prisons and police holding cells easily infiltrated their groups.[32]

A Fall of Student Protest

Despite the ongoing police harassment of Black Power activists, the summer of confrontation had helped BPUM to develop a wide base of support within the city's high schools. By the time school opened in September, BPUM's student activists had formed a council with representatives from high schools and junior highs across the city. Throughout the fall, the council met at the Church of the Advocate to develop its demands and its strategy for broadening support for each school's black student union. Palmer remembers the process as one of assigning specific organizing tasks and then reviewing their results. "Here's the message; here's how you do it . . . . Report back." In addition to organizing the schools, the citywide council also developed mechanisms for getting its message out by word of mouth and leaflet on corners and in housing projects in black working-class neighborhoods across the city.[33]

By the end of October, the student council was ready to take action. On October 26, activists at Gratz High School in North Philadelphia pulled a fire alarm and broke a door chain so that students could exit the school building through a normally locked door to attend a noontime Black Power rally in front of the school. Three hundred students marched in front of the school, listened to speeches by Walter Palmer and Bill Mathis and carried signs with slogans like "the School Board Doesn't Serve the Black Community" and "We Need an Independent School Board." Following the rally, Palmer and leaders of the Gratz student group met with the school's vice principal and Dr. Ruth Hayre, superintendent for the school system's District 4 (which covered North Philadelphia). The students' demands included courses and assemblies on black history taught by black teachers, changes in the school dress code that would allow them to wear African clothes, hats, and jewelry, improvement in the quality and reductions in the price of school food, easing of school discipline, and, reflecting growing opposition to the war in Vietnam, a halt to military recruiting in the school and the requirement that students salute the American flag during school assemblies. During these negotiations, hundreds of students walked out of class and began to chant Black Power slogans in the school halls. In addition, numerous fires were lit in wastepaper baskets. After the police were summoned, the school was closed seventy-five minutes early and the students were ordered to leave the area or face arrest. Fourteen hundred students stayed away from Gratz the next day, but the school was able to return to a normal schedule after it was announced that students would be allowed to wear African clothes and to abstain from saluting the flag if they provided evidence that their objections were based on religious beliefs.[34]

A week later, three hundred black students walked out of classes at Bok Vocational High School in South Philadelphia and met in the school auditorium where seven gave speeches demanding the inclusion of Afro-American history as a major subject in the school curriculum. The students' grievances also included the lack of a single black administrator at Bok and the requirement that they salute the flag. In response, the school's new principal promised to include Afro-American history subjects in "our regular American History course" and to offer a black studies course as a minor elective. The students, however, rejected his proposal.[35]

High schools like Bok, Gratz, and Germantown had long been the focus of interracial tensions that resulted from the changing racial demography of the city. While the student population of each school was more than two-thirds black by 1967, each was located in a neighborhood that was either undergoing massive racial change or, in the case of Bok, feared the loss of a white neighborhood identity. Gratz was located near the border between Nicetown and Tioga, neighborhoods on the western edge of North Philadelphia. The home ward of Mayor Tate, Tioga was one of the few North Philadelphia neighborhoods to maintain a white identity and population through the 1960s. However, racial gerrymandering enabled students from Tioga to attend Germantown High, more than three miles away, and thus to avoid increasingly black Gratz. By 1967, 99 percent of Gratz's 4,200 students were black. At the same time, black migration to Germantown and neighboring Mount Airy—the city's only successfully integrated neighborhoods—along with a white exodus to parochial and private schools had transformed Germantown into a 70 percent black school.[36]

For black students at these and other high schools in neighborhoods experiencing racial transition, the school day was often a series of conflicts with overwhelmingly white school faculty and administrators as well as the dwindling number of white students. At South Philadelphia High School, for example, a white English teacher was reported to have made racially derogatory comments in an April 1967 faculty meeting. Before the teacher could be forced to apologize for having said that blacks are "inferior" and "have smaller brains" and that the best way to increase black parent involvement in the school was to offer them whiskey, fights broke out at the school that led to the hospitalization of twenty-three white students and one black student.[37]

The situation was even more difficult for black students at Bok. Located in an Italian-American working-class neighborhood, students came to

Bok—as they did to the city's two other vocational high schools—from across the city. Unlike the other two schools, however, Bok's student population was more than 80 percent black. Civil rights activists had long argued that the school system tracked the vast majority of its black vocational students into low-paying occupations. Unlike the two other vocational schools, Bok's curriculum included relatively few union-sponsored apprenticeship programs. And even these were reserved primarily for white students. A 1968 *Tribune* study revealed that black and Puerto Rican students held only 18 of the 220 slots in the school's electrical construction apprenticeship program. Meanwhile, a four-year study of black achievement in the Philadelphia schools conducted by a local educational rights group revealed that the average Stanford Achievement Test scores of graduating Bok seniors had actually declined over the course of their years at the school.[38]

For Bok's black students, however, the most difficult problem was often getting to and from school. Most commuted to the school by subway and then faced a more than ten-block walk through a hostile neighborhood to the school. "It's kind of scary," one black student told the *Tribune*, "when you have to move through a place like South Philly by yourself and everybody hates you and you know it. Even the little kids would stop and stare at us like we're some kind of animals 'cause their mommas would tell them that we was animals. They didn't want us to go to school there and we didn't want to go to school there, but we have to." Women students reported being called "black bitches" and having trash thrown at them as they walked to school. "And you better not say anything back," one said, "or they will sick their dogs and cats on you." The neighborhood's white residents, however, insisted that they were the ones being terrorized by the black students. One neighbor complained about black students who "walk[ed] in groups" as they left the school. "You have to move over or get hit and maybe knocked down by them. They curse in front of you. Sometimes they break antennas off automobiles. We can't even sit out on the steps of our homes when they pass; we get called names."[39]

The Possibility of Educational Reform

Despite the problems facing Philadelphia's black high schools, the 1967 protests came amid an atmosphere of optimism about the possibility for racial changes within the school system. In May 1965, voters had approved a revision of the city's Educational Home Rule Charter which shifted the power to appoint members of the school board to the mayor from the board of judges of the common pleas court. That September, Mayor Tate appointed a new nine-member board led by his predecessor, longtime reform mayor Richardson Dilworth. A year later, in January 1967, the new school board thrilled advocates of school reform with the appointment of Dr. Mark Shedd, who had earned a reputation for racial liberalism for overseeing the desegregation of the Englewood, New Jersey, public schools, as the new superintendent of schools. Dr. Shedd assumed his new position on September 1, 1967, and immediately impressed black Philadelphians by enrolling his four children in the predominately black public schools near his family's Germantown home rather than in one of the neighborhood's many prestigious private schools. Shedd, wrote a reporter for the *Tribune*, was "practicing what he preaches about meaningful integration . . . [and] setting an example for white parents throughout the city." While the rhetoric of the Gratz and Bok protests was consistent with the anger of black youth in urban communities across the country, the specificity of the student demands reflected their belief that leadership of the school system was prepared to address their grievances.[40]

In the days following the October 1967 student protests, a committee of adult education reformers organized by BPUM and led by Sylvia Meek, the education specialist for the Philadelphia Urban League, and Mattie Humphrey sought to organize a meeting between the student leaders and Dr. Shedd. Simultaneously, top administrators at the school board asked Charles Askew, a teacher at Germantown High School, to leave the classroom to initiate a process of dialogue with the student activists and with BPUM. As a concession to the students, Askew was given approval to allow BPUM to organize rallies featuring mayoral candidate Cecil Moore and activist-comedian Dick Gregory during school hours at four different high schools in the week before the November 7 municipal election.[41]

On November 3, the last Friday before the election, Moore and Gregory spoke to rallies at Germantown, Gratz, Ben Franklin, and Southern High Schools as well as to a noontime rally in the City Hall courtyard. Publicly, a school board official described the rallies as "real social studies in action." In fact, they were a major concession to the militancy of the black student activists. At Germantown High, Moore urged the students to press the school board to add black history courses to the curriculum. "The Irish have St. Patrick's Day," he said. "The Jews have Yom Kippur and all we have is blue Monday, and if we take that day off, the Man will dock our pay." Claude Lewis, one of the *Bulletin*'s few black reporters, reported that the Gratz students, whom he described as dressed in African clothes and with "natural haircuts," responded enthusiastically, shouting "Black Power" and "tell it like it is, baby."[42]

On election day, Cecil Moore did miserably, receiving less than 10,000 votes of 700,000 cast, while Mayor Tate, and by extension Rizzo, survived the difficult campaign against Arlen Specter, albeit by a margin of less than 11,000 votes. Despite running a vigorous law-and-order campaign—to the chagrin of many of his white liberal supporters—Specter failed to swipe sufficient numbers of the city's white ethnic voters from the Democrats. But if Moore's hopes for reinvigorating black electoral politics were disappointed, his campaign's impact on high school activism was profound. On

November 11, black students at Bok once again walked out of class, this time to attend a meeting to discuss their next steps now that they had rejected the principal's first proposal. The next day, eleven of the Bok student activists were suspended.[43]

According to Walter Palmer, BPUM's student council had always planned to lead a citywide march on the school board building and had already begun to spread the word about the November 17 walkout when the Bok students were suspended. City and school officials seem to have first learned of the march when a flier entitled "Black Students Unite" began to appear at schools across the city at the beginning of the week. The flier called on black students to support the "protest of 16 brothers and sisters expelled for thinking black is beautiful and black is best" by walking out of their classes on Friday and converging on the school board building.[44]

Children or Marauders?

In the aftermath of November 17, public debate focused on the appropriateness of the police actions and whether or not the students had posed a threat to the city. Board of Education president Richardson Dilworth, for instance, charged that "things were under control until Commissioner Rizzo, without our request, saw fit to loose a couple of hundred men, swinging clubs and beating children." Cecil Moore called on black children to stay away from school "until school buildings are relieved of the disciples of an intemperate, sadistic, incompetent policeman like Rizzo." Over the next week, groups and activists across the city's liberal and civil rights communities, including the Philadelphia Urban League, the Fellowship Commission, and the Greater Philadelphia Council of Churches, demanded that Mayor Tate fire the police commissioner. Commissioner Rizzo, in response, evoked the image of a city overrun by marauding black youth. "These children ran through the streets of Center City, beating everyone in their path . . . I leave it to you to judge who was violent and whether these are children."[45]

The events of November 17 clearly reinforced Rizzo's popularity in the city's white ethnic communities. Within hours of the demonstration, Rizzo aides told the press that the police switchboard had received more than three hundred calls in support of the commissioner's actions. What appears to have been a carefully organized campaign to support the police commissioner took place over the days and weeks that followed. Calls of support for Rizzo's stand against Black Power and black teenage lawlessness continually jammed the City Hall switchboards. Twenty-five white teenagers from South Philadelphia held a spirited pro-Rizzo rally, first in front of police headquarters and then in the City Hall courtyard. The Fraternal Order of Police (FOP) collected signatures for a petition that read: "we . . .

support . . . the splendid way in which Commissioner Frank Rizzo and his men handled a near-riot situation last Friday . . . . We also feel that the remarks made by certain members of the Board of Education and the school superintendent were stupid." A *Tribune* photograph captured a uniformed on-duty police officer collecting the signatures of "scores of white persons." Among those issuing public declarations of support for the commissioner were three members of the school board, city council president Paul D'Ortona, John Harrington, national president of the FOP, the national director of Catholic War Veterans, the Philadelphia Committee to Support Your Local Police, and the West Philadelphia Chamber of Commerce.[46]

Key to the mobilization of mass white support for the police was Commissioner Rizzo's masterful use of the media. The commissioner had long viewed the media as a crucial element in his campaign against black militancy. Media coverage of black militancy and urban unrest, he told an October 1967 press conference, "was the best thing that ever happened to the law authorities . . . . I believe that by fully informing the public of the riots we will be able to deal with the rioters with community support. So let them write about the [H. Rap] Browns, the [Stokely] Carmichaels, and the [Cecil] Moores. I encourage it." In the week following the rally, the commissioner blamed the violence of November 17 on both dangerous black militants and the inability of school board president Dilworth and Superintendent Shedd to control unruly teenagers. Dilworth and Shedd, he charged, had allowed "the agitation" to go on "for weeks" and had "permitted [the] cries of Black Power." If school officials "could control their pupils," he argued, "we wouldn't need the police. Dilworth and Shedd are absolutely remiss . . . . Why don't they do their jobs?" At the same time, he expressed absolute confidence in his police officers. The police, he said, "did a beautiful thing." Rizzo concluded the press conference by challenging his opponents' claim to moral leadership. "I am serving notice," he said, "that the Philadelphia police will not permit rule by mob. I am the commissioner and I will make the decisions."[47]

Charles Bowser, whom Mayor Tate had appointed as the city's first black deputy mayor at the same time he promoted Rizzo, has described the public support that Rizzo received as essential to the commissioner's ability to keep his job in the weeks following November 17. According to Bowser, Tate had never liked the commissioner and was prepared to fire him now that he had been reelected. "We've got the bastard now," Bowser remembers the mayor telling him on the phone from vacation in Florida. But the flood of pro-Rizzo calls and letters forced the mayor to ignore those who called for him to fire the commissioner.[48]

The Black Power Student Movement After November 17

While debate over the behavior of the police and student protesters dominated public discussion after the events of November 17, 1967, the demonstration was perhaps most significant for the shift it marked in efforts to improve the quality of public education for black children in Philadelphia. In the weeks and months that followed, black students, parents, and community activists continued to negotiate with the Shedd administration for increased black community participation in the governance of black schools as well for changes in school curriculum and codes of conduct. Despite vigorous opposition from white administrators and teachers as well as from racially conservative politicians, the emerging alliance between black activists and the central school administration would achieve significant reforms in black schooling in the city.

Although Commissioner Rizzo's criticisms led Dilworth and Shedd to seek and receive an injunction barring Walter Palmer and William Mathis from organizing or conducting demonstrations at or near any public school during school hours, the injunction did not prevent the school leadership from continuing to negotiate with the student demonstrators. In the days following the demonstration, black student activists and their adult supporters held a series of closed-door meetings in black neighborhoods across the city to formulate their next steps. One group of thirty students met at the Church of the Advocate to formulate a list of demands and then announced plans for a student-only mass meeting at the Fifty-Ninth Street Baptist Church in West Philadelphia.[49]

By the end of November, negotiations had resumed between the student activists and Dr. Shedd, this time in a private home belonging to a prominent black insurance salesman in the city. The superintendent quickly agreed to organize a series of six retreats in which black students and community representatives could meet with principals from the city's predominately black high schools to discuss racial tensions in the school and their impact on teacher-student relationships. One school district official described the "initial spirit" of the retreats as "one of confrontation, and . . . [verbal] assault on the principals." Still, the retreats resulted in the formation of community-parent-student committees at a number of the high schools whose charge was to work for curriculum changes and improvements in racial climate. For example, Frederick Holliday, the black principal of Gratz, appointed community representatives to a special committee to develop black history curricula for the school. At Ben Franklin High, students, faculty, and parents participated in an all-day planning conference. At a similar meeting at Edison High School, Randolph Scott, second vice president of the student senate, called on teachers and parents to work with the students to ease racial tensions in the 85 percent black school. "We feel," he said, that "the teachers, students, and parents can handle this without Rizzo."[50]

The retreats also led to a change in policy on the formation of black-only student groups within the schools. At Gratz, Principal Holliday provided a basement office to the school's Black Student League. At Germantown

High, students were allowed to establish a club called the Young Afro-Americans (YAA) with David Richardson as their adviser after Richardson helped to settle a gang fight that had erupted at a school dance. Both school clubs sought to use the discourse of racial unity to bridge divisions within black student bodies. At Germantown, for example, the students organized a memorial service for Malcolm X during school hours and limited attendance to black students, teachers, and administrators. The Gratz club addressed a recruitment flier to "All Brothers Who Belong to a Corner" and described the group as "a gang that has realized who the real enemy is and the real enemy ain't no 15-V [the Fifteenth and Venango Streets gang] or 21-W [the Twenty-First and Westmoreland Streets gang]." The flier concluded with a call to revolution. "The revolution is nothing but a BIG gang war."[51]

Not surprisingly, the Shedd administration's strategy of seeking to work with black student activists in the high schools generated significant opposition. In late November, Frank Sullivan, president of the Philadelphia Federation of Teachers (PFT), published an open letter accusing the school administration of failing to deter "disruptive elements in our schools who thrive on disorder and the opportunity to inflict hurt on others." Sullivan charged that a school board directive to high school principals not to carry out "reprisals" against student demonstrators had led to a collapse of discipline in the schools.[52] The police officer assigned to Germantown High claimed that the presence of David Richardson and the Young Afro-Americans club in the school had only made the school's gangs "more cohesive." A new controversy arose in January 1968 after the school district announced plans to hire eleven field agents to act as mediators in racial disputes. Among the proposed agents was Charles Askew, the Germantown High teacher who had served as a school district liaison to BPUM during the fall. Askew had been particularly outspoken in his criticisms of PFT president Sullivan for his hostility toward the student demonstration. An unsigned flier distributed to faculty mailboxes at a number of schools accused Askew of admitting to an "inherent hatred for whites." Under pressure from Mayor Tate and the city council, the school board rejected the appointments of Askew and a second candidate to field agent positions.[53]

Despite the opposition of the teachers' union, black student activists continued to make demands on both the administration of their own schools and the school district as a whole. During the spring of 1968, YAA demanded the removal of three vice principals and nonteaching assistants from Germantown High. The Black Student Council at Olney High School in the racially transitional neighborhoods of upper North Philadelphia issued sixteen demands that ranged from more black history books and courses and an end to police brutality in the school to integration of the school cheerleaders and newspaper staff. Then, in April, a group of black

high school students proposed that they be allowed to take over a summer
school program for middle school students in North Philadelphia. In contrast to teachers and administrators who would continue to "turn off"
black students with curricula that was "irrelevant" to life in the ghetto, the
student activists argued that, with the aid of school custodians and advisers
of their own choosing, they could do a better job of inspiring the younger
students to learn. When the school district argued that it lacked the $2 mil-
lion it would need to fund their proposal, the students replied: "why can't
we have some of [the school budget] to try to help ourselves instead of
spending it all on the same old garbage?"[54]

Decentralization as an Alternative to Desegregation

This period of black student activism took place at a time of heightened
frustration—within both the Shedd administration and the city's civil rights
community—over the persistence of "de facto" segregation in the public
schools.[55] By the time of the November 17 demonstration, both the Shedd
administration and many in the civil rights community had begun to shift
their focus from school desegregation to efforts to improve school quality.
This is not to suggest that Shedd and Dilworth were disingenuous in their
commitment to integrated schools.[56] Rather, the school improvement policies pursued by the school district under their leadership were predicated
on a belief that there was little that the system could do to achieve substantive progress toward desegregation, particularly with a student population
that was nearly 60 percent black. Thus, the district's 1968 Desegregation
Report insisted that the school's prime responsibility was to "provide a successful educational experience for black children, with or without integration." Citing "the black community's demand for community involvement
in its schools," the report argued that decentralization "is the best way to
deliver black children from the clutches of educational failure." Along with
the district's other school improvement programs, decentralization was the
only way to improve racial balance within the district's schools without
causing more white students to leave the system. "The present distribution
of population and location of schools in Philadelphia," the report contended, "are such that integration cannot be achieved . . . by physical or
organizational means alone." Too many white families were choosing to
move to the suburbs or to send their children to one of the city's high-
priced elite private schools or to one of the more moderately priced Catholic schools. In this context, the report concluded, the only way to achieve
substantive school integration would be for the state to erase the "artificial
boundaries" that separated the Philadelphia schools from their suburban
neighbors. Over the next five years, school officials would seek to work with
black student, parent, and community activists to make the public schools
more sensitive to the needs of black students.[57]

The history of efforts to change the school district's teacher transfer policies demonstrates the sense of hopelessness many felt about efforts to desegregate the schools. In 1963, the Pennsylvania Human Relations Commission found that more than half of Philadelphia's public elementary schools had faculties that were more than 80 percent of the same race and ordered the school district to take steps to desegregate its teaching force. The school district agreed to assign new teachers in ways that would promote the desegregation of school faculties, but refused to order the forced transfers of any currently employed teachers. Citing a shortage of 1,200 certified teachers, the district argued that forced transfers would lead to a rash of teacher resignations and early retirements.[58] Instead, the board implemented a voluntary teacher transfer program which allowed teachers to refuse any transfer. During the 1964–65 school year, however, only 94 of the district's 10,600 teachers agreed to change schools. Then, in October 1965, the school board voted to table a proposal from its own Citizen Advisory Committee on Integration to implement a forced teacher transfer program that would have sent low seniority teachers of one race to schools whose faculties were more than 90 percent of the other race. Finally, in December 1967, the state Human Relations Commission ordered the district to implement a mandatory teacher transfer program. The district drafted such a policy but abandoned it in September 1968 in the face of a threatened teachers' strike. Instead, the board adopted a policy of "last resort" that stated that the superintendent could force teacher transfers if and only if voluntary measures failed to produce the necessary result.[59]

In the spring of 1967 a coalition of seventy-five civil rights and black community groups urged Philadelphia voters to reject the school board's request to amend the school district's charter to increase its borrowing authority for school construction. The Coalition for Integrated Quality Education argued that that the capital program, by continuing to build neighborhood schools, would "cement segregation" within the school system. Predicting that two-thirds of schools built under the proposed capital program would be segregated, the coalition distributed thousands of "vote no" fliers throughout the black community.[60] In place of "segregated neighborhoods schools," the coalition urged the school district to adopt a Philadelphia Urban League proposal for education parks that would combine multiple elementary, middle, and high school facilities on a single campus site. As envisioned by their supporters, education parks would bring together students of different races across neighborhood lines, while neutralizing white fears of integration with state-of-the-art facilities and the best quality teachers.[61]

The school board's response to the "vote no" campaign was to announce in March 1967 that it had decided to support a truncated version of the education parks proposal. Specifically, the board added plans for three education parks to the neighborhood school capital program. The first of these parks was to be sited on North Broad Street in the heart of North Philadelphia as part of the city's Model Cities program; the other two would be located in the Northwest section of the city and near the border between North Philadelphia and the primarily white working-class neighborhoods of the lower Northeast. This concession to the demands of the civil rights community won the endorsements of the majority of the city's interracial and white liberal reform groups for the school's capital program. In the May 1967 primary, Philadelphia's voters approved the school debt question by a margin of 57 to 43 percent.[62]

For Superintendent Shedd, the proposal for a "Model School District" in North Philadelphia was the perfect opportunity to shift the focus of debate from desegregation to questions of school quality in the city's black neighborhoods. In a May 1967 speech, Shedd called school decentralization "a logical response to local demands." The creation of clusters of schools "small enough to be manageable," he argued, would lead to increased "chances for individual initiative and satisfaction." School principals and classroom teachers would be able "to develop that pet program or pet idea they have always had," while individual schools would be able to develop programs "with a relevance and sensitivity to local needs not otherwise possible." The combination of modern school buildings, high quality teachers, and community input, he concluded, would enable the North Philadelphia Model School District to develop an educational experience "tailor made" to meet the needs of underprivileged black children. As he envisioned it, the model district would operate autonomously from the rest of the school system, with its own superintendent and an independent school board consisting of community representatives and education experts from Temple University.[63]

Conflicts over the district's boundaries and the level of community participation in its governance ultimately kept the model school district from coming to fruition. Still, the model district was just one component of Shedd's program of administrative decentralization and increased community involvement in the school system. Most dramatically for the future of school politics in the city, the school board decided to open its meetings to the public and to significantly increase the number of public hearings it held. At the same time, the district secured federal funds to hire school-community coordinators to work in schools in the city's poverty areas. In 1967, the district designated four elementary schools as "Community Schools" whose facilities were to be available in nonschool hours for community-oriented programming. In addition, the district turned Hartranft Elementary School in North Philadelphia over to a community corporation for use as a community center. A community-based campaign to prevent the establishment of a "split-shift" school day at all-black Sayre Junior High School in West Philadelphia led to the formation of a Community Advisory Committee at the school. With the support of the central administration, the advisory group negotiated for significant "community control" over school policy, as well the right to run a staff development program that would send "faculty and community members together onto the streets and into the police stations, the bars, the barber shops, and the homes in an effort to make Sayre's teachers and . . . program more relevant to the experiences of the school's children." A similar community committee was established to oversee the development of a new middle school in Germantown. Finally, community activists in the Mantua section of West Philadelphia convinced the central school administration to establish a community-run "small scale" middle school in their neighborhood.[64]

Still, Shedd's decentralization program failed to satisfy advocates of school desegregation. In March 1970, the state Human Relations Commission found the district's school desegregation plan "unacceptable in that it would result only in a minimal amount of desegregation." At the same time, the commission rejected the district's argument that true racial balance could only be achieved through a merger with the surrounding suburban district. Desegregation, the commission insisted, was a local responsibility, "in keeping with the spirit of local control." In October, the commission filed a complaint in state court against the district for "allow[ing] the existence of public schools . . . which are racially segregated." According to the complaint, the percentage of Philadelphia public schools that were 95 percent of one race had risen from 42 to 49 over the previous two years and the percentage of black students in such schools had risen from 54 to 57. The district, the commission argued, could desegregate five thousand students just by altering school attendance boundary lines.[65]

The Bok Crisis and Fissures in Philadelphia's Democratic Coalition

More damaging to Shedd's decentralization program, however, was the almost symbiotic relationship between black student and community activism and white resistance to educational change. Rather than satisfying a universal demand for schools that simultaneously promoted educational achievement and community involvement, the Shedd administration's reform efforts exacerbated the growing racial tensions over education policy in Philadelphia. A prime example of the Shedd administration's inability to defuse racial tensions over the public schools was the crisis that engulfed Bok High School in October 1968. The Bok crisis reflected rising anxieties over issues of control, curricula, and safety in the city's schools. For many white Philadelphians, the events of that October confirmed that school officials were incapable of controlling the city's black high school students and their militant activist allies; increasingly, the law-and-order politics of Police Commissioner Rizzo seemed the only hope for the city. For black Philadelphians, there were two lessons of the Bok crisis, neither of which was particularly novel. First, there were dual standards for police protection for the city's white and black residents. And second, only concerted pressure could force the city government to protect black interests.

So long as white administrators and teachers managed Bok as a school for low achievers, the Italian American residents of the surrounding neighborhood had treated the school's predominately black student population as a minor nuisance. But as black student and community advocates began to demand a greater voice in the school's governance, the area's residents organized to demand that school and city officials respond to their complaints about the behavior of Bok students.

A series of racial conflicts plagued South Philadelphia through the summer and early fall of 1968.[66] Then, on Wednesday, October 2, a group of black youths stabbed a white student from Bishop Neumann, a Catholic high school in South Philadelphia, in an elementary school yard less than five blocks from Bok. False rumors that the boy had died circulated through the neighborhood. Even though the black student arrested for the stabbing did not attend Bok, the incident led neighborhood residents to begin an organizing drive to close the school. "That's when the white citizens gathered," one resident told a reporter, "and decided to voice their opinions." The neighbors made their case against the students both as white citizens and as members of a distinct ethnic group. "Italians are peace-loving people. But you try to touch me or my kid; that's when my Dago blood starts to boil. Touch us and we'll fight back." And fight back they did. The day after the stabbing, neighborhood residents threw rocks at school buses carrying members of the Bok football team to a game at Southern High. During and following the game, incidents of fighting and bottle-throwing broke out among the students. The next day, three to four hundred students from Bok attempted to storm the gates in front of Southern High but were convinced to leave by a vice principal. Two hours later, fights broke out between black students and white neighborhood residents on a number of corners near Bok. To the black students, these incidents were proof that the police were allied with the white neighborhood residents. "A group of black kids coming home from [the] football game were beat up by white kids," one student told the *Tribune*, "And who do you think got arrested? The black kids."[67]

After a quiet weekend, two hundred black students walked out of Bok on the morning of Monday, October 7 to protest the neighborhood harassment. The students headed for the subway and took it to the Muntu Cultural Center, a community center operated by the Black Coalition, the city's newest Black Power organization, in West Philadelphia. At the center, the students met with a number of prominent Black Power activists including Stanley Branche, the coalition's executive director, "Freedom" George Brower of the Young Militants, and RAM's Max Stanford. The students then returned to Bok under the protection of Branche and RAM's Black

Guard. Once back at the school, the students gathered in the auditorium, without the consent of the school administration, to listen to speeches from Branche and other representatives of the Black Coalition. The students then left the school without incident. However, rumors spread through the neighborhood that the Black Panthers had taken over the school.[68]

The next day, the Black Coalition held a press conference in front of Bok to declare that if the police did not provide more protection for the students, then the Black Guard would. Afterward, the coalition's leadership and a group of Bok students met with police and school officials to raise concerns about the lack of police protection for students walking to and from the school as well as about a number of specific incidents of police brutality. Still, a large group of white protesters were waiting for Bok's students as they emerged from the school on Tuesday afternoon. As the protesters threw stones, the police were forced to escort the students away from the school, first on buses and then on foot when they ran out of buses. During the afternoon, fights broke out throughout the area, leading to the arrests of a number of neighborhood residents. That evening, a group of four hundred neighborhood residents marched on the area's police precinct to demand the release of those who had been arrested, the permanent closing of Bok, and increased police protection in their neighborhood. The protesters carried signs reading "White Power Is Boss," "Close Bok Or Else," and "Italian Power." According to one of the march's leaders, Charles Pasquale, an insurance salesman, area residents had petitioned for three years for greater police protection around Bok and the area's elementary schools. Commissioner Rizzo spoke to the crowd, urging them to leave things "to the police," and giving them his "word [that] we're going to give you protection until this is resolved."[69]

Ironically, white opponents of the Shedd administration incorporated the rhetoric of decentralization into their demands. White parents picketing Southern High called for greater parent involvement in the school in order to improve school discipline and protect their children from black student attacks. As proof that their demands were not racially motivated, Bok's neighbors argued that they had no trouble with black students from the local area. "It's not the South Philadelphia colored," one resident told a *Tribune* reporter, "but those youth from North and West Philadelphia who come here and cause trouble."[70] Rather than assure white Philadelphians that the quality of black schools could be improved without threatening the educational experience of white children, Shedd's decentralization plan simply buttressed white fears that blacks were taking over the schools. The more that the school board demonstrated sensitivity to the concerns of black activists the more parent groups from the city's white working- and middle-class neighborhoods charged that efforts to appease the black community were destroying the public schools.

By Wednesday, a clear pattern of protest and counterprotest had emerged. Black students who felt harassed and threatened as they attempted to make their way through South Philadelphia's neighborhoods to Bok and Southern High Schools exacted their revenge once inside the school walls. At ten o'clock that morning four black students attacked a white student with a metal object on the fourth floor of Southern. The victim had to be rushed to a local hospital where he was treated for a possible skull fracture.[71] At the same time, rumors spread that students at predominately black high schools were prepared to avenge the attacks on Bok students by attacking students from predominately white schools. For example, students from West Philadelphia High were rumored to be planning attacks on students from West Catholic High. In North Philadelphia, it was to be students from Gratz and Benjamin Franklin attacking Olney High students. Shortly after noon, a group of three hundred black students from Southern High began marching toward Bok with the expressed intent of supporting their fellow students. Officers from the civil disobedience squad and members of the school district's field staff were able to convince them to return to Southern by promising to arrange a meeting with their principal. At about the same time, other members of the field staff were able to convince members of the Black Student League at Edison High School not to walk out of school. Across town, the principal of West Philadelphia's Overbrook High reported that there had been three assaults on white students by black students. Finally, eighteen blacks—twelve adults and six juveniles—were arrested and charged with carrying concealed weapons in cars that were heading toward Bok and Southern. The police claimed to have found four pistols, two knives, and a gallon of an inflammable liquid.[72]

By 2:45 that afternoon, a crowd of one thousand white adults was blocking the streets in front of Bok. The crowd chanted "We want [George] Wallace," "Burn Bok," and "Come on nigger" to students trying to leave the school for the day. Some carried signs with slogans like "White Is Boss" and "All the Way with Wallace." Neither Police Commissioner Rizzo nor the area's Republican city councilman Thomas Foglietta were able to convince the crowd to disperse. To the white protesters, the violence of black students justified their actions. When Foglietta pleaded that "we're not going to accomplish anything by violence," someone in the crowd responded: "they [the black students] do it." It would take until past 4 P.M. to bus all but one hundred of the school's black students to the Broad Street subway line.[73]

The last group of students, however, insisted on walking through the neighborhood to Broad Street. They would challenge "whitey." As numerous fights broke out, a contingent of thirty police officers sought to separate the two groups and to force the students to return to Bok. Three black students were beaten in the process, one so badly that at first it was reported that he had been stabbed. Finally, Stanley Branche convinced the remaining students to return to the school by arguing that they were outnumbered and outgunned. Twenty-three white protesters were arrested during the melee. Still, Robert Poindexter, the school system's highest-ranking black administrator, charged that the police had failed to respond as forcefully to the white demonstrators as they had on November 17, 1967. "It is especially tragic," Poindexter argued, "since the black students were just beginning to believe that they would get real protection from the police."[74]

At eight o'clock that evening, more than one thousand neighborhood residents met in Bok auditorium with Commissioner Rizzo, Clarence Farmer, executive director of the Commission on Human Relations, and officials from the school district and the Catholic archdiocese. The white residents' demand was simple: close the school permanently. The group chanted "Close down the school or we'll burn it down" and "We want Wallace." A group of young people had to be escorted from the meeting because of, in the words of one journalist, "their shouting and threats." Rizzo was widely applauded when he criticized school board president Dilworth and the other members of the school board for failing to attend the meeting. "I think the superintendent also should be here," Rizzo said, "and I think you people ought to insist that they belong here." At that very moment, Dr. Shedd and the school board were meeting with two groups of community activists—one led by Walter Palmer and the other consisting of twenty white South Philadelphia residents—both of which demanded that the district close Bok and Southern for the rest of the week. After five hours of what one school board official described as "heated discussion," the board acceded to the community activists' demands and agreed to close both schools.[75]

Even with Bok and Southern closed, interracial school violence continued for the rest of the week. On Thursday, three more white students were slashed and five others injured at Overbrook. At 11:30 A.M., two hundred students walked out of Edison, an all-male school, and marched first to Kensington High, their sister school, and then to majority-black Dobbins Vocational High. Meanwhile, fearful white students had to be bused home from Edison. The student protesters' stated plan was to march from Dobbins to South Philadelphia, picking up additional students at Ben Franklin and William Penn High Schools along the way. However, "Freedom" George Brower and other Black Coalition staff members arrived at Dobbins at 3:30 P.M. and succeeded in convincing the group to disperse. Throughout Friday, there were reports that black students from North Philadelphia's public high schools planned to march to Roman Catholic High School, a predominately white school on North Broad Street, to protest the treatment of black students in South Philadelphia. Thirty students wearing Edison High jackets raced through an assembly at Olney, whose student population was 30 percent black, urging the black students to walk out of school. More than four hundred did, but they were then met by large numbers of white students. Scuffles broke out and seven students, three whites and four blacks, were hurt, while four others, three white and one black, were arrested. Eventually, buses had to be brought in to take the black students safely home. Soon thereafter, 1,500 students marched out of Ben Franklin High for a planned march to Bok. However, student leaders, with the support of Walter Palmer and William Mathis, convinced the marchers to return to the school auditorium where they met to discuss problems at Franklin. In return for the march's cancellation, the school principal promised that classes at the school would be canceled on the following Monday so that the students could attend seminars on racial problems in the city schools.[76]

Meanwhile, demonstrations were spreading throughout South Philadelphia's white neighborhoods. The largest took place on Sunday afternoon. A crowd that ranged in size from 800 to 1,300 marched for up to five hours to demand the closing of Bok. A speaker on a sound truck with a "Wallace for President" sticker led the march. The speaker, who refused to give his name to reporters, urged area residents to join the march by appealing to their sense of white racial identity. "We don't care if you're Polacks or Jews. We want Whites!" Many in the march wore "Wallace for President" buttons and chanted "White Power, White Power." Others in the Italian American community looked closer to their ethnic roots for a model of leadership. When Councilman Foglietta returned to the neighborhood on Monday evening to propose a settlement to the crisis that would involve shuttle buses taking Bok students to and from the Broad Street Subway, someone in the crowd called out: "We need a new Mussolini."[77]

Some in the Democratic Party hierarchy were also beginning to take up the neighborhood residents' cause. City Council President Paul D'Ortona declared he would "begin an investigation from top to bottom of the school system" and threatened to delay a $30 million tax package for the school system. An outspoken opponent of the school district's desegregation efforts and a strong supporter of Commissioner Rizzo, D'Ortona framed the issue solely as one of school discipline. "The kids," he charged, "are telling the [school] board how to run the schools. There is no discipline in the schools." Charles Peruto, a party activist and lawyer for the Bok neighborhood residents, called on the school board to expel students guilty of serious misconduct and to exclude "outside agitators" from the schools. After a weekend of demonstrations, Mayor Tate too joined the chorus of school board critics. The school district, he declared, had invited the crisis by allowing "extremists to agitate the children in the auditorium of the schools."[78]

As white protesters marched through South Philadelphia, black adult activists worked feverishly to find a solution to the crisis. On Sunday, one hundred black parents led by the Philadelphia chapter of the National Welfare Rights Organization (PWRO) held a rally at Mayor Tate's North Philadelphia home to demand that the National Guard be brought in to protect their children. On Sunday evening, Mayor Tate met with both members of the school board and a delegation of black leaders led by the Black Coalition's Stanley Branche, while Commissioner Rizzo met with 150 white South Philadelphia residents. Both officials promised that there would be adequate police protection in the area surrounding Bok when it reopened on Monday. Police would protect the black students as they rode public transportation and walked to and from Bok and Southern. In addition, the police would erect barricades in a one-block radius around Bok and would allow only students and school personnel to pass through. The police, Rizzo promised, were "not taking any nonsense from whites or Negroes." Still, the two hundred parents of black Bok students who met at the Black Coalition's offices in West Philadelphia voted to keep their children at home so long as the area remained "unsafe."[79]

The large police presence and high rates of student absenteeism prevented further outbreaks of violence in South Philadelphia on Monday. Only 425 of Bok's 2,059 students and 600 of Southern's 4,100 attended school that day. The police did arrest seven white men in their teens and early twenties who refused to leave an intersection near Bok, but otherwise neighborhood activists cooperated with police requests throughout the day. Meanwhile, the Commission on Human Relations began to convene a series of meetings between students and neighborhood residents in hopes of finding ways to decrease tensions in the area.[80]

Things were not so calm elsewhere in the city. Large numbers of absentee students were reported at Germantown, Edison, Ben Franklin, Olney, Overbrook, and West Philadelphia high schools. At Edison, two hundred students from the Black Students Association conducted a sit-in in the auditorium. In an effort to prevent "a riot," officials at Edison allowed David Richardson, "Freedom" George Brower, and other Black Power militants to speak to the group. Meanwhile, at Ben Franklin, five hundred students participated in a day of seminars. Led by Ronald White, the Franklin students voted to demand that the district replace the school's 80 percent white teaching force with an all-black faculty. Shortly thereafter, nearly half of the school's white teachers left under police protection. Twenty black teachers remained behind to meet with about two hundred students throughout the night. By the next morning, the students had settled on seven new demands. The most significant of these were that (1) the school be renamed "Malcolm X High"; (2) black faculty members be appointed to run the school's academic and athletic departments; (3) "Afro languages" be added to the curriculum as major subjects; and (4) the school board take steps to end the crisis at Bok and Southern.[81]

On Tuesday, Olney High was the focus of protest. The previous day, more than 1,700 students had stayed away from the 70 percent white school. Then, on Tuesday morning, Olney's principal allowed the school's Black Students Union to hold an assembly. The students demanded that all white students and teachers leave the auditorium. David Richardson and at least one black faculty member then spoke to the students. The focus of their complaint was that white students from the school were stoning buses carrying black students as they left the neighborhood. At the same time, a series of fistfights between white and black students broke out in the school's lunchroom. At the request of the school principal, Superintendent Shedd then authorized the use of riot police to end the occupation of the auditorium. The students eventually agreed to leave, but only on school district buses with police protection. The following day, black school board member George Hutt agreed to mediate the situation at Olney. He soon reported that progress had been made on a number of the students' demands.[82]

The final mass protest of the Bok school crisis came on the evening of Tuesday, October 15. At 8 P.M., more than two thousand white residents of South Philadelphia gathered in the Bok auditorium to develop a set of demands to present to the school board. By then, the group had decided to moderate its goals. Instead of calling for the closing of Bok, they sought changes in its curriculum that would increase the school's white student population from 12 to at least 40 percent. They also asked that all black students who lived outside a ten block radius of the school be bused to and from school, that increased security personnel be posted at the school, that a ban on all outsiders from entering the school be established, and that all students who distributed "inflammatory" literature be suspended. Using the language of community control, they insisted that Bok and other South Philadelphia public schools should be "for South Philadelphians." A committee of residents presented these demands to Superintendent Shedd at the school board building at midnight. When he replied that he could only promise curriculum changes that would increase the percentage of white students at Bok to 24 percent and insisted that the school board alone could not bus all of Bok's black students, the South Philadelphia representatives returned to the school and joined another one hundred protesters who had decided to stage an all-night sit-in in the Bok auditorium. Participants in the sit-in spoke in openly racist terms to two white journalists from the *Temple Free Press*, an underground newspaper. "We keep our neighborhood nice," one told the journalists, "and we don't like the filthy way niggers live." Another reveled in the appropriation of protest tactics from the black movement. "If niggers can sit in a school, so can we."[83]

The next morning, CHR Executive Director Clarence Farmer convinced the protesters to leave the auditorium in return for a promised meeting with five members of the school board on the following Thursday. At that meeting, Charles Peruto and Henry Nichols of the school board agreed on the need to increase security personnel at Bok, curriculum changes to recruit additional white students, and stronger disciplinary measures against disruptive students "both in and out of the school," as well as the barring of all outside agitators. Both sides agreed that additional busing would not be needed if these stronger disciplinary measures were adopted. Soon thereafter, circulars were distributed through the neighborhood around Bok praising the renewed relationship between the school board and the community. In the months that followed, the school district instituted significant reforms in the Bok curriculum. Most were designed to attract more white students. However, two union apprenticeship programs that refused to increase their enrollment of black students were ousted from the school and seven others given a month to boost their black enrollments. During the 1968–69 school year, Bok's student population had been 85.2 percent black. By the following year, the percentage of black students had dropped to 76.2.[84]

Like the Ocean Hill-Brownsville controversy in New York City, the Philadelphia school crises of 1967–68 can be viewed as an example of excessive black demands and poorly conceived liberal policies pushing white working-class Democrats into the arms of conservative politicians. As in the debate over busing and neighborhood schools, anxieties over school discipline became evocative issues for those who believed that the liberal wing of the Democratic Party had betrayed the interests of the city's white ethnic voters. Certainly, Frank Rizzo would effectively capitalize on white opposition to Shedd's school reform efforts in his 1971 mayoral campaign.[85] But to solely blame black activists and their white liberal allies for the decline of the New Deal coalition is to overlook the fact that the commitment of working- and middle-class whites to the preservation of localized forms of racial privilege predated the Black Power movement of the late 1960s.[86] In this sense, entrenched white support for racialized hierarchies within public institutions like the Philadelphia public schools was as much a cause of the urban violence of the late 1960s as black radical activism. The violent talk and acts of black activists in Philadelphia were less the spontaneous explosion of a dream deferred than the cumulative result of the constant interracial tensions and violence that existed in the city's schools and on the streets of its working-class neighborhoods. Both sides in the Philadelphia school conflicts—the black students and the white police and neighborhood residents—viewed their own violence as reactive but that of the other side as an inherent part of either, in the case of the black students, their racial makeup or of, in the case of the police and neighborhood residents, their racist beliefs.

*   *   *

Historians of Black Power have tended to depict the movement as consisting of a series of pronouncements from national figures like Stokely

Carmichael and H. Rap Brown, Huey Newton and Maulana Karenga, Angela Davis and Kathleen Cleaver. Stripped of the contexts of time and place, these pronouncements can be constructed into an ideological debate over whether, in the words of scholar-activist Robert Allen, the movement should be "a rebellion for reforms or a revolution aimed at altering basic social forms." For Allen, Black Power activists had to choose between "building a mass revolutionary organization" or succumbing to the neocolonial temptations of black capitalism and elective office, while Harold Cruse argued that declarations of revolutionary intent were at best "romantic escapism" and at worst an attempt to start an unwinnable "race war." What the movement lacked, in Cruse's view, was recognition of the need to win "political and economic power within . . . urban communities, while seeking cultural freedom and equality there and beyond."[87]

In a city like Philadelphia, however, Black Power activists could not afford such a sharp bifurcation of strategic choices. Despite the discursive power of cultural nationalist rhetoric, its critique of efforts to reform state institutions had little relevance for Philadelphia's 150,000 black public school students and their parents. Here again, we can see the importance of community organizing principles to the strategic development of Black Power at the local level. More than the black nationalist critique of integration, it was black students and parents' experiential knowledge of the limited impact of school desegregation that transformed the black nationalist approach to education reform from a marginal demand into a dominant political issue within the city. By combining the demand for black studies courses with the call for community control of the public schools in black neighborhoods, BPUM activists were able to shift the focus of black educational advocacy in the city from school desegregation to efforts to raise the quality of schooling in predominately black schools. The Black Power educational agenda would never completely supersede desegregation. But with the success of the movement against de jure segregation, Black Power advocates were able to establish a political discourse in which questions of integration and separatism had to be debated according to their impact on the average black Philadelphian and on the interests of the black community as a whole.

At its most fundamental, Black Power in Philadelphia challenged the decision-making structures that controlled public and private investment in the city. Decisions that affected the city's black communities, Black Power advocates argued, should be made within those communities, not in government agencies or Center City office buildings. Philadelphia's Black Power activists faced a number of significant obstacles—lack of a consistent vision of how a racially just city might look, inconsistent organizational structures, ongoing police surveillance and harassment, and an increasingly powerful and well-organized white conservative backlash against black activism. Still, the city's Black Power movement was able to present a formidable challenge to the liberal coalition that, though weakened, remained a powerful force in the city. On issues ranging from public education and urban renewal to police brutality and welfare, advocates of Black Power rejected liberalism's faith in antidiscrimination laws and technocratic governance in favor of the principles of community-based leadership, participatory democracy, and racial self-determination.

Chapter 7

The Gender Politics of Movement Leadership

In recent years, there has been a great deal of scholarly attention paid to gender practices and the role of women in the Black Power movement. One thread of this scholarship has emphasized the masculinist aspects of Black Power ideology. For example, E. Frances White, in "Africa on My Mind," her classic study of Maulana Karenga's use of the concept of gender complementarity, demonstrates how black nationalists have valorized patriarchal family forms in response to the ways that both state- and market-based racial discrimination have denied normative/respectable domestic roles to black men and women. In a different vein, Elaine Brown's memoir, *A Taste of Power*, received national attention for its discussion of male chauvinism and misogynistic violence in the Black Panther Party.[1]

A second thread of scholarship examines the leadership roles played by women activists in Black Power organizations. Here again, most of the works have focused on the experience of Panther women. As numerous authors have shown, the national attention that Brown's memoir received for her discussion of intra-Panther male violence overlooked her more extensive discussion of the importance of woman activists to the growth of the Panthers as well as her own rise through the party ranks to become party chair during the period of Huey Newton's exile in Cuba. Moreover, in the years since Brown published *A Taste of Power*, scholars and former Panthers alike have published counternarratives that emphasize the diversity of women's experiences in the party. The weight of this evidence suggests that there was not a single experience of women in the party. Depending on the attitudes of local Panther leaders, the party could be a place of either rigid gender hierarchies and blatant sexual harassment or of remarkable gender equality in which women activists played a multiplicity of roles up to and within the leadership of local party chapters.[2]

This range of gendered contexts across Panther chapters is evident in Mumia Abu-Jamal's recent memoir of his years as a Panther. Abu-Jamal described the Panthers' Philadelphia chapter as a bastion of male dominance. "No women helped found the Philadelphia branch and none held office. When the party's national headquarters sent a deputy field marshall named Sister Love to oversee the branch, there was clear resentment at her presence and, yes, her power." And yet, Abu-Jamal argues, there was also "profound respect" for her position in the party's national leadership. Moreover, when Abu-Jamal moved on from Philadelphia to postings first in the Bronx and then in Oakland, he reported to women activists, all of whom "ran . . . tight and efficient operation[s]." In Abu-Jamal's account, he not only accepted but thrived under the leadership of his female supervisors. He also quotes extensively from "On the Question of Sexism Within the Black Panther Party," an unpublished manuscript written by the late Safiya A. Bukhari, a party leader in Harlem, in order to demonstrate the broad range of leadership roles filled by Panther women. "In a time when other nationalist organizations were defining the role of women as barefoot and pregnant," Bukhari wrote, "women in the Black Panther Party were working right alongside men, being assigned sections to organize just like the men, and receiving the same training as the men."[3]

There certainly were, as Bukhari argued, black nationalist organizations that were more explicitly patriarchal in ideology and organizational structure than the Panthers. In "Elijah Muhammad's Nation of Islam: Separatism, Regendering, and a Secular Approach to Black Power After Malcolm X (1965–1975)," Ula Taylor explores the appeal of the Nation of Islam to Black Power activists, both male and female, in the period following Malcolm X's assassination. Most of Taylor's essay focuses on the attraction of the NOI's conservative philosophy of nation- and wealth-building to activists frustrated by what they saw as the superficial rhetoric of revolution and "effete political resistance" in the Black Power movement. At the same time, she examines why once-politically active women would accede to what Taylor calls the NOI's "gendered prescriptions." For the women Taylor interviewed, the NOI's rigid gender roles offered liberation from a racially and sexually abusive society by restoring "in black men . . . their natural urge to protect black women." The strength, sobriety, and responsibility of Muslim men countered stereotypical images of black men as criminal, shiftless, and sexually irresponsible and, by extension, black women as unfeminine and domineering. For these women, Taylor concludes, "it was both their racial and religious duty to sacrifice self for the liberation project." Through "obedience to all paternal figures," black women in the NOI were contributing to "black redemption" through the restoration of "a responsible, disciplined, dignified and defiant womanhood."[4]

All of the trends discussed in the literature on the gender politics of Black Power were evident in the Philadelphia movement, from the exclusively male leadership of the Black Panther chapter and the ideological complementarity of the Nation of Islam to the presence of effective and respected women activists in groups like BPUM and Philadelphia SNCC. By the 1970s, tensions over the role of women in Black Power organizations would lead to the emergence of the black feminist movement.[5] This chapter, however, explores how movement activists and organizations were affected by the contradiction between masculinist ideologies and the commitment of organizations like BPUM and SNCC to the principles of community organizing and indigenous leadership development. It is the irony of the Black Power era in Philadelphia that a movement committed to the restoration of black masculine leadership in both the community and the home also contributed to the emergence of a very new kind of leadership in black Philadelphia: working-class and predominately female neighborhood activists who for the first time emerged as citywide leaders on issues from welfare rights to police brutality. This chapter examines the paradoxical gender politics of Black Power first by exploring the masculinist politics of a number of Black Power organizations and then by examining the emergence of two black women-led militant organizations of the late 1960s, the Philadelphia Welfare Rights Organization (PWRO) and the Council of Organizations on Philadelphia Police Accountability and Responsibility (COPPAR).

"The Men Were Going to Take Control"

Charyn Sutton's experiences in NSM and SNCC are particularly instructive on the seeming contradiction between Black Power masculinism and the principles of community organizing. Like the women of the NOI, Sutton was drawn to black nationalism by its call for masculine political leadership for the black community. "One of the big issues," Sutton remembers, "was that the men were going to take control. So it was very male-oriented and . . . male-dominated. We thought it was wonderful. We were trying to put forth positive male images in the community." What could be more revolutionary than aiding in the development of a militant black male leadership that would never step down in the face of racist terror or shuffle before white liberal paternalism. Moreover, the restoration of black masculinity was directly linked to overcoming stereotypes of black women as sexual jezebels or as matriarchal and unfeminine. In an interview with the *Tribune*, Philadelphia SNCC staff member Louella Scott linked the call for recognition of black female beauty to Black Power's emphasis on strong male leadership. "It is time," she said, "for the black woman to take a back seat and show her man she's not afraid of being black . . . [by] recogniz[ing] and identify[ing] with the beauty that is particular to the black race."[6]

Despite their embrace of masculinist ideologies, Sutton, Scott, and other women organizers on the SNCC staff were political actors in their own right who had little interest in confining their activism to traditional female roles. As a member of the SNCC organizing staff, Sutton saw her responsibilities as little different from her male co-workers. While acknowledging that the project's leadership was entirely male, Sutton insists that the project's internal "decision-making [process] was collective" and its day-to-day work culture egalitarian. Women did the same work as men and their voices were valued within the organization. Having experienced workplace sexism when she later worked as a newspaper reporter, Sutton is adamant about the respected place of women within Philadelphia SNCC. In her experience, there was no privileging of men over women in the staff's efforts to identify and develop community-based leaders. Sutton and her fellow organizers targeted neighborhood bars and the longshoremen's union, but they also sought to organize women in housing projects and tenements.[7]

Mattie Humphrey's experiences in the Black Power movement seem to have been very much comparable to Sutton's description of the gendered politics within Philadelphia SNCC. On the one hand, she played a crucial role in the development of both the Freedom Library and BPUM and was a featured speaker at numerous BPUM rallies. At the same time, she remembers being "excluded" from "meetings of strategy" within BPUM and only being called on "when they needed somebody with my skills" to carry out specific tasks.[8] The willingness of BPUM's male leaders to take advantage of and even offer public recognition of individual women's political skills seems to have been the cause of the most significant internal tensions in the lead up to the Third National Conference on Black Power in 1968. As I discussed in Chapter 5, Walter Palmer, the conference coordinator, appointed Falakha Fattah, Mattie Humphrey, and a number of other women activists to key positions on the conference organizing committee. According to Palmer, the prominence of these women activists did not sit well with many of the national leaders who believed that "historically [black] women have been out on the front . . . as the result of . . . racism in American society and the attempt to negate maleness." While Palmer's insistence that women activists could not simply be called on to do organizing work for the conference—they must also "be given authority with responsibility"—eventually prevailed, his recollection of the role that women played in the conference planning process would seem to confirm Humphrey's memory that women were called upon if there was a need for their specific skills but that they were rarely if ever included in decision-making or discussions on political strategy.

The Black Coalition

Next to the Nation of Islam, the Black Coalition was perhaps the most explicitly masculinist of Black Power organizations in Philadelphia. In the wake of the 1968 assassination of Martin Luther King, Jr., a coalition of prominent black liberals and white business leaders sought to reach out to a group of black militant activists in hopes of preventing further racial violence in Philadelphia. The willingness of Black Power activists to accept the business leaders' offer to fund a program of black cultural, youth employment and economic development programs was rooted in part in self-interest. They needed to be able to deliver jobs and provide programs if they were to maintain a constituency for their critique of the black community's traditional civil rights and service organizations. Moreover, the business leaders' proposal offered the possibility of salaried movement-oriented employment to activists badly in need of income. Unlike Leon Sullivan's job training and small business initiatives, the Black Coalition would never explicitly endorse market-based solutions to the problems of black poverty. Rather, the coalition's initiatives emphasized racial pride, cultural expression and the development of black-controlled institutions. Still, by turning to the private sector for financial assistance, the coalition's leadership was suggesting, as Booker T. Washington had at the beginning of the twentieth century, that the capitalist class could provide more reliable support for black progress than white-dominated political institutions.[9]

Philadelphia had largely avoided the violence that swept through many of the nation's cities following Dr. King's assassination on April 4, 1968. While Frank Rizzo would claim credit for preventing the violence that engulfed Washington, D.C., and other cities, much credit was also due to Clarence Farmer. A longtime Democratic Party activist whom Mayor Tate had appointed to head the Commission on Human Relations a year earlier, Farmer worked hard to develop relationships with the city's Black Power street activists in the months since the November 17 demonstration. Seeking to prevent a violent reaction to the King assassination, Farmer organized a memorial march and rally on Independence Mall in Center City for the next day. Following the rally, Farmer was meeting with Stanley Branche and a group of militants in his CHR office when he got word of a brewing confrontation between a couple hundred black teenagers and a contingent of police officers in the City Hall courtyard. Working together, Farmer and Branche were able to prevent the confrontation from escalating by convincing both sides to retreat.[10]

Having demonstrated his influence with the city's most prominent Black Power activists, Farmer then approached R. Stewart Rauch, Jr., the president of the Philadelphia Savings Fund Society (PSFS), with a proposal to engage the militants in a community building and economic development project. On April 12, Farmer took a group of black activists, including Stanley Branche and "Freedom" George Brower, to meet with representatives of the city's largest banks, insurance and brokerage companies, utilities, and manufacturers. Also at the meeting were two of the city's leading black attorneys: federal judge and former local NAACP president Leon Higginbotham, and William Coleman, the board chair of the NAACP Legal Defense Fund and the state's attorney on the Girard College case.[11]

The all-male makeup of the PSFS meeting points to the ways in which the Black Power movement's commitment to strong male leadership did not constitute a major break from prevailing practices in both the white business world and in traditional black leadership circles. Except for extraordinary figures like Goldie Watson and Sadie Alexander, political leadership was a male business in postwar Philadelphia, as it was across the country. Women were restricted to behind-the-scenes roles or found opportunities for leadership in the social service and education sectors. But while unremarkable, the all-male makeup of the meeting confirmed the militants' ideological tendency to see their encounter with the city's business elite as a test of manhood. If, in fact, the emasculation of black men was at the core of racial oppression, then the line between extorting funds from the white power structure and being bought and paid for (as Coleman and Higginbotham certainly must have looked to the militants) was thin indeed.

It was at this point that the story of the Black Coalition began to take on the melodramatic elements that often characterized interactions between Black Power activists and "well-meaning" whites. When Farmer and the militants arrived at the PSFS building, they found the police department's civil disobedience squad waiting for them. As Farmer remembers it, he managed both to assure the police officers that there would be no trouble and to convince the activists that the police were there on other business. The militants became even more upset when they arrived at the thirty-third-floor conference room and found Higginbotham and Coleman seated with the white business leaders on one side of the conference table. Farmer and the militants were clearly meant to sit on the other side. According to Farmer, the activists' initial response was to bolt the meeting; intentionally or not, Higginbotham and Coleman had violated the fundamental black nationalist principle of racial unity. Farmer, however, was able to convince them that Higginbotham and Coleman represented the "conscience of the community," and that the two could "talk to those guys [the business leaders] where you and I can't."[12]

The meeting began with the activists making a presentation, in the graphic and profane discourse that often defined black militancy in that era, on the jobs and youth programs that they hoped to start in the black community. The executives then announced that they too would like to make a presentation but that they would first need to caucus. When Coleman also rose to leave the room, the activists were further convinced that he was a race "traitor." When the corporate officials returned, they pledged to provide one million dollars over one year to establish an organization that could oversee the activists' proposed programs. Farmer remembers that many of the activists' initial reaction was less than positive. Someone shouted, "You don't buy us for a million dollars," and others responded, "We want three million dollars!" Farmer then proposed that the activists also leave the room for a caucus of their own. With the assistance of Judge Higginbotham, Farmer was able to convince the majority of the group to accept the offer. He remembers saying: "You guys got to

understand. You have to walk first before you can run. And I think this is a
very generous offer. We're talking about jobs. We're talking about program
money. Here's an opportunity." Although a few still viewed the offer as
insufficient, the majority of the group agreed to return to the meeting.
Finally, the two sides agreed to form a new organization that would be governed by two boards—one made up of the white business executives, the
other of a mixture of black militants and moderates like Higginbotham
and Coleman.[13]

Farmer planned the first meeting of the Black Coalition's "black" board
at a restaurant, with "the bar open." From the beginning, it was clear that
the militant Black Power activists were in fact more hostile to "upper-class
blacks" than they were to the white business leaders. Farmer thus placed a
microphone in the middle of the floor and said, "We need to have a
chance for you guys to recognize" each other. As Farmer remembers it,
"some of the community guys got a hold of the microphone and they
started 'bullshitting' and 'motherfucking' and this, that, and the other."
When some of the ministers present objected, Farmer said, "You've got to
see how mean and mad these guys are. These guys are mad!" Despite the
tensions, a group of fifteen black moderates and militants agreed to serve
on the Black Coalition board. Robert N. C. Nix, Jr., a common pleas court
judge and the son of the city's longtime black congressman, was appointed
board president. Farmer agreed to serve as secretary-treasurer. Others on
the board included Judge Higginbotham, school board vice president Rev.
Henry Nichols, city councilman Charles Durham, lawyer and West Philadelphia community activist Hardy Williams, Stanley Branche, Jeremiah X of
the Nation of Islam, "Freedom" George Brower, and two militants known
to the press only as Hakim and Malik. Branche was appointed executive
director of the Black Coalition with responsibility to oversee the day-to-day
operations; Hakim and Malik were also appointed to the coalition staff.[14]

The breadth of support that the coalition received from the city's corporate community was testament to the level of concern about the potential
for racial violence in the city. Serving as conveners of the white business
group were PSFS's Rauch and Richard C. Bond, chairman of the board of
the John Wanamaker Department Store. The list of business executives
who agreed to contribute to the million dollar pledge reads like a who's
who of the city's business leadership. It included board chairmen and presidents of Bell Telephone, Philco-Ford, the Philadelphia Electric Company,
Tasty Baking Company, Acme Supermarkets, Atlantic Richfield Oil, six of
the city's largest banks, five Center City department stores, five insurance
companies, two pharmaceutical companies and the city's two daily newspapers.[15]

The Black Coalition experiment lasted for a year. Its formation was
announced with much fanfare on May 8, 1968. Rauch declared that the

million dollars was "seed money" with "no ceiling" if the proposed programs proved successful. Branche announced that the coalition had rented a two-story building at Fifty-Ninth and Chestnut Streets in West Philadelphia to serve as its headquarters and that Walter Rosenbaum, a bail bondsman who had long been a supporter of Cecil Moore, had donated a second building on Columbia Avenue in North Philadelphia. The coalition's first project was a jobs program for residents of ghetto neighborhoods. Two job developers and two interviewers were to begin work in each of the offices immediately. A spokesman for the white business leaders promised that fifty jobs would be available by May 15 and hundreds more in the future. By June 3, Stanley Branche was able to announce that the coalition had placed 130 blacks in jobs. No one seemed concerned by the program's resemblance to the youth employment program that Leon Sullivan started in 1959 or to jobs programs that the Tate administration had touted as its riot prevention program the previous three summers.[16]

A second early project of the Black Coalition was a series of meetings with Jewish civic leaders designed to improve black-Jewish relations. The discussions focused on concerns about retail exploitation in the city's black ghettos. Branche and Robert Klein, executive vice president of the black-oriented WDAS radio, issued a joint statement which read: "the meetings of the Black Coalition and Jewish leaders are a joint effort to create new lines of communication and develop affirmative action programs to deal with the current racial crisis." Significantly, Branche and Freedom George Brower were the only militants who actually participated in the dialogues. In early July, the coalition and a group of Jewish leaders announced the establishment of a small business loan fund for black businesses in West Philadelphia's Fortieth and Lancaster retail district. Arranged with the assistance of the Small Business Administration and the Southeastern Pennsylvania Economic Development Corporation, the loans were to be managed by the Black Businessmen's Committee, a group co-chaired by Black Coalition board member Gus Lacy and Harold Treegoob, president of the Lancaster Avenue Businessmen's Association.[17]

As the coalition's executive director, earning a $20,000 per year salary, Branche felt the constant need to defend himself and his staff from charges that they, like the middle-class leaders they had long criticized, now served at the pleasure of their white patrons. In a June interview in the coalition's "air-conditioned" West Philadelphia headquarters, Branche told a reporter:

Some people are saying we used to be militants, but now we've turned into moderates. Don't you believe it, baby. We don't intend to be subservient to anybody, and we don't intend to lessen our protest against the white bigots who consider all black people nothing more than niggers. We're responsible to the black community and nobody else. . . . We're not interested in keeping the lid on anything.[18]

Invited to a closed-door meeting of "Negro leaders" with Republican presidential candidate Richard Nixon in July, Branche told the former vice president, "I ain't nothing but a nigger to you. You can try to fool me if you want to, but to me, you're nothing but a cracker." The coalition director also insisted that the coalition's rank-and-file members were subject to police harassment, despite the support of the city's business community. In August, he met with Police Commissioner Rizzo after charging that the police had beaten four of the group's neighborhood recruiters after they objected to a search of their car. "The cops have become experts at administering savage beatings to black men," Branche told the *Tribune.* "They have learned how to beat victims within an inch of their lives without leaving a scratch on them."[19]

As proof that they remained independent of the white power structure, Branche and the coalition staff could point to the fact that the majority of the coalition's funds went to establish programs that emphasized the development of black pride and cultural consciousness. Of the nearly $400,000 that had been budgeted, $150,000 went to the Black Brigade, a project directed by "Freedom" George Brower and Jeremiah X to clean up ghetto neighborhoods. "We hope to prove that once [these areas are] cleaned up," the NOI minister told a newspaper reporter, "there will be development of black pride on the part of the residents." A second grant of $100,000 was made to establish the Circle of Afro-American Unity, a youth-oriented black history and cultural arts program directed by Hakim at the Muntu Cultural Center in West Philadelphia. Hakim's proposal envisioned a community-based "learning center" which taught everything from basic business and consumer skills to African cultural arts and self-defense. The rest of the Black Coalition funding strategy more closely resembled the grant-making activities of more traditional antipoverty programs. A sum of $26,000 was earmarked for a garment industry job training program in North Philadelphia. The Center for Behavior Modification at Gratz High School received $20,000 for its dropout prevention programs, while the LaSalle College Urban Studies Program was given $4,000 for its gang prevention program. A summer educational and recreational youth program in the Point Breeze section of South Philadelphia received $12,000, while Paul Washington's Church of the Advocate was granted $13,000 to run a summer program on black history. An after-hours medical center in the Mantua section of West Philadelphia received $17,000. What had promised to be a coalition effort between black militants, moderates, and white business executives had evolved into a bifurcated program of black nationalist community development and private sector funding for traditional antipoverty programs.[20]

Almost from its founding, the Black Coalition was plagued by financial scandals and factional battles, both the result, at least in part, of anxieties generated by the group's dependence on black liberal patronage and white corporate funding. For example, two coalition fundraising campaigns led to charges of financial mismanagement. In the first, a motorcade with Muhammad Ali and "black models" toured black neighborhoods and stopped at white-owned stores to ask for donations. In the second, a raffle of a Cadillac, coalition members were seen driving around town in the car at a time when it was supposed to be parked on a West Philadelphia corner. An audit of the coalition's finances revealed that the two drives had resulted in a net-loss of $14,000. In September 1968 a dispute over the coalition's finances exploded in violence after a teacher of Islamic science at the Muntu School of Culture complained of mishandling of funds. According to a police warrant, Hakim and a second member of the coalition staff shot and wounded the teacher. The power struggle at the cultural center erupted again in January. A shootout involving members of RAM's Black Guard left one member critically wounded and two passersby, including a four year-old girl, with minor injuries. Shortly thereafter, an "internal power struggle" in another coalition program led to the arrest of eight coalition staff members on charges of attacking and robbing a dozen program participants.[21]

The collapse of the Black Coalition came quickly. On December 30, 1968, Stanley Branche announced his resignation as executive director, citing his lack of the necessary "education and background" to manage the organization. Saying the coalition "needs someone who knows administration and program designing," Branche defined his qualifications in classic masculinist terms. "I was a fighter." In February, Judge Higginbotham resigned from the coalition board to protest, he announced, the financial mismanagement. When Clarence Farmer and Judge Nix also announced their resignations in April 1969, leaders of the white business group decided it was time to close the coalition. The group promised to fulfill $91,000 worth of remaining programmatic commitments and to cover $12,000 in unpaid bills, including $2,000 of Branche's personal "business-related" debts. The remaining coalition programs were merged with the Philadelphia Urban Coalition, a public-private antipoverty program founded by Mayor Tate.[22]

The Black Economic Development Conference

Equally masculinist in its approach to Black Power politics was the Philadelphia chapter of the Black Economic Development Conference (BEDC). The National Black Economic Development Conference emerged from an April 1969 takeover of the annual conference of the Interreligious Foundation for Community Organization (IFCO), an agency whose mission was to channel church funds to grassroots antipoverty and social justice groups. Led by James Forman, the former executive secretary of SNCC, the activists demanded that IFCO give control of its financial capital to the communities it claimed to serve. In his speech to the conference, Forman called for "a society where the total means of production are taken from the rich and placed in the hands of the state for the welfare of all the people," and urged "black people who have suffered the most from exploitation and racism . . . to protect their black interests by assuming leadership inside the United States of everything that exists." Forman's speech formed the basis of "The Black Manifesto," a document that IFCO's convention delegates ultimately approved. The manifesto demanded that "white Christian churches and Jewish synagogues, which are part and parcel of the system of capitalism . . . begin to pay reparations to black people in this country." Specifically, the manifesto demanded $500 million, the equivalent, the manifesto asserted, of "$15 dollars per nigger." With the money, Forman proposed to establish a southern land bank, black-owned publishing and media cooperatives, training and research centers, a black university, and a fund to support organizing drives among black workers and welfare recipients. And to force these religious institutions to pay reparations, the manifesto called on "black people to commence the disruption of the racist churches and synagogues throughout the country."[23]

BEDC thus emerged as an avowedly socialist group that sought reparations for centuries of racial exploitation in order to fund community-controlled economic development projects in poor black areas. Like the Black Panther Party and the revolutionary union movement that emerged in the Detroit auto plants, BEDC synthesized its Marxist analysis of American racism with a social movement strategy designed to produce tangible gains for the black poor and working classes. Rather than seek financial support from the white business community, BEDC activists sought to force local religious organizations to establish reparation funds by disrupting their religious services and claiming underutilized church properties in black neighborhoods for the benefit of the community.

A week after the IFCO takeover, Forman set the tone for BEDC's combination of macho bravado and brazen confrontational tactics when he interrupted Sunday services at New York's liberal Riverside Church to read the Black Manifesto. Among the activists who agreed to take up Forman's call and to join the twenty-four-member board of the National Black Economic Development Conference was a Chester, Pennsylvania-based activist named Muhammad Kenyatta. As Donald Jackson, Kenyatta had been an active member of both SNCC and the Northern Student Movement. He now became the driving force behind the Philadelphia chapter of BEDC. Paul Washington has described the local BEDC chapter as a "little cluster of reparations activists . . . not a prepossessing group" who continued to earn media attention so long as they "could keep walking down church aisles, forcing white people to struggle with their consciences." Among the local group's to endorse the Black Manifesto was the Citywide Black Communities Council, in whose name Walter Palmer issued a public statement comparing the demand for reparations to the post-Emancipation promise of "forty acres and a mule" and German reparations to the Jewish victims of Nazism.[24]

Philadelphia BEDC operated with the combination of masculinst bravado and politics of personality that was characteristic of so many Black Power groups. Certainly, in the public's mind, Kenyatta and BEDC were indistinguishable. However, the group's internal culture was somewhat different. As Paul Washington has written, BEDC's "small band of activists included some very strong women, whose strength was difficult for Kenyatta to adjust to." Still, it would be a number of years before this kind of masculinist monopolization of power and celebrity would generate a sustained feminist critique from black women activists.[25]

Philadelphia BEDC's masculinist approach to movement activism was evident in the strategies and tactics it used to pursue its goal of reparations. In his theatrical takeovers of church services, Kenyatta was less Robin Hood stealing from the rich to the give to the poor than a "Western" gunslinger and bank robber single-handedly vanquishing the corrupt sheriffs and town fathers. BEDC's first protest action took place on June 3, 1969, when Kenyatta and other group members invaded the Center City headquarters of the Presbyterian Church to demand $20,000 so that it could open BEDC offices in North Philadelphia and Chester. After issuing their demands, the BEDC activists quietly left the building, but not before Kenyatta appropriated a typewriter to be used, he said, to produce educational materials for the children of North Philadelphia. The typewriter was later returned when the Presbyterians agreed to enter into negotiations with BEDC. Two weeks later, Kenyatta read the manifesto to a worship service of the Philadelphia Yearly Meeting of the Religious Society of Friends (Quakers). Shortly thereafter, BEDC disrupted Sunday mass at Holy Trinity Episcopal Church on Center City's Rittenhouse Square. BEDC's influence among liberal church activists can be seen in the description of the event written by Philadelphia's Episcopal bishop, Rev. Robert DeWitt.

After interrupting the service and speaking to the demands of the Manifesto, [Kenyatta] strode to the altar and picked up the alms basin. He flung the money on the floor of the sanctuary, dramatizing the sacrilege of a religious offering to God which belied and denied the weighty matters of the Law of God, such as racial justice. That was religious poetry acted out, worthy of Jeremiah.[26]

BEDC's protest campaign reached a peak when the group occupied Cookman United Methodist at Twelfth and Lehigh Streets in North Philadelphia on July 3. Cookman's white congregation had long ago moved out of the surrounding neighborhood. Instead of a resident pastor, the church shared its minister with three other Methodist parishes. For the most part, Cookman's extensive facilities remained closed to the neighborhood during the week. BEDC took over the church building after negotiations with local Methodist officials failed to produce an agreement that would allow the local community access to the church during the week. For the next eight days, between seventy-five and one hundred black activists remained within the church. On Sunday, BEDC made it clear it would allow the church congregation to hold its regular services. However, only one member of the congregation showed up. In the afternoon, 150 people attended a special worship service led by Rev. James Woodruff, a black Episcopal priest, and featuring a Kenyatta speech. Finally, on July 11, Methodist church leaders requested and received a court injunction requiring the activists to leave the church. When George Fencl's civil disobedience squad arrived to serve the injunction, most of the fifty remaining BEDC members in the church agreed to leave. However, eight ordained ministers insisted on remaining and were placed under arrest. As he was being taken to the police wagon, James Woodruff declared: "This building is God's house and therefore it is the house of the community . . . this church is ours." At a press conference, Kenyatta charged that "the United Methodist Church has put material worth and greed above spiritual worth and honesty."[27]

While protests like the Cookman occupation brought BEDC media attention, it was through negotiations with local church officials that the group was actually able to make progress toward its financial goals. As the presence of black clergy in the Cookman occupation demonstrates, the Black Manifesto's condemnation of church wealth and of the role that religion had played in the justification of racial exploitation and white supremacy resonated with many religious leaders and activists. BEDC's protests became the impetus for a debate over the responsibility of religious institutions toward the creation of racial justice. In an essay entitled "The Church's Response to the Black Manifesto," Rev. Dr. Gayraud S. Wilmore, the black director of the Presbyterian Church's Division on Church and Race, wrote:

Whatever one may think of James Forman's policies and tactics of disruptive confrontation, the church should recognize that this is not the first time that God has called upon the wrath of those outside the church to summon it to repentance and obedience. The great wealth that churches have accumulated may have become a spiritual liability. Rather than help men and women to destroy the dehumanizing, demonic structures which cripple them, most church funds have been used to enhance the welfare of the churches and their members.[28]

BEDC's negotiations with local church leaders began when Paul Washington arranged for Kenyatta to meet with Bishop DeWitt in the rectory of the Church of the Advocate after which the Bishop announced that he supported BEDC's demands for reparations from both the local diocese and the national church. To James Forman's demand that the Episcopal Church provide $60 million in reparations, Bishop DeWitt suggested the national church mortgage the Episcopal Church Center in New York. Also endorsing BEDC's demands were the Council of Black Clergy of Philadelphia, the United Church of Christ Youth Division, and the Wellsprings Ecumenical Renewal Associates, a group of clergy committed to interfaith and interracial dialogue. The support of these religious leaders, however, did not translate into large grants of church funds. The Council of Black Clergy donated $1,000. Church groups in other cities gave similar amounts. Despite Bishop DeWitt's endorsement, the Diocesan Council of the Episcopal Diocese of Pennsylvania initially rejected Kenyatta's demands. Washington then resigned from the council in protest. The Eastern Pennsylvania Conference of the United Methodist Church also rejected a reparations proposal. In August 1969, a walkout of black delegates forced a special national convention of the Episcopal Church to pledge $200,000 to support BEDC's national office. Finally, after nearly a year of cajoling from Bishop DeWitt, the Diocesan Council agreed to establish a $500,000 Restoration Fund for antipoverty projects in the Philadelphia black community. Administered by Jesse Anderson, the Restoration Fund would never make a single grant to BEDC, instead directing its funds to traditional social service agencies.[29]

A year of debate within the Quaker Philadelphia Yearly Meeting produced a similar result. In September 1969, Kenyatta demanded $500,000 from the city's Quaker meetings. After nearly five months of debate, an ad hoc committee of the Yearly Meeting proposed the establishment of a $100,000 fund for black economic development projects. However, the fund was to be managed by a special committee of the Yearly Meeting, not BEDC. All that BEDC would ever receive from the city's Quaker community was $5,000 in individual donations.[30]

As profound as BEDC's challenge to the nation's churches was, the irony of the reparations campaign was that most of the funds that it managed to wrest from religious institutions were directed to the very same social service institutions that had failed to address the crisis of black poverty in America. "The desire in the hearts of many," Paul Washington wrote in his memoir, "to take seriously the commands of the Bible as framed in the Prayer Book's call for restitution was frustrated on the one hand by fear and racist attitudes and on the other by the limitations of the instrument that had been offered to enable restitution."[31] In the end, James Forman and Muhammad Kenyatta's Marxist critique of racial oppression and strategy of confrontation had no more impact on the structures of black poverty in Philadelphia than the pro-capitalist initiatives of Stanley Branche, Nathan Wright, and Leon Sullivan.

Building a Community-Based Movement of the Poor

At the same time that Stanley Branche's Black Coalition and Muhammad Kenyatta's BEDC pursued the vision of a masculinist political leadership for the black community, the logic of the Black Power movement's commitment to community control and indigenous leadership development also produced a very different kind of leadership within the antipoverty and community organizing initiatives that emerged in black Philadelphia during the last years of the 1960s. Two organizations in particular—the Philadelphia Welfare Rights Organization (PWRO) and the Council of Organizations on Philadelphia Police Accountability and Responsibility (COPPAR)—exemplify the way that efforts to establish alternative, community-led organizations that would be capable of forcing the politically powerful to address the problems of black poverty revealed long-hidden forms of working-class women's leadership in the black community.

The welfare rights movement is usually perceived as rooted in the interracialism of the early 1960s.[32] The leadership of PWRO, however, was predominately black and its most active neighborhood chapters were clearly in black areas of the city. Furthermore, the group's maternalist agenda, which insisted that poor women had a right to state support to raise their children, bore a perhaps coincidental similarity to the efforts of masculinist Black Power activists to reinscribe traditional gender roles.[33] Even the interracialism practiced by PWRO looked very different from the colorblindness of the beloved community. The key to PWRO's success within the city's black neighborhoods was its ability to cultivate the leadership skills of black women activists while making use of a staff of primarily white VISTA volunteers as well as allies in the local New Left and among suburban middle- and upper-class churchwomen. This coalition of poor black women and middle-class white activists represented a significant reordering of interracial relationships that had occurred within the mainstream civil rights movement (though not within SNCC, which from its founding was a black-led organization in which white activists played a relatively minor role), a reordering that was at least in part a result of Black Power. Within PWRO, it was clear that the group's strategic decisions were made by the welfare mothers, not their middle-class supporters.[34]

Both local and national welfare rights organizing challenged the stigmatization of aid recipients as unwilling to work, morally disreputable, and the beneficiaries of the state's good will.[35] As Felicia Kornbluh has argued, welfare rights activists employed the "rights talk" of "American constitutionalism" and the civil rights movement to insist that "as citizens, mothers, consumers, and human beings" they had a right to sufficient public aid to support their families and, in the words of one of their leaders, enjoy "perfume once in a while." The welfare rights movement thus challenged not only a long public policy tradition that viewed work as superior to public assistance but also the civil rights movement's emphasis on equal access to labor markets. Kornbluh argues that welfare rights' consumerist position represented a critique of the failure of both government and the market to make it possible for the poor "to participate fully in the post-World

War II consumer economy."[36] The power of the welfare rights organizing discourse lay in its message to welfare recipients that not only should they not have to suffer the stigmatization of being on public assistance but that they had the same right as middle-class mothers to stay out of the waged workforce and focus their work lives on the raising of their children. It was this combination of consumerist and maternalist discourse that made the welfare rights movement's emphasis on working-class women's leadership implicitly complementary to Black Power's masculinist ideology.

The PWRO was formed in the Spring of 1967 as part of the national drive led by George Wiley, the director of the Washington D.C.-based Poverty Rights Action Center and the former associate national director of CORE, to establish the National Welfare Rights Organization. The PWRO's founding conference, entitled the First Welfare Rights Conference, drew three hundred welfare recipients to the auditorium of the Philadelphia Central YMCA on April 21, 1967. According to conference organizers, the attendees represented twenty-seven neighborhood-based welfare rights groups organized through the city's network of settlement houses and neighborhood associations. Buses transported recipients to the conference from five settlement houses, four neighborhood groups, and the offices of five Community Action Councils. The conference's keynote speakers were Wiley and Paul Washington. Workshops were held on topics like "Organizing Rights Groups," "Fundraising," and "Goals and Strategies." Wiley, who would serve as the national organization's executive director until his death, urged the conference attendees to press the state of Pennsylvania to increase funding for public assistance by $60 million and to assist the national organization's efforts to force the federal government to establish a minimum national standard for public assistance. "If we do not get our rights," Wiley said, "we are going to force the Government to grant them as soon as possible."[37]

The local impetus for the establishment of the PWRO had come from an alliance of neighborhood activists, settlement house workers, and social service organization officials who for the previous five years had been seeking to increase the level of public assistance grants in Pennsylvania. In 1962, the Philadelphia Health and Welfare Council (HWC) called on the state legislature to raise public assistance grants by 30 percent and to maintain "the level of payment to a standard at least comparable to that of the community as a whole." After another group, the Pennsylvania Citizens Council, issued a similar report on public assistance elsewhere in the state, the state Department of Public Welfare acknowledged in a 1963 report that its aid programs met "only about two-thirds of the cost of living at a minimum standard of health and decency."[38]

The formation of Citizens Concerned with Public Assistance Allowances in 1964 presaged the shift in welfare advocacy from expert analysis to recipient-led movement organizing. A coalition of community groups and settlement houses formed with the assistance of the HWC, Citizens Concerned's first act was to organize a 130-person march on the state capitol in Harrisburg in February 1964 to demand a one-third increase in public assistance to families. The group's member organizations included community groups and block councils from black neighborhoods in North, West, and South Philadelphia. Groups like the Baldwin Neighbors, the Strawberry Mansion and Wharton Block Councils, and the North City Congress had emerged from well-established settlement houses, while organizations like the Hawthorne Council and the Haddington Leadership Organization had formed in racially transitional neighborhoods to work on urban renewal and landlord-tenant issues. Marie Shumate, leader of the Haddington community group, served as one of the coalition's co-chairs and three of the other five members of the coalition's steering committee were women. Still, few if any of the city's 100,000 aid recipients were active members of Citizens Concerned. In November 1964, Shumate urged the member groups to "let recipients know their rights and try to dispel their fears. We must gain improvements in the rights of recipients."[39]

Although Citizens Concerned brought community-based activists—many of them women—into the leadership of the movement for welfare reform, aid recipients did not begin to play a prominent role in local welfare advocacy until 1966. Partly as a response to the War on Poverty's mandate that antipoverty efforts involve the "maximum feasible participation of the poor," both the HWC and Citizens Concerned began to highlight the participation of "recipients" in their efforts to press for increased state funding for public assistance. In a March 1966 analysis of local welfare reform campaigns, Terry Dellmuth, the HWC's consultant on public welfare, noted that public assistance recipients in the state lacked an organization of their own to "act as a 'lobby' to help influence legislators." Dellmuth called on welfare advocates to emphasize the needs of children on public assistance in an effort to counter "the present negative image of the recipient." As a result, the HWC set out to establish the Crusade for Children as a citywide "coalition of recipients and many civic and religious organizations" committed to raising public assistance in Pennsylvania "to 100 percent of the state-established Minimum Standard for Health and Decency."[40]

Organizers of the Crusade for Children hoped to recruit aid recipients by setting up meetings in the city's network of settlement houses for recipients to discuss their problems with officials from the Department of Public Welfare. Model crusade chapters soon emerged in West Philadelphia, where Marie Shumate had long sought to involve aid recipients in the work of Citizens Concerned, and in the North Philadelphia neighborhoods served by the Wharton Centre. In both areas, groups of aid recipients began to "discuss their problems," study federal and state welfare regulations, and develop strategies for recruiting other aid recipients to the Crusade for Children. Still, the leadership of the crusade remained in the hands of middle-class activists. For example, the crusade's chairman was Rev. Jerry Carpenter of the Greater Philadelphia Council of Churches.[41]

During the summer of 1966, the crusade sponsored two recipient-led protests to demand increases in state assistance grants. On June 8, one thousand welfare mothers and children traveled to Harrisburg to march on the state capitol in order to demand that state legislators raise public assistance grants from 70 to 100 percent of the state's minimum standard. Sponsored by the city agency responsible for coordinating the local War on Poverty, buses for the protest left from twelve neighborhood antipoverty offices. Following the march, Kathryne Dunbar, a mother of eight and leader of the Citizens' Concerned recipient group, served as spokesperson in a meeting with Max Rosenn, the state's secretary of public welfare. Three weeks later, five hundred mothers and children held an all-night vigil in front of the State Office Building at Broad and Spring Garden Streets in Philadelphia.[42]

By then, steps were being taken to establish an independent organization for welfare recipients in the city. In August, a number of Philadelphia welfare activists traveled to Chicago for a George Wiley-organized meeting to discuss the creation of a national welfare rights organization. By the time of the April 1967 conference, members of the neighborhood-based welfare rights groups were ready to establish an independent organization. At a May 11 meeting, the group elected Hazel Leslie to serve as chair of the PWRO Coordinating Committee. A member of the executive board of the Ludlow Community Organization, a neighborhood group on the eastern edge of North Philadelphia, and chair of its welfare rights group, Leslie was raising her eight-year-old niece as a single parent. She had gone on relief after being ordered not to work by her doctor because of her diabetes. Other officers elected were vice-chair Martha Melton, secretary Margaret Campbell, and treasurer Myrtle McCullough, the group's only white officer. Every neighborhood welfare group with ten members who had paid the organization's $1 per year membership dues received two votes on the coordinating committee. By the time of the May 1967 meeting, ten neighborhood groups had qualified as voting members of the coordinating committee.[43]

The PWRO also played a prominent role in the emerging national movement. On June 30, three hundred members of PWRO and supporters from the Health and Welfare Council and the Greater Philadelphia Council of Churches marched in front of the State Office Building at Broad and Spring Garden to protest "insulting treatment of welfare recipients" as part of NWRO's first national day of protest. At the rally, PWRO activists handed out fliers that charged that "caseworkers treat us like dirt . . . [and] do not tell us our rights" and submitted a petition to the County Board of Assistance complaining that "the attitudes and practices of many employees in the Department of Public Assistance [are] grudging, distrustful, judgmental and even abusive." Caseworkers, the petition charged, made unannounced visits to recipients' homes, failed to inform recipients of their basic rights and of benefits to which they were entitled, and did not notify them in writing of reasons for rejection or termination of assistance.[44]

In August, twelve PWRO members attended the first NWRO national conference in Washington, D.C. Following the convention, two hundred members of the local group participated in a 15,000-person Mothers' March on Washington to protest efforts in the House of Representatives to water down the Johnson administration's welfare bill. The convention and march solidified the PWRO members' sense of participating in a national movement. "The Rally in Washington has brought to us the need for more unity," the PWRO newsletter quoted local convention delegate Clara Moore. "If we are to make advancements from poverty we must first make it nationwide. We are under the same roof, fighting the same cause."[45]

By October 1967, the PWRO had 330 dues-paying members. PWRO activists recruited new members at welfare offices across the city by distributing a pamphlet that described in simple terms the benefits programs and eligibility requirements. Many joined the group after receiving assistance from a PWRO activist with a problem that they were having with their benefits. Wearing buttons that declared "Welfare is a right not a privilege," the PWRO activists directly challenged discourteous treatment from caseworkers. "These people can be very nasty," Rosa Lee Williams, president of the Kingsessing WRO chapter in West Philadelphia, told a newspaper reporter. "We just don't want to be treated like dogs just because we have to be on welfare."[46]

The PWRO pursued a multi-faceted agenda. First and foremost was the group's demand for public assistance grants to be pegged at 100 percent of the state's minimum requirement. Equally important to the membership were PWRO's demands for fair treatment from the welfare bureaucracy. The group demanded that different caseworkers evaluate applicants' eligibility for aid and provide services to recipients. The same person, the group argued, could not be effective as both police officer and counselor. The PWRO also called for more selective hiring and better training for caseworkers, recognition that applicants who meet the "means test" have a legal right to aid, regular meetings between officials of the board of assistance and the PWRO, and representation of recipients on the board of assistance. At the same time, PWRO activists worked for a $75 clothing allowance for schoolchildren, an end to discrimination against welfare recipients by landlords and utility companies, and the removal of draconian restrictions on the personal lives of aid recipients, such as the ban on aid recipients' purchasing or improving private homes.[47]

The PWRO won a number of substantial victories very quickly. In 1967, the Philadelphia County Board of Assistance agreed to set up liaison committees to work with the PWRO in every welfare office in the city, although the board refused to give the group official representation on the county board. Working with Community Legal Services (CLS), the War on Poverty's legal assistance program, PWRO was able to reduce the rejection rate for new aid applicants from 50 percent to less than 31 percent by January 1968. During the PWRO's first seven months, the number of aid recipients in Philadelphia rose by 20,000. At the same time, a PWRO-CLS legal suit led to the removal of Pennsylvania's one-year residency requirement for welfare assistance. In April 1969, the state Department of Public Welfare reached an agreement with the PWRO that allowed the group to establish tables in welfare offices from which they could distribute literature and assist applicants and recipients. That fall, the groups convinced the VISTA program to enroll nine members of the organization in their volunteer program and to train them to serve as welfare advocates within welfare offices.[48]

Much of the PWRO's success can be credited to its innovative protest and lobbying tactics. The PWRO's leadership recognized that it had to overcome well-organized opposition to increases in relief spending and a compelling political discourse which accused welfare families of asking taxpayers to support illegitimate babies. They were therefore prepared to use innovative methods to humanize their plight and win public sympathy. To dramatize their inability to buy shoes for their children on their monthly grants, twenty-seven PWRO members went to the Philadelphia Blood Center to sell their blood in November 1967. The action's impact was only heightened when twenty-five of the twenty-seven were rejected because of an iron deficiency in their blood. According to newspaper reports, the PWRO members only laughed when the blood center's director recommended that they eat more red meat and fresh vegetables. A week later, Rev. Jerry Carpenter of the Council of Churches, Rev. David Gracie, the urban missioner for the local Episcopal Diocese, and two other white middle-class activists sold their blood and donated the proceeds to the group. Within days donations of shoes, clothing, and money were pouring into the PWRO headquarters. The PWRO's neighborhood chapters also picketed landlords who refused to rent to welfare families or offered them substandard housing. In March 1968, for example, the *Tribune* quoted Kingsessing WRO chair Rosa Lee Williams as declaring "war against landlords who take advantage of the poor." In May, PWRO representatives met with Gordon Cavanaugh, the city's deputy managing director for housing, to demand that the Department of Licenses and Inspection do a better job of policing slumlords. Specifically, they sought required inspections of all single and multiple family dwellings before they were rented, increased minimum fines for landlords who refused to correct code violations, and a reduction of the number of code violations necessary to declare a building unfit for habitation.[49]

The PWRO's supporters also sought to challenge the public image of welfare recipients in more traditional ways. In January 1968, a wide range of religious and civic organizations—including Catholic Social Services, the Catholic Youth Organization, the Cardinal's Commission on Economic Opportunity, and the Chamber of Commerce—issued public statements supporting PWRO's demand that welfare grants rise to 100 percent of the minimum standard of living. A year later, Bishop DeWitt issued a pastoral letter which called the "claims of the poor . . . just and unconditional" and criticized "a contemptuous view of the poor as incompetent, indolent, and unworthy." "The crushing of people's pride through a welfare system that forces them to live at bare subsistence levels," DeWitt concluded, "is not to be tolerated by a Christian people." In October 1969, Roxanne Jones who had succeed Hazel Leslie as PWRO chair in the spring of 1968, challenged eight hundred civic and political leaders to support their families on a public assistance grant for one month. While the PWRO received no answers from either Mayor Tate or the Republican governor, twenty-three prominent figures agreed to accept Jones's challenge, including David Gracie, black state representative Earl Vann, and Robert W. Reifsnyder, executive director of the United Fund. Jones urged all who accepted her challenge not to cheat if they ran out of money at the end of the month. "If you run into trouble," she told them, "you can go to the Salvation Army."[50]

Essential to the PWRO's growth was the support it received from groups like the Health and Welfare Council (HWC) and the Greater Philadelphia Council of Churches and the networks of liberal allies to which those groups gave the welfare activists access. In addition to the public support from figures like Bishop DeWitt, the PWRO received staff assistance from the Health and Welfare Council until it was able to establish its own staff. Middle-class activists also played a crucial role in the group's legal and legislative activities. For example, the PWRO Coordinating Committee appointed two of its neighborhood leaders, Kathryne Dunbar and Becky Brown to lead a special ad hoc committee to examine housing issues affecting welfare families. Aiding Dunbar and Brown were two "resource persons," Marie Shumate, the Crusade for Children leader who had joined the staff of the Philadelphia Housing Association, and Thomas Gilhool, a lawyer with Community Legal Services. Middle-class supporters were particularly crucial to the PWRO's fund-raising. HWC staff member Sue Hyatt organized a group of suburban churchwomen called Friends of Welfare Rights that raised money for the PWRO and attended demonstrations. Membership dues for associate members were $2 to $5 per year and contributing members made a donation of $25.[51]

The PWRO pursued its most creative protest tactics after Roxanne Jones, a single mother of two, was elected to replace Hazel Leslie—who had stepped down for health reasons—as PWRO chair in March 1968. Six months earlier, Jones had joined the PWRO chapter in South Philadelphia's Southwark Housing Project after a welfare caseworker made her "feel like I had killed someone" for applying for public assistance. She had gone on relief four years earlier after divorcing her husband and quitting her job as a waitress because of high blood pressure. Shortly after her election as PWRO chair, Jones led a PWRO campaign to pressure the state to increase the size of the public assistance grant. On March 27, 1968, eight hundred aid recipients from across the state marched on the state capitol building as the senate appropriations committee debated the governor's proposal to raise relief grants from 71 percent to 90 percent of the minimum family requirement. In a speech to the marchers, Jones declared, "I don't call it being on welfare anymore. I'm getting a subsidy just like those farmers." Shortly thereafter, the legislature approved the governor's proposal.[52]

In April 1968, the PWRO began what would prove to be its most successful campaign, a drive demanding that local department stores offer store credit to PWRO members. The campaign began with a picket line in front of the Lits Brothers Department Store in Center City. By August, four stores—Lits, Wanamakers, Lerner, and Lane Bryant—had all reached credit agreements with the organization. "No longer are we restricted to buying inferior merchandise at high prices in the ghetto," one PWRO member told the *Tribune*. By creating a substantive benefit to membership in the organization, the credit campaign victory led to rapid growth in the PWRO's membership. By November 1968, the PWRO membership had reached one thousand.[53]

PWRO activists, led by Rose Wylie, a widowed mother of six who had lived in North Philadelphia's Richard Allen Homes for sixteen years, were also instrumental in forming the Residents Advisory Board (RAB), the first independent organization of public housing tenants in Philadelphia. Wylie and the RAB worked closely with the Philadelphia Housing Authority under the leadership of liberal reformer Gordon Cavanaugh to resolve tenant concerns. In fact, the RAB achieved its most significant victory when one of its members, Mrs. Kee, was named to the housing authority board. When Cavanaugh left Philadelphia in 1971 for a position in Washington, D.C., Wylie called it "a shock . . . Cavanaugh has always been responsive to tenants. Philadelphia has never had a tenant strike because he and his staff have always worked with us." The RAB's relationship with the city's political leadership was not so cooperative. When Mayor Tate responded to white protests by suspending construction of new public housing units in the Whitman Park section of South Philadelphia in June 1971, RAB activists sought a court injunction against the construction of new luxury townhomes in the elite Society Hill section of Center City. "There's something wrong with a system that allows a mayor to stop the building of homes for

Figure 13. Roxanne Jones of the Philadelphia Welfare Rights Organization negotiates with state officials during a PWRO sit-in at the Philadelphia Offices of the Department of Public Assistance. Urban Archives, Temple University Libraries.

poor people," Wylie declared, "but allows homes for the wealthy to be constructed." That year, Wylie was elected chairwoman of the National Tenants Organization and was named by President Nixon as the first public housing tenant to serve on the National Rent Advisory Board. Wylie accepted the latter appointment even though, she told the *Tribune*, she was opposed to Nixon "in every way."[54]

The PWRO's most confrontational protest campaign took place in November and December of 1968. Even though the state legislature and the governor had approved a bill raising public assistance grants to 90 percent of the minimum standard on January 1, 1969, Roxanne Jones was determined to press for an increase to 100 percent of the standard. On November 14, 250 welfare mothers, children, and their supporters held a sit-in in the Philadelphia offices of the Department of Public Assistance to demand a $50 "Christmas bonus grant" before the increased grant levels began on January 1 (Figure 13). As they sat-in, the mothers and children sang Christmas carols and civil rights songs. "We want $50 additional to provide our children with a decent American Christmas," Jones declared, "more money is needed to insure that the slow starvation inflicted upon citizens in Pennsylvania at this Christmas and for many years will be ended." Working with black state legislators, the sit-in leaders insisted that the state could use its surplus and emergency funds for the special one-time grants. The PWRO activists only agreed to end their sit-in at 2:30 A.M. after the state attorney general threatened to have them forcibly removed. Shortly thereafter, PWRO's black legislative allies sought to amend the welfare bill to move the start date of the grant increases from January 1 to December 1 and to enact the $50 Christmas bonus. As the state House of Representatives debated the proposed amendment, four hundred welfare rights activists from Philadelphia and Chester initiated a second sit-in in the state capitol. Eventually, the amendment was defeated and the welfare rights activists forcibly removed from the capitol, but PWRO and its allies had demonstrated their determination to be heard in the state legislature. By 1971, the group's membership had risen to 3,000, and George Wiley, NWRO's Executive Director, was calling PWRO "the most dynamic local group in the country."[55]

In 1971, the PWRO enthusiastically joined the NWRO campaign against the Nixon administration's Family Assistance Plan (FAP), a proposal to provide a $1600 subsidy grant to families on assistance. In testimony to a U.S. Senate Hearing, Jones attacked the $1,600 figure as insufficient. "I want to know who thought up $1600 a year when Tricky Dick's dogs cost $2700 a year." In their campaign against the FAP Jones and the PWRO turned to both the Black Power and antiwar movements for allies. In 1971, Jones served as co-chairperson, along with Muhammad Kenyatta, of the Pennsylvania People's Coalition for Peace and Justice (PCPJ), an attempt to develop a structured alliance between the white New Left and black activist groups. The PCPJ's platform included an end to the Vietnam War, black equality, and higher welfare benefits. At one Philadelphia antiwar rally, PWRO members carried a coffin with a sign that said "Nixon welfare proposal."[56]

As the 1970s progressed, the rise of antitax conservatives and the impact of economic stagnation on the state's budget stalled PWRO's drive to raise public assistance grants to 100 percent of the minimum standard. In part, PWRO's declining influence was a product of its success. By September 1971, welfare rolls in the city had risen to 312,685, a 166 percent increase since 1967. Between 1968 and 1971, the state's public assistance budget grew from $350 million to more than $1.1 billion.[57] In 1970, Pennsylvania's Republican governor Raymond Shafer announced plans to cut welfare payments by 75 percent in order, he said, to prevent a tax increase. In June of that year, Jones led one hundred WRO members in an angry demonstration at the state capitol to protest Shafer's plan. The governor's proposed cuts were defeated in the state legislature but Jones was arrested and charged with using her shoe to break a window outside the governor's office during the demonstration. She was convicted and sentenced to two months for destroying public property but was released after serving five days when she promised to "refrain from violence." Later, she would declare that her imprisonment had only made her "stronger." "Any time someone in this country works on behalf of social change, at some point he or she will pay a penalty. I've always been prepared for that."[58]

The PWRO and its allies in the national welfare rights movement provided an important challenge to service delivery models of antipoverty work. The welfare reforms of the late 1990s were based on the presumption that the growth of programs like Aid to Families with Dependent Children (AFDC) and food stamps during the 1960s and 1970s had only increased dependency on the state and the concomitant problems of teenage pregnancy and single-parent families.[59] However, in a local economy unable to provide decent paying employment and quality childcare to large numbers of poor mothers, the gains achieved by the PWRO and its allies made a much greater contribution to the quality of life in Philadelphia's poor neighborhoods (as well as the independence of poor women from both bad marriages and degrading domestic work) than the vast array of social services developed during the War on Poverty.

COPPAR and Community Control of the Police

The complex relationship between Black Power's emphasis on masculinist leadership and its promotion of community-based leaders can be seen in the late 1960s campaign for community control of the police. On Sunday, August 30, 1970, Philadelphians opened their newspapers to see the climactic image of the confrontation between black radicals and the police in Philadelphia: members of the Philadelphia chapter of the Black Panther Party (BPP) under arrest and standing naked—symbolically stripped of their manhood—in front of the local party headquarters in North Philadelphia. The previous day, one police officer had been murdered and three wounded in West Philadelphia. Charging that the officer's assailant was a "black revolutionary," Commissioner Rizzo ordered a 5 A.M. raid on Panther offices in Germantown and North and West Philadelphia. Given the Panthers reputation for being well armed, the police arrived with submachine guns and tear gas. Concerned about children who were asleep in the headquarters, Reggie Schell, the Philadelphia chapter's minister of defense, ordered the party members to surrender after the police fired tear gas inside the building. Schell describes what happened next:

Each cop took an individual Panther and placed their pistol up the back of our neck and told us to walk down the street backward. They told us if we stumble or fall they're gonna kill us. Then they lined us up against the wall and a cop with a .45 sub would fire over our heads so the bricks started falling down. Most of us had been in bed, and they just ripped the goddamn clothes off everybody, women and men. They had the gun, they'd just snatch your pants down and they took pictures like that.[60]

Given images like these, it is tempting to view the Panthers, with their discourse and practice of armed self-defense, as the central organization in the movement for community control over the police in Philadelphia's black neighborhoods. But while the Panthers provided an important symbol of the black community's refusal to accept racist and brutal police practices any longer, the more effective challenge to Frank Rizzo's violent version of law enforcement came from a network of community-based activists organized and led by a working-class middle-aged woman. Mary Rouse's style of leadership was the antithesis of the masculinist bravado of the BPP. Her ability to forge the Council of Organizations on Philadelphia Police Accountability and Responsibility (COPPAR) into an effective coalition whose member organizations ranged from the BPP to the ACLU counters the dominant image of the Black Power movement as crippled by racial and gender tensions.

The FOP Campaign Against the Police Advisory Board

The community-based movement against police brutality in Philadelphia emerged in response to the successful campaign of the Philadelphia Fraternal Order of Police (FOP) to press Mayor Tate to abolish the city's Police Advisory Board (PAB). As I discussed in Chapter 4, opposition from the FOP had made the PAB reluctant to overrule the police department's internal disciplinary process in any but the most egregious cases since its founding in 1958. During its nine years of operations, the PAB handled 932 cases but only once did it recommend that an officer be dismissed. All told, the PAB recommended that twenty officers be suspended and thirty officers reprimanded.[61]

Still, the FOP continued to call for the PAB's abolition. In a 1965 lawsuit, the FOP charged that the PAB hindered the ability of police officers to carry out their duties, that it was illegally constituted under the city charter, and that it functioned as a court, rather than as an advisory board. On March 29, 1967, Judge Leo Weinrott of the Philadelphia Common Pleas Court ruled in the FOP's favor, finding that the PAB had been illegally established and ordering the city to abolish the board. Mayor Tate disbanded the PAB even as he approved an appeal of the ruling. For the next two years, the PAB remained dormant. Even after the Pennsylvania Supreme Court overturned Judge Weinrott's decision in June 1969, the mayor refused to reestablish the board. The mayor's reasons for his decision demonstrates the extent to which he had come to view Frank Rizzo's law-and-order policies as key both to his own political popularity and the future of the Democratic machine. In a letter to former PAB chairman,

Mercer Tate—who was not related to the mayor—Mayor Tate argued that "the morale of the Police Department is a matter of primary importance to . . . the community at large." Moreover, he contended that Rizzo and the police department had "been and continue to be receptive to all citizen complaints." The commissioner, the letter concluded, "has promised a full and prompt investigation of every case."[62]

Still, liberal activists continued to press for the PAB's reinstatement. Following the supreme court decision, the Fellowship Commission sponsored the formation of the Citizens for the PAB (Police Advisory Board) to pressure Mayor Tate to reactivate the board. With member groups ranging from the Philadelphia Urban League and the ACLU to the Citywide Black Communities Council and the Paschall Betterment League, a West Philadelphia community organization, Citizens for the PAB reflected the degree to which the city's liberal community was seeking to appear more responsive to black community organizations. However, the efforts of Citizens for the PAB had little impact on the mayor. On December 22, 1969, he issued an executive order dissolving the PAB. In a public statement, the mayor argued that "the continuance of the Police Advisory Board, under current circumstances, actually provokes rather than eases tensions in our city. It appears to be, therefore, in the interest of the public welfare for our entire community that this agency be dissolved."[63]

Even as the city's liberal reform organizations continued to press for citizen oversight of the police, activists influenced by the Black Power analysis of persistent racial inequality began to advocate new approaches to curbing police abuses in the black community. Black activists had long been frustrated with what they viewed as the timidity of the PAB. In the aftermath of the July 1965 incident in which then-Deputy Commissioner Rizzo punched a Girard College demonstrator at the Broad Street State Office Building, a number of activists first submitted and then withdrew complaints to the PAB. In withdrawing his complaint, Dwight Campbell, a member of the NAACP Youth Council, charged that "the powers of the board are not sufficient to handle cases of police brutality." Increasingly, black activists were rejecting the liberal view that police brutality resulted from the racist attitudes of individual officers and instead arguing that the police were the primary enforcers of racial control in a white supremacist society.[64]

Nationally, the most prominent advocate of this view of urban police forces was Black Panther Party founder Huey Newton. To Newton, the police were the "military arm" of the black community's "oppressors." Point 7 of the BPP's platform called for an "immediate end to POLICE BRUTALITY and MURDER of Black people." Citing the failure of "civilian review boards to supervise the behavior of the police," Newton looked to the "organized citizen patrols" that black activists had already begun to organize in a number of cities to follow "the police and observe . . . them in community dealings" for the solution to police abuses in the black community. Influenced by the self-defense language of Malcolm X and Robert F. Williams, the BPP founder decided to go beyond taking photographs and making "tape recordings" to organize armed patrols in order to dramatically demonstrate the black community's right and ability to defend itself against racist police violence. Thus the BPP platform read:

We believe we can end police brutality in our Black community by organizing Black self-defense groups that are dedicated to defending our Black community from racist police oppression and brutality. The Second Amendment to the Constitution of the United States gives a right to bear arms. We therefore believe that all Black people should arm themselves for self-defense.[65]

Frank Rizzo's steady rise through the Philadelphia police hierarchy made the Black Panthers' analysis of the role of the police in black communities seem particularly relevant to Philadelphia. Following Rizzo's May 1967 appointment as police commissioner, CORE leader Bill Mathis charged that the mayor had appointed him "to ride herd on protest elements in the city." The search for new ways of policing the police was heightened even further by the November 17 demonstration. On December 10, 1967, a meeting of one hundred activists who refused to identify themselves or their groups to the media called for a Christmas boycott of all locally-owned stores to protest the mayor's refusal to fire Rizzo. Black Philadelphians were encouraged to buy only essential items from "out-of-town" stores and with each purchase to leave a pledge card that read, in part: "I will not buy any non-essential items until RIZZO IS FIRED!" The activists also distributed anonymous fliers which urged people not to "buy until Rizzo is fired."[66]

The events of 1967 led an ideologically diverse range of Philadelphians to pursue the concept of community control of the police. Following the 1964 riot, the North City Congress (NCC) had received a $600,000 grant to initiate a police-community relations program which included a series of meetings between community residents and police officials. What the NCC leadership believed to have been a productive dialogue broke down following Rizzo's appointment as police commissioner. According to NCC executive director Alvin Echols, Rizzo "showed an unwillingness to accept constructive criticism of police activities . . . and to recognize that give-and-take plays a significant part in building harmony between citizens and police." The NCC later issued a report on police violence that concluded that "there is no way, at present, to insure that police brutality will be redressed, no way to insure that . . . racists and authoritarians will be weeded out [of the department]." The NCC report called for the establishment of police oversight mechanisms that involved the "community's representatives." Alton Lemon, the coordinator of the NCC police-community project, later participated in a Washington, D.C., conference sponsored by the Institute for Policy Studies, a left-wing think tank, which considered three mechanisms for establishing community control over the police: (1) the establishment "of neighborhood commissions with full . . . power over the police"; (2) the creation of "counter-police organizations" to monitor police activity and challenge the political power of police departments; and (3) a shift from a professionalized police force made up of career "beat" officers to a nonprofessional peacekeeping force in which citizens served for short periods of time.[67]

On May 18, 1968, some 241 people representing seventy "citizen and professional groups" attended a conference called "Police Power in a Free Society: Citizen Responsibility and Police Accountability" at Temple University. What was remarkable about the Temple conference was the breadth of city leaders willing to join the search for a new approach to police-community relations. The conference co-chair was Gustave Amsterdam, a leading local business executive who was one of the founders of the Greater Philadelphia Movement (GPM), the leading business group in the urban renewal movement of the 1940s and 1950s. The conference speakers included William Wilcox, the GPM's executive director, Thacher Long-streth, a Republican city councilman and executive director of the Greater Philadelphia Chamber of Conference, and Alvin Echols from the NCC. According to the conference report, participants in the conference largely supported a proposal for the establishment of "civilian policy control boards with powers of investigation both citywide and at the precinct level."[68]

The Black Panther Party in Philadelphia

The Black Panther Party first appeared in Philadelphia in October 1968 when a self-described party spokesman named Terry McHarris issued a statement announcing the formation of the Philadelphia chapter of the BPP. According to McHarris, the local chapter sought "an end to white robbery of the black community . . . an end to police brutality and murder of black people, trial by a jury of black peers, land, bread, housing, education, clothing, justice and peace." By the following spring, the chapter's unquestioned leader was Reggie Schell, a self-described "street nigger," former gang member, and military veteran who had grown up in South Philadelphia and attended Southern High in the late 1950s. After his military service, Schell returned to Philadelphia and began to work in a sheet-metal plant in which blacks were restricted to the foundry and the punch presses and were paid less than white machine workers. Angered by the televised scenes of violent attacks on civil rights demonstrators, he began looking for an organization that would give him "a chance to fight back." Then, in May 1967, he watched the television coverage of the Panthers' armed protest at the California state capitol. Within a year, Schell and some friends had opened the Black Panther offices on Columbia Avenue, just blocks from the center of the 1964 riot.[69]

Early in 1969, national BPP field marshall Don Cox traveled to Philadelphia to inspect the local Panthers and grant them a charter from the national office. During Cox's visit, Schell was named defense captain, the top position in a local Panther chapter. While the Philadelphia Panthers focused their efforts on police brutality and promoting the constitutional right to self-defense, they seem to have rarely used the armed patrolling tactics that gained the Oakland Panthers such notoriety. Rather, they emphasized more traditional forms of advocacy, selling the party newspaper, organizing demonstrations against police brutality, publishing a sixteen-page booklet complete with wanted posters of the police officers who murdered a black high school student, and helping to establish the COP-PAR coalition. According to Mumia Abu-Jamal, who helped to found the Philadelphia chapter as a fourteen-year-old, by the spring of 1970 the local party had grown from fifteen to more than one hundred members and was selling ten thousand copies of the Panther newspaper per week. In addition, the local party started a free breakfast program for children in a building across the street from its Columbia Avenue headquarters with food donations solicited from North Philadelphia merchants. Schell described the breakfast program as a lot of work but very satisfying because "it was our first real program and our first attempt at trying to do something fundamental for people in the community." With the help of a Quaker doctor, the party convinced Philadelphia Yearly Meeting to allow it to open a medical clinic in a building that the yearly meeting owned at Sixteenth and Susquehanna Streets in North Philadelphia. Eventually, the Panthers started a second breakfast program in the Susquehanna building.[70]

Still, the discourse of self-defense remained at the center of Panther organizing in the city. Party members attended weapons classes as well as study groups on Panther ideology. In December 1969, a thousand people attended a memorial service at the Church of the Advocate for BPP members Fred Hampton and Mark Clark who were killed in a police raid on the party's Chicago headquarters.[71] Huey Newton once described the party's armed patrols as a "means of recruiting."[72] Certainly, in Philadelphia it was the party's emphasis on "the gun" that attracted the vast majority of party members. "When people first joined," Schell argued, "the only fundamental change that they thought had to be made was to . . . let the system know . . . that they would fight. Before the party came into existence, black people just were looked on as people who will take a nice little ass whipping." For young men who had grown used to daily harassment from the police, the party's self-defense methods offered the opportunity to protect themselves, their families, and their communities. The party's hypermasculine image of the gun-toting Panther came to represent not only the right to self-defense but all the rights of manhood, including the ability to support and protect a wife and children. As Schell put it to an interviewer in the late 1970s:

I'm talking about a man who's been on the job eight years. He's not satisfied with the wage scale. He's not satisfied with the relationship that the boss has with him . . . he just takes it and takes it . . . because it is essential that he bring home the bread and butter. Now these men . . . are in a constant state of turmoil . . . the Black Panther Party . . . existed as something that was totally opposed to that.[73]

As much as the party's embrace of the gun as a symbol of resurgent manhood spurred on its recruiting efforts among the young men of Philadelphia's poor and working-class black neighborhoods, it also constrained its ability to develop a sustainable long-term strategy for achieving its goals. In particular, the party's commitment to openly discussing and showing its guns contradicted its paramilitary aspirations and left it vulnerable to police harassment. Schell would later acknowledge that the party had begun acquiring weapons before it was "organized well enough to have our security in tact." In this sense, the Panthers became the perfect foil for Frank Rizzo's warnings that armed black revolutionaries were invading the city. In December 1969, a joint FBI-police raid of Schell's sister's home found what the police called a stolen government M-14 rifle. Schell was subsequently indicted by a federal grand jury. As in other cities, the Philadelphia police seem to have taken the Panthers' talk of armed self-defense as a direct challenge. Schell remembers being told by both local police officers and FBI agents "we know you all got guns, motherfucker, but we got the firepower, and we'll kill you." He also describes daily police harassment. "You'd just be walking down the street or driving in the car and he'd pull over, stop, search you, take you down to the station for investigation." FBI agents even visited Schell's mother to warn that other party members were planning to kill her son.[74]

Still, the Philadelphia party continued to grow and was selected by the Panther's national leadership to host its Revolutionary People's Constitutional Convention on September 5–6, 1970. Black Power, antiwar, and other movement activists from across the country had already begun to arrive in the city when the police officer was shot to death on August 29. The subsequent raids on the Panther headquarters caused widespread horror among the city's movement activists. At a press conference two days later, black and white activists, including Muhammad Kenyatta, Sister Falaka Fattah and David Gracie, announced that they were seeking a federal injunction to prevent police harassment of the convention and its delegates. "The Black Panther convention is going ahead full steam," promised one local party member who spoke at the press conference without giving his name. Even though bail for the Panther leadership was originally set at

$100,000, they were freed when the Philadelphia Yearly Meeting and other church groups agreed to post property bail. After Temple reaffirmed its commitment to allow the convention to take place on campus and movement lawyers won their injunction against police harassment, the convention took place without further violence. In the days that followed, the Fellowship Commission called on the U.S. Civil Rights Commission to conduct an investigation of both the police shooting and the Panther raids. In the short term, the raids and the convention led to rapid growth in the local party. In the months that followed, membership in the Philadelphia BPP grew to more than 150.[75]

In a late 1970s interview, however, Schell argued that the convention was in fact the beginning of the party's decline both in Philadelphia and nationally. It marked Huey Newton's first public appearance since his release from prison following the reversal of his conviction for murdering a police officer. The "Free Huey" campaign orchestrated by party leaders David Hilliard and Eldridge Cleaver had enabled the party to grow from a small cadre of activists in Oakland to a national movement with a membership estimated at one thousand in the three years Newton was in jail. Newton was the party's symbolic and ideological leader, but he had little connection to most of the party's membership. As Schell describes it, Newton's speech in Philadelphia was a dismal failure. "What he said just lost people. When he spoke to the people at that session, he spoke . . . way over their head." Schell and other local activists also became increasingly disillusioned with a national leadership that seemed to have lost interest in the party's rank-and-file members. In the months that followed, factional splits divided the party at both the local and national level, climaxing with Newton's expulsion of Eldridge Cleaver and much of the Panther leadership in New York and Philadelphia for advocating urban guerrilla warfare. Believing that the party's advocacy of armed self-defense was leading the party to a war with the police that it could not win, Newton ordered a deemphasis of "the gun" and a shift in strategy to the delivery of services to the poor.[76]

In June 1971, Herman Smith, the BPP's new Pennsylvania coordinator, circulated a letter announcing the party's change in strategy. "We have . . . set aside our purple rhetoric of the past," he wrote, "and are concentrating our efforts on establishing programs that will be of a beneficial nature to our people." Without the masculinist appeal of "the gun," however, membership in many party chapters dwindled. By 1973, the Philadelphia BPP had less than twenty-five members. Meanwhile, Reggie Schell, Mumia Abu-Jamal, and other former members of the Philadelphia chapter had formed the Black United Liberation Front (BULF) early in 1971. While the BULF was able to continue the party's breakfast and prison programs and to start a North Philadelphia gang unity initiative, it too was largely defunct by 1973.[77]

Figure 14. Mattie Humphrey (far left) and Mary Rouse (far right) with fellow activists Novella Williams, Edna Thomas, Alice Walker, and Alice Lipscomb. Urban Archives, Temple University Libraries.

COPPAR

As dramatic as the Panther confrontations with the police were, the most significant challenge to Frank Rizzo's law-and-order approach to urban policing and his campaign of police harassment against black radicals came from the Council of Organizations on Philadelphia Police Accountability and Responsibility (COPPAR), the citywide coalition that the Panther chapter had helped to build. COPPAR was founded and led by Mary Rouse (Figure 14), a community activist with the Kensington Council on Black Affairs, a neighborhood organization in the racially checkerboard and tense working-class neighborhoods of lower Northeast Philadelphia. Rouse first began to work on police brutality issues after one of her sons suffered a police beating in 1966. After the PAB suspended operations in 1967, Rouse formed COPPAR to collect and investigate complaints of police abuse from across the city. "There is no mechanism in the city of Philadelphia today," she said, "where you can take a complaint and get an impartial and thorough hearing." Despite a lack of paid staff or even of telephone service, COPPAR's Operation Alert recruited activists from across the city to observe police conduct in black neighborhoods. In addition, the group provided legal observers for the demonstrations of groups "threatened by police abuse."[78]

The COPPAR coalition could not have differed from the liberal civil rights coalition of the 1940s and 1950s more dramatically. Unlike the Fellowship Commission's roster of professionally led reform organizations, COPPAR's twenty-two member groups included (in addition to the Panthers) neighborhood groups, citywide organizations of the poor, and antiwar groups.[79] COPPAR believed that both political and structural change was necessary to reform police behavior in Philadelphia. COPPAR's position paper argued that the Rizzo-led police department had become "an open and active instrument of political coercion" but recognized that the department's power was premised on "a solid majority of support" in the city for "law and order." "This majority," the paper argued, "has been persuaded . . . that minimal restraints should be placed on the police because otherwise, the 'criminal elements' will overrun the community." Ending police abuses in the black community therefore required efforts to break the law-and-order consensus among the city's white majority. "The majority that now accepts police abuse of power," the COPPAR paper argued, "cannot be moved away from this position until . . . the extent . . . of police mistreatment" is widely known. COPPAR thus proposed to disseminate "the facts on police abuses to a wide audience." The position paper only secondarily focused on "structural reform," the need "to give the people of Philadelphia meaningful control over the conduct of the police." And COPPAR viewed political action as the key to achieving community control over the police. The paper promised that "COPPAR will seek to rally citizens and organizations" to press city officials for reform of police oversight.[80]

As part of its public education efforts, COPPAR and its member groups compiled a large dossier of police brutality complaints and police obstruction of efforts to investigate those complaints. In February 1970, the Germantown Council for Community Control of Police, whose membership included neighborhood groups from both poor and wealthy areas of the Northwest section of the city, published an advertisement documenting nine examples of questionable police activity in the *Chestnut Hill Local,* the neighborhood weekly newspaper in the most affluent section of the city. The ad described the police practice of "turf dropping" in which black youth were picked up and then dropped off on the turf of rival gangs or in white neighborhoods. Commissioner Rizzo, the ad charged, had recently announced that police would no longer use such tactics "only after it resulted in the death of a young man." Previously, the commissioner had denied that turf dropping existed. Most of the incidents cited in the ad involved beatings of arrested suspects and bystanders who protested police violence. "The police have achieved an autonomy in Philadelphia," the ad concluded, that makes "scrutiny of their conduct not only impossible but perilous." COPPAR also published a newsletter documenting police abuses across the city. The October 1971 newsletter, for example, described police harassment of youth activists in Germantown who were working to end gang warfare, including BPUM student leader David Richardson as well as members of the former Brickyard gang who had reorganized themselves into the Brickyard Youth Council. The newsletter charged that rather than assist these antigang efforts, the captain of the Fourteenth Police District had orchestrated a campaign of harassment against the youth activists, including the planting of a Molotov cocktail and a sawed-off shotgun on one black activist.[81]

The COPPAR newsletter also solicited reports of police abuses, such as random car stops and searches, for possible litigation. COPPAR worked with the Lawyers' Committee for Civil Rights Under Law to document what it believed was a significant rise in police shootings of civilians in the weeks following the August 1970 shootings of police officers and the subsequent raids on the BPP's headquarters. According to COPPAR's research, thirteen black Philadelphians were killed by police officers in 1970, almost double the previous high of seven in 1967 and 1969. In 1966, the year before Rizzo became police commissioner, only two blacks were killed by police bullets in Philadelphia. All told, thirty-five Philadelphians were shot by police officers in 1970. Many of these shootings occurred, COPPAR charged, in situations in which "there was no danger of any harm to the policeman." Using this data, COPPAR asked the federal courts for a temporary restraining order against the Philadelphia police for systematically violating black civil rights. In its legal action, COPPAR presented seventy witnesses and 250 complaints of police brutality.[82]

COPPAR's investigations and public education campaigns culminated with public hearings on police-community relations in Philadelphia convened by the U.S. Commission on Civil Rights (USCCR) in March 1971. COPPAR was represented at the commission hearings by Mary Rouse, Rose Wylie of the Residents Advisory Board, Edwin Wolf of the Lawyers Committee, and Maria Bonet of the Puerto Rican Fraternity. Rouse testified that she had faced continued police harassment since she began working on issues of police abuse. "My telephones are tapped," she said, "my mail is censored . . . plainclothesmen follow me [and] people who visit my home." Bonet reported that the police continued to practice "turf dropping," leaving black and Puerto Rican teenagers in the white working-class community of Fishtown and whites on the turf of the Zulu Nation gang. Wylie discussed how police-community relations had changed since she "first moved into public housing [and] there was a policeman on the beat that we all got to know." The Civil Rights Commission's Pennsylvania Advisory Committee concluded that "the rights of minority citizens are not fully respected by the police. The arrest process in too many instances seems to be used as a means of humiliation, harassment, or an instrument of indiscriminate community control." The committee called on the Justice Department to investigate the police department "in as much as the department appears to operate as a system closed to public examination and accountability." In addition, the committee called for the reestablishment of an "external" review board to investigate citizen complaints against the police, as well as the formation of a "nonpartisan citizens' board" with "minority" input "to guide the overall policy of the police department" and the creation of citizens' boards in each police district "to review citizen complaints . . . help determine personnel policies . . . and work in the community to encourage support for law enforcement."[83]

*   *   *

The relationship between COPPAR and the Black Panthers reflected the complex legacy of Black Power masculinism. The male-dominated leadership structures of the Panthers, BPUM, BEDC, and the Black Coalition were not unusual in the local history of black political organization. With important exceptions—most notably Goldie Watson and Sadie Alexander—the city's civil rights leadership had long been an exclusively male club with women activists relegated to behind-the-scenes roles. What was most remarkable in fact about the leadership of civil rights groups in postwar Philadelphia was just how unremarkable male predominance of leadership roles was. Contrary to Black Power's masculinist rhetoric, black women had never been "pushed forward" into black political leadership. The real target of Black Power masculinism was the male leadership of the NAACP, SCLC, and other mainstream civil rights groups that had seemingly failed to fulfill its manly duty to militantly defend black families and communities from racial violence and other forms of racial oppression.

In practice, Black Power's masculinist ideology led groups like Philadelphia SNCC and BEDC to undervalue the tremendously skilled and committed women organizers in their midst. Others, most notably the Panthers and the Black Coalition, followed their own macho rhetoric into what would ultimately prove to be self-destructive strategies. However, the excesses wrought by masculinism should not blind us to the revolution in political leadership that emerged from Black Power's synthesis of community organizing principles with the black nationalist call for a political leadership rooted within poor and working-class communities. By the end of the 1960s, a new coterie of working-class and community-based women activists—figures like Mattie Humphrey and Sister Falaka Fattah, Roxanne Jones and Mary Rouse had emerged to take their place among the citywide black leadership class.

Chapter 8
From Protest to Politics

> The political philosophy of black nationalism means that the black
> man should control the politics and politicians in his own community.
>
> —*Malcolm X*

Given the commitment of Black Power activists to finding collective solutions to the problems facing the black poor and working classes, the War on Poverty provided a logical focus for efforts to establish community control over government programs operating in the black community. The Black Power campaign to establish community control over local antipoverty programs followed a similar trajectory to efforts to win community control over the schools. With the support of sympathetic liberal government officials, Black Power activists and their allies won a number of important victories for the principle that control over government programs to reduce poverty in black communities should reside within those communities rather than within City Hall. These victories, however, depended entirely on the goodwill of government officials and the ability of those officials to remain in power. When more racially conservative politicians replaced the Black Power activists' liberal allies, first on the national level and then in local elections, the structures of community control that had been so laboriously established quickly disappeared.

For many in the city's Black Power movement, there was a clear lesson to be learned from their inability to sustain community control over the local War on Poverty. Without a strategy for controlling the political representatives of the black community, there was little hope for establishing sustainable community control over the public institutions that so influenced life in poor black communities. "Growth Liberalism," as practiced by both Lyndon Johnson and Richard Nixon, responded to the process of private disinvestment in urban industrial economies by investing local government with the financial resources necessary to spur economic development. It is not surprising therefore that black activists and politicians would come to view winning control over city government as the key to gaining the lever-

age they needed to negotiate with the federal government for public investment programs to fight poverty and strengthen the economies of black
urban communities.[1]

Thus, the logic of community control led directly to the reemergence of
Black Power electoral political strategies. Black Power advocates and their
allies won a significant number of important victories for the city's working-
class black neighborhoods in the latter years of the 1960s. But too often,
those victories were rescinded as when conservative politicians replaced liberal government officials at both the local and national levels. For some,
the lesson of these experiences was that political elites were prepared to
use any means necessary to prevent the black community from achieving
self-determination and community control. In this view, continued pursuit
of electoral strategies reflected either persistent naïveté or the triumph of
personal ambition over the commitment to racial justice. But within the
local context of a city like Philadelphia, activists seeking to redress the
problems of the ghetto came to recognize that only by electing supporters
to public office could they hope to sustain black control over public institutions and resources in the black community.

Community Control and the War on Poverty

As numerous scholars have documented, the Johnson administration
developed the War on Poverty on the premise that the primary cause of
continued poverty in the midst of the wealthiest nation in human history
was neither the capitalist economy nor racial discrimination, but rather the
poor themselves. Only a lack of necessary job skills and educational opportunities—and a kind of hopelessness rooted in what academic theorists
called the "culture of poverty"—were preventing poor Americans from
taking advantage of the multitude of economic opportunities available in
the postwar United States. The administration thus proposed to bring an
end to poverty not by providing jobs or redistributing income to the poor,
but by investing in the kinds of social service programs that would enable
the poor to develop the skills and attributes they needed to make it on their
own. It was to be, as Sargent Shriver, the first head of the Office of Economic Opportunity (OEO), put it, "a hand up, not a handout."[2] At the
core of the Johnson's administration's strategy for the War on Poverty was
the Community Action Program (CAP) which provided block grants to
local antipoverty agencies on the theory that local people would best know
how to design antipoverty programs for the local community. The only
requirement placed on these local Community Action Agencies was that
they provide for the "maximum feasible participation of the poor" in the
design and implementation of their programs. Federal officials believed

that this approach would give the poor a greater stake in their communities and thus a sense of hope for their own lives and those of their neighbors.[3]

Thus, the mandate for the "maximum feasible participation of the poor" in local War on Poverty programs provided Black Power activists with the ideal opportunity to fight for community control over the spending of federal dollars in the black community. In fact, as a number of historians have documented, advocates of Black Power and community control were able to have significant influence over Community Action Agencies in places like New York and San Francisco.[4] The situation, however, was quite different in Philadelphia. While the organizational structure of the Philadelphia Antipoverty Action Committee (PAAC) created the appearance of significant participation by representatives of the city's poor neighborhoods, Mayor Tate and the Democratic machine in fact controlled every aspect of the PAAC and its programs. Or to be more specific, Samuel Evans, the black concert promoter and longtime Democratic party activist whom Tate appointed to the PAAC board, ran the antipoverty agency as the black patronage wing of the machine from his position as vice-chairman of the PAAC board.[5] In the words of one observer, the PAAC's primary mission under Evans' leadership was "the maximum feasible participation of Sam Evans."[6]

On February 10, 1965, Mayor Tate announced the formation of the Philadelphia Antipoverty Action Committee with a board made up of five mayoral appointees, representatives of fifteen civic groups ranging from the local chapters of CORE and the NAACP to the Chamber of Commerce and the Catholic archdiocese, and twelve representatives of the city's "poverty community."[7] The representatives of the poor would be selected following an antipoverty election that the mayor scheduled for May 26, 1965. In that election, residents of twelve poverty districts across the city would elect a twelve-member Community Action Council (CAC) to coordinate antipoverty activities in their community. Each CAC was then to select one representative to sit on the citywide PAAC.[8]

The PAAC board, minus the representatives of the poor, held its first meeting in early March 1965. In its first act, the committee agreed to allow the mayor to select an executive director for the antipoverty program based on the recommendations of a six person subcommittee drawn from the PAAC board. The selection process, however, soon devolved into a power struggle between Sam Evans and Cecil Moore. Evans had been a strong supporter of Moore in his role as NAACP president. At the same time, he had long been allied with Mayor Tate and the Democratic organization and he now opposed Moore's candidate to lead the PAAC, Isaiah Crippins, the Philadelphia NAACP's legal counsel. Evans instead proposed Charles Bowser, a black attorney who had done work for the NAACP and had also served on the Police Advisory Board. While Moore called Bowser "a good lawyer," he charged that he "is not identified with the masses of the people." Only the NAACP's candidate, Moore insisted, could be trusted to run the antipoverty program in the interests of the poor. "Crippins comes from the poor," he declared, "works with the poor, and understands the problems of the poor." Moore threatened to resign from the PAAC if Crippins was not selected, making it clear that his goal was to wrest control of the antipoverty program from City Hall. He charged that Evans' support for Bowser represented "an attempt to take the War on Poverty out of the hands of the masses and give it to people whose only interests are their own selfish motives." Evans successfully undercut Moore, however, by proposing that the mayor appoint Bowser as PAAC executive director and Crippins as the program's legal counsel. Eager to mollify activist criticism of his antipoverty efforts without giving up control over the local program to Cecil Moore and the NAACP, Tate accepted. And, much to Moore's consternation, Crippins also said yes.[9]

Charles Bowser's appointment made him the highest-ranking black official in the Tate administration and his $17,000 salary made him the highest paid. The new director's first task was to organize elections for the Community Action Councils. A successful election would make the PAAC the first local antipoverty agency in the country to sponsor direct elections of poor people. By the May 12 deadline, 353 people had submitted nominating petitions with the required fifty signatures. All told, 13,493 people voted in the first-ever CAC election, less than 3 percent of the eligible voters. Turnout ranged from nearly 20 percent in parts of North Philadelphia, comparable to the primary elections earlier in the month, to less than one-half of one percent in the largely white lower Northeast neighborhoods of Kensington, Bridesburg, and Frankford.[10]

The election results demonstrated the disproportionate role of women in community organizations in the city's poor neighborhoods. Women made up 61 percent of the candidates. Community organizations, neighborhood settlement houses, and churches mobilized for the elections. For example, in Area F, on the western edge of North Philadelphia, a coalition of neighborhood block and school parent associations endorsed a slate of twelve candidates "because of their long years of volunteer dedication and meritorious service to the people of our neighborhoods." Nine of the twelve were women. All told, women were elected to 73 percent of the CAC seats. Among the longtime activists elected to their local CACs were Clara Baldwin, the founder and director of the Baldwin Settlement House in North Philadelphia, and Abigail Pankey, president of West Philadelphia's Mantua Housing Committee. While eight of the twelve CACs selected male chairmen, eight of the twelve CAC representatives elected to the PAAC board, in many ways the more important position, were women.[11]

Both the OEO and local movement activists initially praised the PAAC board structure and election process. To David Fineman, CORE's representative to the PAAC, the antipoverty election was evidence "that get-up-and-go, stick-to-it-iveness, shrewdness, and ability to get things done are not the monopoly of the upper economic groups." Johnson administration officials were equally enthusiastic. Less than a month after the election, OEO director Sargent Shriver announced that the city would receive $5.9 million for its antipoverty programs, including nearly $3 million for Board of Education-sponsored preschool programs, $1.7 million for Leon Sullivan's Opportunities Industrialization Centers (OIC), $663,000 for PAAC's central administration, $350,000 to the Department of Recreation for programs "aimed at relieving racial tensions in the city's congested neighborhoods," and $350,000 for the twelve CAC offices.[12]

Soon, however, local movement activists, including the CORE and NAACP representatives to the PAAC board, were charging that Sam Evans was transforming the antipoverty program into a patronage operation for the Democratic machine. Evans had moved quickly during the PAAC's first three months to win control of a majority of votes on the PAAC board. In return for the support of the board's social welfare representatives, he promised to steer the vast majority of the PAAC's funds to their agencies while making it clear that he would block funding to any organization that opposed his leadership of the board. In theory, the presence of representatives of the poor on the PAAC board was supposed to counter the influence of both traditional social service groups and party functionaries like Evans. In Philadelphia, however, the presence of the CAC representatives on the PAAC board only increased Evans's power. The PAAC vice-chairman wined and dined those CAC representatives who supported him; those who opposed him charged that their area councils lost funding. Moreover, it was the OEO's decision to suspend Civil Service requirements, including antinepotism rules, for most jobs in local antipoverty programs—in order to give poor people a greater chance of qualifying for those jobs—gave Evans his most important weapon in his efforts to control the PAAC board. An OEO inquiry would later find that at one point 118 of 144 elected CAC members and 142 of their relatives had received jobs in the antipoverty program or elsewhere in city government. The result of these patronage efforts was that Evans consistently controlled at least nine of the twelve CAC votes on the PAAC board during the program's early years.[13]

As a result of Evans's domination of the PAAC board, the vast majority of antipoverty funds in Philadelphia went to traditional social service agencies rather than to the CACs or other community-based programs. In the PAAC's first year of operation, eighty percent of its funding went to established service programs, including $6 million to the Board of Education, $2 million to OIC, and nearly a million to the Catholic archdiocese's youth leadership programs. As of March 1966, the PAAC board had approved only three of thirty-three proposals it had received from the CACs. "The community action councils have been ready, willing, and able to do their part in mounting a War on Poverty in Philadelphia," CORE's David Fineman wrote, "However, they have been forced into the status of penniless orphans by the established social welfare agencies."[14]

Evans and Bowser, however, were unapologetic for their efforts to forge the CAC representatives into a single bloc. In their view, the War on Poverty was never going to produce sufficient funds to solve the problems of the ghetto. It was therefore crucial to use the antipoverty program to forge a political force in poor black neighborhoods capable of contesting for power within the city's Democratic Party. The fact that most of the PAAC funding was going to service programs for the poor was less important than developing the political skills and capital of the PAAC's representatives of the poor. "We didn't want to give them jobs and give them food and give them houses," Bowser remembers. "We wanted to teach them how to operate so they could get it for themselves." Thus for Evans and Bowser, the goal was to build a political machine that would enable poor blacks to garner the same benefits from participation in the city's political process that members of the city's other ethnic groups enjoyed.[15]

Despite the efforts of both the OEO and local movement activists, Evans and his supporters would never relinquish control of Philadelphia's antipoverty program.[16] Evans boasted that if the OEO "think[s] the poor of Philadelphia don't approve of the way we are handling the program . . . I can pack Convention Hall with poor people who know we're doing a good job." In December 1966, a secret OEO report found that the CACs were so irrelevant to the antipoverty effort in Philadelphia that they had been largely deserted and their staffs left demoralized. In an attempt to reduce the power of the PAAC central office, the OEO then insisted that the PAAC board eliminate Isaiah Crippins's position and demote Bowser's chief aide before it would release additional funds to the program. The PAAC board eventually accepted these requirements but not before Bowser resigned from the agency, charging that the OEO's actions were a "racist" attack on black leadership. The controversy, however, had little impact on Evans's control over the board. Only the collapse of the federal War on Poverty could disrupt Evans' patronage machine. By 1968, congressional cuts had led to a steep drop in PAAC funding. In December of that year, the PAAC board was forced to reduce it budget by $900,000. A year later, the budget was reduced by another million dollars.[17]

Community Control and Citizen Participation in the Model Cities Program

The last of President Johnson's major antipoverty initiatives, the Model Cities Program sought to spur the physical and economic redevelopment of the nation's urban ghettos. Having learned from the PAAC experience, movement activists in Philadelphia were determined to wrest from City

Hall control of the citizen participation component of the local Model Cities program. In this effort, they would enjoy the support of officials from the U.S. Department of Housing and Urban Development (HUD), the federal agency that oversaw Model Cities, who were equally determined to avoid the OEO's mistakes in Philadelphia.[18] This alliance of local activists and federal bureaucrats would transform the balance of power between the Tate administration and North Philadelphia's community organizations.

Mayor Tate had been an early and enthusiastic supporter of the Model Cities Initiative. In testimony before the Housing Subcommittee of the House Banking and Currency Committee, he declared that "the city's goal is to create a floor in the level of physical and social existence below which it will no longer permit human beings to fall." Even as Congress continued to debate the Model Cities legislation, the Tate administration submitted a $600 million proposal to HUD to rehabilitate North Philadelphia, calling its neighborhoods "the single most deteriorated, socially cancerous and economically depressed area in the entire city."[19] When the Model Cities Act finally passed, however, it required cities to first apply for a planning grant to develop a comprehensive redevelopment plan for its target area before seeking development funding. And, as with the War on Poverty, cities had to demonstrate that their planning process would "provide a meaningful role in policy-making to . . . residents" of the target area. In February 1967, the city government submitted to HUD a proposal for a $750,000 planning grant for a nine-hundred-square block area of North Philadelphia. Initially, the Tate administration had planned to use the North Philadelphia CACs as the basis for the citizen participation component of the program. By 1967, however, the city had deleted all references to the CACs, perhaps because the PAAC was by then so discredited within the Johnson administration. Instead, city officials proposed to utilize North Philadelphia's well-established network of block clubs, neighborhood groups, and social welfare organizations for its citizen participation program.[20]

When approached, however, community activists in North Philadelphia insisted on guarantees that they would be able to play a meaningful role in the Model Cities planning process. In January 1967, the North City Congress (NCC), a coalition of fifty-eight neighborhood organizations based in central North Philadelphia, voted to reject the city's request that it appoint representatives to the city's Model Cities Task Force. The NCC voted to participate in the planning grant if and only if the city was willing to give it full "responsibility for developing and maintaining meaningful citizen participation" in the Model Cities program. Alvin Echols, the NCC's executive director, believed that community activists could successfully resist the incorporation of Model Cities into the Democratic machine's patronage operation by organizing a broad-based coalition of neighborhood groups in North Philadelphia to represent the area's residents in the program's planning process. By relying "on existing groups and agencies," Echols argued, the coalition could avoid what he called "the antipoverty trap" in which the representatives of the community could not prevent City Hall from controlling the program's decision-making process. Eager to win HUD's approval of its proposal, the Tate administration conceded to Echols's demand that the organizational structure formed by the area's community organizations be treated as "equal partners . . . in making decisions, setting the goals and policies, and allocating the funds involved in" Model Cities. "For the first time," an NCC statement crowed, "we have the opportunity to influence a major development program from the inside, where our decisions will count."[21]

On February 13, 1967, sixty-six neighborhood representatives approved Echols's proposal to form the Area-Wide Council (AWC) "to involve and organize the community for participation in the MCP [Model Cities Program]." Echols proposed to organize the AWC according to what he called "the 'hub' concept" in order to insure that the council both involved "the greatest number of groups and individuals directly in the decision-making process" and most effectively represented the interests of community residents in the Model Cities planning process. To establish the hubs, the AWC planned to identify "agencies, institutions, and organizations with office space, administrative experience, communications equipment, and connections with individuals and groups around them," in different parts of the North Philadelphia target area to serve as gathering points for community groups and residents interested in contributing to the Model Cities planning process. Each hub was then to form a council representative of its area to work on local redevelopment plans and to appoint members of that council to represent their area on the AWC Steering Committee and its four planning subcommittees: Physical Environment, Education, Human Resources, and Employment and Manpower. To organize the hub structure, Echols hired William Meek as the AWC's executive director. The longtime assistant director of the Wharton Centre, a North Philadelphia settlement house, Meek had chaired the host committee for Martin Luther King's 1966 visit to Philadelphia and was also married to the Urban League's Sylvia Meek.[22]

The AWC was formally established at a five-hundred-person mass meeting on April 20, 1967. By that point, two hundred neighborhood groups had agreed to join one of the council's sixteen hubs. Among the organizations donating space to serve as one of the AWC's sixteen hubs were nine churches (including the Church of the Advocate), three settlement houses, an elementary school, and the Council of Spanish Speaking Organizations. Despite this enthusiastic beginning, the AWC's effort to develop a community planning process was slowed by delays both in congressional appropriations for the Model Cities program and in HUD's review of the city's proposal. Finally on August 17, 1967, Mayor Tate, in the midst of a close reelection campaign, announced that the city would advance the matching funds it was due to provide to the AWC while it waited for HUD to reach a decision on the proposal. The city's grant enabled the AWC to hire the organizing staff necessary to initiate the hub-based planning process. In November, HUD approved a $178,000 Model Cities planning grant for Philadelphia and an additional $100,000 for special projects in the North Philadelphia target area.[23]

As part of his commitment to include the full spectrum of black community activists in the Model Cities planning process, Meek hired BPUM activist Walter Palmer to direct the organizing staff. "Part of our job," Meek told a newspaper reporter, "is to involve ourselves in the community. People should realize that Black Power is a feeling prevalent in the community." As organizing director, Palmer was responsible for hiring a staff of sixteen organizers, one for each hub, and developing a training program for them in community organizing and planning. The only requirement was that the organizers live in the Model Cities area.[24]

Meek's commitment to promoting a sense of community ownership over the AWC led him to approve Palmer's request to use the AWC's mimeograph machine to make fliers for the November 17, 1967, student demonstration. After the march, however, Palmer's presence on the AWC staff and his use of AWC equipment for the student demonstration generated a public scandal that threatened the AWC's position as the community partner in the Model Cities planning process. The director of the federal Model Cities Administration bluntly declared that the AWC's support for the student demonstration was not "legitimate and appropriate parts of model cities planning," while the Tate administration announced that it was sending auditors to the AWC offices to ascertain whether it was spending government funds correctly.[25]

The AWC's Steering Committee, however, affirmed its support both for the student march and for Meek's decision to hire Palmer. Drawing on Black Power's call for community control, the Steering Committee accused the Tate administration of seeking to undercut "citizen participation" in the Model Cities planning process. When the mayor sent an aide to the AWC's November 21 Steering Committee meeting to demand that the AWC refrain from "political action," the committee voted to reject the distinction between its planning mandate and actions like the student demonstration. In order to successfully involve the black community in a long-range planning and development process, the committee argued, the AWC had to be willing to support initiatives like the November 17 protest that sought social change in the short term. Moreover, Meek reminded the Tate aide, the city had committed itself to treating the AWC as "a completely independent community organization—an equal partner with the city."[26]

At its next meeting, the AWC steering committee adopted a policy statement asserting its right to determine the proper mix of "social planning and action" for the organization. "Our leaders can," the statement insisted, "plan best by seeing their limited plans successfully carried out through reasonable and organized community action." The statement concluded that "the interplay between community planning and community participation in securing limited goals must be seen as a necessary part of the total planning . . . required for . . . a Model City Community." While carefully avoiding the confrontational language of the Black Power movement, the AWC statement's evocation of a "model" community within North Philadelphia, its use of words like "we," "our," and "ourselves," and its insistence on total community control of the planning process clearly reflected the influence of those who argued that complete autonomy from white-controlled political institutions was essential to advancing the cause of the black poor. The PAAC had offered the poor the opportunity to participate in the political machine that governed the city. The AWC insisted on the right of poor black communities to govern themselves.[27]

The dispute between the city and the AWC quickly escalated into a fight over money. When the size of its Model Cities planning grant proved to be smaller than expected, the Tate Administration cut the AWC budget from $21,000 to $13,000 per month. The budget cut, Meek complained, "would reduce us to just another ineffectual federal program—nothing more than a buffer between the Government and the community." In response, city officials suggested another agency, such as PAAC, could be found to run the citizen participation component of the Model Cities project. Then, in late December, the city cut off all funds to the AWC when the Steering Committee refused to rescind its policy statement on planning and action. Meek, Palmer and the AWC organizing staff were forced to apply for unemployment insurance so that they could continue to organize the planning process. The Tate administration eventually restored the AWC's funding in March, along with back pay for December, January, and February, but only after HUD officials required the city to obtain AWC approval for every aspect of its Model Cities proposal.[28]

Remarkably, the city and the AWC managed to submit to HUD a joint planning process proposal in early April 1968. However, relations deteriorated further when the AWC learned that the city had in fact submitted two proposals to HUD, one the AWC had approved and one developed entirely by the city's planning office. While Philip Kalodner, the city's Model Cities coordinator, insisted that there were only minor differences between the proposals, the AWC viewed the city's actions as further proof of its lack of a commitment to citizen participation. In early May, the AWC steering committee called for Kalodner to be fired and replaced with a black person with stronger ties to the community.[29]

The Model Cities Act gave the mayor's office final responsibility for the planning process including the right to ignore the AWC. However, the Steering Committee's ties with HUD officials gave it the political strength it needed to prevent the city from disregarding its concerns entirely. By June, pressure from HUD had forced the mayor to reassign Kalodner and replace him with Robert Williams, a former assistant district attorney and school board member. Williams immediately set out to repair relations with the AWC. After ordering an audit of all Model Cities programs, Williams agreed to raise the AWC's funding from $18,000 to $46,000 per month as part of an effort to increase community involvement in the sixteen hub councils. By late August, Williams was declaring that "personality conflicts have been eliminated and philosophical differences resolved." He also professed to be an enthusiastic supporter of citizen participation in the program, "I am only the coordinator of the program," Williams said. "The leadership comes from the Area-Wide Council." Acknowledging that "some of the approaches used in the past in Philadelphia . . . have unintentionally alienated the community," he insisted that "we are going through a wonderful transition" and that the program would soon submit to HUD a comprehensive plan in the areas of housing, human resources, education, and economic development.[30]

On December 31, 1968, the city submitted, with the full support of the AWC, a $49 million application for the Philadelphia Model Cities Program. At the same time, the AWC joined the city in a public education campaign to inform the residents of North Philadelphia about the services available through Model Cities. The application proposed the formation of eight nonprofit corporations to manage the different components of the program. The proposed corporations included a Housing Development Corporation to develop new housing and to rehabilitate the area's existing housing stock; a Community Land Utilization Corporation to acquire vacant lots and "derelict" buildings for sale to private developers; a Model Cities Economic Development Corporation to help area residents to start and expand small businesses; an Urban Venture Capital Corporation to fund labor-intensive industrial development in the area; and an Urban Education Institute to work with the school district on educational reform projects. An April 1969 supplement to the application detailed how the AWC and the city would share responsibility for naming the boards of these corporations. "If a single factor can be isolated from the syndrome of causes that have served to perpetuate the prevailing condition," the supplement read, "it is the absence of any opportunity for Model Cities residents to influence decisions that have had a negative impact upon their community." Thus, the Housing Development Corporation was to be made up entirely of AWC representatives; the only city representative on the Community Land Utilization Corporation board would be the Model Cities administrator; the board of the Model Cities Economic Development Corporation was to consist of eight AWC appointees and representatives of nine other organizations; and the AWC and City Hall were to jointly name the boards of the remaining corporations. Even though HUD indicated that it could only provide $25 million of the $49 million requested, the city and the AWC appeared to be on their way to pursuing a joint physical and economic development program for North Philadelphia.[31]

By the time the city submitted its proposal, however, Richard Nixon was in the White House. Very quickly, the new federal administration made it clear that it intended to restore full control over the Model Cities program to local elected officials. In April, HUD secretary George Romney announced that local government officials must retain "final authority" over the Model Cities programs. Then, on May 27, HUD informed Mayor Tate that the department was denying the city's request for $25 million because of the city government's insufficient role in the program. "Inexperienced community groups," HUD Assistant Secretary Floyd Hyde declared, were not qualified to implement the Model Cities program.[32]

Mayor Tate, of course, was quick to reclaim control over the local Model Cities program. Ironically, the official that he selected to rein in the AWC was Goldie Watson, who had led the left-wing faction in the Philadelphia NAACP in the late 1940s. After losing her public school teaching job because of her refusal to testify before the House Committee on Un-American Activities (HUAC), Watson had opened a dress store in North Philadelphia. She eventually became a key activist in the local Democratic ward organization. In December 1967, Mayor Tate rewarded Watson's work in the party by naming her deputy commissioner of records. Then, in March 1969, the mayor appointed her to replace Robert Williams as Model Cities administrator.[33] On June 9, Watson informed HUD that the city was issuing revised guidelines for the Model Cities corporations. Under this new plan, which HUD had accepted, the AWC would be allowed to nominate not more than one-third of the corporation's board members; the remaining two-thirds would be appointed by the city.[34]

Charging that the Nixon administration wanted to end citizen participation in the Model Cities program and that the Tate administration was engaged in a "power grab," the AWC refused to renew its contract to provide citizen participation to the Philadelphia Model Cities Program. The contract that the city offered the council, William Meek argued, violated the Model Cities Act's citizen participation provisions. The AWC was thus forced to suspend operations on June 30, 1969. Still, the AWC staff and Steering Committee continued to rally public support for its efforts to convince both HUD and the Tate administration to restore the original Model Cities program. Supporters of the council were encouraged to attend protest meetings at eight hub centers on June 25, 1969, and to "register strong protest against the proposed dilution of citizen participation in the Philadelphia Model Cities Program" with their elected officials. In August, the AWC filed a federal suit against the Nixon and Tate administrations, charging that they had violated the citizen participation requirements of the 1966 Model Cities Act. Meek called HUD's decision to deprive the AWC of its equal partnership with the city typical of the "repression of peoples' rights that characterizes the Nixon administration's position on urban problems." In November 1969, however, the federal district court ruled against the AWC. By the time the Third Circuit Court of Appeals reversed that decision on appeal in July 1970, there seemed no way to restore the AWC or its vision of community control over the Philadelphia Model Cities Program.[35]

In place of the AWC, Goldie Watson appointed a thirty-five-member committee to serve as the citizen participation arm of the Model Cities program. In addition, the city sought to revive the sixteen hubs as neighborhood councils. Each council that agreed to a contract with the program received a $25,000 annual grant for staff salaries and overhead.[36] The neighborhood councils' powers, however, remained purely advisory. As Watson would state repeatedly, "there is no community control in Model Cities." The impact of the AWC's exclusion from the Model Cities process was evident when the city presented its revised Model Cities plan. While the AWC had emphasized the rehabilitation of North Philadelphia's housing stock and neighborhood preservation, the city's focus was on the development of abandoned industrial sites. All told, the city had removed two hundred properties proposed by the AWC from the program's acquisition list and added a hundred properties that the AWC had rejected. In its review of the new proposal, the Housing Association of the Delaware Valley (HADV) charged that the city had returned to the discredited urban renewal formula of slum clearance. Inevitably, the HADV predicted, the city's program would lead to the displacement of thousands of households with little provision for their relocation into decent housing.[37]

Back to Electoral Politics

The Model Cities experience had a number of lessons for advocates of community control. First, only the state appeared capable and willing—under the proper political conditions—of providing the necessary resources to address the fundamental needs of the black poor. And second, without political power and control over essential elected offices, struggles for community control remained dependent on the goodwill of white politicians and their bureaucratic appointees. Thus, in the last years of the 1960s, a new generation of black political activists who called themselves black independent Democrats pursued political power as an explicit strategy for defending and advancing the achievements of the local Black Power movement. "Black priorities have moved from integration in the 1950s through the 1960s riots and civil rights movement to control of institutions in the 1970s," declared W. Wilson Goode, a West Philadelphia community activist who would be elected the city's first black mayor in 1983.[38]

In the context of urban deindustrialization and capital flight, there was a strategic logic to seeking political control over the elected offices that managed the public sector "growth machine." Not only was the public sector more vulnerable to popular pressure than private sources of investment, but in an older industrial city like Philadelphia public sector investment appeared essential to the creation of the kind of working-class jobs needed by the majority of black Philadelphians. Thus, Black Power-influenced electoral campaigns shared with movements for community control over the schools and antipoverty programs an emerging spatial strategy of urban black politics which viewed organizational and political control over the ghetto as the best hope for redirecting government resources to the fight against institutionalized racial privilege within local labor and housing markets.[39]

In 1968, a coalition of black movement activists and disaffected Democratic Party workers formed the Black Political Forum (BPF). The BPF's goal was to elect black politicians who were accountable to black community and movement organizations, rather than to the city's white-led party organizations, and committed to defending and extending the victories won by the city's civil rights and Black Power movements. Calling themselves Black Independent Democrats, BPF activists explicitly linked their efforts to establish an autonomous power base within the city's Democratic Party to the Black Power movement's demand for community control. Over the next fifteen years, BPF activists would be elected to the state legislature, the city council, the U.S. Congress, and finally, in 1983, to the mayor's office.

The BPF's founder and first president was John White, Sr., a salesman and longtime West Philadelphia church and community activist with a booming voice and a large, even intimidating, presence. On April 26, 1970, White told the nine hundred black political and community activists who showed up for the BPF's founding convention that the purpose of the new organization was to make the black community's political representatives more responsive to the community's needs and more accountable to their constituents. Specifically, he urged his audience to "let the politicians know that we demand representation." The current crop of black politicians, in White's view, was simply too closely tied to the city's white-led Democratic machine. "Right now, the leaders do not consult the people in the community on anything. They just vote the party line. The people are out of it."[40]

Specifically, John White hoped to bring an end to what he called the "plantation politics" practiced by the Democratic City Committee in its dealings with black voters. Made up of the Democratic leaders of the city's sixty-six wards, the Democratic City Committee is the party's highest governing body. At the time, the City Committee had the final say over the party's candidates for every municipal, state, and federal elected office. In 1970, the vast majority of the party's ward leaders were, as they always had been, white. White and his allies in the BPF charged that the city committee chose candidates in predominately African American electoral districts based not on their records of service to the black community, but rather on their loyalty to the Democratic machine and its white leadership. In other words, white party leaders, not black voters or political activists, were determining the city's black political leadership. The only way to end this kind of "plantation politics," White believed, was to run independent black candidates against the machine's candidates and to defeat them.[41]

To signal its ties to community organizations and the broader black movement, the BPF convention honored nine prominent community-based working-class activists from across the city. The honorees included Black Power activists David Richardson and "Freedom" George Brower, COPPAR's Mary Rouse, Roxanne Jones of the Philadelphia Welfare Rights Organization (PWRO), Rose Wylie from the Residents Advisory Board, and Alice Walker, a parent organizer from Philadelphia Tutorial Project's Educational Self-Help Centers.[42] By identifying their organization with local advocates of welfare rights and community control, the BPF's founders were explicitly linking their efforts to end the machine's control over Philadelphia's black vote to the ideal of community control of poor black neighborhoods and the institutions that served them.

At the same time, the convention was designed to demonstrate the potential impact that a black independent political organization could have on the mainstream political arena. BPF thus arranged for the two leading candidates in the May 1970 Democratic Party primary for governor, State Auditor Robert Casey and Philadelphia businessman Milton Shapp, to speak briefly to the convention. The BPF's commitment to pragmatic political action was also evident in its choice of keynote speaker. Richard Hatcher, the recently elected first African American mayor of Gary, Indiana, urged his audience to "get [its] hands on the levers that control power" and to avoid "suicidal notions of armed revolution or [the] creation of separate black communities." If blacks would adopt the "Irish model of political unity," he concluded, they would soon win "control of many of the nation's cities."[43]

Community Control, Electoral Politics, and the Quest for Political Office

The Black Political Forum's approach to electoral organizing differed from previous efforts to end the Democratic machine's stranglehold on black electoral politics in Philadelphia in three ways. First, the BPF drew directly on the culture and strategies of the Black Power movement to promote its approach to electoral politics. The BPF's founders specifically linked their efforts to elect independent black political candidates directly to the late 1960s campaigns for community control over the schools, police and anti-

poverty programs. "The key characteristic of independent black development," BPF activist Paul Vance told a forum on black electoral activism in
January 1972, "is the achievement of self-sufficiency [through] community
control." Vance, who continued to be a leading member of the Educators'
Roundtable, the pro-Black Power black teachers group, urged community
activists "to politicize their neighborhood and civic organizations" so that
they adopt electoral strategies "as the best means to achieve" community
control.[44]

Second, the BPF's organizers believed that the mass mobilization strategies that had been so central to the achievements of the civil rights movement were not, by themselves, sufficient to defeat the Democratic machine.
Black candidates who were independent of the machine would win elections in Philadelphia when, and only when, the city had a cadre of black
movement and community activists trained in the very electoral organizing
skills that made the Democratic Party's ward organizations so effective.
This was also the message that Richard Hatcher brought to the BPF in their
private meetings before the 1970 BPF dinner. "Mayor Hatcher told us to
organize our community well," Wilson Goode remembers, "pick a good
candidate, and don't expect to win the first time around. Chip away . . .
when you organize right, you'll get it done."[45]

From a West Philadelphia storefront, BPF activists trained potential candidates, street campaigners, poll watchers, and voter registration canvassers
from black neighborhoods across the city. In addition, the BPF held seminars after each election to analyze the returns and the effectiveness of
its candidates' campaign strategies. Leaders of these training sessions
included John White Sr., Hardy Williams, a West Philadelphia attorney and
political activist, Wilson Goode, leader of the Paschall Betterment League,
a West Philadelphia neighborhood organization, and Bernard Watson, a
Deputy Superintendent of Schools. And those attending BPF training sessions in the early 1970s included a number of future elected officials,
including Rev. William H. Gray III, Marian Tasco, David Richardson, Roxanne Jones, Chaka Fattah, and John F. White, Jr., as well as rank-and-file
community activists like former SNCC organizer Charyn Sutton and Shirley
Hamilton, John White Sr.'s neighbor and fellow block captain who would
later serve as Mayor Goode's chief of staff.[46]

Third, the history of independent black political campaigns in the city
encouraged the BPF's founders to believe that they would have a better
opportunity to defeat the machine's candidates by running challengers in
the May Democratic primary elections than by mounting third-party campaigns in the November general elections. In their view, the city's black
movement needed a winning electoral strategy in order to defend and
extend the gains of the civil rights, Black Power, and community control
movements. The Democratic Party primary offered the BPF not only the
best opportunity to defeat the machine, but also the mechanism to control

"the institution" that determined how public sector resources were distributed within the city.[47]

The BPF's first electoral initiative was directed at the Democratic Party's ward committees. Elected every two years in the party primaries, committeemen and committeewomen were the foot soldiers of the machine. Responsible for delivering voters to the polls, they also elected the ward leaders who made up the Democratic city committee (DCC). Electing its activists first as committeemen and -women and then as ward leaders would not only give the BPF an instant street-level organization, but would also begin to undercut the party organization in the city's predominately black wards. In June 1968, BPF activist Hardy Williams upset party loyalist Dorothy Brennan to become leader of the Third Ward Democratic Committee in West Philadelphia. Williams's victory demonstrated the vulnerability of the machine in black neighborhoods and set the stage for BPF campaigns for elected office.[48]

The following year, Williams joined with the other thirteen black Democratic ward leaders to demand that the DCC endorse a black candidate for citywide office in that year's municipal elections. Specifically, the ward leaders urged the DCC to endorse Williams for City Controller and ADA activist Joseph Coleman for District Attorney. For Williams and the BPF, securing the nomination for one of those two offices would have been significant for two reasons. First, with the exception of judgeships and at-large city council seats, the DCC had never endorsed a black candidate for citywide office. Moreover, an endorsement of Williams would have meant recognition for the BPF as an independent power base within the party.[49]

The DCC, however, refused to endorse Williams or Coleman. And, not surprisingly, every one of the black ward leaders except Hardy Williams quickly fell in line and endorsed the party's candidates. The party's refusal to endorse the candidacy of the one black ward leader whose power base lay in the black movement, not the party machinery, and the unwillingness of the black ward leaders to break from the party hierarchy, only underscored the BPF's argument that the Democratic leadership was determined to keep blacks in a subordinate position within the party. Moreover, the 1969 general election proved a disaster for the Democrats. A historically low black turnout led to the reelection of Republican District Attorney Arlen Specter with 59 percent of the vote while his running mate and first-time candidate, Tom Gola, a 1950s-era basketball star, was elected City Controller by a margin of 57 to 43.[50]

Having failed to secure the party's endorsement for public office in 1969, Williams decided to take the machine on directly in the May 1970 Democratic primary by challenging Paul Lawson, the machine-backed state representative in West Philadelphia's 191st legislative district. Located on the south side of Market Street, West Philadelphia's main artery, and encompassing the Third and Sixtieth wards, the 191st District had become overwhelmingly black by 1970. Williams and his campaign managers, Wilson Goode and Paul Vance, took Mayor Hatcher's advice that an effective campaign organization was the key to defeating the machine. As Williams put it, "hard work and not just talk" would win the election. Specifically, Goode and Vance organized a daily door-to-door canvassing operation involving more than four hundred volunteers, most of them high school students.[51] At the same time, Williams focused his campaign on youth and education issues, explicitly linking the growing problem of gang violence in the district to what he charged was Lawson's lack of accessibility to his constituents. Lawson was "never . . . around" for his constituents, Williams declared. "Gangs are a symbol of political default. A responsible official must try to work with the community to aid young people and turn destructive energies into constructive ones."[52]

The Williams campaign faced formidable obstacles. Lawson was the protégé of Isadore Shrager, the longtime Sixtieth Ward leader whom the *Tribune* called "a power of the Democratic City Committee." As the white leader of a ward that by 1970 had become 95 percent black, Shrager epitomized all that the BPF saw as wrong with the Democratic machine. Not only did he maintain firm control over his ward committee, but his endorsement also guaranteed that Lawson, a trade unionist and chairman of the House Labor Relations Committee, would benefit from a strong base of union support. Williams's ward committee, in contrast, was sharply divided between party loyalists and the insurgent candidate's supporters. Against these odds, Williams received nearly 60 percent of the 5,741 votes cast, making him the first black candidate ever to defeat a candidate endorsed by the Democratic City Committee. The *Tribune* called Williams's victory "one of the most stunning upsets in Philadelphia political history." Five months later, Hardy Williams won election to the state House of Representatives against a nominal Republican opponent. Williams's victory validated the BPF's strategic approach to electoral organizing. In two short years, the BPF had succeeded in building a network of community-based activists committed to electoral politics and, now with Williams's election, it had demonstrated its ability to defeat the Democrat machine.[53]

The 1971 Campaign for Mayor

The historic nature of Hardy Williams's victory was almost immediately overshadowed, however, by the 1971 mayoral election, the most important in the city since Joseph Clark and the reform Democrats ended a half-century of Republican municipal rule in 1951. The 1971 election, in contrast, was shaping up as a momentous intraparty struggle between the law-and-order politics of Frank Rizzo, the former police commissioner, and candidates from the party's liberal reform wing. The favorite in the race from the beginning, Rizzo ran a campaign that explicitly accused the city's liberal elites of cowering in the face of black militants. Republican city councilman Thacher Longstreth would later describe Rizzo's campaign message as "I'll stop the black people, who represent crime in the streets and the problems in the school system and whatever else is bad about Philadelphia."[54]

In addition to the endorsement of the Democratic City Committee and widespread popularity in the city's white working- and lower-middle-class neighborhoods, Rizzo's campaign also benefited from a divided opposition. His most prominent challenger was William Green Jr., the thirty-two-year-old son of former New Deal congressman and Democratic Party boss William Green Sr. After the senior Green's death in 1964, his son was elected to fill his congressional seat. In Washington, Green developed a reputation as a mainstream post-New Deal liberal, a defender of government aid to cities and to the poor, and an opponent of the Vietnam War. The irony of Green's candidacy was that the son of the machine boss emerged as the last, best hope for reviving the reform liberalism that had dominated Philadelphia politics during the 1950s.[55]

To Green's left stood David Cohen, a city councilman and party maverick with a strong base of support among younger New Left-influenced party activists and a platform that promised protection of the civil liberties of political protesters, police reform, and support for black community control of public institutions. A longtime Democratic committeeman from a middle-class and increasingly integrated Northwest Philadelphia neighborhood, Cohen first came to prominence in 1966 when he was elected chair of the Seventeeth Ward Democratic Committee on an antimachine platform. A year later, he upset the party's candidate for the Eighth District city council seat. In four years on the city council, Cohen emerged as an outspoken critic of Mayor Tate and Police Commissioner Rizzo. In contrast to Green's mainstream liberalism, Cohen built his campaign around his promise to fire Rizzo. "Philadelphia," he declared, "must end repressive police practices that have made blacks feel as if they are hostages held by some outside power."[56]

Hardy Williams entered the battle over the future of the local Democratic Party in January 1971, just two months after his election to the state legislature. He formally announced his candidacy at the February 1971 Black Political Convention. Organized jointly by BPF activists and advocates of an all-black political party, the convention was an attempt to develop a common platform and a single slate of black, antimachine candidates for the upcoming primary. In the spirit of racial unity, the convention organizers invited Amiri Baraka, Leon Sullivan, Cecil Moore, and Paul Washington to serve as keynote speakers. The goal, said CORE's Bill Mathis, was to overcome the political divisions in the black community by establishing a "structure so sound that it will not matter if some people don't relate to Baraka, Sullivan, or Bill Mathis. Individuals don't matter. What does matter is that we establish a working structure of political accountability." The convention platform, which every candidate seeking the convention's endorsement was required to sign, called for community control over all publicly-funded social service programs and the establishment of a citywide black political organization to select and hold accountable all black candidates for public office. Most important to Williams, the convention endorsed not only his candidacy for mayor but also his rationale for running. Both Sullivan and Baraka defined "Black Power" as control of City Hall. "We have to beat on [black] doors," Sullivan told the convention, "get the people registered and voting and then we'll have Black Power in Philadelphia . . . Black Power is the same as Irish and Jewish political muscle." Baraka called the quest for Black Power "just following the lead of other groups that have already had their turn controlling City Hall" and urged the selection of a candidate "who can appeal to black people, the masses and the middle class."[57]

With the Democratic liberal wing already divided between two candidates, why did Williams decide to run? By its own criteria, the BPF had yet to develop the organizational strength and campaign skill necessary to compete with the machine in a citywide election. Moreover, not only did Frank Rizzo enjoy the support of the party infrastructure—including seven of the sixteen black ward leaders—but Green and Cohen each possessed significantly more political experience and citywide name recognition than Williams.[58] In addition, the two liberal candidates both enjoyed significant levels of support from within the city's black political leadership circles. Not one black elected official or black ward leader would endorse Williams's candidacy.[59] In the years since, Williams has explained his campaign simply as an effort to demonstrate that a black candidate could run a credible citywide campaign. It was, he told Rizzo biographer S. A. Paolantonio, "a straight-up empowerment move." None of Williams's supporters, Wilson Goode would later write, "believed Hardy could win the mayor's office."[60]

Offered in hindsight, Williams and Goode's explanations seek to rationalize a controversial strategic decision that did not work out as they had hoped. Given the BPF's commitment to developing a winning electoral strategy, along with the widespread fear of a Rizzo victory within the black community, it seems unlikely that Williams would have entered the race unless he and his supporters believed he had a reasonable chance of winning a four-way primary contest. Contradicting his earlier point, Goode recalled to Paolantonio that "our view at that time was that there were three whites running and a black and perhaps the black candidate had a chance to win. The strategy was to divide the white vote, pull the black vote, and be able to win the election."[61] Campaign volunteer and former Philadelphia SNCC staff member Charyn Sutton remembers that the feeling among the campaign staff was both that Williams could win a divided pri-

mary and that his candidacy was crucial to the long-term political empowerment of Philadelphia's black community.[62] In a January 1971 speech to the
Philadelphia ADA, Williams had made just this point, arguing that the presence of "a black candidate [in the race] would motivate [voter] registration, a larger turnout in the elections, [and] the hope that the political
system offers a method of change and would offer vehicles to involve the
noninvolved." Pointing to Richard Hatcher's election as mayor of Gary and
Louis Stokes's victory in Cleveland's 1967 mayoral election, Williams urged
the ADA board to reverse the traditional logic of interracial political coalitions. The "best way to beat Rizzo," he told the ADA, "is with [a] good
black candidate as in Gary, Cleveland . . . where white liberals supported
[a] black candidate."[63] A large turnout of black voters—who now made up
40 percent of registered Democrats—combined with at least a portion of
the liberal reform vote (an estimated 15 to 20 percent of the Democratic
electorate), Williams and his supporters believed, might well propel Williams to victory in the primary.[64]

What Williams and his supporters failed to foresee, however, was just how
much the specter of a Rizzo victory would deprive his campaign of the
opportunity to implement the Hatcher/Stokes strategy. Little known outside the candidate's West Philadelphia base and poorly funded, the Williams campaign struggled to bring his message to black voters outside
movement circles. Williams was particularly hurt by a whispering campaign
that asserted that the Rizzo campaign was secretly funding Williams in
order to divide the party's liberal vote along racial lines.[65]

Williams sought the endorsement of the Philadelphia ADA in the belief
that recent changes in the ADA's leadership meant that the group might
well be prepared to support a black candidate as the best way to restore the
reform tradition to City Hall. Not only had Williams, Goode, and John
White Sr. all been recruited to serve on the ADA board over the previous
three years, but the ADA's new president and new executive director, David
Hornbeck and Terry Dellmuth, were white activists with strong ties to the
black activist community. Moreover, Hornbeck and Dellmuth had been
actively working to identify a candidate with a strong base of support in the
black community for the 1971 campaign. "In our opinion here at the
ADA," Hornbeck wrote to one prominent black community leader, "the
best mayoralty candidate will be one who is either black or one who is
closely allied to an identifiable positive response to the problems of low-
income people."[66]

By the winter of 1971, however, it was clear that there was little enthusiasm for Williams's candidacy among the ADA's largely white and middle-
class membership. A January straw poll of the group's membership had
found 106 for Green, 71 for Cohen and 12 for Williams.[67] Hornbeck and
Dellmuth responded to these deep divisions in the group membership by
seeking to delay the endorsement as long as they could. However, the

group's board was finally forced to act in early April after a rump group of longtime ADA activists led by Henry Sawyer, a former city councilman and longtime ally of Joseph Clark and Richardson Dilworth, announced the formation of "Independents for Green".[68] A week later, the ADA board voted to endorse Bill Green out of the "conviction that a united liberal front can defeat Frank Rizzo." While affirming the ADA's "great respect" for both Williams and Cohen, the endorsement asserted that a Rizzo "victory would threaten to tear . . . apart" the city. "Green is the man with the broadest base of support and the man with the strongest chance of beating Frank Rizzo. . . . Blacks, the young, advocates of peace and civil liberties know him [Rizzo] as their enemy."[69]

Two weeks before the election, David Cohen pulled out of the race with a strong endorsement of Green. "The election of Bill Green is not just a stop Rizzo tactic," he declared. "It will put to bed fears of a police state . . . and will clear out every vestige of the old Tate machine. It will be a new day of hope for Philadelphia."[70] Williams, in contrast, soldiered on, despite the increasing anger of the Green camp. "Why should [the] black [candidate] be the one to get out of the race?" he asked in a direct challenge to white activists. Moreover, he insisted that only he could defeat Rizzo. "It is mathematically impossible to beat Rizzo unless the 75 percent of the people who usually don't come out to vote do come out on primary day. Bill Green can't get those people out. I can."[71]

On election day, the worst fears of Green's supporters came true. Rizzo defeated Green by 48,000 votes, while Williams came in third with 50,000 votes—12 percent of the total—the vast majority from North and West Philadelphia's predominately black wards. Still, Green defeated Williams in the city's sixteen majority-black wards by more than 10,000 votes. It can certainly be argued that the Williams campaign provided Rizzo with his margin of victory over Green. Williams's vote total exceeded the 48,000-vote gap between Rizzo and Green by less than 2,000. Without Williams in the race, Green may well have been able to withstand Rizzo's backlash appeal among white Catholic and Jewish middle- and working-class voters.[72]

Still, Hardy Williams had demonstrated that a black candidate could run a serious and effective citywide campaign. His vote total was over 40,000 more than any other black candidate had ever received in a mayoral election. Moreover, his campaign had a significant expressive and experiential impact on black political activism in the city. Thousands of campaign staffers and volunteers had gained valuable campaign experience. And the BPF network had demonstrated to the Democratic Party that a "lesser-of-two-evils" strategy was no longer sufficient to maintain its base of black voters. From then on, black activists and voters would have to be seen as an independent and powerful constituency within the party.

The November general election gave the BPF the perfect opportunity to demonstrate the newfound independence of the city's black voters. After hearing from Rizzo's Republican opponent, Thacher Longstreth, a city councilman and former president of the Philadelphia Urban League, at its August 1971 planning retreat, the BPF endorsed Longstreth and three black Republican candidates for lower office, including Dr. Ethel Allen, a physician running for the North Philadelphia city council seat held by machine loyalist and Rizzo supporter Thomas McIntosh. To support Allen's candidacy, women active in the BPF formed the Black Women's Political Alliance. A week before the election, Hardy Williams announced his personal endorsements of both Longstreth and Allen. Longstreth, he declared, "offers us a chance of hope."[73]

The result of the BPF's efforts was an impressive display of ticket splitting in the city's black wards on election day. Although Rizzo won a narrow 47,000-vote victory, Longstreth swept all but one of the city's black-majority wards. According to one estimate, 64 percent of registered black voters turned out for the election and, of those, 77 percent voted for Longstreth.[74] In addition, Dr. Allen defeated McIntosh by 4,000 votes, a victory she ascribed to a coalition of Democratic, Republican, and independent voters. Of particular importance, she told the *Tribune*, were the efforts of the Black Women's Political Alliance and of supporters of Hardy Williams.[75]

Activists in the Legislature

Hardy Williams's defeat did not impede BPF's continuing efforts to elect independent candidates in black-majority legislative districts. In 1972, David Richardson followed Williams into the state legislature at the tender age of twenty-three (Figure 15). John White Jr., the son of BPF founder John White Sr., joined Williams and Richardson two years later. In the 1976 Democratic primary, Rev. William H. "Bill" Gray III, the thirty-three year-old pastor of North Philadelphia's Mount Hope Baptist Church, challenged Robert N. C. Nix for the congressional seat he had held since 1958. Though Gray lost to Nix that year by 339 votes, he would successfully oust the ten-term incumbent two years later.[76]

The career of each of these legislators was characterized by a fierce commitment to what they perceived to be the interests of the city's black poor as well as a staunch independence from the Democratic Party establishment. Of all of the BPF-affiliated legislators, however, David Richardson proved the most determined to bring movement aspirations and strategies into the legislative process. Following the 1967 student march, Richardson established the Young Afro-Americans of Germantown and opened a neighborhood storefront called the Ebony Shop from which his group sold handmade African clothing and jewelry while preaching racial unity to the

Figure 15. State Representatives Hardy Williams and David Richardson in front of Richardson's Germantown campaign office, 1974. Urban Archives, Temple University Libraries.

area's warring gangs. The Young Afros—as they were known—focused on three goals that were characteristic of Black Power youth organizing in the city: (1) establishing truces between neighborhood gangs, (2) challenging abusive police practices, including those that they charged were designed to instigate tension between rival neighborhood gangs, and (3) pressing for the expansion of the black studies curriculum at Germantown High. During the 1971 public school teachers' strike—a strike opposed by Philadelphia's black activist community—Richardson helped to organize the Germantown Area Schools Project, an alternative educational program for neighborhood children, and continued to teach in the program after the strike was settled.[77]

In the April 1972 Democratic primary, Richardson set out to oust party loyalist and three-term incumbent Francis X. Rush from Germantown's seat in the state house.[78] An Irish Catholic realtor, Rush was ripe for defeat. White flight and black in-migration had transformed Germantown's racial demography over the previous decade.[79] Moreover, the neighborhoods of Northwest Philadelphia had proved a bastion of antimachine and anti-Rizzo sentiment in the 1971 election.[80] But could a twenty-three-year-old black militant whose only electoral experience had come in Hardy Williams's 1970 and 1971 campaigns overcome the advantages enjoyed by a machine-backed three-term incumbent?[81]

From the first, the Richardson campaign took on a social movement ethos. His teenage supporters began canvassing the district three months before the April 1972 Democratic primary. "Some of the people working for Dave," a community activist told the *Bulletin*, "were voting for the first time . . . At last they found a reason to go to the polls. At last they found a man who could relate to them, who convinced them that they count, that they are important." For his part, Richardson couched his campaign in the language of racial unity. Calling for "black family unity and self-help," he declared that: "we need to love black people, but that does not mean hate white people."[82]

Election day confirmed that the Richardson campaign had achieved a political revolution in Germantown. Voter turnout in the state house race was fifteen points higher than in the rest of the city. Not only did Richardson defeat Rush by a landslide, but his supporters won a majority of seats on the district's three ward committees. Richardson credited his victory to the efforts of his youth supporters. "All the kids in Germantown," he told the *Philadelphia Daily News*, "were working for me. They made their parents vote."[83]

Richardson's election made him the most prominent "black militant" in the city. Throughout the 1970s, he sought to infuse his legislative work with social movement strategies and tactics, most often as a way to challenge the policies of the Rizzo administration. One supporter described Richardson's Germantown district office as "the only office around here open 24 hours." Befitting his emphasis on youth issues, Richardson led a series of campaigns to challenge the police department's antigang policies and to reform the Youth Study Center, the city's juvenile detention center.[84] In a 1976 protest against discriminatory treatment of black street vendors, Richardson was arrested alongside Milton Street, the outspoken president of the Black Street Vendors Association. Two years later, Richardson and Street told thousands of protesters that they intended to lead "a poor people's crusade against racial repression in Philadelphia" following a violent confrontation between the police and the black radical sect MOVE.[85]

Richardson also worked to elect independent candidates who shared his movement ethos. Among the Richardson allies elected to public office were West Philadelphia labor leader Lucien Blackwell, elected to the city council in 1975, and Chaka Fattah, the son of Falaka Fattah, who won a seat in the state house in 1982.[86] Perhaps Richardson's most unexpected success came in 1978, when he supported Milton Street, whose combination of economic self-help, outrageous street tactics and virulent attacks on Mayor Rizzo had given him a ubiquitous presence in the local media, in Street's successful campaign to unseat the Democratic incumbent in a North Philadelphia state house district. The following year, Street's younger brother John was elected to represent North Philadelphia on the city council. In 1980, David Richardson was elected chair of the fifteen-member Black Legislative Caucus, and Milton Street ran for and was elected to a North Philadelphia seat in the state senate.[87]

In 1981, Senator Street switched his party allegiance in the state senate to the Republican caucus, thus giving the Republicans control over what had been an evenly divided senate. In return, Street received a senate committee chairmanship. Here was a direct challenge to the BPF's independent Democratic strategy. To Street, his decision to switch caucuses reflected his commitment to the Black Power principle that black politicians should place the interests of the black community above party loyalty. Unlike black legislators who spoke the language of political independence while loyally voting with the Democrats, his act of political independence, Street contended, had produced immediate benefits for his district—a district, as he declared repeatedly, that was the blackest and poorest in the city. "Who is more independent than me?" he asked. "I sit with Democrats, agnostics, Republicans. What difference does it make if I get things done?"[88]

To Street's closest political allies, however, his caucus switch represented the worst kind of political treachery. David Richardson, who ironically had a long record of support for third-party politics and had even discussed switching his party affiliation to the National Black Political Assembly, accused his longtime ally of betraying his constituents. "I don't think it is ethical," he told one of the city's daily newspapers, "for political leaders to change their party affiliation for short-term political gain." Richardson's break with Street was irrevocable. The Republicans were "racist," Richardson declared, and had "absolutely nothing to give" to the black community. What most incensed Richardson was that Street's switch had given Richard Thornburgh, the Republican governor, the votes he needed to pass a package of sweeping welfare reforms. "Thornfare," as welfare advocates derided the governor's reform proposals, established stringent work requirements on "able-bodied" welfare recipients in the state, irrespective of labor market conditions or recipients' family status and job skills. As a result, ninety thousand welfare recipients lost their cash benefits.[89]

Richardson would have to wait until the end of Street's four-year term to enact political retribution on his former ally. In the fall of 1983, he and Bill Gray recruited Roxanne Jones to run for Street's seat in the April 1984 Democratic primary. Jones had stepped down from the presidency of the Philadelphia Welfare Rights Organization in 1973 to found a new statewide organization, Pennsylvania Citizens in Action (PCIA), to continue the push for expanded government assistance for the poor. By the 1980s, however, Jones and PCIA had been reduced to waging a defensive campaign against Thornfare.[90]

In many ways, Jones's candidacy epitomized the ideals of black independent politics in Philadelphia. What she lacked in electoral experience—this was her first campaign and she had never been active in ward-level politics—she made up for with her more than fifteen years of community activism in Philadelphia's poorest neighborhoods and welfare rights advocacy in the halls of the state legislature. And yet her campaign to unseat Senator Street also demonstrated how the boundaries between political independence and party loyalty had collapsed in the fourteen years since Hardy Williams was first elected to the state legislature in 1970. Williams and David Richardson were among the most senior Democrats in the state legislature. Bill Gray was now a member of the Democratic Party leadership in the U.S. Congress. And, as I will discuss shortly, Wilson Goode had been elected Philadelphia's first African American mayor just one year earlier; BPF founder John White Sr. was now one of Mayor Goode's chief aides. As the April 1984 Democratic primary approached, Jones's election became Mayor Goode's top political priority. With control over the State Senate at stake, the Democratic City Committee eagerly endorsed Jones as the candidate most likely to defeat Street. Among her most important financial supporters in the race was Vincent Fumo, a South Philadelphia state senator and ally of former Mayor Rizzo. The Fumo-led Democratic State Senate Campaign Committee provided nearly half of Jones's $26,000 campaign budget.[91]

Convinced that a Republican—even one as independent as he—could not win in North Philadelphia, Street decided to seek the Democratic Party nomination even as he remained a member of the senate Republican caucus. "I believe firmly in the two-party system—just as long as I can be part of both parties," Street joked. "I want to position myself so I can affect the policy of the Democrats in Philadelphia and the Republicans in Harrisburg. . . . Genuine political power brokers don't worry about my label." In response, Jones campaigned as "the true Democrat" in the race, referring to Street only as her "Republican opponent." Conducted in the midst of Jesse Jackson's presidential campaign, the Jones-Street contest was particularly heated, with both candidates trumpeting their activist credentials and accusing the other of selling out to the political establishment.[92]

On primary election day, Jones rode a combination of party support and her popularity with women voters to an easy victory over Street; she received an astounding 61 percent of the vote. Once in the state legislature, Senator Jones joined Richardson in leading the fight against Governor Thornburgh's welfare cuts. Declaring that "it's the poor people who elected me," she immediately proposed legislation to restore to the welfare rolls many of the 68,000 people who lost their benefits as a result of Thornfare. Her bill, however, had no chance of passing the Republican-controlled Senate. During Jones's eleven years in the senate, three different governors would seek major cuts in the state's public assistance programs and in every case she would lead the fight against the cuts. But only once, in 1992, was she able to defeat a proposed cut in welfare benefits.[93]

Movement Goals and the Pursuit of the Mayor's Office

Throughout his eight years in the mayor's office, Frank Rizzo continued to polarize the city along racial, class, and cultural lines. Despite S. A. Paolantonio's portrait of Rizzo as the last of the nation's mayoral power brokers, Rizzo's tenure was in fact marked by racial and political conflict on the city streets and in the smoke-filled backrooms of the local party organization. Rizzo's base of support continued to contract even as his administration succeeded in mastering the politics of growth liberalism, using federal money to significantly develop the city's transportation infrastructure and large nonprofit institutions while delivering jobs to its loyal supporters in the building trades and an eventually budget-busting contract to the city's black-led municipal workers' union. In the 1975 Democratic mayoral primary, the local party hierarchy refused to support Rizzo's reelection, in large part because of his 1972 endorsement of President Nixon's reelection. Instead, the city committee endorsed Louis Hill, a local judge and the stepson of Richardson Dilworth, the legendary liberal reform mayor of the 1950s. While Rizzo easily defeated the charismatically challenged Hill by ten points, the bitter primary did suggest that a candidate capable of adding just enough votes from white ethnic communities to a solid base of blacks and white liberals could defeat the incumbent.[94]

Former deputy mayor Charles Bowser thought he could be that candidate in the 1975 general election. He had the credentials, he believed, to appeal to both the moderate and militant wings of the city's black political community and to voters in upper-income white neighborhoods. To mount his third-party campaign, Bowser formed the Philadelphia Party; Wilson Goode served as coordinator of volunteers for the campaign and John White Sr. and William Meek, the former director of the Area-Wide Council, as campaign strategists. In the end, Bowser was never able to seriously challenge Rizzo, largely because he was only able to raise $200,000 for the campaign. Still, he received 138,783 votes and was able to finish second in the race, ahead of the Republican candidate, city councilman Thomas Foglietta. In just four years, Bowser had added 100,000 votes to Hardy Williams's 1971 vote total.[95]

The stage was thus seemingly set for a black candidate in 1979. A year earlier, Mayor Rizzo had led a drive to amend the city charter to allow him to run for a third term. With Charles Bowser at the helm, the "Vote No to Charter Change" campaign successfully mobilized a broad coalition of blacks and white liberals to defeat the charter change by a two-to-one margin. The breadth of the anti-Rizzo coalition convinced Bowser that he would enjoy his best chance to win a Rizzo-less election as a Democrat. He therefore announced that he would enter the 1979 Democratic primary for mayor.[96]

Bowser's strategy for winning the 1979 primary was premised on the mobilization of a unified black vote and the presence of at least one white liberal and one white conservative candidate to split the still-majority white vote. But Bowser was outmaneuvered on the second count when two of the three white candidates, Albert Gaudiosi and City Controller William Klenk, withdrew from the race and endorsed Bill Green in his second campaign for mayor. Although he won resoundingly in every black ward in the city, Bowser had little hope of defeating a white candidate with solid liberal credentials in a one-on-one contest. Green won the election by nine percentage points.[97]

In an effort to diffuse black anger at Bowser's defeat, Green announced on July 14 that he had reached an agreement with Bowser and Sam Evans to appoint blacks to top positions in his administration. "I have already told community leaders," Green announced, "that I welcome the opportunity to appoint this city's first managing director [the second highest-ranking position in city government] who is qualified, talented and happens to be black." In return, Bowser endorsed the Democratic nominee and Green went on to an easy victory in November.[98]

Shortly after the election, Mayor-elect Green announced that he had chosen BPF founder W. Wilson Goode to fill the position of managing director. Following the 1971 Williams mayoral campaign, Goode had significantly reduced his involvement in electoral politics. For most of the decade, he had served as the executive director of the Philadelphia Council for Community Advancement (PCCA), where he shifted the organization's focus to providing technical assistance for community-based economic development programs. In 1978, then Governor Milton Shapp, a longtime BPF ally, appointed Goode to one of three positions on the state Public Utilities Commission. Arranged by Shapp aide and former ADA official Terry Dellmuth, Goode's appointment reflected both BPF's growing influence within the Democratic Party and the extent to which Goode's reputation as an effective manager had supplanted his activist credentials.[99]

In a few short years, Goode had succeeded in remaking his image from a community-based political outsider to the consummate insider, the very kind of figure who could make the election of the first African American mayor seem a natural next step in the ethnic politics of the Democratic Party's fragile but potentially still effective political coalition. Goode's political makeover does not seem to have been the result of a conscious strategic plan to gain the mayor's office. Rather, it demonstrates that the BPF was, from its origins, a coalition made up of those who sought only to renegotiate relations between the Democrats and the city's black political class and those who saw the achievement of community control over the Democratic Party infrastructure in black neighborhoods as an essential step towards transforming the city's racialized political economy.[100]

In his four years as managing director, Wilson Goode remained largely outside of Green's inner circle. Still, he was able to develop a reputation as an effective city official with a populist touch through his vigorous and highly visible support for the anticrime and community development efforts of neighborhood groups across the city.[101] Thus, when Bill Green unexpectedly announced that he would not run for a second term, Goode was his obvious heir apparent. The entire black political class of the city, from militants like David Richardson to party loyalists, quickly lined up behind Goode. At the same time, a coalition of many of the most prominent business leaders in the city, including the CEO's of Smith and Kline, Provident and PSFS banks, Rohm and Haas, and Arco Chemical Company, formed to support Goode's campaign. And yet in a city that was still 58 percent white, Goode would have to defeat Frank Rizzo, the still popular icon of law-and-order racial conservatism, to claim the Democratic nomination for mayor. Targeting black churches and civic groups in the city's liberal Center City and Northwest neighborhoods, the Goode campaign generated a spirit that reminded many of the movements of the 1960s. In the May 1983 Democratic primary, Goode won a surprisingly easy victory over Rizzo by a margin of 60,000 votes. He received 98 percent of the black vote and nearly 22 percent of the white vote. With Rizzo's endorsement— the former mayor was eager to maintain his influence in the party—Goode won the November general election by 123,000 votes.[102]

Was Goode a community-based political militant who decided as black social movements went into decline in the mid-1970s that the best way to pursue the interests of the black residents of West Philadelphia's working-

and lower-middle-class neighborhoods was to move into the structure of government, first as the head of the state agency that controlled utility rates, then as the city's number two government official, and finally as Mayor? Or was he simply an ambitious technocrat who viewed his movement activism as a means to achieve his career goals and who abandoned the movement's vision of transforming public institutions once he had worked himself onto the Democratic Party's fast track? In the context of the Reagan administration's abandonment of urban concerns and the near total collapse of the left wing of the Democratic Party during the 1980s, it is not particularly surprising that the Goode administration proved unable to bring fundamental change to the city's poor and working-class communities. To give just one example, federal revenue sharing, which had enabled Rizzo to add thousands of workers to the city payroll, had fallen to 0.5 percent of the city budget by the end of Goode's first term.[103] It strikes me as historical wishful thinking to expect the advocates of black independent politics to have foreseen the massive rightward shift in national politics that would begin by the late 1970s.

The 1985 police bombing of the West Philadelphia headquarters of the black radical group MOVE is, of course, the yardstick by which many have judged Mayor Goode's tenure. While a full discussion of the MOVE tragedy is beyond the scope of this chapter, two observations about its meaning for the legacy of independent black politics in Philadelphia do seem in order. On the one hand, Mayor Goode's actions during the crisis clearly reflected his preternaturally cautious approach to governing and his unwillingness to pursue the kind of institutional transformation that the advocates of community control had envisioned during the 1960s. Even in his own account of the MOVE tragedy, Goode acknowledged that he turned full control over the crisis to a police command with a history of racist brutality and a bitter grudge against the confrontational back-to-nature group. And yet, a kind of truncated legacy of community control was at play in the series of events that led up to the police bombing. After all, the mayor's decision to approve the effort to evict MOVE was a direct response to a concerted lobbying campaign by the radical group's black neighbors, lower-middle-class homeowners from the heart of Goode's West Philadelphia political base. Fed up with MOVE's late-night denunciations, broadcast from rooftop loudspeakers, of American materialism as well as with the group's practice of feeding rodents and other household pests, these black Philadelphians expected the city's first black mayor, a politician who began his career as an advocate for the needs of West Philadelphia's black neighborhoods, to be responsive to their concerns about the welfare of their children and the value of their most important financial asset. Responsiveness to the concerns of organized groups of black residents was fundamental to advocates of black independent politics. There are many lessons to be taken from the tragic confluence of an irate black neighborhood group, a politico-religious black nationalist commune, a politically conventional black mayor, and an angry and trigger-happy police department. Each of these forces was, in its own way, the product of the unfulfilled vision of the civil rights and Black Power movements. In the absence of mass political activism for racial justice, what had once seemed the transformative potential of black urban politics was consumed in the same fiery combustion that took the lives of six MOVE members and five of their children as well as the homes and dreams of sixty-one neighboring families.[104]

*   *   *

In his 1965 polemic "From Protest to Politics," Bayard Rustin, the strategic architect of the 1963 March on Washington, argued that the only way that the civil rights movement would be able to turn its legislative achievements into substantive economic gains for the black and poor was to develop an electoral coalition of "Negroes, trade unionists, liberals, and religious groups," the very New Deal coalition that Black Power activists viewed as the prime obstacle to the growth of a truly indigenous black political leadership. And yet, the BPF shared with Rustin the belief that a realistic and effective electoral strategy was essential to achieving the "qualitative transformation of social institutions . . . necessary to satisfy[ing] Negro demands for full inclusion in the nation's socio-economic life." While Rustin charged that those who sought to build "the Negro's independent political power" lacked "a realistic strategy" for changing the nation's "social, political and economic institutions," he still recognized the potential inherent in organizing black electoral power in urban and rural communities with a black majority. "If the movement can wrest leadership of the ghetto vote from the machines," he wrote, "it will have acquired an organized constituency such as other major groups in our society."[105] Thus, the irony of Rustin's "political memo" was that it was black activists most influenced by the emerging Black Power critique of liberalism who proved most effective at developing approaches to electoral politics that served to compliment the protest strategies of the early civil rights movement. Black Power activists in Philadelphia and elsewhere developed electoral strategies that sought not only to elect blacks to represent majority black communities, but then to hold those elected officials accountable to the movement's agenda of fundamental socioeconomic and institutional reform.

It was the desire to defend and institutionalize the economic and programmatic gains achieved by community control activists within the Black Power wing of the Philadelphia movement that gave the BPF its appeal. By the end of the 1960s, Philadelphia's Black Power activists had made significant progress towards the goal of community control. Specifically, community-based organizing strategies had enabled neighborhood activists from black poor and working-class neighborhoods to win significant influence over both the public schools in their communities and the city's Model Cities Program. The turn to electoral strategies came only after conservative victories in both federal and local elections had begun to threaten those achievements.

Moreover, the desire to control federal economic dollars provided the strategic logic behind the BPF's decision to focus on the Democratic Party primaries. The demand for community control was rooted in both Malcolm X's vision of black self-determination at the community level and Rustin's argument that only a fundamental reorganization of government priorities and spending could address the issue of persistent black poverty. While an all-black third party might achieve a form of self-determination, many Black Power advocates in Philadelphia came to see winning community control over the Democratic Party's infrastructure within black communities as necessary for achieving the twin goals of black community control and massive public reinvestment in inner cities. Just as SNCC's 1964 Freedom Summer campaign targeted the Democratic Party as the institution capable of securing black voting rights, BPF advocates saw the party as crucial to the struggle for control over government programs and resources in the urban North.

In the more than thirty years since the founding of the Black Political Forum, black electoral strategies have done little to slow the growth of black poverty and inner-city decay in Philadelphia. It is thus easy to dismiss the vision of a citywide organization of independent black Democrats building on the gains of the local civil rights and black power movements as, at best, hopelessly naive, and, at worst, a facade for the personal ambitions of a small group of political opportunists. But while the dangers of electoral strategies to a mass social movement should not be overlooked, it is crucial, in analyzing the history of black electoral politics in the post-civil rights era, to examine the social movement logic at the root of the Black Power turn to electoral action.

Conclusion

Social movements do not disappear overnight. Rather they dissipate almost imperceptibly as a result of a complex mixture of local and national defeats and changes in political mood. Black Power survived the 1960s in the economic projects of both national organizations like OIC and neighborhood community development groups; in black-controlled cultural and educational institutions like North Philadelphia's Heritage Theater and John Churchville's Freedom Day School; in the continued community organizing and political lobbying of countless neighborhood-based and citywide groups; and even in the armed rejectionism of MOVE. In the 1960s, these efforts had constituted a movement. By the 1970s, movement organizers found themselves increasingly unable to demonstrate to most black Philadelphians that the payoff from social movement strategies was worth either the risk or the effort.

The brief Black Power moment in Philadelphia raises important questions about the life cycle of social movements. Scholars have offered a range of explanations for the rise and fall of movements. Some view ideology as the key determinant of a movement's rise and fall, while others focus on the ability of movement organizers to adapt their strategies to changes in the political and economic context in which they must operate, and still others focus on whether movement strategies effectively make use of the resources and cultural traditions of the movement's key constituencies.[1] The history of the civil rights and Black Power movements in Philadelphia demonstrates how ideology, resource mobilization, and cultural practices combine to determine whether a movement's strategies can convince people to join and then maintain their involvement in the movement. Movements survive and grow so long as their strategies remain both culturally meaningful and politically effective. As the nonviolent protests of the early civil rights movement won dramatic victories in places like Montgomery and Greensboro, suddenly protests seemed to sprout up spontaneously all across the South. Similarly, Black Power prospered so long as its appeal to the desire of African Americans for racial pride and unity was linked to a mobilization strategy that seemed to be increasing African American political and economic power, precisely those areas in which civil rights liberalism had failed. How can we explain how the same ideological positions and strategic initiatives that led to the explosion of Black Power activity in the late 1960s could not sustain the movement in the early 1970s? One could simply cite the changes in economic structures and national political mood to explain Black Power's rapid demise as a social movement. Both of these factors, however, were as evident in the late 1960s as they were in the early 1970s. Just as there is something paradoxical about black nationalism's shift from the dogma of tiny political and religious sects in the 1950s to the cornerstone of Black Power's popular critique of racial liberalism, so too economic factors can provide only a partial explanation for the decline in popular response to Black Power appeals during the 1970s.

What leads large numbers of people to make the seemingly counter-intuitive choice to join social movements, to accept the inevitable disruption of daily routines and to risk even worse (violence, loss of economic well-being, and so on) by taking part in efforts to transform repressive social forms? At the risk of reducing human behavior to positivistic notions of cost-benefit analysis, it is clear that most individuals will not sustain their involvement in a social movement if they do not believe their participation is contributing to the achievement of the movement's goals. The success of social movements is therefore dependent on the ability of their leadership to articulate a message that convincingly links ideology (an analysis of the causes of social injustice and a vision of a socially just world) to a strategy (a proposed set of actions that each individual can undertake to protest injustice) for achieving a goal (a specific remedy to a specific injustice). Such a formulation suggests that social movements should be viewed as a kind of conversation between and among would-be leaders and their potential supporters. In such a dialogue, leaders' efforts to mobilize potential supporters are continually evaluated by the participants as they decide whether their participation in the movement is worth the potential costs and benefits.[2]

It was not simply political and economic context that changed between the late 1960s and early 1970s. What also changed was the belief in the possibility of social change among movement leaders and supporters. At the moment that civil rights liberalism encountered a set of issues for which it lacked an adequate response, the movement was still celebrating two of its greatest victories. Somewhat ironically, given its belief that racism was inherent in white American society, Black Power brought its ideological and strategic message to a black community that believed in its capacity to change the country. In cities like Philadelphia, the Black Power movement led not only to the emergence of new political strategies, but also to a broadening of black political leadership and of the range of issues taken up by movement activists. The Black Power critique of civil rights liberals led to significant changes in the country's approach to racial justice. The federal government's adoption of affirmative action, for example, recognized that it was not enough to protect individuals from racial discrimination; employers and educational institutions had to be forced to diversify their workforces and student bodies. Similarly, it was not enough to allow African Americans to live and eat where they please; racial justice demanded public and private investment in the economic development of black communities.

A decade after it began, the Black Power movement dissipated as African Americans experienced a series of clear lessons about the limitations of their ability to change public policy at the national and local level. Black Power suffered a number of strategic missteps. Most important, it never developed a feasible strategy, either political or revolutionary, for achieving control of political institutions in the black community. However, neither its strategic weaknesses nor the confrontational way it sought to renegotiate cross-racial relations were the primary cause of its failure. At root, Black Power advocates were never able to convince other elements of the New Deal coalition to bear the cost of its agenda for racial justice.

Black Power's greatest contribution to American politics was that it linked the well-known, at least within the black community, nationalist critique of the American polity's ability to fulfill its promise of full citizenship and equality to people of African descent to specific, seemingly plausible strategies for increasing the power of African Americans to control their own destiny and solve the problems of racial discrimination, economic inequality, and mis-education. In the context of rapid decolonization and apparently successful third world revolutionary movements against European and American imperialism, the debate over whether African Americans should pursue strategies rooted in an alliance with other liberal elements in the Democratic Party, economic self-reliance, independent political strategies modeled on the urban politics of white ethnic groups, armed self-defense, or revolutionary violence was not an abstract ideological battle but a high stakes conflict over what to do next. The advocates of Black Power believed that they offered both a more coherent view of white America's addiction to racism *and* more effective strategies for pursuing the goals of the black freedom movement.

Notes

Introduction

1. On the origins of the Philadelphia Plan, see Thomas J. Sugrue, "Affirmative Action from Below: Civil Rights, the Building Trades, and the Politics of Racial Equality in the Urban North, 1945–1969," *Journal of American History* 91, 1 (June 2004): 145–73.

2. Leon H. Sullivan, *Build Brother Build* (Philadelphia: Macrae Smith, 1969), 87.

3. The phrase "a hand up, not a hand out" was a favorite of Sargent Shriver, the director of the Office of Economic Opportunity, the federal War on Poverty agency. Quoted in William H. Chafe, *The Unfinished Journey: America Since World War II*, 5th ed. (New York: Oxford University Press, 2003), 240. On the Johnson administration's support for OIC, see Chapter 3. For a discussion of the class-bound meanings of self-help and racial uplift within the black middle class, see Kevin K. Gaines, *Uplifting the Race: Black Leadership, Politics, and Culture in the Twentieth Century* (Chapel Hill: University of North Carolina Press, 1996), 1–46, 67–99.

4. Sullivan, *Build Brother Build*, 98–148, 161–79.

5. Jeanne F. Theoharis and Komozi Woodard, eds., *Freedom North: Black Freedom Struggles Outside the South, 1940–1980* (New York: Palgrave Macmillan, 2003).

6. The past few years have seen the publication of a number of important studies on civil rights activism in the urban North. In addition to the essays in *Freedom North*, see Rhonda Y. Williams, *The Politics of Public Housing: Black Women's Struggles Against Urban Inequality* (New York: Oxford University Press, 2004); Robert O. Self, *American Babylon: Race and the Struggle for Postwar Oakland* (Princeton, N.J.: Princeton University Press, 2003); Martha Biondi, *To Stand and Fight: The Struggle for Civil Rights in Postwar New York City* (Cambridge, Mass.: Harvard University Press, 2003); Wendell Pritchett, *Brownsville, Brooklyn: Blacks, Jews and the Changing Face of the Ghetto* (Chicago: University of Chicago Press, 2003); Heather Ann Thompson, *Whose Detroit? Politics, Labor and Race in a Modern American City* (Ithaca, N.Y.: Cornell University Press, 2001); Komozi Woodard, *A Nation Within a Nation: Amiri Baraka and Black Power Politics in Newark* (Chapel Hill: University of North Carolina Press, 1999); Suzanne Smith, *Dancing in the Street: Motown and the Cultural Politics of Detroit* (Cambridge, Mass.: Harvard University Press, 1999): James R. Ralph, Jr., *Northern Protest: Martin Luther King, Jr., Chicago and the Civil Rights Movement* (Cambridge Mass.: Harvard University Press, 1993).

7. On the role of the state in the New Deal, see Alan Brinkley, *Liberalism and its Discontents* (Cambridge, Mass.: Harvard University Press, 1998), 37–93. On New Deal housing policies, see Kenneth Jackson, *Crabgrass Frontier: The Suburbanization of the United States* (New York: Oxford University Press, 1985) and Thomas J. Sugrue, *The Origins of the Urban Crisis: Race and Inequality in Postwar Detroit* (Princeton, N.J.: Princeton University Press, 1998) 59–63. On the Social Security Act, see William E. Leuchtenberg, *Franklin D. Roosevelt and the New Deal, 1932–1940* (New York: Harper and Row, 1963), 132–33; Linda Gordon, *Pitied But Not Entitled: Single Mothers and*

the History of Welfare, 1890–1935 (New York: Free Press 1994), 1–14, 253–86. Even the Wagner Act, which labor historian Nelson Lichtenstein has called "perhaps the most radical piece of legislation in twentieth-century American history," only gave workers "the right" to unionize and bargain collectively and, after passage of the Taft-Hartley Act over President Truman's veto in 1947, allowed states to prohibit union shops. Nelson Lichtenstein, *Walter Reuther: The Most Dangerous Man in Detroit* (Urbana: University of Illinois Press, 1995), 50, 261. On the GI Bill and its politics of earned entitlement, see Lizabeth Cohen, *A Consumer's Republic: The Politics of Mass Consumption in Postwar America* (New York: Vintage, 2003), 137–46, 166–73.

8. On the March on Washington Movement and Executive Order 8802, see Jervis Anderson, *Bayard Rustin: Troubles I've Seen* (Berkeley: University of California Press, 1997), 60–87; August Meier and Elliott Rudwick, *Black Detroit and the Rise of the UAW,* (New York: Oxford University Press, 1979), 108–74; and Beth T. Bates, " 'Double V for Victory' Mobilizes Black Detroit," in Theoharis and Woodard, eds., *Freedom North*, 17–40.

9. Gunnar Myrdal, *An American Dilemma: The Negro Problem and Modern Democracy* (New York: Harper and Row, 1944), was the crucial popular text to describe race in America as fundamentally a problem of white society. On the impact of Myrdal's work, see Walter A. Jackson, *Gunnar Myrdal and America's Conscience: Social Engineering and Racial Liberalism, 1938–1987* (Chapel Hill: University of North Carolina Press, 1990).

10. In 1948, Henry Lee Moon, the NAACP's director of public relations, published a civil rights program for the post-World War II era that emphasized the potential power of the growing black vote in the North. See Henry Lee Moon, *Balance of Power: The Negro Vote* (Garden City, N.Y.: Doubleday, 1948).

11. For discussions of black protest movements in other northern cities in this period, see August Meier and Elliott Rudwick, *CORE: A Study in the Civil Rights Movement, 1942–1968* (Urbana: University of Illinois Press, 1973), 182–258; George Lipsitz, *A Life in the Struggle: Ivory Perry and the Culture of Opposition* rev. ed. (Philadelphia, Temple University Press, 1988, 1995), 65–92; Self, *American Babylon*, 180–98; Pritchett, *Brownsville, Brooklyn,* 147–90; Ralph, *Northern Protest,* 7–34; Adina Black, "Exposing the 'Whole Segregation Myth': The Harlem Nine and New York City's School Desegregation Battles," Jeanne Theoharis, " 'I'd Rather Go to School in the South': How Boston's School Desegregation Complicates the Civil Rights Paradigm," and Angela Dillard, "Religion and Radicalism: The Reverend Albert B. Cleage Jr. and the Rise of Black Christian Nationalism in Detroit," in Theoharis and Woodard, *Freedom North,* 65–92, 135–52, 153–76.

12. On the ways that New Deal housing policies reified racial stratification in American society by insuring that patterns of residential segregated were maintained and extended, see Sugrue, *Origins of the Urban Crisis,* 59–63; and Kenneth Jackson, *Crabgrass Frontier: The Suburbanization of the United States* (New York: Oxford University Press, 1985), 190–218. On the exclusion of domestic and farm workers from Social Security during the 1930s and 1940s, see Gordon, *Pitied But Not Entitled,* 275–80.

13. Aldon Morris, *The Origins of the Civil Rights Movement: Black Communities Organizing for Change* (New York: Free Press, 1984), 282. Morris's analysis built from numerous community studies of the southern movement that emphasized its "indigenous" qualities, including William Chafe's classic study of civil rights activism in Greensboro, North Carolina, which not only carefully constructed a decade's worth of local activism in the city but also dissected the peculiarities of the local system of racial domination. William H. Chafe, *Civilities and Civil Rights: Greensboro,*

North Carolina, and the Black Struggle for Freedom (New York: Oxford University Press, 1980).

14. One of the earliest civil rights histories to portray Black Power as causing the downfall of the civil rights movement was August Meier and Elliot Rudwick's 1973 study of the Congress of Racial Equality (CORE). Meier and Rudwick ascribed the mid-decade turn to black nationalism to youthful impatience with the pace of racial change. "In five years," they wrote, "the black protest movement had accomplished more than in all the preceding fifty. Yet with expectations outracing change, many militants had become cynical and bitter about American society." Meier and Rudwick, *CORE*, 329. Even scholars sympathetic to Black Power have accused its proponents of failing to develop a strategic vision for achieving their goals. "While the nationalist wing may criticize the integrationist aims in life," Harold Cruse wrote in 1967, "the integrationists at least have a program which . . . the nationalists do not." Harold Cruse, *The Crisis of the Negro Intellectual* (New York: William Morrow, 1967), 420.

15. Eddie S. Glaude Jr., "Introduction," in Eddie Glaude, Jr., ed., *Is It Nation Time? Contemporary Essays on Black Power and Black Nationalism* (Chicago: University of Chicago Press, 2002), 8. I have taken the idea of Black Power as psychologically liberating from William L. Van DeBurg, *New Day in Babylon: The Black Power Movement and American Culture, 1965–1975* (Chicago: University of Chicago Press, 1992).

16. For similar discussions of Black Power as the basis for social movement organizing, see Woodard, *A Nation Within A Nation*, 91–155, and Scot Brown, *Fighting for US: Maulana Karenga, the US Organization and Cultural Nationalism* (New York: New York University Press, 2003). For an overview of recent work on Black Power, see Peniel E. Joseph, "Black Liberation Without Apology: Reconceptualizing the Black Power Movement," *Black Scholar* 31 (2001):2–19. Another stream of histories demonstrate the ways in which Black Power, far from being discontinuous with the early civil rights movement, emerged from long-standing and continuous forms of black political activism. See, for example, Timothy Tyson, *Radio Free Dixie: Robert Williams and the Roots of Black Power* (Chapel Hill: University of North Carolina Press, 1999); and Robin D. G. Kelley, *Freedom Dreams: The Black Radical Imagination* (Boston: Beacon, 2003).

17. I use the term "black nationalist tradition" because, as numerous scholars have pointed out, the black nationalist thinking can be traced back to very origins of the American nation. On the intellectual history of black nationalism see, Gaines, *Uplifting the Race*, 100–127; Joseph, "Black Liberation Without Apology"; August Meier, *Negro Thought in America, 1880–1915: Racial Ideologies in the Age of Booker T. Washington* (Ann Arbor: University of Michigan Press, 1963); Wilson Moses, *The Golden Age of Black Nationalism, 1850–1925* (Hamden, Conn.: Archon Books, 1978); and Michele Mitchell, *Righteous Propagation: African Americans and the Politics of Racial Destiny after Reconstruction,* (Chapel Hill: University of North Carolina Press, 2004). On the black nationalist view that racism is constitutive of American society, see Michael C. Dawson, *Black Visions: The Roots of Contemporary African-American Political Ideologies* (Chicago: University of Chicago Press, 2001), 21–23, 85–134; and Cornel West, "Afterword," in Wahneema Lubiano, ed., *The House That Race Built: Black Americans, U.S. Terrain* (New York: Pantheon, 1997), 301–3.

18. On the organizing tradition, see Charles M. Payne, *I've Got the Light of Freedom: The Organizing Tradition and the Mississippi Freedom Struggle* (Berkeley: University of California Press, 1995) 67–102, and Barbara Ransby, *Ella Baker and the Black Freedom Movement: A Radical Democratic Vision* (Chapel Hill: University of North Carolina Press, 2003), 239–298. Clayborne Carson, in his groundbreaking 1981 history of SNCC, charged that advocates of Black Power within the organization abandoned

the community organizing strategies that had been key to the group's early successes in favor of ideological sectarianism and inflammatory rhetoric. "Rather than utilizing the creative energy released in the new upsurge of black militancy," he has concluded, "SNCC joined the ranks of social movement organizations throughout history which sought to impose their worldview on people who were struggling to think for themselves." Clayborne Carson, *In Struggle: SNCC and the Black Awakening of the 1960s* (Cambridge, Mass.: Harvard University Press, 1981), 287; see Payne, *I've Got the Light of Freedom*, 338–90 for a similar argument about the decline of SNCC organizing in Mississippi.

19. On Black Power's gender ideologies, see E. Frances White, "Africa on My Mind: Gender, Counter Discourse and African American Nationalism," *Journal of Women's History* (Spring 1990): 73–97; Wahneema Lubiano, "Black Nationalism and Black Common Sense: Policing Ourselves and Others," in Lubiano, *The House That Race Built*, 232–52; and Ula Taylor, "Elijah Muhammad's Nation of Islam: Separatism, Regendering, and a Secular Approach to Black Power After Malcolm X (1965–1975)," in Theoharis and Woodard, *Freedom North*, 177–98.

20. On women activists in the Black Power movement, see Taylor, "Elijah Muhammad's Nation of Islam"; Tracye Matthews, " 'No One Ever Asks What a Man's Role in the Revolution Is': Gender and the Politics of the Black Panther Party, 1966–1971," in Charles E. Jones, ed., *The Black Panther Party Reconsidered* (Baltimore: Black Classic Press, 1998), 267–304; Angela D. LeBlanc-Ernest, " 'The Most Qualified Person to Handle the Job': Black Panther Party Woman," in Jones, 305–34; Kristin Anderson-Bricker, " 'Triple Jeopardy,': Black Women and the Growth of Feminist Consciousness in SNCC, 1964–1975," in Kimberly Springer, ed., *Still Lifting, Still Climbing* (New York: New York University Press, 1999), 49–69; Mumia Abu-Jamal, *We Want Freedom: A Life in the Black Panther Party* (Cambridge, Mass.: South End Press, 2004), 159–84; Stephen Michael Ward, " 'Ours Too Was a Struggle for a Better World': Activist Intellectuals and the Radical Promise of the Black Power Movement, 1962–1972," Ph.D. dissertation, University of Texas, 2002, 223–265.

21. Interview with Charyn Sutton, Aug. 12, 2004, Philadelphia; personal communication with Joan Countryman, July 15, 2004; Abu-Jamal, *We Want Freedom*, 50, 58–59.

Chapter 1. Civil Rights Liberalism in Philadelphia

1. On the liberal reform movement within the Philadelphia Democratic Party, see James Reichley, *The Art of Government: Reform and Organization Politics in Philadelphia* (New York: Fund for the Republic, 1959), and Kirk R. Petshek, *The Challenge of Urban Reform: Policies and Programs in Philadelphia* (Philadelphia: Temple University Press), 1973.

2. On the Philadelphia Republican machine, see Peter McCaffery, *When Bosses Ruled Philadelphia: The Emergence of the Republican Machine, 1867–1933* (University Park: Pennsylvania State University Press, 1993).

3. For a discussion of postwar liberal anxiety about the impact of racial segregation on the U.S. standing in the international community, see Mary Dudziak, *Cold War Civil Rights: Race and the Image of American Democracy* (Princeton, N.J.: Princeton University Press, 2000), esp. 18–114.

4. Richard Kluger, *Simple Justice: The History of Brown v. Board of Education and Black America's Struggle for Equality* (New York: Random House, 1975), 714.

5. For an overview of the history of the NAACP, see August Meier and John H. Bracey, Jr., "The NAACP as a Reform Movement, 1909–1965: 'To reach the con-

science of America,'" *Journal of Southern History* 59 (1993): 3–30. On the Philadelphia NAACP, see "A Brief History of the Philadelphia Branch of the National Association for the Advancement of Colored People, 1954," Philadelphia NAACP collection, box 2, Temple University Urban Archives (TUUA).

6. For a discussion of "discursive framing" and social movement theory, see Doug McAdam, John D. McCarthy, and Mayer N. Zald, "Introduction: Opportunities, Mobilizing Structures, and Framing Processes—Toward a Synthetic, Comparative Perspective on Social Movements," in McAdam, McCarthy, and Zald, eds., *Comparative Perspectives on Social Movements* (New York: Cambridge University Press, 1996), 2–4.

7. Philadelphia Fellowship Commission, "Report to the Community," vol. 2, no. 6, Apr. 1950, Fellowship Commission (FC) collection, box 53, folder 7, TUUA. Civil rights advocates also promoted the charter's antidiscrimination language as crucial to the reform coalition's efforts to revitalize the city's image from one dominated by political patronage and corruption. Among the reform groups that endorsed the civil rights provisions was the Greater Philadelphia Movement, an organization of business executives committed to revitalizing Center City by shifting its economic base from industrial production to white-collar office buildings. On the Greater Philadelphia Movement, see Petshek, *Challenge of Urban Reform*, 35.

8. Michael Omi and Howard Winant, *Racial Formation in the United States: From the 1960s to the 1990s*, 2nd ed. (New York: Routledge, 1994), 11.

9. "In the postwar city," Sugrue writes, "blackness and whiteness assumed a spatial definition. . . . The completeness of racial segregation made ghettoization seem an inevitable, natural consequence of profound racial differences. . . . To the majority of untutored white observers, visible poverty, overcrowding, and deteriorating houses were signs of individual moral deficiencies, not manifestations of structural inequalities." Thomas J. Sugrue, *The Origins of the Urban Crisis: Race and Inequality in Postwar Detroit* (Princeton, N.J.: Princeton University Press, 1996) 9.

10. S. T. Mossell, "The Standard of Living among One Hundred Negro Migrant Families in Phila.," *Annals* 97 (November 1921): 174–75. John F. Bauman, *Public Housing, Race, and Renewal: Urban Planning in Philadelphia, 1920–1974* (Philadelphia: Temple University Press, 1987), 12–13. For the distribution of Philadelphia's black population in 1890, see W. E. B. Du Bois, *The Philadelphia Negro: A Social Study* (1899; Philadelphia: University of Pennsylvania Press, 1996), particularly the map and tables on pages 58 and 59. Mossell would later earn a law degree after finding her academic career blocked by her race and gender. With her husband, Raymond Pace Alexander, she would then form Alexander and Alexander, the city's leading black law firm. The two Alexanders would remain among the city's most prominent civil rights advocates in the 1970s.

11. On the efforts of local industry to recruit black workers during World War I, see Vincent P. Franklin, *The Education of Black Philadelphia* (Philadelphia: University of Pennsylvania Press, 1979), 15–20, and Bauman, *Public Housing, Race, and Renewal*, 12–13.

12. Franklin, *Education of Black Philadelphia*, 21–25. On the murder of the black shipyard worker, see Herbert Hill, *Black Labor and the American Legal System* (Madison: University of Wisconsin Press, 1985), 278; on the Philadelphia NAACP's response, see "Brief History of the Philadelphia Branch"; on the mob violence in 1918, see V. P. Franklin, "The Philadelphia Race Riot of 1918," *Pennsylvania Magazine of History and Biography* 99 (1975): 336–50.

13. W. E. B. Du Bois, "Close Ranks," *Crisis* XVI (July 1918), reprinted in David Levering Lewis, ed., *W. E. B. Du Bois: A Reader* (New York: Henry Holt, 1995), 697; Herbert Shapiro, *White Violence and Black Response: From Reconstruction to Montgomery* (Amherst: University of Massachusetts Press, 1988), 145–57; Adam Fairclough, *Better Day Coming: Blacks and Equality, 1890–2000* (New York: Viking, 2001), 87–108.

14. Mossell, "Standard of Living," 174–75; Du Bois, *Philadelphia Negro,* 97–146, 197–234; Franklin, *Education of Black Philadelphia,* 21–25.

15. "Brief History of the Philadelphia Branch"; Franklin, *Education of Black Philadelphia,* 68.

16. Bauman, *Public Housing, Race, and Renewal,* 12–13, 28–29.

17. Du Bois, *Philadelphia Negro,* 368–84; Roger Lane, *Roots of Violence in Black Philadelphia, 1860–1900* (Cambridge, Mass.: Harvard University Press, 1986), 45–81; Franklin, *Education of Black Philadelphia,* 68–71; and Peter McCaffery, *When Bosses Ruled Philadelphia.* On the black vote in the 1928 election, see Nancy J. Weiss, *Farewell to the Party of Lincoln: Black Politics in the Age of FDR* (Princeton, N.J.: Princeton University Press, 1983), 31, 92. On the Philadelphia NAACP's civil rights lobbying, see "Brief History of the Philadelphia Branch."

18. Meier and Bracey, "The NAACP as a Reform Movement"; August Meier, *Negro Thought in America, 1880–1915: Racial Ideologies in the Age of Booker T. Washington* (Ann Arbor: University of Michigan Press, 1963), 161–170; 181–84. On the nadir thesis, see also Rayford W. Logan, *The Negro in American Life and Thought: The Nadir, 1877–1901* (New York: Dial Press, 1954). On the disenfranchisement of southern blacks, see J. Morgan Kousser, *The Shaping of Southern Politics: Suffrage Restriction and the Establishment of the One Party South, 1880–1910* (New Haven Conn.: Yale University Press, 1974). Among the NAACP's earliest campaigns was an unsuccessful effort to prevent theatrical showings of *The Birth of a Nation.* See John Hope Franklin, "The Birth of a Nation: Propaganda as History," in Franklin, *Race and History: Selected Essays* (Baton Rouge: Louisiana State University Press, 1989), 10–23.

19. "Resolutions, National Negro Conference, 1909," in August Meier, Elliott Rudwick, and Francis L. Broderick, eds., *Black Protest Thought in the Twentieth Century,* 2nd ed. (Indianapolis: Bobbs-Merrill Educational Publishing, 1971), 66. On the founding of the NAACP, see also Fairclough, *Better Day Coming,* 67–85. On African American intellectual and political thought in the early twentieth century, see Meier, *Negro Thought in America;* Kevin K. Gaines, *Uplifting the Race: Black Leadership, Politics, and Culture in the Twentieth Century* (Chapel Hill: University of North Carolina Press, 1996) and the essays in Michael Katz and Thomas J. Sugrue, eds., *W. E. B. Du Bois, Race, and the City : The Philadelphia Negro and Its Legacy* (Philadelphia: University of Pennsylvania Press, 1998).

20. Franklin, *Education of Black Philadelphia,* 71–82; Leslie Pinckney Hill, *Crisis* XXVI (April 1923): 252–54.

21. Genna Rae McNeil, *Groundwork: Charles Hamilton Houston and the Struggle for Civil Rights* (Philadelphia: University of Pennsylvania Press, 1983), 116–17. The NAACP's antilynching campaign never achieved its goal of a federal lynch law, but, as Charles Payne has argued, it contributed to the demise of the white southern practice of public, unapologetic lynchings. Charles M. Payne, *I've Got the Light of Freedom: The Organizing Tradition and the Mississippi Freedom Struggle* (Berkeley: University of California Press, 1995), 54–55. For a compelling recent discussion of the Sweet case, see Kevin Boyle, *Arc of Justice: A Saga of Race, Civil Rights, and Murder in the Jazz Age* (New York: Henry Holt, 2004). On the NAACP's legal activities in the Philadelphia area in this period, see David Alvin Cannon, "The Struggle for Status and Justice: The Life of Judge Raymond Pace Alexander," Ph.D. dissertation, Temple University, 2001, 69–105.

22. Weiss, *Farewell to the Party of Lincoln,* 31, 92–93; Bauman, *Public Housing, Race, and Renewal,* 28–29. On Vare, see McCaffery, *When Bosses Ruled Philadelphia,* 97–188.

23. Weiss, *Farewell to the Party of Lincoln,* 93–94, 185–86; Bauman, *Public Housing, Race, and Renewal,* 30–32; Cannon, "Struggle for Status and Justice, 115–119.

24. Kelly's postelection charge that the Republicans' victory was the result of

vote stealing has been widely accepted by historians of Philadelphia politics. Weiss, *Farewell to the Party of Lincoln*, 228, 293; Reichley, *Art of Government*, 9.

25. Bauman, *Public Housing, Race, and Renewal*, 52–53.

26. My analysis of New Deal racial policies is derived from Weiss, *Farewell to the Party of Lincoln*, 50–59, 136–77, 236–66 and Harvard Sitkoff, *A New Deal for Blacks: The Emergence of Civil Rights as a National Issue* (New York: Oxford University Press, 1978), esp. 42–57. For a study that depicts the New Deal, despite its limitations, as opening up possibilities for racial change in the South, see Patricia Sullivan, *Days of Hope: Race and Democracy and the New Deal* (Chapel Hill: University of North Carolina Press), 41–102.

27. Sugrue, *Origins of the Urban Crisis*, 43–44. Ickes quoted in Bauman, *Public Housing, Race, and Renewal*, 34–47.

28. Weiss, *Farewell to the Party of Lincoln*, 257–66.

29. "Brief History of the Philadelphia Branch." Newman is quoted in Bauman, *Public Housing, Race, and Renewal*, 35–36. Information on the founding of the Young People's Interracial Fellowship is derived from "Address—American Baptist Board of Education, Atlanta, Ga., February 4, 1966," 1–2, and "Marjorie Penney Anniversary Dinner," program, January 8, 1968, in "Marjorie Penney Founder" box, Fellowship House collection, TUUA, and minutes, Board of Commissioners, Jun., 19, 1950, 3, FC collection, box 7, TUUA. Harvard Sitkoff discusses the growing involvement of the leadership of the northern Protestant churches in civil rights issues during the 1930s. See Sitkoff, *A New Deal for Blacks*, 265–66.

30. "Address—American Baptist Board of Education," 1–2, and "Marjorie Penney" program.

31. See minutes, Board of Commissioners, Jun., 19, 1950, 3–4, FC collection, box 7, TUUA for a history of the Tolerance Clearing House.

32. On the Communist Party's involvement in racial issues during the 1930s, see Shapiro, *White Violence and Black Response*, 207–37; Robin D.G. Kelley, *Hammer and Hoe: Alabama Communists During the Great Depression* (Chapel Hill: University of North Carolina Press, 1990), 13–118; and Mark Naison, *Communists in Harlem During the Depression* (New York: Grove Press, 1983), 3–168. Lawyers from the left-wing International Labor Defense actively pursued a number of civil rights cases in the Philadelphia during the 1930's. See Cannon, "Struggle for Status and Justice," 89–94, 101–04. On the Communist Party in Philadelphia, see also Paul Lyons, *Philadelphia Communists, 1936–56* (Philadelphia: Temple University Press, 1982).

33. On the rise of the Popular Front and its impact on civil rights activism, see Kelley, *Hammer and Hoe*, 119–219; Naison, *Communists in Harlem*, 169–286.

34. See minutes, Board of Commissioners, Jun. 19, 1950, 3–4, FC collection, box 7, TUUA.

35. Gunnar Myrdal, *An American Dilemma: The Negro Problem and Modern Democracy* (New York: Harper and Row, 1944), lxix–llxxxiii. On the impact of *An American Dilemma*, see Walter A. Jackson, *Gunnar Myrdal and America's Conscience: Social Engineering and Racial Liberalism, 1938–1987* (Chapel Hill: University of North Carolina Press, 1990).

36. Jervis Anderson, *Bayard Rustin: Troubles I've Seen* (Berkeley: University of California Press, 1997), 60–87; August Meier and Elliott Rudwick, *Black Detroit and the Rise of the UAW* (New York: Oxford University Press, 1979), 108–74; Beth T. Bates, "'Double V for Victory' Mobilizes Black Detroit," in Theoharis and Woodard, eds., *Freedom North*, 17–40. For a discussion of the FEPC's effectiveness, see Hill, *Black Labor and the American Legal System*, 173–84.

37. "Philadelphia Fellowship Commission Report to the Community," May 1955, p. 4, Urban League (UL) collection, box 16, folder 14, TUUA; minutes,

Board of Commissioners, Sep. 18, 1959, FC collection, box 7, TUUA; Arthur Huff Fauset, "United People's Action Committee," *Philadelphia Tribune*, Dec. 18, 1943.

38. Fauset, "United People's Action Committee."

39. "Unions Pledge Job Aid," *Philadelphia Tribune*, Jul. 4, 1942; "Union Takes Arsenal Workers' Case to War Dept. Heads," *Philadelphia Tribune*, Jul. 11, 1942; "FEPC Representative Will Find Complaints Aplenty Upon Arrival," *Philadelphia Tribune*, Oct. 17, 1942; Arthur Huff Fauset, "The Sun Shipyard Proposition," *Philadelphia Tribune*, Jun. 6, 1942.

40. "Shortage of Motormen Offers Opportunity for Colored Men," *Philadelphia Tribune*, Mar. 21, 1942; Arthur Huff Fauset, "UPAC Steps Out," *Philadelphia Tribune*, Apr. 1, 1944. For a summary of the PTC case, see Hill, *Black Labor and the American Legal System*, 274–308.

41. Hill, *Black Labor and the American Legal System*, 274–308.

42. "Philadelphia Seething as Riots Start," *Philadelphia Tribune*, Aug. 5, 1944; "Annual Report of Philadelphia Branch Activities: 1944," NAACP papers, II C 275, Library of Congress (LOC), and "A Brief History of the Council for Equal Job Opportunity," NAACP papers, II C 170, LOC.

43. On the Philadelphia NAACP's membership, see "Brief History of the Philadelphia Branch." On the PTC strike's impact on the Fellowship Commission, see minutes, Board of Commissioners, Jun. 19, 1950, FC collection, box 7, TUUA.

44. "FEPC Mass Meeting to Be Held Sep. 15," *Philadelphia Tribune*, Aug. 15, 1945; "Philadelphia FEPC Bill Introduced in Council," *Philadelphia Tribune*, Nov. 3, 1945; "Drive for FEPC Given Impetus at Mass Meet," *Philadelphia Tribune*, Dec. 1, 1945; "Citizens Bitterly Protest Closing of FEPC Office," *Philadelphia Tribune*, Dec. 8, 1945.

45. Arthur Huff Fauset, "PTC: It Could Be Done," *Philadelphia Tribune*, Sep. 9, 1944; "UPAC Sponsors Housing Meeting at School Bldg," *Philadelphia Tribune*, May 5, 1945; "UPAC Wants Fed. Low-Rent Housing Units," *Philadelphia Tribune*, Jun. 23, 1945.

46. "Annual Report of Philadelphia Branch Activities: 1944."

47. Bauman, *Public Housing, Race, and Renewal*, 57–58; Carolyn Adams et al., *Philadelphia: Neighborhoods, Division, and Conflict in a Postindustrial City* (Philadelphia: Temple University Press, 1991), 9.

48. The committee's research director remembers that Alexander worked with the other attorneys on the commission to insure that its recommendations reflected the constitutional approach to protecting civil rights that the NAACP had developed during the previous thirty years. Interview with Milton Stewart, Mar. 5, 1996, Phoenix, Ariz.

49. The committee report quoted extensively from a letter it received from Secretary of State Dean Acheson. "The existence of discrimination against minority groups in this country," Acheson wrote, "has an adverse effect upon our relations with other countries . . . the gap between the things we stand for in principle and the facts of a particular situation may be too wide to be bridged." U.S. President's Committee on Civil Rights, *To Secure These Rights: The Report of the President's Committee on Civil Rights* 157. On the committee's use of anticommunism to justify government action on civil rights issues, see Mary Dudziak, *Cold War Civil Rights: Race and the Image of American Democracy* (Princeton, N.J.: Princeton University Press), 79–83 and Penny M. Von Eschen, *Race Against Empire: Black Americans and Anticolonialism, 1937–1957* (Ithaca, N.Y.: Cornell University Press, 1997), 109–113.

50. President's Committee, *To Secure These Rights*, 139–73; Martha Biondi, *To Stand and Fight: The Struggle for Civil Rights in Postwar New York City* (Cambridge, Mass: Harvard University Press), 142–47; William H. Chafe, *The Unfinished Journey:*

America Since World War II, 5th ed. (New York: Oxford University Press, 2003), 89–91; interview with Milton Stewart, Mar. 5, 1996. On the 1948 election, see Jack M. Bloom, *Class, Race and the Civil Rights Movement* (Bloomington: Indiana University Press, 1987), 74–86; and Oscar Glantz, "Recent Negro Ballots in Philadelphia," in Miriam Ershkowitz and Joseph Zikmund, II, eds., *Black Politics in Philadelphia* (New York: Basic Books, 1973), 65–77.

51. Dudziak, *Cold War Civil Rights*, 79–83; Chafe, *The Unfinished Journey*, 89–91.

52. Untitled and undated report written by a Spaulding supporter, NAACP papers, II C 406, LOC.

53. "NAACP Elects Jos. Rainey as President," *Philadelphia Tribune*, Dec. 8, 1945; "Rainey Denied Dissension in NAACP Election," *Philadelphia Tribune*, Dec. 15, 1945; "Report of the President of the NAACP for the year ending December 1946," NAACP papers, II C 406, LOC. For a different account of Rainey's leadership of the Philadelphia NAACP, see Berky Nelson, "Before the Revolution: Crisis within the Philadelphia and Chicago NAACP, 1940–1960," *Negro History Bulletin* 61, 1 (January–March 1998): 20–26.

54. "Address of Magistrate Joseph H. Rainey," Jan. 8, 1946, NAACP papers, II C 406, LOC. See also "Joseph Rainey Installed as NAACP Prexy," *Philadelphia Tribune*, Jan. 12, 1946. On antifascism as a key tenet of the black left in the immediate postwar period, see Von Eschen, *Race Against Empire*, esp. 69–144.

55. "Report of the President of the NAACP for the year ending December 1946."

56. See Madeline Bachrach to Joseph Rainey, Dec. 18, 1946, and "Report to Secretary and Committee on Administration," Jan. 27, 1947, NAACP papers, II C 406, LOC. Other members of the CEJO Executive Committee included Raymond Pace Alexander, a lawyer and Democratic Party activist long active in the NAACP, Rev. Luther Cunningham, the branch treasurer, and Charles Shorter, the full-time branch executive secretary who had recently resigned in a dispute with Rainey over his decision to fire a clerical worker. On Shorter's resignation, see "Report to Secretary and Committee on Administration," Jan. 27, 1947. On the politics of the black left during the 1940s, see Martin Duberman, *Paul Robeson* (New York: Knopf, 1988), 296–335; Gerald Horne, *Black and Red: W. E. B. Du Bois and the Afro-American Response to the Cold War, 1944–1963* (Albany: State University of New York Press, 1986) and *Communist Front? The Civil Rights Congress, 1946–1956,* (Rutherford, N.J.: Fairleigh Dickinson University Press, 1988), and Von Eschen, *Race Against Empire*, 69–121.

57. Joseph H. Rainey to Walter White, April 26, 1946, and "Report to Secretary and Committee on Administration," Jan. 27, 1947, NAACP papers, II C 406, LOC; "Foes Seek Ouster of Joe Rainey," *Philadelphia Tribune*, Mar. 30, 1946; "Rainey Upheld 208–15 by NAACP Membership," *Philadelphia Tribune*, Apr. 6, 1946; Untitled and undated report written by a Spaulding supporter, NAACP papers, II C 406, LOC. Rainey had sought but failed to secure the Democratic Party nomination for North and West Philadelphia's Fourth Congressional District. "Machine Union Backs Rainey for Congress," *Philadelphia Tribune*, Feb. 16, 1946.

58. Joseph H. Rainey to Walter White, April 26, 1946, "Report to Secretary and Committee on Administration," Jan. 27, 1947, "Report of the President of the NAACP for the year ending December 1946," and news release, Philadelphia Branch, National Association for the Advancement of Colored People, Jul. 17, 1947, NAACP papers, II C 406, LOC.

59. Memorandum from Mr. Current, re: Philadelphia Informal Meeting, Sep. 15, 1947, NAACP papers, II C 406, LOC.

60. Memorandum to Mr. White from Marion O. Bond, Jun. 26, 1947, NAACP

papers, II C 406, LOC; memorandum to Gloster B. Current from Leroy E. Carter, July 1, 1948, NAACP papers, II C 169, LOC.

61. Raymond Pace Alexander to Walter White, July 18, 1947, and "Save Philadelphia NAACP" flier, NAACP papers, II C 406, LOC; "NAACP and Elks Elections Attract City-Wide Notice," *Philadelphia Tribune*, Dec. 8, 1947; "Rainey Defeats Gay for NAACP President," *Philadelphia Tribune*, Dec. 14, 1947; memorandum to Mr. White from Mr. Current, re: Philadelphia Branch Election," Dec. 15, 1947, NAACP II C 406, LOC. In his letter asking for Walter White's support, Alexander argued that Goldie Watson, whom he did not name but identified as "a very active and dynamic woman identified with a very far left organization who happened to be a school teacher and whose identity you perhaps know," had taken control of the branch's executive board. A similar strategy was successfully used to defeat Rainey's candidacy for the presidency of the Pennsylvania State Conference of the NAACP. See "State NAACP Elects Ambler Man After Bitter Balloting," *Philadelphia Tribune*, Oct. 7, 1947.

62. Memorandum to Mr. White from Mr. Current, re: Philadelphia Branch Election, Dec. 15, 1947.

63. See Theodore Spaulding to Magistrate Joseph H. Rainey, Dec. 22, 1947, Dr. William Bragg to Walter White, Jan. 5, 1948, and Walter White to Dr. William Bragg, Jan. 14, 1948, NAACP papers, II C 169, LOC and memorandum to Mr. White from Mr. Current, re: Philadelphia Branch Election, Dec. 15, 1947.

64. See George B. Morris to Walter White, Feb. 16, 1948, on the formation of the Rainey campaign committee and the reaction of liberals within the chapter, and memorandum from Mr. White to Mrs. Lampkin, Mar. 30, 1948, on support for Wallace within NAACP branches across the country, NAACP papers, II C 169, LOC.

65. "FEPC Enacted into Law by Unanimous Vote of City Council," *Philadelphia Tribune*, Mar. 13, 1948; "A Brief History of the Council for Equal Job Opportunity," NAACP papers, II C 169, LOC; "Civil Rights Laws in Pennsylvania" pamphlet published by the Industrial Race Relations Commission, Commonwealth of Pennsylvania, in NAACP papers, II A 262, LOC; Etta Berg Finkler to National Board of Directors, Apr. 8, 1948, NAACP papers, II C 169, LOC.

66. My assessment of Philadelphia NAACP and the Fellowship Commission is based on a reading of each group's annual reports and newsletters, which are housed in their respective collections at the Temple University Urban Archives. On the shift of NAACP liberals to the Fellowship Commission, see "Report to Secretary and Committee on Administration," Jan. 27, 1947, NAACP papers, II C 406, LOC. The Fellowship Commission's Committee on Community Tension (CCT) provides a prime example of how the commission served a convening function. The CCT, which was founded in 1952, regularly heard reports from officials of the Commission on Human Relations and the police department on incidents of racial and religious violence and the city's neighborhoods and discussed with them options for dealing with those tensions. For an example of these deliberations, see minutes, Committee on Community Tensions, Apr. 4, 1960, FC collection, box 21, folder 3, TUUA.

67. Fair Employment Practices Commission, "annual report 1948–49," Commission on Human Relations (CHR) papers, box 148, folder 1, Philadelphia Municipal Archives (PMA); "FEPC Enacted into Law by Unanimous Vote of City Council," *Philadelphia Tribune*, Mar. 13, 1948.

68. Report of Special Committee, Philadelphia Branch," n.d, NAACP papers, 11 C 169, LOC; memorandum from Mr. White to Messrs. Wilkins, Marshall, Moon, Current, Feb. 4, 1949, NAACP papers, II C 169, LOC; Walter White to Reverend E. T. Lewis, Oct. 24, 1950; see also minutes, Committee on Branches, Oct. 6, 1950;

"Answer to the Charges Submitted by the Director of Branches Against the Philadelphia Branch" and "Suggested Program and Administration Changes"; minutes, Committee on Branches, Nov. 10, 1950; and "Special Board Meeting, Philadelphia Branch," Nov. 6 and 13, 1950, Nov. 6, 1950, NAACP papers, II C 169, LOC. See "Message of the President to the Executive Committee, re: Special Committee's Report, Philadelphia Branch, NAACP" for Lewis's response to the committee's charges, NAACP papers, II C 169, LOC.

69. On Spaulding's strategy, see Theodore Spaulding to Catherine George Smith, Nov. 16, 1950, NAACP papers, II C 169, LOC. See "Anti-Lewis Forces in NAACP Victory," *Pittsburgh Courier*, Nov. 25, 1950 for coverage of the 1950 campaign. For the two slates in the 1950 campaign, see "Official Ballot, Philadelphia Branch," and "Dear NAACP Member," Dec. 12, 1950, NAACP papers, II C 169, LOC.

70. For the Philadelphia NAACP's office statistics, see Philadelphia NAACP, "Annual Report, 1954," NAACP collection, box 2, TUUA.

71. Nancy Kleniewski, "Neighborhood Decline and Downtown Renewal: The Politics of Redevelopment in Philadelphia, 1952–1962," Ph.D. dissertation, Temple University, 1981, 44; Bauman, *Public Housing, Race, and Renewal*, 97–100. See Sam Bass Warner, *The Private City: Philadelphia in Three Periods of Growth* (1968; Philadelphia: University of Pennsylvania Press, 1987) for a discussion of the impact of the ideology of privatism on the governance of Philadelphia. The postwar reform wave also led to the revitalization of a number of progressive-era civic organizations, including the Bureau for Municipal Research, a private research organization, and the Philadelphia Housing Association, an advocacy group for improved housing in the city's poor districts. See Kleniewski, "Neighborhood Decline and Downtown Renewal," and Petshek, *Challenge of Urban Reform*, 16–25, for differing views of the relationship between political reform and urban redevelopment in postwar Philadelphia.

72. Reichley, *Art of Government*, is an account of the reform movement in postwar Philadelphia. On Democratic efforts to win over Philadelphia's black voters in this period, see Cannon, "Struggle for Status and Justice," 174–78, 206–11. On the impact of black voters on the 1947 and 1949 municipal elections, see Charles A. Ekstrom, "The Electoral Politics of Reform and Machine: The Political Behavior of Philadelphia's "Black" Wards, 1943–1969," in Ershkowitz and Zikmund, *Black Politics in Philadelphia*, 84–108.

73. See Petshek, *Challenge of Urban Reform*, 26–36, for a discussion of the charter commission.

74. "Report to the Community," Philadelphia Fellowship Commission, Vol. 2, no. 6, Apr. 1950, FC collection, box 53, folder 7, TUUA. See also the June and October issues of the newsletter. Three members of the charter commission had strong ties to the liberal civil rights coalition. Dr. Tanner G. Duckrey, a black school board official and Sadie Alexander's cousin, and Herbert E. Millen, a black municipal court judge, had both served on the Fellowship Commission and local NAACP boards, while Abraham Freedman was a current member of the commission's board. See minutes, Board of Commissioners, Nov. 21, 1949, FC collection, box 7, TUUA; Philadelphia Fellowship Commission, "Report to the Community," vol. 2, no. 6, Apr. 1950, FC collection, box 53, folder 7, TUUA.

75. Reichley, *Art of Government*, 68–70; Philadelphia Fellowship Commission, "Report to the Community," vol. 2, no. 7, Jun. 1950, FC collection, box 53, folder 7, TUUA; Petshek, *Challenge of Urban Reform*, 35; Cannon, "Struggle for Status and Justice," 206–211. Charles Ekstrom has shown that the city's black wards supported the reform ticket at consistently higher rates than working-class white wards,

though lower than wealthier white areas, just as they had in the 1947 and 1949 municipal elections. Ekstrom argues than the lower rates of black support for reform resulted from a core of voters who remained loyal to the Republican machine's patronage system. See Ekstrom, "Electoral Politics," 84–108.

Chapter 2. The Other Philadelphia Story

1. *Philadelphia Tribune*, Apr. 26, 1955.
2. Manning Marable, *Race, Reform, and Rebellion: The Second Reconstruction in Black America, 1945–1990*, rev. 2nd ed. (Jackson: University Press of Mississippi, 1991), 58.
3. John F. Bauman, *Public Housing, Race, and Renewal: Urban Planning in Philadelphia, 1920–1974* (Philadelphia: Temple University Press, 1987), 154.
4. Dilworth credited black voters with his victory in the 1955 mayoral election. Robert Bendiner, "The Negro Vote and the Democrats," *Reporters* 14, 8 (May 31, 1956). The employment figures are from John H. Strange, "Blacks and Philadelphia Politics: 1963–66," in Miriam Ershkowitz and Joseph Zikmund, II, eds., *Black Politics in Philadelphia* (New York: Basic Books, 1973), 124. See also James Reichley, *The Art of Government: Reform and Organization Politics in Philadelphia* (New York: Fund for the Republic, 1959), 17, 24–27. On opportunities for black workers in municipal government in the post-World War II era, see Suzanne Model, "The Ethnic Niche and the Structure of Opportunity: Immigrants and Minorities in New York City," in Michael B. Katz, ed., *The "Underclass" Debate: Views from History* (Princeton, N.J.: Princeton University Press, 1993), 161–93; and Thomas J. Sugrue, *The Origins of the Urban Crisis: Race and Inequality in Postwar Detroit* (Princeton, N.J.: Princeton University Press, 1996), 110–12.
5. Bauman, *Public Housing, Race, and Renewal*, 154.
6. Carolyn Adams et al., *Philadelphia: Neighborhoods, Division, and Conflict in a Postindustrial City* (Philadelphia: Temple University Press, 1991), 36–38; Kirk R. Petshek, *The Challenge of Urban Reform: Policies and Programs in Philadelphia* (Philadelphia: Temple University Press, 1973), 196; Thomas J. Sugrue, "Affirmative Action from Below: Civil Rights, the Building Trades, and the Politics of Racial Equality in the Urban North, 1945–1969," *Journal of American History* 91, 1 (June 2004): 151; Bauman, *Public Housing, Race, and Renewal*, 84–86. On the city's efforts to revitalize its industrial section in this period, see Guian McKee, "Urban Deindustrialization and Local Public Policy: Industrial Renewal in Philadelphia, 1953–76," *Journal of Policy History* 16, 1 (Jan. 2004): 66–98.
7. See Adams et al., *Philadelphia*, 39–42, for a discussion of the postwar movement of textile and other nondurable industrial jobs from Philadelphia.
8. Bauman, *Public Housing, Race, and Renewal*, 97–105; Petshek, *Challenge of Urban Reform*, 184–231; Nancy Kleniewski, "Neighborhood Decline and Downtown Renewal: The Politics of Redevelopment in Philadelphia, 1952–1962," Ph.D. dissertation, Temple University, 1981.
9. One initiative undertaken by a leading member of Philadelphia's liberal reform movement demonstrates the extent to which the postwar liberal view of the role of government in economic policy prevented any significant response to the labor market changes occurring in aging industrial cities like Philadelphia. Following his election to the U.S. Senate in 1956, former mayor Joseph Clark joined with Illinois senator Paul Douglas to propose federal legislation to aid "depressed areas" in the industrial North. Though Congress passed the bill and it was signed into law by President Eisenhower, the resulting aid packages failed not only to apply sufficient resources to the problem of depressed local economies but—because they

focused primarily on preserving already established businesses and jobs—even to address the structural inequalities that left black and poor communities most vulnerable to the impact of the postwar economic transformation. Sugrue, *Origins of the Urban Crisis,* 6–7.

10. Sugrue, *Origins of the Urban Crisis,* 3–14; W. E. B. Du Bois, *The Philadelphia Negro: A Social Study* (1899; Philadelphia: University of Pennsylvania Press, 1996), 57–58; Kleniewski, "Neighborhood Decline and Downtown Renewal," 45–47; "Philadelphia's Negro Population: Facts on Housing," Commission on Human Relations (CHR) papers, box 148, folder 4, Philadelphia Municipal Archives (PMA).

11. "Philadelphia's Negro Population: Facts on Housing."

12. On the economic development of Bucks County and the NAACP's efforts to press U.S. Steel to increase the percentage of black employees at its plant, see memorandum to Walter White from Clarence Mitchell, Oct. 6, 1953, NAACP papers, II A 161, LOC. On the Pennsylvania fair employment practices law, see Sugrue, "Affirmative Action from Below," 149–50.

13. Bauman, *Public Housing, Race, and Renewal,* 149–53; David W. Bartelt, "Housing the 'Underclass,'" in Katz, *The "Underclass" Debate,* 118–57; "Philadelphia's Negro Population: Facts on Housing," CHR papers; "Testimony Submitted by the Committee on Democracy in Housing to the United States Senate Committee on Banking and Currency, Dec. 18, 1957," NAACP collection, box 16, TUUA; "A Report on the Housing of Negro Philadelphians," Philadelphia Commission on Human Relations, Wharton Centre collection, box 45, TUUA; "The Expanding Ghetto," *Philadelphia Commission on Human Relations Bulletin,* May 1959, NAACP collection, box 4, TUUA.

14. See minutes, Board of Commissioners, Mar. 17, 1952, p. 5, FC collection, box 7, TUUA; press release, Philadelphia Branch NAACP, Sep. 15, 1951, Constance Baker Motley to H. Vashti Norwood, Nov. 5, 1951 and Feb. 18, 1952, memorandum to Mr. Wilkins from Constance Baker Motley, Nov. 9, 1951, memorandum to Gloster B. Current, John W. Flamer from Constance Baker Motley, Feb. 26, 1952, Constance Baker Motley to Jacques Wilmore, Jan. 21, 1953; memorandum to Walter White from Clarence Mitchell, Oct. 6, 1953, memorandum to Arnold de Mille, Robert L. Carter from Constance Baker Motley, Jan. 11, 1955, and "Flash: Bucks County—What Is It Like for Minority Groups," n.d., in NAACP papers, II A 161, LOC. For an overview of the Levittown situation, see Paul Blanshard, Jr., "Roof over Their Heads," *Friends Intelligencer,* Feb. 21, 1953, 98–99.

15. "Philadelphia's Negro Population: Facts on Housing," CHR papers. On federal housing policy and its impact on residential housing patterns, see Bauman, *Public Housing, Race, and Renewal,* 86–87, 95–96; Sugrue, *Origins of the Urban Crisis,* 59–72; and Kenneth Jackson, *Crabgrass Frontier: The Suburbanization of the United States* (New York: Oxford University Press, 1985), 190–218.

16. On the AFSC campaign to find black families to purchase previously owned homes in Levittown, see Richard Taylor and Charlotte C. Meacham to "Friend," Nov. 23, 1959, Urban League (UL) collection, folder 1, TUUA. After purchasing a home in Levittown in 1957, one African American family, the Myers, were harassed by the members of the local "Betterment Society." See minutes, Board of Commissioners, Sep. 16, 1957, FC collection, box 7, TUUA.

17. For a similar discussion of the inability of civil rights advocates to win support for racial reforms in Detroit, see Sugrue, *Origins of the Urban Crisis,* 57–88.

18. Philadelphia Commission on Human Relations, "Annual Report, 1953," CHR papers, box 148, folder 1, PMA. On the breakthrough jobs strategy and civil rights liberals' reliance on persuasive methods to change employer hiring practices,

see Sugrue, "Affirmative Action from Below," 145–173; and William Chafe, *Civilities and Civil Rights: Greensboro, North Carolina, and the Black Struggle for Freedom* (New York: Oxford University Press, 1980), 34–37, 69–70.

19. Commission member Sadie Alexander described Loescher as believing that "you could always settle everything by conciliation," a belief that she ascribed to his Quakerism. Sadie Alexander interview with Walter Phillips, Oct. 20, 1976, Walter Phillips collection, TUUA.

20. Fair Employment Practices Commission (FEPC), "Annual Report, 1948–49," CHR papers, box 148, folder 1, PMA.

21. Alexander interview with Walter Phillips, Oct. 20, 1976; FEPC, "Annual Report," 1951; minutes, Board of Commissioners, Oct. 17, 1949, FC collection, box 7, TUUA.

22. Alexander interview with Walter Phillips, Oct. 20, 1976. On George Schermer's years as a race relations specialist in Detroit, see Sugrue, *Origins of the Urban Crisis*, 5, 77, 87.

23. CHR, "Annual Report,1953," and "Annual Report, 1954."

24. CHR, "Annual Report,1954," and "Annual Report, 1955."

25. CHR, "Annual Report,1954," "Annual Report, 1955," "Annual Report,1956," "Annual Report, 1957," "Annual Report, 1958," and "Annual Report, 1959." On the impact of the CHR's limited enforcements powers and its reliance on citizen complaints and case-by-case investigations of discriminatory hiring practices, see also Sugrue, "Affirmative Action from Below," 148.

26. CHR, "Annual Report, 1960."

27. Memorandum to the executive secretary from Herbert Hill, Apr. 17, 1952 and memorandum to Mr. White from Herbert Hill, Jun. 4, 1952, NAACP papers, A II 342, LOC.

28. Memorandum to Mr. White from Herbert Hill," Jun. 4, 1952.

29. Alexander interview with Walter Phillips; "CHR: Inside Facts," NAACP collection, box 4, TUUA; CHR, "Annual Report, 1955."

30. "Jim Crow's Sweetheart Contract," *Greater Philadelphia Magazine* (Feb. 1963); memorandum to Mr. Wilkins from Herbert Hill, Nov. 15, 1962, p. 14, NAACP papers, III A 180, LOC. The one black member of Local 98 of the International Brotherhood of Electrical Workers was a public schoolteacher, William P. Cannady, who was working as a non-union electrician during a late 1940s summer break when his construction site was unionized. Cannady was the author's grandfather.

31. CHR, "Annual Report, 1953," "Annual Report, 1957," and "Annual Report, 1958"; Burton I. Gordin to Charles Shorter, Aug. 4, 1955, NAACP collection, box 4, TUUA.

32. Sugrue, *Origins of the Urban Crisis*, 114–18; and "Affirmative Action from Below," 154.

33. Burton I. Gordin to Charles Shorter, Aug. 4, 1955; "News from Commission on Human Relations," Apr. 15, 1955, NAACP collection, box 4, TUUA; "Accuse Unions of Bias on City Jobs After Long Probe," *Philadelphia Tribune*, Mar. 16, 1963.

34. CHR, "Annual Report, 1956" and "Annual Report, 1957."

35. CHR, "Annual Report, 1954."

36. Burton I. Gordin to Charles Shorter, Aug. 4, 1955; "News from Commission on Human Relations," Apr. 15, 1955.

37. CHR, "Annual Report, 1959," and "Annual Report, 1960." Two years earlier, the CHR had convinced Waiters Union Local 301 to drop a clause in its union contract that required union consent if the employer decided to change its wait staff from male to female or white to black or vice versa. A 1954 CHR survey of 1,157 hotel and restaurant workers in the city found that blacks worked primarily

as bus help, cooks, and counter servers. Only 21 of the 524 waiters surveyed were black and 16 of those were working in one restaurant. No blacks were observed working as bartenders, captains, cashiers, headwaiters, hostesses or managers. CHR, "Annual Report, 1954," and "Annual Report, 1958."

38. CHR, "Annual Report, 1960."

39. CHR, Annual Report, 1956," "Annual Report, 1958," and "Annual Report, 1960"; Bauman, *Public Housing, Race, and Renewal*, 52–53.

40. "Philadelphia's Negro Population: Facts on Housing." For a discussion on the economics of real estate investment and disinvestment in urban communities, see Kleniewski, "Neighborhood Decline and Downtown Renewal," 26–36.

41. Bauman, *Public Housing, Race, and Renewal*, 97–100.

42. On the shift in the Redevelopment Authority's approach to blighted neighborhoods, see Bauman, *Public Housing, Race, and Renewal*, 127–30, 149–53 and Kleniewski, "Neighborhood Decline and Downtown Renewal," 76–78.

43. Arnold Hirsch, *Making the Second Ghetto: Race and Housing in Chicago, 1940–1960*, (New York: Cambridge University Press, 1983), esp. 9–99; Jackson, *Crabgrass Frontier*, 190–218; Sugrue, *Origins of the Urban Crisis*, 33–55, 181–258

44. CHR, "Annual Report, 1953," "Annual Report, 1954," "Annual Report, 1955," and "Annual Report, 1956."

45. CHR, "Annual Report, 1955," and "Annual Report, 1956."

46. CHR, "Annual Report, 1955," and "Annual Report, 1956."

47. CHR, "Annual Report, 1954."

48. CHR, "Annual Report, 1954."

49. CHR, "Annual Report, 1956," and "Annual Report, 1957."

50. CHR, "Annual Report, 1956."

51. CHR, "Annual Report, 1956," "Annual Report, 1957," "Annual Report, 1958," and "Annual Report, 1959."

52. Bauman, *Public Housing, Race, and Renewal*, 21–47.

53. Bauman, *Public Housing, Race, and Renewal*, 48–53, 67–69.

54. The family of the black veteran was only able to move into the Abbotsford Homes after the police dispersed an angry crowd of white tenants. Bauman, *Public Housing, Race, and Renewal*, 80, 93–96, 121, 127–30.

55. Bauman, *Public Housing, Race, and Renewal*, 127–30.

56. Bauman, *Public Housing, Race, and Renewal*, 127–30, 160–66. On the Fellowship Commission's efforts to counteract white neighborhood opposition to the scattered-site plan, see minutes, Board of Commissioners, Mar. 21, 1955, and May 21, 1956, FC collection, box 7, TUUA. On civil rights groups' support for scattered-site public housing, see minutes, Board of Commissioners, Mar. 21, 1955, FC collection, box 7, TUUA. On homeowner opposition to public housing in white neighborhoods, see CHR, "Annual Report, 1956."

57. Minutes, Board of Commissioners, May 21, 1956.

Chapter 3. Don't Buy Where You Can't Work

1. Leon H. Sullivan, *Build Brother Build* (Philadelphia: Macrae Smith, 1969), 44–52; interview with Leon Sullivan, Mar. 4, 1996, Phoenix, Ariz. On Sullivan's appointment as pastor of Zion Baptist Church, see *Philadelphia Afro-American*, Sep. 9, 1950.

2. On the influence of social gospel theology on black ministers of Sullivan and King's generation, see Taylor Branch, *Parting the Waters: America in the King Years, 1954–63* (New York: Simon and Schuster, 1988), 69–104.

3. Sullivan, *Build Brother Build*, 52, 58–63. During his years in New York, Sullivan

had studied for a master's degree in religion at the Union Theological Seminary, a major center of social gospel theology. Youth violence and gangs had long been a concern of neighborhood activists and social workers in black Philadelphia. For example, the Wharton Centre, a North Philadelphia settlement house, first initiated a gang outreach program in 1945. By the late 1950s, Operation Street Corner, the Wharton center's gang work program was receiving national acclaim. See V. P. Franklin, "Operation Street Corner: The Wharton Centre and the Juvenile Gang Problem in Philadelphia, 1945–1958," in Michael Katz and Thomas Sugrue, eds., *W. E. B. Du Bois, Race, and the City: The Philadelphia Negro and Its Legacy* (Philadelphia: University of Pennsylvania Press, 1998), 195–215.

4. Sullivan, *Build Brother Build*, 62–65; "Zion Baptist to Seat 3rd Biennial Conference," *Philadelphia Tribune*, Jun. 14, 1958. On CCAJD's founding and goals, see also *Bulletin*, Jun. 26, 1953, and "Constitution of the Philadelphia Citizens Committee Against Juvenile Delinquency and Its Causes," and "Program of Citizens Committee Against Juvenile Delinquency and Its Causes" May 21, 1957, Urban League (UL) collection, box 7, Temple University Urban Archives (TUUA).

5. *Bulletin*, Oct. 24, 1953 and Nov. 16, 1954; "Constitution of the Philadelphia Citizens Committee" and "Program of Citizens Committee." CCAJD's criticisms of the materialism of the black middle-class mirrored sociologist E. Franklin Frazier's writings on the subject during the 1950s. See E. Franklin Frazier, *The Negro Family in the United States*, rev. and abr. ed. (Chicago: University of Chicago Press, 1966). On traditions of moral uplift among black elites, see Kevin K. Gaines, *Uplifting the Race: Black Leadership, Politics, and Culture in the Twentieth Century* (Chapel Hill: University of North Carolina Press, 1996). On the juvenile delinquency crisis of the 1950's, see James Gilbert, *A Cycle of Outrage: America's Reaction to the Juvenile Delinquent in the 1950s* (New York: Oxford University Press, 1986).

6. Wilson Moses, *The Golden Age of Black Nationalism, 1850–1925*, (Hamden, CT: Archon Books, 1978), esp. 41–44; "Program of Citizens Committee."

7. On Booker T. Washington's philosophical ties to nineteenth century black nationalists, see Moses, *Golden Age of Black Nationalism*, 49–74, 201.

8. On Sullivan's departure from the CCAJD presidency, see Sullivan, *Build Brother Build*, 63–66; on Moore's career, see biographical sketch of Cecil B. Moore in *Bulletin* clippings file, TUUA; *Philadelphia Inquirer*, May 21, 1958. On Sullivan's recruitment of Moore, see interview with Sullivan, Mar. 4, 1996.

9. See "500 Fight to Halt Taproom Opening," *Philadelphia Tribune*, Jun. 21, 1958; "Strawberry Mansion Council Leads Drive On North Philly Bar," *Philadelphia Tribune*, Feb. 28, 1959. The growing importance of antitavern protests in black Philadelphia was reflected in Mayor Richardson Dilworth's decision in 1958 to publicly denounce bar owners who participated in "organized numbers and narcotics activities." "Blasts Bar Bosses Who Deal In Dope And Digits," *Philadelphia Tribune*, May 10, 1958.

10. Greene and Pickett were selected to serve as committee vice-chair, along with two other black ministers. On the Prayer Pilgrimage, see Branch, *Parting the Waters*, 216–18; John D'Emilio, *Lost Prophet: The Life and Times of Bayard Rustin* (New York: Free Press, 2003), 262–66. On organizing in Philadelphia for the pilgrimage, see minutes, Apr. 29, 1957, NAACP papers, III C 135, Library of Congress (LOC); press release, Philadelphia Citizens Committee, May 3, 1957, NAACP collection, box 30, TUUA; *Bulletin*, May 14, 1957. To publicize the pilgrimage, the Philadelphia committee organized a mass rally at a North Philadelphia church with Randolph and Rosa Parks as featured speakers.

11. On the role of black nationalists in black protest during the 1930s, see Mark Naison, *Communists in Harlem During the Depression* (Grove Press; New York, 1983),

50–51, 100–01, and Charles V. Hamilton, *Adam Clayton Powell, Jr.: The Political Biography of an American Dilemma* (New York: Macmillan, 1991), 89–102. See Manning Marable, *Race, Reform, and Rebellion: The Second Reconstruction in Black America, 1945–1990*, 2nd ed. (Jackson: University Press of Mississippi, 1991), 13–39, for a discussion of the red scare's impact on civil rights activism.

12. See E.U. Essien-Udom, *Black Nationalism: A Search for an Identity in America* (Chicago: University of Chicago Press, 1962), 313–17.

13. Essien-Udom, *Black Nationalism*, 193–195; Claude Andrew Clegg III, *An Original Man: The Life and Times of Elijah Muhammad* (New York: St. Martin's Press, 1997), esp. 14–108.

14. C. Eric Lincoln, *The Black Muslims in America* (Boston: Beacon Press, 1961), 10–17, 180–92; Clegg, *An Original Man*, 106–8, 115–20; Clayborne Carson, *Malcolm X: The FBI File* (New York: Carroll and Graf, Inc., 1991); Malcolm X and Alex Haley, *The Autobiography of Malcolm X* (New York: Ballantine Books, 1964).

15. Carson, *Malcolm X*, 107, 121–23.

16. Carson, *Malcolm X*, 124.

17. Carson, *Malcolm X*, 124–26.

18. "Fisticuffs Mark Muhammad's Visit Here; 3,500 Hear Him Demand Justice for Colored," *Philadelphia Tribune*, Aug. 16, 1960; "Muhammad Sect Charges Harassment in W. Philly," *Philadelphia Tribune*, Oct. 15, 1960. Elijah Muhammad's son Wallace Muhammad was widely expected to be his successor as the chief minister of the Nation of Islam. Details of his career can be found in Essien-Udom, *Black Nationalism*, 75–76, 80–82. While in Philadelphia, Wallace Muhammad maintained the NOI's policy of nonengagement in civil rights issues. When two of his congregants were harassed for moving into a previously all-white neighborhood, he denounced housing discrimination, but called on blacks to "build better communities and reside with their own kind."

19. Interview with Michael Simmons, Apr. 22, 1994, Philadelphia.

20. The flier for the August 13, 1957, neighborhood meeting at Gratz and Norris streets in North Philadelphia asked: "Do You Want a Share of Freedom?" Each neighborhood meeting featured a presentation on national civil rights issues by Calvin Banks, the NAACP field secretary for Pennsylvania, Delaware, and New Jersey. "Philadelphia Branch NAACP News," Jul. 23, 1957, memorandum to Mr. Wilkins, Dr. Morsell, Mr. Current, Miss Black from Calvin D. Banks, n.d.; "Neighborhood Public Information Meeting," Aug. 1, 1957, NAACP papers, III C 135, LOC; "Biographical Sketch, Calvin D. Banks, Program Director, NAACP," n.d., NAACP papers, III A 307, LOC.

21. NAACP newsletter, Jan. 31, 1958, NAACP papers, III C 221, LOC; "Blueprinting the Future for the Negro Citizen," Mar. 29, 1958, Floyd Logan collection, box 2, TUUA; "Design for the Future," n.d., NAACP papers, III C 135, LOC; Dr. Harry Greene and Charles Shorter to Gloster Current, Dec. 19, 1958, III C 193, LOC; on Wilkins's speech to the conference, see *Bulletin*, Mar. 30, 1959.

22. "Where Do Philadelphia's Negroes Stand?" n.d., and "Institute Will Seek Answers to Key Questions Regarding Negro," Feb. 17, 1958, NAACP papers, III C 135, LOC.

23. "Design for the Future"; Greene and Shorter to Current, Dec. 19, 1958.

24. In 1955, Charles Shorter, the executive secretary of the Philadelphia NAACP, acknowledged that the branch had deferred work on a fair housing law in order to support the "pending FEPC legislation." Charles A. Shorter to Henry R. Smith, Jr., May 4, 1955, NAACP collection, box 15, TUUA; minutes, Pennsylvania Equal Rights Council, Feb. 4, 1958, Housing Association of Delaware Valley (HADV) collection, box 182, folder 2002, TUUA; "Organize Statewide Civil Rights Group to Combat All Bias," *Philadelphia Tribune*, Feb. 8, 1958.

25. As of 1957, five states had passed fair housing legislation, in each case narrowly tailored in the way proposed by the Fellowship Commission. Minutes, Board of Commissioners, Mar. 17 and Apr. 25, 1957, FC collection, box 7, TUUA; "We Believe . . . A Credo," in HADV collection, box 171, folder 1677, TUUA; "Report to the Community," October 1956, FC collection, box 53, folder 13, TUUA. In written testimony submitted to the U.S. Senate Committee on Banking and Currency in December 1957, the Fellowship Commission charged that "practically all of the housing . . . receiving FHA [Federal Housing Administration] insurance is limited to whites" and that "FHA programs . . . have actually resulted in an extension of segregation." Testimony before the U.S. Senate Committee on Banking and Currency, Subcommittee on Housing, Dec. 18, 1957, NAACP collection, box 16, TUUA.

26. Minutes, Board of Commissioners, Jun. 20, Sept. 19, Oct. 17, and Nov. 19, 1958, FC collection, box 7, TUUA; memo to affiliate organizations of PERC from Fred Grossman, May 16, 1958, HADV collection, box 182, folder 2003, TUUA.

27. Minutes, Pennsylvania Equal Rights Council, Oct. 3, 1958, HADV collection, box 182, folder 2004, TUUA; minutes, Pennsylvania Equal Rights Council, Nov. 14, 1958, Urban League (UL) collection, box 4, TUUA; Philadelphia Fellowship Commission, special memorandum on housing, Nov. 19, 1958, FC collection, box 7, TUUA; memorandum for Thomas D. McBride, Mar. 13, 1959, FC collection, box 3, TUUA; Thomas D. McBride to Henry R. Smith, Apr. 6, 1959, NAACP collection, box 27, TUUA.

28. Memorandum for McBride, Mar. 13, 1959; minutes, Board of Commissioners, Mar. 13, 1959, FC collection, box 7, TUUA; Council for Equal Housing Opportunities, "Emergency Conference of Organizations for Housing Legislation," n.d., UL collection, box 10, TUUA; "Equal Housing Council Slates Emergency Conference," *Philadelphia Tribune*, Mar. 31, 1959 and "Fellowship Board Urges Changes in Fair Housing Bill," *Bulletin*, Apr. 2, 1959. Maurice Fagan also wrote to newly elected Democratic Governor David Lawrence and to the leading sponsor of the fair housing bill in the state senate, both of whom had previously announced support for the NAACP's position, telling them of the commission's support for a narrower bill. Maurice Fagan to Charles R. Weiner, Mar. 26, 1959, and Maurice Fagan to Roy A. Schafer, Apr. 4, 1959, FC collection, box 3, TUUA.

29. A memo accompanying the open letter predicted that the "proposed change by the Fellowship Commission would serve to perpetuate the existent practice which denies minority groups members the right to housing of their choice." Fagan responded to the NAACP's charges by expressing surprise that the commission's longtime allies had chosen to discuss the disagreement in the press, even though in fact the commission had been the first to discuss its disagreement with the PERC majority in public. Henry R. Smith and Calvin D. Banks to Thomas D. McBride, Apr. 3, 1959, NAACP collection, box 9, TUUA; memorandum to all interested parties from Calvin D. Banks, Apr. 3, 1959, NAACP collection, box 27, TUUA; "Rebuttal Of Bill By NAACP Shocks Fellowship Unit," *Philadelphia Tribune*, Apr. 7, 1959.

30. Walter Gay Jr. to Jefferson B. Fordham, Feb. 16, 1959, HADV collection, box 180, folder 1917, TUUA.

31. Memo to PERC Affiliates from Walter Gay, Jul. 17, 1959, NAACP collection, box 27, TUUA; Philadelphia NAACP, "Annual Report, 1959," NAACP collection, box 30, TUUA; "Many State Legislators Here 'Called on Carpet' by Leaders," *Philadelphia Tribune*, Jul. 7, 1959; Council for Equal Housing Opportunities, "Fair Housing Legislation News," Aug. 6, 1959, UL collection, box 10, TUUA; "State NAACP Demands Senate Act Favorably on Fair Housing," *Philadelphia Tribune*, Aug. 11,

1959; fact sheet, NAACP press conference, Oct. 5, 1959, NAACP collection, box 27, TUUA; "Fair Housing March on Harrisburg," *Philadelphia Tribune*, Oct. 13, 1959.

32. Fellowship Commission, "Report to the Community," September 1961, FC collection, box 53, folder 18, TUUA.

33. Philadelphia NAACP, "Annual Report, 1959"; "Executive Secretary's Report for the Month of December 1959," NAACP papers, LOC III C 136; "Report of the Executive Secretary: A Review of the Highlights of 1958," NAACP collection, box 7, TUUA. The name of the Police Review Board would later be changed to the Police Advisory Board, see Chapters 4 and 8.

34. "Torrid Battle Looms for NAACP Elections, Dec. 8th," *Philadelphia Tribune*, Dec. 1, 1959; "Support These Candidates Because They Believe As You Believe," n.d., NAACP collection, III C 136, LOC; "Obituaries: Harold L. Pilgrim, 85, a Community Leader," *Philadelphia Inquirer*, Jan. 9, 1978.

35. Among the charges issued by the Pilgrim slate was that the chapter leadership had failed to pursue a number of police brutality cases and that it had not adequately serviced the branch's growing membership. "NAACP Policy Attacked, Office Cites Its Record," *Philadelphia Tribune*, Dec. 8, 1959. On Leon Higginbotham's early career, see A. Leon Higginbotham Jr. to Mrs. Justine Smadbeck, NAACP papers, III C 135, LOC.

36. "Strictly Politics," *Philadelphia Tribune*, Dec. 8, 1959.

37. "Daisy Bates Fund Gets Warm Response," *Philadelphia Tribune*, Dec. 15, 1959.

38. "Lawyer to 'Prexy' 19,000 Member Philadelphia NAACP for '60,'" press release, Dec. 15, 1959, NAACP collection, box 17, folder 59, TUUA; memorandum to Robert L. Carter, Gloster B. Current from Calvin D. Banks, n.d., NAACP papers, III C 221, LOC; *Philadelphia Tribune*, Dec. 12, 1959.

39. The Moore complaint included affidavits from branch members who said they never received notice of the election. If these members had known of the election, the complainants charged, the results of the election would have been different. In addition, the complaint charged that nonmembers had been allowed to vote in the election and that Calvin Banks had removed the ballots from the meeting before the election results were certified. "NAACP Candidates Ask for New Local Election," *Philadelphia Tribune*, Dec. 15, 1959; "NAACP Election Reported Set Aside Pending Investigation," *Philadelphia Tribune*, Dec. 29, 1959; "Nat'l Officers Hear 50 NAACP Protestants," *Philadelphia Tribune*, Feb. 6, 1960. Calvin D. Banks to Gloster B. Current, Dec. 15, 1960, NAACP collection, box 30, TUUA.

40. "Nat'l Officers Hear 50 NAACP Protestants"; "Charles Shorter Resigns Effective March 1," *Philadelphia Tribune*, Feb. 20, 1960; *Philadelphia Tribune*, Feb. 27, 1960; "National Office Upholds Local NAACP Election," *Philadelphia Tribune*, Mar. 15, 1960. Two days after Shorter's resignation, Calvin Banks announced the suspension of the Coordinating Council project "because of certain problems in the . . . branch." Calvin D. Banks to Subcommittee, Mar. 1, 1960, NAACP collection, box 26, TUUA.

41. On the sit-in movement, see William Chafe, *Civilities and Civil Rights: Greensboro, North Carolina, and the Black Struggle for Freedom* (New York: Oxford University Press, 1980), 71–101; Aldon D. Morris, *The Origins of the Civil Rights Movement: Black Communities Organizing for Change* (New York: Free Press, 1984), 195–221; and Clayborne Carson, *In Struggle: SNCC and the Black Awakening of the 1960s* (Cambridge, Mass.: Harvard University Press, 1981), 9–25.

42. *Philadelphia Tribune*, Feb. 6, 9, 13, 1960. For an example of the *Tribune*'s weekly sit-in updates, see *Philadelphia Tribune*, Mar. 8, 1960.

43. "Pickets Empty Woolworth's at Peak Store Hour," *Philadelphia Tribune*, Feb.

23, 1960. The pickets came from Temple University, the University of Pennsylvania, Drexel Institute, Swarthmore College, and several high schools. According to one of the picket-line organizers, the committee had contacted students at Lincoln and Cheyney State too late for them to participate in the demonstration.

44. "Boycott Spreads," *Philadelphia Tribune*, Mar. 1, 1960; "F. W. Woolworth Pickets Charge Harassment," *Philadelphia Tribune*, Mar. 8, 1960. The Youth Committee and the local chapter of the ACLU immediately protested the arrests of the black students to police officials. Arthur Bierbaum, the Youth Committee's spokesperson, told the *Tribune* that the committee had consulted with the police before beginning the picket lines and that the police had promised "not [to] interfere as long as the picketing was orderly."

45. "Area Woolworth Stores Picketed by Students," *Philadelphia Tribune*, Mar. 15, 1960; "100 Pickets," *Philadelphia Tribune*, Mar. 29, 1960; "Pickets Advised Not to Picket by Human Relations Comm.," *Philadelphia Tribune*, Apr. 2, 1960; "Phila. Youth Council and College NAACP to Picket Woolworth District Office," *Philadelphia Tribune*, Apr. 9, 1960.

46. "Pickets Advised Not to Picket by Human Relations Comm."

47. "Pickets Advised Not to Picket by Human Relations Comm."; memorandum to community leaders from the Commission on Human Relations, Apr. 8, 1960, Wharton Centre (WC) collection, box 36, TUUA.

48. "National Office Upholds Local NAACP Election," *Philadelphia Tribune*, Mar. 15, 1960; "Phila. NAACP Unit Silent on Counter Revolt," *Philadelphia Tribune*, Mar. 19, 1960.

49. The NAACP's reluctance to allow its branches to undertake local protest campaigns of their own design was well known. Aldon Morris has argued that the creation of local organizations like the Montgomery Improvement Association and Birmingham's Alabama Christian Movement for Human Rights were crucial to the emergence of the southern civil rights movement because they gave southern activists independence from inhibiting control of the NAACP's organizational hierarchy. In Morris's view, Martin Luther King and his coterie of ministerial activists were able to build the Southern Christian Leadership Conference into an effective regional protest organization in part because of the passage of laws in a number of Deep South states that required the NAACP to publish its southern state membership lists. When the NAACP effectively shut down its southern operations to fight these laws in court, local activists like King and Shuttlesworth were freed from the NAACP's cautious tactical instincts. Morris, *Origins of the Civil Rights Movement*, 26–35.

50. Memorandum to all branches, Tri-State Area, from the field secretary, Mar. 31, 1960 and "Flash Bulletin," Apr. 14, 1960, NAACP collection, box 30, TUUA; "NAACP Pickets 13 Woolworth, Kresge Stores," *Philadelphia Tribune*, Apr. 30, 1960. April 23 had been declared "Region II Protest Day" by NAACP's leadership in Pennsylvania, New Jersey and Delaware. See memorandum to Gloster B. Current from Calvin D. Banks, Apr. 14, 1960, NAACP collection, box 30, TUUA.

51. "Don't Buy Segregation" flier, n.d. NAACP collection, box 30, TUUA; *Philadelphia Tribune*, May 10, 14, and 31, 1960.

52. "NAACP Prexy Raps GOP Action on Housing Bill," *Philadelphia Tribune*, Feb. 4, 1961; report of executive secretary, Philadelphia Branch NAACP, Apr. 8, 1961, NAACP papers, II A 68, LOC; press release, Jun. 7, 1961, Floyd Logan collection, box 13, TUUA; "School Board Is Silent in Face of NAACP Suit Charging Bias," *Philadelphia Tribune*, Jun. 10, 1961; "NAACP Hits Bias in Roofers Union," *Philadelphia Tribune*, Aug. 5, 1961. For a discussion of the NAACP's suit, see United States

Commission on Civil Rights, *Civil Rights U.S.A., Public Schools, Cities in the North and West, 1962, Philadelphia: A Report to the United States Commission on Civil Rights* (Washington, D.C.: Government Printing Office, 1962), and Vincent P. Franklin, *The Education of Black Philadelphia*, (Philadelphia: University of Pennsylvania Press, 1979), 200. Racial segregation was pervasive in the city's public schools at the time of the suit. According to the Civil Rights Commission report, 30 percent of the city's elementary schools were at least 99 percent white and 25 percent were at least 97 percent black. To cite one example, the suit charged that the school board had gerrymandered elementary school district lines in Northwest Philadelphia's racially integrated neighborhoods in order to maintain segregated schools. Of the area's sixteen elementary schools, five were more than 80 percent black, five were at least 99 percent white and two others were at least 80 percent white. In addition, the suit charged that black students were districted into older, deteriorating school buildings, while white students were given access to the newest school buildings. Thus, the Emlen School, which was 98 percent black, was built in 1925, while, just across the district boundary, the all-white Day School opened in 1952.

53. Sullivan, *Build Brother Build*, 67; "'Buy Where You're Hired' Campaign Getting Results," *Philadelphia Tribune*, Jun. 11, 1960; *Philadelphia Tribune*, Jun. 18, 1960; "Nation Eyes Selective Patronage in Phila. Area as Job Campaign Shows Results; Pastors Press On," *Philadelphia Tribune*, Jul. 2, 1960; "Negroes Building Boycott Network," *New York Times*, Nov. 25, 1962; Hannah Lees, "The Not-Buying Power of Philadelphia's Negroes," *Reporters*, May 11, 1961. Lees's article provides a comprehensive review of the first year of selective patronage.

54. "Strictly Politics," *Philadelphia Tribune*, Dec. 12, 1959; "Local Human Relations Commission Ends Hearings on Hotel Job Bias," *Philadelphia Tribune*, Jul. 16, 1960. The CHR finally issued a report on discriminatory hiring practices in the hotel and restaurant industry in April 1961, which cited more than sixty restaurants and hotels and three local unions in the city. According to the report, the Horn & Hardart Baking Company and one local union had already reached agreements on fair employment policies with the commission. The CHR gave the remaining restaurants and unions ninety days to submit remedial plans or face action from the city. "Human Relations Commission Issues 13-Month Report," *Philadelphia Tribune*, Apr., 11, 1961; "Human Relations Commission Acts in 1961 on What Negroes Reported to the Them 3 1/2 Years Ago," *Philadelphia Tribune*, Apr. 22, 1961.

55. "'Buy Where You're Hired' Campaign Getting Results." In his memoir, Sullivan has taken more direct credit for selective patronage. According to this version, it was his wife Grace who challenged him to do something about the problems facing African American job seekers in Philadelphia after he returned home one day from a five-and-ten picket line. "If you really want to do something worthwhile," he remembers her telling him, "help your people right here at home. Get them jobs. Then you will be doing something." Sullivan, *Build Brother Build*, 68. Grace Sullivan, on the other hand, argues that her husband's account is more fiction than fact. Interview with Grace Sullivan, Mar. 4, 1996, Phoenix, Ariz.

56. Sullivan, *Build Brother Build*, 67–68.

57. "Ministers Found Breyer Ice Cream Co. Tough Bias Obstacle to 'Melt,'" *Pittsburgh Courier*, Jan. 12, 1963. On the "Don't Buy Where You Can't Work" Campaigns of the 1930s and 1940s, see Naison. *Communists in Harlem During the Depression*, 50–51, 100–01; Hamilton, *Adam Clayton Powell, Jr.*, 89–102; and August Meier and Elliott Rudwick, "The Origins of Nonviolent Direct Action in Afro-American Protest: A Note on Historical Discontinuities," in *Along the Color Line: Explorations in the Black Experience* (Urbana: University of Illinois Press, 1976), 307–89.

58. General Baking cited its union contract as the reason it could not hire black driver-salesmen. Philadelphia NAACP, "Annual Report, 1959," and "Executive Secretary's Report for the Month of December 1959."

59. "Nation Eyes Selective Patronage in Phila. Area as Job Campaign Shows Results; Pastors Press On."

60. " 'Buy Where You're Hired' Campaign Getting Results"; *Philadelphia Tribune*, Jun. 18, 1960; memorandum to Mr. Carter from Judge F. Allen, Jun. 23, 1960, UL collection, box 1, TUUA.

61. *Philadelphia Tribune*, Jun. 18, 1960; "Preachers Reject Baking Firm's Letter: 'Tighten Up' On Retail Stores Boycott," *Philadelphia Courier*, Jul. 2, 1960. See "Pulpit Boycott Rocked Empire of 'Liquid Gold'," *Pittsburgh Courier*, Jan. 5, 1963, for a discussion of the popularity of Tastykake products among black consumers and shopowners and the skepticism that greeted the ministers' call to withhold patronage from the company.

62. "Seeks Assurance on Tasty Baking Co. Hiring Policy" and "Tasty Baking Company Outlines Fair Employment Program," *Philadelphia Tribune*, Jun. 28, 1960; "Tasty Baking Co. Official Denies Job Bias Charge," *Philadelphia Tribune*, Jul. 5, 1960; "Tasty Baking Company Continues Fair Employment Program," *Philadelphia Tribune*, Jul. 12, 1960; "Preachers Reject Baking Firm's Letter"; Lees, "The Not-Buying Power of Philadelphia's Negroes."

63. "Tasty Baking Co. Official Denies Job Bias Charge"; "Pastors Reject Tasty Baking Co. Compromise," *Philadelphia Tribune*, Jul. 9, 1960; "Mighty Blow Fells 'Ole Jim,' " *Philadelphia Tribune*, Aug. 9, 1960.

64. "Seeks Assurance on Tasty Baking Co. Hiring Policy"; Lees, "The Not-Buying Power of Philadelphia's Negroes." Selective patronage did not receive any attention from the white media until the *Wall Street Journal* and the *Reporters*, a weekly newsjournal, ran articles in the late spring and early summer of 1961. "Negro Consumer: He Is Getting More Attention From Big National Advertisers," *Wall Street Journal*, Jun. 30, 1961; Lees, "The Not-Buying Power of Philadelphia's Negroes."

65. *Philadelphia Tribune*, Oct. 4, 1960; "Pepsi Cola Gives In to Ministers; Will Hire Colored," *Philadelphia Tribune*, Oct. 8, 1960; "Ministers claim victory in oil company job drive," *Philadelphia Afro-American*, Jan. 28, 1961; Sullivan, *Build Brother Build*, 83.

66. "Local Ministers Organize for Youth Employment Opportunity," *Philadelphia Tribune*, Jun. 4, 1960.

67. "Spreading Negro Boycott," *Greater Philadelphia Magazine*, 57 (May 1962); Sullivan, *Build Brother Build*, 62.

68. "Philly Blasts Bias with Don't Buy Campaigns," *Philadelphia Courier*. As a teenager living in southwest Philadelphia, Charyn Sutton remembers receiving the charge from her pastor to spread the word about the next selective patronage target to "all the people who didn't go to church [or] who were Catholic (and thus didn't have black ministers)." Interview with Charyn Sutton, Aug. 12, 2004, Philadelphia. One reporter estimated that it took four days for the pastors' announcement of a new selective patronage campaign to reach the unchurched members of the city's black communities. "Spreading Negro Boycott."

69. "Ministers Found Breyer Ice Cream Co. Tough Bias Obstacle to 'Melt' "; Lees, "The Not-Buying Power of Philadelphia's Negroes."

70. "Clergymen Call Off Gulf Boycott; Firm Hires Girls, Others," *Philadelphia Afro-American*, Jan. 21, 1961; "Ministers claim victory in oil company job drive," *Phil-*

adelphia Afro-American, Jan. 28, 1961; "Ministers Found Breyer Ice Cream Co. Tough Bias Obstacle to 'Melt' "; Lees, "The Not-Buying Power of Philadelphia's Negroes."

71. "400 Ministers Blast Job Bias, Launch 'Selective Patronage Program' Against Sun Oil Co.," *Philadelphia Tribune,* Mar. 21, 1961; "Sun Oil Company Gives Its Side in Job Wrangle," *Philadelphia Tribune,* Mar. 25, 1961; *Philadelphia Tribune,* Mar. 28, 1961; Lees, "The Not-Buying Power of Philadelphia's Negroes."

72. Lees, "The Not-Buying Power of Philadelphia's Negroes."

73. "400 Ministers Blast Job Bias"; "Sun Oil Company Gives Its Side," Lees, "The Not-Buying Power of Philadelphia's Negroes"; "Spreading Negro Boycott."

74. "400 Ministers Blast Job Bias"; "Sun Oil Company Gives Its Side"; "Local Pastors Urge No Sunoco Until Your Ministers Say So,' " *Philadelphia Tribune,* May 2, 1961; "30 More Towns Join in Drive Against Sunoco," *Philadelphia Tribune,* May 9, 1961; "Sun Oil Company Fails to Torpedo Preachers' Selective Patronage Drive," *Philadelphia Tribune,* May 23, 1961; " '400 Local Pastors' Cease Boycott on Sun Oil Company," *Philadelphia Tribune,* Jun. 13, 1961; "Negro Consumer," *Wall Street Journal,* Jun. 30, 1961; Lees, "The Not-Buying Power of Philadelphia's Negroes."

75. Sullivan, *Build, Brother, Build,* 76–77. On the ministers' claims about the number of jobs opened up by selective patronage, see "1,000 New Jobs Worth $4 Million Won by Drive," *Pittsburgh Courier,* Sept. 22, 1962.

76. *The 'A' Train: The Community's Action Bulletin,* n.d., UL collection, box 16, folder 17, TUUA. On RAM's founding and its ideology, see Max Stanford, "Who Are the Rams Or What Is a Ram?" *Nite Life,* July 4, 1967, and "Ram Believes That the U.S. Owes Afro-Americans 880 Million Acres of Land," *Nite Life,* July 4, 1967, in *Bulletin* clippings file, TUUA. On the history of RAM, see Robin D. G. Kelley, *Freedom Dreams: The Black Radical Imagination* (Boston: Beacon Press, 2002), 60–109. For more on RAM in Philadelphia, see Chapter 6.

77. Sullivan, *Build Brother Build,* 74–75.

78. Sullivan, *Build Brother Build,* 162–66; interview with Sullivan.

79. Sullivan, *Build Brother Build;* "Zion Baptist Church's Program Develops New Image of Negro in the Metropolitan Community," *Philadelphia Tribune,* Aug. 4, 1962.

80. Sullivan, *Build Brother Build,* 166–70.

81. Sullivan, *Build Brother Build,* 86–94; "Negroes Building Boycott Network," *New York Times,* Nov. 25, 1962; "Slate New Negro Industry Center for Phila. Area," *Bulletin,* Jul. 6, 1963. See also *Bulletin,* Aug. 19, Sep. 15, Sep. 25, 1963, Jan. 27, 1964.

82. Sullivan, *Build Brother Build,* 86–94; "Rev. Sullivan Given $19,000 More for Training Program," *Philadelphia Tribune,* Nov. 23, 1963; *Bulletin,* Aug. 19, Sep. 15, Sep. 25, 1963, Mar. 10, May 18, 1964. On problems with the original training equipment, see Memorandum to Paul Ylvisaker from Clifford J. Campbell, Jun. 23, 1964, Philadelphia Council for Community Advancement (PCCA) collection, box 2, TUUA.

83. *Bulletin,* May 11, 1966.

84. Interview with Leon Sullivan, Mar. 5, 1996; Sullivan, *Build Brother Build,* 99–101; Rev. Thomas J. Ritter to Samuel Dash, Oct. 13, 1964, PCCA collection, box 2, TUUA; "600 Negroes Enroll in New Program Teaching 'Pride and Self-Respect,' " *Bulletin,* Sep. 10, 1964. On the Opportunities Schools, see *Bulletin,* Sept. 22, 1964.

85. Sullivan, *Build Brother Build,* 96; *Bulletin,* Apr. 2, 1965; "Old 19th & Oxford Police Station Sought for School," *Philadelphia Tribune,* Aug. 24, 1963; PCCA staff newsletter, Mar. 20, 1964, HADV collection, box 250, folder 4588, TUUA; "The OIC Story: How Philadelphia Negroes Established a Positive Self-development Program for People Interested in Helping Themselves," n.d., Floyd Logan collection, box 19, TUUA.

86. Sullivan *Build Brother Build*, 84–125; PCCA staff newsletter, Mar. 20, 1964; *Bulletin*, Dec. 18, 1964, May 3, Jun. 24, Sep. 21, 1965, Sep. 8, 1966.

87. Sullivan *Build Brother Build*, 84–125; "Industrialists Arrive for Tour of OIC," *Bulletin*, Mar. 28, 1968; on the growth of the OIC, see "He Is 'Mr. OIC' and That Is All He Wants to Be," *Philadelphia Inquirer*, Dec. 25, 1978.

88. Sullivan, *Build Brother Build*, 98–148, 161–79; *Bulletin*, Jan. 20, Dec. 6, 1966, Jun. 29, 1967; "Johnson Cites OIC as Beacon in Poverty War," *Bulletin*, Jul. 3, 1967; "N. Phila. Center Dedicated to Spur Black Capitalism," *Bulletin*, Nov. 6, 1970. On the Nixon administration's ongoing support for OIC, see "Ford Visits Phila. OIC, Offers Help," *Bulletin*, Mar. 12, 1974.

89. *Bulletin*, Apr. 14, May 25, Jul. 27, Oct. 10. Oct. 17, 1967; Aug. 5, Sept. 11, 1968. "Negro Pioneer: Philadelphia's Rev. Sullivan Preaches Self-Help, Not Protest," *Wall Street Journal*, Apr. 15, 1966.

90. *Bulletin*, Apr. 14, May 25, Jul. 27, Oct. 10, 17, 1967; Aug. 5, Sep. 11, 1968; "Negroes Form Firm to Make Aero Parts," *Bulletin*, Jun. 27, 1968; "Aerospace Firm Trains Disadvantaged," *Bulletin*, Dec. 9, 1968. On Progress Investment Associates, see "Down Many Paths in a Quest for Jobs, Pride—and Profit," *Philadelphia Inquirer*, Dec 2, 1978; "Dreams of Black Capitalism Become Nightmarish Failures," *Bulletin*, Nov. 20, 1980.

91. George Lipsitz, *A Life in the Struggle: Ivory Perry and the Culture of Opposition*, Revised Edition (Philadelphia: Temple University Press, 1995), 227–48.

92. Wahneema Lubiano, "Black Nationalism and Black Common Sense: Policing Ourselves and Others," in Lubiano, ed., *The House That Race Built: Black Americans, U.S. Terrain* (New York: Pantheon, 1997), 232–52; Michael C. Dawson, *Black Visions: The Roots of Contemporary African-American Political Ideologies* (Chicago; University of Chicago Press, 2001), 100–102, 120–32; Marable, *Race, Reform and Rebellion*, 55.

Chapter 4. A False Democracy

1. On the political career and legacy of Adam Clayton Powell, see Charles V. Hamilton, *Adam Clayton Powell, Jr.: The Political Biography of an American Dilemma* (New York: Macmillan, 1991).

2. Until recently, historians have ascribed responsibility for the development of affirmative action almost entirely to government policy-makers. See John David Skrentny, *The Ironies of Affirmative Action: Politics, Culture, and Justice in America* (Chicago: University of Chicago Press, 1996), 136–38, 193–98; Hugh Davis Graham, *The Civil Rights Era: Origins and Development of National Policy, 1960–1972* (New York; Oxford University Press, 1990), 322–45. The best analysis of the role that movement activism played in spurring the federal government's turn to affirmative action can be found in Thomas J. Sugrue, "Affirmative Action from Below: Civil Rights, the Building Trades, and the Politics of Racial Equality in the Urban North, 1945–1969," *Journal of American History* 91,1 (June 2004): 145–73.

3. "16 Critics Called 'Appeasers Who Accept Crumbs of Charity' by Moore," *Philadelphia Tribune*, Jan. 26, 1963. On Robert Williams's critique of nonviolent civil rights protest, see Robert F. Williams, *Negroes with Guns* (1962; Detroit: Wayne State University Press, 1998) and Timothy Tyson, *Radio Free Dixie: Robert Williams and the Roots of Black Power* (Chapel Hill: University of North Carolina Press, 1999), esp. 90–219.

4. *Philadelphia Tribune*, Jul. 9, 1960; "NAACP Seeks 5,000 Members by October 1" and "Local NAACPers Will Accept Goldie Watson," *Philadelphia Tribune*, Jul. 16, 1960. Watson had been stripped of her NAACP membership six years earlier after

her firing from her teaching position in the Philadelphia public schools for refusing to testify before a congressional committee on her alleged ties to the Communist Party. The Pennsylvania Supreme Court reinstated Watson to her teaching position in 1960.

5. In an effort to forestall the controversy over voting procedures that had marred the 1959 elections, the chapter changed the voting process for 1960. Voting machines were rented and the polls were kept open from 3 until 9 p.m. "Moore Charges Naacp Rejected His Dance Plan," *Philadelphia Tribune*, Oct. 15, 1960; Dec. 10 and 17, 1960; Calvin D. Banks to Gloster B. Current, Dec. 15, 1960, NAACP collection, box 30, Temple University Urban Archives (TUUA).

6. "$20,000-Year Post More Significant Than Judgeship, Atty. Higginbotham Says," *Philadelphia Tribune*, Sep. 29, 1962; "Higginbotham Takes FTC Post," *Bulletin*, Oct. 18, 1962; "Lawyers in Battle for NAACP Prexy," *Philadelphia Tribune*, Nov. 17, 1962; "Moore and Akers Blast NAACP Leadership in Opening Campaign," *Philadelphia Tribune*, Nov. 20, 1962; "Clique Controls Local NAACP, Cecil Moore Says," *Philadelphia Tribune*, Dec. 4, 1962; "Cecil Moore NAACP Prexy by Landslide," *Philadelphia Tribune*, Dec. 15, 1962.

7. Moore threatened a boycott of Ford cars if the foundation did not force Dash's resignation or end its financial support for PCCA. "Vocal Fireworks Erupt as Moore Is Sworn in as Local NAACP Head," *Philadelphia Tribune*, Jan. 12, 1963; "NAACP Prexy Outlines Militant Program," *Philadelphia Afro-American*, Jan. 12, 1963; "NAACP Head Demands Negro Direct Social Study," *Bulletin*, Jan. 13, 1963; "Negro Named to Aid Dash on N. Phila. Social Project," *Bulletin*, Jan. 17, 1963; "Negro Named to Million $ Study After Protest by *Tribune*, NAACP," *Philadelphia Tribune*, Jan. 19, 1963; "NAACP Threatens Boycott of N. Phila. Ford Study; See Temple U. Link," *Philadelphia Tribune*, Jan. 22, 1963; "NAACP Head Defends Stand Against North Phila. Study," *Bulletin*, Jan. 23, 1963.

8. "13 Prominent Citizens Rally to North Phila. Study Group Opposed by NAACP Prexy," *Philadelphia Tribune*, Jan. 22, 1963; "Negroes Rap NAACP Head for Boycott Threat," *Bulletin*, Jan. 22, 1963; "NAACP Head Defends Stand Against North Phila. Study"; "Dash Says NAACP Ex-Prexy OK'd Him," *Philadelphia Tribune*, Jan. 26, 1963.

9. Dash also promised to expand the PCCA board from fifteen to sixty in order to add a "sizable proportion" of black leaders. "NAACP Chief Remains Opposed to Dash," *Bulletin*, Jan. 19, 1963; "Negroes Rap NAACP Head for Boycott Threat."

10. Nichols's resignation letter made specific reference to the PCCA debate, charging that "other important matters of branch policy" had been made "prior to any meeting of the Executive Board." Nichols wrote this letter two days after Rev. Mahlon Lewis, his pastor at Greater St. Matthew Independent Church, urged his parishioners not to support the local NAACP as long as Moore remained president. "I can't take Cecil Moore," Lewis told the *Tribune*, "I won't support [the NAACP] under his leadership and won't urge my members to do so." "3 NAACP Board Members Resign," *Philadelphia Tribune*, Jan. 22, 1963; "Tom Burress Ousted as NAACP Executive Secretary," *Philadelphia Tribune*, Feb. 5, 1963; "Burress Leaves NAACP Post, Moore Says He Was Fired," *Bulletin*, Feb. 6, 1963; "NAACP Official Resigns in Protest of Policy Statements Before Meets" and "Pastor Blasts Cecil Moore from Pulpit," *Philadelphia Tribune*, Feb. 12, 1963; "4 Quit Board of NAACP," *Bulletin*, Feb. 12, 1963.

11. "North Phila. Citizens Solidly Behind NAACP Tribune Poll Reveals," *Philadelphia Tribune*, Jan. 26, 1963; "Readers Overwhelmingly in Favor of Cecil B. Moore in NAACP-PCCA Fight," *Philadelphia Independent*, Feb. 2, 1963.

12. "NAACP Head Demands Negro Direct Social Study"; "16 Critics Called 'Appeasers Who Accept Crumbs of Charity' by Moore."

13. "Tom Burress Ousted as NAACP Executive Secretary"; "Burress Leaves NAACP Post, Moore Says He Was Fired"; "3000 Cheer 'New Messiah' Moore at NAACP Rally," *Philadelphia Tribune*, Feb. 26, 1963; "NAACP Pickets on New 24-Hour Alert as Chapter Girds to Put Muscle in Threats," *Philadelphia Tribune*, Mar. 12, 1963; "3000 Bask in Revival Atmosphere at NAACP Met Rally," *Philadelphia Tribune*, Apr. 30, 1963.

14. "NAACP Pickets to Hit PCCA Saturday," *Philadelphia Tribune*, Mar. 23, 1963; "NAACP Pickets Hit PCCA Headquarters; To Picket Homes of 'Infamous 16' Next," *Philadelphia Tribune*, Mar. 26, 1963.

15. "Jim Crow's Sweetheart Contract," *Greater Philadelphia Magazine* (Feb. 1963); Walter C. Wynn, executive director, Council for Equal Job Opportunity, May, testimony before the Commission on Human Relations of the City of Philadelphia, 3, 1963, Fellowship Commission (FC) collection, box 30, folder 23, TUUA; Herbert Hill, "Labor Unions and the Negro: The Record of Discrimination," *Commentary*, Dec. 1959. On the AFL-CIO merger, see also Nelson Lichtenstein, *Walter Reuther: The Most Dangerous Man in Detroit* (Urbana: University of Illinois Press, 1995), 320–54; and Ray Marshall, "Unions and the Negro Community," *Industrial and Labor Relations* 17,2 (Jan. 1964): 179–202.

16. In December 1958, the national NAACP announced that after three years of attempting to work with the AFL-CIO's Civil Rights Department to change union racial policies it would now begin to press independently "for the elimination of discriminatory practices within trade union organizations." Memorandum to Mr. Mitchell from Herbert Hill, May 13, 1958; Roy Wilkins to George Meany, Dec. 19, 1958; "Racism Within Organized Labor: A Report of Five Years of the AFL-CIO, 1955–1960," NAACP papers, III A 179, LOC.; Negro American Labor Council, "Race Bias in the AFL-CIO," Jun. 14, 1961, NAACP papers, III A 180, LOC; "Jim Crow's Sweetheart Contract." On the NALC see Paula F. Pfeffer, *A. Philip Randolph, Pioneer of the Civil Rights Movement* (Baton Rouge: Louisiana State University Press, 1990), 206–39.

17. Jones had been a prominent figure within the city's liberal civil rights coalition for more than a decade. In the early 1950s, he served a term on the Commission on Human Relations as the nominee of the Philadelphia CIO Council. In 1962, Jones publicly criticized the NAACP for filing a decertification suit with the National Labor Relations Board against a Steelworkers local in Atlanta for negotiating segregated employment policies into its collective bargaining contract. The NAACP's actions, Jones argued, could only result in the loss of union representations for black and white workers. Jones was not the only HRC member to have strong ties to Philadelphia's reform community. The committee's secretary was Joseph Schwartz, who was both business manager of Knit Goods Workers Local 190 in Philadelphia and a former chairman of the local ADA. Committee member George Morris, head of the local janitors' union, was a former vice president of the Philadelphia NAACP. The HRC was so closely identified with the city's civil rights groups that it was forced to defend the CHR from the charges of others in the local labor movement that the commission's investigations of complaints of racial discrimination in the building trades and other local unions were overly intrusive. Philadelphia AFL-CIO Council Committee on Human Rights, n.d.; report of AFL-CIO Human Rights Committee of Philadelphia, Dec. 1, 1960; Norman Blumberg, Joseph Kelley to All Affiliates, Phila. Council, AFL-CIO, Jun. 11, 1962; minutes, Sub-Committee, Phila. AFL-CIO Human Rights Committee, Jul. 23, 1962, Ben Stahl collection, box 2, TUUA; "Negro Labor Leader Here Resents NAACP Suits Filed Against Unions," *Bulletin*, Nov. 13, 1962; "NAACP Zeroes in On Union Bias as

Labor Man Cries Foul," *Philadelphia Tribune*, Nov. 24, 1963; Philadelphia AFL-CIO Council Committee on Human Rights, n.d., and Alice M. Hoffman interview with Ben Stahl, Sep. 8, 1975, Ben Stahl collection, box 1, TUUA.

18. Joseph O'Neill and other leaders of the city's Building Trades Council (BTC) refused even to meet with the HRC for nearly two years after the committee's founding. When O'Neill finally agreed to a meeting in June 1962, he insisted that the BTC's member locals were autonomous and that he could therefore do nothing to change their policies. Minutes, Sub-Committee, Phila. AFL-CIO Human Rights Committee, Jul. 23, 1962; minutes, Phila. AFL-CIO Human Rights Committee, Oct. 16, 1962, Ben Stahl collection, box 1, TUUA; James Jones et al. to Executive Board, Philadelphia AFL-CIO Council, Feb. 27, 1963, FC collection, box 30, folder 23, TUUA; "The Honeymoon Between Negroes and Biased Labor Bosses Must End!" and "World Survival Threatened By Jim Crow Craft Unions," *Philadelphia Tribune*, Jun. 19, 1962; "New Negro Weary of 'Waiting His Turn' for Equal Employment," *Philadelphia Tribune*, Nov. 17, 1962; "Wilkins Defies Meany," *Philadelphia Tribune*, Dec. 1, 1962; "Union Bias as Outstanding as a Crap Game at a Church Affair," *Philadelphia Tribune*, Dec. 11, 1962.

19. "Jim Crow's Sweetheart Contract."

20. The CHR had originally given the craft unions until March 25 to respond to its investigation. Its decision to release the report nine days before the deadline suggests that it was feeling significant community and media pressure. "Accuse Unions of Bias on City Jobs After Long Probe," *Philadelphia Tribune*, Mar., 16, 1963; Walter Reeder to Floyd L. Logan, May 13, 1963, Floyd Logan collection, box 3, TUUA; "Phila. Schools Support Biased Unions, Labor Leaders Charge," *Philadelphia Tribune*, Apr. 6, 1963; "Green Is the Color Barring Many Negroes from Craft Unions," *Philadelphia Tribune*, Apr. 13, 1963. The seven crafts cited by Jones and Reeder included the electricians, glaziers, plasterers, bricklayers, plumbers, sheet metal workers, and steamfitters.

21. A number of attempts had been made to establish a CORE chapter in Philadelphia during the 1950s, but chapter activity remained sporadic until 1961. After a six-month "wait-and-see" period, demonstrators from the chapter returned to Horn & Hardart in November 1961 to protest the restaurant's failure to honor the earlier agreement. According to CORE, the restaurant chain had only hired three black waitresses and a cashier since the agreement, only two percent of its waitresses and cashiers were black, and 99 percent of its black employees were employed in "non-public" positions. This time, the chain agreed to hire six black waitresses and three more black cashiers and asked CORE for help in finding qualified individuals for additional positions. Over the next year, the chain hired thirty-two Black waitresses and five cashiers. August Meier and Elliot Rudwick, *CORE: A Study in the Civil Rights Movement, 1942–1968* (Urbana: University of Illinois Press, 1973), 121, 187–88; *Philadelphia Tribune*, Apr. 5, 1960; "Center City Horn & Hardart Hit by Pickets," *Philadelphia Tribune*, Apr. 4, 1961; *Philadelphia Tribune*, Apr. 15, 1961; "CORE Protests Job Bias at Horn and Hardart," *Philadelphia Tribune*, Nov. 18, 1961.

22. Meier & Rudwick, *CORE: A Study in the Civil Rights Movement*, 185, 199; "CORE Charges Midtown Realtor with Bias, Stages Sit-In," *Philadelphia Tribune*, Jul. 14, 1962; "S. Phila. Realtor Hit by CORE Pickets Denies Charges of Rental Bias," *Philadelphia Tribune*, Jul. 14, 1962; "Labor Board to Probe Bias In City Projects," *Philadelphia Tribune*, Mar. 30, 1963; "Mayor Tate 'Unhappy' with CORE Pickets at His Home," *Philadelphia Tribune*, Apr. 16, 1963.

23. "Mayor Tate 'Unhappy' With CORE Pickets at His Home"; "CORE Spokesman Urges City Council Housing Edicts," *Philadelphia Tribune*, Apr. 20, 1963.

24. The 1951 city charter required that all elected officials resign before making a run for higher office.

25. On competition between the liberal and organization Democrats in Philadelphia, see James Reichley, *The Art of Government: Reform and Organization Politics in Philadelphia* (New York: Fund for the Republic, 1959). On Tate's career, see Warren Eisenberg, "Enter the Age of Tate," *Greater Philadelphia Magazine* (Jan. 1964).

26. Memorandum to Commissioners Sadie T. M. Alexander et al., from George Schermer, May 31, 1963, Urban League [UL] Collection, box 16, folder 19, TUUA; "Mayor Tate 'Unhappy' with CORE Pickets at His Home"; "CORE Spokesman Urges City Council Housing Edicts"; "Mayor's Office Sit-In Forces Building Trades Study," *Philadelphia Tribune*, Apr. 27, 1963. On Phillips's career, see Kirk R. Petshek, *The Challenge of Urban Reform: Policies and Programs in Philadelphia* (Philadelphia: Temple University Press, 1973). On the Phillips campaign, see Emily Sunstein interview, Emily Lewis Jones, ed., *Walter M. Phillips: Philadelphia Gentleman Activist* (Swarthmore, Pa.: Portraits on Tape, 1987).

27. "Witness Blasts CHR 'Do Nothing' Job Policy," *Philadelphia Tribune*, May 7, 1963; memorandum to Commissioners Sadie T. M. Alexander et al., from George Schermer, May 31, 1963; "Craft Union Discrimination Is Not Just a Negro Problem," *Philadelphia Tribune*, Jun. 15, 1963.

28. "Witness Blasts CHR 'Do Nothing' Job Policy"; "2,000 NAACP Pickets Demonstrate at City Hall Sat.," *Philadelphia Tribune*, May 14, 1963; "City, Unions Fail to Reach Accord on Ending Job Bias" and "Tells CORE Unions Must Admit Negroes," *Bulletin*, May 15, 1963; "Group Blames Tate's Deceit and Double-Cross for Drastic Action," *Philadelphia Tribune*, May 18, 1963.

29. "Human Relations Unit Gives Report on Discrimination," *Philadelphia Tribune*, May 21, 1963; "Work Resumes on Reyburn Plaza; Electrician Hired," *Philadelphia Tribune*, May 28, 1963; *Bulletin*, Jun. 1, 1963; memorandum to Commissioners Sadie T. M. Alexander, et al., from George Schermer, May 31, 1963. See also Commission on Human Relations, "Annual Report, 1963," CHR papers, box 148, folder 1, PMA.

30. "NAACP Chief 'Not Invited' to Negro Leaders' Meeting," *Bulletin*, May 17, 1963; *Bulletin*, Jun. 1, 1963.

31. "NAACP Chief 'Not Invited' to Negro Leaders' Meeting"; *Bulletin*, Jun. 1, 1963. To this point, Moore and the NAACP had played a relatively minor role in the construction industry controversy, though Moore had publicly endorsed the CORE sit-ins. In a press conference announcing the May 11 support rally for the Birmingham protests, Moore charged that the CHR's public hearings on the construction industry were a "delaying tactic" and urged the city to cancel all of its contracts with contractors that relied on union hiring halls. "NAACP Readies Saturday Protest Demonstrations" *Philadelphia Tribune*, May 11, 1963; "2,000 NAACP Pickets Demonstrate at City Hall Sat."; "NAACP Plaza Sit-in Cancelled with Warning," *Philadelphia Tribune*, May 18, 1963.

32. "NAACP Gives City Until Friday to Oust Biased Unions on City Projects" and "NAACP Launches All-Out War on Bias; Attack 5-Pronged," *Philadelphia Tribune*, May 21, 1963. Moore acknowledged that there were sixty-six unskilled black laborers employed at the site.

33. The city's school construction boom was based in large part on increases in federal spending on education during the Kennedy administration. Sugrue, "Affirmative Action from Below," 153. In October 1962, the Philadelphia Urban League called on the school board to abandon its policy of locating new schools "without regard to the ethnic or religious nature of the school population" and to replace it with "a policy of 'planned desegregation.'" Urban League, "A Statement

on the Proposed Building Plan of the Board of Public Education," Oct. 15, 1962, Wharton Centre [WC] collection, box 41, TUUA; "Board of Education Sets Up $31 Million Program," *Philadelphia Tribune*, Feb. 19, 1963. From the beginning of his presidency, Cecil Moore had promised to focus on the issue of school desegregation. In one of his first acts as branch president, Moore called a meeting of twenty-four of the city's black lawyers to develop a strategy for moving the racial discrimination suit that the branch filed against the school system in 1961 from pre-trial motions to trial. "NAACP Prexy Outlines Militant Program," *The Philadelphia Afro-American*, Jan. 12, 1963; "24 Lawyers Meet; Join in NAACP Suit," *Philadelphia Tribune*, Jan. 5, 1963.

34. Moore also led pickets in front of the law offices of school board president Harry LaBrum to protest the board's insistence that it was powerless to determine who was hired on school construction sites. *Bulletin*, May 20, 22, and 24, 1963; "Bond Issue Only Controversy as Tan Election Hopefuls Shoo-In," "NAACP Gives City Until Friday to Oust Biased Unions on City Projects," and "NAACP Launches All-Out War on Bias; Attack 5-Pronged," *Philadelphia Tribune*, May 21, 1963.

35. Phillips received 44 percent of the vote in high-income white wards. For the bond results, see "Bond Issue Is Okayed Despite Naacp Campaign," *Philadelphia Tribune*, May 25, 1963. For the mayoral election results, see Charles A. Ekstrom, "The Electoral Politics of Reform And Machine: The Political Behavior of Philadelphia's 'Black' Wards, 1943–1969," in Miriam Ershkowitz and Joseph Zikmund II, eds., *Black Politics in Philadelphia* (New York: Basic Books, 1973), 99.

36. *Bulletin*, May 24, 1963; "LaBrum Admits Group's Power to Bar Bldg. Bias," *Philadelphia Tribune*, May 25, 1963.

37. *Bulletin*, May 24, 1963. On blue-collar workers joining the demonstrations when their shifts were over, see interview with Mac Walters, Mar. 7, 1994, Wilmington, Del.

38. "'Average Joes' Star in Demonstrations," *Philadelphia Tribune*, May 28, 1963.

39. "Protest Links Pickets with Common Bond" and "Bricklayer Balks at Crossing Picketers," *Philadelphia Tribune*, Jun. 1, 1963; "Couple Donate Home Near School Site to NAACP," *Philadelphia Tribune*, Jun. 1, 1963.

40. Stanford and Daniels were charged with disorderly conduct, breach of the peace, aggravated assault and battery, resisting arrest and conspiracy. *Bulletin*, May 27, and Jun. 13, 1963; "Camera Taken, Clubbed Says Social Worker," and "Commissioner Apologizes To Irate Crowd," *Philadelphia Tribune*, May 28, 1963.

41. 2,000 NAACP Pickets Demonstrate at City Hall Sat."; *Bulletin*, May 27, 1963; "Tempers Flare; Girl Picket Hit, Dragged by Mob" and "Commissioner Apologizes To Irate Crowd," *Philadelphia Tribune*, May 28, 1963; "Moore Tells Cheering Throng About Family Threats, Increased Demands," *Philadelphia Tribune*, Jun. 1, 1963. Moore had long been close friends with Stanford's father, the owner of a West Philadelphia extermination business whom the *Tribune* called "one of the Nation's top amateur Negro golfers." According to Stanford, his father and Moore had both strongly supported Robert Williams, the dissident former head of the Monroe, N. C., NAACP, in his call for armed self-defense against racist terror in the South. Remarks made by Max Stanford at memorial for Robert Williams, Wayne State University, Nov. 7, 1996.

42. "Human Relations Commission Probe Reveals Rampant Union Bias" and "Commissioner Apologizes to Irate Crowd," *Philadelphia Tribune*, May 28, 1963; "Naacp Charges Mayor with Double-Cross," *Philadelphia Tribune*, Jun. 1, 1963.

43. *Bulletin*, May 28 and 29, 1963; "Naacp Charges Mayor With Double-Cross"; memorandum to Commissioner Sadie T. M. Alexander et al., from George Schermer, May 31, 1963. While Schermer insisted that no agreement had been reached

in Monday's negotiations, he agreed with Moore that Tate's decision to order the police to break through the picket lines was "catastrophic."

44. *Bulletin*, May 28 and 29, 1963; "NAACP Leaders Plead for No Violence; Injuries Mount," "Demonstrators Block Trucks with Bodies," and "Moore Tells Cheering Throng About Family Threats, Increased Demands."

45. "Moore Tells Cheering Throng About Family Threats, Increased Demands."

46. *Bulletin*, May 30, 31, Jun. 1, 1963; "Pact Differs Slightly from Original Offer," *Philadelphia Tribune*, Jun. 4, 1963; "Plumbers Told of School Pact," *Philadelphia Daily News*, Jun. 4, 1963.

47. *Bulletin*, May 31, 1963; "Tan Officers Did Everything To Restrain Pals" and "Police Officer Resents Negro Reporter's Quiz," *Philadelphia Tribune*, Jun. 4, 1963.

48. *Bulletin*, May 31 and Jun. 1, 1963; "Pact Differs Slightly from Original Offer."

49. *Bulletin*, May 31 and Jun. 1, 1963; "NAACP Chief Urges Negroes to Boycott CORE Job Protest," *Philadelphia Inquirer*, Jun. 3, 1963; "Tan Officers Did Everything To Restrain Pals."

50. Not every civil rights activists in the city welcomed the NAACP-Building Trades agreement. Philadelphia CORE president Louis Smith accused Moore of settling for too little. "In exchange for five workers and some publicity," he charged, Moore had "removed all pressure from the unions and the contractors." CORE, Smith announced, would soon bring a group of black electricians and plumbers to the site of the new Municipal Services Building "to test the contractors' good faith" and their willingness to adhere to the original CHR agreement. The following day, however, Smith met with Moore for two hours and forged an agreement to "work together to secure their prime objective—equality." Specifically, CORE pledged to refrain from protests while the NAACP conducted negotiations with the construction industry. *Bulletin*, May 31, Jun. 1, 2, 3, 4, and 10, 1963; "NAACP Chief Urges Negroes to Boycott CORE Job Protest," *Philadelphia Inquirer*, Jun. 3, 1963; "NAACP-CORE Bury Hatchet—In CHR, That Is," *Philadelphia Tribune*, Jun. 4, 1963. The Strawberry Mansion protests inspired similar protests in Brooklyn, Cleveland, and Trenton and Newark, New Jersey during the summer of 1963. Sugrue, "Affirmative Action from Below," 161.

51. Carolyn Adams et al., *Philadelphia: Neighborhoods, Division, and Conflict in a Postindustrial City* (Philadelphia: Temple University Press, 1991); Nancy Kleniewski, "Neighborhood Decline and Downtown Renewal: The Politics of Redevelopment in Philadelphia, 1952–1962." Ph.D. dissertation, Temple University, 1981. Thomas Sugrue persuasively ascribes the unions' opposition to integration to a work and community culture that emphasized loyalty to family and ethnicity as well. Sugrue, "Affirmative Action from Below," 155–56.

52. Three days later, one thousand steamfitters attended a meeting to endorse the local's opposition to the BTC-NAACP agreement. While Dugan suggested he might not follow through on his threat to withdraw the local from the BTC, he reiterated his refusal to participate in the agreement's second round of negotiations. The CHR was the proper agency for negotiations, he argued, and he would not agree to meet with pressure groups. After years of resisting the CHR's investigations, craft unionists like Dugan now viewed the preeminent institution of civil rights liberalism in the city as a necessary buffer against black neighborhood activists who were targeting their protests directly at the union movement. *Bulletin*, Jun. 1 and 5, 1963.

53. "Plumbers Told of School Pact."

54. "AFL-CIO Unity Committee to Handle Racial Issue," *Bulletin*, Jun. 13, 1963.

55. "NAACP Ends Talks on Jobs at School Sites," *Bulletin*, Jun. 17, 1963; *Bulletin*, Jun. 22, 1963.

56. Only the sheet metal workers refused to meet the CHR's demands. "Put Negroes in 15% of Jobs, Bias Plan Told," *Bulletin*, Jun. 20, 1963; "Sit-Ins End After City Acts to Halt Jobs; Court Test Set," *Bulletin*, Jun. 27, 1963; "CORE 55 -Hour Sit-In Victorious," *Philadelphia Tribune*, Jun. 29, 1963. On the commission's agreements, see "CHR, 5 of 6 Unions OK Bias Agreement," *Philadelphia Tribune*, Aug. 20, 1963, and Commission on Human Relations, "Human Relations Bulletin," Summer 1963, WC collection, box 57, TUUA. For an extended discussion of the unions' response to the NAACP's demands as well as the emergence of affirmative action requirements on government-funded construction projects, see Sugrue, "Affirmative Action from Below," 163–165.

57. In Schermer's view, Tate fundamentally misunderstood the role and mission of the CHR, viewing it as the representative of the Negro community rather than as "the forum within which conflicts between the various elements in the population can be resolved." *Bulletin*, Jun. 2, 1963; memorandum from George Schermer, executive director, Commission on Human Relations, to Commissioners, May 31, 1963, UL collection, box 16, folder 19, TUUA; George Schermer to Sadie T. M. Alexander, Jun. 4, 1963, UL collection, box 16, folder 19, TUUA. On Executive Order 1114, Sugrue, "Affirmative Action from Below," 145. On the 1961 Kennedy executive order, see Allen J. Matusow, *The Unraveling of America: A History of Liberalism in the 1960s* (New York: Harper and Row, 1984), 64.

58. Commission on Human Relations, "Human Relations Bulletin," Summer 1963; "Federal Executive Board, Construction Contract Compliance Committee," n.d., FC collection, box 34, folder 1, TUUA. On the slow pace of racial change in the Philadelphia construction industry, see Sugrue, "Affirmative Action from Below," 165–167.

59. On the debate over the Philadelphia plan and the Nixon Administration's efforts to extend it to local markets across the country, see Sugrue, "Affirmative Action from Below," 168. In 1968, city hall and the board of education adopted minority employment programs based on the OFCC model. See Philadelphia Housing Association, memorandum for Board of Directors, May 13, 1968, Housing Association of the Delaware Valley (HADV) collection, box 1073, folder 57, TUUA; and Commission on Human Relations, "City Administration's Philadelphia Plan," n.d., FC Collection, box 34, folder 1, TUUA; Memorandum from H. Louis Evert to Maury Fagan, Jul. 1, 1969.

60. "7,500 at Independence Hall Naacp Rally; Give $1,600," *Philadelphia Tribune*, Jun. 11, 1963; *Bulletin*, Jun. 20, 1963; "Convention Hall Memorial Planned for Slain Evers," *Bulletin*, Jun. 21, 1963.

61. Corleto reported that the overall absenteeism rate for June 24 was 10 percent. Given that black workers constituted about 40 percent of the municipal workforce, his figures suggest that the maximum black absentee rate was 25 percent. On the moratorium, *Bulletin*, Jun. 24, 1963; "4000 NAACP City Hall Pickets Mourn Miss. Martyr Medgar Evers," *Philadelphia Tribune*, Jun. 25, 1963.

62. The NAACP campaign against the Philadelphia post office demonstrated the difficulty that Moore had applying protest strategy to less blatant forms of job discrimination. The postal workers who had first requested NAACP assistance opposed the settlement that Moore reached with the local postmaster. They quickly formed the "Post Office Underground for Equal Job Promotions" to continue to press for changes in promotions within the local post office. By November, these unidentified activists were complaining to Dorothy Anderson, the *Tribune*'s political columnist, that Moore had failed to make effective use of the evidence that they had so "painfully gathered" for him. "40 Demonstrate at Post Office," *Philadelphia Tribune*, Jul. 30, 1963; "NAACP Pickets Still March at Post Office," *Philadelphia Tribune*, Aug.

3, 1963; *Bulletin,* Jul. 31, Aug. 2 and 19, 1963; "Moore Balks at Specifying Postal Bias," *Bulletin,* Aug. 24, 1963; "Underground at PO Formed to Fight Bias," *Philadelphia Tribune,* Aug. 31, 1963; "P. O. Workers Cry: Moore Was Our Man, but He Done Us Wrong!," *Philadelphia Tribune,* Nov. 16, 1963. In December, following a picket campaign at the city's Trailways station, the NAACP reached an agreement with Trailways that was modeled on the Greyhound agreement. *Bulletin,* Dec. 6 and 16, 1963.

63. The thirty thousand estimate comes from *Philadelphia Tribune,* which called the Philadelphia contingent the largest in the march. See "Phila. Sends Biggest Group to D.C.," *Philadelphia Tribune,* Aug. 31, 1963.

64. "Honor 31st & Dauphin Pickets at Naacp Rally," *Philadelphia Tribune,* Jun. 8, 1963; "7,500 at Independence Hall Naacp Rally; Give $1,600," *Philadelphia Tribune,* Jun. 11, 1963.

65. "Sadie Alexander, Austin Norris Deny Moore's 'Part-Time Negro' Rap," *Philadelphia Tribune,* Jun. 8, 1963; "7,500 at Independence Hall Naacp Rally; Give $1,600."

66. According to the *Guardian,* Schwartz did not have a brother. Moore would later claim that he had been referring to a man who referred to himself as Schwartz's cousin. "Cecil Moore takes a look at 'His City'," *Pennsylvania Guardian,* Jun. 7, 1963.

67. "7,500 at Independence Hall Naacp Rally; Give $1,600"; "Moore Is Reported Facing Rebuke by NAACP Chiefs" and "Letter from Bishop Spottswood, Head of NAACP, and Cecil Moore's Reply," *Philadelphia Inquirer,* Jun. 20, 1963.

68. "Moore Is Reported Facing Rebuke by NAACP Chiefs"; "Letter from Bishop Spottswood, Head of NAACP, and Cecil Moore's Reply."

69. *Bulletin,* Aug. 6, 1963. While McDermott refused to make any commitments, Tate did pledge to appoint a black member of the Zoning Commission, though he refused to commit to increasing the number of black police officers. Both candidates insisted that they had no control over their party's nominating process.

70. William J. McKenna, "The Negro Vote in Philadelphia Elections," in Ershkowitz and Zikmund, *Black Politics in Philadelphia,* 78; Ekstrom, "The Electoral Politics of Reform And Machine," 99. Ekstrom's study also found that Tate received 54.8 percent of the vote in the five poorest "largely white wards," 53.3 percent of the vote in Italian wards, and 54.9 percent in Jewish wards.

71. Phil Savage, the NAACP's Mid-Atlantic regional director, defended Moore's comments. "The persons who supported the party deserve some type of recognition," he argued. "Nobody gets shocked when Italians, Irish or anybody else are appointed. There should be no hullabaloo over appointing Negroes." "Negro Leaders Are Split on Moore's Demands for Five Top City Jobs," *Philadelphia Inquirer,* Nov. 10, 1963.

72. "Negro Leaders Are Split on Moore's Demands for Five Top City Jobs."

73. Paul M. Washington with David McI. Gracie, *"Other Sheep I Have": The Autobiography of Father Paul M. Washington* (Philadelphia: Temple University Press, 1994), 32–33.

74. Williams Quoted in "Militant Leaders in Battle for Civil Rights," *Bulletin,* Jan. 24, 1965.

75. Lenora Berson, *Case Study of a Riot: The Philadelphia Story* (New York: Institute of Human Relations Press, 1966), 15; Commission on Human Relations memorandum to community leaders and intergroup health & welfare agencies from Larry Groth, Sep. 3, 1964, FC collection, box 22, folder 16, TUUA.

76. Berson, *Case Study of a Riot,* 16.

77. Berson, *Case Study of a Riot,* 17. On the Philyaw shooting, see minutes, Com-

mittee on Community Tensions, Nov. 1, 1963, FC collection, box 21, folder 6, TUUA.

78. Berson, *Case Study of a Riot*, 17. On the Chester demonstrations, see memorandum to Mr. Roy Wilkins from Mr. Current, Apr. 8, 1964, NAACP papers, III A 68, LOC; Bernard McCormick, "The Insurrectionist," *Greater Philadelphia Magazine* 59 (June 1964).

79. Berson, *Case Study of a Riot*, 17–18; *Bulletin*, Aug. 30, 1964; S. A. Paolantonio, *Frank Rizzo: The Last Big Man in Big City America* (Philadelphia: Camino Books, 1993), 91–93. The report of rock throwing is in "Militant Leaders Clash in Battle for Civil Rights," *Bulletin*, Jan. 24, 1965.

80. Berson, *Case Study of a Riot*, 27–39.

81. Berson, *Case Study of a Riot*, 18–19; Commission on Human Relations memorandum to community leaders and intergroup health & welfare agencies from Larry Groth, Sep. 3, 1964; "Militant Ex-Marine Leads Philadelphia Negroes," *New York Times*, Sep. 2, 1964.

82. "Militant Ex-Marine Leads Philadelphia Negroes." On Georgie Woods, see James Spady, *Georgie Woods: I'm Only a Man: The Life Story of a Mass Communicator, Promoter, Civil Rights Activist* (Philadelphia: Snac-Pac Book Division, 1992).

83. Berson, *Case Study of a Riot*, 19–20.

84. Berson, *Case Study of a Riot*, 16, 20.

85. "Advisory Board Harasses Police, FOP Official Says," *Bulletin*, Jul. 19 and Aug. 2, 1964; Federal Bureau of Investigation Report, Sep. 18, 1964, FC collection, TUUA. Throughout August, Philadelphia had been awash in rumors of an impending riot. The CHR, for example, reported rumors that a New York-group known as the Black Brothers was planning to "create a holocaust in Philadelphia." According to another rumor, six "well-dressed" black men were organizing a teen rumble for the last Saturday in August. Berson, *Case Study of a Riot*, 21.

86. *Bulletin*, Aug. 2 and 3, 1964; Berson, *Case Study of a Riot*, 51.

87. "Fellowship Commission Urges Long-Term Solution to Conditions Responsible for Recent Violence," Sep. 4, 1964, FC collection, box 22, folder 16, TUUA; Brant Coopersmith to Philadelphia ADL Regional Board, B'nai B'rith Lodge and Chapter Presidents, and ADL Chairmen, Sep. 2, 1964, FC collection, box 22, folder 16, TUUA.

88. Berson, *Case Study of a Riot*, 43–45. In her report, Lenore Berson cited evidence that food prices in North Philadelphia stores were only 5 percent higher than in Center City.

89. "Businessmen Urged to Join N. Phila Unit," *Bulletin*, Sep. 3, 1964.

90. "The Goddamn Boss," *Time*, Sep. 11, 1964.

91. Memorandum from Jules Cohen to JCRC Officers, Board of Directors, Member Agencies and Neighborhood Divisions, Aug. 31, 1964, FC collection, box 22, folder 16, TUUA; Coopersmith to Philadelphia ADL Regional Board, B'nai B'rith Lodge and Chapter Presidents and ADL Chairmen, Sep. 2, 1964.

92. *Philadelphia Daily News*, Aug. 31, Sep. 3, 1964; Coopersmith to Philadelphia ADL Regional Board, B'nai B'rith Lodge and Chapter Presidents and ADL Chairmen, Sep. 2, 1964; minutes, Committee on Community Tensions, Sep. 3, 1964, FC collection box 21, folder 7, TUUA; FC collection, box 22, folder 16, TUUA.

93. Paolantonio, *Frank Rizzo*, 73–76. Rizzo didn't publicly voice his criticisms of Leary's riot control strategy until he decided to run for mayor in 1969. *Bulletin*, Jan. 19, 1969.

94. In addition to Rizzo, the mayor appointed three other deputy commissioners: Richard T. Edwards, the city's first black deputy commissioner who was named head of the department's community relations division, and Edward J. Bell and

John Driscoll, two close allies of Leary, who were appointed to run the detective and government relations divisions. Of the four, Rizzo was the only one to oppose Leary's support for the Police Advisory Board and other police reform efforts. Paolantonio, *Frank Rizzo*, 35–73.

95. "Militant Ex-Marine Leads Philadelphia Negroes," *New York Times*, Sep. 2, 1964.

96. "The Goddamn Boss."

97. "The Goddamn Boss."

98. "The Goddamn Boss."

99. Moore also attacked the Police Advisory Board—the centerpiece of the liberal strategy to reform police conduct in the city's black neighborhoods—for its ineffectiveness in the struggle against police brutality. Charging that the PAB was "designed to whitewash crimes of the police," he promised that the Philadelphia NAACP would conduct an independent investigation of the 258 brutality claims rather than forward them to the PAB. "Militant Ex-Marine Leads Philadelphia Negro"; *Bulletin*, Sep. 3 and 9, 1964; "Moore Asks Cut in Riot Area Police," *Philadelphia Inquirer*, Sep. 6, 1964; "The Goddamn Boss"; Berson, *Case Study of a Riot*, 52. Ironically, Moore praised his ally in the NAACP lawyer program, Police Commissioner Howard Leary, as "the most enlightened policeman in the United States" in the same interview.

100. "Moore Rapped by Clergymen for Interview," *Bulletin*, Oct. 10, 1964; *Bulletin*, Nov. 12, 1964. On Nichols's supporters, see *Bulletin*, Feb. 2, 1995, and "Moore Wins NAACP Vote by 5–1 Margin," *Bulletin*, Feb. 7, 1965.

101. *Bulletin*, Sep. 15, 1964; *New York Times*, Sep. 19, 1964.

102. On December 3, a ten-member national investigative committee convened a hearing in the NAACP's New York offices on the various charges and counter-charges affecting the Philadelphia chapter. Among those attending the hearing were forty members of the branch, each carrying a sign reading "Members for Moore." Following the hearing, NAACP executive secretary Roy Wilkins announced that he was ordering a postponement of the Philadelphia branch elections, which had been originally scheduled for December, until after the investigative committee reported its findings to the national board. *Bulletin*, Nov. 12 and 24, Dec. 3, 4, 9, 1964; Jan 5, 7, 15, 18, 24, 1965; "Moore Wins NAACP Vote by 5–1 Margin."

103. *Bulletin*, Jan. 11, 17, 24, 1965.

104. *Bulletin*, Jan. 11, 17, 24 and Feb. 2, 1965. On the original Supreme Court decision, see "Justices' Decision Is Unanimous," *Bulletin*, Jun. 30, 1958. Stephen Girard's will actually mandated that the walls be twenty feet high, a requirement that the campus builders met by sinking the walls ten feet into the ground.

105. *Bulletin*, Jan. 15, 1965.

106. "Moore Wins NAACP Vote by 5–1 Margin." Total branch membership had actually declined, from more than 16,000 at the time of the Higginbotham-Pilgrim election in December 1959 to about 13,000 in February, 1965.

107. "Cecil Moore Calls Election a Mandate," *Bulletin*, Feb. 8, 1965; *Philadelphia Inquirer*, Jan. 31, 1965; Philadelphia NAACP press release, May 10, 1965, NAACP papers, III C 138, LOC.

108. On the formation of Philadelphia Antipoverty Action Committee (PAAC), see "Tate Shakes Up City's Antipoverty Forces," *Bulletin*, Feb. 10, 1965.

109. *Bulletin*, Mar. 15, 1965; "Dr. King Asked to Stay Out of Girard Dispute," *Bulletin*, Jul. 30, 1965.

110. Moynihan, "The Negro Family: The Case for National Action," in Lee Rainwater and William L. Yancey, *The Moynihan Report and the Politics of Controversy* (Cambridge, Mass.: MIT Press, 1967), 39–125.

111. E. Frances White, "Africa on My Mind: Gender, Counter Discourse and African American Nationalism," *Journal of Women's History* 2 (Spring 1990): 73–97.

112. Williams, *Negroes with Guns*, 38–45; Berson, *Case Study of a Riot*, 16, 21; *Philadelphia Tribune*, Sep. 1, 1964; "Fellowship Commission Urges Long-Term Solution to Conditions Responsible for Recent Violence," Sep. 4, 1964.

113. Berson, *Case Study of a Riot*, 21; *Bulletin*, May 1, 1965; "Girard Picketing Ends and Even Police Sing," *Bulletin*, Dec. 18, 1965; "Girard Pickets Described by Police Officer," *Bulletin*, Mar. 16, 1966; "How to Handle Demonstrations," *Time*, Dec. 9, 1966; Frantz Fanon, *The Wretched of the Earth* (New York: Grove, 1965), esp. 29–74. On the importance of struggles for free space in the history of African American activism, see Robin D.G. Kelley, "Congested Terrain: Resistance on Public Transportation," in *Race Rebels*, 55–75.

114. *Bulletin*, May 4, 5, 8, 10, 16, Jul. 12, 13, and 23, 1965; "100 Policemen Are Added to Patrols at Girard College," *Philadelphia Inquirer*, Jun. 26, 1965.

115. "Cold Reduces Picketing at Girard College Wall," *Bulletin*, Dec. 8, 1965; "Girard Picketing Ends and Even Police Sing."

116. Kelley, "Congested Terrain," 55–75.

117. Harold Cruse, *The Crisis of the Negro Intellectual* (New York: William Morrow Press, 1967), 343–44.

118. "SCLC People to People Northern City Tour, July 24—August 4, 1965," Floyd Logan (FL) collection, box 5, TUUA.

119. The most prominent neighborhood activist on the host committee was Alice Lipscomb, president of South Philadelphia's Hawthorne Community Council. On the host committee and King's visit, see mass rally flier, Aug. 3, 1965 and minutes, Steering Committee, Jul. 27, 1965 and Sep. 30, 1965, FL collection, box 5, TUUA; interview with William Meek, Mar. 15, 1994, Philadelphia.

120. Interview with Meek.

121. "Dr. King Asked to Stay Out of Girard Dispute."

122. Interview with Meek; "900 Hear Dr. King; Cecil Moore Absent," *Philadelphia Daily News*, Aug. 2, 1965. On August 1, different editions of Bulletin reported that the visit had and had not been canceled. See "Sponsors Seek New Plan After King Bars Visit" and "King Still Plans to Visit City, Aide Declares," *Bulletin*, Aug. 1, 1965.

123. "900 Hear Dr. King; Cecil Moore Absent," *Bulletin*, Aug. 3, 1965.

124. "NAACP Stands Alone Despite King Appeal for Unity, Moore Says," *Philadelphia Inquirer*, Aug. 8, 1965; *Bulletin*, Aug. 16, 1965; interview with William Meek, Mar. 15, 1994.

125. *Bulletin*, May 10, Jun. 5, 6, and 23, 1965; *New York Times*, Jul. 1, 1965; Commission on Human Relations press release, Jun. 10, 1965, Floyd Logan collection, box 4, TUUA; "Girard Trustees Uncooperative, Chisholm Says," *Philadelphia Inquirer*, Jul. 18, 1965. James Farmer's visit to the Wall took place on May 31, 1965. See *Bulletin*, Jun. 1, 1965. On the CHR's efforts to meet with the Girard College trustees, see also minutes, Board of Commissioners, Jun. 8, 1965, FC collection, box 8, TUUA.

126. *Bulletin*, Jun. 24, & Jul. 8, 1965. On the Fellowship Commission's lobbying effort, see minutes, Board of Commissioners, Sep. 14, 1965, FC collection, box 8, TUUA.

127. *Bulletin*, Jul. 22, Sep. 22, Dec. 17, 1965 and May 20, 1968; "Cold Reduces Picketing At Girard College Wall," *Bulletin*, Dec. 8, 1965; "Girard Picketing Ends And Even Police Sing." On the periodic renewal of the Girard picket line, see *Bulletin*, Oct. 8, 1966.

128. Felicia A. Kornbluh, "Political Arithmetic and Racial Division in the Demo-

cratic Party," Social Policy 26/3 (Spring 1996), 49–63; Thomas J. Sugrue, *The Origins of the Urban Crisis: Race and Inequality in Postwar Detroit* (Princeton: Princeton University Press, 1997), 267.

129. Reichley, *The Art of Government*, 79–80.

Chapter 5. Black Power and the Organizing Tradition

1. On the black nationalist belief in white supremacy's constitutive role in American society, see Michael C. Dawson, *Black Visions: The Roots of Contemporary African-American Political Ideologies* (Chicago; University of Chicago Press, 2001), 21–23, 85–134. On the organizing tradition, see Charles M. Payne, *I've Got the Light of Freedom: The Organizing Tradition and the Mississippi Freedom Struggle* (Berkeley: University of California Press, 1995), 67–102. On the radical democratic nature of SNCC's commitment to community organizing, see Barbara Ransby, *Ella Baker and the Black Freedom Movement: A Radical Democratic Vision* (Chapel Hill: University of North Carolina Press, 2003), 239–98.

2. Clayborne Carson, *In Struggle: SNCC and the Black Awakening of the 1960s* (Cambridge, Mass.: Harvard University Press, 1981), 2, 103.

3. Interview with John Churchville, Feb. 16, 1994, Philadelphia.

4. "Definitive Statement of the Northern Student Movement Coordinating Committee," Student Christian Movement (SCM) papers, box 31, folder 422, Yale Divinity School Archives (YDSA); interview with Joan Countryman, Mar. 16, 1994, New York; "Civil Rights in the North: An Intercollegiate Conference," n.d., Jean and William Bennett papers in author's possession. Cannady would later marry Peter Countryman, NSM's founding executive director. They are the author's parents. On the founding of NSM, see also Peter Countryman to Dear Sir, n.d., SCM papers, box 25, folder 353, memorandum to All Campus Contacts from Executive Director, May 21, 1962 and "Northern Student Movement," Jul. 7, 1963, SCM papers, box 31, folder 422, YDSA; R. W. Apple, Jr., "Ivy-League Integrationists," *Reporters*, Feb. 14, 1963.

5. Interview with Churchville.

6. Ella Baker, "Developing Community Leadership," in Gerda Lerner, ed., *Black Women in White America: A Documentary History* (New York: Vintage, 1973), 351. For more on Baker's critique of charismatic leadership, see Carson, *In Struggle*, 19–30; Payne, *I've Got the Light of Freedom*, 77–102; Aldon Morris, *The Origins of the Civil Rights Movement: Black Communities Organizing for Change* (New York: Free Press, 1984), 102–4.

7. As Charles Payne has written, for Septima Clark, "including everyone in democracy meant that the common assumption that poor people had to be led by their social betters was anathema." *I've Got the Light of Freedom*, 67–68. On Clark and the Highlander Center, see Payne, *I've Got the Light of Freedom*, 68–77; Morris, *The Origins of the Civil Rights Movement*, 141–57; Cynthia Stokes Brown, ed., *Ready from Within: Septima Clark and the Civil Rights Movement* (Trenton, N.J.: Africa World Press, 1980). On SNCC's decision to shift from civil rights protest to voter registration, see Carson, *In Struggle*, 38–82; Payne, *I've Got the Light of Freedom*, 100–131. Since the 1890s, southern states had used a wide variety of officially "nonracial" requirements to prevent blacks from registering to vote. See J. Morgan Kousser, *The Shaping of Southern Politics: Suffrage Restriction and the Establishment of the One-Party South, 1880–1910* (New Haven, Conn.: Yale University Press, 1974).

8. The 1890 Mississippi Constitution required that voters either be able to read or interpret a section of the constitution to the satisfaction of the voter registrar. A 1954 state law gave white registrars even greater leverage to disqualify would-be

black voters by requiring that voters be able to both read and interpret a section of the constitution. See John Dittmer, *Local People: The Struggle for Civil Rights in Mississippi* (Urbana: University of Illinois, 1994), 6–7, 52–53, 70–72.

9. From a field report quoted in James Forman, *The Making of Black Revolutionaries* (Washington, D.C.: Open Hand Publishing, 1985), 275–76.

10. Interview with Churchville; Sherrod quoted in Carson, *In Struggle*, 76–77.

11. Interview with Churchville. On SNCC's decision to concentrate its voter registration efforts in Greenwood during the spring of 1963, see Carson, *In Struggle*, 81, 86–87, and Dittmer, *Local People*, 143–57.

12. Churchville quoted in Carson, *In Struggle*, 195.

13. Interview with Churchville.

14. Interview with Churchville. According to an FBI informant, however, Churchville's return to Philadelphia coincided with Jeremiah X's appointment as minister of the Nation of Islam's Temple No. 12 in West Philadelphia. Churchville, the informant reported, attended the Philadelphia mosque regularly from April 1964 until January 1965. The informant's reports are in the FBI files that Rev. Paul M. Washington obtained through the Freedom of Information Act and which are in the author's possession.

15. Interview with Churchville, Feb. 16, 1994; "A Library Grows in the Riot Rubble," *Bulletin*, Sept. 6, 1964; "Philadelphia—NSM Freedom Library," *Freedom North*, nos. 4 and 5, p. 27, SCM papers, YDSA.

16. Interview with Churchville, Feb. 16, 1994; "NSM Freedom Library Community Project," n.d., Thomas Roderick papers, in author's possession; John Churchville, "The Facts of Life," *Organizer*, Aug, 4, 1965, SNCC papers, Reel 60, item 66.

17. Interview with Churchville; "A Library Grows in the Riot Rubble."

18. Interview with Charyn Sutton, Mar. 5, 1994, Philadelphia.

19. Interview with Churchville; "Philadelphia—NSM Freedom Library." Churchville also organized a parents' association to support the tutoring program. "Parents' Association Dinner Success," *Organizer*, Aug. 4, 1965, SNCC papers, Reel 60, Item 66.

20. Interview with Churchville; interview with Mattie Humphrey, Mar. 12, 1994, Philadelphia; "Philadelphia—NSM Freedom Library."

21. Malcolm X, "A Declaration of Independence," March 12, 1964, reprinted in George Breitman, ed., *Malcolm X Speaks* (New York: Grove Weidenfeld, 1990), 21; "Statement of the Basic Aims and Objectives of the Organization of Afro-American Unity," Jun. 28, 1964, in George Breitman, *The Last Year of Malcolm X: The Evolution of a Revolutionary* (New York: Merit Publishers, 1967), 105–11.

22. Peter Countryman, "The Philadelphia Experiment," n.d., Jean and William Bennett papers in author's possession; interview with Joan Countryman. On the NSM tutorial programs, see also "College Students to Start Pilot Project of Free Tutoring for N. Phila. Pupils," *Bulletin*, Jun. 24, 1962; "Students in Philadelphia Tutor Youths from Minority Groups," *New York Times*, Aug. 5, 1962; "Negroes Helped to Gain College," *New York Times*, Nov. 25, 1962; Apple, "Ivy-League Integrationists"; "Down-to-Earth Idealism," *Time*, May 17, 1963; Lou Anthony, "Tutorials: To Be or Not To Be," *Tutorial Projector*, May 1963, SNCC papers reel 26, item 26. For a discussion of the impact of NSM and the Philadelphia Tutorial Project on student activists in the Philadelphia area see Paul Lyons, *The People of This Generation: The Rise and Fall of the New Left in Philadelphia* (Philadelphia: University of Pennsylvania Press, 2003), 16, 43–49, 170–173.

23. Interview with Thomas Gilhool, Mar. 14, 1994, Philadelphia.

24. Bill Strickland and Dan Schecter, " 'Progress' Must Include People," *Freedom North*, vol. 1, no. 2, SCM papers, YDSA.

25. Interview with Sutton, Mar. 5, 1994; "NSM Freedom Library Community Project." Sutton insists, however, that NSM's shift toward black nationalism "was not necessarily seen as antiwhite as much as it was seen as strategic." While SNCC would eventually expel its last remaining white members, NSM encouraged its white members to form Friends of NSM chapters and to actively organize against racism in white communities. "There was a sense," Sutton remembers, "that we couldn't get anywhere as long as poor whites were venting their frustration against blacks. It made sense to organize poor blacks separately, [to] organize poor whites separately, and then [to] unify them into a common effort, rather than to simply organize poor blacks and leave poor whites out there to be used against the blacks." On the debate over the role of whites in SNCC, see Carson, *In Struggle*, 144–45, 229, 236–42.

26. This assessment of Humphrey's role in recruiting activists to attend the Freedom Library's evening discussions is based on the author's interviews with Paul Washington, Mar. 14, 1994, Walter Palmer, Aug. 10, 2004 and Edward Robinson, Aug. 11, 2004, all in Philadelphia.

27. Interview with Humphrey. Humphrey claimed to have been unaware of Cecil Moore's criticisms of PCCA's lack of black leadership at the time she accepted the position. PCCA's community involvement approach to antigang work reflected the influence of sociologist Richard Cloward's theories about juvenile delinquency in poor communities. On Cloward and the Mobilization for Youth program in New York, see Matusow, *The Unraveling of America*, 110–19, and Michael B. Katz, *The Undeserving Poor: From the War on Poverty to the War on Welfare* (New York: Pantheon, 1989), 83–85, 95–98.

28. Interview with Humphrey.

29. Interviews with Churchville, Humphrey, and Washington; Paul M. Washington with David McI. Gracie, *"Other Sheep I Have": The Autobiography of Father Paul Washington* (Philadelphia: Temple University Press, 1994), 43. Churchville was greatly in need of paid work since NSM's promise of a $25 per week salary had never materialized. Interview with Churchville.

30. Interview with Humphrey.

31. Interview with Churchville; "15 Neighborhood Groups Confer on Phila. School Programs," *Philadelphia Tribune*, Oct. 26, 1965.

32. As described by Walter Palmer, the boundaries of the "black bottom" were Fortieth Street to the west, Lancaster Avenue to the north, Thirty-second Street to the east, and the old Convention Hall to the South.

33. Interview with Palmer.

34. Interview with Palmer. As Palmer remembers it, his use of the term "black people" was so unusual in 1957 that the clerk at the telephone office felt that she needed to check with a supervisor before agreeing to provide a telephone listing for the Black People's University. Palmer would maintain the Black People's University into the 1970s. See "'Black People's University' Opens on 52nd Street," *Philadelphia Tribune*, Apr. 3, 1971.

35. Interview with Palmer.

36. Interview with Palmer. On the Society for the Preservation of Afro-American History, see *Bulletin*, Aug. 28, 1963.

37. Interview with Palmer.

38. Interview with Robinson. On Robinson's career at Provident Mutual Insurance, see also "Black Agents Urged to Up Sales," *Philadelphia Tribune*, May 15, 1971.

39. Interview with Robinson.

40. Interview with Robinson.

41. Charles Sutton and Rev. Paul M. Washington, "Interracial Groups Have 'Planned Swims' At Finnegan Pool," *Philadelphia Tribune*, Aug. 23, 1960.

42. Washington, *"Other Sheep I Have"*, 23–28.

43. Washington, *"Other Sheep I Have"*, 23, 42.

44. Washington, *"Other Sheep I Have"*, 19–39.

45. Washington, *"Other Sheep I Have"*, 33–34.

46. Washington, *"Other Sheep I Have"*, 40–48; interviews with Churchville & Washington.

47. "Statement of the Basic Aims and Objectives of the Organization of Afro-American Unity," June 28, 1964, in Breitman, *The Last Year of Malcolm X*; interviews with Churchville, Humphrey, Washington, Palmer, and Sutton; Washington, *"Other Sheep I Have"*, 26–32; *Bulletin*, Feb. 5, 1966; *Philadelphia Tribune*, Feb. 8, 1966. BPUM's emphasis on intraracial unity across divisions of class, religion, and ideology and, as we shall see, its commitment to the establishment of black community control over public institutions in black neighborhoods placed it within the ideological spectrum of what Michael C. Dawson has called "community nationalism." Michael C. Dawson, *Black Visions: The Roots of Contemporary African-American Political Ideologies* (Chicago; University of Chicago Press, 2001), 100–02, 120–32

48. The transcript of Churchville, Strickland, and Washington's appearance on the Feb. 2, 1996 Joe Rainey show on WDAS was included in Washington's FBI file. See Chapter 1 for a discussion of Rainey's leadership of the left-wing faction of the Philadelphia NAACP during the 1940s.

49. Joseph Rainey Show Transcript, Washington's FBI file. Churchville's comments on the March on Washington closely resemble a critique of the march that Malcolm X first offered in the fall of 1963. See, for example, Malcolm X, "God's Judgement on White America," December 4, 1963, reprinted in Imam Benjamin Karim, ed., *The End of White World Supremacy: Four Speeches by Malcolm X* (New York: Merlin House, 1971), 141–45. On the debate over the March on Washington, see Paula F. Pfeffer, *A. Philip Randolph, Pioneer of the Civil Rights Movement* (Baton Rouge: Louisiana State University Press, 1990), 240–80.

50. Joseph Rainey Show Transcript, Washington's FBI file.

51. Joseph Rainey Show Transcript, Washington's FBI file.

52. Joseph Rainey Show Transcript, Washington's FBI file.

53. Malcolm X, "At the Audubon," November 24, 1964, reprinted in Breitman, ed., *Malcolm X Speaks*, 90.

54. Carson, *In Struggle*, 134–36, 166–68, 186–88.

55. Quoted in Carson, *In Struggle*, 167.

56. *Bulletin*, Feb. 5, 1996; "Anti-White Bias Irritates Cleric," *Philadelphia Tribune*, Feb. 8, 1966; "Church Defends Self Against Bias Charge," *Philadelphia Tribune*, Feb. 22, 1966; Washington, *"Other Sheep I Have"*, 44–46. An FBI informant also estimated that there were twenty to thirty whites in the audience. See Washington's FBI file. Charyn Sutton and Paul Washington agree with Steve Gold that there were no visible objections to Churchville's request. Interviews with Sutton and Washington; interview with Steve Gold, Mar. 9, 1994, Philadelphia.

57. Quoted in Washington, *"Other Sheep I Have"*, 46–47. See also "Anti-White Bias Irritates Cleric."

58. The *Nite Life* editorial is reprinted in Washington's FBI file. According to the *Philadelphia Tribune*, the focus of Bond's speech was on his opposition to the Vietnam War and his efforts to claim his seat in the Georgia legislature. "Anti-White Bias Irritates Cleric."

59. Humphrey and Churchville's letters and the WDAS editorial are contained in Washington's FBI file.

60. Interviews with Churchville and Sutton; "Phila Is a 'Racist City,' Carmichael Tells 2,000," *Bulletin*, Aug. 31, 1966. John Churchville left BPUM in 1967 after expe-

riencing a religious conversion to Christianity. "It was a black Jesus," Sutton remembers, "and it was . . . consistent with [his] politics. It was still nationalist." Interview with Sutton. See also Washington, *"Other Sheep I Have"*, 52.

61. See Chapter 7 for a discussion of gender politics in BPUM and the other black power groups in Philadelphia.

62. "Thursday Night Meet May Settle CORE Postal Dispute," *Philadelphia Tribune*, Jul. 16, 1966. Delegates to CORE's August 1966 national convention in Baltimore passed a resolution defining Black Power as "control of economic, political, and educational institutions and resources, from top to bottom, by black people in their own areas." August Meier and Elliot Rudwick, *CORE: A Study in the Civil Rights Movement, 1942–1968* (Urbana: University of Illinois Press, 1973), 412–19.

63. Interviews with Churchville, Sutton, Palmer; *Bulletin*, Jul. 18, 1966; "'Black Power,' Beauty Unity Rally Themes," *Philadelphia Tribune*, Jul. 19, 1966; "Philadelphians Salute Malcolm X at Police-Guarded Ceremony Here" and "African Dancing, Out-of-Sight Poetry Sparks Tribute to Malcolm X," *Philadelphia Tribune*, Aug. 9, 1966; "Phila Is a 'Racist City,' Carmichael Tells 2,000"; Washington, *"Other Sheep I Have"*, 50–51.

64. "'Black Power,' Beauty Unity Rally Themes."

65. Washington, *"Other Sheep I Have"*, 72–74; "Civil Rights Leaders 'Backing' Black Power Conference to Hilt," *Philadelphia Tribune*, Jul. 13, 1968; "Thousands Attend Black Power Meet," *Philadelphia Tribune*, Aug. 31, 1968; "Black State Planned," *Philadelphia Tribune*, Sep. 3, 1968. Information on the Third National Conference on Black Power is also available in Washington's FBI file, including "Third Black Power Confab to Be Held Aug. 29 in Philly," *Cincinnati Herald*, Jul. 20, 1968; "Calling All Black People" flier, n.d.; and reports from FBI informants. On the Black Power conferences, see also Komozi Woodard, *A Nation within a Nation: Amiri Baraka (LeRoi Jones) and Black Power Politics* (Chapel Hill: University of North Carolina Press, 1999), 84–89, 107–8 and Robert L. Allen, *Black Awakening in Capitalist America* (Trenton, N.J.: Africa World Press, 1990), 157–71.

66. Washington, *"Other Sheep I Have"*, 74–77; interview with Palmer.

67. Washington, *"Other Sheep I Have"*, 74–77.

68. Washington, *"Other Sheep I Have"*, 72–81; Washington's FBI file; Allen, *Black Awakening*, 160–64.

69. Washington, *"Other Sheep I Have"*, 76–77. On the Advocate Community Development Corporation, see "Low Income Families Expected to 'Leap' at 15 New Homes Near 16th and Diamond," *Philadelphia Tribune*, Apr. 3, 1971.

70. On the Black Political Convention, see chapter 8.

71. On the House of Umoja, see D. Fattah, "The House of Umoja as a Case Study for Social Change," *Annals of the American Academy of Political and Social Science* 494 (1987), 37–41. Fattah's son, Chaka Fattah, has represented North and West Philadelphia in the U.S. Congress since 1995.

72. Julius Lester, "The Angry Children of Malcolm X," reprinted in August Meier, Elliott Rudwick and Francis Broderick, *Black Protest Thought in the Twentieth Century*, 2nd ed. (Indianapolis: Bobbs-Merrill, 1971), 469–84.

73. Carson, *In Struggle*, 153–74, 205; Forman, *The Making of Black Revolutionaries*, 460–71; John Hulett, "How the Black Panther Party Was Organized," in Clayborne Carson et al., eds., *The Eyes on the Prize Civil Rights Reader* (New York: Penguin, 1991), 273–78.

74. Interview with Sutton; James Forman, "Philadelphia Black Paper," n.d., p. 1, SNCC papers, reel 32, item 102.

75. See, for example, "Rights Rally Collects $5200," *Philadelphia Inquirer*, Sep. 17, 1962; "SNCC Forming: Student Civil Rights Effort Gains Support," *Germantown*

Courier, Sept. 26, 1963, SNCC papers, reel 34, item 405. In November 1961, Barrett led an interracial student group from Fellowship House that was arrested in a CORE-sponsored sit-in at a segregated restaurant near the state capitol in Annapolis, Maryland. In April 1963, Penney and a group of ten college students were arrested in a similar demonstration in Cambridge, Maryland. "10 From Penna. In Sit-In; 9 To Remain in Jail," *Philadelphia Tribune*, Nov. 14, 1961; "Priest Jailed in Bias Protest in Maryland," *Bulletin*, Apr. 8, 1963.

76. Three months after her shooting, Hall was back in Philadelphia to announce that she was coordinating, as the local representative of Friends of SNCC, a canned food and clothing drive out of the Fellowship House headquarters on Girard Avenue. The food and clothing were to be donated to black families in Georgia and Mississippi who were suffering economic reprisals for attempting to register to vote. In February 1963, Barrett and Hall traveled back to southwest Georgia to work full-time on SNCC's voter registration project and in May of that year Barrett and Hall conducted a nine-day hunger strike in an Albany, Georgia, jail following their arrest for distributing fliers. "We felt," Barrett was quoted in Bulletin, "the time had come when we had to put the total moral weight of our personalities and beliefs on the consciences of Chief Pritchett . . . and the community of Albany as a whole." "Temple Coed Relates Midnight Attack on Georgia Rights Unit," *Philadelphia Inquirer*, Sep. 14, 1962; Joyce Barrett to Family, May, 14, n.d., Fellowship House (FH) collection, TUUA; Horace Julian Bond to Sue Edelman, Nov. 29, 1962, SNCC papers, reel 12, item 1; "Aid Asked for Negroes in Vote Campaign," *Bulletin*, Dec. 18, 1962; "Phila. Women on Probation in Georgia," *Bulletin*, Jun. 5, 1963.

77. Seventeen sets of parents signed an advertisement entitled "Our Children Are in Mississippi Working for Human Rights" that ran in Bulletin on August 9, 1964. "Local Group Considers Aid to Southern Rights Group," *Montgomery Post*, Apr. 22, 1964, SNCC papers, reel 32, item 102; "20 Youths From Phila. Going to Mississippi," *Bulletin*, May 24, 1964; "Parents Seek U.S. Guards for City Students in Miss.," *Bulletin*, Jun. 18, 1964; "Our Children Are in Mississippi Working for Human Rights," *Bulletin*, Aug. 9, 1964. Extensive evidence of SNCC's fundraising efforts in the Philadelphia area can be found in SNCC's microfilmed correspondence. See, for example, SNCC's Sandra Hayden to Atty. Isaiah W. Crippins, May 27, 1963, SNCC papers, reel 34, item 408; Philadelphia Area Friends of SNCC, Apr. 13, 1964, SNCC papers reel 32, item 102.

78. In the year following the 1964 convention, the Philadelphia SNCC office focused its efforts on winning public support for the campaign to press the national Democrats to take action against the party's all-white Mississippi affiliate. Memorandum, Philadelphia Area Friends of SNCC to Pennsylvania Democratic Party Leaders, Sept. 26, 1964, SNCC papers reel 34, item 461; "Civil Rights Unit to Collect 'Poll Tax' From Voters Here," *Bulletin*, Oct 29, 1964; Philadelphia (Penna.) to Philadelphia (Miss.) Conference, A Sister-City Project, n.d., SNCC papers reel 34, item 535.

79. Interviews with Charyn Sutton, Mar. 5, 1994 and August 12, 2004.

80. Interviews with Sutton and Paul Washington. See also Arthur Finch, "On White People in the Movement," *Freedom North*, nos. 4 and 5, 36–39, SCM papers, YDSA, and Don Jackson, "An Open Letter to the ERAP Bulletin," *Freedom North*, nos. 7 and 8, 29–30, SCM papers, YDSA.

81. Interview with Sutton; "Viewpoint Published 'By Youth Itself'," Mar. 1964, FH collection, TUUA.

82. Interview with Sutton.

83. Interview with Sutton.

84. Interview with Sutton; "Philadelphia Freedom Organization," SNCC papers, reel 32, item 102.

85. " 'New Breed' Seeks Change; Vows to Go Down Swinging Not Singing with Young Brainwashed Victims," *Philadelphia Tribune*, Jul. 26, 1966; "Philadelphia Freedom Organization"; interview with Sutton.

86. The Philadelphia Freedom Organization leaflet was reprinted in *The Movement*, vol. 2, no. 10 (November 1966).

87. Interview with Sutton.

88. Interview with Sutton.

89. Interview with Sutton.

90. Forman, "The Philadelphia Black Paper," 1; Stokely Carmichael, "What We Want," *New York Review of Books*, Sept. 22, 1966.

91. "How to Handle Demonstrations," *Time*, Dec. 9, 1966; Paolantonio, *Frank Rizzo*, 93.

92. On Rizzo's scuffle with the Young Militants, see Chapter 4.

93. Interview with Sutton; "Philadelphians Salute Malcolm X at Police-Guarded Ceremony Here"; "Beaten SNCC Worker Claims 'Harassment' After 'Wild Wednesday,' " *Philadelphia Tribune*, Aug. 13, 1966; Forman, *The Making of Black Revolutionaries*, 461–62; Forman, "Philadelphia Black Paper," 3.

94. *Bulletin*, Aug. 13, 16, and 20, 1966; *New York Times*, Aug. 14, 1966; "Six Arrested Following Big Police Rampage," *Philadelphia Tribune*, Aug. 16, 1966; Terence Cannon, "1,000 Cops with Machine Guns 'Find' 2 1/2 Sticks of Dynamite in Philadelphia, Try to Pin it on SNCC," *The Movement*, vol. 2, no. 8 (Sept. 1966); interview with Churchville; Paolantonio, *Frank Rizzo*, 84–85. See Forman, *The Making of Black Revolutionaries*, 460–71, and "Philadelphia Black Paper," for further discussion of the dynamite case.

95. *Bulletin*, Aug. 13, 16, and 20, 1966; *New York Times*, Aug. 15, 1966; Cannon, "1,000 Cops with Machine Guns."

96. *Bulletin*, Aug. 13, 16, and 20, 1966; "3 Are Held, 3 Freed in Dynamite Case," *Bulletin*, Aug. 22, 1966; *New York Times*, Aug. 15, 1966; Cannon, "1,000 Cops with Machine Guns"; "Six Arrested Following Big Police Rampage"; Forman, "Philadelphia Black Paper," 6.

97. *Bulletin*, Aug. 13, 16, and 20, 1966; *New York Times*, Aug. 15, 1966; "Missing SNCC Official Blasted for Leaving Aides Holding the Bag," *Philadelphia Tribune*, Aug. 16, 1966; Cannon, "1,000 Cops with Machine Guns"; Forman, "Philadelphia Black Paper," 6–10.

98. Interview with Sutton; Forman, "Philadelphia Black Paper," 3; *New York Times*, Aug. 15, 1966; Forman, *The Making of Black Revolutionaries*, 462.

99. Forman also announced that he would temporarily direct the Philadelphia project and named Meely "director-in-exile." *Bulletin*, Aug. 20, 1966; Cannon, "1,000 Cops with Machine Guns"; Forman, *The Making of Black Revolutionaries*, 465; Forman, "Philadelphia Black Paper," 6.

100. Cannon, "1,000 Cops with Machine Guns"; "3 Are Held, 3 Freed in Dynamite Case."

101. "3 Are Held, 3 Freed in Dynamite Case"; *Bulletin*, Apr. 22, 1967; Forman, *The Making of Black Revolutionaries*, 467–68, and "Philadelphia Black Paper". Charyn Sutton also remembers that the staff discovered and removed the dynamite just days before the raid. Interview with Sutton. On the disposition of the dynamite case, see United States Commission on Civil Rights, Pennsylvania Advisory Committee, "Police-Community Relations: A Report to the United States Commission on Civil Rights," Philadelphia, June 1972.

102. Forman, *The Making of Black Revolutionaries*, 470, and "Philadelphia Black Paper," 1–2.

103. See Chapters 6 and 7 for a discussion of these issues.

Chapter 6. Community Control and the Schools

1. "Black Power Pickets Battle Police," *Bulletin*, Nov. 17, 1967; interviews with Walter Palmer, Aug. 10, 2004, Philadelphia and Joan Countryman, Mar. 16, 1994, New York. Students at some schools had a more difficult time getting to the school board. Paul Washington's son Kemah and two of his classmates walked out of predominately white Saul Agricultural High School in the far northwest neighborhood of Roxborough during a morning break. However, a school counselor chased the three in a car, returned them to the school and then made sure that all school doors were locked on the inside. Paul M. Washington with David McI. Gracie, *"Other Sheep I Have": The Autobiography of Father Paul Washington* (Philadelphia: Temple University Press, 1994), 63.

2. The Administration building fills a square block just south of the intersection of Twenty-first Street and the Benjamin Franklin Parkway. The actual block is boarded by Twenty-first, Winter, Spring, and Van Pelt streets.

3. "Black Power Pickets Battle Police," and "Dilworth Blames Police; Rizzo Cites Warning," *Bulletin*, Nov. 17, 1967; "Mathis Says He Was a Peacemaker, Not Agitator in Disorders," *Bulletin*, Nov. 21, 1967; Washington, *"Other Sheep I Have"*, 63.

4. Interview with Palmer. Among the sources for the latter version of events is Mattie Humphrey. Interview with Mattie Humphrey, Mar. 16, 1994, Philadelphia. Whether the discrepancy is the result of faulty memories or the student activists, their adult allies, and school officials made a deliberate decision to have the meeting appear to have been spontaneous is unclear to me. Given the amount of preparation that went into developing the student demands and, as I discuss later in the chapter, the pattern of cooperation between the Shedd administration and BPUM activists, I tend to credit Palmer's account. For a version of events similar to Humphrey's, see "Mathis Says He Was a Peacemaker."

5. "Black Power Pickets Battle Police"; "Dilworth Blames Police; Rizzo Cites His Warning"; "Rizzo Cuts All Leaves, Deploys Men," *Bulletin*, Nov. 18, 1967; Washington, *"Other Sheep I Have"*, 64–66; interviews with Palmer and Humphrey; interview with John Churchville, Feb. 16, 1994, Philadelphia; "Report on Clash Between Police and Pupils on November, 17, 1967," Fellowship Commission (FC) collection, box 22, folder 17, Temple University Urban Archives (TUUA).

6. Interview with Palmer; "Black Power Pickets Battle Police"; "Dilworth Blames Police; Rizzo Cites Warning"; "Mathis Says He Was a Peacemaker, Not Agitator in Disorders"; Washington, *"Other Sheep I Have"*, 63. Dilworth would later credit Fencl with keeping "things until control" during the morning.

7. "Black Power Pickets Battle Police"; "Rizzo Cuts All Leaves, Deploys Men"; "Mathis Says He Was a Peacemaker."

8. Washington, *"Other Sheep I Have"*, 64–66; interview with Steve Gold, Feb. 10, 1994, Philadelphia; "Report on Clash Between Police and Pupils on November 17, 1967"; "Black Power Pickets Battle Police"; "Hutt, Nichols Complain About Rizzo to Bowser" and "Mathis and Palmer Are Released; Bail Cut From $50,000 to $5,000," *Bulletin*, Nov. 19, 1967; "Caught Up in a Street Riot: How It Looked to the Victims," *Bulletin*, Nov. 26, 1967; "Nichols Rebuts Rizzo Claim of Pupil 'Mob,'" *Bulletin*, Dec. 13, 1967. For a sympathetic view of Rizzo's actions during the demonstration, see S.A. Paolantonio, *Frank Rizzo: The Last Big Man in Big City America* (Philadelphia: Camino Books, 1993), 91–95.

9. Interviews with Humphrey and Palmer; "Dilworth Says Police Provoked Pupil Rioting," *Bulletin*, Nov. 18, 1967; "Hutt, Nichols Complain About Rizzo to Bowser"; "Cop Brutality Protests Flood Tribune Office," *Philadelphia Tribune*, Nov. 21, 1967; "Caught Up in a Street Riot: How It Looked to the Victims"; "Rizzo Blasts Black

Power, Tells Court of Pupil 'Mob,' " *Bulletin,* Dec. 12, 1967; "Report on Clash Between Police and Pupils on November 17, 1967." According to both Humphrey and Palmer, she was so upset by what she saw through the school board windows that she picked up a log from a fireplace in the meeting room and ran down to the building's front steps where she bumped into Palmer. She then gave the log to Palmer.

10. "Black Power Pickets Battle Police"; "Rizzo Cuts All Leaves, Deploys Men"; "Rizzo Blasts Black Power, Tells Court of Pupil 'Mob' "; "Caught Up in a Street Riot: How It Looked to the Victims"; Washington, *"Other Sheep I Have",* 66.

11. Judge Raymond Pace Alexander would later reduce Palmer and Mathis's bond to $5,000. Interview with Palmer; "Black Power Pickets Battle Police"; "Rizzo Cuts All Leaves, Deploys Men"; "Mathis and Palmer Are Released; Bail Cut"; "Mathis Says He Was a Peacemaker"; "Rizzo Blasts Black Power, Tells Court of Pupil 'Mob' "; "Magistrate Defies DA, Holds Militant for Court," *Bulletin,* Mar. 17, 1968.

12. Interview with Palmer; interviews with Edward Robinson, Aug. 11, 2004, and Thomas Gilhool, Mar. 14, 1994, both in Philadelphia. Since its founding, PTP went through an evolution that in many ways resembled the development of the Freedom Library, albeit without the black nationalist ideological frame. Beginning in its second year, PTP began to shift its focus from recruiting (white) college students as tutors to asking black high school students to serve as tutors for elementary and middle school students. According to Steve Gold, PTP's director at the time, the shift was based on the growing recognition that tutors gained from the tutoring relationship as much if not more than their students. Then, in 1966, PTP board member William Cannady. a guidance counselor at North Philadelphia's Gratz High School, recruited a white Temple University chaplain named David Hornbeck to take the position of PTP executive director. Under Hornbeck's leadership, PTP began to focus as much on parent organizing as on tutoring programs. In Hornbeck's view, tutoring was little more than a band-aid so long as poor black children were being underserved by their public schools. With funding from President Johnson's War on Poverty, PTP's staff and parent activists developed a citywide network of "Educational Self-Help Centers" to serve as both tutoring sites and organizing centers for parents seeking greater involvement in their children's schools. It was in this shared commitment to increasing black community participation in the management of public schools that the BPUM education committee and the Self-Help Centers found common ground. Interviews with Gold, Humphrey, and Gilhool.

13. See William L. Van DeBurg, *New Day in Babylon: The Black Power Movement and American Culture, 1965–1975* (Chicago: University of Chicago Press, 1992), for an excellent account of the confluence of national events that led to the emergence of the Black Power movement.

14. Interviews with Palmer and Robinson.

15. Interviews with Palmer and Robinson. Interview with Elaine Richardson, Aug. 12, 2004, Philadelphia.

16. Interviews with Palmer and Robinson.

17. Interview with Palmer.

18. A 1964 NAACP convention resolution to establish "multiple branches" in cities of more than 250,000 had already been implemented in Houston, Dallas, and Los Angeles. "Moore Silent on Split of NAACP Into 5 Units," *Philadelphia Tribune,* Nov. 2, 1965; "Moore Raps National NAACP Plan to Split Local, Dump Him," *Philadelphia Daily News,* Nov. 4, 1965; "Moore Hits Nat'l Office Plan to Split Local Naacp," *Philadelphia Tribune,* Nov. 6, 1965; " 'NAACP Voted Against Split 291–5'—

Moore," *Philadelphia Tribune*, Nov. 23, 1965; "NAACP Here Votes to Resist Order to Split," *Bulletin*, Dec. 3, 1965; "Judge Reed Calls for NAACP Unity at Meet," *Bulletin*, Mar. 12, 1966; "NAACP Chief Says He'll End Moore's Reign," *Bulletin*, May 10, 1966; "NAACP Orders Moore to Yield Phila. Charter," *Bulletin*, May 20, 1966; "Cecil Moore Predicts Riots in Center City," *Philadelphia Tribune*, May 28, 1966; "NAACP Votes to Split Phila. Chapter; Moore Hits 'Insincerity for Masses,'" *Bulletin*, Jun. 9, 1966.

19. *Philadelphia Tribune*, Apr. 5, 1967; "Savage Says Moore 'Rapes' NAACP Till," *Bulletin*, Apr. 19, 1967; "Moore Admits NAACP Charge," *Bulletin*, Apr. 21, 1967; "Moore's NAACP Domain Being Cut to Pieces as Savage Wields the Axe," *Philadelphia Tribune*, Apr. 29, 1967; "NAACP Shifts Moore to Unity in North Phila.," *Bulletin*, May 17, 1967; "Wilkins Says Phila. NAACP Split Is 'Not an Anti-Cecil Moore Move,'" *Bulletin*, May 21, 1967; "Block NAACP Move to Split Local Branch," *Philadelphia Tribune*, Jul. 5, 1967; "Los Angeles Convention Okays Split of Phila. NAACP Branch After Court Here Sweeps Aside Last Minute Legal Barrier," *Philadelphia Tribune*, Jul. 9, 1967; "Wilkins Ousts Moore as Head of NAACP Unit," *Bulletin*, Jul. 14, 1967; "Cecil Moore Is Suspended by NAACP," *Philadelphia Inquirer*, Jul. 15, 1967; "State Supreme Court Order Delays NAACP Branch Split 6 Months," *Philadelphia Tribune*, Jul. 23, 1967. In September 1968, the NAACP national board confirmed the decision to suspend Moore. "NAACP Upholds Suspension Of Moore as Branch Chief," *Bulletin*, Sep. 10, 1968.

20. Moore had long defended the NAACP's tradition of having a white national board chairperson—even as he criticized the reliability of white liberals. However, after NAACP national board chair Kivie Kaplan publicly attacked his leadership of the Philadelphia branch, Moore called for the national organization to appoint a black board chair. "The white man," he declared, "can walk along side us from now on, but he can never again walk in front of us. The black man is going to lead because this is a black organization." "Moore Raps National NAACP Plan to Split Local, Dump Him," *Philadelphia Daily News*, Nov. 4, 1965; "Moore Plans Rallies to Fight Split in NAACP," *Bulletin*, May 23 and Sep. 12, 1966; "Moore Is Organizing 'Black Unity' Group After Court Rebuff," *Bulletin*, May 23, 1967.

21. "Moore Running for Mayor at Top of All-Negro Slate," *Bulletin*, Mar. 7, 1967; "Cecil Moore Names First 4 Running Mates," *Bulletin*, Mar. 15, 1967; "Candidates Vie with Frug at Teen-Age Charity Ball," *Bulletin*, Mar. 21, 1967; "Moore Opens His Campaign for Mayor; His Slogan Is Moore for Negroes and Whites," *Bulletin*, Sep. 20, 1967.

22. On Rizzo's appointment, see Greg Walter, "Rizzo: A Fearless Cop Has His Work Cut Out for Him in Philadelphia in 1967," *Greater Philadelphia Magazine* (Jan. 1967); and Paolantonio, *Frank Rizzo*, 87.

23. *Bulletin*, Jun. 12, 1967; Walter, "Rizzo: A Fearless Cop Has His Work Cut Out for Him."

24. "Police Halt Moore Rally at 15th, South," *Bulletin*, Jul. 18, 1967; "Moore Threatens Rallies Every Week," *Philadelphia Inquirer*, Jun. 19, 1967; "Moore Speaks to 500 at Two Rallies," *Bulletin*, Jun. 25, 1967; *Bulletin*, Jun. 27, Jul. 7, 9, and 16, 1967; "Excerpts from Speeches made at Cecil B. Moore Rallies," and "Can a Leopard Named Rizzo Change Its Spots?," Rally Flier, Housing Association of the Delaware Valley [HADV] collection, box 107e, folder 41, TUUA; "Saturday, July 1, 1967—Civil Disobedience Demonstration at 16th & South Streets," FC collection, box 58, folder 16, TUUA.

25. "Police Halt Moore Rally at 15th, South"; "Excerpts from Speeches Made at Cecil B. Moore Rallies"; "Moore Speaks to 500 at Two Rallies."

26. "Rizzo Quells Disorders in South Phila.," *Bulletin*, Jul. 27, 1967; "Mayor Bans

Gatherings of 12 or More," *Bulletin*, Jul. 28, 1967; "Rizzo Testifies Mayor's Edict Prevented Riots," *Bulletin*, Aug. 8, 1967.

27. "Rizzo Quells Disorders in South Phila."; "Mayor Bans Gatherings of 12 or More." On the emergency proclamation, see Spencer Coxe, "Philadelphia Authorities Melt Away Rights of Individuals During Long, Hot Summer," *Civil Liberties Record*, Oct. 1967, 3.

28. "Hoover Links Carmichael to Negro Leftist Group," *New York Times*, May 17, 1967; Max Stanford, "Who Are the Rams or What Is a Ram?" *Nite Life*, July 4, 1967, and "Ram Believes That the U.S. Owes Afro-Americans 880 Million Acres of Land," *Nite Life*, July 11, 1967; "Rizzo Quells Disorders in South Phila."; "4 Racists Accused of Cyanide Plot to Kill Hundreds Here," *Bulletin*, Sep. 27, 1967. The SAC memorandum is quoted in Ward Churchill, *Agents of Repression: The FBI War Against the Black Panther Party and the American Indian Movement*, (Boston: South End Press, 1988), 46. On RAM, see Robin D. G. Kelley, *Freedom Dreams: The Black Radical Imagination*, (Boston: Beacon Press, 2002), 60–109. On police harassment of Black Power activists, see also Kenneth O'Reilly, *Racial Matters: The FBI's Secret File on Black America, 1960–72* (New York: Free Press, 1989), 229–360, and Winston A. Grady-Willlis, "The Black Panther Party: State Repression and Political Prisoners," in Charles Jones, ed., *The Black Panther Party Reconsidered* ((Baltimore: Black Classic Press, 1998), 369–389.

29. "Rizzo Quells Disorders in South Phila."; "6th Youth Held Under $10,000 Bail Here on Charge of Inciting to Riot, Conspiracy," *Bulletin*, Aug. 1, 1967; " 'Black Guard' Assailed in Court by DA," *Bulletin*, Aug. 9, 1967.

30. Churchill, *Agents of Repression*, 45–46; "4 Racists Accused of Cyanide Plot to Kill Hundreds Here"; "RAM Plotted to Wreck Hall, Convict Says," *Bulletin*, Sep. 28, 1967; "Police Reveal Arrests of 35 RAM Leaders," *Bulletin*, Oct. 8, 1967.

31. Frantz Fanon, *The Wretched of the Earth*, 29–74; Malcolm X, "The Black Revolution," April 8, 1964, reprinted in George Breitman, ed., *Malcolm X Speaks* (New York: Grove Weidenfeld, 1990), 49–50.

32. "Arise! Awake! Your Future is at Stake!," n.d., Wharton Centre [WC] collection, box 43, TUUA; Stanford, "Who Are the Rams or What Is a Ram?" For an incisive discussion of the presence of informants in black revolutionary organizations, see Mumia Abu-Jamal, *We Want Freedom: A Life in the Black Panther Party* (Cambridge, Mass.: South End Press, 2004), 117–58.

33. Interview with Palmer.

34. *Bulletin*, Oct. 26 and 27, 1967; "Gratz Student Injured During Demonstration," *Philadelphia Tribune*, Oct. 28, 1967; "Negro History Courses Demanded by Students," *Philadelphia Tribune*, Nov. 4, 1967.

35. "Negro History Courses Demanded by Students"; "Police Arrest 5 Student Protest Leaders at Bok; Tension Grows as Faculty Mulls Negro Demands," *Philadelphia Tribune*, Nov. 18, 1967.

36. According to 1969–1970 figures, Gratz was 99.5 percent black and Germantown was 85.4 percent black. Office of Research and Education, School District of Philadelphia, "Enrollment: Negro and Spanish-Speaking Students in the Philadelphia Public Schools, 1969–1970," Floyd Logan (FL) collection, box 4, TUUA.

37. "Alleged Racist Remarks Trigger School Scandal," *Philadelphia Tribune*, Apr. 1, 1967; "S. Phila. High Halts Classes After Incidents," *Bulletin*, Apr. 3, 1967; "S. Phila. High Teacher Apologizes to Negroes," *Bulletin*, Apr. 4, 1967; "23 Whites, 1 Negro Injured In South Philly High Riot," *Philadelphia Tribune*, Apr. 4, 1967. In the 1969–1970 school year, South Philadelphia High School was 51.1 percent black. Office of Research and Education, "Enrollment: Negro and Spanish-Speaking Students."

38. "Bok, Dobbins Accused of Channeling Negroes to 'Low Job' Courses," *Philadelphia Tribune*, Nov. 2, 1968; "Report—Edward Bok Technical High School, May 1963"; "Report—Edward Bok Technical High School," n.d.; Observations Regarding Mr. Samuel Cooper's Rebuttal to the Edward Bok Technical High School Report, Feb. 1967," FL collection, box 4, TUUA. During the 1968–1969 school year, Bok's student body was 85.2 percent black. William T. Kelly, director of vocational education to Floyd L. Logan, May 2, 1969, FL collection, box 12, TUUA.

39. "Whites Foaming with Racial Hatred Accuse Students; Negroes Frightened," *Philadelphia Tribune*, Oct. 12, 1968; "Ten Days of Disorder: Pupils, Neighbors and Faculty Describe Crisis," *Bulletin*, Oct. 20, 1968. See also "Whites, Negroes Disagree on Cause of Bok Tension," *Bulletin*, Oct. 15, 1968, and Commission on Human Relations memorandum re: "Bok School Incidents and Related Events," n.d., FC collection, box 56, folder 2, TUUA.

40. On Dilworth's appointment to the school board, see "View Dilworth as School Board Head With Mixed Emotions," *Philadelphia Tribune*, Sep. 4, 1965; "NAACP Prexy and Minister Blast Choices," *Philadelphia Tribune*, Sep. 7, 1965; "NAACP Blasts Lack of Women," *Philadelphia Tribune*, Sep. 11, 1965; and "School Board Member Calls Dilworth 'Timid,'" *Bulletin*, Nov. 20, 1967. On Shedd's appointment, see "3 Considered by Board for Whittier's Job," *Bulletin*, Nov. 18, 1966; and "D'Ortona Raps Shedd's Action in Disorder," *Bulletin*, Nov. 23, 1967. On Shedd's decision to send his children to black schools, see "New School Superintendent Sending His Children to 90% Negro School," *Philadelphia Tribune*, Sept. 12, 1967.

41. Interview with Humphrey; "City Defends Police Action in Pupil Riot," *Bulletin*, Dec. 11, 1967.

42. "'Vote Black,' Moore Tells Midcity Rally," *Bulletin*, Nov. 3, 1967; "Moore Urges Teaching of More 'Black History,'" *Bulletin*, Nov. 3, 1967; "Candidate Moore Delights Crowds Barnstorming for Black Man's Vote," *Bulletin*, Nov. 5, 1967. For the election results, see *Bulletin*, Nov. 7, 1967.

43. "Police Arrest 5 Student Protest Leaders at Bok; Tension Grows as Faculty Mulls Negro Demands."

44. Interviews with Humphrey, Palmer and Countryman. "Black Power Pickets Battle Police"; "Dilworth Blames Police; Rizzo Cites His Warning"; "Dilworth Says Police Provoked Pupil Rioting." During the march, BPUM posted adult activists, including members of People for Human Rights (PHR), a predominately white New Left organization committed to organizing whites in support of the Black Power movement, outside schools across the city to help guide the students along the pre-planned routes to Center City. For example, PHR activist, and former Northern Student Movement executive director, Peter Countryman was assigned to help guide the students from Germantown High. In an apparent attempt to disrupt the march, police officers detained him and eventually drove him to his in-laws house in Mount Airy to confirm his identity. Interview with Joan Countryman. For a superb discussion of PHR and the politics of white antiracism in this period, see Paul Lyons, *The People of This Generation: The Rise and Fall of the New Left in Philadelphia* (Philadelphia: University of Pennsylvania Press, 2003), 167–92.

45. School board vice president Henry Nichols called on the local television stations to show unedited footage of the demonstration to validate his charges that the police had committed numerous acts of brutality. "If I'm wrong," the school board vice president declared, "I'm perfectly willing to resign. If not, I want the commissioner to resign." Others calling for Rizzo's resignation included black school board member George Hutt, deejay Georgie Woods, the Philadelphia

ACLU, the Citizens' Committee on Public Education, and the American Friends Service Committee. During a bail hearing in which he agreed to release William Mathis and Walter Palmer under a $5,000 bond that had been raised by a committee of clergy and citizens, Judge Raymond Pace Alexander criticized the police commissioner for "unnecessary and unwarranted use of physical violence." The Barristers' Club of Philadelphia, an organization of black lawyers, called on the U.S. Civil Rights Commission to investigate police brutality in Philadelphia. Community Legal Services, a federally funded antipoverty agency, filed suit in federal court on behalf of students who said they were beaten during the demonstration. The suit demanded that Commissioner Rizzo be removed and the police department be placed under federal receivership. Washington, *"Other Sheep I Have"*, 66–69; "Black Power Pickets Battle Police"; "Dilworth Says Police Provoked Pupil Rioting"; "Hutt, Nichols Complain About Rizzo to Bowser"; "Mathis and Palmer Are Released; Bail Cut"; "School Board Member Calls Dilworth 'Timid,'" *Bulletin*, Nov. 20, 1967; "Shedd Restates Schools' Need for Discipline," *Bulletin*, Nov. 21, 1967; "Disc Jockey Asks Mayor Tate to Act," *Philadelphia Tribune*, Nov. 21, 1967; *Bulletin*, Nov. 22, 1967; "Caught Up in a Street Riot: How It Looked to the Victims'; "Charges of Police Brutality Lodged Against Commissioner," *Philadelphia Tribune*, Nov. 28, 1968; "Nichols Rebuts Rizzo Claim of Pupil 'Mob,'" *Bulletin*, Dec. 13, 1967; "'Right of Assembly' Is Seen Issue in Rizzo Ouster Trial," *Philadelphia Tribune*, Dec. 23, 1968; "Police Brutal, Witnesses Say In Rizzo Suit," *Bulletin*, Jan. 2, 1968.

46. "Rizzo Is Praised, Criticized," *Philadelphia Inquirer*, Nov. 18, 1967; "School Board Member Calls Dilworth 'Timid'"; "Shedd Restates Schools' Need For Discipline"; "White Citizens Flock to Sign Petition Backing Commissioner Rizzo's Action," *Philadelphia Tribune*, Nov. 21, 1967; "D'Ortona Raps Shedd's Action in Disorder" and "Rizzo Backers Stage Rally; Leader Knifed," *Bulletin*, Nov. 23, 1967.

47. "Rizzo Lauds Coverage of Riot News," *Philadelphia Inquirer*, Oct. 3, 1967; "Dilworth Blames Police; Rizzo Cites His Warning," *Bulletin*, Nov. 17, 1967; *Philadelphia Inquirer*, Nov. 18, 1967. See also "Black Power Threatens City, Rizzo Says," *Bulletin*, Nov. 23, 1967.

48. Bowser would later claim that Tate might well have fired Rizzo if black leaders had remained quiet. "Henry Nichols made Rizzo," Bowser argues. "If they had never demanded Rizzo's resignation, no one would ever have known how strong he was politically." Interview with Charles Bowser, Mar. 10, 1994, Philadelphia.

49. "Court Orders Wider Ban on School Rallies," *Bulletin*, Dec. 7, 1967, "Hutt, Nichols Complain About Rizzo to Bowser"; "Militant Youths Eject Reporter from Meeting," *Bulletin*, Nov. 20, 1967; Washington, *"Other Sheep I Have"*, 66; interview with Humphrey.

50. "Leaders Paid $350 Each to Discuss Race Problems and the School System," *Philadelphia Tribune*, Dec. 19, 1967; Richard H. de Lone to Charles Simpson, Mar. 8, 1968, FC collection, box 35, folder 29, TUUA; "Shedd Admits He Erred in Letting Militants Speak," *Bulletin*, Oct. 16, 1968; Commission on Decentralization and Community Participation, School District of Philadelphia, "Community Participation in the Schools of Philadelphia," Dec. 1968, Ben Stahl [BS] collection, box III, TUUA; "Remove Racial Slurs, Shedd Orders Gratz," *Bulletin*, May 5, 1970.

51. "Black Militant Gets Mixed Reaction from Germantown Pupils, Faculty," *Bulletin*, Jun. 22, 1968; "150 Teachers 'Rap' at Olney over Hostility Among Pupils," *Bulletin*, Feb. 25, 1970; "Remove Racial Slurs, Shedd Orders Gratz."

52. "Teachers' Union Hits Appeasement of Black Students," *Philadelphia Tribune*, Dec. 2, 1967. Following the union's statement, a group of primarily black teachers that had formed in the aftermath of the November 17 demonstrations and called itself Teachers Concerned secured pledges from 1,300 teachers to resign

from the union if it did not acknowledge the legitimacy of the student demonstrators' grievances. "Teachers' President Is Criticized; Blames Students for Starting Riot," *Philadelphia Tribune*, Dec. 5, 1968; "Teacher Union Changes Stand on Pupil Rally," *Bulletin*, Jan. 2, 1968; "Negro Teachers-Union Row a Misunderstanding?" *Bulletin*, Jan. 7, 1968.

53. Charles T. Askew, "Why the Negro Teachers Are Fed Up with Union," *Philadelphia Tribune*, Dec. 19, 1967; "Circulars Accuse Some Appointees of Being 'Black Power Agitators," *Philadelphia Tribune*, Jan. 9, 1968; "Settlement Looming on Integration Aides," *Philadelphia Inquirer*, Jan. 21, 1968; "7 Accept School Appointments as Racial Field Agents," *Bulletin*, Feb. 6, 1968; Richard H. de Lone to Charles Simpson, Mar. 8, 1968; "Black Militant Get Mixed Reaction From Germantown Pupils, Faculty"; "Shedd Admits He Erred in Letting Militants Speak"; "150 Teachers 'Rap' at Olney over Hostility Among Pupils"; "Remove Racial Slurs, Shedd Orders Gratz."

54. "Community Participation in the Schools of Philadelphia"; "Young Negroes Seek Funds to Run Summer Schools—Minus Supervisors," *Philadelphia Inquirer*, Apr. 28, 1968; "Black Militant Gets Mixed Reaction From Germantown Pupils, Faculty"; memorandum from Millard T. Meers to Dr. Mark R. Shedd, Oct. 10, 1968, FC collection box 36, folder 12, TUUA.

55. In February 1966, both the Philadelphia NAACP and Citizens for Progress, a West Philadelphia community group, publicly called on the Johnson administration to suspend federal funds to the Philadelphia school district because of the school board's unwillingness to institute "a plan whereby Negro children will get an equitable share of the city's resources in terms of schools, materials and teachers." "West Phila. Citizens Group Asks Gov't to Stop School Funds," *Philadelphia Tribune*, Feb. 15, 1966.

56. Shedd's appointment as school superintendent was a direct result of the failure of his predecessor, C. Taylor Whittier, to produce a satisfactory integration program. Civil rights activists were particularly frustrated by Whittier's reliance on voluntary mechanisms to combat segregation. For example, in April 1966, the Rev. Jesse Anderson, chairman of the Philadelphia Urban League's education committee, called Whittier's open enrollment policy, which purported to allow students to attend any school of their choosing, "a damn lie." The Episcopal priest claimed to have repeatedly attempted to enroll black students in white schools only to be told that the schools were full. Anderson further ridiculed the claim of the head of the school board's Office of Integration that the district had never purposively drawn school boundaries in order "to segregate children." "How else," he asked, "did West Philadelphia High get to be an all-Negro school when right behind it the neighborhood is all-white?" "Pastor Calls Phila. 'Open School' Policy 'Damn Lie," *Philadelphia Tribune*, Apr. 14, 1966; "Whittier Says He Will Leave Post Next Year," *Bulletin*, Sep. 22, 1966.

57. The school districted responded to an order from the Pennsylvania Human Relations Commission and the Pennsylvania Department of Public Instruction to "submit [a] plan . . . to eliminate the racial imbalance in their schools" by July 1, 1968, by arguing it should be required only to enact a voluntary desegregation plan and once again cited the demands of black parents and students for community control of blacks school to justify its request. Chronology of Relations Between Philadelphia School District and Pennsylvania Human Relations Commission Regarding School Desegregation, n.d., FC collection, box 35, folder 45, TUUA; Office of Integration and Intergroup Education, School District of Philadelphia, "Summary: Desegregation Report, Philadelphia Public Schools"; Maurice B. Fagan to Charles G. Simpson, Dec. 23, 1966, FC collection, box 4, TUUA. By 1966, the 150,000 white

students attending the city's 90 percent white Catholic schools outnumbered the 110,000 white students in the public schools. For a similar argument about the Shedd administration's approach to school desegregation, see Vincent P. Franklin, *The Education of Black Philadelphia* (Philadelphia: University of Pennsylvania Press, 1979), 201–02.

58. The commission's order was the result of a complaint from the Educational Equality League (EEL), a black-led organization that had fought for equal opportunity for black teachers in the Philadelphia school system for more than two decades. Office of Integration and Intergroup Education, School District of Philadelphia Public Schools, "Progress Report on Integration in the Philadelphia Public Schools," March 1966, FL collection, box 9, TUUA; and "Remarks to the Board of Education Hearings on Task Force Reports: Bishop Robert L. DeWitt, Chair, Citizens Advisory Committee to the Superintendent on Integration and Intergroup Education," Sep. 31, 1966, FC collection, box 36, folder 26, TUUA.

59. The policy of last resort also allowed any teacher forced to shift schools to appeal to an arbitrator on the basis that the transfer would cause "severe hardship." "Teacher Integration Plan Shelved After Clash at Stormy Meeting," *Philadelphia Tribune*, Oct. 16, 1965; "Teacher Integration Issue Too Hot to Handle," *Philadelphia Tribune*, Nov. 6, 1965; "School Board Tables Teacher Integration," *Philadelphia Tribune*, Apr. 14, 1966; "School Board Approves New Teacher Pact," *Bulletin*, Sep. 13, 1966. On the Human Relations Commission suit, see memorandum to All Commissioners from Nathan Agran, General Counsel, Nov. 14, 1967, FC collection, box 35, folder 28, TUUA; "State Human Relations Commission Orders School Integration by 1969," *Philadelphia Tribune*, Dec. 30, 1967. On the revised mandatory transfer program, see "Schools Will Be Open Regardless of Strike; Urge Pupils to Attend," *Philadelphia Tribune*, Sep. 7, 1968; "School Desegregation Plan Drafted, Ready for Board," *Philadelphia Tribune*, Sep. 17, 1968; *Philadelphia Tribune*, Sep. 24, 1967.

60. On the May 1967 "vote no" campaign, see "Negro Clergy Score Schools," *Philadelphia Inquirer*, May 1, 1967; "Board, Urban League Juggle Integration Issue," *Bulletin*, May 7, 1967; "Vote No" flier, n.d., and "A Reply to a WCAU-TV Editorial of May 10, 1967," May 11, 1967, West Philadelphia School Committee (WPSC) collection, box 1, TUUA; and Coalition for Integrated Quality Education, "Why No to the School Charter Amendment," May 1967; West Philadelphia Schools Committee, "Campaign to Defeat Charter Amendment," n.d.; and Flier, Germantown Branch NAACP, WPSC collection, box 2, TUUA. The Philadelphia NAACP had led a campaign against a 1966 school bond issue, but had received very little support from other groups in the black community. See "NAACP Board Votes 'No' To School Loan," *Philadelphia Tribune*, May 7, 1966.

61. Specifically, the Urban League plan suggested that the school district replace its plans for sixty new neighborhood schools with twenty education parks to be built over fifteen years. Sixteen of these parks would be designed to have enrollments that were 70 percent black; the other four would be located in the nearly all-white Northeast section of the city and would be 70 percent white. See Office of Information Services, School District of Philadelphia, "A Digest of Testimony Presented to the Board of Education at Public Hearings Concerning the Proposed 1966 Capital Budget, Apr. 18–21, 1966, FC collection, box 35, folder 10, TUUA; "School Board Urged to Aid Integration, Not Block Path," *Philadelphia Tribune*, Apr. 23, 1966; WCAU-TV editorial, May 10, 1967, WPSC collection, box I, TUUA; Philadelphia Urban League, "What Is an Educational Park," WC collection, box 58, TUUA.

62. "School Loan Question Approved by Voters," *Philadelphia Inquirer*, May 17,

1967; PCCA Schools Project Newsletter, vol. 1, no. 2, Feb. 1967, FC collection, box 4, TUUA; *Bulletin*, Mar. 21, 1967. On the debate over the Urban League's education parks proposal, see Office of Integration and Intergroup Education, School District of Philadelphia, "Minutes of the Meeting of the Citizens Advisory Committee," Mar. 1 and Mar. 23, 1967, FL collection, box 8, TUUA; "Discussion Memorandum on Educational Parks," Mar. 14, 1967, FC collection, box 4, TUUA. On liberal support for the 1967 school debt question see "Dear Community Leader Letter," Larry Groth, Commission on Human Relations, May 20, 1966, WPSC collection, box I, TUUA.

63. Address by Dr. Mark Shedd to the Staff—May 18, 1967," 6–7, FC collection, box 38, folder 11, TUUA; *Bulletin*, Jul. 13, 1967; "Superintendent Hopes Model School District Can Become Reality in North Philadelphia," *Philadelphia Tribune,* Nov. 21, 1967. To those who charged that the model district would only increase school segregation, Dr. Shedd replied that the district's boundaries would be drawn in ways that promoted integration and that the quality of its schools would convince white parents to bus their children to this "dream school district." In contrast, William Mathis and other Black Power activists criticized the model district proposal not for promoting school segregation but for failing to insure substantive community participation in its governance structure.

64. "PCCA: Schools Project Source Book: Change in the Philadelphia Public Schools," PCCA collection, box 1, TUUA; "Community Participation in the Schools of Philadelphia."

65. The commission's complaint began the longest desegregation court case in the nation's history. After the court upheld the commission's order that the school district submit a three-tier plan to eliminate all racially imbalanced schools, the district submitted such a plan on February 15, 1974. The commission, however, rejected the plan and in April 1974 asked the court to appoint a special master to develop a plan for the school district. The court appointed Dr. David H. Kurtzman on June 4, 1974, to improve the school district's desegregation plan. After another year of public hearings, the plan was submitted back to the court on July 7, 1975. "Chronology of Relations Between the Philadelphia School District and the Pennsylvania Human Relations Commission Regarding School Desegregation" and "Desegregation Guidelines for Public Schools," Mar. 29, 1969, BS collection, box 1, TUUA; Pennsylvania Human Relations Commission v. School District of Philadelphia, docket P-697, FC collection, box 11, TUUA.

66. In July, a member of the white 2–4 Counts gangs was shot; the gang promised to kill a black person in revenge. In September, the lack of police protection at a community center dance at Twenty-second and Snyder streets led to an interracial melee with bottles and bricks thrown. Later, a group of black parents marched on the neighborhood police precinct to protest a racial imbalance in police protection in the area. But it was less the big events than the day-to-day small conflicts and the constant potential for interracial violence that set the stage for the events of October 1968. "Discord Grows in South Phila. as Black Pressure Increases," *Bulletin*, Oct. 10, 1968.

67. Memorandum from Meers to Dr. Shedd, Oct. 10, 1968; "Discord Grows in South Phila. as Black Pressure Increases"; "Whites Foaming with Racial Hatred Accuse Students"; "Ten Days of Disorders: Pupils, Neighbors and Faculty Describe Crisis."

68. There were, however, a number of reports from white students over the course of the day that they had been attacked by black students. "Normally white students don't have any trouble with the blacks," one white student would later tell a reporter. "It's just when there's an uprising that it's unsafe to come here to

school." A black student admitted that "a lot of guys would hit white guys in school to retaliate" for attacks on the neighborhood streets. Memorandum from Meers to Dr. Shedd, Oct. 10, 1968; *Bulletin*, Oct. 8, 1968; "Ten Days of Disorders: Pupils, Neighbors and Faculty Describe Crisis." See Chapter 7 for a discussion of the Black Coalition.

69. Memorandum from Meers to Dr. Shedd, Oct. 10, 1968; *Bulletin*, Oct. 8, 1968; "Police Disperse Crowds of Two Races at Bok," *Bulletin*, Oct. 9, 1968.

70. Memorandum from Meers to Dr. Shedd, Oct. 10, 1968; *Philadelphia Tribune*, Oct. 15, 1968.

71. The white student was released from the hospital when the x-rays proved negative. Memorandum from Meers to Dr. Shedd, Oct. 10, 1968; Commission on Human Relations (CHR), "Memorandum to Community Leaders and Members of the Committee on Community Tensions," n.d., FC collection, box 56, folder 2, TUUA; *Bulletin*, Oct. 10, 1968.

72. Memorandum from Meers to Dr. Shedd, Oct. 10, 1968; CHR, "Memorandum to Community Leaders and Members of the Committee on Community Tensions," n.d.; *Bulletin*, Oct. 10, 1968.

73. Memorandum from Meers to Dr. Shedd, Oct. 10, 1968; CHR, "Memorandum to Community Leaders and Members of the Committee on Community Tensions," n.d.; *Bulletin*, Oct. 10, 1968; *Philadelphia Inquirer*, Oct. 10, 1968; " 'All the Way With Wallace,' Heard Amid Tumult at Bok," *Philadelphia Tribune*, Oct. 12, 1968.

74. Memorandum from Meers to Dr. Shedd, Oct. 10, 1968; CHR, "Memorandum to Community Leaders and Members of the Committee on Community Tensions," n.d; *Bulletin*, Oct. 10, 1968; *Philadelphia Inquirer*, Oct. 10, 1968; " 'All the Way With Wallace,' Heard Amid Tumult at Bok"; "Leaders Criticize Cops' Handling of Bok Uproar," *Philadelphia Tribune*, Oct. 12, 1968.

75. School board members Nichols and Hutt opposed closing the schools, arguing that the police should have done a better job protecting the students and would have done so if the situation were reversed and white students were attending schools in a black neighborhood. Instead, they proposed that Mayor Tate declare a limited emergency to prevent public gatherings of twelve or more, as he had done in the summer of 1967 and again following the assassination of Dr. King. Memorandum from Meers to Dr. Shedd, Oct. 10, 1968; CHR, "Memorandum to Community Leaders and Members of the Committee on Community Tensions," n.d.; *Bulletin*, Oct. 10, 1968; *Philadelphia Inquirer*, Oct. 10, 1968.

76. Memorandum from Meers to Dr. Shedd, Oct. 10, 1968; *Philadelphia Inquirer*, Oct. 12, 1968; *Bulletin*, Oct. 14, 1968.

77. "1,000 in South Phila. March to Demand Bok Stay Closed," *Bulletin*, Oct. 13, 1968; "Shedd Asks Peace; 1200 Hold March for 'White Power,'" *Philadelphia Inquirer*, Oct. 14, 1968; "Foglietta Hooted by 'Neighbors,'" *Bulletin*, Oct. 15, 1968; "Dilworth Flying Back to Confer on Schools," *Bulletin*, Oct. 17, 1968.

78. D'Ortona had previously opposed the Shedd administration's proposal to use its powers of eminent domain to evict fourteen white property owners for a badly needed expansion of Gratz High School. Citizens Committee on Public Education in Philadelphia, "Memorandum on City-School District Relations," Mar. 12, 1968, FL collection, box 1, TUUA; "D'Ortona Sees School Tax Endangered by Disorder," *Bulletin*, Oct. 10, 1968; "1,000 in South Phila. March to Demand Bok Stay Closed"; "Mayor Says He'll Propose Solution," *Bulletin*, Oct. 16, 1968.

79. Memorandum from Meers to Dr. Shedd, Oct. 10, 1968; CHR, "Memorandum to Community Leaders and Members of the Committee on Community Tensions"; "Rizzo Warns Whites, Negroes He'll Take No Nonsense at Schools," *Philadelphia Independent*, Oct. 12, 1968; "Women Bok Protesters Want Tate's Apology," *Philadelphia Tribune*, Oct. 19, 1968.

80. Memorandum from Meers to Dr. Shedd, Oct. 10, 1968; CHR, "Memorandum to Community Leaders and Members of the Committee on Community Tensions"; *Bulletin*, Oct. 14, 1968.

81. Leon Bass, the school principal, responded to the demands by praising the students "for the constructive and nonviolent manner in which they are approaching their problems." Memorandum from Meers to Dr. Shedd, Oct. 10, 1968; *Bulletin*, Oct. 14 and 15, 1968; Interview with Palmer.

82. Memorandum from Meers to Dr. Shedd, Oct. 10, 1968; *Bulletin*, Oct. 15, 1968; "Mayor Says He'll Propose Solution."

83. Memorandum from Meers to Dr. Shedd, Oct. 10, 1968; "Group Leaves After Plea by Rights Leader," *Bulletin*, Oct. 16, 1968; "Behind the Scene of White Sit-In Session at Harassed Bok Hi School," *Philadelphia Tribune*, Oct. 19, 1968.

84. Memorandum from Meers to Dr. Shedd, Oct. 10, 1968; CHR, "Memorandum to Community Leaders and Members of the Committee on Community Tensions"; "Group Leaves After Plea by Rights Leader"; "Board Pledges to Keep Order in South Phila," *Bulletin*, Oct. 18, 1968; "Negro City Official Praised for Easing Tension at Bok Hi," *Philadelphia Tribune*, Oct. 19, 1968; "Unions Booted Out Bok After Apprentice Bias Is Exposed by Tribune," *Philadelphia Tribune*, Nov. 26, 1968; William T. Kelly, Director of Vocational Education to Floyd L. Logan, May 2, 1969; "Enrollment: Negro and Spanish-Speaking in the Philadelphia Public Schools, 1969–1970."

85. On the role of school issues in the 1971 mayoral campaign, see "Tate's Appointee to School Board Could Influence Course of Education," *Bulletin*, Jun. 6, 1971.

86. See Chapter 4, note 128.

87. Robert L. Allen, *Black Awakening in Capitalist America* (Trenton, N.J: Africa World Press, 1990), 1, 274; Harold Cruse, *The Crisis of the Negro Intellectual* (New York: William Morrow Press, 1967), 344, 391, 447–48.

Chapter 7. The Gender Politics of Movement Leadership

1. E. Frances White, "Africa on My Mind: Gender, Counter Discourse and African American Nationalism," *Journal of Women's History* 2 (Spring 1990): 73–97; Elaine Brown, *A Taste of Power: A Black Women's Story* (New York: Pantheon, 1992).

2. See Brown, *A Taste of Power*, 356–76. Examples of recent scholarship on women's experiences in the Black Panther Party include Angela D. LeBlanc-Ernest, "'The Most Qualified Person to Handle the Job': Black Panther Party Women, 1966–82," and Tracye Matthews, "'No One Ever Asks What a Man's Place in Revolution Is," in Charles E. Jones, ed., *The Black Panther Party Revisited* (Baltimore: Black Classic Press, 1998), 305–34, 267–304, respectively. Memoirs that emphasize the relative gender equality within the Panthers include Regina Jennings, "Why I Joined the Party: An Africana Womanist Reflection," and Miriam Ma'at-Ka-Re, "'I Got a Right to the Tree of Life:' Reflections of a Former Community Worker," in Jones, *Black Panther Party Revisited*, 258–65, and 135–45, respectively; and Kathleen Cleaver, "Women, Power, and Revolution," in Kathleen Cleaver and George Katsiaficas, eds., *Liberation, Imagination, and the Black Panther Party: A New Look at the Panthers and Their Legacy* (New York: Routledge, 2001), 123–27.

3. Mumia Abu-Jamal, *We Want Freedom: A Life in the Black Panther Party* (Cambridge, Mass.: South End Press, 2004), 181. The quote from the Bukhari manuscript is on page 173.

4. Ula Taylor, "Elijah Muhammad's Nation of Islam: Separatism, Regendering, and a Secular Approach to Black Power After Malcolm X (1965–1975)," in Jeanne

F. Theoharis and Komozi Woodard, eds., *Freedom North: Black Freedom Struggles Outside the South, 1940–1980* (New York: Palgrave Macmillan, 2003), 177–95. For a poignant discussion of one black woman activist's response to the masculinism of Black Power, see Cythnia Griggs Fleming's superb biography of Ruby Doris Robinson, SNCC's administrative director from 1966 to her death from cancer in 1968. Even as Robinson rose to a top leadership position in SNCC, she professed to *Ebony* magazine her commitment to male political leadership and her desire to return to the role of wife to her husband, who as a mechanic on the staff of the SNCC motor pool reported to her. Cythnia Griggs Fleming, *Soon We Will Cry: The Liberation of Ruby Doris Smith Robinson* (Lanham, Md.: Rowman and Littlefield, 1998), esp. 143–81.

5. On the origins of the black feminist movement within the movements of the 1960s, see Robin Kelley, *Freedom Dreams: The Black Radical Imagination*, Boston: Beacon Press, 2002) 135–56; Kristin Anderson-Bricker, " 'Triple Jeopardy,': Black Women and the Growth of Feminist Consciousness in SNCC, 1964–1975," in Kimberly Springer, ed., *Still Lifting, Still Climbing* (New York: New York University Press, 1999), 49–69; Stephen Michael Ward, " 'Ours Too Was a Struggle for a Better World': Activist Intellectuals and the Radical Promise of the Black Power Movement, 1962–1972," Ph.D. dissertation, University of Texas, 2002, 223–265.

6. Interview with Charyn Scott, Mar. 5, 1994, Philadelphia; " 'Black Power,' Beauty Unity Rally Themes," *Philadelphia Tribune,* Jul. 19, 1966; " 'New Breed' Seeks Change; Vows to Go Down Swinging Not Singing with Young Brainwashed Victims," *Philadelphia Tribune,* Jul. 26, 1966.

7. Interview with Scott. Charyn Scott's experiences in Philadelphia SNCC correspond closely to the experiences of black women SNCC organizers in the rural South in the years before the group adopted Black Power. As Winnie Breines has recently documented, black women in SNCC tended to reject the argument of white women activists like Casey Hayden that women were treated as second-class citizens in the organization. From the perspective of many black women, the organization viewed them as effective and trusted organizers. Many, in fact, were named leaders of their own organizing projects. Until Ruby Doris Robinson's election as SNCC administrative secretary in 1966, however, women were completely excluded from the top leadership posts in the organization. Note?

8. Interview with Mattie Humphrey, March 12, 1994, Philadelphia.

9. Interview with Clarence Farmer, April 14, 1994, Philadelphia. On the founding of the Black Coalition, see "20 Civic Leaders Offer $1 Million for Ghetto Jobs," *Philadelphia Inquirer,* May 10. 1968.

10. Interview with Farmer. According to Walter Palmer, he was able to head off a similar black youth-police confrontation in North Philadelphia with the assistance of Temple University president Marvin Wachman who opened the university's largest auditorium to a Palmer-organized speak-out. Interview with Walter Palmer, Aug. 10, 2004, Philadelphia. On Mayor Tate's issuance of an Emergency Proclamation following the King assassination and Rizzo's claim to have prevented a race riot, see S. A. Paolantonio, *Frank Rizzo: The Last Big Man in Big City America* (Philadelphia: Camino Books, 1993), 96–97.

11. According to Farmer, "Freedom" George Brower showed up for the meeting with gaping holes in the soles of his shoes. Interview with Farmer; *Bulletin,* May 9, 1968 and "20 Civic Leaders Offer $1 Million for Ghetto Jobs."

12. Interview with Farmer.

13. Interview with Farmer; *Bulletin,* May 9, 1968 and "20 Civic Leaders Offer $1 Million for Ghetto Jobs"; "15 Projects Financed by Black Coalition," *Bulletin,* Jul. 28, 1968.

14. Interview with Farmer; *Bulletin*, May 9, 1968; "20 Civic Leaders Offer $1 Million for Ghetto Jobs"; *Bulletin*, Sep. 12, 1968. Hakim was Edward Anderson, the young brother of Philadelphia SNCC activist George Anderson, who had been arrested during the police department's summer of 1967 round up of RAM activists. See "6th Youth Held Under $10,000 Bail Here on Charge of Inciting to Riot, Conspiracy," *Bulletin*, Aug. 1, 1967; Malik Yulmid had dropped out of St. Joseph's College for financial reasons. "Dispute Flares over Demise of Year-Old Black Coalition," *Philadelphia Inquirer*, Apr. 10, 1969.

15. Also contributing to the pledge—presumably in smaller amounts—were the Greater Philadelphia Movement, the Greater Philadelphia Chamber of Commerce, the Southeastern Pennsylvania Economic Development Corporation, and the Episcopal Diocese of Philadelphia. "20 Civic Leaders Offer $1 Million for Ghetto Jobs"; "32 Phila. Firms Back Self-Help for Negro Poor," *Philadelphia Inquirer*, May 12, 1968.

16. *Bulletin*, May 9 and Jun. 3, 1968; "20 Civic Leaders Offer $1 Million for Ghetto Jobs"; "32 Phila. Firms Back Self-Help for Negro Poor."

17. "Black Coalition, Jewish Leaders Join Bias Fight," *Philadelphia Inquirer*, Jun. 28, 1968; *Bulletin*, Jul. 7, 1968. Other participants in the dialogue were Judges Nix and Higginbotham, Clarence Farmer, Henry Nichols, Gus Lacy, and councilman Charles Durham from the Black Coalition and Murray Friedman, regional director of the American Jewish Committee, city councilman David Cohen, Rabbi David Clayman, Emily Sunstein, chair of the Philadelphia ADA, and attorneys Robert Greenfield and Theodore Mann.

18. "Black Militancy to Continue" *Philadelphia Inquirer*, Jun. 16, 1968. See also "Preventing Riots Is Not Black Coalition's Job, Says Branche," *Philadelphia Tribune*, Jul. 27, 1968.

19. "Nixon Blasted by Rights Leader," *Philadelphia Tribune*, Jul. 20, 1968; "4 Members of Black Coalition Say Cops Beat Them," *Philadelphia Tribune*, Aug. 13, 1968; "Dispute Flares Over Demise Of Year-Old Black Coalition."

20. "Black Militancy to Continue"; "15 Projects Financed by Black Coalition"; "Dispute Flares over Demise of Year-Old Black Coalition."

21. "Dispute Flares over Demise of Year-Old Black Coalition"; *Bulletin*, Aug. 30, Sep. 12, Nov. 21, 1968, and Jan. 8, 1969.

22. Interview with Farmer; *Bulletin*, Jan. 8 and Apr. 9, 1969; "Dispute Flares Over Demise Of Year-Old Black Coalition"; "Bowser Ready to Quit Tate, Lead Civic Unit," *Bulletin*, Apr. 27, 1969; "Tate Confirms Bowser's Plans to Quit at Hall," *Bulletin*, Apr. 30, 1969.

23. "The Black Manifesto," in Robert S. Lecky and H. Elliott Wright, eds., *Black Manifesto: Religion, Racism, and Reparations* (New York: Sheed and Wright, 1969); "Reparations Demand Stirs Church Furor," *Bulletin*, Aug. 3, 1969.

24. "Black Community Council Endorses 'Reparations' from Christians, Jews," *Bulletin*, Jun. 23, 1969; "Reparations Demand Stirs Church Furor"; Paul M. Washington with David McI. Gracie, *"Other Sheep I Have": The Autobiography of Father Paul Washington* (Philadelphia: Temple University Press, 1994), 87–88. According to Walter Palmer, the Citywide Black Communities Council was founded to bring together community organizations that would have been reluctant to join an explicitly Black Power organization. Interview with Palmer.

25. Washington, *"Other Sheep I Have"*, 87–88.

26. *Bulletin*, Jun. 4 and 19, 1969; DeWitt quoted in Washington, *"Other Sheep I Have"*, 89.

27. *Bulletin*, Jul. 3, 1969; "Blacks to Let Whites Enter Seized Church," *Bulletin*, Jul. 6, 1969; "Negroes Hold Own Services in Occupied Church," *Bulletin*, Jul. 7, 1969; "20 Sit In at Methodist Offices, Hit Church Ouster of Blacks," *Bulletin*, Jul. 11, 1969; "Rights Group Ends Sit-In at Church Office," *Bulletin*, Jul. 12, 1969.

28. Gayraud S. Wilmore, Jr., "The Church's Response to the Black Manifesto," *Philadelphia Yearly Meeting News* 7, no. 7 (September 1969).

29. Washington, *"Other Sheep I Have"*, 89–98; interview with Paul M. Washington, Mar. 14, 1994, Philadelphia; "Reparations Demand Stirs Church Furor"; "Wrice Rejects Reparations If Result Divides Blacks," *Bulletin*, Feb. 1, 1970; *Bulletin*, Dec. 17, 1969 and Apr. 5, 1970.

30. Washington, *"Other Sheep I Have"*, 89–98.

31. Washington, *"Other Sheep I Have"*, 96.

32. See, for example, Thomas Jackson, "The State, the Movement, and the Urban Poor,: The War on Poverty and Political Mobilization in the 1960s," in Michael B. Katz, ed., *The "Underclass" Debate: Views from History*, (Princeton, N.J.: Princeton University Press, 1993), 426. On the NWRO, see Nick Kotz and Mary Lynn Kotz, *A Passion for Equality: George A. Wiley and the Movement* (New York: W. W. Norton, 1977); Felicia Kornbluh, "To Fulfill Their 'Rightly Needs': Consumerism and the National Welfare Rights Movement," *Radical History Review* 69 (Fall 1997); and Kornbluh, "Black Buying Power: Welfare Rights, Consumerism and Northern Protest," in Jeanne F. Theoharis and Komozi Woodard, eds., *Freedom North: Black Freedom Struggles Outside the South, 1940–1980* (New York: Palgrave Macmillan, 2003), 199–222.

33. For a superb discussion of the relationship between poor black women's organizing in the urban North and the Black Power movement, see Rhonda Y. Williams, *The Politics of Public Housing: Black Women's Struggles Against Urban Inequality* (New York: Oxford University Press, 2004).

34. *Straight Talk*, vol. 1, no. 11, Sept. 20, 1967, Housing Association of the Delaware Valley (HADV) collection, box 326, folder 6286, Temple University Urban Archives (TUUA); interview with David Gracie, Apr. 24, 1994, Philadelphia.

35. For example, unwed mothers were excluded from Philadelphia's public housing projects as a threat to the moral upkeep of those communities until May of 1968. "Doors of Public Housing Are Opened to Thousands of City's Unwed Mothers," *Philadelphia Tribune*, May 28, 1968.

36. Felicia Kornbluh, "To Fulfill Their 'Rightly Needs,'" 78.

37. First Welfare Rights Conference flier, n.d., West Philadelphia Schools Committee [WPSC] collection, box 1, TUUA; "Organize Selves to Gain More Relief, Poor Told," *Bulletin*, Apr. 22, 1967.

38. Minutes, Health and Welfare Council, Public Assistance Committee, Oct. 19, 1962, Health and Welfare Council (HWC) collection, box 14, folder 3, TUUA; Commonwealth of Pennsylvania, Department of Public Welfare, "Public Assistance Allowances Compared with the Cost of Living," March 1963, HADV collection, box 107e, folder 58, TUUA. On the Pennsylvania Citizens Council, see the *Council Reporter*, vol. 2, no. 3, January 1964, (Urban League) UL collection, box 16, folder 19, TUUA.

39. "Concerned Citizens of Philadelphia Will March on Harrisburg" flier, Feb. 18, 1964, and Urban League of Philadelphia, "Health and Welfare Services Newsletter," March 1964, Wharton Centre [WC] collection, box 4, TUUA; Citizens Concerned with Public Assistance Allowances, "Fact Sheet," Feb. 27, 1964, HADV collection, box 175, folder 1777, TUUA; "Aim for Next Assembly Meet in Harrisburg," *Bulletin*, Apr. 4, 1964; Citizens Concerned with Public Assistance Allowances, "Background and Policy Statement," Nov. 6, 1964, and memorandum to Health and Welfare Council's Committee on Public Assistance and the Pennsylvania Citizens Council from Citizens Concerned with Public Assistance Allowances, Nov. 6, 1964, HADV collection, box 325, folder 6275, TUUA. On the Haddington Leadership Organization, see "Haddington Leadership Organization Active on Commu-

nity Front in 1967," *Philadelphia Tribune,* Jan. 16, 1968. On the number of aid recipients in Philadelphia, see "Petition Demands 'Rights and Respect' For Persons Getting Public Assistance," *Bulletin,* Jun. 30, 1967, and memorandum to Public Welfare Committee from Terry Dellmuth, Oct. 13, 1967, HADV collection, box 325, folder 6263, TUUA.

40. Ironically, it was the involvement of groups like the Health and Welfare Council in the mayor's antipoverty task force two years earlier that civil rights activists had cited as proof that the city administration was not serious about involving the poor in the local War on Poverty. "Meeting of Some Philadelphia Area Organizations Interested in Public Assistance," Mar. 7, 1966, UL collection, box 16, folder 15, TUUA; minutes, Citizens Concerned with Public Assistance, Mar. 29, 1966, HADV collection, box 105, folder 314, TUUA; Citizens Concerned with Public Assistance, "A Statement Relating to Present Department of Public Welfare Grants," Jun. 8, 1966; HADV collection box 105, folder 315, TUUA.

41. Crusade for Children, "A Study Document on Welfare Rights Goals," n.d., minutes, Citizens Concerned Public Assistance, May 12, 1966, and minutes, Crusade for Children, Oct. 27, 1966, UL collection, box 16, folder 25, TUUA; "1,000 Welfare Mothers, Kids March on Capitol; Charge Food Stamps Make Situation Desperate," *Philadelphia Tribune,* Jun. 11, 1966.

42. "Political Use of Antipoverty Funds Is Charged," *Philadelphia Inquirer,* Aug. 16, 1965; "PAAC Plans 2d Harrisburg Bus trip To Push for Higher Relief Payments," *Bulletin,* May 17, 1966; Crusade for Children flier, Jun. 8, 1966, UL collection, box 16, folder 25, TUUA; "1,000 Welfare Mothers, Kids March on Capitol"; "All Night Vigil at State Bldg.; Protest Planned," *Philadelphia Tribune,* Jun. 28, 1966.

43. George Wylie to Welfare Rights Leaders and Organizers, Oct. 31, 1966, UL collection, box 25, folder 12, TUUA; *Straight Talk,* vol. 1, no. 5, May 19, 1967, HADV collection 107e, box 58, TUUA; "Women on Relief Would Like a Raise," *Bulletin,* Oct. 22, 1967. On Leslie, see memorandum to Members and Friends of the Ludlow Community Organization from Ludlow Executive Board, n.d., UL collection, box 16, folder 17, TUUA.

44. *Straight Talk,* vol. 1, no. 7, Jun. 23, 1967, HADV collection, box 325, folder 6280, TUUA; "Petition Demands 'Rights and Respect' For Persons Getting Public Assistance"; "Bishop Defends Welfare Protest as Basic Right," *Philadelphia Inquirer,* Jul. 1, 1967; "Women on Relief Would Like a Raise."

45. *Bulletin,* Aug. 27 and 28, 1967; *Straight Talk,* vol. 1, no. 11, Sept. 20, 1967.

46. *Straight Talk,* vol. 1, no. 11, Sept. 20, 1967; "Women on Relief Would Like a Raise"; "Group Protests Treatment by Welfare Aides," *Philadelphia Inquirer,* Dec. 9, 1967; "Filling in the Relief Gap," *Philadelphia Inquirer,* Jan. 15, 1968; United Neighbors News, n.d., HADV collection, box 107e, folder 52, TUUA. On VISTA volunteers, see *Bulletin,* Apr. 22, 1970.

47. Philadelphia Welfare Rights Organization, "Why Public Assistance Grants Should Be At 100% of a Current Standard of Health and Decency," n.d., HADV collection, box 326, folder 6287, TUUA; *Straight Talk,* vol. 1, no. 7, Jun. 23, 1967 and vol. 1, no. 11, Sept. 20, 1967; "Petition Demands 'Rights and Respect' For Persons Getting Public Assistance"; "Bishop Defends Welfare Protest As Basic Right"; *Bulletin,* Aug. 24, 1967; "Women on Relief Would Like a Raise"; "Group Protests Treatment by Welfare Aides"; "Relief Recipients Map Drive for More Funds," *Bulletin,* Dec. 28, 1967; Terry Dellmuth to Rosa Lee Williams, Jan. 17, 1968, and minutes, Subcommittee on Housing for Welfare Recipients, Feb. 15, 1968, HADV collection, box 325, folder 6281, TUUA; Philadelphia Welfare Rights Organization, "Summary of Goals," n.d., HADV collection, box 326, folder 6286, TUUA; Roxanne Jones to Mrs. Dolbeare and Mrs. Shumate, n.d., HADV collection, box 326, folder 6287, TUUA; Kornbluh, "To Fulfill Their 'Rightly Needs,'" 84–85.

48. "Petition Demands 'Rights and Respect' For Persons Getting Public Assistance"; memorandum to Public Welfare Committee from Terry Dellmuth, Oct. 13, 1967; "Filling in the Relief Gap"; "State Grants New Power to Rights Group," *Bulletin*, Apr 24, 1969; "Welfare Recipients Here Turn Tables, Work for VISTA Among Poor," *Bulletin*, Dec. 19, 1969.

49. "Women on Relief Would Like a Raise"; *Bulletin*, Nov. 9, 1967 and Mar. 9 and 27 and May 11, 1968; "Minister Sells Blood for Funds to Feed, Cloth DPA Families; Claims Relief Checks Too Small," *Philadelphia Tribune*, Nov. 14, 1967 and Mar. 16, 1968; "Welfare Mothers Ask Help to Change Law," *Philadelphia Inquirer*, Nov. 17, 1967; *Philadelphia Tribune*, Jul. 13, 1968; *Philadelphia Inquirer*, Jan. 6, 1968; "North Phila. Realtor's 'In Middle' of Feud with Welfare Mothers," *Philadelphia Tribune*, Jan. 30, 1968; Terry Dellmuth to Rosa Lee Williams, Jan. 17, 1968; "Residents Picket Realtor; Demand He Make Repairs," *Philadelphia Tribune*, Mar. 30, 1968; "New City-Wide Tenants' Council Vows Fight for Better Housing," *Philadelphia Tribune*, Aug. 24, 1968; "Report on Activity of the Kingsessing Welfare Rights Group," n.d., HADV collection, box 326, folder 6286, TUUA.

50. "Clergy Support State Rise in Relief Grants," *Bulletin*, Jan. 19, 1968; "Bishop DeWitt Urges Higher Welfare Grants," *Bulletin*, Jan. 5, 1969; "23 Try to Live a Month on State Relief Grants," *Bulletin*, Oct. 2, 1969.

51. Roxanne Jones would praise the Friends of Welfare Rights for giving "us so much help and support." *Straight Talk*, vol. 1, no. 11, Sept. 20, 1967; "Women on Relief Would Like a Raise"; "Group Protests Treatment by Welfare Aides"; "100 Percent over 1968 Standard Goal of WOR," *Philadelphia Tribune*, Oct. 26, 1968; "Leader of Welfare Sit-In Calls Herself Nonviolent," *Bulletin*, Nov. 17, 1968; interview with Gracie. On the establishment of Community Legal Services, see Philadelphia Antipoverty Action Committee (PAAC), "Summary of Programs Funded by OEO," n.d., HADV collection, box 221, folder 3051, TUUA; "Year of War on Poverty Ends on a Note of Discord," *Bulletin*, May 29, 1966.

52. Philadelphia Welfare Rights Organization, "Why Public Assistance Grants Should Be at 100% of a Current Standard of Health and Decency," n.d., HADV collection, box 326, folder 6287, TUUA; "Clergy Support State Rise in Relief Grants." On Jones's tenure as chair of PWRO, see Lou Antosh, "Fighting to Liberate The Fountain of Welfare," *Philadelphia Inquirer Magazine*, May 16, 1971. Hazel Leslie died of a heart attack on July 8, 1968. *Philadelphia Tribune*, Jul. 13 and 20, 1968.

53. PWRO's credit campaign also inspired the national organization's national boycott of Sears when the national retailers refused to create a similar credit program for welfare families. *Philadelphia Tribune*, Jul. 13 and 20, 1968; "Wanamaker and Lerner Agree To Give Relief Clients Credit," *Philadelphia Tribune*, Aug. 20, 1968; "Leader of Welfare Sit-In Calls Herself Nonviolent"; Kornbluh, "To Fulfill Their 'Rightly Needs,'" 84–85, and "Black Buying Power," 205–15.

54. Interview with Thomas Gilhool, Mar. 14, 1994, Philadelphia; "Tenant Sworn into PHA by Judge Stout," *Philadelphia Tribune*, Mar. 23, 1971; "Sues to Overrule Tate's Order to Halt Building of the Whitman Project," *Philadelphia Tribune*, May 29, 1971; "Many Sorry Cavanaugh Resigned Housing Job," *Philadelphia Tribune*, Oct. 12, 1971; "Mrs. Rosetta Wylie Elected to Top Post," *Philadelphia Tribune*, Nov. 16, 1971; "Woman Named by Nixon to Rent Advisory Board Poor Tenants Advocate," *Philadelphia Tribune*, Nov. 27, 1971.

55. "100 Percent over 1968 Standard Goal of WRO," *Philadelphia Tribune*, Oct. 26, 1968; "500 Reliefers in Sit-In Sing Carols, Demand $50 Christmas Bonus," *Bulletin*, Nov. 14, 1968; "Shafer OKs Meeting on Yule Grants," *Philadelphia Inquirer*, Nov. 16, 1968; "'Sit-ins Demand $50 Per Person Grant for Christmas," *Philadelphia Trib-*

une, Nov. 16, 1968; "Leader of Welfare Sit-In Calls Herself Nonviolent," *Bulletin*, Nov. 17, 1968; "400 on Relief Sit In at Capitol for Yule Bonus," *Bulletin*, Nov. 19, 1968; *Bulletin*, Nov. 15, 21, and 26, 1968; *Advance: Newsletter of Health and Welfare Council, Inc.*, vol. 6, no. 3 (Jan.–Feb. 1969), Fellowship Commission [FC] collection, box 54, folder 15, TUUA; "111 Phila. Delegates to Join in WRO Conference," *Bulletin*, Jul. 21, 1971.

56. "Welfare Group Faintly Praises Nixon Reform Plan," *New York Times*, Aug. 22, 1969; "1,500 on Plaza Join National War Protest," *Bulletin*, Apr. 15, 1970; "Nixon's Dogs Are Target at Hearing on Welfare," *Bulletin*, Nov. 19, 1970; "Philadelphians Lead Service for Dr. King," *Bulletin*, Apr. 5, 1971; "The Family Assistance Plan Called 'Racist, Dehumanizing,'" *Philadelphia Tribune*, Jun. 12, 1971; "Black, White Women Await First Coalition Conference," *Philadelphia Tribune*, Mar. 6, 1971.

57. "Anger Grows over Rising Welfare Cost," *Bulletin*, Nov. 8, 1971. For examples of the conservative backlash against welfare spending and the response of the PWRO, see "Courts Eyed in Budget Crisis," *Bulletin*, Jul. 11, 1973; "Blacks Fail to Gain Access Given Whites," *Bulletin*, Nov. 18, 1973; "Welfare Group Plans March on Harrisburg," *Bulletin*, May 18, 1974; "Shapp Booed in Protest," *Bulletin*, Jun. 3, 1975.

58. "Bishop DeWitt Urges Higher Welfare Grants," *Bulletin*, Jan. 5, 1969; "Hearing Is Halted After Row," *Bulletin*, Jun. 2, 1970; "Welfare Aide Unruffled by Arrest Warrant," *Philadelphia Inquirer*, Jun. 4, 1970; "Roxanne Jones Released; Will End Violence," *Bulletin*, Dec. 5, 1970; "Welfare Recipients Protest Proposed Cuts in Harrisburg," *Philadelphia Tribune*, Aug. 17, 1971; Antosh, "Fighting to Liberate The Fountain of Welfare," Hardy Williams served as Jones's lawyer in the "shoe" case; his fee was covered by Bishop DeWitt. Interview with Gracie.

59. Michael B. Katz, *The Undeserving Poor: From the War on Poverty to the War on Welfare* (New York: Pantheon, 1989), 125–235. For an example of the new right critique of government aid to the poor, see Charles Murray, *Losing Ground: American Social Policy, 1950–1980* (New York: Basic Books, 1984).

60. Schell's quote is from an interview conducted by Dick Cluster and published as "A Way to Fight Back: The Black Panther Party," in Dick Cluster, ed., *They Should Have Served That Cup of Coffee* (Boston: South End Press, 1979), 65. Lieutenant Fencl would later insist that the police had not ordered the Panther members to strip in public. Minutes, Board of Commissioners, Sep. 15, 1970, FC collection, box 8, TUUA. See also "Kunstler Accuses Rizzo of Trying to Gag Black Militants," *Bulletin*, Sep. 1, 1970; Abu-Jamal, *We Want Freedom*, 194–96. On the photograph of the strip search, see "Black Panthers: Little Left," *Philadelphia Daily News*, Mar. 24, 1975.

61. Crime Commission of Philadelphia, "Analysis of Police Disciplinary Process," FC collection, box 43, folder 2, TUUA.

62. On the FOP suit, see Committee on Community Tension, memorandum for Emil F. Goldhaber, Sep. 9, 1965, FC collection, box 4, TUUA; minutes, Board of Commissioners, Oct. 12, 1965, FC collection, box 8, TUUA; memorandum to Peter Hearn et al. from Maury Fagan, Apr. 13, 1967, FC collection, box 4, TUUA; "Police Brotherhood May Seek Referendum in Bid to Abolish Advisory Board," *Philadelphia Inquirer*, Nov. 27, 1966; "Citizen Police Board Ordered Abolished by Judge Weinrott," *Bulletin*, Mar. 30, 1967; "Police Advisory Board Upheld by High Court," *Philadelphia Inquirer*, June, 28, 1969; James H. J. Tate to Mercer D. Tate, Sept. 30, 1969, FC collection, box 18, folder 19, TUUA.

63. Committee on Community Tensions, memorandum for Dr. J. Otto Reinemann, Secretary, Apr. 7, 1967, FC collection, box 4, TUUA; Memorandum to Citizens for the Police Advisory Board from Mark Hyman, Oct. 3, 1968, Citizens for the Police Advisory Board, press release, Oct. 9, 1969, and James H. J. Tate to Mercer

Tate, Dec. 22, 1969, FC collection box 22, folder 20, TUUA; memorandum for Judge Emil F. Goldhaber, chairman, Committee on Community Tensions, Nov. 11, 1969, FC collection, box 4, TUUA; Citizens for the Police Advisory Board, Sponsoring Groups, n.d., FC collection, box 22, folder 21, TUUA; Office of the Mayor, news release, Dec. 22, 1969, FC collection, box 23, folder 3, TUUA.

64. Dwight Eisenhower Campbell to Clarence Farmer, Jul. 26, 1965, Police Advisory Board [PAB] collection, box 3, TUUA.

65. Huey P. Newton, *Revolutionary Suicide* (1973; New York: Writers and Readers Publishing, 1995), 116–120. For Malcolm X and Robert Williams's influence on Huey Newton, see Newton, *Revolutionary Suicide*, 112–13; and Hugh Pearson, *The Shadow of the Panther: Huey Newton and the Price of Black Power in America* (Reading, Mass.: Addison-Wesley, 1994), 28, 109.

66. "CORE Leader Joins Attack on Rizzo, Calls Him Racist," *Philadelphia Tribune*, May 27, 1967; "Anti-Rizzo Meeting Votes for Toyless 'Black Xmas,'" *Philadelphia Tribune*, Dec. 12, 1967; "Rizzo Must Go!" flier, n.d., HADV collection, box 107e, folder 50, TUUA.

67. "North City Congress Says Rizzo Severs Police-Community Ties," *Philadelphia Tribune*, Dec. 23, 1967; "Police Acts Only Mirror Our Society, Says Civil Leader," *Philadelphia Tribune*, Jun. 4, 1968; Arthur Waskow, "Community Control of the Police," n.d., and Council of Organizations on Philadelphia Police Accountability and Responsibility (COPPAR) Funding Proposal, PAB collection, box 2, TUUA.

68. "Philadelphia: Conference on Police Power in a Free Society," May 18, 1968, Americans for Democratic Action [ADA] collection, box 38, folder 22, TUUA.

69. According to Schell, he joined the gang as a result of having to fight his way to school through white neighborhoods. Still, he insists that it was not until he entered the service that he encountered "true" racism, the "deep intent to control and to dominate you because you happen to be someone else." See "A Way to Fight Back," 41–69. For McHarris's announcement, see "Black Panthers Unit Brands Branche and Jeremiah X 'Fronts,'" *Philadelphia Tribune*, Oct. 12, 1968. On the founding of the Philadelphia chapter and Schell's emergence as its leader, see Abu-Jamal, *We Want Freedom*, 46–63; Washington, *"Other Sheep I Have"*, 126–128. On the BPP protest at the California State Capitol see Bobby Seale, *Seize the Time: The Story of the Black Panther Party and Huey P. Newton* (New York: Random House, 1970), 153–66. The best recent surveys of the history of the Black Panther Party are Charles E. Jones, "Reconsidering Panther History: The Untold Story," and Nikhil Singh, "The Black Panthers and the 'Underdeveloped Country' of the Left," both in Jones, *Black Panther Party Reconsidered*, 1–24, 57–105 respectively.

70. "A Way to Fight Back" 41–69; Abu-Jamal, *We Want Freedom*, 69, 179–80, 194–98; Washington, *"Other Sheep I Have"*, 126–28; House of Representatives, Committee on Internal Security, *The Black Panther Party: Its Origin and Development as Reflected in Its Official Weekly Newspaper, The Black Panther Black Community News Service* (Washington D.C.: U.S. Government Printing Office, 1970), 88–89; "Doctor Backs Panthers at Quaker Parley," *Bulletin*, Mar. 31, 1970.

71. Washington, *"Other Sheep I Have"*, 127. For a photo of Abu-Jamal speaking at the Hampton memorial, see Abu-Jamal, *We Want Freedom*, 251.

72. Newton, *Revolutionary Suicide*, 120.

73. "A Way to Fight Back," 41–69.

74. "A Way to Fight Back," 41–69; House of Representatives, Committee on Internal Security, *The Black Panther Party*, 33–34; "Black Panther Proclaims Rights to Carry Weapons," *Bulletin*, Dec. 5, 1969. See also "Two Injured Fighting Police in City Hall Courtyard," *Bulletin*, Sep. 30, 1970.

75. Interview with Gracie; Abu-Jamal, *We Want Freedom*, 72–76; Washington,

"Other Sheep I Have", 132–134; "A Way to Fight Back," 41–69; "Kunstler Accuses Rizzo of Trying to Gag Black Militants," *Bulletin*, Sep. 1, 1970; *Bulletin*, Sep. 5 and 6, 1970; minutes, Committee on Community Tensions, Sept. 4, 1970 and Fellowship Commission Conference with Mass Media, Sept. 8, 1970, FC collection, box 61, folder 26, TUUA; minutes, Board of Commissioners, Sep. 15, 1970, FC collection, box 8, TUUA; Daniel B. Michie, Jr., Esq. to The Rev. Theodore M. Hesburgh, Sept. 25, 1970, FC collection, TUUA; "The Black Panthers: The Growl Grows Softer," *Philadelphia Inquirer*, Dec. 31, 1973.

76. See Abu-Jamal, *We Want Freedom*, 205–26, for a discussion of the Panther split. For an excerpt from Newton's speech at the Philadelphia convention, see Newton, *Revolutionary Suicide*, 295–96. On the BPP leader's decision to shift from self-defense to what Newton called survival programs, see Brown, *A Taste of Power*, 241–267 and David Hilliard and Lewis Cole, *This Side of Glory: The Autobiography of David Hilliard and the Story of the Black Panther Party* (Boston: Little, Brown, 1993).

77. "Dear Sirs" letter from Herman Smith, coordinator Black Panther Party, Pennsylvania Chapter, June 24, 1971, HADV collection, box 107e, folder 51, TUUA; "The Black Panthers: The Growl Grows Softer"; "New Panthers: Breakfasts, Not Bullets," *Bulletin*, Jul. 19, 1972. On the BULF, see "Committee of 1,000 Is Formed," *Philadelphia Tribune*, Jan. 16, 1971; "Ex-Gang Members Blast Black City Officials and Threaten to Close Down North Phila," *Philadelphia Tribune*, July, 17, 1971; "A Way to Fight Back," 41–69; Abu-Jamal, *We Want Freedom*, 233–34.

78. Minutes, Citizens for the PAB, Mar. 3 & May 26, 1970, FC collection, box 22, folder 22, TUUA; "New Group Sends 20 Observers to Watch over Police Behavior," *Bulletin*, May 10, 1970; *Philadelphia Tribune*, May 19, 1972; "The COPPAR Newsletter," n.d., ADA collection, box 38, folder 22, TUUA; Pennsylvania State Advisory Committee of the U.S. Commission on Civil Rights, "Police-Community Relations: A Report to the United States Commission on Civil Rights," June 1972, 55–57.

79. Among COPPAR's member groups were the Spring Garden Community Service Center, the South Philadelphia Community Concerned Committee, the Westside Community Council of Germantown, the Residents Advisory Board of the Philadelphia Housing Authority, the Philadelphia ACLU, the Lawyers' Committee for Civil Rights Under Law, Philadelphians for Equal Justice (PEJ), a white activist group formed to oppose police harassment of black activists, and the antiwar group Philadelphia Resistance. "New Group Sends 20 Observers To Watch Over Police Behavior"; *Philadelphia Tribune*, May 19, 1972; COPPAR funding proposal; "Police-Community Relations: A Report to the United States Commission on Civil Rights," 50–51.

80. COPPAR funding proposal; "New Group Sends 20 Observers to Watch Over Police Behavior."

81. "The Truth Behind Charges of Police Brutality," *Chestnut Hill Local*, Feb. 5, 1970; COPPAR newsletter, Oct. 1, 1979, HADV collection, box 107e, folder 52, TUUA; "The COPPAR Newsletter," n.d., ADA collection, box 38, folder 22, TUUA.

82. "The COPPAR Newsletter," n.d., ADA collection, box 38, folder 22, TUUA; "Police-Community Relations," 45–47, 55–57.

83. "Police-Community Relations," 6, 15–17, 45–47, 50–51, 55–56, 85–87.

Chapter 8. From Protest to Politics

1. For a discussion of the opportunities and constraints inherent in urban government in the 1970s, see Adolph Reed, *Stirrings in the Jug: Black Politics in the Post-Segregation Era* (Minneapolis: University of Minnesota Press, 1999), esp. 79–116. On

growth liberalism, see John Mollenkopf, *The Contested City* (Princeton, N.J.: Princeton University Press, 1983), esp. 139–79; and John R. Logan and Harvey L. Molotch, *Urban Fortunes: The Political Economy of Place* (Berkeley: University of California Press, 1987), 50–98. On the centrality of federal aid to Frank Rizzo's economic policies during the 1970s, see S.A. Paolantonio, *Frank Rizzo: The Last Big Man in Big City America* (Philadelphia: Camino Books, 1993), 154.

2. Quoted in William H. Chafe, *The Unfinished Journey: America Since World War II*, 5th ed. (New York: Oxford University Press, 2003), 240.

3. The best historical studies of the war on poverty are Allen J. Matusow, *The Unraveling of America: A History of Liberalism in the 1960s* (New York: Harper and Row, 1984), 243–71; Michael B. Katz, *The Undeserving Poor: From the War on Poverty to the War on Welfare* (New York: Pantheon, 1989), 79–123; and Thomas Jackson, "The State, the Movement, and the Urban Poor: The War on Poverty and Political Mobilization in the 1960s," in Michael B. Katz, ed., *The "Underclass" Debate: Views from History* (Princeton, N.J.: Princeton University Press, 1993), 403–39.

4. Both Matusow, *The Unraveling of America*, 243–71, and Jackson, "The State, the Movement, and the Urban Poor," 407, discuss the range of local War on Poverty programs. On the War on Poverty in Philadelphia, see "Poor Lacked Power in Philadelphia," *New York Times*, Nov. 6, 1965.

5. The board's first chairman was C.F. McNeil, executive director of the Health and Welfare Council. He was later succeeded by Dr. John O. Reinemann, the representative to the PAAC board from the city's juvenile court. Neither man seems to have exercised significant influence over the board. *Bulletin*, Apr. 15 and Nov. 12, 1965.

6. Quoted in Matusow, *The Unraveling of America*, 257. Matusow acknowledges that urban party machines dominated CAAs across the country, but argues that the "radicalism" of the community action component of the War on Poverty was "the exception that proved the rule" of liberal orthodoxy within the Great Society. Matusow, *The Unraveling of America*, 270. In contrast, Thomas Jackson argued that agencies like PAAC should be seen as the norm for the War on Poverty. "The War on Poverty, long on rhetoric and short on results, basically continued a tradition of top-down hierarchical reform that benefited mainly the middle class, leaving control of social policy in the hands of local elites and perpetuating the exclusion of minorities and the poor from decisions affecting their lives." Jackson, "The State, the Movement, and the Urban Poor," 407.

7. "Indigent Win Role in City's Antipoverty Bid," *Philadelphia Inquirer*, Feb. 6, 1965; "Tate Shakes Up City's Antipoverty Forces," *Bulletin*, Feb. 10, 1965. The Tate administration's two previous efforts to establish a local War on Poverty agency were rejected by the Office of Economic Opportunity because of a failure to adequately involve the poor or other community representatives in the program design. *Bulletin*, Oct. 19, Nov. 26, Nov. 30, and Dec. 14, 1964, and Jan. 1, 1965; "Another Try for Antipoverty Funds," *Bulletin*, Dec. 30, 1964; "Labor Attacks Tate Plan for Poverty War," *Bulletin*, Jan. 29, 1965; "Mayor Defends Antipoverty Program," *Bulletin*, Feb. 8, 1965. Allen Matusow has ascribed Tate's reluctance to structure any involvement of the poor in the antipoverty program to a desire "to convert the program into a source of political patronage." However, I think the mayor's most immediate motivation was to exclude local civil rights activists—in particular Cecil Moore and the leadership of Philadelphia CORE—from the program. Tate's eagerness to include social welfare agencies in the antipoverty program suggests that he was more interested in turning over the programs to city's social service professionals than in using it to reward his political supporters. Matusow, *The Unraveling of America*, 256.

8. City of Philadelphia, "Executive Order 1–65," Feb. 22, 1965, Greater Phila-

delphia Federation of Settlements (GPFS) collection, box 68, Temple University Urban Archives (TUUA); minutes, Philadelphia Antipoverty Action Committee, Mar. 5, 1965; GPFS collection, box 69, TUUA. The twelve poverty districts were established according to data from the 1960 census. While everyone residing in one of the poverty districts was eligible to vote in the elections, only those residents whose income fell below a certain limit, which varied according to family size, were eligible to run in the elections. "City Defines 12 Pockets Of Poverty," *Bulletin*, Mar. 26, 1965; Charles Bowser, "Philadelphia Antipoverty Action Committee Statistical Survey of Candidates of the May 26, 1965 Election," n.d., GPFS Collection, box 72, TUUA. In addition to electing a representative to the PAAC, each CAC received a $25,000 budget for neighborhood programs. "Antipoverty-War Troops Complain About Cramped 'Command Post'," *Bulletin*, Nov. 28, 1965; "Troubles Plentiful, Furniture Scarce, At Typical Action Council Office," *Bulletin*, Feb. 27, 1966; "Antipoverty Unit Runs 13 Projects," *Bulletin*, Jun. 16, 1966.

9. Interview with Charles Bowser, Mar. 10, 1994, Philadelphia; "City Antipoverty Group OKs Tate's Picking Director," *Bulletin*, Mar. 6, 1965; "Poverty Unit Proposes Bowser as Executive," *Bulletin*, Apr. 2, 1965; "Moore Insists Poverty Post Go to Crippins," *Philadelphia Inquirer*, Apr. 3, 1965; "Dispute Perils Poverty War, Aides Contend," *Bulletin*, Apr. 4, 1965; "Moore Sees Selfish Motives Behind Selection of Bowser," *Bulletin*, Apr. 5, 1965; "Cecil Moore Says Poverty Fight Is 'Not for Power, But for People,'" *Bulletin*, Apr. 9, 1965; "Both Bowser, Crippins Get Poverty Jobs," *Bulletin*, Apr. 13, 1965; "Crippins Takes Poverty Job Despite Moore's Disclaimer," *Bulletin*, Apr. 14, 1965; "Poor Lacked Power in Philadelphia."

10. To publicize the elections, the PAAC sponsored town meetings in each of the poverty districts to explain the purpose of the CACs and the antipoverty program. Interview with Bowser; "War on Poverty Vote Hailed Here as Success," *Bulletin*, May 27, 1965; Bowser, "Philadelphia Antipoverty Action Committee Statistical Survey"; "Report on Town Meetings," n.d.; and David Fineman, "The Community Action Councils—A Philadelphia First: A Freedom Report of the Philadelphia Chapter, Congress of Racial Equality," n.d., GPFS Collection, box 71, TUUA; "300,000 Urged to Attend Meetings Wednesday on Poverty Program," *Bulletin*, Apr. 25, 1965.

11. Others elected to the PAAC board as representatives of the poor included Milton Ibach, a roofer with four children, Ida Mae Watkins, a *Tribune* typist who described herself as active in a number of civic groups, Mayme James, a widow and street vendor, Virginia Pryor, a real estate saleswoman from the Haddington section of South Philadelphia, and Jean Crutchfield, a waitress and mother of two who had been active in community affairs. "Local Leaders Plan to Keep Control of Poverty War," *Bulletin*, Apr. 27, 1965; "War-on-Poverty Vote Hailed Here as Success," *Bulletin*, May 27, 1965; "12 Are Picked For Seats on Poverty Unit," *Bulletin*, Jun. 8, 1965; Philadelphia Antipoverty Action Committee, Community Action Council Representatives, Jun. 8, 1965, Housing Association of Delaware Valley [HADV] Collection, box 275, folder 4717, TUUA; "Area F Preferred Antipoverty Council Slate," Urban League [UL] Collection, box 16, folder 21, TUUA. On Abigail Pankey, see "Meeting Is Told Politicians May Grab Poverty Funds," *Bulletin*, Jan. 19, 1965, and "W. Phila. Unit Rejects City Poverty Plan," *Bulletin*, Feb. 4, 1965. On the organization of the CAC offices, see "Resident Participation," n.d., GPFS Collection, box 69, TUUA; "U.S. Gives City $5.9 Million to Fight Poverty," *Bulletin*, Jun. 23, 1965.

12. Bowser and Evans both claim that the OEO turned down the initial OIC proposal and only approved it after it was rewritten by the PAAC staff. Interviews with Bowser and with Sam Evans, April 15, 1994, Philadelphia; Fineman, "The Community Action Councils—A Philadelphia First"; "Present Members of PAAC," n.d., GPFS paper, box 77, TUUA; "U.S. Gives City $5.9 Million to Fight Poverty"; "Poor Lacked Power in Philadelphia."

13. Samuel Yarborough, the PAAC representative from North Philadelphia's Area D worked as a $9,000 per year administrator in the PAAC central office. Also employed in the PAAC office was Alison Bryant, the PAAC representative from Area F and a former substitute teacher in the city schools. In response to the OEO inquiry, Charles Bowser insisted that all of the CAC board members and their relatives had been hired on their merits and that council members should be allowed to lift themselves out of poverty. "Poor Lacked Power in Philadelphia"; "PAAC Urged to Put Salaried Workers Under Civil Service or Merit System," *Bulletin*, Jan. 25, 1966; "Year of War on Poverty Ends on a Note of Discord," *Bulletin*, May 29, 1966; "Philadelphia's Plan to Give Poor a Voice in Poverty Drive Called a Failure," *New York Times*, Jul. 17, 1966; "Most Elected Aides on PAAC Panel Turn Up on Payroll," *Philadelphia Inquirer*, Jul. 20, 1966; "Woman Critic of PAAC Gets Seat on Its Board," *Bulletin*, Sep. 20, 1966; "PAAC Official's Dual Role Threatens Funds, U.S. Says," *Bulletin*, Jan. 19, 1967; "New Philadelphia Story: Hard Times Befall a 'Model' Antipoverty Program," *New York Times*, June 26, 1967.

14. Interview with Bowser; "Poor Lacked Power in Philadelphia"; *Bulletin*, Jan. 6, 1966; "Fired Aide Again Blasts Poverty Setup," *Bulletin*, Jan. 20, 1966; "City Hit for Lack of Support to Poverty Units," *Bulletin*, Mar. 28, 1966; "Year of War on Poverty Ends on a Note of Discord"; Mrs. Anderson Page to Dr. John O. Reinemann, Dec. 16, 1966, GPFS Collection, box 73, TUUA; "Mrs. Page Quits PAAC Committee, Says Evans Usurped Her Authority," *Bulletin*, Dec. 19, 1966; "PAAC Names New Chairman of Review Unit," *Bulletin*, Dec. 21, 1966.

15. Evans and Bowser were never reluctant to use the PAAC infrastructure to support the political activities of the Tate administration and the Democratic machine. In August 1965, Bowser joined members of a North Philadelphia CAC on two chartered buses for a trip to the state capitol to protest Republican governor William Scranton's veto of $17 million in state welfare spending. Bowser and others insisted that the buses had been chartered with private funds. Then, in September 1966, the PAAC sent buses full of protesters to Washington to oppose cuts in the Neighborhood Youth Services program. Even after the OEO ruled that PAAC employees could not be paid for participating in electoral activities, the PAAC leadership urged them to volunteer in support of four city bonds on election day in November, 1966. Interviews with Bowser and Evans; "Political Use of Antipoverty Funds Is Charged"; "PAAC Plans 2d Harrisburg Bus Trip to Push for Higher Relief Payments," *Bulletin*, May 17, 1966; *Bulletin*, Sep. 23, Oct. 28 and 30, 1966; memorandum to Council Chairmen, PAAC Representatives, CAC Office Staff from Miss Barbara L. Weems, Oct. 28, 1966, GPFS Collection, box 70, TUUA; "New Philadelphia Story: Hard Times Befall a 'Model' Antipoverty Program."

16. In March 1966, the OEO changed its positions and issued a directive banning elected representatives of the poor and their close relatives from holding paid positions in antipoverty programs. However, the agency was forced to suspend its ruling after the PAAC laid off nearly five hundred workers. At a July 1966 public hearing sponsored by the Philadelphia ADA, CAC members who felt isolated from the PAAC central office charged that "everything is controlled downtown" and that "nothing is happening" in their neighborhoods. That month, PAAC held a second set of CAC elections. This time, an insurgent group calling itself the Maximum Participation Movement (MPM) and led by a University of Pennsylvania sociologist named Arthur Shostak formed slates of candidates to challenge Evans's supporters. Of the MPM 's forty-two candidates, however, only six were elected. *Bulletin*, Apr. 3, Jun. 29 and 31, 1966; "Year of War on Poverty Ends on A Note of Discord"; "Unit Threatens to Boycott City Poverty Elections," *Bulletin*, Jun. 5, 1966; "PAAC Is Said to Fail To Reach Poor in Slums," *Bulletin*, Jul. 15, 1966; "PAAC Goes Secret," *Phila-*

delphia Inquirer, Jul. 16, 1966; "Philadelphia's Plan to Give Poor a Voice in Poverty Drive Called a Failure," *New York Times,* Jul. 17, 1966; "Most Elected Aides on PAAC Panel Turn Up on Payroll," *Philadelphia Inquirer,* Jul. 20, 1966; "U of P Sociologist Enters Slates in Antipoverty Election Campaign," *Bulletin,* Jul. 20, 1966.

17. Weems assumed the position of acting director of PAAC following Bowser's resignation. Interview with Bowser; "PAAC Is Said to Fail To Reach Poor in Slum"; "U of P Sociologist Enters Slates in Antipoverty Election Campaign"; "26,000 Poor Vote in PAAC Election Here," *Bulletin,* Jul. 23, 1966; "Bigger Vote Turnout of Poor Shows Their Faith in Democracy, U.S. Says," *Bulletin,* Jul. 24, 1966; "Rival Faction and PAAC Chart Collision Course," *Bulletin,* Aug. 5, 1966; "Poverty Official Here Denounces Federal Control," *Philadelphia Inquirer,* Oct. 26, 1966; "Apathy Found in Poverty War Here," *Philadelphia Inquirer,* Dec. 26, 1966; "PAAC Oks Federal Guidelines; Moore Quits with Blast at U.S.," *Bulletin,* Dec. 28, 1966; "PAAC Official's Dual Role Threatens Funds, U.S. Says," *Bulletin,* Jan. 19, 1967; "No Regrets, Bowser Says, Praising PAAC," *Bulletin,* Jan. 22, 1967; "Rejected Aide to Direct War on Poverty Here," *Bulletin,* Jan. 30, 1967; "Tate Names 31 to New Antipoverty Commission," *Bulletin,* Feb. 20, 1968; "New Poverty Agency Elects Same Officers in 3 Minutes," *Bulletin,* Mar. 13, 1968; *Bulletin,* Apr. 16, Aug. 6, Dec. 11, 1968, and Mar. 25, 1970.

18. In October 1966, HUD official Ralph Taylor told a Philadelphia audience that the "demonstration [model] city programs must be planned and operated by local people, based on their own evaluation of their total need." "A Note on Social Planning," *Bulletin,* Nov. 4, 1966.

19. In its proposal, the Tate administration pledged to build 14,700 new public housing units and to rehabilitate 28,000 substandard dwelling units in the area. The proposal also included plans to build twenty-two new public schools in the area, all of which would be available for community use in the evenings and on the weekends, a $9 million revolving investment fund for economic development, and $49 million to job training programs. *Bulletin,* Mar. 21, 1966; "Proposal to the Department of Housing and Urban Development by the Honorable James H. J. Tate," Mar. 21, 1966, HADV collection, box 107e, folder 50, TUUA.

20. "Proposal to The Department of Housing and Urban Development by the Honorable James H. J. Tate"; minutes, Committee on Citizen Participation, Jan. 30, and Feb. 2, 1967, HADV collection, box 107e, folder 50, TUUA; "15 Named to Oversee Model Cities Program," *Bulletin,* Feb. 9, 1967; "Jobless Rate of 11 Percent Shocks City Economist," *Bulletin,* Feb. 21, 1967; *Bulletin,* Feb. 26, 1967.

21. Minutes, Committee on Citizen Participation, Jan. 30 and Feb. 2, 1967, and Philadelphia Crisis Committee, "Chronological Fact Sheet on Model Cities Controversy," n.d., HADV collection, box 107e, folder 50, TUUA; North City Congress, "What Is the Model Cities Program?" n.d., UL collection, box 16, folder 24, TUUA. On the North City Congress, see "Testimony to PAAC Hearing: Mrs. Bertha Brown, Jul. 5, 1967," GPFS collection, box 77, TUUA.

22. Interview with William Meek, Mar. 15, 1994, Philadelphia; minutes, Temporary Committee to Design AWC Structure, Feb. 13, 1967, HADV collection, box 107e, folder 50, TUUA; "Area Council Fights Change in Model City Plan," *Philadelphia Inquirer,* May 9, 1967; "Testimony to PAAC Hearing: Mrs. Bertha Brown"; "Statement of the Temporary Steering Committee of the Area-Wide Council (AWC): Mrs. Emily Clark," Jul. 5, 1967, and minutes, Temporary Steering Committee of the AWC, Aug. 9 and 24, 1967, HADV collection, box 107e, folder 50, TUUA. On the neighborhood meetings that led to the formation of the AWC, see the Turner staff logs for Jan, 11 and Feb. 6–14, 1967, HADV collection, box 107e, folder 50, TUUA. For an example of the work of the AWC Planning Committees, see Working Paper no. 1, AWC Standing Committee on Physical Environment, Aug. 3, 1967, HADV collection, box 107e, folder 50, TUUA.

23. Interview with Meek; minutes, Temporary Committee to Design AWC Structure, Feb. 13, Jul 24, Aug. 9, 24, and 31, 1967, "Area-Wide Council" flier, Apr. 20, 1967, and "Area-Wide Council Staff Resume Summary," n.d., HADV collection, box 107e, folder 50, TUUA; City of Philadelphia Press Release, Aug. 17, 1967, HADV collection, box 107e, folder 49, TUUA; Area Wide Council Press Release, Sep. 21, 1967, *Bulletin* clippings file, TUUA; *Bulletin,* Apr. 21 and Nov. 16, 1967.

24. Interview with Meek; interview with Walter Palmer, Aug. 10, 2004, Philadelphia; "Area-Wide Council Staff Resume Summary."

25. Interview with Meek; "Leaflets Made in Model Cities Headquarters," *Bulletin* Nov. 18, 1967; "Negro Leader Hails Student Protest Here," *Bulletin,* Dec. 4, 1967; "Court Orders Wider Ban on School Rallies," *Bulletin,* Dec. 7, 1967; Temporary Steering Committee of the Area-Wide Council, Emergency Meeting, Nov. 21, 1967, HADV collection, box 107e, folder 50, TUUA.

26. Temporary Steering Committee of the Area-Wide Council, Emergency Meeting, Nov. 21, 1967.

27. Working Draft of Policy Statement by Area-Wide Council, Nov. 24, 1967 and Area-Wide Council of Model Cities Program, General Meeting, Dec. 7, 1967, HADV collection, box 107e, folder 50, TUUA; "Model Cities Unit Pledges Attack on 'Unrest in N. Phila.,'" *Bulletin* Dec. 8, 1967; "Phila. to Get Request for Model Cities Funds," *Philadelphia Inquirer,* Dec. 10, 1967.

28. "Phila. to Get Request for Model Cities Funds"; *Bulletin,* Dec. 11 & 13, 1967; "Model Cities Unit Rejects City's Reduced Budget Plan," *Bulletin,* Dec. 15, 1967; *Philadelphia Inquirer,* Dec. 20, 1967; "Restoration of Model Cities Funds Sought," *Bulletin,* Dec. 28, 1967; Achtenberg Logs, Dec. 1–6, 1967, Mar. 20–Apr. 5, Apr. 8–May 2, H. Ralph Taylor to Cushing N. Dolbeare, Jan. 30, 1968, and Area-Wide Council Meeting at Strawberry Mansion, Feb. 28, 1968, HADV collection, box 107e, folder 50, TUUA; *Bulletin,* Jan. 6, 1968. Still, the AWC and the Tate administration continued to feud. In April, 1968 Alvin Echols called Model Cities a "golden ghettoes program," that seeks to maintain de facto segregation. After the AWC refused to provide the city with minutes of its meetings, one Tate aide charged that "a very narrowly based, very militant group [was] controlling the AWC staff." The aide said he was "not at all satisfied that the Area-Wide Council really represents the whole North Philadelphia community." *Bulletin,* Apr. 17 and 18, 1968; "Model Cities Group Insists on Bigger Role in Reform Planning," *Philadelphia Inquirer,* May 26, 1968.

29. *Bulletin,* Apr. 9, 1968; Achtenberg Logs, Mar. 20–Apr. 5, Apr. 8–May 2, May 3–16, 1968, minutes, Executive Board Meeting of the Area-Wide Council, May 3, 1968, and Position Statement of Area-Wide Council Board, May 9, 1968, HADV collection, box 107e, folder 50, TUUA.

30. The staff of the regional HUD office in Philadelphia included Terry Chisholm, the African American former executive director of the Commission on Human Relations (CHR), and Yvonne Perry, a former staff member with the Philadelphia Council for Community Advancement (PCCA). Achtenberg Logs, May 3–16, 1968, HADV collection, box 107e, folder 50, TUUA; *Bulletin,* Apr. 9, Jun. 20 and Jul. 4, 1968; "New Model Cities Directed Feels "Crises Stage Is Past," *Bulletin,* Aug. 26, 1968; "Residents and Officials Committed To Making 'Model Cities' a Success," *Bulletin,* Sep. 5, 1968.

31. The other three corporations were a Housing Multi-Service Center to provide housing services; a Model Cities Community Foundation to provide low interest loans for commercial developments; and a Health Services Corporation to improve health services in the area. "Model Cities Program Geared to Make Living Conditions Better for Many Thousands," *Philadelphia Tribune,* Dec. 21, 1968; North

City Area-Wide Council, Inc. v. George W. Romney, and William R. Meek to Mrs. Dolbeare, Jun. 19, 1969, HADV collection, box 107e, folder 50, TUUA; "Ghetto Needs Entrepreneurs," *Philadelphia Inquirer,* Jan. 12, 1969; *Bulletin,* Jan. 17 and May 7, 1969.

32. In July 1968, Robert H. Baida, deputy assistant secretary for Model Cities at HUD, spelled out the agency's position in greater detail. HUD was seeking to distinguish "between citizen control and participation . . . . The Model Cities program is not to be controlled by citizen groups. Control and responsibility rests with the local government." *Bulletin,* Mar. 12, 1969; Floyd H. Hyde to James H.J. Tate, May 27, 1969, and HUD News, "Model Cities Contract Tendered to Philadelphia, Pennsylvania," Jun. 30, 1969, HADV collection, 107e, box 49, TUUA; "Model Cities: The Philadelphia Story," n.d., HADV collection, box 107e, folder 49, TUUA; Philadelphia Crisis Committee, "Chronological Fact Sheet on Model Cities Controversy."

33. After his election as mayor in 1971, Frank Rizzo named Goldie Watson to the post of deputy mayor, making her the highest-ranking African American official in his administration. "Goldie Watson Another Negro Woman 'First' for This City," *Philadelphia Tribune,* Dec. 30, 1967. For Watson's view of the Model Cities controversy, see memorandum from H. Louis Evert to Maury B. Fagan, Sep. 10, 1969, FC collection, box 4, TUUA, and minutes, Philadelphia Committee on City Policy, Sep. 30, 1969, HADV collection, box 107e, folder 50, TUUA.

34. North City Area-Wide Council, Inc. v. George W. Romney; "Model Cities: The Philadelphia Story"; Philadelphia Crisis Committee, "Chronological Fact Sheet on Model Cities Controversy"; "Citizens Sue U.S. for Curbs in Model Plan," *Bulletin,* Aug. 17, 1969.

35. North City Area-Wide Council, Inc. v. George W. Romney; "Model Cities: The Philadelphia Story"; Philadelphia Crisis Committee, "Chronological Fact Sheet on Model Cities Controversy"; William R. Meek to Mrs. Dolbeare, Jun. 19, 1969, and North City Area-Wide Council, "Dear Organizer and Friend of Area-Wide Council," Jun. 25, 1968, HADV collection, box 107e, folder 50, TUUA; "Model Cities Council To Sue City, US Govt. For Program's Control," *Philadelphia Tribune,* Aug. 5, 1969; "U.S. Sued on Grant for Model Cities," *New York Times,* Aug. 16, 1969; "Citizens Sue U.S. for Curbs in Model Plan"; "Bigger Voice in Model Cities Won by Areawide Council," *Bulletin,* Jul. 15, 1970; "Plan for Philadelphia Is Ruled a Violation of Model Cities Act," *New York Times,* Jul. 19, 1970.

36. Nineteen of the thirty-five advisory committee members were former members of the AWC or one of its hub councils. Beetle Log, Aug. 22, 28 and Sep. 19, 1969, Dolbeare Log, Jun. 12, 1970, and minutes, Philadelphia Committee on City Policy, Sep. 30, 1969, HADV collection, box 107e, folder 50, TUUA.

37. The Philadelphia Housing Association changed its name to the Housing Association of the Delaware Valley in 1969. Beetle Log, Aug. 22, 28 and Sep. 19, 1969, Dolbeare Log, Jun. 12, 1970, minutes, Philadelphia Committee on City Policy, Sep. 30, 1969, and Housing Association testimony on Model Cities renewal plan, Nov. 18, 1969, HADV collection, box 107e, folder 49, TUUA.

38. Goode quoted in memorandum to Committee on Black Political Development from Robert J. Sugarman, Feb. 9, 1972, Americans for Democratic Action [ADA] papers, box 38, folder 3, TUUA.

39. For discussions of the urban politics of space, see Robert Self, " 'To Plan Our Liberation': Black Power and the Politics of Place in Oakland, California, 1965–1977," *Journal of Urban History* 26, 6 (Sep. 2000): 759–92, and Logan and Molotch, *Urban Fortunes,* 17–49.

40. *Philadelphia Tribune,* April 15, 1970; "Black Political Power in Phila. Has Come Far in a Generation," *Philadelphia Inquirer,* Nov. 16, 1998. "In for the 'Long

Haul': John White, Raised in Politics, Civil Rights," *Philadelphia Inquirer*, Feb. 23, 1999. On John White, see "J. White Sr. Dies," *Philadelphia Inquirer*, Sept. 16, 1999; "Farewell Brother: John White Sr. Dies; He Helped Bring End to 'Plantation Politics,'" *Philadelphia Daily News*, Sep. 16, 1999; "A Legend Eulogized at His Funeral: John White Sr. Remembered as Great Leader," *Philadelphia Inquirer*, Sep. 21, 1999.

41. "Farewell Brother: John White Sr. Dies"; "A Legend Eulogized at his Funeral."

42. The remaining honorees were Bertha Brown, president of Our Neighbors Association, Robert Russell, Executive Director of FOLK, and Novella Williams of Citizens for Progress. *Philadelphia Tribune*, April 15, 1970.

43. Richard Hatcher quoted in *Bulletin*, Apr. 27, 1970. Turnout for the dinner would have been even higher, the Forum's organizers charged, had not Mayor Tate ordered leading black Democrats to stay away. For a discussion of the impact of Mayor Hatcher's visit on the Black Political Forum, see W. Wilson Goode with Joann Stevens, *In Goode Faith* (Valley Forge, Pa.: Judson Press, 1992), 104–05.

44. Vance's remarks are summarized in a memorandum to the Committee on Black Political Development from Robert J. Sugarman. At the time, Vance was a middle school principal in the Philadelphia school system. He would go on to serve as superintendent of schools in Montgomery County, Maryland and in Washington D.C. On Vance's career, see Bernard C. Watson, *Colored, Negro, Black: Chasing the American Dream*, (Philadelphia: JDC Books, 1997), 112–19, 126, 261. For an early articulation of the potential for black electoral politics to address issues of poverty in the urban North, see Robert Vernon, "Black Ghettos Need Political Power," *Illustrated News*, Aug. 24, 1964. For a survey of postwar racial politics in Philadelphia with a somewhat different emphasis, see Carolyn Adams et al., *Philadelphia: Neighborhoods, Division, and Conflict in a Postindustrial City* (Philadelphia: Temple University Press, 1991), esp. 124–53.

45. Goode, *In Goode Faith*, 104–5.

46. Watson, *Colored, Negro, Black*, 137–38; "Farewell Brother: John White Sr. Dies"; interview with Charyn Sutton, Aug. 12, 2004, Philadelphia. On Wilson Goode's background in community organizing and antipoverty work, see Goode, *In Goode Faith*, 92–102 & 109–120 and Paul M. Washington with David McI. Gracie, *"Other Sheep I Have": The Autobiography of Father Paul M. Washington* (Philadelphia: Temple University Press, 1994), 140. Bernard Watson would go on to serve as vice president for academic administration at Temple University and then as president of the William Penn Foundation.

47. For a discussion of independent black politics in Philadelphia that is narrowly focused on Wilson Goode's election as the city's first black mayor, see Bruce Ransom, "Black Independent Politics in Philadelphia and the Election of Mayor W. Wilson Goode," in Michael B. Preston, Lenneal J. Henderson, Jr., and Paul L. Puryear, eds., *The New Black Politics*, 2nd ed., (New York: Longman, 1987), 256–89.

48. "Jack Saunders Says," *Philadelphia Tribune*, Mar. 7 and 14, 1970. For a profile of a black party loyalist, ward leader and city councilman, see "Decent Housing Uppermost to Councilman Campbell," *Philadelphia Tribune*, Feb. 7, 1970.

49. "Negro Dems Name D.A., Controller Choices," *Philadelphia Tribune*, Feb. 15, 1969.

50. "Democrats Hurt by Failure to Endorse," *Philadelphia Tribune*, Nov. 8, 1969.

51. Watson, *Colored Negro, Black*, 136; Goode, *In Goode Faith*, 104–6; "Jack Saunders Says," *Philadelphia Tribune*, Mar. 7 and 14, 1970; *Philadelphia Tribune*, May 16, 23 and June 5, 9, 1970.

52. Three months earlier, the popular principal of West Philadelphia High School had complained that twenty-one youth gangs had overrun the school. "21

Youth Gangs Have School Reeling, West. Phila. Principal Moans," *Philadelphia Tribune*, Feb. 7, 1970.

53. Williams received 3,408 votes to 2,333 votes for Lawson. "Jack Saunders Says," *Philadelphia Tribune*, Mar. 7, 14, and June 5, 13, 1970; *Philadelphia Tribune*, May 23, 1970; Paolantonio, *Frank Rizzo*, 111–17; Goode, *In Goode Faith*, 105.

54. Thacher Longstreth with Dan Rottenberg, *Main Line WASP: The Education of Thacher Longstreth* (New York: W.W. Norton, 1990), 253. On the Rizzo campaign, see Paolantonio, *Frank Rizzo*, 102–22.

55. On the Green campaign, see memorandum to ADA Board Members from Dave Hornbeck, Jan. 18, 1971, ADA papers, box 38, folder 2, TUUA; Paolantonio, *Frank Rizzo*, 113–15. On Rizzo's endorsement by the Democratic city committee, see Paolantonio, *Frank Rizzo*, 111.

56. "Cohen Says He Will Fire Comm. Rizzo, if Elected Mayor," *Philadelphia Tribune*, Mar. 15, 1971. On David Cohen's career, see "David Cohen, in City Hall," *Distant Drummer* 60 (November 21–29, 1969), in FC papers box 51, folder 5, TUUA. On Cohen's support for black activist demands, see "Cohen Backs NAACP Probe of Police Here," *Bulletin*, May 8, 1970. On the Cohen campaign, see memorandum to ADA Board Members from Dave Hornbeck.

57. Memorandum to ADA Board Members from Dave Hornbeck; "Convention Planned Here to Form Black Political Unit," *Bulletin*, Feb. 5, 1971; "Black Political Convention Planners See Rizzo's Candidacy as Good Omen," *Philadelphia Tribune*, Feb. 6, 1971; "Hardy Willliams' Real Intention Subject of Crystal Ball Gazing," *Philadelphia Tribune*, Feb. 9, 1971; "Black Political Convention: No Place for Personal Advancement Candidates," *Philadelphia Tribune*, Feb. 13, 1971; "Black Convention Ignores Machine Politicians," *Philadelphia Tribune*, Feb. 16, 1971; Washington, *"Other Sheep I Have"*, 155.

58. "Right On! By Pamala Haynes," *Philadelphia Tribune*, Mar. 16, 1971.

59. For example, Rev. M. Lorenzo Shepard, the son of Marshall Shepard and a longtime ally of Cecil Moore, ran a "Green for Mayor" headquarters from his West Philadelphia church. See "Green for Mayor Headquarters Opened by Group Headed by Mt. Olivet Pastor Rev. Shepard," *Philadelphia Tribune*, Jan. 12, 1971. On black support for Green and Cohen, see also "Green Surrounded by Black Followers as He Announces Candidacy for Mayor," *Philadelphia Tribune*, Mar. 2, 1971; "Rizzo a 'Tyrant and Bully' Black Labor Leader Says, New Political Unit Throws Support to Bill Green," *Philadelphia Tribune*, Mar. 16, 1971; "Congressman Asserts Vote for Williams Helps Rizzo," *Philadelphia Tribune*, May 15, 1971; "Right On! By Pamala Haynes," *Philadelphia Tribune*, May 11, 1971. On Williams's failure to win the support of a single black elected official, see "Jack Saunders Says," *Philadelphia Tribune*, Mar. 20, 1971.

60. Williams quoted in Paolantonio, *Frank Rizzo*, 113; Goode, 106.

61. Goode quoted in Paolantonio, *Frank Rizzo*, 113.

62. Interview with Sutton.

63. Williams quoted in memorandum to ADA Board Members from Dave Hornbeck. See also "Williams Says He Has Good Chance to Win Mayor Race," *Philadelphia Tribune*, Mar. 16, 1971. On the Williams campaign, see *Philadelphia Tribune*, Apr. 10, 17, 1971; "Center City Citizens for Hardy Williams," n.d., ADA papers, box 38, folder 4, TUUA; Paolantonio, *Frank Rizzo*, 111–17; Goode, *In Goode Faith*, 106; Watson, *Colored, Negro, Black*, 136–37.

64. For similar discussions of the Williams campaign strategy for winning the primary, see Watson, *Colored, Negro, Black*, 137; "Jack Saunders Says," *Philadelphia Tribune*, Mar. 2 and May 11, 1971.

65. Williams would eventually be forced to publicly deny reports of secret ties

between the Rizzo camp and his campaign. "Link to Rizzo Is Denied by Williams as Primary Nears," *Philadelphia Tribune*, May 15, 1971. On rumors of the Rizzo campaign's support for Williams's candidacy, see also "Right On! By Pamala Haynes," *Philadelphia Tribune*, May 15, 1971; Paolantonio, *Frank Rizzo*, 112–13; Watson, *Colored, Negro, Black*, 137.

66. Memorandum to Jack Adler, et al., from David Hornbeck, June 22, 1970, ADA collection, box 38, folder 3, TUUA; David W. Hornbeck to Dr. Leon Sullivan, Pastor, n.d., ADA collection, box 38, folder 2, TUUA. Of the eighty-one ADA board members in 1971, sixteen—eight whites and eight blacks—had strong ties to movement organizations. See ADA Board Membership List, n.d., ADA collection, box 38, folder 2, TUUA.

67. Memorandum to ADA Board Members from David Hornbeck, January 27, 1971.

68. "Green: Democrat for Mayor," press release, Apr. 5, 1971, ADA collection, box 38, folder 4, TUUA. At the time, Sawyer was one of seven "honorary chairmen" of the Philadelphia ADA. Thirteen of the twenty-six members of the Independents for Green committee were current ADA board members. ADA Board Membership List, n.d., ADA collection, box 38, folder 2, TUUA.

69. "ADA Endorses Bill Green in the Democratic Primary," Apr. 11, 1971, ADA collection, box 38, folder 4, TUUA. The ADA's failure to endorse Williams did not prevent the BPF from joining with the ADA and four other white liberal reform groups to endorse three anti-organization candidates for at-large positions on the city council, two of whom were white, in the 1971 Democratic Primary. See "Philadelphia's Six Independent Democratic Organizations Have Endorsed," flier, n.d., ADA box 38, folder 4, TUUA.

70. "Scores Sob as Cohen Pulls Out of Race and Throws His Support to Green," *Philadelphia Tribune*, May 8, 1971.

71. Memorandum to ADA Board Members from David Hornbeck, January 7, 1971; "Scores Sob as Cohen Pulls Out of Race and Throws His Support to Green"; Paolantonio, *Frank Rizzo*, 114. On Green's anger at Williams, see "Verbal War Between Williams, Green Grows Hotter, Hotter," *Philadelphia Tribune*, Apr. 17, 1971 and "Green Wants No Rerun of Williams Clash," *Bulletin*, Feb. 17, 1972.

72. "Rizzo's Big Victory: How, Why, and What It Means," *Philadelphia Tribune*, May 22, 1971. See also "Jack Saunders Says," *Philadelphia Tribune*, May 25, 1971. Cecil Moore received 8,971 votes in his 1967 independent campaign for mayor, just 1.2 percent of the votes cast in that November's election. "Specter Loses by Only 10,892 in 73 Percent Turnout," *Bulletin*, Nov. 8, 1967.

73. "Longstreth to Make Pitch to Black Political Forum; Rizzo Decides to Warm Bench," *Philadelphia Tribune*, Jul. 31, 1971; "Longstreth Vows He Will Appoint More Blacks to His Cabinet than Democrats, if He Is Elected Mayor," *Philadelphia Tribune*, Aug. 3, 1971; "Black Political Forum Endorses Longstreth, Republican Ticket," *Philadelphia Tribune*, Sept. 21, 1971; "Longstreth to Get my Vote: Hardy Williams," *Philadelphia Tribune*, Oct. 26, 1971; "McIntosh Beaten by Anti-Rizzo Tide, Dr. Allen Says," *Philadelphia Tribune*, Nov. 9, 1971; interview with Charyn Sutton. On Longstreth's efforts to win black votes, see "Thacher Longstreth Banking on Black Vote to Beat Rizzo," *Philadelphia Tribune*, May 22, 1971; "Moore Comes Out 'Fighting' For Longstreth, Raps Rizzo," *Philadelphia Tribune*, Oct. 2, 1971; "Rev. Leon H. Sullivan Endorses Longstreth for Mayor; Rizzo's Election Will Divide City, Minister Asserts," *Philadelphia Tribune*, Oct. 23, 1971. On McIntosh's support for Rizzo, see "8 Ward Leaders Bank on Frank Rizzo," *Philadelphia Tribune*, Sept. 25, 1971.

74. "Blacks Voted Against Frank Rizzo but Supported His Running Mates," *Philadelphia Tribune*, Nov. 6, 1971; Paolantonio, *Frank Rizzo*, 116–21; Longstreth, *Main*

Line WASP, 249–261. Estimates of the black vote are based on an analysis of ten wards in which 90 percent or more of registered voters were black. See Goode, *In Goode Faith*, 106. In the twenty-three wards with black majorities, Longstreth defeated Rizzo by 74 to 26 percent.

75. "McIntosh Beaten by Anti-Rizzo Tide, Dr. Allen Says"; "Jack Saunders Says," *Philadelphia Tribune*, Nov. 2, 1971.

76. On John White, Jr.'s political career, see "In for the 'Long Haul': John White, Raised in Politics, Civil Rights," *Philadelphia Inquirer*, Feb. 23, 1999. On Gray's victory over Nix, see Watson, *Colored, Negro, Black*, 141.

77. Interview with Palmer; interviews with Edward Robinson, Aug. 11, 2004 and Elaine G. Richardson, Aug. 12, 2004, both in Philadelphia. On the Young Afro-Americans, see "Black Militants Get Mixed Reaction from Germantown Pupils, Faculty," *Bulletin*, Jun. 25, 1968; "5 Groups Bid for Grant to Control Gangs," *Bulletin*, Sept. 9, 1969; "Private Black School System Goal of Young Afro-Americans," *Philadelphia Tribune*, Feb. 23, 1971; "The Incident," *Community Forum: A Publication of the Urban Studies and Community Services Center of LaSalle College* (Spring-Summer 1969) in the Police Advisory Board [PAB] collection, box 2, TUUA; Organizational List, n.d., FC papers, box 62, folder 8, TUUA. In the late 1960s and early 1970s, six black youth gangs operated in Germantown: Clang, Somerville, Dogtown, Haines Street, Brickyard, and Pulaskitown. See Nancy Loving, "Somerville in the Streets," *Community Forum: A Publication of the Urban Studies and Community Services Center of LaSalle College*, (Spring 1970), PAB collection, box 2, TUUA; "United Progressives, Brickyard Youth Council Fight Gang Warfare and Crime in Wister Area," *Philadelphia Tribune*, Nov. 2, 1971.

78. "Rep. Rush Plans Vigorous Campaign in Face of District Reapportionment," *Bulletin*, Feb. 21, 1972; "Rights Veteran Running for Legislature," *Bulletin*, Feb. 27, 1972.

79. By 1971, black voters outnumbered white voters in Northwest Philadelphia's 8th Councilmanic District 51,887 to 38,358. "Jack Saunders Says," *Philadelphia Tribune*, Mar. 9 and Apr. 6, 1971

80. On the anti-Rizzo sentiment in Northwest Philadelphia, see *Philadelphia Tribune*, Apr. 6, 1971. Ironically, Rizzo, who was born in South Philadelphia, moved with his family to Germantown as an adolescent and would live in the Northwest section of the city for the rest of his life. Paolantonio, *Frank Rizzo*, 33–36.

81. This description of Richardson's electoral experience is based on my interview with Charyn Sutton.

82. "Rights Veteran Running for Legislature," *Bulletin*, Feb. 27, 1972; "Blacks Celebrate Victories over 'Machine' in Legislative Races" and "Richardson Upsets Rep. Rush in 201st," *Bulletin*, Apr. 27, 1972.

83. "Richardson Upsets Rush in 201st"; "Upset House Winner Credits Youth Drive," *Philadelphia Daily News*, Apr. 27, 1972.

84. "Squabbling Rizzo Calls Gang Probe 'Worthless'," *Philadelphia Inquirer*, Jun. 23, 1973; "Rizzo Opposes Blacks, Legislator Charges," *Bulletin*, Aug. 20, 1974.

85. "Legislator Seized in Vendor Protest," *Bulletin*, Jul. 20, 1976; "1,000 Black Join Boycott At the Gallery," *Bulletin*, Aug. 25, 1978; "Funeral Services Set for State Rep. David Richardson," *Philadelphia Tribune*, Aug. 22, 1995. On the 1978 MOVE-Police Confrontation, see Paolantonio, *Frank Rizzo*, 224–27, and Washington, *Other Sheep I Have*," 178–181. On Milton Street's career as a community activist and politician, "Philadelphia Poor Taking Over Houses To Fight City Decay," *New York Times*, Jun. 12, 1977, and Kia Gregory and Mike Newell, "Brother from Another Planet," *PhiladelphiaWEEKLY.com*, July 2, 2003.

86. On Lucien Blackwell's career, see Paolantonio, *Frank Rizzo*, 233–34; Goode

In Goode Faith, 210, 281–282, 304. On Chaka Fattah's career, see Goode *In Goode Faith,* 278. Ironically, Blackwell and Fattah would face each other in two different campaigns for William Gray's seat in the U.S. Congress. Following Gray's 1991 retirement from Congress, Blackwell defeated Fattah in both the special election to complete Gray's term and in the simultaneously held Democratic primary for the following term. Two years later, however, Fattah ousted Blackwell from the seat. Fattah is currently in his fifth term as the representative for Philadelphia's Second Congressional District. On the Fattah-Blackwell races, see "Fattah to Face $1M Libel Lawsuit: Legal Wrangling Beginning to Overshadow the Issues," *Philadelphia Tribune,* Mar. 25, 1994; *Philadelphia Inquirer,* Sept. 12, 1994.

87. "Brothers Picket and Protest Way to Power," *New York Times,* Jan. 1, 1980; "Riots Predicted in Welfare List Purge," *Bulletin,* June 5, 1980. After serving on the Philadelphia City Council for twenty years, John Street was elected mayor of Philadelphia in 1999. Gregory and Newell, "Brother from Another Planet."

88. *Philadelphia Inquirer,* Jan. 11, 1984; Gregory and Newell, "Brother from Another Planet." On Street's claims that his caucus switch enabled him to better serve his constituents, see *Philadelphia Inquirer,* March 20 and Apr. 6, 1984.

89. "Party-Crossing Talk Raises the Ire of Rep. Richardson," *Bulletin,* Mar. 9, 1981; *Philadelphia Inquirer,* Apr. 6, 1984; *Philadelphia Daily News,* May 20, 1996. On "Thornfare," see "Riots Predicted in Welfare List Purge," *Bulletin,* Jun. 5, 1980.

90. On Jones's career with the Philadelphia Welfare Rights Organization, see *Philadelphia Tribune,* Jul. 13 and 20, 1968; "Leader of Welfare Sit-In Calls Herself Nonviolent," *Bulletin,* Nov. 17, 1968; Lou Antosh, "Fighting to Liberate The Fountain of Welfare," *Philadelphia Inquirer Magazine,* May 16, 1971; "111 Phila. Delegates to Join in WRO Conference," *Bulletin,* Jul. 21, 1971; Felicia A. Kornbluh, "To Fulfill Their 'Rightly Needs'": Consumerism and the National Welfare Rights Movement," *Radical History Review* 69 (Fall 1997). On PCIA's campaign against welfare cuts, see "Riots Predicted in welfare list purge" *Bulletin;* Washington, *"Other Sheep I Have",* 83–84.

91. "Activist to Oppose Sen. Street: Welfare Activist Backed by Party," *Philadelphia Inquirer,* Jan. 11, 1984; *Philadelphia Inquirer,* Apr. 6, 1984; Watson, *Colored, Negro, Black,* 141. On Goode's support for Jones's candidacy, see *Philadelphia Inquirer,* Mar. 20, 1984.

92. *Philadelphia Daily News,* Jan. 6 and Apr. 6, 1984; "Street to Jones: Let the Voters Decide, *Philadelphia Daily News,* Mar. 23, 1984; *Philadelphia Inquirer,* Jan. 11, 1984, "Donnybrook: Jones and Street Act Like Politicians," *Philadelphia Inquirer,* Feb. 23,1984; "Two Street Wars Steal the Spotlight," *Philadelphia Inquirer,* Apr. 2, 1984.

93. Throughout her tenure in Harrisburg, Jones was a vociferous critic of the state's job training and placement programs for welfare recipients. The state's programs, she argued, put too much emphasis on placing recipients unskilled low-paying jobs over providing the education and training that they needed to get out of poverty. *Philadelphia Inquirer,* Apr. 11 and 12, 1984, Jan. 2, and Jun. 25, 1985, Mar. 15, 1988, Apr. 18, 1992, Jun. 22, 1993, and Jan. 24, 1996; *Philadelphia Daily News,* Aug. 21, 1986, Jun. 9, 1994, Mar. 19, 20, 21, and 28, 1996; "Roxanne Jones: A Fighter Mourned," *Philadelphia Tribune,* May 21, 1996.

94. Paolantonio, *Frank Rizzo,* 147–63, 180–87. On Rizzo's mayoralty, see "For Mayor Frank Rizzo, One Issue Has Been Enough," *New York Times,* Aug. 19, 1979. S. A. Paolantonio argues low black turnout was a major factor in Rizzo's victory. According to Paolantonio, supporters of Charles Bowser—angry that the city committee had passed over their candidate—plastered North Philadelphia with signs that read "Bowser in November" in the days before the May primary. Paolantonio, *Frank Rizzo,* 185.

95. Watson, *Colored Negro, Black*, 138; interview with Bowser; *New York Times*, Sept. 29, 1975; "Black Political Power in Phila. Has Come Far in a Generation," *Philadelphia Inquirer*, Nov. 16, 1998; "In for the 'Long Haul': John White; Raised in Politics, Civil Rights," *Philadelphia Inquirer*, Feb. 23, 1999; Charles Bowser, "White Sr., Led Attack on Plantation Politics," *Philadelphia Tribune*, Sept. 21, 1999.

96. Paolantonio, *Frank Rizzo*, 223–29; Ransom, "Black Independent Politics," 259–60.

97. *New York Times*, June. 19, 1979. See also "The Philadelphia Primary: Is Rizzo Right?" *New York Times*, May 14, 1979; Goode, 141–42; Paolantonio, *Frank Rizzo*, 231–34, Ransom, "Black Independent Politics," 260–62.

98. "Bowser Accused of Stealing Show," *Bulletin*, July 15, 1979. Green's announcement was in part in response to Republican candidate David Marston who had already pledged to appoint a black managing director. Goode, *In Goode Faith*, 142; Paolantonio, *Frank Rizzo*, 233–34.

99. The Green campaign leaked Goode's name to the Philadelphia media as the likely managing director before the election, but his appointment was not officially announced until after the election. Goode, *In Goode Faith*, 121–159. Goode appointed John White Sr. to be his chief deputy in the Managing Director's office. "In for the 'Long Haul': John White; Raised in Politics, Civil Rights."

100. "In for the 'Long Haul': John White; Raised in Politics, Civil Rights."

101. Goode, *In Goode Faith*, 167–75, and Ransom, "Black Independent Politics," 262–265.

102. "Election of Black Mayor in Philadelphia Reflects a Decade of Change," *New York Times*, Nov. 10, 1983; Goode, *In Goode Faith*, 167–87; Paolantonio, *Frank Rizzo*, 266–86, Ransom, "Black Independent Politics," 265–78. Population data is from U.S. Bureau of the Census, *City and County Data Book* (Washington, D.C.: Government Printing Office, 1983). On the Goode campaign's movement ethos, see quotes from campaign staff members in Ransom, "Black Independent Politics," 265–66.

103. Paolantonio, *Frank Rizzo*, 312–13. On the impact of cuts in federal urban spending during the 1980's, see Linda Williams, "Black Political Progress in the 1980s: The Electoral Arena," in Preston et al., *New Black Politics*, 129–31.

104. For Wilson Goode's discussion of the MOVE crisis, see Goode, *In Goode Faith*, 160–65, 207–51. Paul Washington and Charles Bowser both describe the tensions between MOVE and its neighbors as well as between MOVE and other black activists in the city. See Washington, *"Other Sheep I Have"*, 183; Charles W. Bowser, *Let the Bunker Burn: The Final Battle with MOVE* (Philadelphia: Camino Books, 1989), 94–95. Bowser and Washington were both members of the Philadelphia Special Investigations Committee (PSIC) appointed by Mayor Goode to investigate the MOVE bombing. The PSIC's final report described the mayor's hands-off approach to the police operation as "grossly negligent" and an "abdication of his authority.' No government official was ever charged with criminal wrongdoing in the bombing. Bowser's recounting of the PSIC's deliberations is instructive on issues of moral and legal culpability. Bowser, *Let the Bunker Burn*, 158–75.

105. Rustin was particularly critical of "black militants" and their " 'no-win' policy" of exposing "the hypocrisy of white liberals," a clear reference to the independent political strategies of groups like the BPF. Bayard Rustin, "From Protest to Politics: The Future of the Civil Rights Movement," *Commentary* 39,1 (Jan. 1965): 25–31.

Conclusion

1. On the question of social movement sustainability, see Aldon Morris, *The Origins of the Civil Rights Movement: Black Communities Organizing for Change* (New York:

Free Press, 1984), 275–90, and George Lipsitz, *A Life in the Struggle: Ivory Perry and the Culture of Opposition*, rev. ed. (Philadelphia: Temple University Press, 1995), 227–47.

2. See Morris, *Origins of the Civil Rights Movement*, 283–86, for a discussion of the interdependence of leaders, organizers, and "followers," within a successful social movement.

Index

Acknowledgments

I first learned the importance of history at my grandparents' dining room table. At family gatherings during the heady days of the late 1960s and 1970s, stories of the ancestors were interwoven with contentious debates over the issues of the day and lessons about the importance of education. All errors of fact and interpretation in these pages are mine alone. But the spirit of inquiry and passion for social justice with which I have attempted to write belongs entirely to those who came before me, in particular my grandparents, Virginia B. Cannady and William P. Cannady, Jr., and my parents, Joan C. Countryman and Peter J. Countryman.

The generous support of many individuals and institutions made this book possible. The initial research was conducted with fellowship support from the Ford Foundation and Duke University. I am particularly grateful to the University of Michigan for a generous publication subvention award as well as for the research support that I received from the Provost's Office, College of Literature, Science, and the Arts, Rackham School of Graduate Studies, Department of History, and Program in American Culture. I also benefited greatly from the opportunity to attend a civil rights history workshop sponsored by the University of Houston History Department and a conference on black politics at the University of Rochester's Frederick Douglass Institute. It has been my privilege to be able to work with Robert Lockhart and the University of Pennsylvania Press. Bob's skills as a reader, his patience, resourcefulness, and vision have all been crucial to my ability to complete this book.

Throughout my research, I benefited greatly from the knowledge and assistance of Margaret Jerrido, George Brightbill, Beverly Galloway-Wright, and the staff of Temple University's Urban Archives. Thanks are also due to the reference staffs of the Philadelphia Municipal Archives, the University of Pennsylvania Archives, and the Library of Congress. I owe a huge debt of gratitude to the many Philadelphians who agreed to share their memories of the 1960s with me and who helped me to identify other people with whom I should talk, in particular Charles Bowser, Kitty Caparella, John Churchville, Joan Countryman, Samuel Evans, Clarence Farmer, Gillian Gilhool, Steven Gold, David Gracie, Mattie Humphrey, Elaine Richardson, Edward Robinson, Tom Roderick, Michael Simmons, Leon Sullivan, Grace Sullivan, Mac Walters, and Paul Washington. I am especially grateful to Thomas Gilhool, William Meek, Walter Palmer, and Charyn Sutton for their guidance in establishing the scope of this study.

It has been my great privilege to have the opportunity to learn from an extraordinary group of historical scholars and teachers. In high school, William Koons and Patricia Reifsnyder introduced me to the work of historians and to a world of historical scholarship beyond the textbooks. Yale was an extraordinary place for an undergraduate to pursue the study of history from the bottom up. David Montgomery, George Chauncey, Cornel West, William Cronon, and David Scobey were not only superb teachers, but they all took time from their busy schedules to encourage my interests in social movement history and politically relevant scholarship.

It was as a graduate student at Duke University that I first began to consider the questions that would come to shape this study. As a scholar, teacher, mentor, and critic Bill Chafe has influenced my growth as an historian in innumerable ways. I have depended on his careful readings and insightful commentary at every stage of this project. Larry Goodwyn's vision of democratic scholarship and Raymond Gavin's guidance and scholarly rigor have helped to shape every aspect of this book. As my first graduate school adviser, and now as my colleague at the University of Michigan, I have relied on Julius Scott's wise counsel more than he can know. Special thanks as well to my graduate school colleagues from whom I have learned so much over the years, in particular Herman Bennett, Leslie Brown, Alex Byrd, Ann Farnsworth-Olvear, Kirsten Fischer, Christina Greene, Charles McKinney, Deborah Montgomerie, Jennifer Morgan, Andrew Neather, Stephanie Smallwood, Tim Tyson, Anne Valk, Lisa Waller, and Stephanie Yuhl.

Numerous colleagues read and commented on all or part of the manuscript. I am particularly indebted to Thomas Sugrue and Komozi Woodard for their thorough readings of the entire manuscript and crucial suggestions for revisions. Gina Morantz-Sanchez agreed to read and reread my work more times than I can remember and always responded with thoughtful comments and suggestions. John Carson and Robert Self also read the entire manuscript carefully and with great insight. I am also grateful to Charlie Bright, Reginald Butler, Richard Candida-Smith, Cathy Cohen, John Dittmer, Geoff Eley, Tom Fujita-Rony, Kevin Gaines, Barry Gaspar, Fred Harris, Andrew Highsmith, Scott Kurashige, Matt Lassiter, Earl Lewis, Kate Masur, Maria Montoya, Charles Payne, Ahmed Rahman, Barbara Ransby, Linda Reed, David Roediger, Hannah Rosen, Bill Rosenberg, Damon Salesa, George Sanchez, Barbara Savage, Jeanne Theoharis, Mills Thorton, Tim Tyson, Maris Vinovskis, Penny Von Eschen, Stephen Ward, and two anonymous reviewers for the *Journal of Urban History* for their thoughtful comments on my work.

Jess Rigelhaupt, Carla Vecchiola, and Kidada Williams provided crucial research assistance in the last years of the project. I have benefited enormously from Michele Mitchell's scholarly insights into the gender politics of black nationalism. Karen Miller has been a friend, teaching colleague, and fellow student of race and urban politics. Long conversations with Jeanne Theoharis, along with a jointly planned conference panel on the civil rights movement in the North, were crucial to the development of my thinking on this project. I cannot thank her enough.

I do not know how to thank the many friends and family members whose support I have relied on during the many years that I have worked on this project. Brian Glick, Sue Novick, and Steven White were always there when I called. Phil Deloria, Manal Houmani, Terry McDonald, Richard Meisler, Sonya Rose, George Sanchez, Abby Stewart, Alan Wald, and Margaret Walsh generously offered sage and timely career advice. Mary Cannady, Karen Countryman, Carole Marks, and Julie Yanson are aunts extraordinaire on whom I can always depend. My in-laws, Jose Ceballo and Ana Ramos, have shown great patience with the vagaries of academic life and pride in the work of their daughter and son-in-law. My mother and stepfather, Joan Countryman and Edward Jakmauh, have supported every decision that I have made, always understanding as I have moved in and out of the academy. Their commitment to making teaching and learning a part of every day life has always been an inspiration to me.

My children, Elisia and Miguel Ceballo-Countryman, have endured long hours of "Daddy's working on his book." That Daddy's book is older than they are remains for them a source of wonder and mystery. They are my daily reminder of the importance of researching and recounting the stories of those who have worked and continued to work to build a more just world for all children and families.

My final and most important thank you goes to my wife, Rosario Ceballo. Despite the pressures of her own academic career, she has always been willing to contribute her talents as a thinker and reader to this project. Simply put, I could not and would not have finished it without her love, insight and support. This book is dedicated to her.